Nora

BOOKS BY BRENDA MADDOX

Beyond Babel: New Directions in Communications
The Half-Parent: Living with Other People's Children
Who's Afraid of Elizabeth Taylor?
Married and Gay
Nora: The Real Life of Molly Bloom

Nora

The Real Life of Molly Bloom

Brenda Maddox

Houghton Mifflin Company

B O S T O N

1988

Copyright © 1988 by Brenda Maddox.

ALL RIGHTS RESERVED.

For information about permission to reproduce
selections from this book, write to Permissions,
Houghton Mifflin Company, 2 Park Street,
Boston, Massachusetts 02108.

Library of Congress Cataloging-in-Publication Data

Maddox, Brenda.
Nora : the real life of Molly Bloom / Brenda Maddox. p.   cm.
Bibliography: p.
Includes index.
ISBN 0-395-36510-4
1. Joyce, Nora Barnacle, 1884–1951.   2. Joyce, James, 1882–1941 —
Biography — Marriage.   3. Authors, Irish — 20th century —
Biography.   4. Wives — Ireland — Biography.   I. Title.
PR6019 .O9Z7184   1988
823'.912—dc19
[B]   88-3023
CIP

Printed in the United States of America

A 10 9 8 7 6 5 4 3 2 1

To Bruno

Her image had passed into his soul for ever . . .

James Joyce,
*A Portrait of the Artist
as a Young Man*

Acknowledgments

Many people contributed to this book, two above all: my daughter Bronwen, who encouraged me to write it, and Bernard McGinley, whose generosity and encyclopedic knowledge of Joyce, Joyceana, bibliography, and libraries were a constant source of advice and inspiration. No one helped more.

I am also indebted to Canon Padraic O Laoi, Nora's Galway biographer, and to Miss Jane Lidderdale, O.B.E., goddaughter of Harriet Weaver and guardian of Lucia Joyce, who gave me valuable perspective on the two most important women in Nora Joyce's adult life. A stroke of good fortune also led me to the fashion historian Miss Jane Mulvagh, who examined the photographs of Nora's clothes with the eye of an archaeologist. It is quite coincidental that Miss Mulvagh, author of the *Vogue History of Twentieth Century Fashion*, is also a relative of the late Willie Mulvagh of Galway, the boyfriend of Nora Barnacle of whom James Joyce was most jealous.

Constant support and encouragement have come from my literate agents, Hilary Rubinstein of A. P. Watt in London, and Georges and Anne Borchardt of Georges Borchardt, Inc., in New York; from my skilled and sympathetic editors, Christopher Sinclair-Stevenson and James Woodall at Hamish Hamilton and Robie Macauley and Sarah Flynn at Houghton Mifflin; and from my husband, John Maddox. Their enthusiasm for Nora never slackened.

For helpful conversations and hospitality, I am indebted to many people, including the late Richard Ellmann and Mrs. Ellmann, Mr. and Mrs. Ken Monaghan, Mrs. Patricia Barnacle Hutton, Ira B. Nadel, Mr. and Mrs. John J. Slocum, Mr. and Mrs. Dáithí O Ceallaigh, Stelio Crise, Fritz Senn, and A. Walton Litz. I owe particular thanks to Stan Gébler Davies and Bernard McGinley for the loan of their personal collections of books about Joyce, and to Vivien Igoe for sharing her great knowledge of Joyce photographs.

Rough drafts of portions of the manuscript were read by Shari and Bernard Benstock, Ruth Bauerle, Eilis Dillon, James Card, Noel Riley Fitch, Ira Nadel, Arnold Goldman, Jane Lidderdale, Dr. J. B. Lyons, and Bernard McGinley. They offered many valuable criticisms and suggestions on perspective, style, and interpretations. What errors remain are my own.

I am grateful to The Bodley Head and Random House, Inc., for permission to reprint extracts from *Ulysses: The Corrected Text;* to Jonathan Cape Ltd. and Viking Penguin, Inc., for permission to reprint extracts from *Dubliners, Exiles,* and *The Critical Writings of James Joyce;* and to Faber & Faber Ltd. and Viking Penguin, Inc., for permission to reprint extracts from *The Letters of James Joyce,* edited by Richard Ellmann, and *Finnegans Wake.*

I also owe thanks to the estate of Harriet Shaw Weaver, for permission to quote from her unpublished letters, and to Frederick Dennis for permission to quote from Sylvia Beach's papers.

Among others who kindly consented to the use of unpublished material are Bozena Schaurek Delimata, Moune A. Gilbert, Patricia Barnacle Hutton, Frederick Joyce, Mrs. Nelly Joyce, Ken Monaghan, Betsy and Tina Jolas, Oliver D. Gogarty, Roderick Power, Enid Kastor Rubin, John Slocum, and Arthur J. Wall.

Every effort has been made to trace copyright holders, and I would be grateful to hear from any who have escaped my notice.

The Joyce archive is a scattered one. I would like to thank the librarians and staff of the following libraries and museums for making their collections available to me and, in some cases, permitting me to reproduce letters or photographs: the Poetry/Rare Books Collection of the University Libraries at the State University of New York at Buffalo; the Manuscript Room of the British Library (Harriet Shaw Weaver papers); the Butler Library at Columbia University (Bennett Cerf papers); the Department of Rare Books, Cornell University (the Joyce Collection); the Houghton Library, Harvard University; the National Library of Ireland; the Berg Collection and the Jewish Division at the New York Public Library; the Public Library at Camillus, New York; the Joyce Museum; the Special Collections Department of the Northwestern University Library (Helen Nutting diaries and Nora Joyce correspondence); the Firestone Collection and Manuscript Division of the Princeton University Library (Sylvia Beach papers); the Special Collections Room of the Morris Library at Southern Illinois University (the Dr. Harley K. Croessmann and Charles A. Feinberg Collections, and the Herbert Gorman papers); the Special Collections at the Stanford University Libraries; the Civici Musei di Storia ed Arte, Trieste; the Beinecke Rare Book and Manuscript Library at Yale University (the John and Eileen Slocum Collection); the Manuscript Room at Trinity College Library, University of Dublin (Patricia Hutchins and Thomas McGreevy papers); the Humanities Research Center of the University of Texas at Austin (Helen Kastor Joyce, Lucia Joyce, and J. F. Byrne papers); University College, Dublin (Constantine Curran papers); the James Hardiman Library, University College, Galway; the Manuscript Room of University College, London (Lucia Joyce bequest and James Joyce Collection); the Department of Special Collections, University Research Library, University of California, Los Angeles (Myron Nutting Oral History); and the Zentralbibliothek, Zurich (Paul Ruggiero papers).

I would like to thank many people for interviews, letters or other personal assistance on this book. In Britain: Diana Athill, Derek Attridge, Brian Behan, Mary Breasted, Richard Brown, Mrs. M. Burbidge, Mrs. Henry Carr, Dr. Anthony Clare, Moira Gaster, Arnold Goldman, Patricia Barnacle Hutton, Nelly Joyce, Colin MacCabe, Dermot B. Mulvagh, Richard Ryan, Graham Smith, Ted Smyth, Susan Swift, and Thérèse Wright.

In France: Georges Belmont, Iphrène Benoît-Méchin, Odette Bernard, Marcel Bouboule, Evelyne Shapero and Leo Chardonnet, Nino Frank, Moune A. Gilbert, the late Maria Jolas, Kathy Knorr, Jean Lambert, the late Dominique Gillet Maroger, and Anne-Marie Pacquet.

In Ireland: Maureen Charlton, Mr. and Mrs. Patrick Collins, Peter Costello, Noreen Craughwell, Bozena Delimata, the Rev. Mother Mary Doyle, Mr. and Mrs. Desmond Fisher, Patrick Friel, Stan Gébler Davies, Oliver D. Gogarty, Dr. Patrick Henchy, Patrick Hennessy, Vivien Igoe, Norma R. Jessop, John Kelleher, Mary Rose Kelly, Jim Kemmy, His Excellency Eamon Kennedy, Maureen Kenny and Thomas Kenny, Dr. J. B. Lyons, Nancy McCarthy, Christopher Murphy, K. A. Murray, Robert Nicholson, Sen. David Norris, Ulick O'Connor, Riana O'Dwyer, Sean O'Faolain, Joe O'Halloran, Donal O Luanaigh, Sean O Mordha, D. B. O'Neill, the late Arthur Power, Roderick Power, the late E. G. Quin, John Ryan, Nuala Silk, Gerard Treanor, and Arthur J. Wall.

In Italy: Aldo Bernadini, Dr. Grazia Brava, Stelio Crise, Evelyn Mulvagh Odierna, and Lorenzo Quaglietti.

In Switzerland: Pfarrer Hans Canoni, Rainer Diedrichs, Thomas Fleiner, Dr. Senta Frauchiger, Klara Heyland, Rita Jotterand, Jacques Mercanton, Mrs. Paul Ruggiero, Fritz Senn, Dr. Heinrich Straumann, Pfarrer Johann von Rotz, Mrs. Maria Zöbeli-Gerhardt, the late Mrs. Hulda Zumsteg, and Gustav Zumsteg.

In the United States: Berenice Abbott, Floyd Abrams, Deirdre Bair, the late Maurice Beebe, Bernard and Shari Benstock, Ellen Bentley, David Binder, James V. Card, Alan M. Cohn, Robert A. Day, Eilis Dillon, Wilson Dizard, Walter Engel, Noel Riley Fitch, Grete Hartley, Judith Hayes, Cathy Henderson, Eleanor Herrick, Maureen Howard, Jean Kimball, David Koch, Nita Krevans, A. Walton Litz, James Longenbach, Jane

Marcus, Jonathan Miller, Sigrid P. Perry, Mrs. Raymond Porter, Mary T. Reynolds, Edda Ritson, Enid Kastor Rubin, Elizabeth Curran Solterer, Bonnie Kime Scott, and John and Eileen Slocum.

Elsewhere: Elfin Bettinger, Francis Evers, Hans Walter Gabler, and Ira B. Nadel.

I would also like to thank the following institutions for assistance: Kennys Bookshops and Art Galleries, Galway; Gotham Book Mart, New York City; the sound archives of the BBC; the Superintendent Registrar's Office of the Western Health Board of Ireland; the Consular Section of the British Embassy, Paris; the Diocesan Office of the Cathedral, Galway; the press office of the Irish Embassy in London; the Locarno Official Tourist Board; the Galway Family History Society; the Mairie du 6e Arrondissement, Paris; the Union Française des Arts du Costume; the office of the Stadtpräsident, Zurich; H. M. Customs and Excise Office Archives; the Office of the Revenue Commissioners, Ireland; the Irish Railway Record Office; the Public Record Office of Ireland; the Irish Tourist Board; the Public Record Office of England and Wales; and St. Bridget's Hospital, Ballinasloe, Galway.

Contents

Illustrations

Following page 204

Galway, c. 1895–1900. Probably Nora and her grandmother or mother. (Courtesy of Cornell University Libraries.)

Presentation Convent, Galway. (Courtesy of Kennys Bookshops and Art Galleries, Galway.)

Galway fish market. (Courtesy of the Board of Trinity College, Dublin.)

Willie Mulvagh. (Courtesy of Dermot Mulvagh.)

Michael Healy. (Courtesy of Cornell University Libraries.)

Galway corset advertisement, 1902. (Courtesy of the British Library.)

Grafton Street, Dublin. (National Library of Ireland)

Finn's Hotel. (Photograph by Peter Harding, RTE.)

Nora, Giorgio, and Lucia in Zurich. (Courtesy of the Poetry/Rare Books Collection, State University of New York at Buffalo.)

The Schaureks. (Courtesy of Mr. and Mrs. Ken Monaghan.)

Roberto Prezioso in naval uniform. (Courtesy of the Fototeca Civici Musei di Storia ed Arte di Trieste.)

30 Universitätsstrasse, Zurich.

Lucia with Zurich schoolmates. (Courtesy of Maria Zöbeli-Gerhardt.)

James Joyce, 1904. (Courtesy of the Poetry/Rare Books Collection, State University of New York at Buffalo.)

Nora in *Riders to the Sea* costume. (Courtesy of Jimmy Joyce.)

Nora by Tullio Silvestri. (Courtesy of the Poetry/Rare Books Collection, State University of New York at Buffalo.)

Nora by Frank Budgen. (Courtesy of the Poetry/Rare Books Collection, State University of New York at Buffalo.)

James Joyce. (Courtesy of Berenice Abbott and Commerce Graphics Ltd., Inc.)

Nora by Myron Nutting. (Courtesy of Northwestern University Library.)

James Joyce in Trieste. (Courtesy of the Joyce Museum, Sandycove, Ireland, and Bord Fáilte.)

Introduction

My curiosity about Nora began years ago at Harvard when John Kelleher, in his seminar on Anglo-Irish literature, mentioned that the Joyces spoke Italian at home. My own grandparents were immigrants to America from Ireland and Italy, and I was intrigued by this Irish family who had gone east, not west.

The revised edition of Richard Ellmann's monumental biography of Joyce, published in 1982, reawakened my curiosity. I put the book down longing to know more about Nora. How had she managed the passage from Galway to Trieste, Zurich, and Paris? How had she survived Joyce, whose monomania destroyed many of his friendships and, as far as one can judge, blighted his children? Why was she always so funny?

The Joyces' marriage also presented many unanswered questions. How did a convent-trained girl have the courage in 1904 to run away with a man who refused to marry her? Why, after cohabiting for twenty-seven years, did the Joyces bother with a civil wedding in 1931? What did Nora feel when her young son took up with a Jewish-American divorcée eleven years his senior? And, as she did not give a damn for the printed word, what did she see in Joyce?

Others interests fed this book. As home affairs editor for *The Economist*, I wrote about Northern Ireland and Ireland and made many trips there: the visit of Pope John Paul II was another stimulus for this book. I watched with fascination the long-running Irish debate on contraception, abortion, divorce, and illegitimacy. Whatever problems women have, Irish women have them worse. I began to see Nora Barnacle as typical of a certain kind of Irish girl — desperate to escape from her circumstances, unequipped with anything but strength of character and charm.

The Joyce saga touched more personal ground — my maternal grandparents' elopement in 1908 and the sudden descent into schizophrenia of a member of my family — but I needed none of these to set me to work. Nora Barnacle is a reporter's dream: an unexplored corner of the Joyce story. She has a legion of admirers, people, like me, who always wanted to know more.

When I first spoke to Richard Ellmann, Joyce's biographer, about a biography of Nora, he was skeptical. There were few letters, he said, Joyce and Nora having so rarely been apart, and their friends were dead. There was not even material, he ventured, for a feminist treatise.

Ellmann changed his mind well before his death in 1987 and generously told me that he had come to appreciate that there was a study of Nora waiting to be done; he kindly offered suggestions, names, addresses, and answers to questions I put to him. When he telephoned me in December 1986 to say that he had been stricken with motor neuron disease, he inquired, in spite of his difficulty in speaking, whether I had been able to trace a surviving daughter of Joyce's Aunt Josephine, Mrs. William Murray.

Ellmann died in May 1987. I did not have a chance to discuss with him the points on which he and I differed. Except one. Visiting the Ellmanns at their home in Oxford in 1985, I gave him a copy of an article of mine that was about to appear in the *New York Times Book Review* called "Could Nora Cook?" "She couldn't," he said, smiling, only to be contradicted by his wife. "Nora *could* cook," said Mary Ellmann, author of *Thinking About Women*. "She could cook *chicken*. And she was funny." With that last Ellmann agreed. He had always been amused by Nora's report to Joyce on a new flat she had inspected: "That place wasn't fit to wash a rat in."

There have been many sources of new information for this book. The principal one has been the great mass of unpublished letters in the Joyce collection at Cornell University and in the Harriet Shaw Weaver papers in the British Library. There was also valuable material in the Herbert Gorman collection at Southern Illinois University, and much insight into Nora to be found in the papers of Lucia Joyce and Helen Kastor Joyce at the Humanities Research Center at the University of Texas at Austin.

The memoirs of Paris of the 1920s and 1930s, and the notes from which they were prepared, were another source. Nora was often there, sometimes in material discarded by authors and editors concentrating (and why not?) on her husband. Some of the excisions nonetheless would fit very well into a feminist tract. To give just one example: the Joyces' friend, the art critic and writer Arthur Power, in preparing his book *Conversations with James Joyce,* described how the Joyces spent their evenings in Paris: "After going to the theatre they often call in on the way home at the café [Café Francis]." His editor changed the sentence to read in the singular: "After Joyce goes to the theatre he often calls in . . ."— an alteration that presents the carefree artist as out on the town on his own while his drone of a wife waits to nag him when he gets home.

James Joyce scarcely took a step without Nora. His dependency was stressed by some of their old friends who were still alive when I began this book: Arthur Power, Maria Jolas, and Moune (Mrs. Stuart) Gilbert. There was also a younger generation to interview, people now in their seventies, who knew the Joyce family well and shared their reminiscences with me. Particularly informative on Nora were Constantine Curran's daughter, Elizabeth Solterer, who had been a frequent visitor to the Joyces' household in Paris; Evelyne Shapero Chardonnet, the niece of Nora's best friend, Kathleen Bailly; and Iris Wise, the stepdaughter of James Stephens.

Then there were Nora's letters. Joyce had reasons of his own for insisting that she did not write any. He knew better. "I have *thirteen* letters of yours," he boasted six weeks after they had met in the summer of 1904. Nora did write letters; the problem is that few people, Joyce apart, kept them. Fortunately, enough have survived to show her enormous influence on Joyce's writing style. She wrote as she talked; she was spontaneous, direct, humorous, and, when she chose, vulgar. She was not shy of calling a penis a prick. She was also a good reporter.

As a reporter as well as biographer, I have been gratified to find how much new, and often unexpected, information lay waiting in public documents. I am indebted to the record offices of Trieste, Zurich, Paris, London, many parts of the United States, Dublin, and, above all, Galway for answering my requests for documents.

This then has been a work of excavation. As a result, I have used more footnotes than I would like in order to identify the sources of my information. I have not used Joyce's fiction as a source of biographical fact. Self-denial has been a strain, however, when dealing with an author who once said, "Imagination is memory." Joyce, perhaps above all other authors, used his life as the raw material of his art. From the time he met Nora, her memories were as useful as his own. Where the parallels between the life and the work are striking, I have pointed them out. Where Joyce himself made the connection explicit, as in his notes to *Exiles,* I have used the information more freely.

I have not invented any quotations for Nora. I have written "Nora thought" or "she wondered" only when I had evidence that she did so. Where I have speculated on her thoughts and feelings, I have tried to make it clear to the reader.

I began this book liking Nora. I finished in awe of her. Nora's life was shaken by the major political and social forces of the first half of the twentieth century — two world wars, the struggles of Irish and Italian nationalism, the emancipation of women, even the anti-Semitism of New York society. With her strength, wit, and calm, she survived them all, just as she survived thirty-seven years with James Joyce and taught him what life was about.

Nora was ordinary. Nobody who loves Joyce will need to know how much that conveys. She was funny, passionate, courageous, spontaneous, and articulate. She talked and talked. Her voice can be heard in all Joyce's major female characters. I hope I have done her justice.

BRENDA MADDOX

PART I

Lily

The men that is now is only all
palaver and what they can get out of you.

— "The Dead"

1

❈

Exit from Finn's

To this day departures by sea from Ireland are noisy, anxious affairs. The air is filled with wailing as children protest at being edged forward in step with piles of shopping bags and suitcases. Parents, tired and irritable, worry about getting a seat, even about getting on at all (ferries across the Irish Sea can be crowded), but know they cannot afford to fly. The flight to England takes only an hour but costs more than twice as much. Yet the long journey by boat and connecting train is hardly faster at the end of the twentieth century than it was at the beginning; the overnight crossing through Holyhead still tips passengers bleary-eyed into London's Euston Station in the morning.

Family parties are still large (a group of seven or eight is not uncommon), the sexes still very separate. Once aboard, the men forge ahead with their teenage sons and aim straight for the bar, the video games, or the duty-free shop, while the wives, clutching last year's baby and a toddler or two, hunt for places and shriek at the older ones wandering away. Long before the boat sails, all the seats are full, the aisles are piled with luggage, and some passengers are already asleep or drunk.

A glance can swiftly sort out the crowd into holiday makers, white-collar workers, at home on either side of the Irish Sea, and young laborers off the land, going to England to find work on building sites. In any boatload there will probably be women intent on services unobtainable in Ireland and also young people leaving Ireland forever.

In every young Irish mind, the question of emigration is inescapable as it has been since the Great Famine of the 1840s. If not, why not? And

3

the young do not leave only for a job or better pay. Ireland, although there are now some who live there happily while defying its conventions, is still a priest-ridden land: no divorce, little secular education, almost no escape from prying eyes and gossip. Outside Dublin, the tolerance that British and other foreign residents enjoy is rarely extended to native dissidents.

In the past every boat that left Ireland was launched with tears. "American wakes" were held at the home of someone leaving to cross the Atlantic, and the next day at the docks there were anguished scenes as families were torn apart, as mothers looked on faces they would not see again, and brothers and sisters said goodbye, those staying resentful at being left behind to look after the old parents and reproaching themselves for not daring to go.

On the Saturday evening of October 8, 1904, shortly before nine o'clock, a tall young woman with a very straight back walked up the gangway of the night boat from Dublin. She had thick red-brown hair, high cheekbones, and dark blue eyes set off by black lashes and thick black brows. Her heavy hair was drawn over her ears and fastened with long pins, the better to fit under her wide-brimmed hat. She wore a borrowed coat against the chill October wind.[1]

Her boat was leaving from the North Wall, one of the Dublin quays along the river Liffey, and there was a great press of people, illuminated by the light streaming through the portholes, as well-wishers and mourners mingled with the passengers. Those who were not weeping were joking and enjoying the drink that was being passed around.

There was no one to weep at Nora Barnacle's departure, but she did not care. She had not told her family in Galway that she was leaving Ireland, nor her employers at Finn's Hotel in Dublin. If any of them had had a hint of what she was doing, they would have tried to stop her and might have succeeded for, at twenty, she was still a minor and she was running off with Jim Joyce.[2]

Nora herself had no cause for grief as she was not making the passage to America, from which few returned, and those not until they were rich or old, but only to London and Paris, then on to Zurich — wherever that might be. Geography had not been her strong suit at school in Galway. She had failed the subject three years running.[3]

Through the crowd she could see Jim, surrounded by the relatives and friends who had come to see him off. Jim liked to think of himself as friendless and alone,[4] but, as Nora could see, that was far from the truth. There he stood, with his weeping father, John Joyce; his Aunt Josephine, who had helped look after the large Joyce brood after their mother had died; his eldest sister, Poppie; and his younger brother, Stanislaus. Stanislaus, Jim had told Nora, was the only one of the family who understood him.[5]

All except John Joyce knew that Nora and Jim were running away together, but they made no sign of recognizing her. She and Jim had agreed not to approach each other until the boat sailed. John Joyce was supposed to believe that his son was traveling alone. Jim had lived in Paris for four months in late 1902 and early 1903 but had been called home because his mother was dying. Now — as far as his father knew — Jim was merely returning to the Continent to resume where he had left off. John Joyce, broken-hearted at saying goodbye to his eldest and favorite son, did not protest. He agreed with Jim: "No one with any self-respect stays in Ireland."[6]

Nora had self-respect, and courage. It was the second time in a year that she had run away and much easier than the first. When she had left Galway, she had been utterly alone. She had slipped out of her Uncle Tommy's house and taken herself to Dublin, not knowing a soul.[7]

Now she was embarked on the greatest adventure of her life. What would they say at Finn's when they realized she was gone? They would be angry at being short-handed at the weekend, and they might telegraph her family in Galway.[8] The proprietress was bad-tempered enough perhaps even to inform her family that Nora had run off with an unemployed writer best known for his love of drink and inability to hold it.

Nora wished that Jim had made a better impression at the hotel when he came to see her. He used to come into the bar wearing a straw hat and dirty canvas shoes. As she watched him, seeing the poor way he was dressed, she wondered if she were wise to entrust her life to him.[9] Given her choice, she would have preferred to make her life with a shop owner, a doctor, a schoolteacher, almost anything but a writer, but she loved him deeply.[10] She was sure that, with his experience of Continental living and command of several languages, he would soon find work for them both.

Nora refused to fear the future. Jim had accused her of not appreciating the difficulty of what they were attempting, but he had also recognized her impatience. If anything, it was she who had pushed him into their running away together. She had nothing to lose. She could not go back to Galway. There was nothing for her in Dublin.

She was under no illusion. Jim was not going to marry her. He had not even said that he loved her, although she had often confessed her love for him.[11] What he had said was, as she interpreted it, almost as good: that he had never felt as close to any other person and that the fact that she had chosen to share his life filled him with great joy.[12] He was convinced that he would be one of the greatest writers of his time — an ambition that meant less to Nora than the confidence with which he held it. She was a good judge of men, and his words rang true.

A passionate girl, she was eager to be alone with Jim. She was curious about the ways of love. There were things in her past Jim knew nothing about,[13] but a night in bed with a man was an experience she had not tried.

Four Saturdays before, just as they were deciding to go away together, Jim had had his second short story published in an Irish newspaper.[14] He had written it that very week and in it he wrote of Eveline, a Dublin girl of nineteen — almost exactly Nora's age — going to the North Wall on a dark and misty night, intending to run off with a sailor named Frank. In the story, Frank seized her hand and the boat blew its warning whistle. Eveline froze. She recalled the promise she had made to her dying mother, that she would look after her father.

— Come!

All the seas of the world tumbled about her heart. He was drawing her into them; he would drown her. She gripped with both hands at the iron railing.

Eveline stayed, powerless to break her ties with the past. Nora went, without a backward glance.

2

The Man-Killer

. . . She's from Connacht, isn't she?
— Her people are, said Gabriel shortly.

— "The Dead"

ONE WARM AFTERNOON in Paris in the early 1920s Nora Joyce was walking with her daughter, Lucia, and a young American friend in the Tuileries Gardens when the girls spotted a vendor selling ice cream. They ran over and bought some, giggling as they went. They knew they were too old to be eating in public and risking stains on their dresses. To cover her embarrassment, Phyllis Moss, Lucia's friend, said, "What *will* Mrs. Joyce think of us?"

In her low Galway voice, Nora replied, "You have no idea what simple people I come from."[1]

Nora was born in March 1884 in the west of Ireland, which Dublin's Anglo-Irish literati were beginning to romanticize but from which the natives were clamoring to escape. A succession of famines took the population of Ireland from 8 million in 1840 to 3 million in 1920, and nowhere was emptying faster than the Gaeltacht — the Irish-speaking counties of the west and northwest. Connaught (or Connacht, as it is sometimes spelled), the western province encompassing the counties of Galway, Mayo, Sligo, Leitrim, and Roscommon, was losing more to the emigrant boats than to the graveyard; it also had the lowest birthrate in Ireland.

The city of Galway, in contrast to its hinterland, was a place of life and bustle. It had a population of fifteen thousand and was the port, marketplace, and administrative center for the whole vast expanse of Connaught. Galway City had been gaslit since 1837; piped water ran under its streets, into the houses and the backyard communal water closets of the crowded tenements.

7

The city dreamed of regaining its seventeenth-century eminence as the second port in Ireland, but the shallow Galway Bay, about whose sunsets exiles sang and wept, frustrated the dream by continually silting up. In 1860 when the ship *Indian Empire* tried to enter, it hit the Marguerite Rock at the harbor entrance.[2] Nonetheless, the dredging continued. As Galway was the port in the British Isles nearest North America, it cherished hopes of being designated a "mail port" through which fast steamers, connecting with five trains a day, could speed letters and parcels between Canada and London.

Along the city streets soldiers were everywhere. The Renmore military barracks a mile outside of town housed the Galway militia of the Connaught Rangers. The Rangers, with their scarlet uniforms piped in green, were very popular, and many Galway families kept a picture of the Rangers on their walls.

The military and maritime presence in the city attracted considerable wealth. There were fine houses on the banks of the river Corrib and elegant shops boasting clothes as fashionable as those to be found in Dublin or London. The same elements attracted plenty of prostitutes as well, and Galway's main street, Shop Street, had a sixpenny side and a three-halfpence side. Galway was also a city of beggars, widows, and orphans. Its tenements were some of the worst in Europe. As a succession of small famines followed the great one, people driven off the land poured starving into the city, where there was nothing for them except the workhouse or the immigrant ships. From Dublin, Galway City looked wild and uncultured, as remote as Cheyenne seems from New York.

But Galway saw itself differently — "more Spanish than Irish in general character," according to the *Galway Year Book* in 1902.[3] Its long trade with Spain was reflected in houses with Moorish architecture. The city also boasted a Spanish Arch and a Spanish Parade where Spanish merchant families had once promenaded. It also called itself the "City of Tribes" in honor of the fourteen Galway families directly descended from the clans that had fiercely resisted Oliver Cromwell and his troops in 1651. These tribal names, with two exceptions, are not widely associated with Irish ancestry: Athus, Blake, Bodkin, Browne, D'Arcy, Deane, Ffont, Ffrench, Kirwan, Martin, Morris, and Skerrett. The exceptions are Joyce and Lynch.

Galway City is the gateway to the Joyce Country — a desolate and wild region of grazing land, bog, and mountain stretching westward to the pounding Atlantic. James Joyce had never set foot in this part of Ireland when he met Nora; his own Joyce line came from Cork in the southwest. The name of Lynch carried more urban associations. Lynch's Castle, a fine old mansion in Shop Street, was the home of a Galway mayor, James Lynch-Fitzstephen, who, the year after Columbus discovered America (memories are long in Ireland), executed his own son by hanging him from a window of the Old Jail. The high-principled mayor felt he had no alternative because his son had murdered the hot-blooded Spaniard who was his rival in love. The verb *to lynch* came to have its own meaning in the American South, but in Galway the name retained the sense of betrayal.

Nora Barnacle was born in March 1884 on either the twenty-first or the twenty-second (church and state records disagree).[4] Her birth took place in the Galway City Workhouse, not because her family was penniless — they were not — but because the handsome limestone-terraced institution, which had sheltered more than a thousand people during the Great Famine of 1847–48, later served as general hospital for the city. Her parents were Thomas Barnacle, a baker, and Annie (short for Honoraria) Healy, a seamstress and dressmaker. Annie, a tall, handsome woman of twenty-six, was the daughter of a shop owner, Patrick Healy, and Catherine Mortimer Healy; the Mortimers had some pretensions to gentility.

In 1884 Tom and Annie Barnacle had been married for three years and already had a daughter, Mary. After Nora, they were to have three more daughters before producing the long-awaited son, Thomas, who was followed by yet another girl, Kathleen, in 1896. One other boy died in infancy. All of the children, except Nora and Kathleen, were born at home. The fact that Annie Barnacle went to a hospital for her second child suggests a problem with the birth; so does the timing of Nora's baptism — immediately after the birth.[5] Her name was registered as *Norah*. That is the way Mrs. Barnacle spelled her daughter's name all her life and the way Nora spelled it until she met James Joyce.

Tom Barnacle, thirteen years older than his wife, came from a line of Galway bakers and was well skilled at his trade by the time he married. Although he did have a few years of schooling, he was illiterate. At his marriage to Annie Healy in 1881, he had to sign the register with an X. Being unlettered, however, did not distinguish him from one-third of the population, and he was earning enough to pay the priest the decent-sized fee (one pound ten shillings) most middle-class families offered for a wedding.

In 1904, when James Joyce's father heard the surname of the girl with whom his son had run away, he exclaimed, as unable as his son ever to resist a pun, "Barnacle? She'll never leave him." In Galway, however, there can have been few people who bothered with the joke.

In the west of Ireland Barnacle was a common enough surname. It was derived from "barnacle goose," a large seabird that lives in the Arctic wastes and visits British and Irish estuaries in the winter. The way people in Galway still pronounce it — "Bearnacle" — carries a whiff of the origins of the bird's name: *bernekke* in Middle English and *bernaca* in medieval Latin. The goose was a fabled bird, long regarded with suspicion because it was believed to come from a shell that grew like a fruit on a tree and then dropped into the sea for nourishment.

In the twelfth century, the Welsh churchman Giraldus Cambrensis, on a visit to Ireland, saw (or so he claimed) more than a thousand barnacle geese enclosed in shells and hanging by their beaks from trees. He also observed that the Irish took advantage of this oddity to classify the bird as fish, not meat, thereby allowing themselves to eat it during Lent when meat was forbidden. In *Topographia Hiberniae,* Giraldus describes this as a symbol of deceitfulness — not of the bird but of the Irish.[6]

The name, however, is better known in the English translation of its original Irish form: *cadhan* (or, *O cadhain*). This became O Cadhain, then Kane, O Kane, and Coyne. There were Kanes and Coynes aplenty in Nora's Galway just as there were other Barnacles. Today the name survives in the west of Ireland (and in Boston, Massachusetts) as Barnicle.[7]

James Joyce never made his father's mistake. He had studied Irish for a year, with no particular enthusiasm — he disagreed with his teacher, the rabid nationalist Patrick Pearse, who did not believe that Irish writers should write in English — but the Barnacle-Cadhain-seabird connection is one he would have made.[8] Among the many tributes to Nora in his work are the many, often hidden, references to seabirds and geese, which he tucked into the text, much as medieval monks wove their favorite flowers and animals into their illuminated capitals. Among the notes for *Finnegans Wake,* he scribbled "glorious name of Irish goose."[9]

But the important fact in Nora's background was not whose daughter she was but whose niece. Her uncle Michael Healy was a prominent figure in Galway. The younger and cleverer of Nora's mother's two brothers, he did well at the Patrician Brothers' secondary school and went on to win a place in Her Majesty's Civil Service in 1883. Not long before, the British Civil Service had begun to fill its posts through competition rather than patronage, a move that assisted the entry of Catholics as well as Jews, Methodists, and others.

Michael Healy rose rapidly through the ranks. Starting as boatman second class in the Galway Customs Office, he was sent for five years to Liverpool. By the time Nora was an adolescent, he had returned to become collector of customs, enjoying modest power, total security, and a healthy income.[10] His name was listed among Galway's prominent citizens in the much-thumbed directories such as Kelly's and MacDonald's. He never married.

Nora's other maternal uncle was Thomas Healy; Uncle Tommy, Nora called him.[11] A tall, muscular man, he worked as a handyman and then also became, like Nora's father, a baker. Tom Healy married late, in the Irish manner (in 1898, when he was thirty-nine), and until his death in 1926 did little to distinguish himself — apart from a dramatic intervention in Nora's life in 1904 that changed the course of modern literature.

Both the Healys and the Barnacles and all their known forebears spent their entire lives in Galway City, scarcely venturing farther into the countryside than to Menlo Castle on the outskirts for the annual games on four Sundays in May, or to the pleasant bathing resort of Salthill, a two-mile tram ride out of the city.

Nora Barnacle, therefore, was irretrievably urban — not a barefoot peasant from the moorland like J. M. Synge's Pegeen Mike, desperate for any stranger to talk to, but a city girl, street-smart, with a ribbon in her hair, a sharp tongue in her head, and an uncle in the civil service. All the events of her early life, her homes, her schools, her jobs, her adolescent flirtations and griefs, took place within the narrow confines of the center of Galway, with its strong smells of the fish market and the stables, of peatsmoke, boiling potatoes, and cabbage. All Galway's landmarks — Lynch's Castle, the Old Jail, the cathedral, the railway station, the docks, O'Brien's Bridge, and Nun's Island — were places she passed every day.

It was a foretaste of the life she would share with James Joyce. As she accompanied him from city to city across Western Europe, and went on holiday in the finest resorts, the last thing either wanted was to get away from people.

Nora's mother had married beneath her. Like Joyce's father in his own marriage, she never forgot it. But whatever the social differences between the Barnacles and the Healys, property ownership was not one of them. In turn-of-the-century Ireland, Catholics had not yet advanced very far toward the status of homeowner. Neither the Barnacles nor the Healys had a permanent home.

Before Nora left Galway in 1904 her parents had changed address seven times — another pattern that was to mark her later life. As their brood grew, Annie and Thomas Barnacle peregrinated through a tight circle of tenements and small houses at shabby addresses in the heart of Galway: Abbeygate Street, Raleigh Row, Newtownsmyth. They came to rest sometime after 1896 in a one-up, one-down artisan's dwelling in an L-shaped back street near Lynch's Castle called Bowling Green. Part of a terrace, or row of houses, the little house contained a main room with a fireplace out of the side of which a staircase led to the single bedroom. Houses like it in which families of eight, nine, ten, or more lived can be seen today in the Ulster and Welsh Folk Museums in Belfast and Cardiff. In the nineteenth-century Celtic world, sleeping arrangements were as casual as mealtimes, and no one fussed about crowding or improvising.

It is to this small terrace house at 8 Bowling Green (formerly number 4) that literary tourists come to stare at "the home of Nora Barnacle." But the house was mainly the home of Nora's mother, who lived there from 1899 until her death in 1939. Nora spent much of her childhood elsewhere.

When Nora was two, her sister Bridget (also called Delia or Dilly) was born, followed in 1889 by twin girls. At one or another of these births (accounts vary and there is no written record) Nora was sent to live with her maternal grandmother, Catherine Mortimer Healy. This was Nora's first exile and the one that most shaped her personality.

In leaving the crowded nest, Nora gained many material advantages. She probably had better food than was served at her mother's table, where there were so many mouths to feed. At her Grandmother Healy's, she enjoyed lemonade and currant cake, a piano, and pictures on the walls, which were decorated with holly and ivy at Christmas. Her grandmother was kind to her. When her best friend, Emily Lyons, left for America and Nora wept inconsolably, Mrs. Healy gave her a new pinafore to wear and sat her down by the fire with bread and butter. Michael Healy tried to cheer her up with a new pair of buttoned-up boots.[12] Her grandmother also taught Nora (as she had taught Nora's mother) good table manners and the polite forms of speech. But Nora never forgave her mother for shutting her out.

Mrs. Healy's house was on Whitehall, a dead-end extension of St. Augustine Street, near the docks. It was a noisy building fronting the street and at the back looked out on the back entrance to the Castle Military Barracks where the cavalry was billeted. Nora thus was only a few minutes from her mother at Bowling Green and saw her often, probably turning up many days at tea time, a bread-and-butter meal washed down by endless cups of tea — another custom to which she clung across Europe.

Being sent to be fostered, common as that practice was, broke Nora's bond with her mother. She was her own woman from then on, independent, with some bitterness but without self-pity, and conscious from an early age of the qualities with which she would make her way in the world: amiability and stoicism. Ironically, it may have been Nora's singularly pleasing disposition and humor (traits common in second children) that marked her out for fostering. A grandmother may be willing to help out by taking a grandchild into her home, but she will prefer one who is easy to manage and provides good company.

All evidence is that by the age of five Nora was well on her way to becoming the typical Galway woman of the nineteenth century. The Galway-born writer Eilis Dillon has described such women as "tall, muscular and resourceful [because] deserted by disease and emigration . . . with a better sense of humour than the men" but also with "a depressed quality in their minds which makes them accept a bad situation."[13]

It is part of the myth of the chambermaid who ran off with the artist that Nora was ignorant and untutored. "Just think!" tourists have been heard to say at the Joyce Musuem in the Martello tower at Sandycove. "She was illiterate!" The belief adds to the *frisson* of the genius with the dunce, but it is false. Nora went to school until she was twelve — the usual leaving age of that time. She had the maximum schooling that was available without fees to girls of that day. Many of both sexes had less.

Galway, said the *Galway Year Book,* with a firm Protestant air, had four "nunneries . . . devoted to the instruction of the female children of the poor, to the education of the higher classes and the relief of the indigent."

It was at one of these, the Convent of Mercy, that Nora began her education in 1889 when she was five. The convent, of gray limestone like the Workhouse, was in the quarter of Galway known as Newtownsmyth, just behind Bowling Green. Nora's mother had been a pupil there before her. In October 1892 Nora passed into its junior or "national" school where she studied the three Rs as well as grammar, geography, needlework, music, and drawing.[14] Those who equate Nora with Molly Bloom in *Ulysses* should note that she got good grades in spelling and writing.

These were not the brightest of girls perhaps. All, Nora included, repeated years (Nora did the fourth year twice), but the reason was as often economic as academic: many stayed on at school until their families needed them to go to work or work could be found for them. Yet even if they had been intellectually gifted, they would not have been treated any differently. The aim of the school was to prepare girls for the reality ahead, which was the same whether they emigrated or stayed in Ireland: housework. For girls there was no free secondary education comparable to that available to bright boys like Nora's uncle, Michael Healy. Nora never had a hope or a thought of it.

Young women of her generation did occasionally go to take university degrees, but these came from well-to-do families who could afford to send them to convent preparatory schools. Even within the impoverished Galway Catholic society in which Nora lived, there were subtle gradations. Shopkeepers and tradesmen felt superior to those who worked with their hands or lived on charity. Thus Nora Barnacle, with a baker for a father and her Healy connections, was a cut above her classmates at the Mercy School such as Cissey Casey, whose father was a porter, or Bridget Fahy, who was an orphan.

Nora left school in April 1896 at the age of twelve. The Mercy sisters found her a good job: porteress at the Presentation Convent even nearer her mother's and grandmother's homes. The Presentation Order was considered to carry a higher social rank than the Sisters of Mercy, and it is solid testimony to Nora's appearance and affability that the Mercy sisters put her forward to open the Presentation's door. To act as go-between between the silent world of the cloister and the rough world outside was not inappropriate training for what Nora's future held in store.

About the time that Nora left school, Mrs. Barnacle, exhibiting the strength of her breed, threw her husband out. Tom Barnacle had a familiar failing. He drank. His habits had cost him his own bakery shop, but, a journeyman baker, he was much in demand as a free lance at bakeries from Galway City to Oughterard, fourteen miles away.

James Joyce later made much of the irresponsibility of the father-in-law he had never seen. "Papa drank all the buns and loaves like a man," he wrote to his brother Stanislaus (as if he himself were in the habit of bringing home a full pay packet every Friday night). But Barnacle the Baker, a thick-set man of about five foot nine, was liked in Galway for his good humor, his story telling, and his geniality. As Nora's local biographer, Canon Padraic O Laoi summarized Barnacle's Galway reputation, "True, he took a drink but he never disgraced his family." [15]

Nora, grumbling many years later to her youngest sister about the difficulties of being married to a writer, said, "He's a weakling, Kathleen. I always have to be after his tail. I wish I was married to a man like my father." [16]

Nora was obviously fonder of her father than Joyce cared to admit. He could tolerate no thought of a rival for Nora's affections. When he was alarmed by her nostalgia for the men of long ago, Joyce should have put Tom Barnacle at the top of the list.

Barnacle was good with children. Jim Byrne, the baker with whom he lodged in Oughterard, allowed him to look after his daughters, and they remember how he told them ghost stories by the fire. Nora may well have enjoyed the same treat. Joyce's Eveline is a girl who has a father who drinks, yet "Sometimes he could be very nice. Not long before when she had been laid up for a day, he had read her out a ghost story and made toast for her at the fire."

With her father gone, Nora saw her Uncle Michael become the male head of the household. Joyce told Stanislaus that "the mother's family are 'toney.' " [17] The Healys did put on airs. They had a penchant for being photographed by R. W. Simmons, Galway's most fashionable photographer, a man who justified his high prices with the slogan "A bad photograph is dear at any price." Simmons, who had a high-ranking clientele, headed by the Duke of Connaught, photographed Michael Healy several times. [18]

Simmons also took the picture that gives the best guess at what Nora looked like as she entered adolescence. It shows a tall young girl — as tall as the older woman beside her — with heavy black eyebrows, a generous but firm mouth, and shoulders held squarely back. She has a big bow in her wavy hair, which hangs girlishly loose, and wears an ugly, ill-fitting coat but also fine, apparently new, pointed boots. [19] Although the photograph, found among the Joyce papers in Trieste, bears no identification, several features mark the girl as Nora: the large hands, big-knuckled as a man's, the shape of the brows, the line of the mouth, and, above all, the strabismus or slight cast to the left eye that led Joyce to call her his "sleepy-eyed Nora." The tall, gray-haired woman standing at her side, to judge from her protective attitude and fine clothes, including a lapel watch and bracelet, could be Nora's grandmother, Catherine Healy.

The Healys' patronage of Simmons also reveals their politics. Simmons was well known as a unionist. No true Irish nationalist would have patronized him, according to Eilis Dillon.[20] The Healy family, especially Michael with his civil service position, were lifelong supporters of the British Crown. It was a loyalty Nora retained.

Nora was a very pretty girl. There are, as Norman Mailer wrote of Marilyn Monroe, a half dozen of her in every small town — girls with the looks and manner to make heads turn and tongues wag. Her most striking feature was her hair. She had a fresh complexion with high color, and the set of her eyes, which tilted downward at the outside corners, gave her a mocking air, with a touch of sultriness added by the droop to the left lid. And, like her mother, she had superb carriage. Nora walked with her head held high, arms swinging, with a long and confident stride. "We are all Irish, all kings' sons," says Mr. Deasy in *Ulysses*.[21] Nora walked royally ("like a queen," Joyce would later say), with classless Irish assurance, looking everybody straight in the eye.

Her pride, however, covered a sense of rejection and probably some guilt. Like many children sent from home, she may have felt that she had done something to deserve it; she may even have felt responsible for her father's leaving as well. But as a pretty girl she sought the time-honored solace: attracting a stream of admirers from an early age.

She had little difficulty, considering her charms. These included her voice. It was remarked upon by almost everyone who met her in later life: low, resonant, strong, and rich, with the tones of the Irish west.[22]

Nora had many admirers when young, including two who died. Her first serious crush, when she was approaching thirteen, was on a boy called Michael Feeney.[23] He was sixteen and a half and a schoolteacher. (Nora, in spite of her protestations, liked clever men.) She had known him all her life for he lived nearby, on William Street West. In February 1897 he fell ill with typhoid, followed by pneumonia, and was removed to the Workhouse where, after seven days, he died. He was buried at Rahoon Cemetery, two miles from Galway City.[24]

Nora was distraught with grief. It was a terrible winter for her. Only six weeks earlier, on New Year's Day, her beloved grandmother had also died — of bronchitis, at the age of sixty-seven, in the house they shared at Whitehall.[25] The only real home Nora had known was gone, and, with Emily Lyons gone to America, she had lost everybody she really loved.

What happened to her next is unclear. By 1901, when the decennial census was taken, she was living at her mother's home at 8 Bowling Green. Her profession (later to find echoes in the work of James Joyce) was listed as "laundress."[26] By 1904 she is known to have been living with her Uncle Tommy, but their address is not known. In 1897, when Mrs. Healy died, Tom Healy was still unmarried and living in a room on New Docks Street, not far away but unlikely to have been a home in which to accommodate a niece. Nora herself gave the only clue to her residence during the years around the turn of the century when she told a friend in Paris that during her girlhood for four years she lived at the convent.[27]

If Nora did go direct from her late grandmother's house to the Presentation Convent, it means that the events upon which Joyce drew for the background of his most famous short story, "The Dead," took place just before her thirteenth birthday. The details of her life in that year fit the story well.

In the closing pages of "The Dead," considered by many to be the finest short story in English, Gretta Conroy, a red-haired Irishwoman from the west, bursts into tears thinking of a boy she knew long ago. Her pompous husband, Gabriel, a Dubliner well known in intellectual circles, is stricken. He had been about to reach out to make love to his wife. Patronizingly, he asks who the young man was:

— It was a person I used to know in Galway when I was living with my grandmother, she said.

Gabriel coldly asks Gretta if she perhaps intends to visit this former lover when she visits Galway.

— He is dead, she said at length. He died when he was only seventeen. Isn't it a terrible thing to die so young as that?

Gabriel asks how the boy came to die so young. Was it consumption?

— I think he died for me, she answered.
A vague terror seized Gabriel at this answer as if, at that hour when he had hoped to triumph, some impalpable and vindictive being was coming against him, gathering forces against him in its vague world.

Gretta continues, without being asked. The boy's name was Michael Furey.

— It was in the winter, she said, about the beginning of the winter when I was going to leave my grandmother's and come up here to the convent. And he was ill at the time in his lodgings in Galway and wouldn't be let out, and his people in Oughterard were written to.

Furey, Gretta says, was a gentle boy with whom she used to go out walking. He had a very good voice but delicate health. Trying to control herself, she describes how she heard gravel thrown up against her window and ran down into the garden,

> and there was the poor fellow at the end of the garden, shivering.
> — And did you not tell him to go back? asked Gabriel.
> — I implored of him to go home at once and told him he would get his death in the rain. But he said he did not want to live. I can see his eyes as well as well! He was standing at the end of the wall where there was a tree.
> — And did he go home? asked Gabriel.
> — Yes, he went home. And when I was only a week in the convent he died and he was buried in Oughterard, where his people came from. O, the day that I heard that, that he was dead!

The proximity of Michael Feeney's death in February to that of Nora's grandmother on New Year's Day and the occasion of her leaving her grandmother's home make Feeney a closer model for the fictional Michael Furey than Nora's later admirer, Michael Bodkin, who has been widely cast in the part. Feeney's age — he was five months short of seventeen when he died — is more deserving of Gretta's "Isn't it a terrible thing to die so young as that?" — than Bodkin's. Bodkin died at twenty.[28] Furthermore, the names sound alike. The shift from *Feeney* to *Furey* is the kind of association of sounds that Joyce liked — what psychologists call a *Klanglink*.

The Presentation Convent, moreover, could have provided the setting for the famous scene. Nora's grandmother's house had no garden, but the nuns' garden behind the convent is spacious and penetrable, with the river Corrib running through it and with scalable walls. Boys still come in and steal the apples.[29] (In the story Joyce placed Gretta's grandmother's house on Nun's Island, a part of central Galway surrounded by the river and the canal.)

Life was cruel to the people of those times and to Nora. There is no doubt that she was very taken with the darkly handsome Michael Bodkin, who also died. Bodkin, whose father ran a sweetshop on Prospect Hill, went to work for the gas company after dropping out of the local university. Stricken with tuberculosis, he, like Michael Feeney, succumbed to the bleak midwinter and died on February 11, 1900. He too was laid to rest at Rahoon. Nora was then nearly sixteen.

In all likelihood, Joyce fused Nora's memories of her two lost friends. It hardly matters where he got the facts for "The Dead." Joyce rearranged and patterned his materials to suit his art and his ear. To understand Nora, however, it is important to know that as early as the age of twelve she was left without close maternal supervision and simultaneously began to see herself as a woman of dangerous sexual power. In fact, Joyce may have merged the two lovers into one not only for dramatic effect but for credibility. Few readers would have believed that a girl could have had two admirers who died, including one when she was as young as twelve.

Joyce, by the time he came to make notes for his highly autobiographical play, *Exiles,* implied that Nora had had two lovers who died, although he gave the names differently. The main female character, Bertha, is modeled on Nora. In Joyce's notes the entry under "N. (B)." says: "Bodkin died. Kearns died. At the convent they called her the man-killer. . . ."[30]

The man-killer jibe must have struck home. Nora had at least one other conquest on her conscience that the convent knew nothing about. When she was sixteen, a good-looking young priest had taken a liking to her and invited her to tea at the presbytery. During the visit, he pulled her onto his lap and began to explore under her dress with his hand. Nora broke away only to be told that it was she who had committed a sin. When she told it in confession, the priest said, she was not to say that the culprit was a priest but rather "a man."[31]

Nora was not fooled. Self-reproach was not her habit. Her mother could not bring her to heel. Mrs. Barnacle was an erratic disciplinarian. She had instilled good manners and tidiness into her girls and adamantly refused to allow any of them to wear make-up. But she had her own weaknesses (she used snuff heavily) and, still fresh in Galway memories, failed to curb Kathleen, who earned a local reputation for a rough tongue and hard drinking.[32] Annie Barnacle leaned heavily on her brothers, particularly Michael, who supported her large brood after she sent her husband packing.

It fell to Tom Healy, prompted perhaps by his new wife, Bedelia, to try to discipline his adventurous niece. He took to walking around Galway at night, swinging his blackthorn stick and looking for Nora. As he prowled, he whistled the Irish air "My Mountain Maid, Arise." Nora froze in dread when she heard it floating through the night.[33]

Nora would not be kept in. With her best friend, Mary O'Holleran, she found ways to escape. With Mary, she would dress up in men's clothes, hair tucked under a man's cap, and explore the streets of Galway and Eyre Square. Nora had the height, the swagger, the confidence, and the heavy brows to pass in the dark for a good-sized boy. Once they even spotted the dreaded Uncle Tommy; Mary said "Good evening" in a deep false voice and got away with it.

Cross-dressing was no light matter at the turn of the century. In Paris women were forbidden by a strictly enforced ordinance to wear male attire. In Ireland, the nationalist Fianna organization, wanting to dissuade the beautiful Countess Markiewicz (born Constance Gore-Booth of Lissadell) from marching with them, passed a resolution saying that it was an offense to participate in a public occasion except in a Fianna uniform. The determined countess outwitted them by getting a tailor to make her a uniform. Her boldness, however, extended only to the waist; below the soldier's jacket she wore a skirt.[34] For Nora, pulling on trousers and a cap took some daring and revealed an acceptance of the masculine elements in her personality.

Seeing how swiftly marriage could turn into disillusion and drunkenness in no way stopped Galway girls from dreaming about their true love. They played many superstitious games whose object was to reveal the name of their future husband. The games, classic examples of ancient marriage-divination rites, took on greater importance in the primitive west than in Dublin — not surprising, for the raw materials were nearer to hand. Mary O'Holleran described them in an interview for Richard Ellmann's biography of Joyce.

Nora and her girlfriends would fill their mouths full of wheat and run around the neighborhood, listening at doors. If a boy's name was mentioned, it was he who was to be their husband.[35] They would buy a penny's worth of pins, stick nine into an apple, throw the tenth away, and put the apple in their left stocking. They tied the stocking with their right garter and then went to bed, hoping to dream of their future husband.

The games rose to a pitch on Halloween. Nora and Mary would go into a strange garden and steal a head of cabbage. They would take the cabbage into a field, find a dunghill, and, standing on it and eating the cabbage, would look into a mirror. There they hoped yet again for a glimpse of the face of their future husband.

Most of the girls would eventually be rewarded with what Joyce contemptuously described to Nora as "red-headed louts."[36] Nora, as she looked into her mirror, must have hoped to see a vision resembling her dark and handsome lost lover, Michael Bodkin, not the long, humorous, bony countenance of James Joyce. But the ritual prepared her to expect a great change to come into her life out of the blue on one important day. No marriage manual could have been more instructive. It is a mark of Nora's character that as she played these games of destiny, she would burst out laughing, her head thrown back.

Nora was a pious girl and went to Mass regularly. When at school she belonged to the Sodality of the League of the Cross and, upon leaving, she joined the Sodality of the Sacred Heart. She went regularly to its meetings, went to confession at least once a month, and took communion in the cathedral on Sodality Sunday.[37] But she did not live in fear of the confessional. She was a tearaway, as wild as a respectable girl could be. She swore easily, sprinkling her conversation with "God" and "damn," and with her girlfriends, giggling in the dark, used to practice saying dirty words.[38] She was not embarrassed by her body; annoyed by the profusion of her pubic hair, she trimmed it back.[39]

Nora liked practical jokes and did not stop short of shoplifting. There was a sweetshop on Prospect Hill run by a Mrs. Francis, who was nearly blind. Nora would go in with Mary, order a ha'pennyworth of sweets and, while the old woman was fumbling around, put a pound weight on the scale. Sometimes they would simply pinch the sweets while the old lady's back was turned. The prank that most delighted them made a young neighbor, Jim Connell, their victim. Jim, who could not read, had been telling everybody about the letter he was expecting with the papers for his passage to America. Nora and Mary went out and bought the largest envelope they could find, filled it with a large card holding licorice sweets, and posted it to Jim Connell. When Connell received his official-looking envelope, he was so excited that he ran across to the O'Hollerans' to have his papers read to him. When he saw the trick that had been played on him, he was so furious that he blamed his fiancée and broke off the engagement. Nora and Mary, trying to contain their laughter, had to run and hide. They dared not, Mary remembered, "be seen for a week."[40]

Little is known of how Nora passed the years between leaving school and leaving Galway. There are no employment records. However, she seems not to have spent the whole time at the convent. She may have worked at O'Gorman's Bookbindery (why else would Joyce have sent O'Gorman's an autographed first edition of *Ulysses*?). She may have worked as a domestic for a doctor's family, but there were so many Barnacle sisters that no one is sure. That she did washing and ironing for a living, as the census report says, is probable. She was always good with clothes and linen, perhaps a skill acquired from her mother, who was a dressmaker. Many of her photographs suggest a facility with fabric, ribbons, and starched ruffles. Even as a girl, she liked good clothes and admired them on others. She was always well groomed.[41] As she grew into a young woman, she learned how to manage her heavy hair by pinning it into a chignon; she was good at ironing ruffles and tying bows. She liked to pin scented handkerchiefs into her clothes so that she exuded a scent of balsam or roses as she walked.

One day as Nora crossed O'Brien's Bridge there in her path stood a dapper young accountant with insolent eyes. Nora knew who he was. His name was William Mulvagh (pronounced "*Mul*-vey," almost in one gulp, with the accent on the first syllable).[42] He had gone to the country grammar school. The Mulvaghs were the only Protestants living on Mary Street. His sister was married and lived in Oughterard. Would Nora go out with him?

Nora did not know what to say. She was not wildly attracted to him, or so she told Mary, but girls in Galway needed a boyfriend if they wanted to go out in the evening or to dances. Nora loved dancing, particularly the dances held at the crossroads outside the city.[43] After consulting Mary, she decided that she would accept Mulvagh's invitation. He was a useful escort. Three years older than she, he had a job as an accountant at Joe Young's Mineral Water Factory (Nora never reached beneath her in her choice of suitors).

To walk out with Mulvagh meant deceiving Uncle Tommy. He had forbidden her to go out with Mulvagh because of his religion. Nora found a way. Enlisting Mary as conspirator, she would say in the evening that she was going to church. Then she and Mary would stroll together to the Abbey Church on Francis Street, and Nora would slip off to meet Willie, leaving Mary to wait alone (no doubt wondering what they were getting up to). When Nora returned, they would go to Mary's home, and Nora, laughing, would scatter the booty Willie had presented to her — chocolates and cream sweets — all over the O'Hollerans' table. Willie was very much in love with Nora.

What Nora and Willie did in the dark can never be known. However, the line "Mulveys was the first"[44] is well known to readers of Molly Bloom's monologue in *Ulysses,* although what Mulvey achieved is unclear. Nora was as aware as any Irish girl of the danger of premarital pregnancy. To have a child out of wedlock was ruin; to be known to have risked it was almost as scandalous. As Stanislaus Joyce was later to write about the Ireland of his boyhood, "If a couple is known to have had intercourse before marriage, it is remembered against them all their lives."[45] Galway was not as puritanical as Dublin, and its priests married many an expectant couple. Whatever the means used to avoid illegitimate births — emigration, infanticide, and suicide were the only other alternatives for the desperate; there was no contraception or abortion — they worked. The illegitimacy rate in Galway was next to nil. In 1901 Galway City registered only 11 bastards out of 895 births.[46]

On balance, it seems as if Willie Mulvagh may have been the first to instruct Nora in the art of pleasing a man without losing her virtue. In *Ulysses* Molly Bloom gives her own account of her initiation by Mulvey, the first man to put his tongue into her mouth: ". . . how did we finish it off yes O yes I pulled him off into my handkerchief . . ."[47]

Nothing interested Joyce more than Nora's sentimental education, as "The Dead" proves. In the case of Willie Mulvagh, whose very name Joyce bestowed on Molly Bloom's first lover (changing it only to read as pronounced), posterity is entitled to suspect that the young man from the mineral water factory and Nora Barnacle ventured further in their embraces than Nora revealed to her girlfriend waiting in the Abbey Church's pews.

Whatever was going on was too much for Nora's Uncle Tommy. He learned that she had been seeing Mulvagh, against orders, and caught her one night on her way home. "Well, my girl," he declared. "Out again with your Protestant!"[48] Annie Barnacle was there, and when Tom ordered her out of the room, Annie let her daughter down by obeying her brother rather than by remaining to protect her daughter. With Annie out of the way, Tom beat Nora with his thorn stick until she fell to the floor, clutching his knees and begging him to stop.

That, at least, is the story Nora told James Joyce. There are reasons for believing that it was not the whole truth.

It was common for young people to be beaten in turn-of-the-century families but not because they had consorted with someone of a different religion. The Galway of 1904 was not the Belfast of today. Relations between Protestants and Catholics in Galway at that time were excellent. Families of both religions lived side by side and visited each other's homes. On the solemn occasion when new nuns were received into the order of the Sisters of Mercy, the convent always invited Protestants to witness the ceremony.

That Nora's family should have told people that Nora left town because she was punished for going out with a Protestant only proves, according to Willie Mulvagh's daughter, simply "what a rough lot they were."[49] If Nora wanted to convert Willie, she had only to try. He became a Catholic when he married three years later, as did his brothers in turn.

It seems more likely that Nora was punished because her sultry glances and headstrong ways were making her an embarrassment to her family. By 1904 Michael Healy had reached the eminence of collector of customs, with a fine salary of perhaps £150 a year.[50] He was a man with a reputation to consider. He may even have persuaded his brother to take disciplinary action. (Although Michael Healy in later years generously assisted James Joyce, he is remembered in Galway as having been very strict with Nora.)[51] Tom Healy, for his part, may have equated Protestantism with libertinism; his niece was going out with a young man who did not need to confess to a priest.

In the story as she told it to Joyce, Nora concealed any worry her uncles had about her sexual magnetism. Yet she may have been alarmed by her own power herself. The deaths of Feeney and Bodkin were on her mind. So was her sin in tempting a priest beyond his strength. She may also have sensed an incestuous longing behind Tom Healy's rage.[52]

One week after the beating Tom Healy had no niece left to thrash. There were several domestic service agencies in Galway; one of them, run by a Mrs. Finn on Lower Dominick Street, was right in Nora's daily path. Any of them could have provided information about work in Dublin. Nora took her chances. From what she had seen of life, the words of the prayer to the Virgin at the end of the Mass were true: life was a vale of tears. In Dublin it could be no worse. She slipped out of the house and out of Galway. She did not bother to say goodbye to "her Protestant" or to her mother.

3

The Summer
of 1904

"CHANCE," James Joyce once said, "furnishes me what I need. I am like a man who stumbles along; my foot strikes something, I bend over and it is exactly what I want."[1]

On Nassau Street in Dublin on June 10, 1904, chance furnished him Nora Barnacle. Joyce, then twenty-two, saw Nora and accosted her, much as Willie Mulvagh had the year before on a Galway bridge.

Love at first sight is grossly underestimated; a single glance can take the whole person. Not that Joyce could see very much. In 1904, although he had had trouble with his eyes all his life, he was not wearing glasses, for a doctor had advised him that going without might strengthen his sight. All he could have made out as he peered nearsightedly at the tall young woman was her figure, her hair, and her stride. The way she moved, arms swinging, was enough to win him. *Sauntering* was to be one of his favorite words for it; *proud* was another, by which he meant a confident woman, one whose hips could be seen moving beneath her skirt.[2]

It was part of the genius of James Joyce myopically to pick from a crowd the woman essential to his art. With the same sureness with which all his life he took what he needed, he introduced himself. Her voice and her broad, open face told him she was from the west, and his delight can be imagined when he heard that she had a name out of Ibsen. Ibsen was Joyce's idol, for the honesty and realism of his plays and especially for his understanding of women. (All literary Dublin knew that Joyce, when only seventeen, had published an article on Ibsen in the respected London *Fortnightly Review*. When from the dark north a grateful letter had come to the review's editor from the Master himself, Joyce's friends and teachers began to realize that perhaps James Joyce was more than an arrogant prophet of his own artistic destiny.)[3]

The very sound of Nora's name appealed to Joyce as well. A trained singer with a fine light tenor voice, he always warmed to the vowel sounds of $\overline{oo}$ and $\overline{o}$. (He was later to draw on them in choosing names for his children, Giorgio and Lucia, and for two of his principal literary creations, Molly and Leopold Bloom.) Would Nora have sauntered so easily into his soul if her name had been Bridget or Mabel?

Nora too liked what she saw: a slim young man with soft, dark brown hair, a long, thin face, jutting chin, and intense, pale, almost translucent blue eyes.[4] The thrust of his jaw tilted his whole face up; he looked at her with a cocky, expectant charm. Because of his slenderness and erect bearing, Joyce looked taller than he was. At five foot ten he was about the same height as Nora's father and not much taller than Nora herself. His name also fell happily on her ears: two alliterative monosyllables, the second of which (like Bodkin's) was one of Galway's fine family names. She agreed to meet him the following Tuesday evening at 8:30 beside Sir William Wilde's house at the corner of Merrion Square, a local landmark and close to where she was working but far enough away for her to be unobserved.

Nora had landed on her feet in coming to Dublin. She had found a job at Finn's Hotel on Leinster Street, the eastern extension of Nassau Street. Small (with only twelve rooms) and shabby but respectable and central, Finn's occupied the first two of the row of red brick eighteenth-century houses that forms part of the wall around Trinity College, Ireland's Protestant university. From her room high up in Finn's, Nora could look down into the heart of what Joyce's wealthy friend Oliver St. John Gogarty (one of the few Catholics to hold a degree from Trinity at that time) called "Trinity swank."

Dublin's most elegant shops, on Kildare, Dawson, and Grafton streets, were nearby. Within a few minutes Nora could walk to gaze at the latest fashions in the windows of Brown Thomas or at the cakes piled high at Bewley's Café, and she could sense the nearness of the Continent as travelers went to and from the boat-trains at Westland Row Station, around the corner and behind Finn's.

Finn's Hotel bordered the turf that Joyce and his friends called their own. They were students or graduates of University College, Dublin, the Jesuit institution on nearby St. Stephen's Green, and they lounged around the National Library on Kildare Street, arguing with each other and watching the street scene.

Joyce was at a loose end. In 1902 he had received a lazy "pass" degree from University College in what were considered women's subjects, French and Italian. During his university years, he had failed to display the dazzling brilliance he had shown at his preparatory school, Belvedere, where at fifteen he had come in first in all of Ireland in English composition. After taking his degree, he had spent some months in Paris, trying to study first medicine, then law; he then tried his hand at literary journalism. It was a miserable time, and he suffered from hunger and terrible toothaches. But since returning to Dublin and especially since his mother had died in August 1903, he had surrendered to dissipation, working fitfully at teaching and writing and doing nothing to help his father with the burden of supporting nine younger children.[5]

Yet Joyce's friends treated him with wariness and respect. They feared the power of his pen and his conviction of his own greatness.

It is possible that Joyce and his crew knew Nora by sight. He had three close friends in 1904: Gogarty, then a medical student; Vincent Cosgrave, also a medical student; and John Francis Byrne, the model for Cranly in *A Portrait of the Artist as a Young Man*. It is likely that the arrival on the scene of a statuesque and sexy redhead with no visible escort would have caught the notice of such practiced girl watchers. In later years Byrne was to maintain that their mutual friend Cosgrave introduced Nora to Joyce.[6]

Nora often told the story of how she met Joyce, and she did not always tell it the same way. Sometimes she had him wearing a sailor's cap and looking like a Swedish sailor; at others she remembered him in a big, white sombrero and a long overcoat that hung down to his feet. (As Joyce was affecting both costumes that summer — the bohemian garb, round, wide-brimmed hat and flowing tie, brought back from Paris, and the "yachting" outfit — she probably saw a lot of both.) To her sister she said he had looked strange, severe, very much like a little boy with a whiff of Michael Bodkin about him. And she never forgot his shabby shoes.[7]

At Finn's Nora could only have been earning a shilling or two a week, but the money mattered less than the provision of board and room. The proprietress of Finn's knew she was supplying an alternative to the emigrant ships and that girls in Dublin were lucky to find any work at all. Joyce's many sisters were endlessly applying and reapplying for jobs, and his sister May, sixteen and still living at her father's home in 1907, was delighted to win a place "at business" for three shillings a week: "The position is not a very good one, but the best feature of the thing is that I have all my meals there, breakfast, dinner and tea, and at each meal we get the best of everything."[8]

Nora had no illusions about the perils of the unprotected penniless female. The very names of charitable institutions around her were a warning: The National Hospital for Consumption for Ireland was just along Leinster Street from Finn's, past the ironmonger's and cleaner's. There was the Asylum for the Female Blind of Ireland, the Retreat for

Respectable Protestant Poor, St. Patrick's Hospital for Idiots and Luna-
tics, the Female Orphan House, and the Protestant Association for the
Education and Support of the Destitute Orphans of Mixed Marriages.

Her hours at Finn's were long, but, in theory at least, Nora had every
other evening free. Sometimes she had two or three free nights in a row.
If things were busy, however, she had to sacrifice her night off and sometimes had to work until two o'clock in the morning, even though there
was breakfast to be served in just a few hours.[9]

Nora is remembered as a chambermaid; however, she not only made
beds but also waited on tables and, because she was personable and competent, worked at the bar. (It was a duty carrying higher status for it
involved handling money, but the term *barmaid* would be much used
against her in later years.)[10] In every way at Finn's she enjoyed greater
independence and companionship than she would have as a servant in a
private house.

Nora was lonely in Dublin, though, and she was not used to loneliness.
The city, with its trams, theaters, commuters, and floating population,
was a metropolis compared to friendly Galway, where she seemed to
know everybody. Often her natural good spirits gave way to fits of gloom
and odd aches and pains.[11] Her free time hung heavy. Unless she spoke
to strangers she would have had no friends at all, except the girls at the
hotel.

In Dublin, far more than in Galway, Nora was vulnerable to unwanted
male attentions. One of the guests at Finn's, a Mr. Holohan, cast lewd
eyes upon her and propositioned her, showing her a condom invitingly.[12]
Nora was unimpressed. Joyce's story "The Dead" is opened by a sharp-
tongued serving girl, Lily. Lily's bitter words — "The men that is now is
only all palaver and what they can get out of you" — sound like Nora's.
If they did not drop straight from Nora's lips, they undoubtedly were in
her mind. Wariness of the male was Nora's strategy for survival.

When a well-mannered, well-spoken, amusing, and unthreatening young
man stepped into her path one day in Dublin, therefore, Nora was quite
happy to accept his invitation to meet him one evening.

But she did not appear. Joyce took himself to the appointed place at
the appointed time and waited until he gave up. A man more sure of
himself with women would have gone round to the hotel to find out what
had gone wrong. Joyce instead wrote Nora a letter. Its first words, ironically prophetic, convey the haze through which, even at twenty-two, he
peered at the world:

60 Shelbourne Road
June 15, 1904

I may be blind. I looked for a long time at a head of reddish-brown hair and
decided it was not yours. I went home quite dejected. I would like to make

an appointment but it might not suit you. I hope you will be kind enough to make one with me — if you have not forgotten me!

James A Joyce.[13]

Nora had not forgotten him. Most probably she failed to keep the rendezvous because she could not get the evening off and had no way of letting him know. Once she had received his letter with his address, however, she was able to accept his second invitation and that time did not disappoint him.

Was the day of their first date Thursday, the sixteenth of June, 1904? Probably. That is the best that can be said. There is no evidence from letters or diaries that June 16 was the day that divided the lives of Nora Barnacle and James Joyce into before and after — none, apart from the date of the action of *Ulysses*.

To Richard Ellmann, the literary evidence that Nora and Joyce first walked out together on June 16 was overwhelming. "To set *Ulysses* on this date was Joyce's most eloquent if indirect tribute to Nora," says Ellmann. "It was the day upon which he entered into relation with the world around him and left behind the loneliness he had felt since his mother's death."[14]

Herbert Gorman, an earnest American writer who danced around Joyce in the late 1920s and 1930s, trying to prepare an authorized biography, tried to find out from Joyce himself. When Gorman timidly submitted a biographical questionnaire to the then-great author, he received (in what looks like Nora's handwriting) answers to all the queries but one:

Q: Why did you pitch on June 16, 1904 for Bloomsday? Was it the day you met Nora?
A: Reply later.[15]

Gorman never received his answer. In his book, published in 1941, he concluded that there was "no evidence that anything unusual happened to Joyce six days after his first meeting with Nora Barnacle."[16]

The origin of the date obviously was something Joyce did not want known — perhaps because the association was too personal and too shocking.

When Nora joined him at the corner of Merrion Square for their first meeting, Joyce did not take her to any of the theaters or cafés in the center of Dublin, but rather to the east, past the docks and toward the harbor, to the area, deserted at night, known as Ringsend. The attraction between them was immediate, and Nora, who had to be back at Finn's by half past eleven, wasted no time. To Joyce's grateful astonishment, she unbuttoned his trousers, slipped in her hand, pushed his shirt aside, and, acting with some skill (according to his later account), made him a man.[17]

Another man might have congratulated himself on his luck and pressed for a quick seduction. Instead it was Joyce who was seduced. Nothing in his experience, from his pious mother to the Jesuits, had prepared him for the frankness and directness of Nora's sexual approach. Instead of losing respect for her, he fell in love for life.

In his heart, however, Joyce knew that young girls do not do such a thing for the first time unless they have been instructed by a man. The year before, reviewing some romantic novels, he had used the phrase "a girl of wayward habits," so he was well aware that there was a category of girl between his prim sisters and the brazen whores of the Kips — Dublin's brothel quarter, where he had been accustomed to find his sexual gratification.[18]

Five years later his suspicions would burst out and he would remind her accusingly how readily she had embraced him, how shamelessly she had touched him first and let her hands wander over his body. Had she never, he asked belatedly, touched a penis before her fingers made their way to his?[19]

That Nora should have acted so boldly with a stranger on the first date suggests the possibility of a mild form of soliciting. It cannot be ruled out; prostitutes did ply their trade on Nassau Street.[20] Nora was very short of money, and Ringsend was not the place where a nice girl would expect to be taken for an evening of social conversation. In Galway, where Nora's reputation is just recovering from the disgrace of her having lived unmarried for many years with the notorious author of a dirty book, there is still speculation about the legendary meeting in the street. "She made herself an easy mark," they say, "picking up a man like that."[21]

If Nora was intending to exchange favors for money, she had the wrong man. Joyce was a genius of a scrounge. It was more likely that he took money from her. Another of the short stories in Dubliners, "Two Gallants," written the following year, portrays a conceited young Dublin blade who has a servant girlfriend. The girl, believing him to be "a bit of class," yields to him on the first date, then later gives him a gold coin. "But what if she gets pregnant?" asks his envious friend. "She's up to the dodge" is the confident answer.

Nora, from her Galway encounters, knew how to dodge pregnancy. She acted as she did, in all likelihood, because she craved companionship and was eager to please. Their own private feelings that first night at Ringsend are suggested in a passage early in Ulysses, where the voice and thoughts of Stephen Dedalus, Joyce's alter ego, mix with the voice of a girl he has picked up:

Touch me. Soft eyes. Soft soft soft hand. I am lonely here. O, touch me soon, now. What is that word known to all men? I am quiet here alone. Sad too. Touch, touch me.[22]

system. There were five deliveries a day, with the first collection at quarter past one in the morning. Joyce, who liked to write in the small hours of the morning, took full advantage of the service. After he came in from seeing Nora, he would stay up writing long, painful, self-revealing letters ("It is only fair that you should know my mind on most things") and took them to the box, confident that she would get them in the morning. Both of them relied on letters posted before lunch to make or cancel a date that same evening, as Nora did in her first rushed letter of June 23 to let him know that she could not meet him.[30]

Their exchange of correspondence that summer disproves any suggestion that Nora was illiterate. The long, self-analytical letters he wrote her that summer reveal far more directly even than *A Portrait of the Artist* Joyce's state of mind as a young man; they are not the type of letters addressed to an inferior intelligence. Joyce wooed Nora with words, and he wanted hers. On July 12 he begged her to write him. Nora obliged. By early September he was able to boast that he had collected thirteen letters from her.[31]

Nora was not long in learning that Joyce, with his intense imagination, found many ordinary things extraordinary. Women's garments, for example, he seemed to find as exciting as their bodies. One evening he stole one of her gloves and took it to bed with him. He wrote her coyly that "it lay beside me all night — unbuttoned — but otherwise conducted itself very properly — like Nora."[32] He knew she would catch the double meaning of *unbuttoned*. At the same time, he gave Nora her first instruction on the use of letters as erotic objects when he asked her to take his letter into bed with her.

On July 21 he gave her a pair of gloves to compensate for the glove he had stolen. He knew how much new ones cost; he knew from his sisters how expensive such small luxuries were.

As the summer wore on and he became more and more attached to Nora, Joyce showed the first signs of suspiciousness. She had three free evenings in a row that he could not account for. Where would she be, he wanted to know, that she could not meet him on Saturday, Sunday, or Monday?[33] There is no record of her answer.

In spite of their absorption in each other, Joyce and Nora were conventionally formal in their written forms of address. Joyce, for whom all words had near-magical power, attached particular taboos to the use of his first name. Even though by July 8, for example, he could greet her as "Little Pouting Nora," he signed off as "J.A.J." Even when he told her that he was becoming closer to her than to anyone he knew because when he was with her he dropped his usual cynicism, he could not decide what to sign himself and so did not sign anything at all.[34] Sometimes he hid behind fey pseudonyms: W. B. Yeats or Vincenzo Varnutelli. It was September before he could bring himself to write "Jim" — a confession of

intimacy that, as much as anything, signified his formal commitment to
Nora. Nora accepted the privilege proudly and ostentatiously called him
"Jim" in front of the friends who called him (as was the custom) only by
his surname. Yet when signing her name for him she too was restrained
by convention. Her letter beginning "My Precious Darling" ended "N
Barnacle"; another opening with "my dearest" closed "with kisses Norah Barnacle."

Much has been made of the social difference between James Joyce and
Nora Barnacle, yet, with the enormous exception of their educations,
were they so different? Joyce had experienced the two great fears of Irish
life — hunger and eviction — and Nora had had a far from comfortable
life in Galway. Both came from drunken fathers disappointed at having
too many daughters (John Joyce had produced six out of ten, Tom Barnacle six out of eight), fathers who did not trouble themselves unduly
about supporting the large brood they had sired. For both John Joyce
and Tom Barnacle, breadwinning consisted of moving the family to cheaper
quarters. The Joyces were even more nomadic than the Barnacles; between the years of James Joyce's birth and the time he met Nora, his
family had moved thirteen times.

Both had suffered the brutality of a loveless home. Joyce's mother,
downtrodden as she was, was no soft disciplinarian herself. (One of her
punishments, the young Joyce boasted to a friend, was to stick her children's heads into the toilet bowl and pull the chain.)[35] Both had lived at
close quarters with zealous members of religious orders. Both had joined
holy sodalities. Both had a strong sense of ritual and loved celebrating
holidays. Most important, both had been thrust from the nest early. Joyce,
at six, had been sent to boarding school; the early pages of A Portrait
convey the childish longing for mother, the fear of wetting the bed, and
the yearning for the holidays of a child away from home.

Sexually too they were similar, rebels by the standards of their families.
Joyce's first sexual encounter had been with a prostitute when he was
fourteen. By the time he met Nora he had had a bout of venereal disease,
and, to judge from his correspondence with Gogarty, in February 1904,
a recurrence.[36] Even his sister Poppie knew that, as Stanislaus confided
to his private diary, "Jim and Charlie whore."

Joyce was ripe for rescuing. During his four months in Paris he had
been tormented by fantasies of homosexuality and sadomasochism and
did not know where his instincts, unrestrained, might lead him.

He did know they imperiled his art. In Nora he sensed his rescuer — a
woman who would save him, satisfy him, and forgive him. "You were to
my young manhood," he later told her, "what the idea of the Blessed
Virgin was to my boyhood." (In Stephen Hero, Joyce's autobiographical

novel that became *A Portrait,* it was "to Mary, as to a weaker and more engaging vessel of salvation" that Stephen prayed.)[37]

A decade earlier, Joyce and Nora might have been separated by an economic gulf. John Joyce had started life well-off; his own mother had been widowed early and had never remarried, leaving John, her only child, with an independent income from family properties in Cork.

For his rapid financial decline, John Joyce never ceased to blame his marriage into a family of lower station, the despised Murrays. But it was apparent to everyone else that his own extravagance was his ruin. In 1894 he was forced to sell the Cork real estate (for £1,875) to pay off debts. From then on he sank faster and deeper into debt, leading his family into increasingly shabby quarters, until by 1904 the small house in which he and nine children were squeezed was hardly more commodious than the Barnacles' cramped cottage at Bowling Green, Galway. Joyce summed up the father of Stephen Dedalus in *A Portrait* as a

> medical student, an oarsman, a tenor, an amateur actor, a shouting politician, a small landlord, a small investor, a drinker, a good fellow, a storyteller, somebody's secretary, something in a distillery, a tax-gatherer, a bankrupt and at present a praiser of his own past.[38]

By 1904, in fact, the annual income (about £150) of Nora's upwardly mobile Uncle Michael was more than double that of Joyce's father. By 1904 John Joyce, after cashing in part of his pension to buy a house and then losing the house, received only £70 a year in pension.

It was in their respective mothers' responses to their fate that Nora's experience most differed from Joyce's. Annie Barnacle and May Joyce were nothing alike. Mrs. Joyce, before dying of cancer at the age of forty-four, produced a child almost every year. Taking into account several miscarriages as well, there were few stretches in her adult life when she was not pregnant. She followed the teachings of her church absolutely. She did not refuse to perform her conjugal duties, whatever her condition. Stanislaus, who grew far more anti-Catholic and anti-Irish than his elder brother ever became, was revolted by his mother's passivity. "She ought to have rebelled," he wrote later. "But in that hateful country and hateful times in which she lived it would have required very considerable strength of character, which she did not possess."[39] Once May Joyce had considered leaving her husband; she told her priest, who was furious and sent her back.

Annie Barnacle, in contrast, not only threw her husband out when she could take no more of him but applied for a legal separation order that enabled her to receive, in addition to the support she received from her brother Michael, twelve shillings and sixpence a week from the state.[40]

Mrs. Barnacle, to be sure, never lived in fear of the physical abuse that May Joyce suffered. Stanislaus recalled his father (whom he loathed) lunging at their mother, shouting, "'Now, by God, is the time to finish it!'" The younger children ran screaming from the room, but James quick-wittedly "sprang onto his [father's] back and overbalanced him so that they tumbled on the floor."[41] When a police sergeant called at the house a few days later to discuss the row, the noise of which had reached the neighbors, Stanislaus interpreted it as the final slide to the lower classes: "We were, at last, on the same level as the navvies and farm-labourers around us."

Sensitive as he was to his own family's decline, Joyce was acutely conscious of slights to Nora. Someone may have called her "countrycute" (a jibe applied to Gretta in "The Dead"). Joyce did not spare Nora's feelings. "Certain people who know that we are much together often insult me about you," he told her, as if it would not hurt her feelings.[42] Nora may have sensed, from Joyce's hostility to Lady Gregory and her circle, how many of his supposed admirers looked down on him.

Anglo-Irish Dublin literary society was very exclusive; W. B. Yeats froze a man who came to his salon uninvited. To people from Protestant professional or landed backgrounds, Joyce, from the Catholic urban, lower middle class, looked distinctly seedy. George Moore, the novelist and playwright, later described Joyce as nothing but a beggar.[43] When Joyce's works later gave offense because of their coarseness, many like Moore shrugged as if they could expect no better.

There was a snobbery among Irish Catholics as well. Joyce had attended two famous schools, Clongowes Wood College in County Kildare, as a boarder, and, later, Belvedere College in Dublin, because his father, immensely proud of his son, insisted that he have the best. Both schools were run by Jesuits. In between, poverty forced Joyce to attend a school run by the less elegant Christian Brothers, but his father took him away, unhappy that his son should be keeping company with "Paddy Stink and Mickey Mud." But at the better schools Joyce was among the poorer boys, and in later years the rector of Belvedere was to say of Joyce, "It was a mistake to educate a boy here when his background was so much at variance with the standards of the school." His father, said the rector, was a "bounder."[44]

Joyce's medical friend Oliver Gogarty was a rarity among Catholics because he came from three generations of medical men. Gogarty was free, says his biographer, Ulick O'Connor, "from that sense of inferiority and insecurity that affected Catholics of his generation."[45] His Trinity degree and time at Oxford had given Gogarty an overcompensating arrogance. He was patronizing toward Joyce when they were friends and later scathing. Joyce was "not top drawer," said Gogarty. "He was not from any drawer at all."[46] He pitied Joyce, Gogarty said, seeing him torn between "a miserable background and sumptuous education," with his father an alcoholic and his mother "a naked nerve." Gogarty also (as many would later) saw something petty bourgeois in Joyce's excessive courtesy: "He had the formal and diffident manners of a lay brother in one of the lower orders of the Church."[47]

Given his background, it is not surprising, therefore, that Joyce found middle-class Dublin girls coy, unattainable, and condescending. Joyce never felt comfortable with such girls, he told Nora. He found them artificial and insincere.[48] The salon he knew best was that of the Sheehys. David Sheehy was the member of Parliament for Galway, and he had two sons and four daughters, of whom Joyce was for a time enamored of the prettiest, Mary. He spent many evenings in their drawing room at Belvedere Place, just off Mountjoy Square, singing and playing charades. It was the highest he rose in genteel Dublin society. Yet the four Sheehy sisters thought he was uncouth, if amusing and talented. *Farouche* was the word that Hanna Sheehy later chose to describe him — that is, wild and savage. Their mother had to give him a clean shirt when he came to her "evenings." But, Hanna recalled, there was also something "terribly serious about him."[49]

Stanislaus, who was seldom invited out into Dublin society, even to the Sheehys', believed that Mary Sheehy was the only other girl who ever aroused any flicker of emotion in his brother James, but that "compared with the 'wild, radiant' enduring passion, of which he soon after showed himself to be capable, it could not be called love."[50]

Stanislaus knew condescension when he saw it. He felt that the Sheehy girls, the "wise virgins" of society, were excited by his brother's genius and wild ways. The way that the girls flattered Jim made "the dullard" (as Stanislaus referred to himself) envious, but "they will not meet him on the highways alone, nor will they marry him."[51]

After dreaming of gentle, well-bred girls with cool hands, therefore, Joyce unhesitatingly chose as his life's partner a tough, unpolished, rootless, provincial girl unburdened by family, a Catholic girl without a Catholic conscience.

To pretend, however, that Joyce was immune from serving-girl fantasies himself would be wrong. His family, when Joyce was about thirteen and they were still prosperous, employed a hoydenish serving girl of twenty-three or so. One day Joyce playfully pulled her over his knee and spanked her. The incident would have been forgotten had not Stanislaus been called for interrogation by the Jesuit rector of Belvedere. The rector probed for evidence of immorality in Stanislaus's brilliant, wayward brother, and Stanislaus blurted out the story from the past. "Such was (and is) the dominance of the priest in Irish life that it never entered my head that he had no right to do so," Stanislaus said. The rector, naturally, took the tale straight back to Joyce's mother and told her her son was inclined to evil ways. She, unsurprisingly, blamed the girl, who had left their service long before. Joyce's father went to see the rector, who warned him, "That boy will give you trouble." "No, he won't," said John Joyce, in words that came back to taunt him, "because I won't let him." (James, however, just laughed and called Stanislaus a fathead.)[52]

Joyce undoubtedly was attracted by Nora's simplicity. "I have *enormous* belief in the power of a simple honourable soul," he once told her.[53] But he was also excited by the serving girl's vulnerability and availability — a theme he made good use of in *Dubliners*. The sharp-tongued Lily in "The Dead" shows that he did not regard them all as stupid. But as Joyce told Mary Colum, an Irish writer friend, "I hate intellectual women."[54] By moving Nora to a series of unfamiliar environments and retaining the power of the purse, he kept her, in a sense, in servitude.

Joyce liked to think that all women were instinctive, mindless creatures. "Do you notice," he asked Stanislaus once, "how women when they write disregard stops and capital letters?"[55] It was a self-serving observation. At University College he attended its women's affiliate, St. Mary's University College, and met many young women who understood the niceties of punctuation and a good deal more. Hanna Sheehy and Mary Colum (then Mary Maguire) were among them, but in general he avoided what he called "female fellows." When a woman undergraduate at the college received a postcard with a rude message on it and assumed that James Joyce had sent it, she wrote him to protest. Joyce replied icily that it was inconceivable that he, James A. Joyce, had written such a postcard as he never communicated with women students unless they were family friends. The truth was that by the time he reached the university, his family had sunk so low that there were no women students who were family friends.

But Nora knew that she had caught a literary man who loved her words as well as her body and (as he kept insisting) her soul. "Write to me, Nora," he begged. He did not try to interpret his writing for her, but he made sure she knew that he was becoming recognized. He published two love poems, both inspired by her. She learned them by heart. On August 13, on the anniversary of his mother's death, he sent her a copy of the *Irish Homestead* containing his first published short story, "The Sisters," about a mad priest. He did not try to interpret it for her (which was just as well; its symbolism still puzzles scholars); all he said was that it was "by me (Stephen Daedalus)."

Three days later, however, as if she realized that she had to rise to his standard, Nora went out and bought some decorated writing paper, with purple violets and bright green leaves, the kind that her mother liked, and in her best handwriting and striving to express herself with great dignity she wrote him a formal love letter:

> Leinster Street
> 16 August 1904

My Dearest
My loneliness which I have so deeply felt, since we parted last night seemed to fade away as if by magic, but, alas, it was only for a short time, and I then became worse than ever. when I read your letter from the moment that I close my eyes till I open them again in the morning. It seems to me that I am always in your company under every possible variety of circumstances talking to you walking with you meeting you suddenly in different places until I am beginning to wonder if my spirit takes leave of my body in sleep and goes to seek you, and what is more find you or perhaps this is nothing but a fantasy. Occasionally too I fall into a fit of melancholy that lasts for the day and which I find almost impossible to dispel it is about time now I think that I should finish this letter as the more I write the lonelier I feel in consequence of you being so far away and the thought of having to write write *[sic]* what I would wish to speak were you beside me makes me feel utterly miserable so with best wishes and love I now close —.
Believe me to be ever yours XXXXXXX

> Norah Barnacle[56]

This loving if stilted letter did much to tarnish Nora's later reputation. Joyce showed it to Stanislaus, saying that J. F. Byrne, to whom he also had shown it, said that Nora must have copied it from a letter-writing book. (Byrne, a great supporter of Nora's, later denied he would have said anything so cruel.)[57] It is the only letter of Nora's to have been reproduced in facsimile among Joyce's collected letters and in Ellmann's biography and to be displayed at the Joyce Museum in the Martello at Sandycove south of Dublin tower — probably because it is on flowery notepaper. Ellmann used the letter as a key to Nora's character, saying that Nora's "artifice in the face of his own attempt at total sincerity gave Joyce a hint for the amorality of woman."[58]

But Joyce, having had so many other letters from Nora, knew how she had departed from her own genuine prose style. The way she wrote to him in her late-night letters, the words rushing off the page, must have given him his first intimation of the use he might make of the warm, unpunctuated outpouring of a passionate woman on the verge of sleep:

Dear Jim
I feel so very tired to night I can't say much many thanks for your kind letter which I received unexpectedly this evening I was very busy when the Post-

man came I ran off to one of the bedroom's to read your letter I was called five times but did not pretend to hear it is now half past eleven and I need not tell you I can hardly keep my eyes open and I am delighted to sleep the night away when I cant be thinking of you so much when I awake in the morning I will think of nothing but you Good night till 7 P.M. to morrow eve

Nora xxxxxxxxx[59]

Such lines show why the Joyce scholar Phillip Herring has argued that Nora must be considered the main stylistic influence on the long interior monologue of Molly Bloom with which Joyce ended *Ulysses*.[60]

In order to have copied her letter of August 16, Nora would have to have found a model that expressed exactly what she wanted to say, for in her stilted letter she said exactly what she said in her more spontaneous letters and what she said to Joyce every time she saw him: that she thought of him every minute, awake or asleep, and was depressed without him. The first words of the August 16 letter are particularly significant: "My loneliness which I have so deeply felt . . ."

Nora was lonely not only because she was in love but because she had no alternative to that love. She was alone in the world. Joyce was all the life she had and her only hope for the future. While Joyce was diverting himself by showing her love letters to his friends, she kept his to herself, reading them over and over in her small room, trying to understand them.

By late summer, he was proudly escorting her in public. He was eager that she should hear him sing in a concert on August 27 in which he was to appear on the same program as the celebrated John McCormack in Dublin's finest hall, the Antient Concert Rooms. As he had spent the entire week rehearsing and was nervous, he did not try to bring Nora to the concert himself but instead delegated Vincent Cosgrave as substitute.

Cosgrave was only too willing to oblige. About five foot eight, strong and animated, almost always dressed in gray tweed and a cap, he was four years older than Joyce and more outwardly interested in women and seducing them than any of the crowd except Gogarty, whose preoccupation was more grossly anatomical. Cosgrave was a perpetual medical student — Gogarty called him a "chronic medical" — someone who liked living in hospitals.[61] That summer Cosgrave was working as dresser (assistant) to Sir Thomas Myles, a dashing and famous surgeon. He had already pressed his attentions on Nora. (Gogarty later recalled that Cosgrave "caused jealousy by walking out with Miss Barnacle, who had beautiful auburn hair.")[62] Nora, however, assured Joyce that she had not been interested.

If Cosgrave had wanted to pay court, the opportunity was there. By the time Joyce mounted the platform and began to sing, however, Cosgrave's chances were gone. The beauty of Joyce's singing moved Nora deeply. Some of the songs he chose, "In Her Simplicity" and "My Love Is from a Far Countree," seemed aimed straight at her.[63] Nora wholeheartedly agreed with the reviewer from the *Freeman's Journal* that Mr. Joyce possessed a sweet tenor voice (although the critic found the voice inclined to force on the high notes) and that he used it with "artistic emotionalism." Many years later, when Nora would tell their European friends, "Jim should have stuck to singing," she was not only disparaging the craft of writing — which she was — but thinking back to Joyce's evening of musical triumph in the first weeks of their love.

Joyce was still talking desultorily about leaving Ireland, perhaps for England. Nora, once more taking the initiative, began to press him to take her too. She was quarreling with the proprietress of the hotel and had nowhere to turn. Her life in Dublin would be bleak indeed without Jim. He tried to restrain her, calling her "my dear simple-minded, excitable, deep-voiced, sleepy, impatient Nora." [64]

The idea that they might leave Ireland together slowly took shape in his mind. Joyce was tempted but terrified. He was in no position to acquire a dependent, especially one who, if she reverted to type, might try to nag him into a conventional married life. With cruel honesty, as if to dispel any false sweetness suggested by his songs, on August 29 he told Nora exactly what he was like and what he was going to be like. Nora was severely shaken. She had little time to recover for he then wrote her a letter, ostensibly an apology for the agony he had seen come into her eyes, but really to spell it all out again.

> I may have pained you tonight by what I said but surely it is well that you should know my mind on most things? My mind rejects the whole present social order and Christianity — home, the recognised virtues, classes of life, and religious doctrines. How could I like the idea of home? My home was simply a middle-class affair ruined by spendthrift habits which I have inherited. My mother was slowly killed, I think, by my father's ill-treatment, by years of trouble, and by my cynical frankness of conduct. . . . I cursed the system which had made her a victim.

What he said next hurt her more. Nora's religion was part of her life. Joyce had teased her for her piety. But now he attacked the Church. He had left it, he said, when he was sixteen, because of "the impulses of my nature," but he now hated it:

> I make open war upon it by what I write and say and do. I cannot enter the social order except as a vagabond. I started to study medicine three times, law once, music once. A week ago I was arranging to go away as a travelling actor. I could put no energy into the plan because you kept pulling me by the elbow. The actual difficulties of my life are incredible but I despise them.[65]

Nora heard his confession of the worst about himself and went into Finn's with a shrug of pained indifference. She understood perfectly well what he was saying. He wanted her body. ("I know what's talking now," she told him.) He would never be her husband. As for her dreams of a settled family life with a nice home with curtains and furniture and neighbors, he would never give them to her. He rejected the whole idea.

But she had listened to all that he had said — "No human being has ever stood so close to my soul as you stand" — and she could discern another message. He needed her, Nora Barnacle. No other woman would do. He needed not only her love but her strength and her teasing. In his need lay her security. Was he asking her to run away and live with him? She still was not sure.

Elation alternated with despair. Joyce broke the news to his sister Poppie that he was in love with Nora. He told Stanislaus also. Stanislaus agreed that he understood his brother, although he did not entirely like what he understood. Resigned as he was to being in his brother's shadow, Stanislaus fought constantly to protect himself. Joyce was outrageously indifferent to interests other than his own. Stanislaus's own prospects had been blighted by the family's decline; he received an education inferior to his brother's, although he clearly had considerable intellectual ability of his own. No Clongowes Wood boarding school for him, although Stanislaus knew that it provided, as he said later, "the best education the country had to offer a boy of [Joyce's] class and religion."[66] No university either.

There was another Joyce brother, Charles (a fourth, George, had died). Charles, like Stanislaus, was able to attend Belvedere when John Joyce persuaded the rector to take his boys without fees. At nineteen Stanislaus was studying to become an accountant, a sober, cautious profession to which his personality was adapting itself.

About his brother's first steady girl, Stanislaus was of two minds. Nora was not worthy of Jim, he thought. She had magnificent hair, Stanislaus conceded, but a "common expression" on her face and on her lips. He shuddered to hear her call Joyce "my love" in public.[67] As a companion for Jim, however, Nora was to be preferred to Gogarty. Stanislaus loathed the suave medical man, with good reason: Gogarty had called him a jackal and thick-lug.

When Joyce cursed the "system" that destroyed his mother, he meant not only the Catholic Church but the bitter state of relations between the sexes in Ireland. The pattern was for long engagements (for those who married at all), preceded by calculating financial settlements. Once married, the men sought the company of their mates while the women remained at home, had large families, and doted on the eldest male child, giving him the strongest dose both of love and of guilt about sex. (The heavy burden of sexual guilt has been suggested as one of the possible reasons for Ireland's high rate of schizophrenia.)[68]

There were some advantages for those belonging to the supposed inferior sex. Irish women were not pressed to idealize their mothers or to suppress their natural instincts to the same extent. In consequence, Irish men envied their freedom to be passionate. This envy is well expressed in the words of the Irish ballad, "Sure 'tis the women are worse than the men. / They were sent down to Hell and were threw out again."[69] Nora, as an Irishwoman singularly distant from her mother, had a personality unusually free of conflict. Such people are devastatingly attractive to those (like Joyce) wracked with sexual guilt. What Nora did, she did, with few regrets.

As the summer progressed, Joyce was more rootless than ever, moving from place to place — a furnished room, the home of relatives, his father's squalid house. In early September he moved into the Martello tower on the coast south of Dublin, on which Gogarty held the lease. The tower was part of a string of fortifications built around Ireland in the early nineteenth century as a defense against Napoleonic invasion.

Nora cannot have been happy about the move. Joyce had never introduced her to his most distinguished friend.[70] But she knew that Gogarty was wealthy and that he shared a house in Dublin and a villa in the country with the formidable widowed parent he called The Mother. Nora knew of The Mother too. Mrs. Gogarty came from Galway; her family, the Olivers, were prosperous millers with a house in Eyre Square and owned a bakery where Tom Barnacle once worked.[71] Gogarty had been expecting Joyce to move in since July 22. Joyce's courtship of Nora may have been the cause of the delay, for the tower was eight miles southwest of Dublin.

At the start of his stay in the tower, with its magnificent view of gray-green Dublin Bay, Joyce was content, even cozy. On September 12 he wrote Nora:

The Tower, Sandycove

Dear Nora It is such a dreadful morning that I suspect we shall not be able to meet tonight. It is pouring rain here and the sea is flying up along the rocks. I should like to sit down here at the fire by myself, but I have to go into town shortly to meet Mr Cosgrave. It is just possible that it may become fine by evening, and if so, I shall expect you, but do not come out unless it is fine. I hope you are getting better every day. Have you found that place on the map? If we don't meet tonight — tomorrow at 8. Jim.[72]

The reference to a map suggests that they had been talking, idly perhaps, about going away, but he had reproached Nora for her impatience and years later even permitted his much-censored biographer, Gorman, to say that Nora Barnacle had been "a force violently pushing him toward flight."[73]

Nora, left alone that evening, wrote to Jim:

> I hope you did not get wet if you were in town to day I will be expecting to see you 8-15 to morrow evening hoping it will be fine I feel much better since last night but feels [sic] a bit lonely to night as it is so wet I was reading your letters all day as I had nothing else to do I read that long letter [about rejecting the Church and the social order] over and over again but could not understand it I think I will take it to you to morrow eve — and perhaps you might make me understand it
> no more at present from your loving Girl
>
> Nora XXXX
>
> excuse writing in haste
> I suppose you will be lighting the fire when you get this[74]

As far as is known, Nora never reproached Joyce for leaving the Church. She kept her views to herself. It was harder for her to understand why, if he could say that he had never regarded anyone as he regarded her, he could not say that he loved her. She had told him of her love many, many times. His excuse was that his life had made him very reserved. She was not to be disheartened. The closest he could come to the declaration she craved was a reworking of Aquinas: "If to seek to secure that person's happiness in every way is to 'love' then perhaps my affection for you is a kind of love."[75]

Their courtship put a strain on his relations with Gogarty. Joyce was the kind of person who can have only one close friend at a time. Byrne had been succeeded by Cosgrave, Cosgrave by Gogarty, and Gogarty by Nora, and Gogarty did not like being superseded. All of Joyce's cronies had read his published poems, and some took to referring to Nora with a phrase from one of them: "the companion," taken from the line "His love is his companion."[76]

Gogarty had still another grudge against Joyce. Joyce had written a savagely satirical poem called "The Holy Office," which he was circulating. In it he mocked a good many of the influential people who recognized his talent and who had tried to help him. Joyce accused Lady Gregory, J. M. Synge, George Moore, and others of the literati of hypocrisy, and he ridiculed Gogarty for snobbery. Joyce had nothing but contempt for the Irish Literary Revival. Comparing himself to Satan, he saw himself as "self-doomed, unafraid, unfellowed, friendless and alone," writing about the harsh reality of Irish life while they frolicked in the Celtic twilight: "That they may dream their dreamy dreams / I carry off their filthy streams."[77]

The final break between the two young men came in the middle of the night of September 14. They shared the tower with a strange Englishman from Oxford named Chenevix Trench. That night, dreaming that he was being attacked by a black panther, he awoke and grabbed the revolver that he kept beside his bed, and shot into the dark. Gogarty, not to be outdone, grabbed his own rifle and shot down all the pots and pans that were hanging near Joyce's head. Joyce, as Gogarty well knew, was so frightened of thunder that he would hide under a table during a storm.

Deeply shaken, Joyce scrambled into his clothes and fled from the tower, even though it was in the middle of the night and he had to walk nine miles in the dark to his cousin's where he took refuge. He never returned, even to collect his things (he made a friend do it for him), yet immortalized his few days there in the opening scene of *Ulysses*.

Coincidence or not, it was on the night of that long day that Joyce seems to have formally invited Nora to run away with him. It was not quite what she could call a proposal. He asked very obliquely: "Is there one who understands me?" Nora did understand him and had her answer ready. He was asking her to go away with him. He was not asking her to marry him. She said yes.

The following night, Joyce confirmed their engagement in a letter written with the voice of a man who has turned his back on his country:

> While I was waiting for you last night I was even more restless. It seemed to me that I was fighting a battle with every religious and social force in Ireland for you and that I had nothing to rely on but myself. There is no life here — no naturalness or honesty. People live together in the same houses all their lives and at the end they are as far apart as ever. Are you sure you are not under any misapprehension about me? Remember that any question you ask me I shall answer honourably and truly. But if you have nothing to ask I shall understand you also. The fact that you can choose to stand beside me in this way in my hazardous life fills me with great pride and joy.[78]

It was not the declaration of love Nora craved, but it was the truth. Every promise he made to her that summer he kept. He held out a vision of "the hazardous life" that awaited her, but he also said he hoped to be worthy of her love and to return it, and he assured her that any happiness that might be his he wanted to share with her.

Once committed, they fell silent and uneasy with each other. Joyce also began to question Nora. He was curious about the Healy connection. "Are your people wealthy?" he asked. Nora grew distant — perhaps he was after money — but Joyce excused himself lamely, saying he was only trying to find out if she "would be deprived of comforts she had known." Nora did hold out the hope (perhaps to deter Joyce from changing his mind) that her grandmother might have left her something in her will.

Joyce broached the idea of eloping with Nora to J. F. Byrne. Byrne, himself unconcerned with the formalities of marriage, questioned Joyce about the depth of his feeling for Nora and, assured, said, "Don't wait, and don't hesitate. Ask Nora, and if she agrees to go away with you, take her."[79]

Joyce carried the news to his aunt, Mrs. Josephine Murray. The wife of his maternal uncle, Aunt Josephine had warmly done what she could to mother the nine Joyce children after May Joyce died, even though she had six of her own. She tried to talk him out of the project, as he had no means of supporting Nora, but when he added that he did not plan to marry her — that as he had lost his faith he was not going to let any man utter meaningless words over him, but that he and Nora would not be any less married for the lack of a ceremony — Mrs. Murray did not object. Although a devout Catholic, she was an understanding woman, and besides, she, like Joyce's sisters, hoped that Nora would settle Jim down. "If you don't believe in something, there is no point in doing it," she told him, and promised to do what she could to help.[80]

It was the kind of move that might have taken months of planning. Joyce tried to accomplish it in a few weeks. Once again the impressive postal services of the day played their part. Joyce combed the newspapers, wrote away for jobs for himself and Nora, and waited for replies. Seizing at any possibility, he answered, among others, an advertisement placed by the Midland Scholastic Agency in the small Lincolnshire town of Market Rasen. Although the agency was hardly likely to be the nerve center for European job opportunities, it was seeking English teachers to work on the Continent — just what Joyce was looking for.

On September 17 the agency answered with a letter from an E. Gilford. Miss Gilford stated that she had reserved a job for him as an English teacher in "a Berlitz School 'Continent' " but was withholding the particulars until he forwarded her two guineas.

Joyce, after telegraphing officials in Market Rasen and receiving an assurance that Miss Gilford was of good character, trustingly sent her the hefty sum she asked.

For Nora the wait was agonizing. Each day brought new possibilities. One day she thought she might be going to Paris, the next to Amsterdam. In answer to one of his letters Joyce found a job for Nora in London but none for himself. The practical details in his letters alternated with increasing tension. They did not know what to say to one another. He found himself babbling even in his letters:

And yet why should I be ashamed of words? Why should I not call you what in my heart I continually call you? What is it that prevents me unless it be that no word is tender enough to be your name? Jim.

Write if you can find time.[81]

Nora could hardly find time. She had to keep on with her duties at the hotel, without giving a sign of agitation, keeping all her plans to herself. On September 27 she wrote:

Dearest Jim I hope your cold is better I notice you have got very silent lately I felt last night as if I had not seen you at all in consequence of you having to leave me so early when I came in I thought I could get to retire and not think of you so much but there was a great spree here and I need not tell you I did not like going amongst people whom I did not care for it was two o Clock when I got to bed I sat all the time like a fool thinking of you I longed for the time to come when I would not have to leave you

Dear Jim I feel so lonely to night I dont know what to say it is useless for me to sit down to write when I would prefer to be with you I hope you will have good news when I see you to morrow night I will try and get out 8-15 Giving you all my thoughts till then   Nora[82]

On October 4 Joyce was at last able to give her the news she wanted. Miss Gilford had at last divulged the name of the country (Switzerland) in which his new job lay and even that of the city (Zurich). Exhilarated, Joyce put out of his mind another letter he had received, one from the Berlitz School in London warning him that it had no agents in the United Kingdom and that he should beware of dealing with strangers.

"The boat is really beginning to whistle for us," he wrote Nora. His only real worry was that Nora's mother or uncles in Galway might get wind of their plans and try to stop them. He broke the news to his father that he was leaving Ireland but did not mention Nora.

Nora appreciated the enormity of her decision even though Joyce feared that she did not. By running away unmarried, she too was breaking with the social order and was committing an open act of rebellion. She was burning her bridges and she had no way of supporting herself abroad if Joyce left her. In a non-English-speaking country she was unlikely to find work even as a domestic servant. Her courage, like his, was fortified by bitterness at those who had let her down.

The fare to Zurich was three pounds and fifteen shillings, seven pounds and ten shillings for two, plus a pound to send their trunk. Joyce was not shy of borrowing from those he had ridiculed. Lady Gregory gave five pounds, George Russell, his publisher, ten shillings. His father gave something — seven pounds, he later claimed. Although Joyce had not yet been paid for his three published poems, he pocketed another guinea for a new short story, "After the Race," and they were ready to go. They left in their wake a flood of rumor and scorn that only increased with Joyce's later fame. George Russell said he pitied the poor girl, whom Joyce would certainly abandon. Another former friend, Francis Skeffington, thought Nora's future even more dubious than Joyce's own. Cosgrave told him he would never make anything of her. Women had their own suspicions as to how Nora had persuaded Joyce to take her with him. Mrs. Kathleen Behan, mother of Brendan and Dominic, writing many years later, said,

> All that talk about being our conscience! He only wanted to leave his family, but he ran straight into another. She was supposed to be in a peculiar condition before he left Ireland with her. I wonder, was she, or did she make it all up?[83]

As they turned their backs on Ireland, at twenty-two and twenty, Joyce and Nora had enormous courage. But so had 37,413 other people from Ireland that year.[84] Apart from the fact that he was going to forge the uncreated conscience of his race and that Nora had put aside a life of religious training to go as his unwed bride, they were absolutely typical Irish emigrants. If Nora described herself as a servant in any form, she would have been part of the largest emigrant category: female domestic servants from Connaught. The main difference was their destination. They were going to make their lives as "the Joyces" in countries where — *Yoice? Tscheuss? Zois?* — hardly anyone could pronounce their name.[85] Their letters remained behind, but in time these too would leave Ireland.

PART II

Bertha

As I have the name
I can have the gains.

— *Exiles*

4

Signora Joyce

IN THE MORNING of the third day after leaving Dublin, as soon as they had reached Zurich and found a Gasthaus near the station, Nora gave herself to Joyce. It was their first opportunity, as their first nights of freedom had been spent traveling. Joyce could not wait to tell Stanislaus back in Dublin. Even though he had an appointment at four o'clock at the Berlitz School to learn the details of his job, he dashed off a letter to Dublin with the news: *"Elle n'est encore vierge, elle est touchée."*[1] In the next breath, enjoying the double meaning, he asked his brother to touch their mutual friends for enough shillings to make a pound and to send it to him.

It was just as well that they had celebrated promptly because the Berlitz director turned out never to have heard of James Joyce nor of E. Gilford of Market Rasen, Lincolnshire, neither of which mattered as there was no vacancy in any case. However, Joyce's charm and tenacity soon had the director offering to tap the whole Berlitz network in southern Europe and to promise a job, somewhere in Switzerland or Italy, in the next eight or ten days. He would pay their fare to get to it.

There was no alternative but to wait, eking out their loan capital. Nora got her first taste of living in a hotel with a writer. Joyce plunged himself deep into his autobiographical novel while Nora wandered about the shops, wondering whether her mother would advertise her disappearance in the newspapers and running over in her mind her thoughts of her new life.

Had she really been a virgin? Doubt continued to torment Joyce. He

49

looked for, and was gratified to find, a few spots of blood on the sheets, but it could have been menstrual blood.[2] Nora had been having her period the previous day when they had stopped in Paris, and Joyce, setting out on his rounds, had left her in a park, the Parc Monceau, near the Gare Saint-Lazare where their boat-train had arrived. For him the fact that "her boot was pinching her," the euphemism he used for menstruation, was a convenient excuse to leave her behind. Her presence would have embarrassed him as he had to try to scrape up more money. He called upon a French psychotherapist whom he had known in his student days, who gave him sixty francs, and upon two eminently shockable Catholic friends from University College, Constantine Curran and James Murnaghan.

Later, however, obsessively running over the evidence for Nora's possible infidelity, Joyce reminded her accusingly there had been very little blood when she gave up her virginity. He had come to realize what Nora had known all along: that men could not tell the difference between menstrual blood, hymeneal blood, or any other kind. As Molly Bloom says in *Ulysses*,

> . . . and they always want to see a stain in the bed to know your a virgin for them thats all thats troubling them theyre such fools too you could be a widow or divorced 40 times over a daub of red ink would do or blackberry juice . . .[3]

There was no way he could know unless Nora chose to tell him whether she had attempted the complete sexual act before.

If Nora's period had indeed lingered on until the following day, they would have consummated their union under less than ideal conditions, and Nora's inhibition would explain Joyce's teasing remark to her years later, that she had been cold at first.[4] A chambermaid knows what other chambermaids notice.

Many years later John F. Byrne, the only friend with whom Joyce appears to have discussed his doubts about Nora's purity, said that Vincent Cosgrave, whom Byrne believed to have introduced the couple to each other, may well have had carnal knowledge of Nora before she met Joyce, but not after. "Joyce had no reason to demand virginity from his wife as he was no virgin himself," Byrne said.[5]

The Berlitz man in Zurich was as good as his word. Eight days later, Nora and Joyce emerged in the echoing neoclassical railway station at Trieste, which was then an Austrian city. Once again Joyce left Nora sitting in a public garden — the dusty park facing the station — but this time he did not return. Hours passed as she sat, like an unclaimed parcel, exposed to the leering glances of the sailors and workers from the port nearby. If she had not realized it before, she knew then that she was dependent, for every morsel she ate as well as for every word of communication with the strange world around her, on the young man who had asked her to believe in him instead of in God. It is impossible to think that she did not pray.

Suddenly Joyce was back, and he had a very good excuse: he had been arrested. Walking through the Piazza Grande, he had happened upon an argument between some drunken English sailors and the Triestine police. As he spoke Italian, he offered to be of assistance, only to find himself carted off to jail with the sailors. He was released only by the grudging efforts of the British consul. (As Irish, Nora and Joyce were British subjects.) Joyce swiftly made amends to Nora. He found them a room in the lovely Piazza Ponterosso, a square of pink-fronted houses overlooking the blue-green canal and market stalls full of gaudy vegetables and flowers — a wonderful vista for Nora's first glimpse of the Europe south of the Alps. Joyce also showed himself to be completely at home. He charmed "loans" out of total strangers and even managed to earn some petty cash by tutoring two private pupils in English. But the Berlitz network let them down again. Another promised job turned out to be a mirage, and with their money running out, there was no place cheap enough for them to live. They moved four times in two weeks.

As before, Berlitz, having dashed their hopes, came to the rescue. There was a job, if they would board a steamer and travel farther into the unknown, down the coast of what is now Yugoslavia. Just as unexpectedly, their luck turned. By the end of October 1904, Nora and Joyce found themselves settled at last in their first ménage, a furnished room, with pots, kettles, and pans, in Pola, 150 miles to the south of Trieste, where Berlitz was opening a new school.

Pola, the Austro-Hungarian Empire's largest base on the Adriatic, was multilingual, with a corrupted form of Italian dominating the Serbian and German (the official language). It was in Italian that in the local paper Berlitz heralded the arrival of James A. Joyce, B.A., the second English teacher on its staff, and implored all those who had been turned away before to return and register for lessons. Joyce's first pupils were Austrian naval officers trying to learn Italian. Joyce was not badly paid — two pounds a week for sixteen hours' teaching — and he had plenty of time for writing and for Nora.

Their domestic life began as it was to go on: a series of bad rooms at good addresses. Starving as they often were, the Joyces never lived in a slum nor even in working-class neighborhoods comparable to their addresses in Ireland. Joyce always looked for quarters in the central parts of European cities favored by foreigners — a great boon to today's Joyce scholars — near the piazza, the station, the banks, and the cafés with their international clientele reading foreign newspapers on sticks.

For Nora and Joyce, their daily routine was newlywed bliss. He delighted in giving Stanislaus the details:

> We get out of bed at nine and Nora makes chocolate. At midday we have lunch which we (or rather she) buys, cooks (soup, meat, potatoes and something else) in a locanda [inn] opposite. At four o'clock we have chocolate and at eight o'clock dinner which Nora cooks. Then off to the Caffé Miramar to read the newspapers . . . and we [come] back about midnight.[6]

Joyce could read the French and Italian papers, of course, but Nora grabbed the *Daily Mail*, which she read across Europe all her life.

Nora loved playing house. Not for the Joyces the Continental reluctance to invite friends into their homes. They entertained those whom they met at the school: the Francini-Brunis,* a handsome Italian couple in their twenties, who loved singing and who had also eloped; Eyers, the other English teacher; and the school secretary, a Yugoslavian spinster named Amalija Globocnik. Nora made an English pudding for them all.

Nora went to work on Joyce too. With her curling iron, she styled his hair *en brosse,* so that it looked thicker and more European. She loved his looks. "You have the face of a saint," she told him. She saved him money by rolling his cigarettes, using Turkish tobacco, and smoked them herself (they were both heavy smokers).[7] Although she urged Joyce to finish his book and become famous so that they could return to Paris, Nora was delighted with her new life and asked Joyce how Stanislaus could bear to live in Ireland. Why did Jim not help his brother, she demanded, to go abroad? Joyce conveyed the wish to his father but kept up the pretense that he was traveling alone.

Joyce needed no such pretense with tolerant Aunt Josephine. He asked his aunt, when writing to Nora, if it did not offend her, to address the letter to "Signora Joyce."[8] By that title Nora was known to their new acquaintances. The Berlitz proprietor at Pola, a fellow socialist and presumed freethinker to whom Joyce had confided that he and Nora had no wedding certificate, gave sensible advice: simply to sign all the certificates as if they did. The procedure was easy and it worked. Wife's name: Nora. Maiden name: Barnacle. Birthplace: Galway. In that document-free time, passports were not necessary, and their claim to be married was taken at their word.

---

* Alessandro Francini added his wife's surname to his own, making it Francini-Bruni, but Nora, James, and Stanislaus Joyce always referred to the couple as the Francinis.

The respectability of their physical appearance was another matter. Since their trunk had not arrived, they could not change their clothes. Day after day, Nora wore the dress in which she had walked out of Finn's. They were not forgiven their shabbiness. When they arrived on the pier at Pola from Trieste, their official greeter from Berlitz was so shocked that, as he told others later, he contemplated "suicide or assassination." Their friend Francini later recalled what they had looked like on arrival. Francini's memory, although colored by Italian hyperbole and the envy that infected Joyce's old friends once he became famous, was probably not too far off the mark:

> Ragged and tattered as a beggar, [Joyce] dragged along nonchalantly a hyena of a suitcase that had lost its fur. . . . From every rent in it things hung dangling in the breeze but he did not trouble himself to tuck them in. Mrs. Joyce, a little to one side, almost lost in a wide-brimmed straw hat and a man's overcoat that hung below her knees, looked like a pile of rags. Erect and motionless, she shifted her glance from one man to the other, without a trace of expression on her face.[9]

Erect and motionless. That was how Nora survived that day and all the troubles to come. She drew herself up, but she also drew into herself. It was to prove her best defense against Joyce.

But she could not use it often. They spent most of their time together. Nora was no intellectual companion, to be sure, but she was far from boring. She had a sharp tongue, a talent for ribald observation, and a repository of lore from the west of Ireland that Joyce had never heard. She sang for him old Irish songs, "Old Tom Gregory, Had a Big Menagerie," in which he enjoyed the sexual innuendo, and "The Lass of Aughrim"; that melancholy song of a servant girl abandoned with her baby by her lover had its own double meaning for them both. She taught Jim the words and, with no other companion but him, talked and talked.

She might as well have been talking into a tape recorder. Her Jim was interested in every scrap from her past, all about Galway, her sisters, the nuns, her boyfriends, the food, even her fantasies, and soon the details were making their way to Dublin. Stanislaus learned all about Barnacle the baker "who drank all the buns and loaves like a man," about the curate with the roving hands, and Uncle Tom with his blackthorn stick. As she babbled on, Nora could never have dreamed that Joyce was telling Stanislaus *everything:*

> Uncle Michael supports Mrs and the children, while Papa bakes and drinks in a distant part of Connacht. Uncle M is very rich. Papa is treated very contemptuously by the family. Nora says her mother would not lie with him.

Nora has not lived at home but with her grandmother who has left her some money.

She has told me something of her youth, and admits the gentle art of self-satisfaction. She has had many love-affairs, one when quite young with a boy who died. She was laid up with news of his death.[10]

In his phrase about the "gentle art," Joyce managed to imply that masturbation was a lesser sin for the female. He and his brother both felt guilty about masturbation and Stanislaus was later to classify it, with drunkenness, as one of the afflictions of the Irish.[11]

By the same token, Joyce tantalized his celibate brother with scenes from married life. "I really can't write," Joyce ended one letter. "Nora is trying on a pair of drawers at the wardrobe. Excuse me." In another, he listed all he had been doing: teaching English, learning German, writing a novel, a book of poems (to be called *Chamber Music*), more short stories . . . "Jaysus. I think I'm a hell of an industrious chap lately. And then Nora!"[12]

Nora's experiences, in many ways so much more traditionally Irish than his own, quickly found their way into the stories he was writing at the table in their little room. They would go into a collection he would call *Dubliners*. Joyce revised "Eveline" to give more of the view from inside Eveline's head; his fictional nineteen year old now knew that her father's violence "had given her the palpitations." The walls of Eveline's home were improved to sport a colored print of "the promises made to the Blessed Margaret Mary Alacoque." (The Blessed Margaret Mary founded the devotion of the Sacred Heart to whose sodality Nora had belonged in Galway.) A continuing puzzling detail about the story, a west of Ireland phrase muttered by Eveline's dying mother — "Derevaun Seraun! Derevaun Seraun!" — may also have come to Joyce via Nora.[13] The ordinary speech of people in Galway was full of Irish expressions, and old Catherine Healy, at whose house Nora had been living, could have mumbled such a phrase when she died. Joyce, seeking realism, was always uncomfortable in inventing details for his fiction and preferred to draw from real evidence, and it is certain that the curious phrase came from nothing in his own experience.

In November 1904, just after they had settled into their room with no stove (the reason Nora had their food cooked at a café), Joyce began to write a story called "Hallow Eve" (retitled "Clay" when it was published as part of *Dubliners*). In it he wrote of Maria, a tiny, aging spinster who works in a Dublin laundry. Maria leaves work expecting to spend a pleasant evening with a friend whom she knew as a young man and who now has a family and children. But her evening is ruined when she is drawn into the children's fortune-telling games. Blindfolded, Maria gropes for the ring (a sign of marriage), but the children trick her into dipping her hand in a bowl of clay (a symbol of death — all she can expect).

Joyce was too original a writer to have begun this story simply because Nora, homesick on Halloween, was sitting around their room in Pola moaning about what they were doing in Galway that night. But closeted with such rich lore, he was too clever to let it go to waste. The games in "Clay" are the very rituals of marriage divination that Nora and Mary O'Holleran played on Halloween in Galway. The "two next-door girls" who play the prank on poor blindfolded Maria are no crueler than Nora and Mary had been to the hapless blind lady who kept the sweetshop on Prospect Hill. (The story also contains more than a bit of grief for the plight of Joyce's many sisters, some of whom clearly would never find husbands and were doomed to spend lonely lives in dreary jobs in Dublin.)

Nora tried to adjust herself to the fact that she had chosen (she considered herself "married") a man who earned his living by putting ink onto paper. It was not easy. He showed her a magazine from London (*The Speaker*) that had published one of his poems and scolded her when she managed to lose it.

She tried to follow what he was reading and to give him her own opinion. She read George Moore's short story "Mildred Lawson," and she put down the book in disgust. "That man doesn't know how to finish a story," she said. She read the Dublin paper *T.P.'s Weekly* and the name of Ibsen caught her eye. "Is that the Ibsen you know?" she asked Jim. She interested herself for the first time in questions of theology. "Is Jesus and God the same?" she asked him. She tolerated his writing because she expected that it would allow them eventually to live a rich life in Paris. (She was quite right, but neither of them would have believed how long they would have to wait.)

In his letters to Stanislaus, Joyce portrayed Nora as a naive little primitive. " 'Tell Stannie I am axing at him!' " he quoted her as saying. He patronizingly described how Nora delighted in the cinema (a technical marvel in which that part of the world was very advanced) and could not contain herself when a cruel Lothario threw his betrayed girlfriend into a river. "Oh, policeman, catch him!" she cried aloud. And she expressed herself in that Irish inverted form of speech that Joyce was to use repeatedly in *Ulysses:* "Divil up I'll get till you come back!" When he had stomach cramps, she prayed to God "to take away Jim's pain." (She did not risk his anger, however, by praying in church or by consoling herself with the one custom common to Galway and Pola, going to Mass.)

Nora's lack of sophistication was not the whole truth. Joyce was so frightened of so many things — fights, being alone, dogs, as well as thunder — that Nora thought he was childish. She called him "simple-minded

Jim." She quickly learned how to manipulate his dependence. One night she decided to punish him, apparently for staying out all night without telling her. When they went to the Caffé Miramar, she avoided his gaze and sat staring stonily ahead. Joyce scribbled her a desperate note:

> Dear Nora For God's sake do not let us be any way unhappy tonight. If there is anything wrong please tell me. I am beginning to tremble already and if you do not soon look at me as you used I shall have to run up and down the cafe. . . . When we go home I will kiss you a hundred times. Has this fellow annoyed you or did I annoy you by stopping away? Jim [14]

"This fellow" may have been Eyers, the other English teacher at the school. He had said that Nora was not worthy of Joyce, and once he had made Nora cry. Joyce had thrown him out. In that foreign environment, it took a fellow Briton to discern the incongruity between Joyce and Nora. To the rest, Nora and Joyce were a matched pair, "the Irish couple."

They lived on their charm. Their sense of fun and occasion attracted many friends; they gave good parties, usually with music. Even for their first Christmas in a cold, small room they rented a piano so that they could have singing. (From Dublin Stanislaus contributed a plum pudding.)

Their charm drew the Francinis, who, early in 1905, invited them to share a house. Nora and Joyce were glad to move into a sunny apartment with shuttered windows, a warm stove, and a writing desk. Even so, they ate out every night, and the Francinis, living on the same income, felt they could not afford to join them.

Then, as later, the Joyces were poor with style. One of the many reasons that Nora never left Joyce, although she frequently threatened to do so, was that she enjoyed the life he gave her. In their attitude toward domestic economy, Nora and Joyce were as one in believing that money is for spending and that living well is the best revenge on the past.

Their constant dining out all their lives gave rise to the story that Nora could not cook. She could. She cooked the plain Irish food they both preferred, especially sweets, puddings, and cakes, but she gladly accompanied Joyce out in the evening because it meant less work for her and because Joyce, after a day's solitary writing, liked to get out, to see and be seen.

Joyce complained to Stanislaus that Nora had no friends, but she soon was on close terms with Clotilde Francini. Clotilde, who was housebound with a young child, welcomed Nora's company and found her full of fun. [15] Clotilde, who was Florentine and spoke a pure Italian, began tutoring Nora, who ambitiously dreamed of learning to speak the language as well as her husband did. Clotilde also undertook Nora's education in Italian cooking and in fashion. Nora, newly conscious of her educational inferiority, asked Joyce to teach her the geography she had failed to learn at the convent and to give her lessons in French as well, in preparation for the day when they could return to Paris.

But in one area of their lives she needed no tutoring. Nora took to sexual intercourse with enthusiasm and imagination. Often she took the lead, as she had in their courtship. Even on that first night in Pola, when to their official greeter earlier that day she had looked so bedraggled and withdrawn, she was wildly passionate in bed. Joyce was delighted but slightly overwhelmed. One night, naked, she straddled him like a horse, urging, "Fuck up, love! fuck up, love!"[16] Her behavior fulfilled all his dreams of domination by a fierce woman, and that Nora could release such fervor only three weeks after initiation left him with a lasting sense of awe at the banked fires of female desire.

The true curse of Edwardian women, menstrual rags, which needed to be washed and boiled and dried, did not plague her. Nora became pregnant at the first opportunity — the end of October 1904. Joyce craved a family, or at least to be a family man. There is no record that he and Nora ever discussed it. In their experience, the equation of man plus woman equals baby was incontrovertible. It was then that they began to feel their isolation. Nora was still out of touch with her mother. The only way she had let Annie Barnacle know that she had left Ireland to make a new life with a man was to drop her a postcard from Paris. "Delightfully vague," Joyce wrote Stanislaus. Isolated with Nora and cut off from his friends, he poured all that he could not share with Nora into private letters to his brother. Stanislaus read them carefully and added them to his collection.

Nora, Joyce told Stanislaus, was "adorably ignorant" about the facts of childbirth, but so was he. He asked Stanislaus to sit down with Cosgrave and study some books on midwifery, and he requested his Aunt Josephine to write Nora a letter of instruction. He went on to confide touchingly in Mrs. Murray that, easily disillusioned as he was, he had been "unable to discover any falsehood in this nature which had the courage to trust me." He had not left Nora, he reminded his aunt, as his cynical friends had predicted he would do.

On the second of February Nora celebrated Joyce's birthday (his twenty-third) for the first time. With the Englishman Eyers and Fräulein Globocnik, the Berlitz School secretary, they took a steamer excursion to the island of Brioni. It was Nora's introduction to the solemnity with which Joyce regarded any birthday. He had learned from the Jesuits the habit of ritual. To him sacred days required appropriate ceremony, and his own anniversary was the supreme holiday in his personal liturgical calendar.

After this outing Joyce remarked to Stanislaus that Fräulein Globocnik had taken a fancy to him. Flattered, he decided that there might be something in him that was attractive to women. Yet he noticed more than he knew, for in describing the Berlitz secretary to his brother, he called her a "melancholy little Androgyne," discerning the type of woman to whom he was particularly attractive. Nora, with her strong stride, mannish eyebrows, and big-knuckled hands, had many androgynous qualities herself.

Joyce liked to think of Nora as uneducated: it made her seem all the more his creation, and it was not until his long years of near-blindness began a decade later that he openly acknowledged his dependence on her. In the early months of their life together he apologized for her seeming inadequacies. He told Stanislaus that he admired her character, which was in many ways more admirable than his own. He told Stanislaus of Cosgrave's jibe that he would never make anything of her but declared that "in many ways in which Cosgrave and I are deficient she requires no making at all."

As Joyce's literary go-between in Dublin, Stanislaus had many assignments. One of them was to break the news to Cosgrave that his name in Joyce's novel was the evil-sounding "Lynch." His greatest service of all was to act as Joyce's correspondent.

Joyce, as his previous summer's exchange of letters with Nora showed, needed to explain himself on paper almost as a daily purgative, and, with his emotional needs satisfied, he needed to talk about his work. On that subject, Nora was no use. She did not, Joyce wrote his brother, care "a rambling damn" for art; with one side of his nature "she will never have any sympathy."

The charge was not entirely justified, for when he read Nora a chapter of his novel she found it remarkable. What is more, she knew his poems by heart. Nonetheless, the sight of Joyce copying from his notebook into his novel irritated her. "Will all that paper be wasted?" she wanted to know. Joyce mentally compared himself to Heine — an artist with an uneducated mistress.

As the months went by, Nora and Joyce became depressed and homesick and got on one another's nerves. Joyce drank more and more. There were many arguments. Nora tried to pass them off as lovers' quarrels but began to understand that she had thrown her lot in with a man with the same weakness as her father and that she was condemned to long hours, even years, of loneliness. Had they emigrated to Boston or to Melbourne, she would have found herself in an Irish enclave or at least among people who could speak English. Instead she had landed in a curious foreign corner of Europe that no one had ever heard of, full of mosquitoes, men in britches, and strange, oily food she could scarcely keep down in the queasy months of early pregnancy.

Even Joyce did not want their Dublin friends to know that they were in a backwater "down towards Turkey," as he thought of it. But Gogarty found out and spread the news: "The bard has fled to Pola on the Adriatic; a slavey shared his flight."[17]

All the time their minds were half in Dublin, Joyce trying to get his "Holy Office" distributed to those whom it was intended to insult, Nora wondering what they were saying at the hotel. When Stanislaus reported back that "all they said at Finn's was that 'Miss Barnacle had gone away,' " she was bitterly disappointed. Her great act of defiance had been forgotten.

In one of his letters, Stanislaus hinted that Joyce should be wary of Cosgrave, and he also wrote critically of Nora but Joyce would have none of it:

> Cosgrave . . . was, so far as I can remember, guilty of no duplicity towards me. . . . You are harsh with Nora because she has an untrained mind. She is learning French at present — very slowly. Her disposition, as I see it, is much nobler than my own, her love also is greater than mine for her. I admire her and I love her and I trust her — I cannot tell how much.[18]

As Nora's pregnancy advanced, Joyce began altering himself. He bought a new brown suit, a scarlet tie, and (realizing that he did after all need glasses) a pince-nez. The unkempt Dublin bohemian was giving way to the slightly dandified Italian man of family, someone who, as he saw himself in various letters home, was "a very pretty man." The progress of *Dubliners* also mimicked that of pregnancy; the subjects of the stories moved from childhood to adolescence to political, religious, and married life. The crowning touch of couvade was supplied when Joyce pronounced himself to Stanislaus as "about to produce a baboon baby by sitting for six hours on a jug full of soda water." The gross image reveals an infantile, and male, confusion about the exact orifice in the female from which babies emerge.

By Easter they were transferred to the Berlitz School in Trieste. Joyce hated the Berlitz regime where the proprietor locked up his bachelor of arts certificate to prevent him applying for other jobs; but he and Nora loved the large and beautiful city, with its green, wooded hills running down to the Adriatic, its cosmopolitan liveliness, its fountains, its fine piazzas open to the sea, and its opera house, the Verdi. The first monument to be erected to the composer, the Verdi attracted the finest international singers, who found Trieste was a convenient stopover on the route between Milan and Vienna.

Waiting for her baby, Nora still did not want anything to do with her family in Galway. Her mother, however, had found out where she was and with whom. By no means as indifferent to her daughter as Nora believed, Mrs. Barnacle was desperate to get her back. From Galway she shrewdly wrote and asked for help from the one woman she knew of in Dublin who was acquainted with James Joyce, Gogarty's mother (an Oliver from Galway). There was not much the formidable mother could do. Gogarty was much amused and joked to Joyce's brother Charlie, "They are probably having masses said for Nora's soul." [19]

Nora was thriving and, for the moment, content. They celebrated her twenty-first birthday in March; five months pregnant, she was an adult at last. She sang while she was dressing, and Joyce delighted in describing for his brother her uninhibited girlish behavior:

> At present she is licking jam off a piece of paper. She is very well, wears a veil now and looks very pretty. Just now she came in and said "The landlady has her hen laying out there. O, *he*'s after laying a lovely egg."
> Jaysus! O Jaysus! [20]

They returned to the Piazza Ponterosso and found a room at number 3. Nora lazed about, reading the odd magazine or book Joyce had left lying around. When Joyce tried to write, she daubed him with inky paper. Joyce was amused. Their landlady, when she noticed Nora's thickening waist, was not. She gave them a month to get out. The directors of the school also were appalled at Nora's condition and told Joyce he must be mad. Only a few doors from the school — which was on the dark and narrow via San Nicolò but almost as near the port, the opera house, and the fine, blue-domed Greek churches that fascinated Joyce — they found a landlady willing to take them in. A kindly Jewish woman with a great respect for education, Signora Canarutto was delighted to house a member of the staff of the distinguished establishment.

Joyce was still pleased with himself for having had the courage to reject the institution of marriage. He justified it again in a letter to Stanislaus:

> But why should I have brought Nora to a priest or a lawyer to make her swear away her life to me? And why should I superimpose on my child the very troublesome burden of belief which my father and mother superimposed on me? [21]

He saw himself as a socialist. He had an unsocialist interest in earning money, he confessed, with his engaging candor, but, "If I made a fortune it is by no means certain that I would keep it."

The Francinis had also been transferred to Trieste. Nora was very grateful. They were all hungry a good deal of the time but at least had the comfort of starving together. The weekly stipend from Berlitz was good pay by Dublin standards (about one pound fifteen shillings; in Dublin, Stanislaus was looking for a job for fifteen shillings a week), but the costs of room and board were also heavy. Joyce often borrowed on his pay in advance and every Saturday morning was first in line to collect what was left of what Berlitz owed him. Taking a large coin with the head of the Empress Maria Theresa on it, Joyce, according to Francini, "would turn it — first heads, then tails — in the palm of his thin, rigid hand and bring it up to his malicious eye; then with contempt he would put it in his pocket and spring away into the unknown."[22]

Nora was exasperated that Joyce would not do what he could to bring in more money. He wasted time on foolish things like entering a newspaper competition but otherwise spent every spare moment writing. To her satisfaction, the Francinis agreed with her that Jim's voice was so fine that he could solve their financial worries if only he would sing professionally.

Nora decided that the time had come to try to collect her inheritance from her grandmother, Catherine Healy. Not surprisingly, Stanislaus drew the assignment. Joyce instructed his brother to look up the will of Catherine Mortimer Healy, who had died between 1895 and 1897. His request shows that although Nora could not remember what year her grandmother had died, she was still too alienated from her mother to write and ask. It also makes clear that Joyce was well aware of how very young Nora had been when she left her grandmother's house. The dates he gave Stanislaus gave Nora as ten, eleven, or twelve at the time of Mrs. Healy's death.

But there was no money waiting for Nora. If she had led Joyce to dream, like one of his "Two Gallants," that he had settled down with "a good simple girl with a little of the ready," she disappointed him. Mrs. Healy had died without making a will, and Stanislaus's searches were doomed to fail. Nora told Joyce she could not believe it. Stanislaus insisted she must have made a mistake.

Their living standard was as contradictory as it would remain. They went to the opera regularly, and, in their appreciation of that art at least, they were equally matched. Joyce insisted on maintaining the habits of a gentleman as far as he could, and it galled them both, from their cheap seats high in the gallery, to look down upon the heads of some of Joyce's wealthy pupils.[23] At the Berlitz School Joyce, with his natural elegance and sharp wit, so quickly acquired a following of noblemen, editors, merchants, and young women of good family, all with time on their hands and a wish to learn English, that he was tempted to set up as a private teacher. But as Berlitz forbade private teaching, he could not give up his job. Their domestic economy was too uncertain.

Nora was, as he had learned in Pola, not prepared to make the petty economies of the careful wife with a profligate husband. They still took many meals out. She refused to cook in a shared kitchen and dreaded shopping — for good reason. Trieste, Joyce observed to Stanislaus, was the rudest place he had seen:

> It is hardly possible to exaggerate the incivility of the people. The girls and women are so rude to Nora that she is afraid to go out in the street. Nora can speak about thirty words of Triestine dialect (I tried and failed to teach her French) and so whenever she goes out I must accompany her and I have often to spend an afternoon looking for a very simple thing at a reasonable price.[24]

Swiftly they had learned that they had landed in the land of *la bella figura*. As Joyce lamented,

> The Trieste people are great "stylists" in dress, often starving themselves in order to be able to flaunt good dresses on the pier and she with her distorted body (Eheu! peccatum?) and her short four crown skirt and hair done over the ears is always nudged at and sniggered at.[25]

His own new brown suit was not well received. Eyers, the annoying Englishman at the school, who had also been shifted from Pola to Trieste, said to Joyce, "I often notice that eccentric people have very little taste: they wear anything. I give you a tip. If you have no taste you go in for grey. Stick to grey. Doesn't matter what kind — always looks gentlemanly."[26]

Confronted with his new responsibilities and frustrations, Joyce resumed heavy drinking. Nora was in despair. She could hardly go out and look for him. One night she sent Francini, who found Joyce lying in a gutter in the Old City. Joyce always complained that Nora found him no different from other men. To her he was not. Swollen with pregnancy, in a strange climate and culture, she had a man no better than her mother's and no legal tie through which to claim support for herself and the child if he left her.

The baby was due in August; Nora's heaviest months coincided with her first experience of intensely hot weather. She lay on the bed all day weeping. She could not make baby clothes, she said, even though Joyce went out and bought the sewing patterns. No, she did not want to go back to Galway, she insisted; yes, she did want to have the baby.

Joyce, however, confided to Stanislaus his suspicion that "she is one of those plants which cannot be safely transplanted." He knew that she needed a woman's company, especially in her first pregnancy; she had, apart from the Italian-speaking Francinis, nobody to talk to but him and the other English teacher, who had insulted her. Sometimes when she sat with the two men in the café, she did not utter a word the whole evening. Joyce wondered "what strange morose creature" she would bring forth from her tears. He still loved her; perhaps the only right thing was to take her back to an environment suitable to her temperament — in other words, Ireland. They both were consumed with visions of Irish food; Nora longed to see a kettle on the side of a fire. They could not continue to live as they were. As Joyce poured out all his woes to Stanislaus, he reminded himself of her bravery in leaving with him from the North Wall and of her loving understanding of his character:

> I have certainly submitted myself more to her than I have ever done to anybody and I do not believe I would have begun this letter but that she encouraged me.[27]

Joyce had conceived an extraordinary plan, which he spelled out. He and Nora would return to Dublin and, with Stanislaus, take a cottage in the suburbs. They would finance it with Joyce's savings from Berlitz, with the money he expected from the publication of *Dubliners,* and with Stanislaus's own earnings. The only thing he was not sure of, Joyce said, was his brother's attitude toward him and his "companion."

It is hard to say which of the two was more ignorant of the facts of childbirth. All Nora could keep down was beer. Joyce blamed her indigestion on the Italian food. He began to realize how truly alien their personalities were from each other; she cared nothing for his art yet, he mused to his distant brother:

> Once when we were both passing through an evening of horrible melancholy, she quoted (or rather misquoted) a poem of mine which begins "O, sweetheart, hear you your lover's tale." That made me think for the first time in nine months that I was a genuine poet.[28]

Perhaps, Joyce concluded with renewed hope, if each could accept the other's entirely different personality, they might be happy together. However, he removed the words "to Nora" from the first poem in *Chamber Music.*

The phrase *nine months* occurs in Joyce's letters again and again — another reminder of how the exact time of their exile coincided with Nora's pregnancy.

Every day Nora took her lunch with the Canaruttos, while Joyce took his at a café. On July 26, while she was eating, Nora began to feel pains. She said nothing until Joyce returned. Together they tried to diagnose the symptoms and failed. Joyce finally summoned the Canarutto women, who were less uncertain about what was happening. They called the midwife and shifted the furniture around so that they could get at the bed. Joyce left to fetch one of his pupils, who was a doctor, then gratefully accepted the invitation of the men of the household to join them for dinner. No wonder Joyce always found Jews hospitable.

By nine o'clock, nine months and sixteen days after they had first made love in Zurich, Nora had delivered her baby. *"Un bel maschio,"* announced the old Jewish aunt in Trieste dialect ("A fine boy"). It was a sure way of learning a language, and Nora learned. The women marveled at her bravery. During labor, Nora had made hardly a sound; her composure gave way only when she heard that it was a boy, and she clapped her hands in delight. Guided by the midwife, she put the baby to her breast, saw that she had plenty of milk, and that he was going to be no trouble.

Joyce was equally delighted. He would pick the baby up and sing operatic arias to him. When the infant listened attentively, Joyce concluded, accurately, that the child had inherited his father's voice. They named him Giorgio — George, for Joyce's brother who had died. Nora herself called her son, in a good blend of Italian and English, Georgie.

Joyce sent a telegram to his own home, "Son born Jim." If he also sent one to Bowling Green, Galway, it has not survived. Nora awaited reaction from Dublin and Stanislaus duly supplied it: "Aunt Josephine says I should say 'Bravo, Nora!' " and "Cosgrave says it is good news and that he will bear it in person to Skeffington"; but he then went on lengthily to discuss Joyce's novel. Nora was disgusted. Stannie's letter, she said, was all about books.

Nora herself wrote the news of the birth to Cosgrave, on a card carrying a picture of herself. He replied by writing to Joyce:

Dear Joyce, Nora has just reminded me of my rudeness in leaving your last card unanswered; but you know my indolence. I had half a letter written after receipt of your novel but was unable to continue so I consigned it to domestic uses. . . . I regret not having been the first to communicate the joyful intelligence of Nora's delivery to Skeffington. Meanwhile accept congratulations and give them to Nora for me. Hope the B. is doing well. I am unable to say anything about your novel as I have lost the continuity. Please send some more soon to Charlie and I will do my best to help you with criticism. Meanwhile why in the name of J——— Lynch. Anything but that. . . .
    . . . I write to Nora tomorrow. Is that a tinted photograph of her on the card. If so, compliment her for me. She looks much healthier than in Brown Dublin.[29]

Nora, in the confines of their little room on the via San Nicolò, tried to cope with their infant and their lack of money. She did the one thing she could do to help: she resorted to her old profession as a laundress. One day, impatient for a piece of scrap paper on which to list the clothes she was washing, she grabbed the first page of a new story Jim was working on. Called "A Painful Case" it began, "Mr James Duffy lived in Chapelizod because he wished to live as far as possible from the city of which he was a citizen . . ." Nora turned it over and did her own writing on the back:

10 rags, 2 chemises, 1 blouse, 3 towels, 3 Pr drawers, 3 vests, 4 Petticoats, 1 belt, 1 shirt, 3 Pinafores, 1 Pr trousers, 1 bolster, 2 pillow, 2 sheets, 2 Pr socks . . .

There were several other items. Joyce rescued the page. He needed it for sending to Stanislaus, who read the story and returned it to his brother, "with appendage."[30]

Joyce boasted in later years that Nora had taken in washing in the years of their extreme poverty, but he did not say that she had done so three weeks after her first accouchement.

Pleased as he was with the baby, Joyce reacted jealously to fatherhood. His fear of betrayal by Nora may in fact date from Giorgio's birth. An eldest son, Joyce had been his mother's favorite and had found Nora in less than a year after his mother's death. Now Nora had replaced him within the year. Joyce distanced himself from the child by writing home that "he has dark blue eyes, which he doesn't get from me"; he stepped up his campaign to persuade Stanislaus to join him at Berlitz. And he gave himself over more than ever to feelings of persecution. All he wanted from life, he declared, was some pen and ink and peace of mind to sharpen his pen and "write tiny little sentences about the people who betrayed me and sent me to hell."

Like many a new father, he found himself attracted to other women, and like many a teacher, he had a ready supply of eager admirers. One of these was Baron Ambrogio Ralli, who lived on the via di Scorola, and another, who lived two doors away, was Anny Schleimer, the young daughter of an Austrian banker. Anny was a year older than Joyce and studied with him in the autumn of 1905. Through her mother, Emilia Baumeister, she was part Jewish, and was reserved, refined, and accomplished in music. One day Joyce kissed her and suggested that she marry him. Whether he was serious or not (he was, after all, legally free to marry), Anny was captivated and told her father. Her English lessons came to an end. Signor Schleimer was horrified at the thought of his daughter involved with a miserable language teacher. Joyce continued to write to Anny, however, and in later years sent her his books, which she guarded jealously and showed to visitors at her home in Trieste. She never married.[31]

Joyce was thinking of leaving Nora, beyond a doubt. In December 1905, with Giorgio nearly five months old, he wrote to Aunt Josephine that as soon as he received some money from his writing, which would happen within two years at the latest, he intended to change his life:

I have hesitated before telling you that I imagine the present relations between Nora and myself are about to suffer some alteration. I do so now only because I have reflected that you [are] a person who is not likely to discuss the matter with others. It is possible that I am partly to blame if such a change as I think I foresee takes place but it will hardly take place through my fault alone. I daresay I am a difficult person for any woman to put up with but on the other hand I have no intention of changing. Nora does not seem to make much difference between me and the rest of the men she has known and I can hardly believe that she is justified in this. I am not a very domestic animal — after all, I suppose I am an artist — and sometimes when I think of the free and happy life which I have (or had) every talent to live I am in a fit of despair. At the same time I do not wish to rival the atrocities of the average husband and I shall wait till I see my way more clearly.[32]

Joyce had sent *Dubliners* to Grant Richards, a publisher in London. "I do not think that any writer has yet presented Dublin to the world," he wrote to Richards. "It has been a capital of Europe for thousands of years, it is supposed to be the second city of the British Empire and it is nearly three times as big as Venice." Joyce hoped there might be a market for "the special odour of corruption which, I hope, floats over my stories."

As he waited for Richards's response, Joyce kept adding to the collection. In the spring of 1906 he completed "A Little Cloud," the story of a young husband who feels slighted by life, who hates his job, and who, coming home after a bad day, tries to read some Byron:

> It was useless. He couldn't read. He couldn't do anything. The wailing of the child pierced the drum of his ear. It was useless, useless! He was a prisoner for life.

Little Chandler's despair is complete when his young wife enters and, paying no attention to him, clasps the child in her arms and walks up and down murmuring, "My little man! My little mannie!"[33]

Giorgio's birth presented Nora and Joyce for the first time with the practical problems of illegitimacy. Joyce liked to say that it did not matter whether a child took its father's or its mother's name because paternity was a legal fiction. All the same, when he registered the birth a year later, he persuaded the Austrian imperial lieutenant for Trieste to check the box marked "legittimi" rather than "illegittimi" on the birth certificate.[34]

He found Stanislaus a job teaching English at the Berlitz School and a room at the Canaruttos'. Stanislaus might do worse than "winter in Trieste," he wrote debonairly, offering visions of opera and carnival, roast chestnuts and new wine.

In October came the news he craved. Stanislaus accepted the invitation. Stanislaus's only regret in emigrating, he wrote, was in abandoning his sisters to life alone with their drunken father. "What can you do?" Joyce retorted. He sent Stanislaus one hundred crowns for the journey (about four pounds). (Joyce was never miserly with his money, merely extravagant.) Joyce told his brother to bring his manuscripts, their only hope for the future, and to dress magnificently because of the "cursed, stupid snobs who patronise these schools."

In Dublin, John Joyce feigned indifference to the impending loss of his second son. When Stanislaus asked for some money for travel, his father told him to go to hell for it. Yet when the time came for Stanislaus to get on the boat, just a year after Nora and Joyce had sailed away, he was not denied the traditional farewell. The last brother left behind, Charlie, re-layed the scene to Trieste:

> The day you left there was much weeping and wet eyes. When we returned from the boat Aunt Josephine, thoughtfully enough, took Poppie down to the North Strand [Aunt Jo's house], where, I have no doubt, they had a gala lamentation. Cosgrave remained with me all day.[35]

Charlie went on to describe how he had followed Stanislaus's instructions about shipping the accumulated correspondence and his other papers to Trieste:

> I have packed up all the books. I put as many as would fit into the trunk also all the letters. The music, I brought that up to my room also. Aunt Josephine wants to know: may I bring her down her letters and can she burn them? I see you left Jim's Epiphanies behind — was this a mistake?[36]

You might, Charles concluded forlornly, "tell Jim I am still alive."

Stanislaus, who took such care with his brother's papers, took precautions of a different kind with the personal letters of his parents. One day, finding his father's love letters to his mother, he burned them all unread. He truly cut his ties with the past. Unlike Joyce, who made three visits to Ireland after going into exile, Stanislaus (although he lived longer) never returned and never looked upon his despised father's face again.

Two brothers, one wife. A common rural family pattern and also the psychological triangle that Joyce always seemed to create in relationships; neither a recipe for domestic tranquillity. When Stanislaus arrived at Trieste's central station after his long trip, he was shocked. Joyce received him very coolly. Of Stanislaus's new clothes, Joyce said merely that his brother was so changed that he would not have recognized him if he passed him on the street. He then told Stanislaus that he and Nora were broke. Was there any money left from the journey?

Nora was equally unwelcoming. Still nursing Giorgio, she spoke mainly with Jim, often in Italian. "If Nora has forgotten how to speak English, what language does she speak?" asked Aunt Josephine in answer to Stanislaus's complaining letter home.[37] Nora scarcely knew Stanislaus except by sight, but she could see that his addition to their household on the via San Nicolò was a mixed blessing. Stanislaus, about two inches shorter than Joyce, stocky, square-faced, and solemn, was a middle-aged twenty, a man unsure of himself with women and eager for meals on time. Glad as she was of a voice from Dublin, Nora recognized that Stannie would be a drain on her energies, an intruder on their privacy — he had a bedroom next to theirs — and a sender of telltale letters back to Ireland.

Nora was not the type to hold things back just because a third party was present. Shortly after Stanislaus arrived, she and Joyce had a terrible fight about a new hat. Stanislaus duly reported it; Aunt Josephine was shocked:

> To say the least of it the hat episode would have driven any other man to drink it must have been very trying to Jim. I would not have at all imagined Nora was so particular but perhaps Austrian milinery *[sic]* is ugly in any case she should have taken something to please Jim It certainly was enough to ruffle him for the day but I can't understand why you should be made the target. Jim says in his letter to me he is never alone. I think it must be very trying for you all to be living in one room but after all there are times when one likes a little solitude . . .[38]

Aunt Josephine did not know Nora very well. Even in Galway Nora had had a passion for style, fabric, cut, and line, especially in hats, and she saw herself now in a position to exercise it.

Joyce had a weak spot for her cravings. Nora was the only one who could wheedle money out of him. Sometimes she took a quiet polite approach — "Please leave me another five crowns as I must get a little velvet for my dress," she said in a note one day.[39] At other times she helped herself from Jim's pockets. One day Joyce angrily complained to his brother that Nora had taken some money to pay the bootmaker. "Why don't you take the money back from her?" Stanislaus asked. "Because I amn't strong enough" was the frank reply.[40]

Stanislaus was disturbed to see how Nora bossed Jim about; she even had him peeling vegetables, he wrote home. "Where is the art in that?" asked Aunt Jo crossly.[41] A worse shock was Joyce's drinking. Stanislaus had been dismayed by Joyce's carousing in Dublin, and now saw that his brother was behaving even worse, throwing away money needed for Nora and the baby. Joyce seemed to have forgotten all about the intellectual companionship Stanislaus was going to supply; he seemed to care only about Stanislaus's paycheck.

Aunt Josephine tried to do what she could as a long-distance marriage counselor and wrote separately to Nora and Jim. "Matrimony has its little drawbacks," she said, accepting their fiction that they were man and wife.[42]

And in every important respect they were. For their first Christmas as a family of four, Nora made, as she did every year after, with great ritual, a plum pudding. They had a dismal New Year's Eve, however, all three of them sour about how their lives had turned out. In the New Year Aunt Josephine, worried that Nora might become pregnant again, wrote her the long-promised letter of maternal advice:

> 4 Northbrook Villas
> Jany 8th 1906

My dear Nora

Thank you for your letter I know it must be hard to write now. Your son is teething probably & consequently very uneasy it is as bad for the Baby as a toothache for an adult. [?] the poor little fellow must be suffering his own share I hope you make Jim & Stannie share in the nursing. He must be very engaging now. I am delighted you are in good health Keep so if you can remember though you do not see your monthly courses you may conceive again & if this occurs you must at once wean Georgie Dont let me alarm you I am only putting you on your guard . . . I am Vy glad you had a pudding it must have been a great treat for the Boys whenever you can I know you will let me know how the Baby is thriving With [?] wishes for the New Year may it be a happy and successful one for you & Jim

> Sincerely yours
> Aunt Josephine[43]

To Stanislaus and Joyce she spoke out of the other side of her mouth. She had heard from both her nephews how bad-tempered Nora could be.

Things eased for Nora when in February the Francinis once again invited them to share a house (or a "quarter," as it was called, a section of an apartment building) on the via Giovanni Boccaccio. Although in an unfashionable area on the hill behind the station, the new address offered more room for the four of them, and Aunt Josephine was pleased to hear that Nora was back with such nice people. Nora had begun to appreciate the benefits of Stanislaus's presence. He handed over most of the forty crowns a week he earned at Berlitz. He could also take direct action on Jim's drinking. Stanislaus would sling his brother on his back and bring him home from the cafés of the port and the Old City. (Joyce was never at any time in his life a belligerent drunk but rather a floppy public one. As he weighed so little, he was often carried home by friends and put to bed. The next day when he awoke, he was complaining — his eyes hurt, and so forth — but he was not, by all accounts, surly.)

In a monologue with which he diverted his pupils, Joyce linked his drinking to Nora's fertility:

> My wife, if nothing else, knows how to produce children and how to blow soap bubbles. . . . We have George the First. If I don't watch out she is liable to stick me with a second heir to the dynasty. No, no, Nora, my girl, I have little appetite for that game. Therefore, as long as there are bars in Trieste, I think it is better for your husband to spend his nights out, dangling like an old rag.[44]

This limp metaphor suggests that Joyce saw drunkenness as a form of birth control. He disapproved of contraception (as does Stephen Dedalus in *Ulysses*). For all his hatred of the Church, he never criticized its stand on artificial birth control (which was not the social or theological issue in the very early twentieth century that it later became). He blamed his mother's many pregnancies on the refusal of the priest to allow her a separation from her husband.

Nora and he certainly did not want another child at that time. The only preventive measures available were douching (difficult in their cramped quarters) or coitus interruptus. Perhaps Nora expected that breast feeding would prevent pregnancy. She fed Giorgio herself until he was nineteen months old.[45] Whatever her technique, it was effective for a time, for she did not conceive in 1906.

Stanislaus's arrival meant closer ties with the Joyces back in Dublin. The little household on the via Boccaccio was in such constant contact with Dublin a thousand miles away that sometimes it seems as if they were a family separated by a street instead of half of Europe. Stanislaus may have wished the distance were greater, as he received a steady barrage of demands from Dublin for money.

The sisters in Dublin were much closer to Stannie than to Jim. Jim, as the eldest, had been away so much, at university, in Paris, and then in Trieste, that he was a remote figure to the younger ones. The oldest sister, Poppie, of course knew Jim better than the rest and was very hurt that he had not once written to her since she had helped him and Nora make their getaway. "He treats me as a person completely to be ignored," she complained to Stanislaus, who understood very well what she meant.[46]

It was not only money the girls and Charlie wanted. Shoes, clothes, and teeth were constant themes in Joyce family correspondence. As May Joyce explained to Stannie,

> We are all very well here, excepting Charlie whose health is not at all as good as it might be Charlie gets little or no air as he has neither boots nor clothes. If you have any clothes worth the price of the carriage they would be a great God-send. Charlie would be annoyed if [he] heard of my saying

this so please dont mention it in any letter to him . . . Poppie is saving up to buy herself clothes and teeth. I am going to have my own teeth seen to before they go too far. . . .

Your affectionate sister

May[47]

Stanislaus sent what he could, and soon Charlie was apologetically asking for a cast-off suit. (The ease and cheapness with which both ends of the Joyce family shipped old clothes, shoes, and books across Europe is yet another tribute to the postal services of yesterday.)

Such letters from home made it clear to Nora that she had to hold on to Jim. There was nothing to return to in Ireland. Charlie himself wished he had the money to emigrate. Stanislaus, for his part, began to think he had made a mistake. He had moved to Trieste only to make himself a prisoner, a responsible man torn between two spendthrift families. He could not begin to think of getting married himself (and indeed did not marry for another two decades).

Nora cannot have been happy to see money flowing back to Dublin. For all those starving months, she had believed what Joyce told her: that as soon as *Dubliners* was published the money would start rolling in.

In London Grant Richards had at last agreed to publish *Dubliners,* and Joyce was furious when Richards refused him an advance on royalties. Richards was adamant; the trouble he said, was that *Dubliners* was about Ireland and books about Ireland did not sell. (Joyce wrote back saying that he had no idea of the book's prospects, but that if it sold at all in England it might then be published in America "where there are some fifteen millions of my countrymen.")[48]

By 1906 Joyce's dream of wealth had begun to fade. In February Richards announced that he could not bring out *Chamber Music* unless Joyce paid the costs. And in March, after a contract for *Dubliners* had been signed, Richards sent a bombshell: the English printer would not set the book into type. Under English law, printers as well as publishers were responsible for obscenity and libel in the books they produced. The printer did not wish to take the risk of publishing the sexual innuendoes in one of the stories, nor the word *bloody* in another, especially as it referred to Queen Victoria as "that bloody old bitch."

Joyce stood his ground. If he erased everything in his book that gave offense, what would be left? The title, perhaps. He would like to see the book in print and to have the money in his pocket but not if it meant prostituting his art. The criticism's worst effect, Joyce said, was that it has "brought my own writing into disfavour with myself."

In truth, the criticism's worst effect was to make him drink more. It also unleashed the full savagery of Nora's tongue. Aunt Josephine, drawn in once more, loyally defended Jim — her side of the family — and blamed

Nora. Joyce's short temper was understandable, for "he has got so many rebuffs from Fortune lately," wrote Aunt Jo,

> but honestly Stannie I can't understand Nora surely it is a monstrous thing to expect Jim to cook or mind the Baby when he is doing his utmost to support both of them surely she can make as good an attempt as Jim it seems very soon for her to be so disappointed I wonder does she know what it is to be with a person with a scurrelous tongue from which you are never safe there is some excuse for Jim drinking it is the old story of finding forgetfulness. Perhaps there is some excuse for Nora being irritable but she could not have expected her life to be all roses and you may rest assured she will never send any of these letters home this constant threatening must be very trying to both of you. She thinks her life unhappy now what does she think it would be with her own people. . . .[49]

Aunt Jo hoped that there was no chance of "Georgie being rivalled at present." That, she said, "would be the climax."

Nora had, as Aunt Josephine's letter shows, been moved by her mother's pleas and had begun at least to draft letters home. As she composed one of these, saying that she was returning home to Galway because she was living with a man who could not support her, Joyce, looking over her shoulder, said, "If you're going home at least write 'I' with a capital letter." Nora's riposte was unanswerable; "What difference does it make?" she demanded.[50]

Nora knew her mother. As the few surviving letters of Annie Barnacle show, the first person pronoun was one of the few words that Nora's mother did not dignify with a capital letter.

Joyce and Stanislaus might have resisted sending their letters of woe back to Dublin had they realized the use their father was making of them. John Joyce gleefully read them out in bars to "let people see what blackguards the Jesuits could 'turn out'!" He told everybody that he had not had a penny from the boys in Trieste.

Since Charlie Joyce knew that Stanislaus was starving himself and going without new clothes in order to send money home, he burned to hear his father's ingratitude. Charlie, dressed in Stanislaus's castoffs, saw himself as "neither a genius nor an artist but the brother of both or at least one" and said he was grateful to them both for "having taught me much and rooted many evils out."[51] (Charlie was another of the family's heavy drinkers.) The least he could do, Charlie felt, was to tell Stanislaus the fate of a gift of ten shillings that Stannie had sent from Trieste:

> Pappie came home drunk last night. I know this must be hard for you to hear; but tho I tell it it is no easy task. So you see that the whores that can afford to belittle you and wish to kick your arse can also afford to drink your scanty money. I hope sincerely that I may be near on some occasion when these gentlemen are amusing themselves at yours or Jims expense.[52]

So poor that he had not even a pair of suspenders ("I am wearing a tie for a belt — to hold up my trousers"), Charles sympathized with the plight of his brothers in Trieste. Some of their troubles were not of their own making.

The Berlitz School was coming apart at the seams; the manager had absconded, and at least one of the Joyce brothers' jobs was in jeopardy as there did not appear to be enough work for two English teachers. At one point the administration considered sending Stanislaus to Pola. "It is a rather painful thing to think that you or Jim or both should starve or approach starvation in a foreign country so far from home," wrote Charles. "It seems that the Joyces are doomed to live and die in uncertainty."[53]

Word of Joyce's straits reached his old friend Gogarty. By 1906 a successful surgeon, Gogarty wrote from the Waldorf-Astoria in New York, suggesting that Joyce come to America, where, Gogarty assured him, he would not fail to make money rapidly. Joyce refused (as he always would do) to consider America. Instead, he spotted a small advertisement in a Rome newspaper asking for young men proficient in foreign languages to work in a bank.

Desperate to finish his novel, Joyce decided on a radical move. He would take Nora and the baby to Rome. There, at double pay for shorter hours, he would finish his book on the making of an artist (himself). He did not trouble himself to find out what Roman working hours were.

So Nora and Joyce packed up, leaving Stanislaus, seven months after Joyce had implored him to be at his side, alone in a strange foreign city. They left also unpaid bills from the baker, the tailor, and even Francini, their landlord. Giving Stanislaus elaborate instructions as to how he was to face all these creditors, Joyce promised, if things went well in Rome, to send for him.

5

Madonna
and Child

ALL HIS LIFE Joyce gave reasons for uprooting his household — overlapping, often contradictory reasons and rarely the real ones. Nora learned to shrug and put up with each new upheaval. There was no stopping him once he had made up his mind.

In retrospect it is apparent that Joyce needed to go to Rome to clear his head. His autobiographical novel, at one thousand pages, was out of control. *Dubliners* had not been published, and he had ideas for improving it; he was dissatisfied with his charming poetry and knew he was not really a poet. Rome was a time of incubation from which his great work of the next seven years emerged and from which he extracted from Nora some of her most powerful contributions. It was also the period in which their union was cemented. At twenty-two and twenty-four, cut off from everybody but one another, each learned to tolerate the other's alien temperament, to delight in their child, and to live as Italians. But that did not stop them from hating every minute of it.

In Rome they made no close friends. The monuments bored them; Joyce said Rome reminded him of a man who makes his living by exhibiting his grandmother's corpse. They did not even like the wine. Joyce's hours at the bank, far longer than they had expected — from 8:30 in the morning to 7:30 in the evening — canceled out the very purpose of moving to Rome, and they still had no money. As Joyce was paid monthly, they were in debt from the start and never caught up with the extra expenses of travel and settling in.

Never since Finn's had Nora been so lonely. Joyce left home at seven in the morning in order to read at a café before the bank opened. She was shut in, still nursing Giorgio, in virtual solitary confinement. The only breaks in the day were the two-hour Roman lunchtime, when she carried Giorgio to meet Joyce at a café, and at five o'clock, after Giorgio's nap, when she took him to a café and had coffee by herself.

The capital city did have a few saving graces. The Romans loved children. Giorgio was showered with gifts of biscuits and fruits as he sat in a little highchair in restaurants, clapping his hands with delight as each new dish arrived. Rome also offered plenty of music. Giorgio, riding on Joyce's shoulders, went to open-air brass band concerts in the Piazza Colonna and even accompanied them to the opera. (The Joyces were furious when the audience told the boy to keep quiet.) There was also their new pleasure, the cinema.

Baedeker recommended that travelers look for accommodation in the "foreigners' quarter" between the via del Corso and the via del Tritone, and Joyce found them a room on the small unpretentious via Frattina near the Spanish Steps.[1] Joyce's job at the bank, which was on the corner of the Piazza Colonna, was within walking distance, as were nine picture houses.

In her long empty hours, Nora would put on her hat and take Giorgio to sit in the dark and watch the flickering films that were then the rage of Italy and France. Their themes were dear to Nora's heart — elopements, marriage brokers, harems, lover's revenge; the hit of the year was *Cavalleria Infernale*, a drama based on the Rome Riding School.[2] For twenty centesimi Nora indulged in the daydreams of the solitary wife.

She brooded also on her memories of Galway. When Joyce took her to the outskirts of Rome to visit Shelley's tomb, Nora responded with a string of morbid romantic associations that moved him deeply. Later he recorded them in his notes for his highly autobiographical play, *Exiles* (in which Richard is the name he gave himself and Rahoon is the name of the cemetery outside Galway):

> Rome is the strange world and strange life to which Richard brings her. Rahoon her people. She weeps over Rahoon too, over him whom her love has killed, the dark boy whom, as the earth, she embraces in death and disintegration. He is her buried life, her past . . .[3]

That Joyce, when he came to write the play, chose Rome to represent their many places of exile shows that the Eternal City, above all others, made them feel most foreign.

Joyce himself was haunted by visions of Ireland. He longed for a breakfast of bacon and eggs. He dreamed of suspending the laws of time and space so that he might drop, just for an hour, into the middle of Dublin. He even wished there were an Irish club where he and Nora might go to meet their countrymen, of whom, they were certain, there were plenty in Rome.

The main event of Nora's morning was the arrival of the post. There were letters from Trieste, letters from Ireland, and, much-awaited, the Irish newspapers. One day Nora found some good gossip to take to Joyce at lunchtime and, hurrying to meet him, bumped into him in the street. "Guess the latest, guess who's married?" she asked, holding out the newspaper. It was Gogarty; he had married Martha Duane, a wealthy girl from a Catholic land-owning family in Galway. The news renewed their awareness of their own irregular status and made seem unbridgeable the gap between Joyce and Gogarty. "I suppose he wouldn't dare present me to his wife," Joyce wrote his brother. "Or does the poor mother accompany them on the honeymoon?" When Joyce later noticed that Gogarty had published two newspaper columns written on his honeymoon, he joked that the new Mrs. Gogarty could not be very good company — as if he himself had spent his own honeymoon showing Nora the sights of Zurich rather than working on his novel.

Nora and he were getting deeper and deeper into debt. They turned to the obvious source of help. Nora shared in the chore of writing begging letters to Stannie.[4] It was a bizarre form of assistance, as Stanislaus had to telegraph the money, and to wire forty lire cost eight. Stanislaus, still struggling to pay the debts Joyce had left behind, had new instructions for creditors: tell them he had gone to Scotland. Stanislaus was very fond of Giorgio (one of the reasons he subsidized his profligate brother), and Nora kept him apprised of his nephew's progress:

> He is well able to run about he is able to say a lot he has a good appetite he has eight teeth and also sings when we ask him where is Stannie he beats his chest and says non c'e piu.[5]

It was this interpolation into a long letter of Joyce's that caused Joyce to make his famous libel on the female sex for its indifference to punctuation.

Giorgio, as Nora's note indicated, was learning Italian as his first language. He could say "*Addio*" and "*Appetito*"; he commanded, "*Abba*," for "*A braccia*" ("Pick me up"), and "*Ata!*" for "*A terra!*" ("Put me down"), two phrases that, Joyce noted, he alternated rapidly. Giorgio was also quick with an "*O Gesu Mio*" and "*Brutto, brutto*," amusing his parents in some compensation for the trouble he caused by pulling all their papers about and hiding their shoes and hair brushes.

One reason they were always short of money was their enormous appetites. They were always hungry. Giorgio ate like a grown man. Joyce himself, uncharacteristically, thought of nothing but food. And Nora, as a nursing mother who was always teased by her husband for her too-girlish body, did not stint herself. Nora's usual dinner, Joyce boasted to his brother, was two slices of roast beef, two Italian meatballs, a tomato stuffed with rice, salad, and a half liter of wine. Sometimes, Joyce said, they divided a whole roast chicken between them, plus a plate of ham, and still went to bed hungry. At the end of this recital, he asked Stanislaus to send fifty lire because he was about to run out of money again.[6]

On October 8 the little family went into the country to celebrate what Joyce, overflowing with pleasure in Nora and their child, called "the anniversary of the day of my espousal and of the day of the gladness of my heart." He described for Stanislaus "the full and exact list of what we ate":

10.30 a.m. Ham, bread and butter, coffee
 1.30 p.m. Soup, roast lamb and potatoes, bread and wine
 4. — p.m. Beef-stew, bread and wine
 6. — p.m. Roast veal, bread, gorgonzola cheese and wine
 8.30 p.m. Roast veal, bread and grapes and vermouth
 9.30 p.m. Veal cutlets, bread, salad, grapes and wine[7]

His salary, he feared, would not sustain them for the winter. Still yearning for Irish food, he taught the cook in their house to make tripe and onions with white sauce in the English fashion.

They needed money also for clothes, especially Nora's. Joyce, who had been supplementing their income by giving language lessons at one lira an hour (thus consuming spare hours he ought to have used for writing), spent twenty-eight lire to buy Nora a skirt, two blouses, and two combs. Although his own trousers were worn so thin in the seat that he had to keep his long coat on all day at the bank, he bought only a shirt and a hat for himself.

After two months, they decided that they must economize. They would eat at home. Joyce gave Nora fifty lire and told her to try to make it last for two weeks. But in two days she had spent half, simply stocking up on staples such as oil, candles, coal, coffee, and sugar. Joyce did not scold her; he saw the logic of the investment:

So I think we have begun at last. The only thing is the plan is risky for, if I cannot get a pupil before the end of the month we have nowhere to get credit. But I prefer even to risk this as I am determined to save money.[8]

Still, he portrayed himself to Stanislaus as living on nothing but soup in order to economize, but added (as if he knew he were presuming too much on his brother's sense of responsibility) that Nora and Giorgio were being fed properly. Stanislaus, in any case, could not have re-proached Joyce for idleness. A note from Nora begged Stannie "to tell Jim not to be doing so much as he doesnt have a minute to himself."[9]

On December 2, they had a familiar experience: eviction. The land-lady, who had given them notice three weeks before, declared that she would not let them spend one more night at the via Frattina. As Joyce had three hours of teaching after he finished at the bank, Nora put on her hat, picked up Giorgio, and spent two hours in a cinema, then moved to a restaurant to wait for Jim to finish teaching. Then they all began the rounds of looking for a place to spend the night — "like the holy fam-ily," Joyce said. Unlike the holy family, however, they had a big dinner first and then made the search by hired car. (The car was necessary in order to protect Nora's hat.) The third hotel they tried accepted them, and they stayed for four nights, spending more than half a month's rent in that time.

During the day, Nora, carrying the heavy, squirming child, went from place to place, up and down staircases, looking for new rooms. She learned that Romans, so fond of other people's children in restaurants, did not welcome them as tenants. After one rebuff, she was so furious that she sent a stinging and ungrammatical letter to Joyce at the bank. Joyce got a laugh out of it and sent it on to Stannie.

Their search ended on the via Monte Brianzo, parallel to the Tiber, when they took a room on the top floor, with access to a kitchen. (They had compromised in their efforts at economizing: they ate lunch at home and were without wine, but in the evening went out to a *trattoria* and enjoyed themselves.) The room was spartan: a stone floor, a bureau, a small table, and one bed. In bed they slept, Joyce thought fit to report to Stanislaus, "lying opposed in opposite directions, the head of one towards the tail of the other."

In *Ulysses*, Molly Bloom, whose husband also insisted on this unortho-dox sleeping posture, has a great deal to say on the matter.

In December they prepared for a bleak Christmas, with no friends, no piano, and no cash. Nora, expecting some payments that did not mate-rialize, had been up to her old tricks and paid some bills. "Tomorrow we dine on paste [pasta]," Joyce said on a Christmas Eve postcard to his brother. "I suppose you couldn't relieve the agony at all?"[10]

Out of their hunger and homesickness came the richly laden Christmas table of "The Dead." Joyce conceived the idea for the story while in Rome, inspired in part by Nora's reverie, the city's funereal atmosphere, and their sense of exclusion from Roman life. After completing *Dub-liners,* his portrait of the ugliness of life in his native city, he felt that he had not been fair to Dublin's tradition of generous hospitality. When, therefore, a few months later, he decided to add "The Dead" as the final, longest, and most important story in the book, his description of a Dublin Christmas buffet table was almost pornographic in its vision of pure pleasure:

> A fat brown goose lay at one end of the table and at the other end, on a bed of creased paper strewn with sprigs of parsley, lay a great ham, stripped of its outer skin and peppered over with crust crumbs, a neat paper frill round its shin, and beside this was a round of spiced beef. Between these rival ends ran parallel lines of side-dishes: two little minsters of jelly, red and yellow; a shallow dish full of blocks of blancmange and red jam, a large green leaf-shaped dish with a stalk-shaped handle, on which lay bunches of purple raisins and peeled almonds, a companion dish on which lay a solid rectangle of Smyrna figs, a dish of custard topped with grated nutmeg, a small bowl full of chocolates and sweets wrapped in gold and silver papers and a glass vase in which stood some tall celery stalks.

Joyce was not the only member of his family who could describe a Christmas dinner, or convey, with poignant echoes of the Great Famine, the horror of having the Christmas feast spoiled. Old John Joyce was masterly on the theme. In that same month of December 1906 he asked each of his exiled sons, could they spare a pound? They obliged, Joyce borrowing his from Stanislaus but insisting that the money be routed through Rome to Dublin so that he himself would get the credit. The old man was eloquent in his humble gratitude. Thanks to his boys, he effused, "what looked likely to be red herrings on the Saturday became Turkey and Ham, Goose and bacon, Plum Pudding, etc. and punch."[11]

In the event, the Joyces' Roman holiday was not as bad as they had feared. On New Year's Eve they invited a Welsh teacher and his girl-friend to dine with them (Joyce never liked to spend New Year's Eve alone), and the young woman, a manicurist, responded by inviting them to lunch in her elegant flat on New Year's Day and diverting them by telling them she had done the nails of Edward VII.[12]

Nora, who always liked giving presents, scraped together enough to buy one for the old servant on the floor below. The two had become friends as Nora listened to the woman's stories of quarrels with her mistress.

If Joyce had intended their top-to-toe sleeping arrangement to be contraceptive, it was too late. In the New Year Nora discovered that she was pregnant again. Her morale was very low. She had weaned Giorgio; Joyce seemed interested only in his writing and in news from Dublin. He was away from home most of the time; he spent his evenings teaching, studying in the Biblioteca Vittorio Emanuele, or drinking. She was worried about him:

Dear Stannie Jim posted a letter to day he had no time to finish it. He is at the bank till half past seven he has only half an hour for dinner lessons at eight he never has time to eat anything properly stuffing it down his throat he ought to give up the school it is not worth the time. Georgie is so awfully fond of Jim. . . . Nora.[13]

In her loneliness she clung to Giorgio. Lines in *Exiles* suggest that she would take Giorgio and climb to the roof of their building on via Monte Brianzo and stare at the dome of Saint Peter's and the tiled roofs and roof terraces of the Rome skyline.[14] She developed a closeness to Giorgio and a dependence upon him from which neither she nor the boy ever escaped.

Joyce never admitted any sense of rivalry with his son. He idealized his own father, and he idealized Giorgio. When old John Joyce died in 1931, Joyce wrote, "I was very fond of him always, being a sinner myself, and even liked his faults. Hundreds of pages and scores of characters in my books came from him."[15] Joyce, according to Richard Ellmann, disagreed with Freudian views of the Oedipus complex, "probably because he found little trace of it in himself."[16]

Joyce did, however, recognize that he was more distant from the boy than Nora was and felt excluded from their intimacy. He noticed that Giorgio would not let him and Nora talk to each other. For Stanislaus he sketched a family scene: "A young man with snivelling nose sits at the little table: on the bed sit a madonna and plaintive infant."[17] He also said,

Certainly Georgie is the most successful thing connected with me. but he's only a small part mine. I think he rather likes me, however. When I come to eat he pulls over the chair and says 'Se' (sede).[18]

Joyce was more easily able to see the effect of isolation upon Nora. In *Exiles*, Bertha, the Nora character (that is, the young, red-haired, common-law wife of Richard, an arrogant Irish writer), says,

Heavens, what I suffered then — when we lived in Rome! . . . I used to sit there, waiting, with the poor child with his toys, waiting till he was sleepy. I could see all the roofs of the city and the city and the river, the Tevere . . . . . . It was lovely, Dick, only I was so sad. I was alone, Dick, forgotten by you and by all.[19]

Joyce knew that plunging Nora, only twenty-two, into such a strange environment had disoriented her. She was his portable Ireland, yet he had sacrificed her Irishness to the needs of his art. In *Exiles*, Richard, having returned to Ireland, is complimented by his friend, Robert, at having wrought a miracle in Bertha:

ROBERT: You have made her all that she is. A strange and wonderful personality.

RICHARD *(darkly):* Or I have killed her.
ROBERT: Killed her?
RICHARD: The virginity of her soul.[20]

Joyce, in his life as in the play, did not seem to grasp that motherhood also had transformed Nora's soul. He had in one sense lost Nora permanently, not to the dead but to the living; the rival whom he could not vanquish was his own son.

Nora, trying to win Joyce back, tried harder than before to keep up with his intellectual interests. She read *Hedda Gabler* twice (and forgot it as soon as she had read it, Joyce told his brother). She pleased him more with her contempt for a new book of stories by one of his University College acquaintances. Nora found these stories tiresome rubbish.[21] In her view of the unlovely reality of Irish life, she agreed with Jim.

In an impassioned letter to Stanislaus, Joyce gave his own artistic credo, a warning that when he came to write about love between men and women, he was going to write what he knew and not

> lying drivel about pure men and pure women and spiritual love and love for
> ever: blatant lying in the face of the truth. I don't know much about the
> "saince" of the subject but I presume there are very few mortals in Europe
> who are not in danger of waking some morning and finding themselves
> syphilitic.[22]

In mid-February Nora, fed up with their room, went out and found them a better one on the Corso. She could defend her interests in Italian by then. One day when Joyce gave her a gold coin to exchange, she set out for the post office only to be restrained by the landlady, who told her it was fake. It took two trips to the post office, but Nora made them take it.

Accepting that the Corso room might make Nora temporarily content, Joyce gave notice to their Monte Brianzo landlady. He then changed his mind and gave notice at the bank instead. He wanted to get out of Rome altogether. Unfortunately, the landlady from the Corso, wanting her rent, tracked the couple down at a restaurant and made a scene that can easily be imagined. Joyce finished by having to pay both women. (Later, when declaring that each nation could be identified with one of the seven deadly sins, Joyce put Italy down as Avarice.) He toyed with the idea of moving the three of them to Marseilles. He knew, he said, that Stanislaus would like him to settle down at the bank, and in twenty years have a career, a flat, a servant, children at school, a bank account. Such a life, however, would also leave him with "a great fear of everything in me." Instead he would leave Rome for an unknown destination. Stanislaus might have guessed what it would be. The next news he had was a telegram: "Arrive eight get room."

They arrived. When Stanislaus saw Nora, Joyce, and Giorgio on the platform at Trieste, with just one lira among them, he knew well the truth of a line in a begging letter he had received a few weeks before: "Remember there are three people now. And I suppose it will be worse when there are four. . . ."

Just as two years earlier, Nora had to go through the last months of pregnancy in the heat of the Triestine summer. In the summer of 1907, with her baby expected in July and Giorgio to chase after, she saw Joyce fall ill and carried to the city hospital with rheumatic fever.

Since their return, they had enjoyed a measure of good news. Joyce had wangled a few hours a week back at Berlitz. He also had enhanced his standing in Trieste with a series of public lectures on Ireland; his audience easily saw the parallels between Ireland's struggle for independence from England and Italy's from Austria. His talks were published as articles in the city's excellent newspaper, *Il Piccolo della Sera.* Better still, *Chamber Music,* his collection of thirty-six poems, had been published. It had not brought them any money, but it had good reviews and was a genuine book. Even though *Dubliners* was no nearer publication, Joyce was a published author at last.

Nora wrote to Aunt Josephine about Jim's illness, and Aunt Josephine wrote straight to Jim in his hospital bed.

June 4, 1907

My poor Jim

Nora's letter confirmed my worst fears such a terrible illness . . . how I wish I could nurse you (no offense to Nora) poor thing it must be hard on her to see you suffering . . . It is a grand thing your little son is so strong and good he must miss you so much I wonder how he will react [?] to his rival I wish Nora was near her time [?] but she will be grand this time . . .[23]

Jim's mission in life, Aunt Jo was loyally convinced, was to write, and she grieved over all the obstacles in his way.

How Nora made her way to the Ospedale Civico di Trieste on July 26 — they were living back on the via San Nicolò, directly over the school — is not known. Probably Stanislaus escorted her. She told the Francinis later that her baby girl had been born "almost in the street." The birth occurred just one day before Giorgio's birthday; late July would be an occasion for a joint celebration for many years. Joyce heard the news in another ward of the hospital and was happy to be able to bestow the name he had kept in waiting for two years: Lucia, the patron saint of light. To this was appended Anna, a form of Annie Healy's name, and the names were registered as Anna Lucia, an inversion of the intended order that persisted for many years. When Nora took the child home (to a room that had to be reached by walking through Stanislaus's own room), the hospital gave her twenty crowns, a standard payment made to women who gave birth in a free ward. From Dublin Aunt Josephine wrote exuberantly,

A thousand welcomes to the little lady who has opened her eyes in Trieste. I am sure she will bring you and Nora all kinds of good luck (which . . . has shirked you a bit lately).[24]

When Nora first saw her daughter, her heart must have skipped a beat. The infant, well formed in every other way, had a cast in one eye, like Nora's sister Peg. Peg (one of the twins born to Annie Barnacle in 1889) was so self-conscious about it that she used to run and hide so that people would not see her.[25] As an imperfection, Lucia's squint was slight; nonetheless, it was much more pronounced than Nora's own sleepy left eye. Nora and Joyce believed that a defect in a girl was more worrying — a possible blight on her chances in love — and Lucia Joyce herself would in later years become obsessed with the flaw in her appearance.[26]

The rest of the family in Dublin were not very happy about the newborn's name. They were not sure how to pronounce it. (The Joyces always used the Italian form: "Lu-*chee*-a.") Poppie asked, "What on earth made you call her that? Pappie wanted to know were you quite mad when you selected that."[27] In the manner of an older sister, Poppie also took it upon herself to urge Joyce to stop changing his lodgings.

News of Joyce's severe illness also reached Vienna, where Gogarty was working. Gogarty sent Joyce a patronizing, medical-man letter, saying, "I am sorry you had so little time in bed to fight that rheumatic fever; at least six months are necessary to ensure the safety of the cardiac valves." He enclosed a pound (roughly equivalent to fifty today) to help out, as well as an invitation to join him in Vienna at Gogarty's expense. Since Gogarty's wife had just given birth to a ten-pound child in Dublin, she had remained in Ireland, and Gogarty would have appreciated the company of an old and literary friend.

In spite of his new child, Joyce abruptly resigned from the Berlitz School in the autumn of 1907 because of a change of management and because of its ban on private teaching. He toyed with various wild schemes — to sell Irish tweeds in Trieste, to emigrate to South Africa, to teach in Florence, to win a professorship back in Ireland at the Royal University (the subject of the plot of *Exiles*), to become a singer — but in the end threw in his luck by embarking on a career as a private teacher to polite and haughty Triestines who seemed very ready to help him with influence and occasional loans. He was very popular, and women students continued vulnerable to his well-mannered flirtatiousness, so different from the local machismo, although they also found him at times nasty and insolent. One night Joyce joined a few of his students after class and went with them to one café after another. He asked one of the girls to dance. As he danced with her — "lightly and gallantly," she recalled — a rose on her dress fell to the floor. Joyce retrieved it and returned it, saying, "I seem to have deflowered you."[28]

But he was not welcome everywhere, for he was acquiring a terrible reputation as an *umbriaccio* (drunkard).

One young woman of good family wanted to take English lessons from Joyce, but her father refused to let her study with "that drunk."[29] Another later recalled that Joyce once arrived drunk at the lessons she had at the home of a friend and suddenly collapsed onto the marble floor. The friend, who was in love with her *professore inglese,* tried to wipe his face, but her scandalized mother pulled her back. Joyce was so pleased with himself when he revived that they all thought he had done it on purpose.[30]

Many people found Joyce's drunkenness amusing, especially as it was confined to the social hours of the evening.

Stanislaus was not amused by Joyce's behavior. Nor was Nora, ever. "Yes, go now and get drunk. That's all you're good for. Cosgrave told me you were mad. Faith, I tell you," she stormed, unleashing her worst threat, "I'll have the children baptized tomorrow."[31] But she did not. The Joyce children were not baptized and were listed on official forms, like their father, as *senza confessione.*

Morale in Trieste was not boosted by news from Dublin. The letters from Dublin kept up a steady tom-tom of despair. Eileen had failed an examination for the Telephone Office; Charlie was trying to find a way to get to America and still wanted Stanislaus's old suit. The world of Dublin was just as Joyce had portrayed it in *Dubliners.* The rich got richer; Gogarty was flying through the streets in his motorcar. For the rest jobs were few, employers unforgiving, the slightest sexual misstep ruinous, and fathers still irresponsible, especially the Joyces' own. John Joyce was in arrears in rent on their new house. He begged the brothers to bring Charlie to Trieste. May, stuck behind a desk for five shillings a week, asked, "Are we always to be the same paupers that we are now? It is simply miserable this eternal want of money." She later declared, "He is a terrible little no-good is my Pappie."[32]

When Christmas came round again, John Joyce was no better off than in previous years, but he started his money-raising campaign earlier, on December 14: "Now that we are without a penny for the next fortnight and so could you send a pound or two I suppose I need not remind you that I *never* refused either of you *when I had money.*" It would be the last Christmas he would bother them, he assured them, because he was going into hospital and was sure to leave "feet-foremost." He signed it

"A happy Xmas Your fond Father," and lived another twenty-four years.[33]

Stanislaus, it seemed, was able to remain sober and responsible, and apparently chaste. Charlie was not so successful. Soon Trieste had more bad news from Dublin: Charlie had got a girl into trouble. What to do? Aunt Josephine was reliably unshocked. The important thing, she confidentially reported to Nora, Jim, and Stannie, was "to keep the truth from those who don't know."[34] Charlie agreed and told no one but Vincent Cosgrave. Cosgrave gave solid advice. If there was a choice, he said, of going to jail or to marry, marry.[35]

Charlie happily made his choice. He admired his new wife. Tall, fair-haired, and twenty, she had not tried to trap him, he believed. "She said she did not mind how hard she had to struggle as long as I was her husband," he proudly wrote to his brothers. Charlie found a job in Brookline, Massachusetts, as a bill-sticker, and within a week of the wedding he and his pregnant bride had sailed away. John Joyce took great pleasure in describing the familiar scene for his older sons:

> The "usual rabble" came to see him off. There was the usual weeping, real and feigned. . . . And Jim would be glad to hear that your friend Cosgrave retains all that suave, yet unmistakeable, appreciation for a pint and even when parting it occured to me that he was holding his lower lip out for more.[36]

That left John Joyce with six unmarried daughters on his hands. They were, from oldest to youngest: Poppie (Margaret), Eileen, May, Eva, Florrie, and Baby (Mabel). He found Poppie (who had been running the house) insolent and pressed her to go ahead with her plan to depart for a convent in New Zealand.

But Nora had her own miseries. By the summer of 1908 she found that she was pregnant once more. On August 4, 1908 (the date is known because it was recorded precisely in Stanislaus's diary), she had a miscarriage. Joyce later claimed to be the only one who regretted the fetus's "truncated existence." Nora's reaction is not known. She and Joyce certainly could not afford another child. That very month Stanislaus had confided to his diary that he had saved his brother and family from starvation six times and had walked out on them after a row about four hundred crowns. (Although he still took his meals at Nora's table, Stanislaus never, apart from a few months after the First World War, shared quarters with them again.) Jim and Nora could not even afford to move to a new flat because their landlady would not release their furniture. Aunt Josephine did not censor her own views when writing to Nora. Word had reached her that Lucia was not an easy baby:

I was sorry indeed to hear of your dangerous illness but dont think me very inhuman if I say I am glad now that it is over because you cannot possibly be strong enough to carry another baby besides I imagined you have just [?] your hands full in the 2 you have & my poor Jim what a lot of trouble he is having. . . . You will have to be very careful also particularly (whenever you are pregnant again) at the time you miscarried you will always be subject to a recurrence at that time. Giorgio must be a lovely Boy now and a great source of pleasure to his father you will find after a time the little girlie will be very good . . .[37]

It was advice wasted. Nora never became pregnant again.

Poverty and unhappiness were easy to write about in letters home, a settled love and sexual compatibility almost impossible. The lean years in Trieste were not all misery or ugliness. Nora kept her commonsense wit, as on the night when Joyce asked her, "Where will you meet me?" "You'll meet me in bed, I suppose," she replied.

And their poverty, as always, was relative. A photograph of Nora with Giorgio as a toddler and an unidentified short, stocky older woman, for example, shows her beautifully dressed, fuller in the face than in later years but also tranquil, pleased with her child.[38] Her hair is in a chignon. She is wearing an elegantly cut, light-colored costume, with wide collar and elongated lapels. With it she wears a high-necked blouse, adorned at the neck with a pin. Giorgio too is wearing what looks like the height of fashion, with high leather boots (perhaps bought in Rome) and a double-breasted coat with an unusual lined collar. Their poverty seems to have expressed itself in a lack of ready cash but not, thanks to Joyce's talents, in an inability to wangle credit.

The same photograph shows that Nora well fits Robert's description of Bertha in *Exiles:* "a strange and beautiful lady," graceful, cordial, distant, with soft features and a flair for fashion. (Bertha carries her cream gloves knotted around the handle of her parasol.) In "The Dead" too, Gretta is elegant, drawing her husband's admiration by the formal beauty of her clothes and the color of her hair:

> If he were a painter he would paint her in that attitude. Her blue felt hat would show off the bronze of her hair against the darkness and the dark panels of her skirt would show off the light ones.

Joyce thought his wife was beautiful and was pleased that other men were attracted to her.

Among these men was Stanislaus. He was attracted to Nora and found her indifference hurtful. He kept his thoughts to himself and confided them only to his diary.[39]

Joyce's other troubles were mounting. *Dubliners* was rejected again;

he suffered an attack of iritis. Letters from London made it clear that the publication of *Dubliners* was more remote than ever. It is a measure of his faith in himself and sense of purpose that, during those angry, anarchic months when his "home" — rooms shared with two babies, an angry wife, and a resentful brother — was in an uproar, he recast *Stephen Hero* into *Portrait of the Artist,* conceived *Ulysses* and *Exiles,* and finished "The Dead."

Sympathetic as the sisters were to their first little niece and nephew, they still could not, three years after what John Joyce called his son's "miserable mistake," bring themselves to mention Nora by name. May thanked him for "Mrs. Joyce's photo & Georgies"; she found Giorgio "a fine little boy not at all like Jim rather like his mother I think." John Joyce a few months later was delighted to receive a photograph of "Lucia and Mother." Charlie wrote from Brookline, "Who is Lucy like — you or Mrs. Joyce?"

Poor Aunt Josephine, for all her efforts, was hurt to receive no photograph at all.

It was time to heal the breach between Ireland and Trieste. In the winter of 1908 Joyce decided on a plan. As Nora had her hands full with the two children, he decided that in the summer he would send Stanislaus back to Dublin, with Giorgio, counting on the handsome child to win over the family. John Joyce was overjoyed with the news and asked Joyce to teach the child some English as "personally I should wish to convey myself intelligently to the young gentleman nor would I wish him to return to you with the idea that his auld grandfather was a bloody auld Cod." John Joyce also tried to tempt his son back to Ireland. "Do you intend to spend the balance of your life in Trieste? . . . Don't you think you ought to aspire to something higher?" (He suggested an interpretership.)

But in the spring of 1909 Joyce's feelings of persecution, exacerbated by the continuing row over the language of *Dubliners,* were almost out of control. He got it into his head that his family in Dublin did not wish to receive his little son. He wrote an angry letter to his father; its unreasonableness can be judged by the bewildered response of his sister May:

44 Fontenoy Street
3rd June 1909

Dear Jim,
Pappie told us part of the contents of your letter. What do you mean by saying that no one seemed to welcome the idea of Stannie's and Georgie's visit? To put it very mildly that's not true. When Poppie heard of the visit first she wrote you saying how delighted we all were at the prospect of seeing Stannie & little Georgie. Pappie, to my own knowledge, wrote three letters

on the subject. Aunt Josephine & Eileen & I wrote also several times, but perhaps we dont count I cannot understand your saying that the visit is not welcome. Why on earth do you pay any attention to Pappies talk of going into hospital? I thought you knew him better. He is precisely the same as when you saw him last he is not one bit changed except perhaps that he is oftener sober. . . . Do you think that between us we could not care for & make little Georgie happy? If you think this you make a mistake. He will have too much petting & attention if I'm a judge, Pappie was rather crazy about that little photo of him so that I cant imagine how he will contain himself when he sees the child himself. It would be a terrible disappointment to us all if they did not come over. The children would never forgive it I was thinking what could have made you write that letter . . . *Is Nora better?* What the dickens is the matter with Stannie that he wont write to anyone? Eileen received the money & it was very good of him to send it, it was a great boon to them at home but why did he not write to Aunt J. when he heard she had been so ill? You boys always were rum 'uns.

Your affectionate sister May [40]

When the train drew into Westland Row on July 29, 1909, the entire Joyce family was lined up. Out stepped the long-awaited Giorgio, accompanied not by his uncle but by his father. "Where's Stannie?" the family asked. Joyce assumed, quite rightly, that his father was even happier to see him.[41]

Joyce quickly scribbled a postcard to Nora, asking her to instruct his sisters about Giorgio, and he set himself to wait for her reply. The trip was the first time in five years that they had been separated, and he was rapidly beginning to suffer withdrawal symptoms.

6

Away Alone

FROM THE NIGHT they left Dublin, Nora and Joyce were almost never apart until his death in 1941. An exception was the year of 1909 when Nora stayed in Trieste while Joyce made two trips back to Ireland. The letters he and Nora exchanged then went straight to the heart of the mysterious bond between them.

Nora disliked letter writing. She wrote only when compelled by necessity, courtesy, or force of feeling, as when she had fallen in love. In late July 1909, when Joyce left with Giorgio for Dublin, she did not write to him right away. She was busy with Lucia, who was then a difficult two year old, and with preparing meals for Stanislaus. (The dining out stopped when Joyce was away.)

Nora was happy that Jim and not Stannie had made the trip. Jim could accomplish much in Dublin. The London publisher, Grant Richards, had let him down over *Dubliners,* backing out after three years of negotiations over the wording of the stories. In Dublin Jim was going to see a new publisher, George Roberts of Maunsel, who seemed interested. Jim was also going to look into the possibility of getting a job — at a university or in the civil service — which would allow them all, Stannie too, to return to Ireland. Best of all, Jim was going to take Giorgio to Galway to meet her mother and they would both meet her mother for the first time. Nora's long rift with her family would be ended.

She waited to hear how pleased their families were with Giorgio. He had grown into a handsome, well-formed child, with dark blue eyes, a high forehead, and grave mien. It would be lonely for her without the two of them for a few weeks, but life was going to be easier when they returned, for Nora had persuaded Jim to bring one of his sisters back to Trieste to give her a hand with the children. She then would be far freer to go out in the evening to the opera and cafés. They had moved twice since Lucia was born. Their latest flat was on the second floor of an apartment building on the via Scussa, in a pleasant residential area, near the public garden, the Municipal Opera House, and fine shopping streets. Giorgio had a room of his own that an extra person could share.

Within a few days two communications arrived from Dublin: a post-card for Nora, announcing that Joyce and Giorgio had arrived safely, then a newsy letter for Stanislaus. Joyce, after five years' absence, had been received with that critical condescension accorded those returning to a small world from a large one. Family and friends all pronounced upon his appearance, variously judging him to look thin, melancholy, older, foreign, mature, ecclesiastical, and blasé. Only Vincent Cosgrave was unstinting with his compliments; he found Joyce "in splendid health."

Joyce took the opportunity to relay to Stanislaus some of the scurrilous Dublin gossip he had picked up that Synge was rumored to have had syphilis when he died.[1] The letter concluded with the plea that Nora should write to him. He wrote it on August 4.

A few days later Nora received a letter from Jim dated August 6. Its opening words must have struck her like a fist in the face. "Nora I am not going to Galway nor is Georgie."

In short brutal sentences, Joyce laid out a case against her. He accepted it all as true and knew that he could never trust her again. He had learned only an hour before that in their sacred summer of 1904 she had betrayed him, that "At the time I used to meet you *every second night* [underlined] you kept an appointment with a friend of mine . . . You stood with him: he put his arm round you and you lifted your face and kissed him."[2] How much farther had the embraces gone? Joyce was, he said, weeping and sobbing in grief and humiliation as he wrote. All he could see was Nora's face raised to kiss "another's." Was their own life together to be finished? She, the only person he had ever trusted, had deceived him. His love was dead. Yet he begged three times that she write to him.

Joyce did not bother to enlighten Nora about the identity of her accuser. When he spoke of having heard the story "from his lips," he knew that she knew he meant Cosgrave. The pieces fell into place. Among his friends, Cosgrave knew her best. Cosgrave was the only one to write to Nora personally and to have had the audacity to refer to her to Joyce by her first name — a familiarity that, by Joyce's standards, was tantamount to a hand inside her dress. With hindsight, Joyce could recall Cosgrave's attempt to dissuade Nora from eloping and also Cosgrave's reputation as a fast-talking medical man experienced with women. When, on the afternoon of August 6, 1909, Cosgrave had taken Joyce aside and boasted that he too had enjoyed Nora's favors five years before, Joyce unhesitatingly believed him.

Nora did not have much time to recover. A second letter arrived, written at half past six in the morning following the first. Joyce had scarcely slept. With controlled hysteria and uncharacteristically coarse language, he threw questions at her. Was Giorgio really his child? (During the long night he had recalled how little blood there had been on the sheets when he and Nora first had intercourse and had calculated that Giorgio's birth nine months and sixteen days later allowed the possibility that Nora might have been pregnant already at the time.) The interrogation continued: had she been fucked by anyone before him? Had she lain on the ground to kiss "that other"? (Joyce's refusal to write "Cosgrave" shows the magical power he attached to names.) Had she touched Cosgrave in the same intimate way as she had touched him?[3]

All the suppressed doubts of five years burst forth. Nora's sexual confidence, it was belatedly obvious to Joyce, had not sprung from nowhere; she had sauntered over to him a little too easily in June 1904. He had been the last to realize that people were laughing at him for choosing a girl known to have been enjoyed by other men.[4]

Nora's response was total silence. Whatever her reasons — hurt, anger, inability to defend herself in writing, or guilt — she sent not one word to relieve Joyce's agony. Instead, she showed the accusing letters to Stanislaus, who set about forming his own reply.

In Dublin meanwhile, Joyce was distraught. He needed to confide in someone; the obvious person was J. F. Byrne, who had been his best friend until superseded by Cosgrave. Joyce's friendship with Byrne had formed at University College where Joyce, as the younger of the two, had admired Byrne's calm, athletic skill and maturity. (Byrne was the model for Stephen's friend Cranly in *A Portrait*.)

That summer Byrne was living in a brick Georgian terraced house at 7 Eccles Street on the north side of Dublin and, as he had already had a visit from Joyce and little Giorgio, was not expecting another. Byrne was therefore astonished when Joyce burst into his home unannounced:

I have always known that Joyce was highly emotional, but I had never before this afternoon seen anything to approach the frightening condition that convulsed him. He wept and groaned and gesticulated in futile impotence as he sobbed out to me the thing that had occurred. Never in my life have I seen a human being more shattered and the sorrow I felt for him then and my sympathy were enough to obliterate forever some unpleasant memories. I spoke to him and succeeded in quieting him; and gradually he emerged *de profundis*. He stayed for dinner and supper and spent the night in my house. The following morning he was up early, fully out of the gloom, and after breakfast he went off, humming as he went.[5]

What had Byrne said to such healing effect? In later years he could not remember. According to Joyce, however, Byrne told him that Cosgrave's story was "a blasted lie," probably a plot concocted by Cosgrave and Gogarty to destroy Joyce's happiness with Nora.

Joyce accepted Byrne's theory eagerly and joyfully. He left the house, as Byrne recounts, with his peace of mind restored. Joyce was even more reassured a few days later when he heard from Stanislaus. Stanislaus revealed that he had been keeping a secret for five years: that in 1904 Cosgrave had confessed that he had tried to take Nora away from Joyce and had failed. Cosgrave had asked Stanislaus to swear not to tell his brother, and Stanislaus had kept his word — apart from dropping veiled hints in a letter to Jim that Cosgrave was a treacherous friend. For Joyce, Stanislaus's letter corroborated Byrne's theory.[6]

But what did Byrne really say to Joyce? The incident of August 6, 1909, merits a close look as it is central to understanding the relationship between Nora and Joyce, as well as the origins of *Ulysses*. (Out of relief and gratitude to the place where his "marriage" was reborn, Joyce made Byrne's address at 7 Eccles Street the Dublin home of his modern Odysseus, Leopold Bloom.)

It is clear that Byrne reassured Joyce on the basis of speculation rather than information. Byrne did not know whether Cosgrave's story was true or not; he himself had never even met Oliver Gogarty. His words to Joyce were emotional first aid, spoken to calm a friend as a parent might offer a child a less painful explanation for an imagined insult. Neither was Byrne himself objective in the matter. He had encouraged Joyce to take Nora away in 1904, and he wanted to patch up the rift between them as quickly as possible.

As for Cosgrave's motives, if indeed he invented the whole story, they are as hard to fathom as Iago's. Joyce in 1909 was no Othello, no colossus, only a young writer desperately seeking publication. Nora was no Desdemona but an Irish emigrant who took in washing in Trieste. Joyce convinced himself that Cosgrave and Gogarty wanted to shatter his domestic happiness out of envy and out of fear of what he might someday write about them — yet they had seen nothing of his life with Nora, and the books in which they would feature were (apart from *Stephen Hero* in which Cosgrave was Lynch) as yet unwritten.

Joyce nurtured the thought of "those bowsies" conspiring against him and Nora, but to do so required him to overlook a great deal. It required him to believe that Gogarty, a successful surgeon with a busy practice, met Cosgrave after Joyce's unexpected return and plotted to break Joyce's trust in Nora. It required him also to believe that both men wanted revenge against him — Gogarty for the imbroglio over the tower and Cosgrave for the pseudonym of Lynch. It also required Joyce to decide that Gogarty had been lying when, as he and Joyce parted during their meeting the previous week, he had shaken Joyce's hand and said, "I don't care a damn what you say of me so long as it is literature."[7]

With hindsight and access to Joyce's family letters now at Cornell, it is clear that Joyce was in a high state of paranoia that summer. He had returned to Dublin bristling, ready to take offense. *Dubliners,* the book he had counted on to make his name and to let his countrymen know how he saw them, was nowhere near being published. The young son of whom he was so proud was widely known to be illegitimate. (Joyce's sensitivity on this score had already been shown when he wrongly accused his father and sisters of not wanting to see Giorgio.) Joyce's paranoia only increased when he re-entered the Dublin gossip mill. He sensed rejection on every side. Where he did not find it, he created it.

Separation from Nora had removed his anchor to reality; besides, his friends were much changed. The years in life between the ages of twenty-two and twenty-seven are long ones, and many of his old circle who had remained in Ireland had risen in society, married, and prospered. Constantine Curran was a lawyer; Joyce found him "disposed to be unfriendly." Thomas Kettle, another University College friend, was a member of Parliament and about to marry the girl Joyce had so admired, Mary Sheehy. Gogarty was established as a surgeon, with a fine house in town, another in the country, and consulting rooms on Ely Place.

It was not true that Joyce's old friends ignored his return. Gogarty had tried to repair the breach. He invited Joyce to lunch but then had to send the kind of professional excuse that should not offend a friend but invariably does:

> I find that at 1 o'c. there is a patient coming who cannot come at any other time. I will be glad if, in view of this, you will forgive a little postponement of the lunch. I will let you know. Yours. O.G.[8]

When Joyce did go around to Gogarty's room and found himself looking out at a splendid rose garden, he refused (as he boasted in a letter to Stanislaus) "grog, wine, coffee, tea." He also turned down the kind of invitation that a returned exile might welcome — a chance to drive down to Enniskerry, a pretty village twelve miles from Dublin, to meet Gogarty's wife (the woman to whom Joyce had believed Gogarty would never present him).

Joyce was invited to dinner by another of the Sheehy girls, Hanna, who had just married his friend Francis Skeffington. Joyce refused. Yet when

Hanna's parents, the senior Sheehys, whose house on Belvedere Place he had so often visited as a young man, did not get in touch with him, he smarted from the slight. He knew himself to be in the land of betrayers; he was being treated only as he expected. In one of his public lectures on Ireland in Trieste two years earlier, he had told his audience that the Fenian movement for Irish nationhood would never succeed "simply because in Ireland, just at the right moment, an informer always appears." [9]

In his own life, two years later, almost on cue, the informer had appeared — only it was Nora, not Ireland, who was the victim.

The chances are high that there was some truth in the tale Cosgrave poured into Joyce's ear — words full of innuendo spoken softly at lunchtime, possibly in a crowded pub — and that Joyce fashioned them into the story that he craved to hear. Nora, while working at Finn's, did have free evenings for which Joyce could not account.[10] Joyce also knew that he was exaggerating when he charged Nora with seeing Cosgrave *every second night;* he himself had occasionally seen her several nights in a row, and sometimes her free time was canceled and she did not have her planned evening off. That Cosgrave and Gogarty could have lied about Nora out of sheer malicious glee is possible. It was not inconsistent with their cruel Irish wit. But Joyce himself was not shy of a half-truth when he wanted to pay off an old score. While in Dublin that summer, when he heard the news that the chauffeur of Gogarty's car had run over a child in a road accident, Joyce reported to Trieste, "Gogarty killed a child last week." [11]

A more realistic interpretation of the known facts about the courtship of Nora Barnacle would be that Cosgrave had indeed escorted Nora out on a few evenings in 1904 (Joyce had arranged one himself) and that on one or more of these occasions, before she seriously committed herself to Joyce, she had allowed Cosgrave to fondle her and to progress in his advances at least as far as Willie Mulvagh had done in Galway.

Byrne in later years carried his speculations further — that Nora had given herself to Cosgrave but that their relationship finished when she fell in love with Joyce:

> To my knowledge, Joyce neither could, nor should have thought of himself as a "cuckold." It was Cosgrave who introduced Joyce to Nora and, when Joyce was visiting me in Eccles Street in 1909, Cosgrave told him he had had carnal knowledge of Nora *before* he introduced Joyce to her — *not* afterwards. This is the reason why Joyce should not have regarded himself as a "cuckold." And, indeed, Joyce himself was no virgin when he went from Dublin with Nora. As a matter of fact, Joyce should not have been otherwise than grateful to Cosgrave for being the person who had brought him and Nora together — that same Nora being the young woman who, as Jim himself told me, took in washing during Joyce's illness in Trieste to help make

money for herself and family. Nora was a splendid, outstanding helpmate for James Joyce. She was a great girl and woman. This is what everyone ought to know now; and this is all they need to know.[12]

Byrne, in retrospect, did not believe Stanislaus's story of Cosgrave's confession of being rebuffed by Nora. To Byrne, the difference in the men's ages was too great. Cosgrave, a worldly twenty-six at the time, would not have confided a sexual failure to someone of twenty, as Stanislaus then was, Byrne said.

The glaring truth in the whole shadowy episode is that Joyce could not have written *Ulysses* without the surge of fear and relief that he derived from it. He had a need to feel deceived (the critic Leon Edel has called him "The Injustice Collector") for which world literature is the richer.[13] This need, exacerbated by the bitter frustration of remaining unpublished, blinded the Joyce of 1909 to any clear view of the motives of people around him. He saw treachery everywhere, and perhaps had since childhood. (Some Joycean scholars have detected the theme of betrayal in the opening pages of *A Portrait,* written in the distorted language of infancy, where Stephen Dedalus sees himself as "baby tuckoo" — in other words, a baby cuckoo or baby cuckold, a nice little boy born to be betrayed.)[14]

To satisfy his persecution fantasies, Joyce needed to feel not only that Nora had concealed from him her loss of virginity *before* she met him; he had also to believe that she had betrayed him *during* their own courtship. The two love affairs of 1904, as he organized them in his mind exactly five years later, had to be concurrent, not consecutive.

It is interesting to compare Joyce's insistence that Nora had betrayed him *"every second night,"* rather than *before* she met him, with a long debate Stephen Dedalus holds with himself in the Proteus episode of *Ulysses.* Stephen, walking along Sandymount Strand, ponders the difference between audible experience, in which symbols come one after the other, and the visible, in which they appear all at the same time. Stephen asks himself why audible forms of art, like music or literature, which flow through time, cannot be like the visual arts, painting or sculpture, which exist in space and in which time does not exist. Stephen distinguishes the two as *nacheinander* (one after the other; the audible) and *nebeneinander* (next to each other; the visible).[15]

In his own art, Joyce resolved the dilemma by writing *Finnegans Wake,* a book set outside time and outside history, with no beginning and no end, but he never resolved his personal uncertainty about the sequence of events in Nora's sexual past. There is no evidence that she ever enlightened him.

Although Byrne restored Joyce's peace of mind shortly after Cosgrave destroyed it on August 6, Joyce cruelly took nearly two weeks to do the same for Nora. Not until August 19 did he write to apologize for falsely accusing her. Then he did so by asking disingenuously why she had not written: "Are you ill?"

He went on to say that Byrne had convinced him that Cosgrave's story was a fabrication. Then followed a series of staccato one-sentence paragraphs, again not his usual epistolary style. He was worthless. He would now try to be worthy of her. He had just sent her three large bags of shell cocoa. His sister Poppie was leaving Ireland (for a convent in New Zealand). He had just signed a contract for *Dubliners*. No man was worthy of a woman's love. She was not to read the crazed letters he wrote. He would be acclaimed one day, and she would be at his side. He closed with four lines from his poem "My kiss will give you peace now."[16] The letter, full of love, contrition, and longing for reconciliation, contains one jarring note: a desperate plea for her to send him even one word denying Cosgrave's claim. Apparently he was still not entirely convinced of her innocence.

Only then, after she had been "forgiven," did Nora begin to write to Joyce, and she did so with great shrewdness. She offered not one word of denial or defense. Instead she told him that she had been reading *Chamber Music*. She added, touching a raw nerve in a jealous man, that Stanislaus had been very kind to her in the upset of the previous few weeks.

Joyce responded with a passionate redeclaration of love. When he met her, she was far from the ethereal beauty he dreamed of in his youth but, by revealing to him a deeper beauty, had become his fulfillment and his inspiration. His poems, therefore, were for her.[17]

Cruel as he had been to her, he said, at least he had not killed her generous warmth and spontaneity. He congratulated himself that he had taught her much and that she was a more sensitive person than when he met her. He was to keep his promises, to bring his sister Eva back with him and to go to Galway to see her mother and her family, but he dreaded the visit. Any hint or mention of her past might revive his torments of jealousy. He knew he was unreasonable, but there was nothing he could do to control his terror. He was, he said, absurdly jealous of the past.[18]

Joyce knew that Willie Mulvagh still lurked in Galway and he was not sure how many other former boyfriends as well. Joyce's panic, coming two years after completion of "The Dead," shows that as an effort to exorcise the past, the story was a failure. Joyce never conquered his fear of Nora's old loves.

Accusation, contrition, reparation. On August 22, Joyce changed key. He reminded Nora that in "The Dead" he had described her body as "strange and musical and perfumed." (His remark is a sign that Nora had read his story and that she knew that she was the model for Gretta

Conroy.) Then he said something strange — that *she* owed *him* compensation in some form for having inspired the jealousy still burning in his heart: "Your love for me must be fierce and violent to make me forget *utterly.*"[19]

It was as if he were the injured party and hers the responsibility for making amends. Relief released in Joyce a torrent of erotic fantasy. He dreamed of her that day in all kinds of poses, from the maidenly to the obscene. She was to have no secrets from him — no privacy of the body any more than of the mind — he was to be her master. And, he added, he was bringing her a special gift.

He then dropped an explicit hint about the kind of compensation he required from her, something she could provide for him even before he returned to Trieste: a letter of a kind that he himself dared not send to her.[20]

Nora, to judge from Joyce's subsequent correspondence, granted his wish. She did understand him. At about the same time that Joyce reached Galway and was sitting at the kitchen table in Bowling Green, talking to her mother, and going to look at the house in Whitehall where she had lived with her grandmother, Nora sat down in Trieste, presumably after her little daughter was put to bed, picked up her pen, and wrote him an obscene letter.[21]

For the remainder of his time in Dublin, Joyce could think of little but his reunion with Nora. He did manage to tend to his business affairs and to badger Stanislaus for money for him and Eva.[22] He held out to Stannie prospects of prosperity just around the corner: in the next year (1910), with both of them teaching private pupils, plus the publication of his book, they would make a good living and he and Nora would take a honeymoon.

His letters to Nora were of a different nature. She was writing to him almost daily now, letters that were an aid to masturbation. He was highly upset, he wrote her on September 2, "on account of doing what I told you." As the correspondence progressed, he reminded her how crude speech offended him. Yet he wondered if perhaps even his letters had gone too far. In the morning when he remembered what he had posted to Trieste the night before, he felt disgusted with himself. But, at least, he consoled himself, Nora now knew the very worst about him and that she held the secret of holding him forever.[23] Or, of punishing him. A new masochistic craving began to surface. Why, he demanded, had she not disciplined him sooner? That night he had an insane new fantasy —that she would flog him, with her eyes blazing with anger.[24]

He wondered if he were out of his mind as he alternated between visions of her as a madonna and as an insolent whore. He feared he might disgust her, but it was she, he reminded her, who always led the way. He recalled the night in Pola when she had urged him on. He wanted her to know him at his worst and to think of him as the weak, impulsive fellow she loved who needed her to make him strong. "I gave others my pride and joy," he ended. "To you I give my sin, my folly, my weakness and sadness."

Joyce expected Nora to play both virgin and whore. But Nora had her own contradictions to hold in balance. She thought Joyce was childish, but he was master of her fate; she loved him and desired him but despised him for not providing for his family. Each, therefore, was prisoner of the other. The present Joyce had bought for Nora summed up his dependence: a necklace of ivory cubes on which he had inscribed "Love is unhappy when love is away," a line from the ninth poem in *Chamber Music*. Joyce meant it literally when he implored her to save him "from the badness of the world and of my own heart!" Nora rescued him from the isolation of his imagined depravity by indulging in it with him, as when he confessed to a wish to kiss her somewhere, not on the mouth. He left it to her to guess where.[25]

One of the thoughts about which he felt ashamed was his jealousy of his own children. He resented sharing Nora with Giorgio and Lucia. He needed her entirely for himself, and amid the clutter of sadomasochistic and sacrilegious images he sent her was a cry (almost straight out of Ibsen's *Little Eyolf*): "Our children (much as I love them) must *not* come between us." He even went further and longed to become one of them. If he could shelter in her womb, if he were part of her soul, "then I will indeed become the poet of my race."[26]

Joyce, as he went about Dublin, was by no means as despised as he pretended. *Dubliners* was set to come out the following March. At a reception at the Gresham Hotel he was introduced as the great writer of Ireland's future. His mind, however, was in bed with Nora. He urged her to take every day the cocoa he sent, to make her figure as voluptuous as his fantasies.[27]

He wanted her to wear black underwear and to think about ways to excite him. His sensual longing extended also to thoughts of his return journey; how the train from Venice would wind along the beautiful Adriatic coastline, pass the promontory on which stands the white castle of Miramare, and then, *"la nostra bella Trieste,"* the city they had discovered together, their real home.

August turned into September, and the time came to enact the dream. Eva was packing, with her sisters around, helping her, and busy with all the practical details of their return, Joyce was no longer tormented by fierce erotic fantasies and turned to practicalities. He wrote Nora continually, sometimes twice a day. He began to worry that Nora would nag him about bills when he returned. He hoped her hair would not be untidy, full of ashes from stoking the fire. She was not to cry when he saw her; he wanted to see her beautiful eyes clear. And thoughts of bed gave way to thoughts of table. "Will you make me a nice cup of black coffee in a nice small cup?" he said. "Ask that snivelling girl Globocnik how to do it. Make a good salad, will you? Another thing don't bring garlic or onions into the house."[28]

He had so much to tell her of Dublin, he promised, that he would be talking to her every minute of the night when they were not otherwise occupied. (This message to Nora was enclosed in a letter to Stanislaus, whom Joyce trusted not to open it.)

The long-awaited day came. Joyce, with Eva, arrived in Trieste on September 13. Nora put on a good gray dress with a blue underblouse and came rushing out to meet him. "Jim!" she called in her husky voice. The exuberance of their reunion irritated Stanislaus. Suppressing his attraction to Nora, hurt that she took little notice of him, he was disgusted when he saw the necklace proclaiming, "Love is unhappy when love is away." Stannie muttered, "So is love's brother."[29]

If she had been expecting that the scenes of their correspondence were to be acted out immediately, Nora was disappointed. When night came and she approached Joyce, with her long red hair streaming down over her white chemise with its blue ribbons, she had to wake him. Her willful, erring, jealous lover was asleep.[30]

Five weeks later Nora was by herself again. Joyce was back in Dublin. He was nothing if not enterprising. Four well-to-do Triestines had backed him in a new business venture he had dreamed up, inspired by his sister Eva upon her arrival in Trieste. How was it that Dublin — a city of half a million people who loved theater and music halls — lacked the new form of entertainment that was sweeping the rest of urban Europe? In his scheme to open Dublin's first moving-picture house, Joyce saw his chance for solid and swift profit at last.

Try as he would, however, Joyce still could not read Nora's mind. He was continually suspicious of her reservations about him and her true views about her religion. One day while they were out shopping a priest passed them. Joyce, testing Nora, asked if she did not feel revolted by the very sight. "No, I don't," she said — a little too shortly and drily for Joyce's comfort. He fell into a gloom. Was she his ally, or was she secretly against him? There were many times when she disappointed him. She was rude to him at *Madame Butterfly* when all he wanted was the pleasure of hearing the music in her company. Another night when he came home late from the café, bursting to tell her of all he hoped to achieve with his writing, she wouldn't listen. She was tired and wanted to go to sleep.[31]

When the time came for him to return to Dublin, their parting had not been friendly. As Nora walked out the door of their flat to see Jim off at the station, she was so angry because he had come home late that she called him an imbecile (probably spitting out the insult in its powerful four-syllable Italian form). She faced a long separation. Jim would not even be home for Christmas. Yet as she stood on the platform as his train pulled out, she turned her head so that he would not see her weep.

This time it was Nora who was driven to write first. Nothing came from Dublin; Jim was punishing her for her bad-tempered farewell. She used her humblest voice. Was he tired of her? Why had he ever been interested in an ignorant little Galway girl?

Her tactic worked and Joyce replied at length. He would never be tired of her; he simply wanted her to be politer to him. She was to remember that with all the work involved in setting up the cinematograph he would be very busy. But:

> You are my only love. You have me completely in your power. I *know* and *feel* that if I am to write anything fine and noble in the future I shall do so only by listening at the doors of your heart.[32]

Two days later he was writing to say he was so much a part of her that he hoped they would live like one person and even die at the same time.

It would take a harder-hearted woman than Nora to be unmoved by such protestations. Nora may not have appreciated Joyce's later books, but in their personal relations she constantly warmed to the beauty of his words.

She also liked the way he wooed her with presents and care about her appearance. He wrote that she was to be dutiful and drink her fattening cocoa and also to pay some of her dressmaker's bill in preparation for having a new dress made out of the yards and yards of Donegal tweed he was sending her. (Probably he got the cloth wholesale. One of his peripheral commercial activities in Dublin was to find an agency to handle the export of Irish tweed to merchants in Trieste.) She was to have an ensemble made exactly as he wished: the coat to reach nearly to the hem of the skirt and (recreating the colors he had associated with Gretta Conroy in "The Dead") to be lined with dark blue or bronze satin, and with its collar, belt, and cuffs to be made of blue leather.

Nora, who basked in Joyce's interest in her wardrobe, shared with him his love for fur (Joyce seemed to believe in its healing as well as its erotic properties). When he returned, she would also have, as he described with great delight, a hat, stole, and muff of gray squirrel. He had selected them himself: the hat decorated with violets at the side, and the stole and muff lined with violet satin. There would be more, he promised. If the cinema succeeded, she would have more fine clothes than she ever dreamed of.

For an immediate gift, he sent Nora several pairs of gloves and announced in advance what his Christmas present to her would be: her own copy of *Chamber Music,* hand copied onto parchment by himself.

Nora had lost none of her sense of humor. She wrote an arch thank-you letter in the style she had used as a chambermaid at Finn's Hotel:

dear Mr Joyce how can I thank you for your kindness the box of Gloves which you sent me are lovely and a splendid fit it was a great surprise to get such a nice present I hope you are quite well and will be very pleased to see you I hope you will write to me and let me know when I am to meet you again at present I am rather busy and cant get out for some time I hope you will excuse me and accept many thanks   Nora Barnacle[33]

For a few weeks into November the correspondence between Dublin and Trieste continued routine. There was plenty of news to report. From Trieste to Dublin Stannie wrote of Eva's homesickness, his own and Giorgio's health, the opera, and the arrangements for teaching Joyce's language pupils in his absence. From Dublin to Trieste Joyce sent the electrician's estimate for the new cinema (to be called the Volta), literary gossip, and the usual litany of bad news about the family: their father in the hospital, Charlie destitute in Boston, their sisters (five remained at home) facing eviction.

Such mundane exchanges were cut short by two abrupt communications to Joyce from Trieste. The first was a telegram from Stanislaus: "wire £4 writ landlord." The second was a letter from Nora.

She was leaving him. She was taking the children and returning to Galway. His false promises and total inability to protect his family like a man disgusted her. *He* disgusted her. It was as if the threat of eviction had broken their bargain; she could put up with his odd sexual proclivities only as long as he looked after her and the children.

Joyce, who often teased Nora, never laughed off her threats to leave him. This time he groveled. He wrote imploringly to her, calling himself a swine, a low wretch; he agreed that Nora and the children should not live with such depravity. He had worn down her love. She should abandon him to the gutter from which she had rescued him. He would give her two-thirds of his income.

More to the point, he paid the rent. He wired a pound and seven shillings, nearly fifty-seven Austrian crowns, to Trieste, enough for one month of the overdue rent if not for two, and he also barked long-distance commands to Stanislaus, to do everything possible, even sell the furniture, to keep Nora and Georgie and Lucia from eviction.

Nora's anger vanished. Swiftly she showed him another Nora, the little country girl. It was her turn to apologize. She sent two letters that moved Joyce so deeply that when his backers from Trieste arrived in Dublin to supervise the Volta project he booked them into Finn's Hotel, which, he said, impressed them very much (even though it was hardly Dublin's finest).

Finn's was unchanged. "The place is very Irish," Joyce wrote Nora. "The disorder of the table was Irish, the wonder on the faces also, the curious-looking eyes of the woman herself and her waitress." He later persuaded the waitress to let him go upstairs to see where Nora had lived in 1904. There he indulged in a bath of fantasy, looking at the little servant's room where Nora had read his love letters and decided to go away with him.[34]

Nora made another move; she seemed always to be one jump ahead of him. In her letters she abandoned her humility for an erotic aggressiveness. Initiating a new round of salacious correspondence, she threatened to punish him if he failed to obey her instructions.

During the short time Joyce was in Trieste between journeys, from September 13 to October 18, 1909, he and Nora had resumed their sexual relations, with him even more insistent than before that there be no veil of shame between them. He began to exact from Nora some of the exercises of which he had dreamed during their summer's separation. He taught her to make what he called "filthy signs" and "whorish gestures" to excite him. His demands did not stop there. He persuaded her to defecate while he lay under her and watched. Nora was too embarrassed even to look at him afterwards. Even her embarrassment pleased him.[35]

Joyce had what H. G. Wells later called a cloacal obsession. *Cloaca* means sewer in Latin. Somewhere between his training at the hands of his mother and his experience at Clongowes Wood, where he was afraid of wetting the bed and where bullies could push boys into the cold slime of the "square ditch" (the cesspit), Joyce came to find everything connected with excretion unusually pleasurable. Moreover, if the Freudian view be taken — that the unconscious associates defecation with spending money or with childbirth — Joyce had formidable influences within his own home. His father's wild extravagance was the very opposite of anal retentiveness; Joyce himself linked his father's "spendthrift habits" with his own and with "any creativity I may possess." As for his fertile mother, fat brown things popped from her body with a regularity that must have awed her impressionable eldest child.

How Jim came by his obsession was no concern of Nora's. The quirk of personality, combined with a fetish for women's underclothes and furs, was part of the reality of the man she had chosen.

She put up with Joyce's oddity and manipulated it for her own protection and satisfaction. Joyce's peculiar sexual tastes gave her a hold on him that in some ways compensated for his power over her.

She engaged in their obscene correspondence also to keep him away from prostitutes. Joyce had had a venereal disease when she met him. He might, she feared, return to consorting with Dublin whores when he was away from her; he might renew his infection and possibly pass it on to her.[36]

He, for his part, was worried about her sexual appetite. If she was unable to bear the frustration until he returned, she might, he feared, turn to another man.

Both were prepared, therefore, for a new round of masturbatory correspondence when the second separation followed so swiftly upon the first. Back in Dublin, he seems to have survived for about ten days before lustful longing poured itself into a letter.[37] Nora directly raised her old worry about prostitutes, but he assured her that she could supply all that they could, and he hoped his letters were being equally preventive for her.

Nora's actual letters to Joyce in those highly charged weeks have never surfaced. However, Joyce so faithfully echoed her own words in his letters, which have been published,* that it is possible to reconstruct Nora's own. These began with the frank declaration, late in November 1909, that she was longing to be fucked by him.[38]

Joyce placed her letter on the table before him, fixing his eyes on the word, which was, he said in his letter of December 2, "like the act itself, brief, brutal, irresistible and devilish." He replied in a frenzy of obscenity, reminding her later (what Nora knew very well) that he never used obscene phrases when speaking and that he intensely disliked dirty jokes. Yet, he told her, she transformed him into an animal.

Their correspondence then entered an extraordinary phase. He always seemed to be inviting her to lead the way, as when he said he imagined things so dirty that he could not write them until he saw how she wrote herself. He also made it clear, with graphic description, that he was overwhelmed by thoughts of her flushed face, mad eyes, and lustful inventiveness. He described her sexual practices: the way she used her fingers, fondling and tickling his balls or stuck up in his rectum.[39]

If Nora was offended by any of his obscenity, she was mollified by other passages containing exquisite lyrical expressions of his love for her character and her beauty. She thanked him for the lovely name he called her: "My beautiful wild flower of the hedges! My dark-blue, rain-drenched flower."

There was no stopping him now. A man who believed he would be the greatest writer his country ever produced saw himself with the chance to write high pornography. Joyce also seized the opportunity to rehearse the techniques he was going to use in his future writing. He was going to tell the truth. He demanded of himself — and of Nora — exactly what Freud was asking of his patients in the new art of psychoanalysis: to put every thought, however shameful, into words without flinching.

The wonder is not that James Joyce could do it, but that Nora Barna-

---

* See the Appendix.

cle, schooled only at the Convent of Mercy, confidently matched him and, by his own judgment, sometimes bettered him.

In his letters he listed all the things that she had done first — used the first obscene word, touched him intimately in the dark. Yet this train of thought revived yet again his nagging doubts about her experience.

Astonishingly, three months after the Cosgrave trauma, which he had pretended had settled the question forever, he began all over again to question her about her past in words that suggest that Nora had confessed to something. Had "that person" had his hands inside Nora's body? How far inside?[40] Had she come? Had the other person? Had she assisted? Was he, Joyce, to believe that his was the first penis she ever touched?

No prosecuting attorney could have been more meticulous. The precision and persistence of Joyce's new questions suggest that possibly, upon his return to Trieste in September, Nora had conceded having allowed Cosgrave's hands to wander into forbidden territory in 1904. Yet Joyce was still insisting that he must be told all. She must not be afraid to tell him everything: his desire for her would not slacken even if he knew that she had been enjoyed by half the young men in Galway.[41]

He would love her always, Joyce insisted, because the things he had written and told her he could never tell another woman. Nora knew truth when she heard it. Tighter than marriage vows, their obscene exchanges bound them to each other. Nora knew also that she was faithful to Joyce, but she was also practical. She kept him on tenterhooks. One can imagine her saying, "There is no need to tell the man everything."

Nora began maneuvering to her own advantage. Instead of answering his new inquisition, she provoked him with a picture he could not resist. She was so short of money, she said, she was going around without underclothes.

As if she had pressed a key, she released a new rush of fantasy and money. Joyce sent her a banknote to buy drawers and described the long-legged frilly undergarments he loved. The drawers, he said, would be improved if she would discolor them with a brown stain. He dreamed of squirting semen on her face, of buggering her.[42]

Nora pressed on. She told him to masturbate twice when he read her letter. When he returned, she said, she would fuck him off and she wanted him to lick her cunt. She said she did like "being fucked arseways." Could he remember, she asked, the night when they did it for so long "backwards"?[43]

Joyce remembered indeed. The stream of his associations — his December 8 letter spoke about farts spluttering out of her backside — is almost unreadable in its exaltation of fetid odor.

The letters were designed as aids to self-stimulation, yet Joyce could not indulge in it until two and three o'clock in the morning after exhausting days organizing the cinema. He wrote them in the room he had in the small house at 44 Fontenoy Street that he shared with his family, and there is nothing erotic in their physical appearance. They are neat letters. The first was on a small, blue sheet folded like a card, the rest on larger, cream-colored paper, written in small, careful handwriting, with hardly a word crossed out. They give no sign of having been written during the act of masturbation; indeed the clarity of the filthiest passages, compared with the more mundane, suggests that Joyce may even have copied them from rough drafts he wrote during the day. Nonetheless, their contents are punctuated by exclamations of relief. In one letter Joyce confessed that the need to change his trousers prevented him from catching the last post.

Nora's own sexual tastes do not seem to have been anal, but she wanted to hold her man, she wanted to extract money, and she loved sexual games. Once he complained when her letter was unexpectedly cold; he sent another banknote. He was in bliss when she told him "she wants me to roger her arseways and wants me to fuck her mouth and wants to unbutton me and pull out my mickey and suck it off like a teat." He was dazzled by the dirty words she used, wished he could see her lips "spluttering" (a word he favored for Nora almost as much as *sauntering*) the obscene words. He was also awed by her own talent for pornography, in which she described going at herself in the "closet."

The closet — the Continental-style water closet, with its floor-level facilities — was probably the only place where Nora could find privacy in the family flat. He also admired how she could say just what he wanted to hear: "You say you will shit your drawers, dear, and let me fuck you then . . ."[44]

Nora boasted that she could outdo him at this writing game, and he conceded her superiority, especially when she described the use to which she could put her tongue (and, he said explicitly, he knew she did not mean fellatio). "Write more and dirtier, darling." He also instructed her, as he had five years before, to use the letters as erotic objects in themselves. She was to hold them beneath her, break wind upon them and perhaps do worse, then send them to him, "my darling brown-arsed fuckbird."

As in August, the focus of the erotic correspondence shifted as the pace intensified. By mid-December 1909, after writing about a half dozen of the letters, Joyce descended to infantile and masochistic images. He revived the wish to be flogged; if his filth offended her, he asked her to bring him to his senses "with the lash as you have done before." He wished that Nora, or a stronger version of her, with a full bosom and big fat thighs, would rip off his trousers and beat him as if he were a naughty child.

He paid a tribute to the ingenuity of her lust but went on to suggest possibilities himself: on the stairs, on the kitchen table, in the water closet; with only her hat and stockings on, with a flower sticking out of her bottom; or, like a man, like a nursemaid with her soldier . . . Always she was to be the dominant partner, he the passive recipient.[45]

He continued to combine his basest images — Nora atop him grunting like a sow doing her dung — with the most lyrical — "my love, my life, my star, my little strange-eyed Ireland." [46]

In his letter of December 20, Joyce gave in to his most florid anal fantasy: a girl with her white drawers pulled apart and "a fat brown thing" protruding from her bottom. That same letter, which recorded his orgasm, also marked the turning point in the correspondence. From then on in his letters he rose to the surface, floating on blissful thoughts of hearth and home. He dreamed of putting up posters to decorate the kitchen walls, of hanging new red curtains, and sitting in a comfortable armchair. Childish visions of favorite foods, Irish and Italian, danced in his head. He wanted polenta, stewed eels, mashed potatoes, roast beef, macaroni and pot roast, *torrone* . . . The only warm, brown image intruding upon his reveries then was of the kind of new linoleum he wanted for the kitchen. His longing had taken him, in the space of a month, from vagina to anus to womb.

The dirty letters were over. Joyce and Nora never corresponded in that manner again. During the rest of his stay in Dublin, Joyce confined his letters to boyish poetic effusions of love ("a million kisses to my darling dew-laden western flower, a million million kisses to my dear Nora of the curls"). He was preoccupied with the opening of the Volta on December 20 and with plans for Christmas. Mrs. Barnacle had sent him a turkey. Busy among the Christmas crowds, he nonetheless found time to send Nora some music and her promised copy of *Chamber Music,* with the Joyce family crest worked into its cover. He asked her to keep some of the special Italian Christmas candies so that Eileen could taste them when they both reached Trieste in January.

The fires of jealousy were not entirely extinguished. Joyce suffered a bad attack of anxiety one day in Dublin when he met a policeman from Galway whose sisters had known Nora at the Presentation Convent. What might the stranger not let slip about Nora's past? Fortunately, the policeman remembered Nora only as "the Barnacle girl with the red curls and the proud walk."

For Nora too the dirty revels were ended. She was back where she had begun: with no money and Christmas approaching. Once again she sent Joyce the other kind of letter at which she was becoming adept: she had had enough; she was taking the children and going back to Galway; this time she meant it.

Once again the tactic worked. Fourteen crowns arrived by wire on

Christmas Eve, followed by more abject purple prose: "My little mother take me into the dark sanctuary of your womb." Nora sent Christmas greetings in return, and with them she enclosed, without a word of explanation, a wedding congratulations card. Now that she had satisfied his secret cravings, the card suggested, perhaps he might attend to hers.

The "dirty letters," as they are known to Joyce scholars, are still dirty today, a sexual revolution later. Excrement still smells; soil still suggests pollution and infection. For the most part, the letters are not erotic; the imagery is too lavatorial, childish, and repetitious. Those who read them in *Selected Letters of James Joyce* tend to think, with Molly Bloom in *Ulysses,* "O Jamesy let me up out of this pooh."[47] But the letters are important, for understanding not only Joyce but Nora too, her personality and also her contribution to *Ulysses.* When Joyce had Molly Bloom say,

> Ill drag open my drawers and bulge it right out in his face as large as life he can stick his tongue 7 miles up my hole as hes there my brown part then Ill tell him I want £1 or perhaps 30/- Ill tell him I want to buy underclothes . . .[48]

he had Nora's letters for guidance. The passage, as much else, showed that Joyce had been listening, as he promised Nora, "at the doors of your heart."

The dirty letters raise many questions that remain unanswered. Did Nora and Joyce regard anal sex as a form of birth control? For all that Joyce claimed that they had no bodily secrets from one another, in all the explicitness of their letters about sex there is no mention of the possibility of pregnancy. And where did Nora store the letters in Trieste? Joyce had warned her to keep them to herself. Yet when the post arrived at the via Scussa, Eva and Stannie must have asked, "Letter from Jim, Nora? What does he have to say?"

Later in her life, when Nora complained about her husband's fondness for obscenity, few realized that she derived her opinion from stronger evidence than the pages of *Ulysses.*

As a form of communication between husband and wife for relieving sexual frustration by the least undesirable method, the Joyces' 1909 correspondence was far from unique. The works of Peter Gay on nineteenth-century sensuality show that Victorian prudery was only superficial. Excretory preoccupations were also common, as is shown by the following passage from a letter written in the United States in May 1904:

> I was almost wild with desire as I came along hither in the train today. I wished that your bladder were filled with urine to bursting, and you could,

to save your life, relieve yourself only by urinating into my mouth until you had entirely emptied yourself and I was totally filled with your urine to bursting . . .[49]

The writer was the proper Bostonian Godfrey Lowell Cabot, writing to his wife Minnie at 4:12 in the morning while on a business trip to West Virginia.

For Nora the dirty letters were an exercise in fluency and in control. She proved to Jim that she could match him on paper, and she proved to herself that she had her curious man firmly under her thumb. For her the most memorable line in the whole correspondence may have been the declaration of total surrender on or about December 13: "I will never [*never* underlined four times] leave you again."

7

A House of Joyces

WITHIN THE SPACE of three months, Nora, who had scarcely spoken a word of English to a woman in five years, found herself in a household with two girls from Ireland. In Dublin people had warned Joyce against bringing a sister-in-law into the house, but Eva's arrival in October 1909, followed by Eileen's in January 1910, gave Nora just what she wanted, companionship and help. The Joyce sisters were a strong whiff of Catholic Ireland. They went to Mass regularly and remembered holy days of obligation. "Pray for me!" Nora would call out as Eva and Eileen left for church while she stayed in bed with Jim.[1] Jim was less relaxed about their practice and would not let the *cattolicissime*, as he called them, take Giorgio or Lucia with them.

Eighteen-year-old Eva, the more religious of the two, had been selected by their eldest sister in August 1909 as the one to return to Trieste with Jim because Poppie hoped that Eva might prove a good influence. Eva's stern conscience, however, worked against her adjustment. Joyce and Nora enjoyed the rich mixture of cultures found in Trieste, where there were many Greeks (who Joyce believed brought him luck), as well as Jews, Serbs, Austrians, and Italians, but Eva did not. Homesick from the minute she arrived in Trieste, Eva could not forget that Nora and Jim were not married. She believed, moreover, that her brother had got himself into a false position from which he could not extricate himself. Nora's earthiness shocked her. In August 1910 they moved into a bigger apartment nearer the center. One day, after working to arrange the furniture, they all fell into chairs to admire the effect. Suddenly Nora picked up a chamber pot and placed it triumphantly upon the highest piece of furniture in the room. Eva winced. None of the Joyce girls, she felt, would do anything so common.[2]

Eileen was more Nora's type. Sharp-tongued and good at mimicry, with thin, angular good looks and piercing eyes of Joycean ice-blue, Eileen had no misgivings about her new home. She was proud of her voice and had ambitions as an opera singer. Trieste, for her, was just a step toward her true destination, Milan.[3] She had eagerly helped Joyce prepare for the journey, working at the Volta cinema when it opened and happily accepting the warm coat and gloves he bought her for their journey. Joyce, improvident but generous, was appalled at the way his sisters were living in Dublin and would have brought them all to Trieste had he been able. He promised Nora that in a year or so they might import one of her sisters as well, probably Delia.[4]

Nora may have been under similar pressure from Galway, although no letters survive. Life in Ireland held prospects just as bleak for her brother Tom and her five sisters as it did for the Joyce clan, and they all were to emigrate, most of them permanently. Yet Nora never brought any of them into her Joyce household except as a visitor, and never to Trieste.

For their part Joyce and Stanislaus had set up what amounted to a Joyce commune in Trieste. The sisters left behind dreamed longingly of joining it. It was in many ways a lively place. Giorgio and Lucia made everyone laugh. There was much singing around the rented piano. Saint Patrick's Day was a grand occasion, celebrated with almost as much ceremony as Christmas and Joyce's birthday. Nora, Eileen, and Eva did the cooking together. Nora roasted chickens stuffed with mashed potatoes, sautéed onion, and a touch of cinnamon, her specialty.[5] She also prepared the annual Christmas pudding for which they all, Joyce included, scoured Trieste for the ingredients. Right in the midst of all their activity in the kitchen sat Joyce. He liked to work there, where the light was best, and would sit there reading, with his feet propped up on the table, or writing, with his papers spread across it. Their chatter never bothered him.

It was genuine family life, which meant that there were many arguments, usually about money. Stanislaus was the scapegoat, the odd man out. Living in his own room on the via Nuova, he took his meals with the others and paid board, more than his share, to subsidize his sisters. Often, however, when he arrived in the evening, he would find that the others had already finished eating and had gone out, taking the children, leaving him to eat alone. He felt rejected and exploited, supporting two families; he was even asked on occasion to contribute to Nora's bills for clothes. Stanislaus knew that Nora, Jim, and his sisters made fun of him behind his back, yet whenever they were short of money they ran to him. Even little Giorgio regarded Stanislaus as the family meal ticket. "We've had nothing to eat today," the child scolded his uncle one day, meeting him in the street. "Keep that in your head." Worse to Stanislaus was the way they all conspired against him. Eileen once tricked him into giving her money for a new blouse and then handed it over, by prearrangement, to Jim for housekeeping bills.[6]

Stanislaus confided his bitterness and sexual frustrations to his diary.[7] He believed that his brother was a genius and that his own role in life was to keep the genius from starvation and alcoholism. A thousand miles away Aunt Josephine, with her usual perceptiveness, sensed the tensions in Trieste and scolded Stanislaus for having a low opinion of himself. "It is well that there are so many others who think differently," she said, more with affection than conviction.[8]

Needless to say, Joyce's excursions into commerce had not swathed Nora in cloaks, dresses, and furs. "How did you finish up with the Volta?" his father asked. "Swindled, I presume?"[9] Joyce felt that he had indeed been swindled for he had been promised 10 percent of the profits. However, as there were no profits and the business was sold at a loss that summer, his backers felt justified in giving him nothing.

The familiar shortage of money did not deter Nora any more than Joyce from dressing as well as their credit with tailors and dressmakers would permit. Family photographs taken in Trieste belie the tales of penury being sent back to Dublin. A studio portrait of Eva and Lucia, for example, shows both the three-year-old girl and her aunt sporting enormous hats whose layered ruffles speak of expensive workmanship. It is as if the Joyces needed, in their dress, to proclaim their equality with the snobs whom Joyce had to teach.

The hauteur of Trieste mercantile society rankled Joyce. Joyce enjoyed, and made maximum use of, the patronage of counts, barons, merchants, and professional men. Yet stimulating as he was, no one thought he was a genius; in their eyes he remained a member of a lower class. One sign was that his wife had to work. Another was the modesty of his flats. What is more, Joyce made his rounds in many places without Nora. One Triestine put Nora's absence down to a lack of the appropriate wardrobe. "You had to have the right clothes," she said.[10]

Joyce did enter fine houses, such as the elegant Villa Veneziani with its tiled floors and walls hung with portraits, but only as a teacher. It was the home of Ettore Schmitz and his proud and beautiful wife, Livia. The Schmitzes never received Joyce socially. Livia Schmitz employed Nora to do her ironing (which Nora did at her own home and returned when it was finished). The Schmitz family thought Eileen more refined than Nora and, in order to help Joyce financially, employed Eileen as a governess for their daughter. But the sense of social distance was very great. Joyce, who regarded Signora Schmitz as a model of the beautiful gentlewoman, never forgot that he never crossed the threshold except as an employee and that Livia Schmitz snubbed Nora when she saw her in the street.[11]

The Joyces were not so lowly that they could not employ help of their own. "We didn't come to Trieste to cook for you," Eva and Eileen told Stanislaus. In the autumn of 1910 Joyce hired a young village girl named Mary Kirn as a maid and child minder, luring her away from another job by offering higher pay. Mary Kirn enjoyed working for the Joyces. Not only was she paid regularly (another sign that Joyce was no miser), but she received tips from the wealthy Triestines who came for lessons and who had to be admitted at the street door and led the three flights upstairs to the Joyce apartment.[12]

Mary liked Nora, whom she found always laughing and full of fun. She admired the way Nora would try to tease Joyce out of his gloom. She learned from Nora how to prepare the midday meals. Although Nora had mastered many Italian dishes, she and Joyce preferred Irish food, and for lunch they ate a very traditional combination of bacon, cabbage, and potatoes, washed down with hot tea. Nora spent her afternoons practicing the piano, at which she worked very hard. She also tried to improve her Italian, as Jim was giving her lessons.[13] While doing her ironing, Nora would talk of home, saying, "Oh, you should see how the clothes dry in Ireland, Mary."

Nora had her hands full with Lucia. The child was difficult and often ill. She suffered from boils on her neck, and Nora was mortified. "Don't say anything about this to anybody," she instructed Mary. Nora was not unskilled at home remedies, however; when Lucia had mumps, Nora made a poultice of bread and milk and strapped it to the child's neck. (In her later years Lucia was convinced that this treatment had caused the small scar on her chin about which she was acutely self-conscious.)

Nora loved Lucia, but, like many an Irish or Italian mother, she favored her son. Joyce, in turn, favored his daughter and used to rock her to sleep with a lullaby, *"C'era una volta, una bella bambina, che se chiamava Lucia . . ."* Nora had not breastfed Lucia as she had Giorgio, something Joyce always regretted.[14] She never felt as close to her daughter as to her son, partly because when Lucia was born in 1907 Nora, with an invalid husband, a two-year-old son, and no money, was exhausted in a way she had not been in the weeks following Giorgio's birth.

Still, Giorgio could do no wrong in Nora's eyes, although she often scolded Lucia. Once when the girl sat her doll on a chair it fell off and broke. "Butter hands," Nora snapped. Joyce tried to have the doll repaired.[15]

Nora, nonetheless, left Mary to do much of the caring for Giorgio and then was hurt to find that he had shifted loyalties. During the summer of 1911 Mary took Giorgio and Eileen to visit her family in the country, then found that Giorgio refused to return home. Nora and Joyce both were very upset, and Joyce met at least eight trains in vain. Sternly, he wrote to Mary, ordering her to bring Giorgio back the very next day and to tell Giorgio that his father was very sad because he didn't want to come home anymore. If Giorgio acted up, Joyce instructed Mary, she was to call a policeman to make him obey.[16]

As part of her easy chatter with Mary Kirn, Nora mentioned that she had had a miscarriage and said that she could have no more children. She did not say whether she meant that she was unable to bear another child or whether she had been advised to avoid further pregnancy. She and Joyce never touched on the subject in their correspondence about sex. His plea that their children should not come between them suggests that he was just as afraid of new claims on Nora's attention as of claims on his purse, yet he was of two minds on the subject: in later years, especially when in his cups, he would speak longingly of the wish for a bigger family. (The unending sense of loss of a dead child — Leopold and Molly Bloom's little Rudy — runs through *Ulysses*.) It is even possible that Joyce's reference to the "truncated existence" of Nora's third child reflects a suspicion that she had, with some help from her Triestine women friends, aborted it.

Nora is known to have suffered from gynecological difficulties. When Giorgio and Lucia were very young, she took them with her to Visinada, a village known for its healthy climate, but the trip was a failure. The children were ill, and there was nothing to buy, as she complained in a letter to Jim:

> Dear Jim
> I did not enjoy myself in the least since I came here Lucy has been ill all the time and when she got better Georgie took ill last night he was vomiting all night and is feverish to day I did not sleep a night since I came with Lucy every time she would look at the wild look of the place she would begin to cry she wont go to Gina so that I have to carry her about all day the food is very heavy so that's probably what upset Georgie you need not bother sending me pocket money and I dont intend to stay any longer than Monday so I hope you will kindly arrange for it I intend to go back by the steamer I hope your eyes are better there are no shops here cant buy anything no more at present hoping Stannie is well
>
> Write soon
>
> Nora
>
> still continues[17]

The last two words look like a husband-wife code for some kind of vaginal discharge, and Nora's circumspection in using it shows that she was more alert than was her husband to the possibility that, in their crowded household, private letters were read by other than the intended recipient.

Nora and Joyce themselves argued a great deal. One day, in a fit of rage at her, Joyce took the manuscript of *Stephen Hero,* threw it into the fire, and stormed out of the room. Nora, Mary, and Eileen leaped to rescue it. "This book will make him famous," Nora told Mary. "I'm going to hide it so he won't destroy it." [18] Joyce was too shrewd to have thrown to the flames a work he considered important. He was well on his way to turning *Stephen Hero* into *A Portrait of the Artist as a Young Man.* Nonetheless, he was grateful to his home fire brigade and told his sister Eileen that there were passages in it that he could not have rewritten.

Nora could see how cynical and gloomy continual rejection by publishers was making Jim. She tried to tease him out of it, but he was convinced that he could not finish *A Portrait* until *Dubliners* had seen the light of day. Yet two years after the Dublin publisher George Roberts had contracted to bring out the book there was still no sign of it. In Dublin the Joyce family looked expectantly at the bookstands every month and were disappointed.

In Trieste, Joyce was acquiring a fair reputation as an expositor of English literature and Irish politics. The editor of Trieste's *Piccolo della Sera,* Roberto Prezioso, one of Joyce's earliest pupils, asked him to contribute articles to the paper, and in 1912 Joyce was invited to give two public lectures on "Idealism and Realism in English Literature."

In one of these Joyce gave unsuspecting Triestines a glimpse into the ideal and reality of his relationship with Nora. He spoke about William Blake, a writer with whom he felt great affinity, and described the powerful attraction that existed between Blake and his wife Catherine, "a totally uneducated woman." Joyce narrated the details simply, like an adult telling a child a story with a double meaning:

> Like many other men of great genius Blake was not attracted to cultured and refined women. Either he preferred . . . (if you will allow me to borrow a commonplace from theatrical jargon) the simple woman, of hazy and sensual mentality, or in his unlimited egoism, he wanted the soul of his beloved to be entirely a slow and painful creation of his own, freeing and purifying daily under his very eyes, the demon (as he says) hidden in the cloud. Whichever is true, the fact is that Mrs. Blake was neither very pretty nor very intelligent. In fact, she was illiterate, and the poet took pains to teach her to read and write. He succeeded so well that within a few years his wife was helping him in his engraving work, retouching his drawings, and was cultivating in herself the visionary faculty. [19]

In the early years of their life together, Joyce continued, as if it were of great importance to understanding Blake, "there were discords, misunderstandings easy to understand if we keep in mind the great difference in culture and temperament that separated the young couple."

Nora, to Joyce's dismay, never became a Catherine Blake. She kept herself aloof from his work, from an instinct for self-preservation as well as from a natural indolence. She assisted him when she had to; when there was no one else available, she took dictation, wrote to publishers and patrons, and read tedious books aloud, but she would not embark on any of the programs of self-improvement that he suggested. She shared with him a love for music and a growing store of knowledge about opera. For the rest, apart from trying to learn languages, Nora felt no more need to prove her intellectual ability than her sexual fidelity.

Nora had become, with maturity and experience, more elegant. She, like Joyce, wore evening dress when they went to the opera, and she dressed her dark red hair with ribbons.[20] Joyce very much enjoyed watching other men admire her. Having turned thirty in 1912 and ever more immersed in his writing, he began to indulge in the thrill of imagining Nora in the embrace of another man. He went as far as encouraging her to invite their advances. Voluble, frank Nora, he knew, would tell him exactly what transpired.

Nora, as before, was ready for sexual adventure, although she was profoundly puzzled to find Joyce pushing her toward the very deception he said he most feared. She feared, understandably enough, that he was merely getting tired of her. However, like many a femme fatale who sees her fourth decade approaching, she was worried about losing her own charms, and she gladly seized opportunities for reassurance.

Their unspoken conspiracy soon claimed its first victim. Prezioso, the handsome, worldly editor of the *Piccolo,* was much taken with Nora. Prezioso had the charm and overconfidence that came from being a member of an aristocratic Venetian family, an important and dashing leading figure in Trieste, and a former naval officer. The Joyces may have been unaware that Prezioso, as emotional as he was good-looking, was rumored to be bisexual and to have a romantic attachment to Aldo Mayer, the son of the *Piccolo*'s founder.[21] But he was also a ladies' man and found Nora, with her high color and Irish vivacity, an exotic flower in his corner of the Adriatic. Prezioso, who had been close to Joyce since 1905 when he had provided introductions at the time of the move to Rome, began to drop around to the via della Barriera Vecchia apartment to see Nora. Joyce was usually busy giving lessons, either behind closed doors in the living room or in a pupil's home in some other part of the city.

The fact that Nora was Joyce's woman was certainly part of her attraction for Prezioso. Joyce was not ignorant of the psychological vagary called troilism in which a homosexual desire for someone is expressed in sharing, or dreaming of sharing, a partner. Strong hints of this can be found in *Ulysses* and even more openly in Joyce's play, *Exiles,* for which he began making notes late in 1913.

Prezioso's fascination with Joyce extended to all things Irish and grew in part from it, because of the nationalism issue. For Prezioso, Nora was "Irlandina," or Little Ireland, and in mid-1913 he wrote his "Little Ireland" notes and a postcard when he was away.[22] By that time, in spite of his editorial duties at the newspaper, as well as a wife and two children, Prezioso seemed to have endless time for lounging around the apartment, gazing at Nora, and for staying on for dinner. With his Latin urbanity, he saw a familiar domestic scene: a passionate woman with a frail and preoccupied husband. One day he decided to try his luck. *"Il sole s'è levato per Lei,"* he declared beguilingly ("The sun rises for you").[23] He may have kissed her.

Whatever passed between them remained their own secret. Nora, however, did tell Joyce that Prezioso was trying to seduce her. Joyce, like an actor fed his cue, sprang into his favorite role: the man betrayed. Encountering Prezioso in the street one day, he made a furious scene. Their mutual friend, the painter Tullio Silvestri, passing by was astonished to see Prezioso weeping. The visits to Nora ceased, and the friendship between Joyce and one of his staunchest supporters in Trieste was ended.

Prezioso's attentions stirred Nora deeply. She was flattered. Another highly intelligent man had found her irresistible, and she told a friend of Prezioso's extravagant Latin compliment linking her with the rising sun.[24] But the old man-killer nerve had been touched. Three years later she was still dreaming of Prezioso, weeping in the street, shattered at having broken a friendship for love of her.[25]

However much he luxuriated in suspicions of Nora's infidelity, Joyce continued to indulge in his own dreams of adultery. Sometime between 1911 and 1914 he fell obsessively in love with another of his wealthy pupils, Amalia Popper, the daughter of a Triestine Jewish merchant. In Trieste, where there were many Jews fleeing Russian persecution, Joyce had decided that Jewish women were unusually sensual. Devouring Signorina Popper with his eyes, Joyce was transfixed by her olive skin, her delicate eyelids, her long, coiled, dark hair, her clacking high heels, and her rich, warm furs.

The fact that the infatuation probably began even before Joyce followed Nora to Galway in the summer of 1912 (Ellmann places it somewhere between late 1911 and 1914) suggests that it was no more than a settled married man's wishful thinking and that while Nora's thoughts were straying to Prezioso in 1913, Joyce's too were elsewhere. But Joyce felt everything with extraordinary intensity and used all his feelings as the raw material of his art.

Elements of the tormented *affaire manquée* found their way into a prose love poem, *Giacomo Joyce*. This short work, not published until after Joyce's death and the only one of his writings to be set in Trieste, shows Joyce in his early thirties torn between his desire for a forbidden beauty and his terror of the dangers of giving way to his erotic imagination. Certain elements in it echo his earlier attraction to the part-Jewish Anny Schleimer, who, unlike Amalia Popper, had had an appendix operation such as is vividly imagined in the text:

> The surgeon's knife has probed her entrails and withdrawn, leaving the raw jagged gash of its passage on her belly.[26]

Giacomo Joyce ends with a surrealistic nightmare from which the narrator drags himself with two despairing cries. One is a confession of impotence: "Write it, damn you! Write it! What else are you good for?" The other is a despairing cry, a prayer to his wife to rescue him: "A starry snake has kissed me: a cold nightsnake. I am lost! — Nora! — "[27]

Joyce's frustration was as social as it was sexual. Signorina Popper was typical of Joyce's students, wealthy and leisured, and the way that these attractive young girls, as much as their parents, treated him as a servant rankled him. Sometimes they were unsubtle in their reminders of his status. Once, when Joyce was teaching one of his female pupils in her home, as he packed up his books and made ready to leave, the girl pointed to the clock above his head: the hour for which she had paid still had five minutes to run.[28]

In July 1911 Eva broke ranks. She returned to Dublin, telling herself that she was getting nowhere in Trieste. It is more likely that the freer sexual climate of Trieste overwhelmed her, for when back in the safety of Dublin she raved to her sisters about the dashing and handsome men of Trieste.[29]

Stanislaus agreed to pay her fees at a Dublin technical college where she could study typing and bookkeeping in the evenings after working during the day. Wrenching herself from Nora, Jim, and the children was painful. She hated to say goodbye to Lucia. "I never took such a fancy to any child as I did to her," she wrote to Stannie to tell Nora.[30]

Letters from Dublin soon reminded Nora of the folly of dreaming of "home." On Eva's first night back she did not even have a place to sleep. Her sisters found her temporary lodgings, but she was turned out of those by the end of the week because her father had not paid the rent. He was furious at the reappearance of another mouth to feed. Her sisters too were puzzled at her return. Whenever they needed something it was to Trieste they turned, and it was usually Stanislaus who responded. He even sent the youngest sister, Baby, money to buy a new costume.

But Baby did not wear it for long. Shortly after Eva's return, Baby fell ill of typhoid and died within a week. The sad account sent to Trieste by May Joyce, describing Baby's last hours, shows that James Joyce was not the only writer in the family.* May blamed their father: "Pappie is a thorough no-good & the quicker we are all to do without him the better. He does nothing but drink & fight & groan." May said that there would have been enough money for them all to be properly nourished if he had not squandered it, and she asked Stanislaus to send more.[31]

The tragic tale from Dublin only served to widen the gulf between Joyce and Stanislaus. Stanislaus, hating his father passionately, agreed with May and felt more pressed than ever to send part of his wages back home. Joyce, equally sympathetic with the girls' suffering, knew more than ever the importance of conserving his money for Nora, Giorgio, and Lucia. Besides, he alone among them loved his father, admired his extravagance, and treasured every scrap he could remember of the old man's wit.

In September 1911 Nora's life became freer when Giorgio started school. She and Jim were very proud of their handsome child, who even at a tender age revealed a splendid singing voice. But parental pride was wounded by Giorgio's first report card from his school on the via Parini: unsatisfactory in every single subject.[32] (Not because he was badly behaved — he got top marks in deportment.) Giorgio suffered from several handicaps. Coming from an immigrant home, Giorgio could not match his schoolmates in command of Italian. He was also, like his father, extremely nearsighted at a very early age. At seven Giorgio began wearing glasses all the time, much to the dismay of his doting aunts, who felt that spectacles spoiled his looks. (Joyce himself, who had increasing trouble with iritis, was now wearing lenses so thick that, according to the Irish writer James Stephens, who met him in Dublin in 1912, his blue eyes looked nearly as big as the eyes of a cow.[33]) But with eyes and voice the resemblance between father and son seemed to end. Giorgio's real difficulty was that, like his doting mother, he was content with what life sent. Joyce never openly blamed Nora. To a friend, however, he mocked Giorgio's ambition to work with horses. How odd it is, he would say, "the father an intellectual, the son a stableboy."[34]

By the spring of 1912, Joyce, who was barely on speaking terms with

---

* "From the beginning she was very quiet during her illness & it was very hard to know whether she knew she was so bad at all or not . . . her throat was sore & it was almost impossible to understand what she was saying & it seemed to excite her to talk. The next Sunday (the Sunday before she died [)], when we went into the ward she was asleep . . . Pappie stood looking down at her & she suddenly woke with a start & stared at us for a minute Then after a minute . . . she commenced to talk but all we could understand was 'May, I am dying, I am dying, its a positive fact . . .' Stannie, have you ever seen an animal in pain, do you know the look they have in their eyes? well it was with just that look that our little sister followed us out of the ward after we had said goodbye to her. I will never forget her & it is always of her lying there in bed that I think of her . . ."

Stanislaus, decided to take Nora and the children away from Trieste and move to Italy. His patience was exhausted from the long hours and uncertain income of teaching private pupils and from the endless family rows. A teaching job in the Italian public schools, he decided, would give him security and allow him time to get on with his writing. However, such a post required a certificate that could only be obtained through a competitive examination at the University of Padua. To sit it Joyce would have to be away from Nora for about a week. From his 1909 experience in Dublin, Joyce was aware of the strain this imposed on his nervous temperament. He circumvented it by staying in Padua for just one night, between the two written papers, then returning to Trieste until summoned back to Padua for two more examinations.

It is a mark of Joyce's lack of snobbery that neither in his language teaching, in his Padua examinations, nor in his various curious business ventures did he think of himself in any sense as slumming. He threw himself wholeheartedly into whatever was the task at hand. In Padua he produced two remarkable essays (which were rescued many years later and published), one on the Renaissance in literature, the other on Dickens. Confidently he settled back in Trieste to await his high marks. Nora could not wait. She was longing to see her mother again. Her uncle Michael Healy sent her money for a ticket. Once the school year had ended (with Giorgio winning a *molto buono* in arithmetic and singing), she picked up Lucia and set out for Galway.

When she stepped off the boat-train at Westland Row Station on July 8, 1911, Nora was the embodiment of the exile's dream: the triumphant return in fine clothes. She had a charming Italian-speaking child in tow, and she breathed Continental sophistication. A row of Joyces lined up to meet her. Among them was Joyce's brother Charlie, who only two months before had made the other kind of exile's return — he had failed abroad and come home to stay. Charles Joyce, like many others, hoped that when Parliament passed Asquith's Home Rule bill, there would be many new jobs in Ireland.*

John Joyce led the welcoming party. It was his first meeting with Nora. Since becoming reconciled with his son in 1909 and meeting his grandson, the old man had begun writing to Nora, sending his love to her and to "Georgie Porgie." She sent him gifts at Christmas. With his droll sense of humor, John Joyce had decided that the right touch for celebration would be a dinner at Finn's Hotel. A day or two later, he and some of the others swept Nora and Lucia out to Howth Head, the beautiful

---

* Home rule was stalled by the resistance of Ulster Unionists and postponed by the outbreak of war in 1914.

promontory on the north side of Dublin Bay. There they spent a pleasant afternoon, enjoying tea and sandwiches and hearing Lucia sing. Then, as tourists will, they all signed a postcard and sent it to Jim.

Nora next got down to her main business in Dublin: visiting Joyce's publisher, George Roberts at Maunsel & Company. She had promised Jim to find out what was stalling *Dubliners*. However, his father and brother did not want to entrust her with such an important errand, so they went along as well. As soon as she reached Galway, Nora sent Joyce a vivid but discouraging report:

> I feel very strange here but the time wont be long slipping round till I am going back to you again well Jim I am sure you would like to know something about your publishers well on Tuesday your Father Charley and myself went in and just pinned that charming gentleman well I asked what he ment [sic] by treating you in such a manner but your Father then began to speak so that Roberts took no further notice of me only spoke to your father he made some excuse saying he was very busy and said to call again and so Charley and myself called twice the next day but I am sorry to say he kept out of our way but Charley will do all he can he says he will watch him every day then he will write to you. I am afraid it will be a job to get any definite answer on my way back i will call again I hope Charley will be able to do something . . . Good-bye love and keep well Nora
>   love to Georgie[35]

Nora wished that Joyce could have come with her on the trip, but it was out of the question. Uncle Michael had no spare funds left. He had spent, Nora wrote Joyce, "a buckett full of money getting a bone cut out of his nose."[36] And she knew there was no money to spare in Trieste. Their postal savings account in Trieste, which once reached a high point of one hundred Austrian crowns, was, by mid-1912, down to one.[37]

If Joyce had received her letter, he would have noticed how Nora used *he* indiscriminately, to refer first to George Roberts, then to his brother Charlie. It was a habit of hers he was later to employ to great effect in Molly Bloom's soliloquy in *Ulysses*. But Joyce was not in Trieste when the letter arrived. He had already left for Ireland.

For the first day or so after Nora's departure, Joyce had been cheerful. He boasted to Schmitz how he and Giorgio were enjoying their bachelor existence without the females in the family.[38] Yet almost immediately Joyce was back at the Villa Veneziani, begging Schmitz for money to follow Nora to Ireland. Schmitz (who later became, largely through Joyce's encouragement, the celebrated Italian novelist known as Italo Svevo) took pity on him and paid for a block of lessons in advance.

Without Nora, Joyce had become distraught. He literally could not sleep without her. In a wrathful postcard that crossed her first long letter from Galway, he gave her a magisterial scolding almost as fierce as that of 1909 for not having written to him:

> Having left me five days without a word of news you scribble your signature with a number of others on a postcard. Not one word of the places in Dublin where I met you and which have so many memories for us both! Since you left I have been in a state of dull anger. I consider the whole affair wrong and unjust.
>
> I can neither sleep nor think. I have still the pain in my side. Last night I was afraid to lie down. I thought I would die in sleep. I wakened Georgie three times for fear of being alone.
>
> It is a monstrous thing to say that you seem to forget me in five days and to forget the beautiful days of our love.
>
> I leave Trieste tonight as I am afraid to stay here — afraid of myself. I shall arrive in Dublin on Monday. If you have forgotten I have not. I shall go *alone* to meet and walk with the image of her whom I remember.
>
> You can write or wire to me in Dublin to my sister's address.
>
> What are Dublin and Galway compared with our memories? Jim[39]

That Nora's letter survived in spite of Joyce's absence is a measure of how meticulously Stanislaus saved Joyce's correspondence as he did all letters from Dublin. During the summer of 1912, however, Stanislaus had other worries on his brother's behalf. Joyce had rushed off leaving behind four eviction notices he and Nora had been served. They had known their tenancy was in danger and had even looked at thirty new flats. They had done nothing about moving, however, as Joyce believed the landlord, by subsequent friendly behavior, had indicated that he was not serious about getting them out. Joyce was wrong.

Nora, in Galway, could not have cared less. She was the talk of the city. As she wrote triumphantly to Eileen:

> well what have you to say to Jim now after all our little squabbles he could not live without me for a month can you imagine my joy when I received a telegram from London a week after Jim and georgie on their way it seems to me that he can do wonders. he sent me a wire from the boat and it out on the deep sea at midnight. but to make a long story short he arrived in Galway on a Tuesday night with Georgie all the people here were talking about him for running after me. . . .[40]

Nora's view of Joyce was, in many ways, exactly his own. He was poor childish simple Jim, yet at the same time a miracle worker, able to vault over obstacles like distance and money. To have him and both children with her in Galway was an unexpected pleasure — they were an Irish family in Ireland at last, as she related to Eileen in the picture she sent of August in Ireland:

now dear Eileen I am only giving you a sketch as I will be telling you all
when we meet now I suppose you would like to know how we spend our
day we would enjoy it more if we had not such bad weather every second
day rainy when its not raining we usually go to the beach in the morning.
the air is splendid here and the food Jim Georgie and myself are sleeping in
my Uncle's Lucia sleeps with mother you'd be surprised at how homely she
has got every night about ten or so when we are leaving Mother's we say
good night to Lucia and she goes up to bed singing she is wonderful she is
as rosey the two children love the place they are out all day they dont give
themselves time to eat Jim is also very much improved and myself they say
to me O you are getting a show you are so fat well I think I have got a little
fat, to tell you the truth I dont go out much I stay with Mother nearly all the
day . . .[41]

Annie Barnacle believed that her daughter was a married woman. Nora
had bought herself a wedding ring, and Joyce himself wore one on the
appropriate finger (to ward off blindness, he said). Annie Barnacle was
glad to see him again. On his previous visit she had sung "The Lass of
Aughrim" for him and was moved by the way he glowed when he spoke
of her daughter. Joyce, for his part, was impressed by Michael Healy.
Nora's uncle was the father Joyce, at thirty, could have used: upright,
competent, respected, and ready to reach into his pocket to help out a
young couple in need. The two men formed a respectful friendship that
lasted until Healy's death in 1936.

The trip was the honeymoon Joyce had promised Nora. They went to
the Galway Races, five days at the end of July that marked the height of
the city's social season. By himself Joyce cycled the fourteen miles to
Oughterard and visited the graveyard of "The Dead." (He may also have
discovered that the actual graveyard that loomed so large in Nora's memory was at Rahoon, only two miles from Galway City.)[42]

Nora accompanied Joyce on a boat journey thirty miles out to sea to
visit the Aran Islands where Joyce saw for the first time the Irish peasants
of whom J. M. Synge wrote. (He had come to admire Synge's *Riders to
the Sea,* which Synge had first shown him in Paris in 1903, and he would
read it aloud to Francini, who did not speak English, just for the sound
of the words.) As the two of them walked about on the island of Inish-
more, an old woman invited them into her cottage. She gave them bread
and salted butter, and many cups of hot tea. There was a young man by
the fire. Nora asked how old he was.[43]

The answer was straight out of Synge: he did not know but did know
that he would soon be old. Why had he not taken a wife? Perhaps, the
young man answered, because there were no women for him. And why
not? At that blunt question, he removed his hat and hid his face in its
soft wool. Upon leaving, Nora, who seems to have acted as interpreter,

offered to pay for the tea, but the old woman pushed them out, asking them if they were trying to dishonor her house.

Joyce enjoyed himself so much that he turned to journalism, something he disdained in later years. He sent two articles, one on the islands, the other on Galway, to the *Piccolo*, which printed them in August 1912. (The break with Prezioso, judging from correspondence, seems to have occurred later, perhaps in early 1914.)

"The City of the Tribes" revealed how struck Joyce was by the Spanishness of Galway and its inhabitants, an association that he would work into the character of Molly Bloom in *Ulysses;* Molly is a hot-blooded woman born in Gibraltar, a blend of Spanish and Irish. The same article also contains echoes of Gabriel Conroy's guilt in the "The Dead" for never having made the journey westward to his wife's region, the true Ireland. As Joyce informed the readers of the *Piccolo:*

> The lazy Dubliner who travels little and knows his own country only by hearsay, believes that the inhabitants of Galway are descendants of Spanish stock and that you can't go four steps without meeting the true Spanish type, with olive complexion and raven hair. The Dubliner is both right and wrong. Today in Galway the black eyes are scarce enough, and the raven hair, too, since a Titian-red predominates for the most part. The old Spanish houses are falling to ruins, and clumps of weeds grow in the protruding bay windows. Outside the city walls rise the suburbs . . . but you have only to close your eyes to this bothersome modernity for a moment to see in the twilight of history the "Spanish City."[44]

The article gave Joyce occasion to tell to a new audience the story of the terrible Lynch, the mayor who, after a farewell kiss, "hanged his son from the window beam before the eyes of the horrified crowd."

The Joyces' trip should have been a romantic return to their native land. Instead it became a bitter experience that left them determined to reject Ireland forever. From Trieste Stanislaus was obliged to relay the disappointing news that Joyce had not secured an Italian teaching certificate after all. The Paduan authorities had written him to say that, although his examination scores were outstanding, fifty points above those of his nearest competitor, the Higher Council of the Italian Ministry for Education had ruled that his Irish university degree was invalid under Italian rules.[45] Stanislaus soon had more bad news. The landlord at the via della Barriera Vecchia had not been bluffing about eviction and had ordered that the entire contents of the flat — which included Joyce's manuscripts and their sister Eileen — be cleared out by August 24.

Joyce could have borne both blows had there not been ominous news about *Dubliners.* In Dublin George Roberts was getting cold feet, just as Grant Richards had in London before him. As time went by he was becoming increasingly alarmed about the rumored immorality of the book. He was even more concerned about the possibility of being sued for libel by the proprietors of all the pubs, restaurants, and other establishments whose actual names Joyce had used in his stories. Every time Joyce conceded a point — even to the dropping of an entire story, "An Encounter," because it was about a pervert — Roberts thought up a new difficulty. By mid-August, when Joyce was in Galway, Roberts was threatening to back out altogether.

Joyce decided to go to Dublin himself to force a showdown over the book. Never had his paranoia had so much justification. He began to believe that there was a jinx over everything he tried to do.

Nora said goodbye, grieving to see him so frustrated. He had spent an afternoon at the Galway Races pouring out his heart to her about *Dubliners*. Knowing the ordeal that awaited him in Dublin, after he left she sent him a telegram in the Italian-English that was their own private language: "Courage Angelo Mio."[46]

He needed it. The encounter with Roberts was worse than Joyce had feared. Roberts asked him to put up a thousand pounds against possible lawsuits; otherwise he would not publish. Joyce ran from lawyer to publisher and back, trying all kinds of schemes to bring about publication, while at the same time writing instructions to Stanislaus on moving his things out of the flat and into a neighbor's if the landlord would not relent. Joyce's coolness toward his brother faded from necessity.

Nora soon had pitiful letters. Joyce was in just the condition he had come to Ireland to avoid: on his own, without Nora at his side. In long letters to Galway, he shared with her all the details of his negotiations with his publisher, even making copies by hand of the letters he had written to put his own case. He told of his despair, in terms he felt she could understand, when he thought

of the book I have written, the child which I have carried for years and years in the womb of the imagination as you carried in your womb the children you love, and of how I had fed it day after day out of my brain and my memory.[47]

Not surprisingly, amid all his other persecutions, his old jealousy came back. Her telegram had not sufficed. Why had she not written him a letter? What was she doing in Galway without his eye on her? Willie Mulvagh (still an accountant at Joe Young's Mineral Water Factory) and the lascivious priest were never far from his mind.

Joyce kept his sense of humor this time, however. He wrote to Nora, quoting a glowing review of *Chamber Music,* and asked her, "Can your friend in the sodawater factory or the priesteen write my verses?" Joyce seems to have assumed that Nora preferred a poet to a lesser mortal.

Even at that dark hour, though, he held out the lure of celebrity to Nora as if it were something she herself was striving for: "I hope that the day may come when I shall be able to give you the fame of being beside me when I have entered into my Kingdom."[48]

With no idea how he would find their return fare to Trieste, Joyce made plans to escort Nora to Dublin's most important social event, the Royal Dublin Society's Horse Show, in the last week of August. He booked a hotel for them both and, wanting to show Nora off, instructed her on looking her best. She could get her hair done in Dublin, he wrote her. She was to wear her tight lilac blouse, brush her teeth, and "be sure not to break your hats especially the high one." If she did not look well, he said, he would send her back to Galway — an unlikely threat, especially as he added, movingly, "I wish you were here. You have become a part of myself — one flesh." While they were separated, he urged her to be happy, to eat, and to sleep: "You can sleep now. Your tormentor is away."[49] His remark is clear evidence that the Joyces' sexual relationship continued strong at least until 1912.

Joyce did not hesitate to rub in this fact to his unmarried brother. Nora wished to join him in Dublin, he wrote to Stanislaus, for understandable reasons.[50] He seemed to ignore how the burden of supporting him and his family kept Stanislaus a bachelor. Aunt Josephine did not ignore the problem, however. She wrote and advised Stanislaus to "grasp a little domestic happiness if you can and I know well how happy you could make the one you select. I would like to hear you were married."[51]

When Nora at last said goodbye to her mother and returned to Dublin, she quickly agreed with Joyce that "its a horrible place." She yearned to return to Trieste. But for their first (and as it turned out only) appearance in Dublin as a married couple, they dutifully made the expected rounds. Nora did not like Aunt Josephine, in spite of all the older woman's efforts, and reacted to her as to a mother-in-law. She did not warm to Aunt Jo's daughters either. "I thought Id never get my heels out of Murrays I dont like any of them now," she confided to Eileen.[52]

The trouble was that Aunt Josephine had a proprietorial air toward her nephew Jim. One night Joyce had come in disconsolate about the prospects of his book. He went upstairs to console himself by playing the piano. "Ah, do go up to him," said Aunt Jo. "Can't you see all that is for you!" Nora refused. "I would much prefer, Aunt Josephine," she said shortly, "that he came down to eat the chop you kept for him."[53]

If Nora and Joyce had realized what Aunt Josephine's daughters had done when their backs were turned, they would have been even less friendly. The Murray girls, scandalized at the circumstances of the Joyce children's upbringing, took Giorgio upstairs to the bathroom and surreptitiously baptized him in the name of the Father, Son, and Holy Ghost.[54] Nora did not have much use for Joyce's Dublin sisters either. One night when they were all at Aunt Josephine's house, Charlie mentioned that his wife, Mary, would like to join them to hear Jim sing but could not leave the babies. (Charlie and Mary had come back from America with three children under the age of four and were living in a single room.) Joyce asked his sister Florrie to go to Charlie's to baby-sit for half an hour so that Mary could get out. Florrie refused. Nora, without a word, got up, put on her hat, and went and relieved Mary.[55]

The following Sunday it was arranged that the whole clan, twelve in all (fifteen, counting Charlie's children) should have dinner at Charlie's. Nora was appalled at the thought of Mary cooking for that army and said Mary should have some help. But none of the Joyce sisters volunteered. Charlie was disgusted. He wrote glowingly to Stanislaus how kind Nora and Jim had been to him and Mary, even buying them fruit and wine (news that was unlikely to have pleased Stanislaus, faced with the financial mess in Trieste).

The prospects for *Dubliners,* meanwhile, went from bad to worse, even though the text had been set into type and the pages printed. At the end of August 1912 George Roberts was so terrified of all the hidden dangers that the book might contain (he asked Joyce if there was more to "The Dead" than met the eye) that he spoke of suing Joyce for the cost of all the time and labor he had invested. Joyce in desperation offered himself to assume the responsibility for publication and to buy a thousand copies himself. He had, however, forgotten about the printer's risk of prosecution for obscenity. The printer belatedly (prompted, Joyce suspected, by one of his own old enemies) decided that he had been mistaken ever to touch such an immoral book and refused to hand over the printed pages to be bound. Instead, to be sure that no one could ever bind them into a book, he destroyed the pages and broke up the type. *Dubliners* was not to issue from Dublin. "I'm sure you will agree with Jim as I do," Charlie wrote to Stanislaus sarcastically, "that Ireland is a nice country."[56]

Nora and Joyce left Ireland next morning. Joyce was never to set foot there again. On the way back to Trieste, he poured his fury into a scatological poem, "Gas from a Burner." In it, with gross anal imagery, he mocked "This lovely land that always sent / Her writers and artists to banishment / And in a spirit of Irish fun / Betrayed her own leaders one by one." He had it printed, then posted it to Charlie to distribute. In Dublin, Eva and Florrie, getting their first taste of guilt by association with the dreadful immoral writer James Joyce, begged Charlie not to touch it. He took the risk. It was a small act of courage, but Charlie was grateful to Nora and his brother Jim, and he performed it.

The knowledge that in his native land he was branded, perhaps forever, with the mark of immorality made Joyce laugh. To Ettore Schmitz, whose loan had made the journey possible, Joyce declared, "What is cer-

tain is that I am more virtuous than all that lot — I, who am a real mo-
nogamist and have never loved but once in my life."[57]

Upon their return in September 1912 fortune relented. Joyce won a job
at Trieste's commercial high school and taught there in the mornings. In
the afternoon private pupils flocked to him. He and Nora enjoyed a rise
in their standard of living. Stanislaus had rented an apartment in a new
block on the via Donato Bramante, a road that opened onto the Piazza
Vico and led uphill to the focal point of Trieste, the castle of San Giusto.
They invested in new furnishings, including some replicas of antique Danish
furniture (part of Joyce's Scandinavian craze). The living room held the
grand piano over which they hung some framed photographs of works
by a sculptor they both admired. Nora's handwritten parchment copy of
Chamber Music stood on an open lectern.

The austere calm of the drawing room, the only part of the flat to
which the language students were admitted, was shattered in late afternoon when the two children rushed in shrieking from school. (Lucia had
started school in 1913, and Joyce and Nora were delighted to see how
bright she was. She got top marks in everything except handwriting.)
However, both children spoke in the harshest form of Triestine street
dialect. Nora, one of Joyce's students observed, could silence them with
a glance and him as well. He was slightly awed by her: "cordial, well-
mannered, amiable . . . the guardian angel of the household, a truly
beautiful woman."[58]

An even more generous compliment was paid Nora by the painter Tullio Silvestri. Joyce had commissioned Silvestri to paint Nora's portrait,
allowing her for the first time to visit an artist's studio and present herself
to be painted — a heady experience far more flattering than serving as a
writer's model. Silvestri, pleased with the picture, declared Nora the most
beautiful woman he had ever seen.[59] His portrait captured, at a time in
her life from which few photographs survive, her composed and radiant
face.

Joyce loved the portrait and hung it on the wall in their new apartment, along with the family portraits that John Joyce had sent from Dublin. The exhibition created the intended effect on his visitors. "Joyce had
been born a gentleman," said Francini later, "as one could easily see from
the portraits hanging on the walls of his apartment."[60]

In 1913 from London came word that Grant Richards had had second
thoughts and was willing to publish *Dubliners* after all, the costs being
reduced because Joyce had shrewdly garnered a complete set of page
proofs before the Dublin debacle. Another letter from London just before
Christmas presented the prospect of further publication. Ezra Pound, an

American poet unknown to Joyce, wrote pleasantly upon Yeats's recommendation to ask if, by any chance, Joyce had any manuscripts he wanted published. Joyce sent the incomplete *A Portrait of the Artist as a Young Man*. Pound loved it and arranged for it to appear, in serial form, in a London magazine, the *Egoist*, which specialized in avant-garde literature.

"It seems a crime not to get you paid for it," Pound apologized cheerfully.[61] But Joyce was so desperate to get his work known and reviewed that he would have paid for publication himself. That year on his birthday, Nora and he had real cause to celebrate, for the first installment of the novel — with its bedtime-story opening, "Once upon a time and a very good time it was . . ." — appeared in the issue dated February 2. The following June, ten years after Joyce had written the first of its stories, "The Sisters" and "Eveline," *Dubliners* was published at last. None of the feared lawsuits appeared. Joyce was no longer just an artist but an author.

None of this success meant that the Joyce household was any better managed. Nora was furious with Joyce for buying a number of extra dining room chairs. They did not need the ones they had, she scolded. But Joyce had bought them, not for diners, but for his own arms and legs, which he liked supported as he sprawled and wrote. Nora's own fecklessness with money irritated Livia Schmitz. While other women saved their children's clothes from season to season, storing winter clothes in summer, Signora Schmitz said later that Nora Joyce simply threw Giorgio's and Lucia's away and bought new ones when the time came.[62]

The Joyces were no better with creditors when they were friends or relations. Joyce did not pay Silvestri the ninety crowns he owed for Nora's portrait. He did not send his sister May the money he had promised to reimburse her for buying him an overcoat before he left Dublin. ("I dont know what he means by treating people in such a way unless indeed he is of opinion that being so extraordinarily clever manners are superfluous," May wrote to Stanislaus, hoping that he could collect the money for her.)[63] And Nora herself was getting dunning letters from bill collectors. In July 1913 she received a stern notice to pay a shipping bill unless she wanted to face further expense and annoyance.[64] It may have been the bill for transporting the portraits from Dublin — a sign that when Joyce's credit ran out he was not above incurring debts in his wife's name even though she was perfectly capable of running them up herself.

With his two books on their way into the world, Joyce turned to his long-projected sequel to *A Portrait*. It was to be the story of a modern Odysseus, whose wanderings, before he finally returned home to his wife, would take him far and wide through his known world, the city of Dublin. But almost as though he had to remove a cork from the bottle of his imagination, Joyce in 1914 labored on a play about love, loyalty, and imagined adultery.

All Joyce's works are autobiographical but none more so than *Exiles*. It is faintly embarrassing to read about "Richard Rowan," a writer who returns to Ireland after nine years' exile with his common-law wife, "Bertha." Bertha, when they left Ireland, had been a simple, uncultured, Irish country girl. With them upon their return is little "Archie," a child with Continental manners who calls his father "Babbo."

The plot, such as it is, concerns the attempt of a journalist and an old admirer of Bertha's, Robert Hand, to take her away from Richard. Life abroad has transformed Bertha into an elegant, sensuous woman of the world, all the more alluring to other men because, as is well known in the Dublin to which she returns, she is still legally free. Her relationship with Richard, moreover, is uneasy. He is cold and cruel to her; she fears he may be tired of her and may prefer instead Robert's cousin Beatrice, an intellectual young woman who comes to teach Archie the piano.

Robert, ostensibly Richard's best friend, is a blunt-speaking journalist, a coarse foil to the introverted, sensitive writer. He makes advances to Bertha. She reports these to Richard in vivid detail and he cross-examines her like a priest. She says Robert kissed her:

RICHARD: Your mouth?
BERTHA: Once or twice.
RICHARD: Long kisses?
BERTHA: Fairly long. *[Reflects.]* Yes, the last time.
RICHARD *[Rubs his hands slowly; then]*: With his lips? Or . . .
    the other way?
BERTHA: Yes, the last time.

When Richard, a glutton for punishment, asks her if she had been excited, Bertha says candidly, "He has not nice lips . . . Still, I was excited, of course. But not like with you, Dick."[65] When Robert proposes to Bertha an assignation at a cottage near Dublin, Richard tells Bertha she is free to keep it. When she arrives in evening dress, Richard is waiting. He has already told Robert that he will leave the two of them alone together. As Robert helpfully absents himself, Richard once again tells Bertha that she must make up her own mind. He leaves. As the curtain falls on act 2, Bertha faces the adoring Robert. The door to the bedroom is open.

When the curtain rises on the third act, Bertha has returned home, and Robert is preparing to leave Ireland. Did they or did they not make love? Richard is not sure. Neither was Joyce. He would ask friends what they thought happened.

In the play, Bertha offers to tell Richard "the truth." Yet her words are ambiguous; she says that she has been true to him. Richard brushes aside her attempts to explain. He says he can never be sure. Whatever Bertha says, he insists he will retain "a deep wound of doubt which can never be healed."

Nora was not oblivious to the fact that she was being turned into literature. Joyce used to read out passages of his work to her and Eileen in the evening, and they were among the first to hear the first pages of *Ulysses*. The parallels in *Exiles* between Prezioso and Robert Hand can hardly have escaped her. Nora would also have recognized lines in the play from Joyce's own love letters to her: "Why is there no word tender enough to be your name?" and "Your face is a flower — a wild flower blowing in a hedge."

There are vestiges too of Vincent Cosgrave in Robert Hand. When Robert jealously asks Bertha, "The first night we met, we three together. Why did you choose him?" one may wonder if J. F. Byrne was not correct in saying that Cosgrave introduced Joyce to Nora and was astonished to lose her to him. And Robert, shades of Cosgrave, guiltily recalls advising Richard against eloping with the girl who was not his equal. Robert, moreover, congratulates Richard, as Cosgrave did Joyce, for the improvement he has wrought. Robert says to Richard in the play, "She is yours, your work."

In *Exiles* the theme of troilism is blared in trumpets. Robert (who, it must be noted, bears the same first name as Prezioso as well as his profession) explicitly confesses the homosexual attraction for Richard underlying his desire for Bertha: "And that is why I, too, was drawn to her. You are so strong that you attract me even through her."[66]

In *Exiles* Nora may also have recognized words of her own. Bertha retains a capacity for coarse speech in spite of her sophistication: "As I have the name I can have the gains," she hurls at Richard. If she is only a mistress and not a wife, why should she not be allowed freedom? If Richard really loves her, why does he push her toward another man? Most telling, for those who would look for insight into Nora in the words of Bertha, is Bertha's statement that she is unhappy. She declares that she has given up everything for Richard — religion, family, her own peace:

> Happy! When I do not understand anything that he writes, when I cannot help him in any way, when I don't even understand half of what he says to me sometimes![67]

One critical interpreter of *Exiles*, Robert M. Adams, has remarked on Bertha's odd, provocative indifference to Robert's wooing.[68] Nora's own powerful passivity certainly tantalized Joyce; he manipulated it but never with confidence. Nora conveyed to Joyce precisely what Adams found in *Exiles* — that the idea of a man's remaking a woman according to some learned ideal of his own is inherently ridiculous. Nora, in spite of the veneer that Joyce helped to apply, remained herself. Joyce knew it. "My wife's personality," he said ruefully to friends, "is absolutely proof against any influence of mine." [69] Joyce's defeat was Nora's victory. Richard's grudging surrender to Bertha is the resolution of *Exiles*.

In an introduction to the play written in 1951, the Joyces' long-time friend Padraic Colum appraised Bertha's character:

> Bertha exists through her tenderness, her pride, her capability of sorrow for a past, which is also the sorrow of exiles, and her resentments which come out of her awareness of her own simplicity. . . . She is not really concerned with principles, and she looks on philosophical discourse as a game that engages men's wandering minds. She is neither shocked nor thrilled at Richard's break with the order she was brought up in and his dedication to the creation of a new order. Being a woman, she has in herself an immemorial and universal order . . . more fundamental than the order Richard would destroy or the order he would create. [70]

Colum could just as easily have been describing Nora and James Joyce.

For years after it was published in 1918, *Exiles* was regarded as Joyce's only failure. The London Stage Society at first turned it down, one member penciling in the comment book, "Like Strindberg at his worst." [71] But revivals — such as the British National Theatre's production, directed by Harold Pinter at London's Mermaid Theatre in 1970, and a French production in the Théâtre du Rond-Point in Paris in 1983 — have brought out meanings of interest to audiences of today: how to reconcile fidelity with freedom, love with friendship, trust with doubt.

The character of Bertha is a counterbalance to Molly Bloom; she is a version of Nora as Joyce saw her upon her return to Ireland in 1912, in Robert Hand's words, "a strange and wonderful personality."

For all their erotic turmoil, Nora and Joyce passed three settled, comfortable years at the via Bramante. Eileen Joyce remembered them as the happiest of her life. Joyce read aloud to her and Nora in the evening and sang so beautifully that people would stand in the street to hear the beautiful tenor voice floating out over the night air. Eileen too had found Trieste a second home. She picked up Italian quickly and soon was very Italian in her manner, using her hands extravagantly as she talked. From time to time she thought of returning home for a visit, but her sister May wrote that, although Eileen would be welcome, "I hope she intends going back to Trieste as it would be madness for her to try to stay here." [72] By 1914 Eileen had no intention of abandoning her exile. She had fallen in love with one of Joyce's pupils, Frantisek Schaurek, a tall, fair bank clerk from Prague, who was working in Trieste, and in the spring they became engaged. From Dublin, John Joyce wrote to Joyce, in a resurgence of parental feeling, asking to be assured that Eileen would take no step to mar her future as she was the only one of his daughters who had never given him any insolent backtalk.[73]

In August 1914 the First World War broke out. The Austro-Hungarian and German empires were fighting the Allies, Italy on their side. Trieste was seething with divided allegiances. Joyce's immediate worry was the interruption of the mail to London; it was impossible to continue sending chapters of *A Portrait* to the *Egoist*. He circumvented the problem, however, by sending his envelopes to Italy and Switzerland, where they were forwarded to London. This ruse was the subject of the first letter Joyce ever received from the woman who, next to Nora, did most to change his life: the selfless London feminist and freethinker, and founder of the *Egoist*, Harriet Shaw Weaver.

Trieste had turned into an armed camp. The piazzas bristled with soldiers and echoed with the sounds of the Hapsburg imperial anthem, to the sullen anger of the Italian-sympathizing population. Stanislaus, unlucky as always, was picked up by the police in January 1915 and interned in an Austrian castle for the duration of the war. His offense was to be an outspoken irredentist — in favor of uniting Trieste with Italy — and to associate with one of Trieste's leading supporters of irredentism.

It was without Stanislaus, therefore, that on April 12, 1915, Joyce, Nora, their children and their friends all walked in the wedding procession of Eileen and Frantisek Schaurek (whom the family called Frank) along the short distance from the via Bramante to the magnificent fifteenth-century cathedral of San Giusto.[74] There Nora watched the marriage ceremony she never had, while Joyce, putting aside (not for the last time) his anti-Catholic scruples, acted as best man.

Joyce and Nora hoped to remain in Trieste, even though the commercial high school had shut and many of his private pupils had gone to war or stopped lessons. Nevertheless, when the Italians declared war on Austria in May 1915, a partial evacuation of the city was called for and all foreigners were suspect. It was time to go. Eileen and Frank headed for Prague, where he had been called into the Bohemian army.[75] Nora and Joyce held on until August when, with the help of Joyce's titled pupils, they obtained safe conducts to the Swiss border.

Thus Nora, at thirty-one, packed up the children and followed Joyce to a new country with a new language. There were no Joyces left in Trieste, the city that Joyce believed he and Nora had discovered with their courage. None of them knew that they were saying goodbye to a life they would never see again, one that they would remember as an idyll of sun and blue sea before their lives were shattered by war and a book called *Ulysses*.

PART III

Molly

I knew more about men and life when I
was 15 than theyll all know at 50 . . .

— *Ulysses*

8

Second Exile

NORA HAD NEVER lived in a city like Zurich — Protestant, orderly, clean. When she threw away a piece of paper in a hallway, no less than a policeman made her pick it up. The whole city was so spotless Joyce joked that you could eat off the pavement.[1]

Few cities give such a sense of security. Sitting at the western end of Lake Zurich, it is rich yet small, neat yet grand. Every place of importance is within easy reach of the center, yet there is no need to walk: trams stand ready as taxis to crisscross the city and to climb from the shimmering lake high into the wooded hills.

Yet Zurich was hardly its usual self in the summer of 1915 when the Joyces arrived. It was teeming with foreigners, war profiteers, refugees, and spies. There were so many from Central Europe that the Bahnhofstrasse was nicknamed the Balkanstrasse, and there were revolutionaries of every kind: the Dadaists, Jung, and (until he boarded a sealed train for St. Petersburg) Lenin. Zurich in 1915 was not a bad place from which to break the mold of the English novel.

Few were better prepared than were Nora and Joyce for life as refugees. After a week at their old honeymoon hotel near the station, they moved three times in the first eight months, always to furnished rooms. All the newly accumulated worldly goods of which they were so proud, the portraits, the Danish furniture, and all of Joyce's manuscripts and papers, had been left in the Trieste flat.[2] Their first stop was on Reinhardstrasse, where Nora found the kitchen better supplied with mice than pots and pans.

At thirty-three and thirty-one, although still penniless, they were hardly the bedraggled unsophisticates of 1904. They had two half-grown children and Joyce enough of a literary reputation to be invited into *Who's Who 1916*. Filling out the form, Joyce chose to list his occupation as teacher in the Trieste Commercial High School, but he was overly modest. With *Chamber Music* and *Dubliners* published in book form and the serialization of *A Portrait* (in twenty-five installments) continuing in the *Egoist,* with Yeats declaring him a genius and Pound lobbying for him in New York, Joyce knew that he may have left Trieste as a teacher but he arrived in Zurich as a writer.

Their early weeks in Switzerland were cushioned by a gift of fifteen pounds from Nora's uncle, Michael Healy.* Mr. Healy had sent the money, representing almost a month of his own salary, knowing how poor they would be in Zurich, where Joyce had no job and no pupils. He thought Joyce would do better to return to Ireland to seek employment: "I need scarcely tell you that you will be as welcome as the flowers of May."[3] But he had the wrong man.

Residence in bureaucratic Switzerland meant filling out endless forms. In the process certain errors crept into their biographical records that would remain. Nora lost two years from her age; her birth year (whether by error or by her own choice is not known) was recorded as 1886 rather than 1884. Her birthday became March 25. At the same time, both she and Joyce shed their androgynous middle names. (When Nora was born, her middle name was registered as Joseph, and Joyce's, for some reason, possibly a simple misspelling, went down as "Agusta.") While children in Catholic countries often have second names taken from a saint of the opposite sex, the Zurich clerks meticulously altered Nora's and Joyce's respectively to Josephine and Augustine. Their fictitious wedding date appeared as it did in documents in Trieste — October 8, 1904, the day they had sailed from the North Wall.[4]

Giorgio and Lucia, who were ten and eight, found that they had arrived just in time for the new school year, which began in mid-August. They hated going to school in a strange language. In the morning Joyce had to drag them by the hand to the schoolhouse on Mühlebachstrasse. With so many foreigners in Zurich the Joyce children were not alone in their predicament: one of Lucia's classmates was from Colorado. But the Swiss standards were unyielding, and within five days Giorgio was sent down, from the fourth class to the third, leaving him humiliatingly just a year ahead of his younger sister.[5]

At the school, where the foreign European children were listed by native city, the Joyces' children were described as coming from Dublin.

---

* The sum was not as small as it now sounds. It was worth about $72 then, and in 1988 about 26 times as much, roughly £400, or $750.

Giorgio and Lucia reinforced this Irish identity, in spite of their fluent Italian and almost nonexistent English, by telling everyone that they were Irish and must not be called Englander.[6] It did not matter. At school Giorgio acquired perforce a German first name — Georg — and both were expected to speak German.

In a time of fierce national allegiance, the position of Nora and Joyce was as ambiguous as Ireland's own. They were British subjects with British passports whose homeland was Ireland and country of residence was Austria. In order to secure permission to go to Switzerland, Joyce had had to promise the Austrian authorities that he would not take sides in the conflict. This was a promise he readily gave, not only because he wanted to remain in their good graces, but also because he had strong political reservations about the war and about the British Empire. He had every reason to believe that they would all resume life as before in Austrian Trieste as soon as the war (which was expected to be short) was ended.

Thus the family of four, cut off from Eileen and Stanislaus, as well as from their familiar Triestine environment, was culturally and linguistically unique. The trouble was that this isolation, so fruitful for the artist, was not as beneficial to the artist's family.

The family's disorientation was intensified by an internal split along language lines. Nora and Joyce usually spoke to each other in English. They addressed the children in Italian — *"Porta del legno," "Vade al letto."* And the children had their private patois, first their Triestine slang, and then, even more exclusive, for their parents found it harder to follow, the Zurich dialect of *Schwyzertütsch.*[7]

However, the gregarious Joyces did not lack friends for long. The children soon mastered the new language. Giorgio became the clown of the class; Lucia entertained her schoolmates with stories of beautiful Trieste and of Galway, where her grandmother had a rocking horse as big as a real horse.[8] For Nora and Joyce, there were fellow Triestines fleeing the war, and the usual cosmopolitan crowd of businessmen and admirers eager to be taught English by a clever and amusing Irish writer.

Soon Joyce had something better than pupils — patronage. The efforts of Yeats in London had secured for Joyce a grant of seventy-five pounds from the Royal Literary Fund. Yeats persuaded Edmund Gosse, the writer and critic, who was an official of the fund, that Joyce was living in great penury in Zurich. Gosse gave his backing to the grant, even though he disapproved of the fact that Joyce had not made any statement of support for the Allied cause. (Nor had Yeats, for that matter, Gosse noted.)

Thus the immediate financial pressure was eased, although Joyce still had no secure source of income. He was happy, therefore, to receive yet more money from Nora's uncle, who had sent another nine pounds toward their expenses in moving from Reinhardstrasse to Kreuzstrasse. The selfless Michael Healy actually thanked Joyce for "having had the good sense to let me know how things stood so that I might be of assistance."[9] And he soon sent another five pounds, with apologies for not sending more because of the heavy demands placed on his income. Michael Healy was not exaggerating. His assistance to his sister's children extended even to their spouses. Nora's eldest sister, Mary, had married William Blackmore, a soldier in the British Army who was so determined to go to America and avoid the trenches that he was prepared to desert. Healy, however, ever-loyal to the Crown, bought Blackmore out of military service so that he could emigrate with honor.[10]

Nora needed to equip her family for life in Switzerland. Joyce, thanking his uncle-in-law for his generosity, spelled out what Nora had bought with the money: "a lot of flannels and other clothes which the children need in this climate and a hat which she finally selected from the few hundred which were shown to her."[11]

That is not all that Nora bought. The move north of the Alps necessitated a whole new wardrobe for them all, and Nora always liked to change with the times. Wartime shortages and the entry of women into the work force had swept the Edwardian ruffles, parasols, and pale colors that Joyce so loved into the bin of history. In Zurich Nora equipped herself with a dark, military-style overcoat with large collar, epaulets, and wide lapels. Her new hats (she needed more than one) were brimless toques or sailor hats. For afternoon and evening she bought an austere silk dress with covered buttons along the shoulders (another military touch), a white collar, and demure velvet bow. Her hemlines rose and her waistlines dropped — and she saw that Lucia's did as well. One photograph shows both Joyce females in lace, Nora in a lingerie-style blouse and turned-back "harlequin" hat, and Lucia in an elaborate party dress with lace trim. Another shows Lucia at school, far more elaborately dressed than the other girls; they are in plain dresses with their hair drawn severely back, while she stands out in a carefully detailed dress and a number of accessories: a necklace, a wristwatch, and an enormous hair bow.

Nora did not ignore, as some well-dressed wives do, the appearance of the males in her family. She saw to it that Joyce and Giorgio were always immaculate in well-cut trousers and well-tied cravats. In a typical Joyce family complaint about looking threadbare, Joyce told Michael Healy, "I am to be seen in a shell-cocoa-coloured overcoat which an absent-minded German left behind him."[12] But as so often the photographs belie the letters. A picture taken shortly after his arrival in Zurich shows Joyce looking as handsome as an actor, debonairly strumming a guitar and wearing a smart blazer, a waistcoat with brass buttons, and a light-colored silk tie. In truth, in Nora's hands Joyce had become a clothes-horse. He was never foppish — she had to nag him for not changing his shirt or for not shaving when he did not feel well — but he did cut a figure in Zurich because of his clothes and the easy grace with which he wore them.[13]

Separation meant correspondence. In her first year in Zurich, Nora had never been so moved to put pen to paper. She wrote to her mother in Galway about the children, about the news from Eileen and Stanislaus, and about the progress of Jim's work. Mrs. Barnacle, who had even less interest in literature than did her daughter, had great sympathy for Joyce and his difficulties; she urged Nora to try to cheer him up. "Dear Norah," she wrote. "i think you never fret that is Why you Look So young but When you Look at Jim so Despondent i am sure you feel it . . ."[14]

But the war had touched even Bowling Green, Galway. In December 1915 Nora's brother Tom had answered the call, even though Michael Healy offered to pay his way so that he could join his sister and her husband in America if only he would change his mind. Mrs. Barnacle was broken-hearted at the departure of her only son. Her difficulties with writing did not inhibit an impassioned letter to Nora:

> i feel So Worried that i Do not care for Writing your Letter made me feel so Bad and poor Gorgie [Giorgio] — how he is always speaking a Bout Tom Well Dear Norah i Did not Like to tell you in Last Letter i know you Will be sorry to here Tom Left his office just Two Weekes Before Christmas Day and Went and joined the army he gave me a sad Christmas Dinner — We Done all We could Do To keep him Backe but he Would not stay uncle Tolde him That he would sende out to Mary but he Would not Do What he Was Tolde . . . at present he is only geting a shilling a Weeke he sined me Half his pay than I am geting seperation allowance, that i get 12-6- a Weeke my heart nerely brakes When i Thinke of him . . . i got him medlers scaphlers and [?] and sewed them together and got a prayer book and got them all Blessed i thinke only my prayers he would be gone to france longe ago than God help me pray for him and get Gorgie and Lucy also to pray There is nothing like prayer i tell you . . . Loving Mother[15]

Nora heard also from Stanislaus. He wrote to her often, especially early in his internment. Once, when he felt a reply was overdue, he wrote to Joyce saying, "A letter from Nora would be very acceptable."[16] In his relations with Nora, Stanislaus adopted the joking technique by which brothers traditionally keep their distance from a brother's wife. He roared with laughter when Nora advised him to learn German. *"Sei tu tanto studioso?"* he teased her ("Are you so studious?").[17]

Stanislaus revealingly confided to Nora that he dreamed of her. Once, when the camp corporal saw her photograph and asked if she was his wife, he confessed, "I said yes, and looked grave — important I mean of course. Many people suspect me of a wife . . . Evidently I am not such a fool as I look." Stanislaus also extended an avuncular eye on the postcards the children had sent him and observed that Lucia wrote better and more correctly than did Giorgio.[18]

In his camp Stanislaus was not badly treated. His main problems were a wrist sprained playing tennis and a shortage of costumes for amateur theatricals. Nora shopped zealously for him, and he thanked her for "everything very thoughtfully selected."[19] She sent fruit, books, sweets, tins of biscuits, dried milk, even cigars, which, as a nonsmoker, he used for barter. She sent him so much cocoa that he passed the excess over to Eileen. He was contemptuous of the family back in Ireland. Nora's uncle, Michael Healy, Stanislaus complained, was the only one in both their families conversant enough with German not to address him as *Absender* (sender — the word that they copied from the return address in his letters to them). "They really are the most amazingly unsophisticated lot," he said. "I wonder do they know there's a war on somewhere."[20]

The war had also driven the Francinis from Trieste back to Italy, where Alessandro had been recruited for military service. Clotilde also wrote to Nora: "I have dreamed of you so many times, always happy and merry, that I have prayed that it might be real."[21]

Nora missed Eileen most of all. The move to Zurich had revived all her memories of loved ones lost. Her longing for Eileen expressed itself in a vivid dream, which she told to Joyce, as she did almost everything that was on her mind. He, as usual, listened avidly. Although he claimed to disdain the new psychoanalysis that was all around them, he actually made careful notes.

In her dream of Eileen, Nora was lying alone on a hill amid a herd of silver cows. One of the cows spoke, "making love" (according to Joyce). A mountain torrent appeared, then Eileen; then the cow died "of its love."[22]

Joyce saw frank homosexual yearnings in the dream and expressed surprise that his wife had shown no abhorrence at being made love to by a female beast. "Here," he commented to himself, "there is no fear of goring or of pregnancy."[23] This would appear to be a strong suggestion that Nora feared sexual intercourse because she was afraid of another pregnancy. He added associations of his own — of *silver* with Prezioso, of *cow* with a loose woman, and of the dream of death with Nora's old familiar story: "Her lovers are all posting to death, death of the flesh, death of youth, death of distance, of banishment or of a despair lit only by her memory."

Nora had the comfort of knowing that Eileen missed her just as much. From Prague Eileen wrote longingly, calling her "dearest Nora" over and over again: "How often I long for your company you were always so cheerful and still so calm Will the time ever come again I wonder I suppose you have quite forgotten me."[24]

Married only two months, Eileen too had moved to a strange city, without family or friends. She had to learn Bohemian (Czech) and Czech cooking. Before long she was taken ill — probably from a miscarriage — but Eileen wrote that she would save the details to tell Nora in person:

I am always thinking of you and how and what you are doing, sometimes I even wish foolishly wish [sic] to meet you although I know it is impossible. I sincerely hope that it wont be much longer before we do meet . . . When we meet I will have so many dishes to teach you amongst them many sweets. We often say, "You can imagine how Jim would like that" and for you I have learnt to make apple roll.[25]

Eileen longed for the day when they would all return to Trieste and she and Nora could cook their little dinners in Jim's honor as before, even though she — like Nora — could not understand his work:

Give my best love to Jim and tell him that although I don't understand much still that nothing makes me happier than when I hear good news of his writings and know that you both are happy.[26]

The "good news" concerned the Royal Literary Fund grant from London and the imminent publication of *A Portrait* in book form in New York. Eileen, like Stanislaus, sensed that more than a world had come between them and James Joyce. The grant with its royal label impressed even Joyce's father. John Joyce put his anti-British views to one side, spread the news around Dublin, and congratulated his son on "such an Honour from His Majesty" (King George V), although it was nothing of the kind.[27] Stanislaus saw the seventy-five pounds for what it was — recognition of a promising new writer by the London literary establishment — and also something more: his release from responsibility for nurturing his brother's genius and his family.

During their first year in Zurich, Nora and Joyce both began to complain a great deal of ill health. Mainly they blamed the climate. They were experiencing bitter winter cold for the first time in their lives and were learning that the alternative to snow and ice was gray skies and damp. Joyce suffered from rheumatism, tonsillitis, and possibly colitis,[28] and Nora from "nerves" and occasionally a "nervous breakdown" (as did Joyce from time to time). It is difficult to put these complaints into modern perspective, but they seem to have been talking about feelings of depression, expressed in anxiety, insomnia, and fits of weeping. They both, with their contemporaries, firmly believed in "a change of air" as a cure.

In outward appearance, however, Nora at thirty-one was the picture of health and a very pretty woman. A formal photograph for which she sat in Zurich shows her mocking eyes and provocative mouth set off by a dark brimmed hat. The Viennese writer Felix Beran, one of the many foreign artists to take refuge in Zurich, described how, sitting in the little garden of his pension, he looked up from his writing and saw the Joyces for the first time:

The unknown lanky man with the eyeglasses came directly to me. He was leading a little girl by the hand. Close behind him came a lady, apparently his wife, young, with lovely dark eyes. A lusty little youngster was dragging at her right hand.[29]

In Zurich Joyce grew better known, and Nora became more visible. In Trieste Joyce's cronies had been men who left their women at home in the evening. Zurich was different. Bourgeois Swiss society kept the sexes less separate, and besides, Nora's children were older and she was freer to go out. Also, in Zurich there was no Stanislaus to stop Joyce from drinking too much and to bring him home. Nora had to do it herself.

Nora had her hands full just feeding her family. For five months there were no potatoes. There were shortages of bread, meat, and, infuriating in the land of Alpine herds and pastures, a scarcity even of butter and milk. The refugees blamed the Swiss for selling the products to the belligerents to make nitroglycerine; the Swiss blamed the refugees for eating all the bread.

The Joyce family life settled into a new routine. Joyce worked entirely at home. At midday Nora cooked lunch for him and the children. In the evening he went out to a café, where Nora joined him; he liked the Weisses Kreuz, the Terrasse, or, his favorite (where he had a regular table behind a curtain), the Pfauen on Bellevue Platz. Nora easily accepted the blend of actors, poets, painters, and musicians that Joyce collected around him. Like many Celts, she was unimpressed by rank, and she had no sense of awe. The young American composer Otto Luening found her friendly, warm-hearted, and very Irish. When Nora joined the party, he noticed, it became more relaxed. She chatted easily, and if she had a question to ask, she asked it. Never bored in restaurants, she cast her irreverent eye on the other diners, particularly the women. Joyce often listened more than he talked and made notes. If Giorgio was with them, they would look on tolerantly as he, in a well-mannered way, roamed about the restaurant.[30]

One Triestine habit they kept was going to the opera or to the theater. They did not take the children with them, to the rage of Giorgio and Lucia, who would shout from the window (in Italian), "You are locking us up here like pigs in a sty!"[31]

A frequent companion was Ottocaro Weiss, a young and handsome Triestine Jew who was studying political economy at the University of Zurich. Nora and Weiss enjoyed each other's company, although his interest at first was in her husband. With Weiss she could talk in Italian, and they shared a common appreciation of Wagner, whose music Joyce disliked. "Wagner stinks of sex," Joyce would say.[32]

The attentions of Weiss, about ten years her junior, were a welcome reminder to Nora that she had not lost her powers of attraction even though she was the mother of a son approaching adolescence. That Nora suffered these anxieties is suggested by the most sexually explicit of her dreams that Joyce recorded:

Fully dressed, shitting in her grandmother's garden
Mary, her sister, bids the lover wait
The lover has a puce face
His hair in curling papers
He is bald
He sits outside a strange house
A woman no longer young is also there
The woman puts her leg up
Her cunt is hairless
Georgie passes smoking a cigarette
Anger
She follows him home
A quarrel about smoking with Eileen and Stannie
She screeches with anger
Her lover expects her to dinner.[33]

The richness of the imagery suggests much about Nora's constant efforts to link her past and her present, and also about her sensual love of
smoking, a possible cause of the quarrel with Eileen and Stanislaus. That
such powerful images could be conveyed from wife to husband reveals
the extraordinary depth of intimacy between Nora and Joyce. However
artfully Joyce wrote it down, the dream was Nora's.

Her wish to tell her dreams may have come from listening to Weiss,
whose brother, Dr. Edoardo Weiss, had been the first Freudian psychoanalyst in Italy. Weiss talked much about the subject and was acquainted with Jung.[34]

Before he was called up for Austrian military service, Weiss took some
fine photographs of the Joyces in 1915, including what was perhaps the
first photograph of the four Joyces in a restaurant.[35] They are seated all
in a row, with Nora positioned strategically between her husband and
the children, who are sitting like little adults, with very straight backs.
Giorgio, with his little steel-rimmed glasses, looks old beyond his years.

In Zurich Nora also made new friends of her own. When a British actor,
Claud Sykes, approached Joyce about the possibility of writing a film
script, Joyce asked him to bring his wife around to meet Nora. Sykes's wife
was small, pert, English actress, whose stage name was Daisy Race. She
was a year younger than Nora and provided just the gossipy, lively, English-
speaking companion that Nora longed for. Close as the two women became,
however, Nora never addressed her friend as anything but Mrs. Sykes.

Nora's physical circumstances continued to improve as money continued
to appear in various currencies from various sources and various donors.
Miss Weaver in London, who was now editing the *Egoist* herself, was
determined to look after Joyce, about whose health and working condi-

tions she, prompted by Pound, was very worried. In late 1915 she sent him fifty pounds as "royalties" for serializing *A Portrait of the Artist as a Young Man*, even though it had earned none. The money was her own.

Harriet Weaver, then aged thirty-nine, was a doctor's daughter with a very strong social conscience. Although she enjoyed an independent income derived from her late mother, she believed that to live on inherited wealth was to live on usury.[36] In James Joyce, who believed that the world owed him a living, she found the ideal partner to lift the burden from her conscience. In December 1915 he warmly thanked her for her gift, and also for her efforts to bring *A Portrait* out in book form in London, for, he said, "I am writing a book *Ulysses* and want the other out of the way once and for all."[37]

Other funds began to appear in small, then not-so-small, amounts. From New York an Irish-American lawyer named John Quinn sent Joyce ten pounds (then worth nearly fifty dollars). Then in August 1916 from the British Civil List under the control of the prime minister, H. H. Asquith (or rather his private secretary, Edward Marsh, who had read Joyce's books), he was awarded the substantial grant of one hundred pounds.

The largesse served to improve the Joyces' standard of living. In Zurich as in Trieste they shared flats with strangers with whom they ended up good friends. By 1917, disliking their third set of rooms at 54 Seefeldstrasse down near the lake, because it was small, damp, and on the ground floor, they accepted an offer from Paul Ruggiero. He was a bank clerk who had been taking English lessons, and the Joyce family was glad to move into a flat belonging to a pupil's father. The new flat was on the same convenient street, parallel to the lake, but with larger rooms. There were two drawbacks: only two of the five rooms were available to the Joyces, and it cost three times as much as their old address.

Sleeping arrangements in wartime Zurich being hardly any more ideal than those in prewar Ireland, the Joyces had little privacy for the sexual side of their relationship. They put Giorgio to sleep on a camp bed in the living room and took Lucia into their room.[38] However, Nora and Joyce liked the new home at 73 Seefeldstrasse and thought it, at 120 Swiss francs (about five pounds) a month, well worth the price.[39] As usual, they were amusing, diverting neighbors and soon made fast friends of a young composer and a leading operatic soprano with whom they shared the premises.

The two gifts to Joyce from Britain appeared on either side of the event that was to become sacred to Irish patriots: the Easter Rising in Dublin in 1916. Joyce could hardly be anti-English when he was living on English largesse and when the most sympathetic patron he was ever to have, Harriet Weaver, was in manner, in principles, and in sensibility, as she wrote to Joyce, "hopelessly English."[40]

In truth, Joyce was uninterested in politics in the narrow sense. He had learned in 1916 of the death of two old friends. Francis Sheehy Skeffington was shot in Dublin, and Tom Kettle was killed in British uniform during the Battle of the Somme.* Both men had married Sheehy sisters, and Skeffington, a feminist, had added his wife's surname to his own. As to the outcome of the Great War, Joyce professed such unconcern that his friend the English painter Frank Budgen teased him. If Joyce was ever asked what he did during the Great War, Budgen said, he could say "I wrote *Ulysses*." And when Joyce was asked if he did not support Ireland's struggle to be an independent nation, he countered, "So that I might declare myself its first enemy?"[41] He felt profoundly that to be Irish was to be not-English, although he knew from his classes with Patrick Pearse many years before that to be anti-English was not in itself to be pro-Irish.

He knew that by writing in English, he enclosed himself in the English literary tradition. He was soon to find his own way to escape from that tradition.

Joyce was also restrained from the excesses of Irish patriotism by the constant support of Michael Healy. Healy was a remarkably tolerant man. While a singularly devout Catholic, he had unqualified admiration for the great labor and total conviction that Joyce put into his writing.[42] Healy's respect continued even after Joyce became notorious for the obscene language used in *Ulysses*.

As Joyce's fame grew, Nora's relatives had to come to terms with the fact that Nora's husband was a writer. They could not avoid Jim's books because he sent them all copies. When Nora's sister Mary, then living in Utah, received hers, William Blackmore, her husband, used the opportunity to sing the praises of America to Joyce:

> You are pretty close to those warring nations. This country is keeping out of it pretty well. We have a pretty good President — he does not believe in war if he can keep out of it. I like this country well but Mary is always wanting to go back to the old country. . . . It would be nice if you strayed around this way sometime. . . . I guess I will finish as I have to read a little of your Book before I go to bed.[43]

Nora in 1916 had to worry about her mother, left almost alone in Galway. Only the youngest, Kathleen, remained at home. The worst blow for Annie Barnacle came when Michael Healy, because of lack of trade in the port of Galway, was transferred to Dublin. She wrote heart-rendingly to Nora:

---

* Sheehy Skeffington's death was particularly cruel. Trying to prevent looting during the Easter Rising, he had been arrested by the British and while in custody was shot on the orders of a British officer. The officer was later found to be mad.

i was so Troubled a bout uncle That id Did not know What To Do he going
from Galway When he Went i thought all the World Was Dead to me and
than he Was in Bad health Well he Was to go to Business on Last Wenesday
But it Must Be Light Worke the Custom House is only a Mile and a Haff he
takes the train and then this terrible War. Poor Tom out in France i sent him
his Boxes on Tuesday Butter Cocacoa [sic] cooked ham Biscuits Tea Milke
and all these things God help him this War is Terrible i got masses for him
also poor Sarah Homans Husband is Dead and Berrid he nearly Dide in the
street the night he Was Dead she had not the price of a candle the Friends of
his had to go Around With The hat and there was 30 pounds colected What
Will She Do With 7 children Mrs Standas you know the Nun you Liked She
is Revern Mother now you Aughtr to Write to her . . . i hope you got the
children to pray for Tom loving Mother good bye[44]

Annie Barnacle naturally assumed that Nora was still practicing her religion.

Joyce read these letters from home to Nora. He took Annie Barnacle's
moving account of the collection taken for the widow and her seven or-
phaned children and put it into *Ulysses,* where the mourners for Paddy
Dignam take up a collection for his widow.[45] This anecdote was not the
only contribution made to *Ulysses* by Nora's family. Michael Healy,
hearing of Joyce's rheumatism, had strongly advised Joyce to carry a
potato in his pocket to ward off rheumatism, and Joyce not only followed the advice himself but put a potato in Leopold Bloom's pocket for
the same purpose.[46]

In March 1917, as if the heavens had opened, there arrived an even
bigger gift, with no official label — in fact, with no label at all. A firm of
solicitors in London informed Joyce that he was to receive two hundred
pounds in four installments from an anonymous supporter. Joyce did not
recognize the name of the firm — Slack, Monro and Saw — as Harriet
Shaw Weaver's and had no idea where the money came from. In any
event, he needed the money, for he had a new claim on his purse.

Joyce's eyes had troubled him since his severe bout of rheumatic fever
in 1907. Since reaching Zurich they had been inflamed, and he was treated
for inflammation of the iris (iritis). Early in 1917, however, while walking along the street, he was struck with glaucoma, a swelling and increased tension of the eyeball. He could not walk for the pain.*

For the first time in ten years, Nora found herself with an invalid for a
husband. And without Stanislaus or any other alternative, she did what
she most loathed: acted as Joyce's secretary. Their income depended on
the increasing tide of correspondence with publishers, lawyers, and pa-

---

* The experience resulted in a poem, "Bahnhofstrasse," published a decade later in *Pomes
Penyeach:* "The eyes that mock me sign the way / Whereto I pass at eve of day . . ."

trons, and above all with Miss Weaver. Nora had come to see Miss Weaver as someone who shared her loyalty to Jim.

In the letters, the words Nora used sometimes show that she was taking Joyce's dictation as when she thanked Miss Weaver for her "heroic efforts on my husband's behalf."[47] But when he was too ill to help she chose her own. To John Quinn, she almost wept: "I feel he must go into hospital at once to be operated."[48]

Quinn shot back some sound American advice:

Now, Mrs. Joyce, please remember this: that I have had a very great deal of experience in picking out specialists in medicine as well as in law. . . . Nothing is more important than getting the right doctor . . . All I can do is to urge Joyce as strongly as I could to get the best eye specialist or two of them that he can possibly get in Switzerland.[49]

Dutifully Nora read the little literary magazines on Joyce's behalf for something Jim might want to hear about — such as an essay by Arthur Symons or news that Pound was going to include an essay on *Ulysses* in a new book.[50] And when Joyce's correspondents wrote to her, she had to read out tedious details about manuscript proofs and corrections and had even to convey bad news. Mr. Knopf in New York, of whom neither she nor Joyce had heard, had read a copy of *Exiles* and did not care to publish it.[51]

Joyce, in the event, although he believed an operation to be unavoidable, postponed it "due to fear and also to the fact that the eye to be operated upon is mine."[52] The pain had subsided, and he was able to return to his more pressing concerns: getting *Exiles* published and writing *Ulysses*.

By 1917 both Nora and Joyce had begun to regard Harriet Weaver, whom they had never seen, as a second mother.[53] Miss Weaver received one of the first hints that the Joyces were beginning to be worried about Lucia. On July 18 Joyce said, "I wrote you a letter a few hours ago but my daughter who is an 'absentminded beggar' lost it somewhere in the street. So I repeat it here."[54] To drop a letter is something any ten year old might do, but the photographs of the girl taken in Zurich about that time show a disturbing expressionlessness, a blank-eyed lack of any reaction to the experience of being photographed. Nora, also apprehensive about her daughter, had another vivid dream that she reported to Joyce about that time. In it, Nora saw a newly discovered play by Shakespeare in which there were two ghosts, and she feared that Lucia might be frightened.[55]

Nora was worried about her own problems. Her "nerves" were bothering her, and her hair was falling out. In early August, as Joyce was better, she took off to Locarno on Lake Maggiore in Italian Switzerland.

Promising to get the children back in time for the mid-August reopening of school, she left Joyce behind to write *Ulysses* and feed the cat.

It was not a cheap holiday — a week at the Pension Daheim cost more than half the month's rent for their flat on Seefeldstrasse — nearly five Swiss francs a day per person.[56] But there was money in the bank, and Nora wanted to spend it: she knew more was to come. John Quinn had promised another twenty pounds for the manuscript of *Exiles*. Nora wished the promised money would arrive from Quinn so she could decide how long to stay; anyway, she felt that Joyce ought to be glad to have them out of the house. "I hope you are writing Ulisses," she wrote to him, "without us to bother you."[57] (She spelled the name of this book — as he pronounced it — in its Italian form, but added an *s* at the end: *Oolisays*.)[58]

This break from one another's company was one of the rare periods after 1909 during which Nora and Joyce were separated long enough to correspond. They did so with a frequency and attention to domestic detail that reveals them in the state where monogamy becomes monotony. Nora wanted her blouse from the dry cleaner. She made a sardonic remark about the intentions of one of their wealthy Triestine friends: "Tripcovich probably has got six children somewhere else and just wants to chuck Miss Mordo."[59] She also gave a graphic account of Locarno:

> Dear Jim: Thanks for the money also your letter of this morning with enclosures for which I send you back by return I am glad you got the money [one of the anonymous fifty-pound installments] so that you wont have anything to worry about I hope you will make the best of your time. we are alright as I told you before the food could not be better and more than we can eat and the bedroom is alright it has a balcony now that the weather is much better we will be able to take some nice walks yesterday and it was quite lively to hear the men calling out the prices and making as much noise as they could just like in Triest [German spelling] they are just like Italians lively and dirty and disorderly it is quite different from Zurich.[60]

There was a new coolness between them. Not that, with Nora away, Joyce was any less solicitous than ever. "Thank you for letter, telegram and postcard," Nora began one of her letters to him.[61] (He had telegraphed to inquire about her health, and she had wired in reply, "*Grazie Sto benissimo.*")[62] But she did not save his letters. He kept hers, undoubtedly noticing that in not one of them does she use any term of endearment stronger than "dear." If she sent love in closing, it was usually the children's.

Nora taunted him with suggestions that she was looking for companionship among other guests at the pension. With cruel wit, in one of her letters she aimed at his weak point and also at one of the main themes of

Ulysses (the adultery of a sexually unsatisfied wife) by opening a letter with the words "Dear Cuckold."[63] And she told him that "we had a little dancing to day after lunch [I] danced also."[64]

Dancing? Cuckold? How did Nora dare to write this to the man who, only five years before, had raced across Europe to keep an eye on her?

The difference was *Ulysses*. It was more than a book; it was a whole private world into which Joyce had withdrawn, taking his libido with him. Nora's bold attempts to stir his old jealousy suggest a desperate attempt to get him back.

But Nora was determined to enjoy herself, regardless. She climbed to the top of the Madonna del Sasso, a hill topped by a monastery. She went rowing on Lake Maggiore, she danced, ate extremely well, and tolerated the children's winding up the gramophone constantly. And she read the pornographic book he sent her — "I am very glad to get it," she said, "especially because its by Masoch."[65] In pornography as in music, they had similar tastes.

The weather at Locarno was terrible. Nora's own illnesses and phobias had begun to mimic Joyce's, and she, like him, was eloquent about thunderstorms:

> It began last night about half past nine we were in the dining room with a few people and as it had been raining all day the people did not expect it and all of a sudden it came on lightening thunderbolts I thought it was our last I was almost stiff with fright about twenty minutes then it poured and we went to bed about half past ten but I did not sleep then a hurricane began and lightening which lasted till halfpast five this morning it makes a most awful impression because it cuts off the electric light so that I was groping about all night in the dark room so you can imagine how I am today . . .[66]

Nora's rest cure was helped by the independence of the children. At twelve and ten they were old enough to look after themselves much of the day and were well behaved, thanks to Nora. A tough parent, she knew how to lay down the law; Giorgio and Lucia could get anything they wanted out of their father. They did, however, wrestle with each other, as Nora wrote Joyce, in her characteristic frank language:

> The children want to go home about thursday to have two or three days before the school begins I havent any trouble with them except in the morning before they get up its a regular game with them they have a boxing match in the bed and of course I have to pull the two of them out on the floor Georgie is very shy he is afraid of his life I might see his prick so that he rolls himself up in the quilt now I must wash my hair its the only trouble it continues to fall out very much hoping
> this will find you well
> best love from
> children Nora[67]

Joyce seemed to be surviving fairly well on his own, working ceaselessly on the three opening episodes of *Ulysses*. For once he worked better with Nora away. Alone during the day, he talked to the cat and the cat talked to him. He repaid her by writing her into Leopold Bloom's first appearance in *Ulysses:*

> — Mrkgnao! the cat cried.
> . . . Wonder what I look like to her. Height of a tower? No, she can jump me. . . .
> — Mrkrgnao! the cat said loudly.[68]

The addition of an extra *r* in the cat's second cry shows how intently Joyce listened to his pet.

He telephoned Nora often and seemed glad to have her out of the way, but Nora was worried about the bill:

> as I told you before I dont mind staying here but I dont think the children will remain longer than saturday so that I dont know what to do, and then of course its very expensive. I suppose you must be very tired waiting Quinn's money if it arrived I could know better what to do, in any case you better send me one hundred and thirty 130 *[sic]* crowns and that will pay our train and the pension, my hair is a little better the people say its best to go to a doctor that its probably from always thinking but since I came here I dont think so much so that I may get better by degrees in any case Im not going to worry any more. I hope you are well and writing something I read a little everyday . . .[69]

However, Giorgio and Lucia got their wish for a speedy return to Zurich. On August 18 Joyce suffered a new attack of glaucoma so painful that he had to undergo an immediate operation. Nora rushed back to be at his bedside.

The crisis plunged Nora anew into the duties of literary secretary. In replying to correspondence, she took care to punctuate properly but, in her distress, did what she would otherwise never have done and referred to her husband by his nickname, as when she wrote to Ezra Pound:

> Dear Mr. Pound. I was too upset to write till now. Jim was operated on Thursday. Professor Sidler told me the operation was complicated and difficult. Unfortunately after it Jim fell into a nervous collapse which lasted three days. I was allowed to see him yesterday and he is getting better slowly. He begs you if you have got no reply to cable again to Mr Quinn and will send you the amount when he is out again.[70]

When he did come home, they tried to resume normal life at 73 Seefeldstrasse, but Joyce did not make a good recovery, and Nora was not feeling well either. In October he suffered, as he told Miss Weaver, three or four collapses that he feared were due to heart failure but the doctor said were due to further nervous breakdowns.

A warmer climate for the winter it must be, Joyce decided. They would all return to Locarno and might remain there, perhaps for the duration of the war. They gave up their rooms, packed up their things, put the cat in a traveling basket, and moved out of Zurich. Paul Ruggiero told Ellmann of seeing the four of them running to catch the train just as it left the station.[71]

The move was another disastrous step in the education of Giorgio and Lucia Joyce. The Joyces loved their children — but loved them rather than reared them. They gave no thought to preparing them for careers or for marriage, and never hesitated to pull them out of school when they felt the need of a change of air or when Joyce sought a different atmosphere in which to work.

In Locarno Giorgio and Lucia entered the local school, which meant resuming their schooling in Italian. The family at first tried the Villa Rossa, then moved back to Nora's pension of the previous August, the Daheim, near the lake and the central piazza. Joyce, among whose gifts was the ability to work anywhere, even in small, impersonal hotel rooms, with his notes in a suitcase, completed the first three episodes of *Ulysses*. He sent them to their friend Claud Sykes to be typed. (Ezra Pound was arranging serialization in an avant-garde magazine in New York, the *Little Review*.) He also read bits aloud to Nora, who did not care for it at all.[72]

She may have been shocked by the language, even though she used many of the words herself in ordinary speech. She probably thought that there were better ways to describe Dublin Bay than "the snotgreen sea. The scrotumtightening sea." But she never failed to encourage him to keep on, or to try to ensure that he had the conditions he needed to work. Her interest in his work was partly motivated by self-interest in his advancement and partly by her unflagging concern for every aspect of his well-being. As she had expressed it that summer:

> I'm glad to hear your book is selling I hope you are writing Ulisses dont stay up too late at night I suppose you havent bought any clothes for yourself be sure and do so . . .[73]

In the pleasant atmosphere of Locarno Joyce found time again to indulge his prim roving eye. One evening at the pension he met a young German woman, a doctor recovering from tuberculosis. Like Nora, Dr. Gertrude Kaempffer was tall (Joyce told Stanislaus he liked big women). Like Amalia Popper she had long, slender hands. Joyce was intrigued and sought to escort her home to her hotel, but her friends intervened. Mrs. Joyce would not be amused, they said.[74] Joyce had to content himself with a chance meeting in front of the casino.

Later Joyce sent the baffled young doctor two letters in which he said he was in love with her but also burdening her with a tale of his first sexual experience. As a child, he told her (using far more felicitous language), the sound of his nursemaid urinating in the woods caused him to masturbate.

Dr. Kaempffer did not care to know. A year later when she met him accidentally on the street in Zurich, her original impression was confirmed: a gifted but melancholy and sickly man. She rejected his invitation to meet.

One of the confidences Joyce wrote to the bemused young doctor was that he found it exciting, when lying with a woman, to be in danger of discovery. He could unconsciously have been referring to his own children. By 1917 the Joyces were constantly having to choose between having Lucia share a room with them or with her brother, who, as Nora's dream and letter indicated, was becoming sexually self-conscious about his organ. The consequences to all four of such close proximity can only be guessed.

A Joyce scholar and expert on the background of *Ulysses,* A. Walton Litz of Princeton, has suggested that the active sexual life of the Joyces ceased around this period.[75] As Joyce plunged deeper and deeper into his own erotic imagination, he lowered, as he had said to Stanislaus in 1906, "a bucket into my own soul's well, sexual department," and everything he drew up he put into *Ulysses.* The novel changed course (according to Litz) between 1917 and 1920, sharply turning away from naturalism and heading into the surreal phantasmagoria of the brothel scene in which every form of sexual perversion whirls past. It seems likely that there was nothing left — from that department — for Nora. In this light, Joyce's furtive correspondence with Dr. Kaempffer, like the 1909 correspondence with Nora, looks like yet another warm-up exercise for *Ulysses.*

There can, of course, be no objective evidence, only the hints that escape through their own words. Something had happened. Nora's calm cheerfulness was giving way to tears and anxiety. As Joyce wrote to Claud Sykes,

> Please convey my wife's excuses for her taciturnity both to Mrs Sykes and Mrs Bleibtreu from whom she had a card today. She has been constantly ill and has even had very bad nervous breakdowns here so that I really do not know what to do — whether to go to Z[urich] on the offchance of finding a flat or leaving this pension and looking for a flat here. Instead of doing her good the stay here has made her much worse.[76]

Nora gave her own view on what was wrong to Daisy Sykes when they moved back to Zurich in January 1918: "Jim never spoke a word to me at the Pension Daheim."[77]

9

➤✳✳◀

Artists
and Models

BACK IN ZURICH the Joyces settled into a new flat on Universitäts-strasse, just a few minutes from the Zentralbibliothek and the Pfauen Café. Its only disadvantage was that Giorgio and Lucia had to change schools yet again, as Zurich required children to attend the school nearest their home. They blamed the weather in Locarno for their unexpected return. Nora had been right when she observed to Jim in August, "I fear that the climate is not much different than Zurich." [1] He had swiftly learned that Locarno's social and intellectual climate was considerably worse.

Any doubts about Zurich vanished in February. Joyce answered a mysterious invitation to visit the Eidgenössische Bank and learned something to his advantage: an American woman living in Zurich was so convinced that he was a literary genius that she had placed 12,000 Swiss francs (then worth £480) in an account for him, to be paid out in monthly allowances of 1,000 francs (£40). The admirer was revealed as Mrs. Edith McCormick, the daughter of John D. Rockefeller. Since 1913 she had been living in a flat in the Old City, dispensing benefaction to musicians, writers, and, above all, to the psychoanalyst Carl Jung.

Joyce called on Mrs. McCormick to thank her. It is certain that he made a good impression, for he was drawing attention in Zurich at that time for his raffish elegance, cool eyes, little mustache, pince-nez, impeccable blazer, round black hat, and narrow gray trousers. [2] His natural confidence, moreover, was bolstered by his growing international reputation. A *Portrait* had established him as a new force in modern literature, and the appearance of the first chapters of his new novel, *Ulysses,* in the American *Little Review* was eagerly awaited. *Exiles* was about to be published in New York and in London; his poems also were becoming known.

Joyce and Nora now had, counting the anonymous quarterly stipend from London, a monthly income of 1,500 Swiss francs. They were comfortably off, even more than today's equivalent of the sum suggests, for at that time the Swiss franc was weak in relation to British and American currencies. But Joyce, fortified with a regular income, soon found a new way to live beyond it. Not only did he teach less and drink more, he entered into a plan, suggested by his actor friend Claud Sykes, to set up a company to perform plays in English. It would be a patriotic contribution to the war effort. Sykes, as an actor, would be the director, and Joyce, with his experience of the Volta cinema and of textile exportation, the business manager.[3]

All the belligerent nations with a presence in neutral Zurich were competing in cultural propaganda. Joyce was conscious of a vague debt to the British Crown because of the patronage he had received and because he had declined an invitation to register at the consulate for possible military service. (He declined with some asperity; he sent back the letter of the consul general, A. Percy Bennett, with the message that Mr. James Joyce was returning a document addressed to him in error.)

He was pleased, therefore, to be able to go to the British consulate and ask for its official blessing for his own company, to be called the English Players. As usual, his stated motives were bolstered by private ones — he saw a possible way to get *Exiles* performed. The play, so close to his heart, had been rejected for performance everywhere. W. B. Yeats, his great supporter, had even turned it down for the Abbey Theatre. Another hope lay behind the venture: profit. Joyce and Sykes were sure the Players would repay their own investment many times over. They persuaded some of their friends to buy shares.[4]

There was nothing selfish in the effort Joyce put into the English Players. Although he was responsible only for the company's finances, he threw himself into every aspect of the venture — choosing the plays, the costumes, and the cast, coaching and prompting, selling tickets, giving the cast party. His final grand gesture, picking up the Players' outstanding debt of eleven thousand francs, belies assertions that Joyce spent the First World War in Zurich in great poverty.[5] That he found time for such a preoccupying activity during the most intensively creative period in his life speaks volumes for his stamina. Joyce was physically frail but, until his eye operations sapped his strength, tireless. During the three months preceding the Players' first production in May 1918, Joyce completed three episodes of *Ulysses* — "Calypso," "Lotus-Eaters," and "Hades" — taking Leopold Bloom from his breakfast and visit to the public baths to Paddy Dignam's funeral in Glasnevin Cemetery.[6]

The play Joyce and Sykes chose for the first production was *The Importance of Being Earnest*, by Oscar Wilde — a source of particular pleasure to Joyce because Wilde was Irish. The best English plays have been written by Irishmen, he liked to say.[7] (His Irish loyalties, it must be stressed, were cultural, not political. He never forgave his countrymen for persecuting Charles Stewart Parnell, long before they turned their attentions to betraying him.)

From their experiences in Trieste and Dublin, Nora knew that Joyce was litigious; in his dealings with publishers and landlords who offended him, she had seen how, in the English phrase, he ran to law at the drop of a hat, but she had yet to learn that his litigiousness, like his extravagance, would only increase with his reputation.

When the Wilde play had been performed to general acclaim, Joyce paid all the actors; he gave 30 francs to the professionals and 10 francs to the amateurs, simply to cover expenses. One of the amateurs, however, Henry Carr, a tall, former British soldier who worked at the consulate, was furious at receiving the smaller sum — thrown at him, he thought, like a tip. As Algernon Moncrieff, Carr had been the star of the show and had been so enamored of the part that he had spent 150 francs on new clothes the better to play it. He demanded reimbursement for his costume; Joyce countered by pointing out that Carr actually owed him money, as he had not paid for all the tickets to the performance he had been given to sell.

The farcical row that ensued between Carr and Joyce has deservedly been enshrined in Tom Stoppard's play *Travesties*. Its true cause lay deeper than money. Carr, fighting in France, had been severely wounded in the groin by shrapnel and bore scars that would last all his life; the Germans, who held him prisoner for three years, had released him precisely because he was no longer fit to fight — as the British authorities had acknowledged by giving him a noncombatant job at the Zurich consulate. A short-tempered man, Carr was enraged by the sight of the cool Irishman who made no secret of the fact that he did not care how the war came out.[8]

Joyce asked for the 25 francs due on the tickets; Carr counterdemanded the 150 he had spent on clothes. When Joyce refused, Carr called him a cad and a swindler. He said he would see that the consulate withdrew any backing for the English Players and what was more that if he saw Joyce again he would wring his neck and throw him downstairs.

Joyce went straight to a lawyer. He filed two lawsuits: one to recover the 25 francs (a pittance compared with what he was lavishing on the Players out of his own funds), the second for threat of assault and libel. The legal actions were a severe drain on Joyce's health and emotional energy at a time when he had none to spare. Nora nursed him when he was bedridden with iritis in both eyes for nine weeks that summer. All the same, by October he managed to complete the next two chapters of

Ulysses. These were "Aeolus," set in the offices of the *Evening Telegraph,* and "Lestrygonians," set mostly in Davy Byrne's pub, where Bloom has lunch and thinks of the decline of a loving relationship. In the end he got no satisfaction, for although he won the first suit, he lost the second, but not before many months of haggling. Joyce even wrote to Lloyd George to protest at the injustice of his brutal treatment in a British government office while he was doing so much for British culture in Zurich. The British prime minister, who had somewhat more pressing matters to consider in 1918, seems not to have replied.

Early in the controversy, Bennett, the acting British consul general, took Carr's part against Joyce. Joyce was so angry that he became outspokenly anti-British and pro-German — sentiments Nora never shared, because of her uncle's job and her brother's service in the British Army. But Joyce wanted a more lasting revenge. He wrote Bennett and Carr into *Ulysses.* Carr is one of two loutish, drunken British soldiers who knock Stephen Dedalus down. Bennett is Carr's superior officer. Joyce made the foul-mouthed Carr the voice of British patriotism: "I'll wring the neck of any fucking bastard says a word against my bleeding fucking king." [9]

The Carr contretemps, which dragged on to a second trial in February 1919, worked to Nora's benefit. As the English Players were out of favor with the British establishment in Zurich, Joyce and Sykes had to scale down their plan. For their next production, they decided upon a triple bill of one-act plays. For one of these Joyce chose Synge's *Riders to the Sea,* set in the Aran Islands. Despite his response to it on reading the manuscript in 1903, Joyce had come to like the play very much. As far as he knew it had never been performed on the Continent. In the part of Cathleen, one of the daughters of the old woman whose last son is drowned in the sea, he cast Nora.

Nora threw herself into the part. She had always had a touch of the actress and, at social gatherings where she felt at ease, often played the role of raconteuse, while Joyce listened appreciatively, hiding his smile behind his hand.[10] Her posture, appearance, and, above all, her voice were perfect for the part, as Daisy Sykes probably told her. As it turned out, the play was virtually a family production: Giorgio and Lucia played children in the crowd, and Joyce himself contributed an off-stage tenor.[11]

The performance took place on June 17, 1918. From her first words, the opening line of the play, "She's lying down, God help her, and may be sleeping, if she's able," Nora set the pace for the rest to follow. Otto Luening found her performance remarkably convincing, and Sykes, her director, thought she was splendid.[12]

When photographs were taken of the production, Nora posed in character. Her picture was one of the best ever taken of her. In Aran costume and bare feet, with a hand on her hip and a saucy smile on her face, she is the embodiment of confident sensuality and of amused awareness of the absurdity of acting. She thoroughly enjoyed herself, all the same, and from then on always liked to talk about the theater. Daisy Sykes was only one of the actresses among her close friends. Another of the English Players' troupe, Evelyn Cotton, an English actress who appeared as the Hon. Gwendolen Fairfax in the Players' production of *The Importance of Being Earnest* and Lady Sims in Barrie's *Twelve Pound Look,* was a lifelong friend and was to prove a mainstay of the last years of Nora's life.

It is often thought by those who know Joyce only by the notoriety of *Ulysses* that he must have been a great libertine and womanizer. To the contrary, he was not only monogamous but uxorious. His shady reputation is not entirely misplaced, however, because he was sexually mischievous, both with Nora's virtue and with his own. In writing *Ulysses,* Joyce was drawing for the first time, not on his adolescence but on his maturity, not on his memories but on his daily life as a husband and father. Everything, from the cat to Henry Carr, was grist to his mill. So too were far more personal and delicate matters. Into his book he wove strands such as the sexual rivalry between an overripe mother and a blossoming daughter. (In *Ulysses,* Milly, the daughter of Leopold and Molly Bloom, is fifteen. Bloom is troubled by incestuous longings for this younger version of his wife.) Nora knew, if Lucia did not, that she was constantly under Joyce's intent gaze and that when his own life's experiences ran thin, he did not hesitate, for his book's sake, to enrich them with hers.

The small matter of putting his wife briefly on the stage, for example, touched that chord in Joyce that wanted Nora desired by other men. Just as in *Ulysses* Joyce made Leopold Bloom show the photograph of his wife (a professional singer) to Stephen Dedalus, he himself sent the picture of Nora in peasant costume to Forrest Reid, drama critic of the *Belfast Telegraph:* "I enclose also a photograph of my wife who took a part in Synge's play. As she was born within sight of Aran I think Synge's words were spoken with the genuine brogue."[13]

The wish to exhibit his wife, Joyce was well aware, masked at the very least yearnings toward adultery. (Joyce and Nora thought of themselves as married, as did all their friends.) Thus an act of infidelity was tantamount to the sin of adultery, as Joyce spelled out. In his notes for *Exiles,* Joyce explains why Richard thrusts Bertha into the arms of Robert, the journalist:

Richard, unfitted for adulterous intercourse with the wives of his friends because it would involve a great deal of pretence on his part rather than because he is convinced of any dishonourableness in it wishes, it seems, to feel the thrill of adultery vicariously and to possess a bound woman Bertha through the organ of his friend.[14]

In pursuit of that vicarious thrill, Joyce in 1918 and 1919 hoped that Nora would be strong where he was weak. He did not want the thrill merely for its own sake. He needed the experience for *Ulysses,* the story of a cuckold. Leopold Bloom wanders the streets of Dublin on June 16, 1904, keeping helpfully out of the way while his voluptuous wife, Molly, commits adultery with her business manager, Blazes Boylan.

Nora knew what Joyce wanted; she also knew that she was being used and resented it. As so often, she translated Joyce's own beautifully worded but veiled thoughts into plain words, with terrifying accuracy. One night, leaving a café with Frank Budgen, as Joyce lagged some way behind, Nora burst into tears. "Jim wants me to go with other men," she told Budgen, "so that he will have something to write about." [15]

There could be no clearer statement of their relationship. Nora was imagining nothing. Another of their Zurich friends, the newly married sculptor August Suter, watched with disapproval the way that Joyce introduced Nora to "Jews and Greeks" with the intention of "playing with his wife's virtue." But Suter, like Budgen, could see that Nora refused to play her part, that she was not a coquette. She truly loved Joyce and was steadfastly loyal in the face of her husband's odd demands. [16]

The Joyces made many new friends in Zurich, including Fritz Fleiner, professor of law at the university, and his wife. Of them all, they enjoyed Frank Budgen most. He swiftly became the closest friend they were ever to have. Budgen was that rare individual who could appreciate both the life and the work. He was English, self-educated, widely read, and sturdily good-looking, with a broad forehead and narrow, perceptive eyes. (Budgen later served as the model for the sailor on the Players cigarette box.) He had become a painter after running away to sea. During World War I, he was employed at the Ministry of Information in Zurich. When they first met at dinner in the summer of 1918 (at the height of the Carr furor), Joyce suspected Budgen of being a spy sent by the British consulate to watch him.

During the Joyces' remaining seventeen months in Zurich, Nora, like her husband, came to rely on Budgen. She often scolded him for encouraging Joyce to drink too much, but she was grateful when Budgen carried Joyce home on his broad back. And Joyce found Budgen a far more congenial sounding board than Stanislaus had been for his ideas of what he was trying to do in *Ulysses.* To a painter, Joyce's theories made perfect sense. "I have all the words," Joyce said one day. "What I am seeking is the perfect order of the words in the sentence."

Budgen asked what the words were. Joyce replied patiently,

I believe I told you that my book is a modern Odyssey. Every episode in it corresponds to an adventure of Ulysses. I am now writing the "Lestrygonians" episode, which corresponds to the adventure of Ulysses with the cannibals. My hero is going to lunch. But there is a seduction motive in the Odyssey, the cannibal king's daughter. Seduction appears in my book as women's silk petticoats hanging in a shop window. The words through which I express the effect of it on my hungry hero are: "Perfume of embraces all him assailed. With hungered flesh obscurely, he mutely craved to adore." You can see for yourself in how many different ways they might be arranged.[17]

It was to Budgen that Nora also expressed what she thought of *Ulysses*. Contrary to the legend that she never read a word of Joyce's work, she knew perfectly well what was in *Ulysses*, just as most people who live with an author have an idea of what the latest book is about. And what she knew she did not like. "What do you think, Mr. Budgen," she asked mockingly, "of a book with a big, fat, horrible married woman as the heroine?"[18]

Budgen retorted that there was nothing wrong with being fat and married; it was a welcome change from the sylphlike heroines of most books. But Joyce was stung that Nora did not appreciate that *Ulysses* was a comic novel. He was furious one morning when Nora inquired, "What is all this about Irish wit and humour? Have we any book in the house with any of it in? I'd like to read a page or two." To Budgen, with exasperation, Joyce said, "This is what my wife reads," and pulled romantic novels from the bookcase.[19]

Budgen at that time was a bachelor, and their remarks to him were made very much as from the far side of a great divide. To him, Joyce unburdened all his views of woman as an unthinking animal creature. One night in conversation, he disputed Budgen's claim that Christ was a "complete all-round character." The Savior was a bachelor, Joyce pointed out, and never lived with a woman — "one of the most difficult things a man has to do."[20]

Unable to push Nora into infidelity to rehearse a scenario for *Ulysses,* Joyce in late 1918 and 1919 made a bizarre and imaginative attempt of his own.

In late October 1918, the Joyces moved across Universitätsstrasse to new quarters above an ophthalmic shop. The back of their flat at number 29 looked out at the back of houses facing Culmannstrasse. Joyce conceived one of his voyeuristic passions for a young woman who lived in number 6 Culmannstrasse (a building since renumbered). Her name was Marthe Fleischmann and she was his erotic ideal: big, dark, Jewish-looking. He told Budgen, his unwilling confidant, that he had fallen in love with his neighbor when he had seen her rising from the lavatory seat and pulling the chain.

If Joyce did glimpse Marthe in her bathroom, he must have strained his eyes very hard. The two buildings are not positioned directly opposite one another; besides, by 1919 Joyce's sight was so reduced that he used to carry papers over to the window and bring them close to his eyes in order to read. The story that he told Marthe is more plausible — that he had seen her on the street and that she reminded him of a girl he had once seen on the seashore in Dublin (the "bird-girl" whose vision is at the climax of *A Portrait*).

He watched Marthe, he introduced himself, he wrote furtive letters, amusing himself by signing his name with the same kind of Greek letter *e*'s that he was to use for Leopold Bloom's clandestine correspondence with a Martha Clifford in *Ulysses*. His efforts achieved some progress. Joyce boasted to Budgen that he had visited Marthe in her rooms, seen her in her nightgown, and had discussed with her the subject of female underwear. ("Every reader of Joyce," Budgen later remarked, "will be well aware of the kind of mid- to late-Victorian lingerie he admired.") [21]

However, Marthe had a protector (so-called), a Zurich engineer. Although she liked to insist that their relationship was merely platonic, she suffered the boredom, idleness, and sense of subordination of a mistress. With her days spent in smoking and reading novels, she was diverted by Joyce's letters (and he by standing at his rear window and trying to watch her reading them).

The letters Joyce wrote Marthe, sometimes in German, sometimes in French, were lightly romantic, with just a trace of crudeness. (Marthe discreetly tore one dirty word off the end of a page.) They echo faintly Joyce's early love letters to Nora:

> I imagine a misty evening to myself. I am waiting — and I see you coming towards me, dressed in black, young strange and gentle. I look into your eyes, and my eyes tell you that I am a poor seeker in this world, that I understand nothing of my destiny, nor of the destinies of others, that I have lived and sinned and created. . . . Perhaps you understand the mystery of your body when you look at yourself in the mirror, where the wild light in your eyes comes from; the colour of your hair? [22]

Joyce decided to mark his intrigue with Marthe with a ceremony on his personal holy day, his birthday. He asked Budgen if he might bring the young woman to visit Budgen's small studio. Budgen, who did not like being assigned a role in a plot to deceive Nora, tried to dissuade Joyce. Joyce was immovable. To desist, he said, "would be spiritual death for me." [23]

Budgen, to whom Joyce had confided his artistic conviction that imagination is memory, understood what Joyce was trying to do: to arrange a model of certain events about which he was writing, much as a painter might compose a scene in his studio, with live models, in order to see the light and spatial relationships in their true intensity. Indeed, Budgen had interpreted Nora's tearful complaint about Joyce's invitation to "go with other men" as just such a literary exercise on Joyce's part, and, as one artist to another, he agreed to cooperate. He went so far as to oblige Joyce by making the studio seem even more bohemian by drawing on the wall a large charcoal sketch of a nude with a very large bottom. Joyce did his own scene setting. He brought, to heighten the atmosphere, a Jewish bracketed candlestick, a menorah. In the late afternoon of February 2, 1919, he led Marthe into the artist's den.

Budgen noticed at once that Joyce's Dark Lady was broad in the beam and had a limp: "hard to imagine her giving a display of her undies for Joyce's benefit."

Marthe, led around the studio by candlelight, gave polite, bourgeois exclamations of admiration at the various sculptures and sketches. With much amusement, Budgen noticed Joyce receive "the reproachful smirk he fished for when he pointed to the massive bum in the drawing I had made to order." Joyce, then, vastly satisfied with the whole performance, saw that Marthe was warmly wrapped in her coat and took her out into the night.

Whatever took place subsequently between Joyce and his Junoesque neighbor, he was back home at 29 Universitätsstrasse in time for dinner. His friend Paul Ruggiero, who was of Greek origin, was cooking Middle Eastern dishes as part of the great feast with which Nora always celebrated February 2. During the evening, Joyce took the opportunity to whisper to Budgen that he had that day "explored the hottest and coldest parts of a woman's body." (He did not say what they were.) Budgen concluded that Joyce had contented himself merely with a manual exploration of Marthe and that Nora never suspected what had been going on. If Joyce had indeed embarked on an attempt at adultery, it was the second time within a year that he failed.

Marthe did not come out of the entanglement so lightly. Subject to frequent attacks of anxiety and depression, she could not keep the flirtation secret from her protector. He called Joyce in for a showdown. Joyce brazened out the scene, he assured Budgen, with "that suave human diplomacy, that goodness of heart, that understanding of others, that timidity which yet is courage" — in short, all his Bloomlike qualities. But he must have been frightened. He was so afraid of violence, he complained to Budgen, that he could not even put a fist fight into *Ulysses*. He certainly distanced himself from the effect on Marthe. In June he wrote Budgen, "M—— in a madhouse or Nervenanstalt but now back again threatening suicide."[24]

The incident was simply a blip on the screen of his domestic contentment. In the same letter, Joyce said how pleased he was with the portrait

Budgen was painting of Nora. He pronounced Budgen's sketch for it "a delicate and provocative object." They were not the words of a man bored with his wife.

Nora was delighted to have her portrait painted yet again. Sitting as a painter's model was one of the pleasanter aspects of life as the wife of an artist. Budgen found her a superb sitter: serene and patient, "a stately presence." What impressed him most, he added, was her absolute independence:

> Her judgments of men and things were swift and forthright and proceeded from a scale of values entirely personal, unimitated, unmodified. In whatever mood she spoke it was with that rich, agreeable voice that seems to be the birthright of Irish women.[25]

Budgen captured these qualities on canvas, and something of what he knew of the Joyce marriage as well.

It is no wonder, perhaps, that Nora hated the portrait. (At some point in her later life, she tore it from its frame.) Budgen had not flattered her as Silvestri had done in Trieste. Budgen admired her, but he was not in love with her. His portrait shows a sensual face with full lips, high, almost oriental, cheekbones, and heavy oval eyes: a woman sulky but pleased with herself, hot-tempered, a bit indolent, and very Irish.

The Fleischmann episode came to light when Marthe sold her letters after Joyce was dead. Budgen published his own account of the incidents two decades later. The letters were of particular interest because of the details that made their way into *Ulysses:* Marthe's name and limp, the exoticism and tawdriness of the clandestine correspondence, and the Greek *e*'s.

What remained hidden was that during this same period Ottocaro Weiss may have been in love with Nora. Claud Sykes, whose wife was Nora's best friend, confided to Herbert Gorman (Joyce's authorized biographer) in the 1930s that he knew he was treading on delicate ground in saying so, but he believed that Weiss was in love with Mrs. Joyce and that his overtures had been repulsed. Gorman, working with Joyce as censor, naturally did not break the confidence.[26] Sykes was not alone in observing Weiss's attachment to Nora. Lucia Joyce also noticed, although she was only twelve at the time, that Mr. Weiss was fond of her mother (whom she thought of as a very pretty woman). She was also aware that her father quarreled with Weiss about her mother.[27]

Weiss spent much time with the Joyces in 1919. He had returned to Zurich from military service in January, just when Joyce was most preoccupied with his voyeuristic love affair with Marthe. Weiss may even have suspected that Joyce had arranged some sort of rendezvous, for he asked

Joyce why he wanted the seven-branch candlestick and his curiosity could not have been satisfied by Joyce's answer, *"Per una serata nera"* ("For a black mass").[28]

Weiss accompanied the Joyces to parties and concerts that year. With his sister Paula, he escorted them to the Rheinfall at Schaffhausen and took Nora and Paula across the turbulent river in a small excursion boat, while Joyce, making sarcastic comments, waited in the café, eating tomatoes and watching them fight the current. Weiss sat with Nora and Joyce at the private dinner party held to wait by the telephone for news from Munich of the reaction to *Exiles,* which was having its first performance there in August 1919. (The play flopped; one Munich newspaper critic called it "an Irish stew.")[29] And when Joyce gave a party to celebrate the hanging of Budgen's portrait of Nora, Weiss donned a dinner jacket for the occasion, much to Budgen's amusement.[30]

The suppression of any mention of the Weiss attachment is an example of the distortions of fame. Because of Joyce's celebrity and the continual quest for the backgrounds of *Ulysses,* the Fleischmann escapade was chronicled and written into the record of Joyce's life and the history of *Ulysses.* Because Nora was considered unimportant, because a woman's reputation was so much more easily tarnished by rumor than a man's, and also because Weiss himself, by the 1930s when Gorman was collecting biographical information on Joyce's past, was an important figure in international banking and insurance, his youthful fondness for a married woman (and her husband's resentment of it) remained buried in unpublished notes in libraries hundreds of miles apart.

Yet in the real lives of Nora and James Joyce, the flirtations with infidelity were simultaneous and related. Weiss, in fact, seems to have been the man toward whom Nora complained that Joyce was pushing her.

Just like Richard and Bertha in *Exiles* (which the English Players never did perform), the Joyces were a couple engaged in a connubial game for two players. The various third parties, who were drawn in and hurt, Prezioso, Marthe Fleischmann, and Weiss (perhaps also even Vincent Cosgrave, whose side of the Joyce story was never told), could not realize what pawns they were.

Why did men like Prezioso and Weiss address their attentions to another man's wife? Possibly because Joyce had become impotent or sexually indifferent, conscious as Odysseus of the suitors surrounding his wife while he was occupied elsewhere.

Ulysses is full of references to the unsatisfactory sex life of the Blooms. Leopold Bloom hardly gave his wife, for more than ten years, any embrace more ardent than a kiss on the bottom. In the "Cyclops" episode, the blatherers in Barney Kiernan's pub make great sport of Bloom's supposed impotence:

— Do you call that a man? says the citizen.
— I wonder did he ever put it out of sight, says Joe.
— Well, there were two children born anyhow, says Jack Power.
— And who does he suspect? says the citizen.[31]

In *Ulysses* Molly Bloom commits adultery, but Joyce does not describe the scene. He showed it only in Bloom's imagination and in Molly's reverie. The only sexual climax in *Ulysses* comes from an act of masturbation. Bloom satisfies himself, excited by the sight of Gerty MacDowell revealing her knickers while gazing at fireworks: "O! then the Roman candle burst and it was like a sigh of O!"[32]

Indeed, the one ordinary human activity conspicuous by its absence in *Ulysses* is copulation. All that people do in a routine day is in the book, including every bodily function from defecation to nose picking — every routine act, in short, except the one necessary for the survival of the species and the only form of sexual expression condoned even for the married by the Roman Catholic Church. Why is there no fucking in *Ulysses?* the British critic Colin MacCabe has asked.[33] The speculation is irresistible that Joyce excluded it from his book because he had excluded it from his life.

The key to many a marriage lies in the bank book rather than the bed. The way two people organize their money is often their most personal secret, the way in which they differ from all other couples and face the world as a united front. Nora and Joyce, in their attitudes toward money (apart from the occasional row over the size of a tip or the price of a hat) were as one. Nora never doubted for a minute that Jim was entitled to generous patronage or that she as well as he was entitled to spend it rather than hoard it.

In May, Joyce took Budgen off to Locarno as part payment for Nora's portrait. (He was willing to travel without Nora as long as he had someone to look after him.) Nora was alone with the children in Zurich when a letter came from Monro Saw and Company (formerly Slack, Monro and Saw) in London. With the children looking over her shoulder, she read unbelievable good news: a client of the firm, who had asked to remain anonymous, wished to settle on Joyce a five-thousand-pound war bond that yielded 5 percent interest a year. Nora was jubilant. The money, she joyfully told Giorgio and Lucia, would pay for their education.[34] She rushed to telegraph the news to Locarno, employing as usual the formal language she thought appropriate to the medium of wire: "hearty congratulations Nora Joyce."[35]

When Joyce received the message he rushed off, without telling Budgen why. He arrived in Zurich to find Nora, who had come to meet him, dancing an Irish jig on the steps of a tram.[36] Their money worries were over; they had reliable income at last.

The donor was Harriet Weaver; the gift had been on her mind for some time as she searched for a way to alleviate Mr. Joyce's financial difficulties. More appropriate than a regular allowance, which she considered an undignified form of subsidy, she decided, would be the transfer of some capital. Mr. Joyce could then live on the interest and plan sensibly for the future.

Her solicitors politely tried to dissuade her. The junior partner in the law firm wrote her. He wondered, before they informed Mr. Joyce about her very generous proposal to settle from four thousand to five thousand pounds capital on him, "whether you would like to have a talk with my partner before actually taking the step. Two heads are well known to be better than one."[37] It was a delicate way of saying that the firm's senior partner, Fred Monro, had guessed that Joyce was a spendthrift.

Miss Weaver was not to be halted. She went ahead, insisting that her lawyers observe her wish for anonymity. Joyce bombarded Monro Saw with courteous questions as he and Nora strove to guess who the patron might be. John Quinn? No, the money was in sterling. Lady Cunard, perhaps?

Fred Monro (an old friend of Miss Weaver's), carrying out instructions, naturally refused to divulge the information — until, that is, gossip from Zurich reached him that Joyce had received a gift "from some lady."[38]

Miss Weaver concluded that her secret was out. She was quite wrong. The lady in question was Mrs. McCormick. Joyce had never told Miss Weaver about the monthly thousand francs he had been enjoying for a year and a half from a rival female patron.

Miss Weaver accordingly confessed her secret on July 6, 1919. Shyly and at the end of a business letter, she begged Joyce's forgiveness for her own deviousness:

> Perhaps I had better add that it was I who sent the message through Messrs Monro, Saw & Co and that I am sorry I sent it in the way and in the form I did. It is rather paralysing to communicate through solicitors. I fear you will have to withdraw all words about delicacy and self effacement. I can only beg you to forgive my lack of them.[39]

Miss Weaver, with her sensitive conscience, knew that she was guilty of something more than excessive modesty. She had enjoyed the cat-and-mouse thrill of watching Joyce try to guess the source of the money, and she silently reproached herself for this self-indulgence.

Giorgio Joyce, now fourteen, also knew the source of their good fortune, but he told his school friends otherwise. To them he boasted that his father had been working five years on a big book, that it would take five years more to finish, and that its name was *Odysseus* or *Ulysses*. So where does the money come from? asked Giorgio's friends with Swiss practicality. When his father wanted money, young Joyce declared, he simply wrote to an English lord and got a hundred pounds.

The boys were also curious to know what a writer looked like, so Giorgio led them home. Home was unremarkable in every respect — the friendly mother, the smell of cooking, the piano — except the writer himself. In his black coat, thick glasses, and little pointed beard, Joyce, the boys decided, looked like the devil himself.[40]

Joyce also received other money that year. From New York Padraic and Mary Colum had collected one thousand dollars (about two hundred pounds) from wealthy friends and cabled it to Joyce. Nora again was able to be the bearer of glad tidings. She rushed to give the news to Joyce, who was with his acting group, only to have one of the English wives remark wickedly, "And so, Mrs. Joyce, you open your husband's mail?" It was a story Nora later liked to tell on herself.[41]

With the war over in November 1918, the other members of the Trieste Joyce clan reassembled. Stanislaus returned from prison camp. Eileen and Frank (with a small daughter and expecting another child) came back from Prague. They all took an elegant (thanks to Frank's job at a bank) flat together on the via Sanità, just off the main piazza, and waited. Cartons of books arrived from Zurich but no Nora and Jim.[42] "Have you decided to remain permanently in Zurich?" wrote Aunt Josephine. She also reported the embarrassment that *A Portrait* was causing his family in Ireland. One reviewer had called the book a study in garbage, and Eva, Florrie, and May were bitter; they did not like the family references.[43]

But Joyce, suffering from nerves, overtiredness, and unfinished business with the English Players, hung on in Zurich. He also had to wait for permits to re-enter Trieste. In the interval, for the first time since they had left Trieste, he failed to keep up the rent payments on their old flat at the via Bramante. The landlord, true to type, issued an ultimatum, and soon Stanislaus was writing to his brother in a familiar vein:

> The packing up and moving out of a flat ankle-deep in dust has been a week's dirty work for Frank and Eileen. It has cost me nearly three hundred lire. I have just emerged from four years of hunger and squalor, and am trying to get on my feet again. Do you think you can give me a rest?   Stannie.[44]

Stanislaus was to get his answer but not right away. Two months later Joyce replied, saying that he had sent money but that it had been returned by mistake, and could Stannie send him his dinner jacket?[45]

In fact, Joyce had intended that he, Nora, and the children leave at the beginning of October. Accordingly, on the first of the month he went to draw his regular allowance from Mrs. McCormick, only to be told that there was no money in his account. The American heiress had, without warning, cut off the payments.

Stung, Joyce asked to see Mrs. McCormick. When she refused, he sent her, hoping she would relent, a gift of the manuscript of *Ulysses*. She did not. In a brisk note, dashed off in bold American handwriting with a broad-nibbed pen, Edith McCormick told him she was sure now that the war was over that he would find publishers and recognition.[46] How to explain her sudden change of heart? Joyce later blamed Jung for influencing Mrs. McCormick; Jung, he claimed, wished to psychoanalyze him to cure him of his money-wasting habits. But at the time he found a less abstract motive. A certain person, he told Claud Sykes, "for sinister reasons of his own," had gone to Mrs. McCormick and told her that James Joyce was wasting her money by carousing in riotous nights at the Pfauen.

The person whom Joyce suspected was Ottocaro Weiss. There had been, in Weiss's later words, "a little coolness about money," but the underlying tension, as Sykes gathered, was jealousy over Nora.[47] That seems to have been the occasion of the row that made an impression on Nora's daughter.[48]

Even so, Weiss tried to repair the friendship. He approached Joyce, who was sitting in the Pfauen with Nora and some friends. Joyce froze him out, refusing to ask him to sit down. Nora, even though she herself did not believe that Weiss had informed against Joyce, sat there impassive.

Joyce never forgave Weiss. He saw him as yet another one of the betrayers who appeared, with ominous regularity, to undermine his lonely struggle to achieve his artistic destiny. Joyce's anger was in no way weakened by his knowledge that he himself had encouraged Nora to take a lover.

Nora herself was still feeling unwell. Before returning to Trieste, she took herself to Dr. Adalbert Panchaud de Bottens, a specialist in internal medicine and a cardiologist.[49] Given her history and later gynecological difficulties, she may have been suffering from the complaint that Joyce gave Molly Bloom, when he wrote the "Penelope" episode of *Ulysses* two years later, irregular menstrual periods. There is no one but Nora from whom Joyce could have gleaned the thoughts of a woman whose period catches her by surprise:

> O patience above its pouring out of me like the sea . . . I dont want to ruin the clean sheets I just put on. I suppose the clean linen I wore brought it on too damn it damn it . . .[50]

They held on in Zurich well into the beginning of the new school year. Giorgio had matured during their time in Switzerland. He had developed a beautiful operatic voice and would sing from *Il Trovatore* or *Rigoletto,* accompanying himself on the piano. In August he had begun a course at the gymnasium, leading to a certificate. But on October 19, he was taken out of his school and Lucia out of hers. All four clambered aboard a train that would take them back through the St. Gotthard Pass not just to their old city but to a new country. Trieste had been transferred to Italy at the war's end. They had already reached Milan when Stanislaus received a telegram: "We arrive tomorrow evening at seven."

10

"Circe" Goes
to Paris

NINE MONTHS LATER they were all back on a train, changing city yet
again. It was Ezra Pound's idea that Joyce should visit Paris. He persuaded Joyce during two days on the Lago di Garda, where he was va-
cationing. Joyce came to meet at last the American poet and literary editor of the *Egoist* who brought him publication and patronage. Joyce,
who did not dare to travel by himself for fear of thunder, brought fifteen-
year-old Giorgio with him — as "a lightning-conductor," he told Pound.
Giorgio had shot up and, over six feet tall, bespectacled, and serious, was
a fitting protector for his father.

The two writers liked each other at once, although they could not have
been more different. Pound played to the hilt the part of the swashbuck-
ling artist for which nature had endowed him. He was burly with a handsome head and thick tawny hair. He affected velvet jackets, an open-
necked shirt, and a single earring, and he draped his long legs carelessly
over chairs and sofas. When he first saw Joyce, Pound thought "cantan-
kerous Irishman," then revised his opinion. Joyce, he decided, was sensitive, pleasing, exhausted, but stronger than he looked; stubborn, but
not unreasonable, with a concentration and absorption passing Yeats's.
Yeats, for whom Pound had been secretary before the war, "had never
taken on anything requiring the condensation of *Ulysses.*"[1] Joyce, who
had only reluctantly agreed to make the short trip because (he warned
Pound) he was poor and shabby, nonetheless readily accepted Pound's
suggestion that he show his face in Paris, the center of the literary uni-

verse. He told Pound, and Pound agreed, that the best thing until *Ulysses* was finished was to stick it out in Trieste.

But Joyce had been unable to re-root himself in Trieste. He hardly spoke a word to anyone. He spent most of his time sprawling across two beds, writing the final chapters of *Ulysses,* while Nora read the *Daily Mail.* The family flat, although well appointed, was noisy and full to bursting. There were eleven living there in all. In addition to the four arrivals from Zurich, it housed Eileen and Frank Schaurek, their tiny daughters (newborn Eleanora, named for Nora, and two-year-old Bertha or Bozena, named for the heroine of *Exiles*), Stanislaus, a cook, a children's nurse, as well as Frank's prized collection of antiques and ancient coins. Stanislaus did not want to live with his brother any longer, while Joyce was angry to see them all using his Danish furniture, even though they had done him a favor by rescuing it from the old flat. He and Nora searched Trieste to find a new flat of their own but did not have the lump sum for a down payment. Relations were so strained that the Joyces had to cook for themselves, and the two families ate separately — so much for Eileen's dream of "our little dinners together." Trieste had lost (for Joyce) its vitality. As part of Italy, a country well supplied with ports, it was no longer the cosmopolitan commercial center it had been under Austria. Joyce found the place provincial, and he did not even like the climate anymore.[2]

For their part, Nora, Giorgio, and Lucia were glad to return to an Italian environment (although the children were put back in school yet again, and Joyce, abandoning any attempt to continue Giorgio's formal schooling, engaged a private tutor for his son). They looked up old friends — the Francinis were back — and were happy to be near the sea. The flat on the via Sanità was at the best address they ever had in Trieste (it is today the local headquarters of the Italian electricity board), and from its balcony they could watch processions in the street. Nora and Lucia went for an outing to the nearby bathing resort of Barcola in an open tram. Nora sat in the sun — with her red-haired complexion, she did not like to take too much of it — while Lucia swam; one Sunday they went to Venice and saw San Marco. Eileen got to work on their children's English.[3] But Nora too missed the sophistication of the friends they had left behind in Zurich. "We have not got over the loss of your company," Nora wrote Budgen warmly.[4]

Joyce also had good reason to be restless. He was moving into the most difficult episodes of *Ulysses.* To judge from the trouble they caused the censors (the U.S. Post Office had burned three issues of the *Little Review* containing episodes of *Ulysses*), Joyce must himself have been unsettled as he explored the limits of his artistic imagination. His first months in Trieste were spent completing "Nausicaa," with Bloom, Gerty, and the fireworks. Probing Bloom's guilty, incestuous impulses toward his adolescent daughter, Milly (deflected onto the figure of Gerty MacDowell), Joyce must have been acutely sensitive to his own arousal by his daughter's approaching puberty.[5]

Joyce lived each episode so intensely in his imagination that when working on the next episode, "Oxen of the Sun," set in a maternity hospital, his head was so full of images of half-born fetuses, swabs, and the smell of disinfectant that he could not eat.[6]

The climax of *Ulysses* lay ahead: "Circe," set at midnight, when all the images, sacred and obscene, of Bloom's and Stephen's past rise to haunt them in Bella Cohen's Dublin brothel. To complete it, Joyce knew he had to get away from the Schaurek flat. His intention, when they got on the train in Trieste, was to find a place in England, Wales, or even Ireland where Nora and the children could have a long holiday and live cheaply while he finished "Circe," then to return in September.[7]

The patronage Joyce had received only served to increase his sense of grievance at having to think about money at all. More than ever, he indulged his habit of writing self-pitying, begging letters. He complained to Pound, before they met, that his children had not slept in a real bed since they left Zurich; they were forced to sleep on hard beds in the living room in the sweltering heat. As for himself:

> I wear my son's boots (which are two sizes too large) and his castoff suit which is too narrow in the shoulders, other articles belong or belonged to my brother and to my brother-in-law. I shall not be able to buy anything here. A suit of clothes, they tell me, costs 600–800 francs.[8]

In a postscript Joyce asked Pound not to imagine that his letter was "a subtly worded request for secondhand clothing." It was, of course, exactly that, and Pound set about providing the requested articles. Such letters did not spring only from the monomaniacal self-absorption of a genius; they were a son's direct imitation of his father. The lament to Pound echoed almost verbatim one Joyce had received from John Joyce in Dublin six months earlier. "I am in a *dreadful state* for clothes and boots," Joyce senior wrote his eldest son. "The prices now charged here are *quite prohibative [sic]* as far as I am concerned."[9]

Triestine prices did not deter Nora. Before they left on holiday, she went down to the Corso, Trieste's main shopping street, and paid a visit to Giaconi's stylish hat shop (*"confezione accuratissima"* — finest workmanship), where she had an account.[10]

When they arrived at the Gare de Lyon on July 19, 1920, Joyce told his family that after a week or two they would leave Paris and move on to London.[11] But Pound, who was a superb fixer, found them a place to stay for the summer. It was a small flat on the fifth floor of an apartment

building in Passy. The Joyces were welcome to use this servants' flat —
on the understanding, said Ludmila Bloch-Savitsky, later to be the French
translator of *A Portrait,* who offered it until the end of September — that
they were under no illusions about its comfort and were prepared to
make allowances. There was no bathtub and no electricity. There was
gas in the kitchen, which was very small; there were only a few plates,
two casseroles, and some blankets. And, although there was one excellent double bed, there were no single beds for the children. Madame
Joyce would be obliged to complete what was lacking by renting some
beds. The flat, in sum, was only to be taken as a last resort if the Joyces
found nothing else.[12]

Number 5 rue de l'Assomption sounded quite different when described
to Stanislaus. "Admirer of mine has placed 3 room flat, furnished, at my
disposal for three months."[13] And once Joyce was assured of a roof over
his head, thoughts of the British Isles faded, and he told his friends that
three months was how long he would stay in Paris.[14] Joyce did not dream
of delegating Nora to finding the missing furniture. She had not the command of French or the knowledge of Paris for such a task. He delegated
it instead to Pound, with an air of reproach: there were no sheets or
blankets, and a table would have been helpful. Pound deftly passed the
assignment on to the French literary agent Jenny Serruys ("For Christ's
sake, get him a bed for his too large son to sleep on . . ."), apologetic
that the Irish genius from Trieste came encumbered with wife and teenage children. Thus freed, Nora and Joyce went shopping for a Burberry
raincoat.[15]

Their errand was undertaken for Stanislaus, who rashly had given his
brother the money for the purchase. Joyce looked into the matter and
informed Stanislaus that Burberry's was laying in autumn and winter
stocks.[16] That was the last Stanislaus ever heard of his raincoat or his
money. Joyce implied that his brother did not need such a garment, as he
himself was wearing a secondhand army overcoat, another gift from "an
admirer of mine."[17]

Like Stanislaus, he knew his brand names. He contemplated ordering
a Tress hat from London and brogues from Norwell in Perth, Scotland.
In spite of his shabbiness, he wore ornate rings on his hand.

They were so cramped in the servants' flat that Nora was delighted
when Budgen turned up one day and took Giorgio and Lucia swimming
in the pool at the Pont de Grenelle. Both children were good at sports.
Nora was less grateful when Budgen and Joyce headed to a café just as
they had done in Zurich. The hours slipped by, and it was after midnight
when they made their way back along the quiet street. They tried to keep
their voices low, and like most who have been drinking, they failed. The
sound, according to Budgen, pierced the fearful hollow of Nora's ear. A
top-story window suddenly opened and Budgen saw a woman's face ap-

pear: "a pinkish splodge . . . and out of it winged words spoken in a magnificent Irish brogue descended upon me":

> This sort of thing had got to stop. I was to take note that what I thought I could do in Zurich I was not going to do in Paris. That, and more to the same effect.
>
> I heard every word she said: I thoroughly agreed with the view she expressed. But at the same time, I couldn't for the life of me understand why she had nursed her wrath and kept it warm for me only. On reflection, however, I decided that Joyce probably heard the rest of it within four walls.[18]

Pound, who had himself arrived in Paris only two weeks before, also organized a party at which Joyce could meet everybody who mattered in the literary world. For Joyce and Nora, it was as if they were arriving on a stage. Until then, buried in Trieste and Zurich, they had been Voices Off. Few British and fewer Americans had had a look at the author of *A Portrait* and the astonishing chapters of the new book appearing in the *Little Review*. But Pound, whose judgment on new writers was greatly respected, spread the word: "Our James is a grrreat man."[19]

The party — a buffet — was held at the home of André Spire, a French publisher. Nora was terrified as they walked in. "I don't speak a word of French," she told Pound's English wife, the former Dorothy Shakespear. Mrs. Pound reassured her that there were plenty of English speakers present. She introduced Nora to a small boyish woman, about Nora's own age but dressed, unlike any woman Nora had ever met, in a severely cut velvet blazer and a shirt with a flowing tie. Relaxing, Nora confided that she could not cope in French. "Now if it had been Italian . . ." The Joyce family, she said, spoke Italian at home.[20]

She was speaking to Sylvia Beach, a minister's daughter from Princeton, New Jersey, who ran a bookshop on the Left Bank. Sylvia was jittery herself. Like all those dedicated to the cause of the avant-garde in literature, she had been dazzled by Joyce's work. When she walked into the party (accompanying her good friend Adrienne Monnier, but not having been invited herself), she had not even known that Joyce was in Paris. When she heard that her idol would actually be present, she nearly went home. It was a relief to be able to begin with the wife: a tall, pretty woman with curly red hair, neither stout nor thin, a friendly manner, and a very Irish voice.

When Sylvia got up her courage to meet the writer himself, she found him taking refuge in the library, drooping against a bookcase. Joyce was hardly any more at ease among the French literati than was Nora, fearing (correctly, as it turned out) that he would create a bad impression by not making the appropriate obeisances toward Corneille and Racine.[21] To her opening, "So this is the great James Joyce?" he replied, extending a limp, boneless hand, "James Joyce."

Sylvia, who had a good ear, was struck by the strong Irish pronunciation in his speech, as in his wife's, and noticed that he had trouble with *th*. He said *t'ing* for *thing* and pronounced *book* and *look* to rhyme with *spook*. His manner was both courtly and shy, yet he swiftly shifted from the formal to the highly personal when he heard the bark of a dog. "Is it coming here? Is it feerce?" he asked her (again using the long vowel sound). The small goatee he wore on his chin, he explained, was intended to conceal the scar of a dog bite he had suffered as a child.

His coloring was sandy, his hair brushed straight back from his brow, and he had freckles; his bearing was graceful, if stooped, and his blue eyes, such as could be glimpsed through the thick glass of his lenses, had the intensity of an artist. He wore rings on his hand. She thought he must have been very handsome as a young man and invited him to visit her bookshop. He warmed to its name, Shakespeare and Company.

Nora was left to fend for herself in a drawing room full of French intellectuals arguing furiously over the merits of Claudel, Gide, and Valéry. She did not realize that they had met the new Stanislaus in their lives, a person who would put her own well-being second to theirs. Joyce sensed it, however. He was around at Sylvia's bookshop the next morning, wearing tennis shoes and carrying an ashplant. Sylvia was more smitten than even the day before and thought him the most distinguished man she had ever seen. She showed him the facilities of the shop, the little English-language literary magazines, the letterboxes she kept for frequent customers, and her excellent lending library. Joyce became one of her "bunnies" (Sylvia's little nickname for her *abonnés,* or subscribers), and he began by taking out a book he hardly needed to read: *Riders to the Sea.*[22]

Deep into the complexities of "Circe," Joyce soon realized that he would have to stay put until he finished *Ulysses,* even though he did not have a hope of a publisher. He did not know where to go next.[23]

No writer before had so boldly tried to set onto the page the irrational, bizarre, and shameful fantasies of the unconscious. Few writers have labored under such difficulties. While he was extending the frontiers of the novel — incorporating dramatic dialogue, snatches of song, and disembodied voices, causing Leopold Bloom to change sex and Stephen Dedalus's dead mother to rise from the grave in her moldy grave clothes — Joyce had to shut his ears to his adolescent children's whining: How long are we staying? Will we have to learn French? Will we have to go to school?

Uncertain as to whether they were going back to Trieste or forward to London (which appealed to Nora), Giorgio and Lucia were more isolated and frustrated than ever before. They cocooned themselves in low German, which caused people to stare at them. Joyce, in a letter to John Quinn in New York, expressed his first open anxieties about his children's future. Outside the family, Joyce noted with dismay, they did not exchange a word with anybody for three months. Giorgio, "to all intents and purposes a man, as tall as I am and much hungrier," had given up the idea of studying medicine and was sinking, Joyce noted, "into a state of listlessness. I do not know what to do about my daughter."[24]

Both young Joyces impressed everyone with their good grooming. Nora saw to that. Giorgio in particular was remarked upon for his impeccable toilette: clothes perfectly pressed, cuffs trimmed back to hide the frayed edges, collars starched and flat. Their English, however, little better than their French, was accented and unidiomatic. "I don't want to make you an experience," Lucia said one day to an American family friend, meaning that she did not want to send her on a wild-goose chase by misdirecting her.[25]

Joyce, nonetheless, was depressed by what he felt was their poverty and shabbiness. Yet he did own shoes that were not made of canvas and soon was cured permanently of complaining about the state of his footwear by his formidable contemporary T. S. Eliot.

Not long after Joyce's arrival in Paris, Eliot, another of Pound's London protégés, was planning a brief trip to Paris, and he too wanted to meet Joyce. Pound, who had returned to London, offered to provide him with an introduction, and to facilitate a meeting gave him a parcel to deliver.

Eliot wrote Joyce, informing him of the parcel, and inviting him to dine with himself and Wyndham Lewis on the evening of August 15, 1920. Joyce arrived at the Hôtel de l'Élysée, correctly dressed in a dark suit and wearing black patent shoes and a straw hat. Giorgio was with him. Eliot made a pompous little performance of handing over the mysterious bundle and placed it in the center of the hotel table at which they were sitting. Joyce tried to untie the string but failed. He asked his son in Italian for a knife. Giorgio, annoyed, answered in Italian that he did not have one. Eliot joined the search, and eventually a pair of nail scissors was procured. The papers were peeled off and there, for all to see, was a pair of Pound's old brown shoes. As Wyndham Lewis reconstructed the scene:

"Oh," said Joyce faintly, and again, "Oh." He turned away, and sat down again, placing his left ankle upon his right knee, and squeezing, and then releasing, the horizontal limb.[26]

Then in Italian Joyce commanded Giorgio to go home and tell Mama — to be sure to tell Mama — that Babbo was not coming home to dinner, and incidentally, to take the shoes with him.

The scene between father and son, said Lewis, was stormy, with many passionate asides: "a good imitation of an altercation between a couple of neapolitan touts, of the better order." It ended with fifteen-year-old

Giorgio, "eyes blazing with a truly southern ferocity," rushing away with the parcel beneath his arm — but not before bowing from the hips to the gentlemen from London and shaking hands with formal politeness. At the end of the evening, Joyce, as if he had been the host, insisted on paying the whole bill, including tips and taxis.

That is the last time Joyce allowed himself to complain about his footwear. From then on, photographs show the Joyce family beautifully shod; their collective array of dancing pumps, lounging slippers, spats, two-tone sports shoes, lace-up gillies, and glacé kid pumps with diamanté buckles, double T-straps, or cut-out insteps could serve as an illustrated history of French footwear fashion between the wars. Even in his poorest days, Joyce is likely to have worn tennis shoes because they were comfortable, and he continued to do so for walking around Paris until Nora threw them out in disgust.[27]

As the agreed-upon date for the Bloch-Savitskys' return neared, Joyce began moaning about his forthcoming "eviction." He wrote to one literary admirer that he had "received notice to quit this flat (if you can call it so)".[28] He said that they all would be glad to move as the place was damp and no more than a matchbox. Lucia complained that the furniture was stuck together with spit.[29] Postwar Paris was having a *crise de logement,* and no one found housing easy. However, Joyce's demands — six rooms in the Odéon quarter — made it hard to house them. None of this inconvenience deflected Joyce from his task; his concentration, as Pound noted, was prodigious. By September 20, working without the case of books he needed and which had failed to arrive from Trieste, he had written six drafts of "Circe."

In London Harriet Weaver had still not laid eyes on James Joyce. She heard his complaints about poverty with sympathy and alarm, but she knew nothing of his style of living, and certainly not that he drank heavily. She determined, say her biographers, to give him "a mode of life settled enough in which to write."[30] If Miss Weaver was Joyce's distant but loving mother, Sylvia, with whom Miss Weaver was now in regular correspondence, had taken on the role of nanny.

Miss Weaver believed (and she was right) that Joyce was at the height of his creative powers. Determined that he not be slowed down by the practicalities of existence, she resolved to provide him with money in a more accessible form than that of the five-thousand-pound war bond she had given him the year before, from which he drew just over sixty-two pounds every three months. He could not touch the principal without the consent of a British official, the public trustee.

In the summer of 1920, however, Miss Weaver had inherited some more money, a settlement of two thousand pounds from her aunts, which yielded one hundred pounds a year in interest. She passed the gift straight over to Joyce. Because she knew how short he was of funds to settle his family in Paris, she wanted him to have access to the capital as well as the interest and took care not to put the gift into the restraining hands of the public trustee. That done, she felt content. Before long, she was certain, the royalties from *Ulysses* would start coming in and he would be as self-supporting as his growing reputation promised. She had no idea that her Mr. Joyce spent every bit of his money as soon as he laid hands on it or that he worked best in conditions of chaos.

The Joyces held out at the Bloch-Savitsky flat, which they were to leave in September, until the first of November. Then, again under Pound's aegis, they moved to a residential hotel at 9 rue de l'Université in the Latin Quarter. The small hotel, now the Hotel Lenox, was popular with writers and intellectuals; T. S. Eliot had stayed there during his Paris sojourn before the war. It was also within walking distance of Sylvia's bookshop, which Joyce, like many other writers, was using as a combination of bank, post office, coffee shop, library, and home away from home.

Moving into the hotel, Joyce returned to Jenny Serruys the borrowed bed and mattress. If he found a flat, he told her, he would like to borrow them again and meanwhile was retaining two blankets to comfort him.[31]

Joyce's express concern was for what the lack of privacy meant for finishing his book. He had no desk. He wrote sitting in an armchair with a suitcase propped over the arms for a flat surface.

Convenient as the address was, however, Nora could not pronounce it. Nora had trouble with the French diphthongs. Accustomed to the pure Italian vowels, she had trouble saying *neuf*. She pronounced it *neff*. Some new friends, an American book illustrator, Richard Wallace, and his wife, Lillian, an English writer, told her to rhyme it with a word that falls trippingly off the Irish tongue: *turf*. It worked. Gratefully, when she wrote to Lillian, Nora headed her letter "Turf rue de l'Université" and signed it, laughingly, "from us Irish."[32]

Nora wanted to find a flat so that they could have their meals at home. Far from having any kitchen facilities at the hotel, however, she and Jim did not even have a bedroom to themselves. Joyce felt, as at Locarno, that they must save money by taking only two rooms. Lucia was thus confined with her parents once again, and at a more awkward age (she was thirteen in 1920) shared a bedroom with her parents; only Giorgio had his privacy.

Unable to cook, they had to dine out. The sight of the Joyces at table is part of the Joyce legend. It gave rise to the belief that Nora could not cook. "There are too many restaurant pictures, too many eating pictures," says Tom Gallacher in his play, *Mr. Joyce Is Leaving Paris*. In fact, almost all the expatriate colony ate out all the time. The question was where? While the Joyces lived at this address, they used to dine nearby at Michaud's. It was sheer necessity, Joyce maintained to John Quinn in New York:

We are obliged to eat in a popular restaurant, both lunch and dinner. The food is bad, the cooking worse and the wine is worst of all. The restaurants are chockfull but only for two hours because at nine o'clock (which was my dinner hour) they close the restaurants and go to sleep under the tables. By a slight effort of imagination you may behold me and my family in the middle of one of those institutions patiently waiting for a vacant seat at some table. If I were alone, rather than enter one, I would buy food and eat it in the street.[33]

Once again he exaggerated. When the young Ernest Hemingway and his bride, Hadley, arrived in Paris early in 1921, trying to stretch their money so that they could travel and stay in Europe as long as possible, they envied the Joyces' style of life. As Hemingway wrote to the American writer Sherwood Anderson, who had given him a letter of introduction to Joyce,

The report is that he and all his family are starving but you can find the whole celtic crew of them every night in Michaud's where Binney [Hadley] and I can only afford to go about once a week.[34]

Hemingway and Hadley stared long enough to get a good view of the Celtic crew:

Joyce peering at the menu through his thick glasses, holding the menu up in one hand; Nora by him, a hearty but delicate eater; Giorgio, thin, foppish, sleek-headed from the back; Lucia with heavy curly hair, a girl not quite yet grown; all of them talking Italian.[35]

For Nora, one of the additional hardships of hotel life was that she had to get out of the way in the afternoon so that Joyce could write. An extremely orderly writer, Joyce carried his voluminous notes, revisions, little scraps of paper, and books of reference around in a small valise and boasted that he could work anywhere. To her great pleasure, she found that there were shops that sold phonograph records where, for a small fee, she could sit and listen to opera all afternoon. One day she took with her their friend from Zurich, August Suter, the Swiss sculptor who had moved to Paris. That evening in Michaud's, Joyce asked where they had gone. Suter told him and remarked on what a Wagnerian Nora had become: Wagner's operas were all she wanted to listen to. Joyce retorted that Wagner was obscene.

That was too much for Nora. "Oh, there are many obscenities in your book too!" she burst out. (Or, "Oh, *es gibt viele Schweinereien auch in*

Deinen Buch!" according to Suter. It is not clear whether the three spoke English or German together.) Joyce wanted appreciation for his own untraditional work but would not tolerate her own preference for something other than Verdi and Puccini.[36]

The winter of 1920 came, and the hotel was freezing. Joyce wrote on, wrapped in blankets. On December 1, to be warm and to have a piano for Christmas, they moved into a furnished flat at 5 Boulevard Raspail in the seventh arrondissement. It was expensive. But the Joyces had a larger family than most of the new arrivals, a problem compounded by Joyce's own convictions. He insisted on bourgeois comfort in the Odéon quarter. That the rent — three hundred pounds a year — was more than his income from Miss Weaver's two capital gifts did not alarm him. Joyce demanded only that the address be a good one, a tribute to his art. Gleefully he wrote to Budgen, once they had moved into their first quarters of their own, "By the way, is it not extraordinary the way I enter a city barefoot and end up in a luxurious flat?"[37]

A new Irish friend was a Europeanized young writer and art critic named Arthur Power. Accepting Joyce's invitation to meet his family, Power stumbled into the flat and found it dark and gloomy,

> typical of the sort which was let to foreigners, with any kind of furniture thrown in to make it up. A huge floppy lampshade dominated the living room, reminding one of a ballet dancer's skirt. It plunged the whole room into darkness so that everything seemed to be lost in a Dostoevsky gloom.

Power was not well received on his first visit. He was on his way to a party, and his pockets were clanking with bottles. Nora, Giorgio, and Lucia glared with hostility at a drunken Irishman come to take their husband and father away. Giorgio was particularly grim. They relented when they saw that Power was among the more sober of Joyce's café acquaintances, and he soon found himself invited to supper.

> I remember how pleased I was to be friends with this pleasant Irish family, with Georgio just coming into being a man and Lucia, younger than Georgio, silent and super-sensitive, and finally Mrs. Joyce, warm-hearted and gay.[38]

During the meal the conversation constantly returned to the subject of Dublin. Power was astounded. To be cosmopolitan was his ideal, and their Irishness impressed him; without knowing then that Giorgio and Lucia had hardly seen Ireland, he thought to himself that this Irish family had adapted itself remarkably well to the Continent. He did detect in Nora a certain nostalgia for Galway.

Another visitor to the Raspail flat also liked Nora's good looks and

affability. Robert McAlmon, one of the best-known figures in the growing Parisian colony of young American writers, thought when he saw her
that, whatever was wrong with Joyce's sight, it was clear that he had
used his eyes in picking his wife. McAlmon found Joyce surprisingly provincial, a Dublin Irishman who could not believe that to others (including
a minister's son like himself) questions of theology were of no interest
whatsoever.

Joyce, weeping in his cups, told McAlmon that he wanted more children. (He was then thirty-nine and Nora thirty-seven.) His father had
sired a large family; his grandfathers before him had produced from twelve
to eighteen apiece. By the grace of God, Joyce swore, he was still a young
man and would have more children before the end.

McAlmon was shocked and told Joyce, hinting not too subtly at the
plight of Lucia and Giorgio, that if one is to produce children one had
better have the money to educate and care for them in their formative
years.[39]

Their move to Paris was marked by an intensifed social life. Paris was the
crossroads to everywhere. Irish and British friends, such as Frank Budgen
and the Sykeses, most of whom had returned to live in England, looked
them up in Paris. Joyce became a mandatory stop for visiting luminaries;
he and Nora had dinner with the Yeatses. There was much to attract the
whole family out to both theater and opera. They all went to see John
McCormack, Nora no doubt reminding the children, as she did everybody, that their father had once shared a platform with him. Joyce next
day wrote him a fan letter. Prominent in their social life were two new
elements: homosexuals and Americans.

The Joyces seemed not to notice homosexuality. Although Joyce was
alert, for literary purposes, to strains of it in Nora and himself, he was
indifferent to it in their friends. Sylvia Beach was devoted to her partner
and roommate, Adrienne Monnier, who ran her own bookshop. Although everybody assumed they were lovers they were in no way lesbians
in the grand style of the Left Bank in the 1920s.

Sylvia dressed in severe, tailored clothes, she herself said, because she
was a businesswoman. Even though she preferred the company of women,
particularly single women, she had a girlish awe of charming men. She
adored Hemingway (who noticed that she had pretty legs), and she
worshiped Joyce. Sylvia was honest when she declared the three loves of
her life to have been Adrienne Monnier, her bookshop, and James
Joyce.[40]

Adrienne Monnier's shop, La Maison des Amis des Livres, was across
the rue Dupuytren from Sylvia's Shakespeare and Company. She and
Sylvia were utterly complementary. If Sylvia was full of the girlish zeal of
an American minister's daughter, Adrienne had the stolid shrewdness of

the daughter of a Savoyard mountain farmer. Her style of dress was even more individual than Sylvia's. Shaped like a Russian doll — perhaps because she was a superb cook — she swathed her bulk in a gray skirt reaching to her ankles and a white fichu. No one saw Adrienne's legs. Sylvia's hair was bobbed, Adrienne's not. If they contrasted in their appearance and pace — Sylvia, quick and sharp; Adrienne, reflective and slow — they were as one in their passion for their trade: bookselling, with special attention to cultivating authors.

Robert McAlmon, like Sylvia Beach, was a homosexual. A gaunt, handsome man with a cruel wit, he had, as a young writer in Greenwich Village, made a marriage of convenience with Bryher, a young English writer who was in love with the American poet H. D. (Hilda Doolittle). The marriage was more than convenient because Bryher (whose real name was Winifred Ellerman) was the daughter of one of the wealthiest men in England. McAlmon, even before the divorce settlement that gave him the nickname of McAlimony, had lots of spending money. He soon was giving Joyce thirty pounds a month "to tide him over." Joyce found McAlmon a spirited and witty drinking companion. Hemingway did too at first but gave up the friendship because McAlmon could not hold his drink and was sick in public.[41] But he treated Joyce, twenty years older and a cult hero, with more respect than he did McAlmon.

Americans were another matter. The attraction was mutual, and the cultural misunderstanding was great.

Many Americans who met the Joyces in Paris did not grasp that they were seeing a family that was in some ways Italian and for the most part Irish. There was nothing American — or English — in their attitudes toward education, entertaining, home furnishings, clothes, work, or debt. Myron Nutting, for example, marveled at how late in the evening the Joyces ate dinner (eight or nine o'clock) and at the way in which they entertained friends by inviting them to restaurants rather than to their home.[42] Nutting puzzled, as did Ezra Pound, that Joyce's hands were so limp "that you felt he would be no good as a handyman, fixing things around the house." Sylvia Beach too appreciated do-it-yourself: Pound made a table with his own hands, and she showed it off with pleasure to Joyce. Joyce was unimpressed. Why would Pound, a poet, bother to do that when a workman could do it in a week?[43]

This tone of reproof for the Joyce household for not being like others enveloped Nora: why could she not save Joyce from his excesses by good household management? She seemed neither to prepare meals nor to economize nor to keep the books. The American wives (and American scholars later) did not see how much Joyce and Nora had in common. Accustomed to a country where higher education was available for women, they believed that clever men should have clever wives. Nora was a great disappointment to most of them.[44]

Sylvia Beach soon accepted that "Mrs. Joyce," as she always called her, was the source of Joyce's inspiration but that Mrs. Joyce was not to be bothered with anything but running the Joyce ménage. She did not buy opera tickets or train tickets. She did not hunt for books for Joyce. She did not take dictation. Nora's responsibilities were to feed Joyce, hold his hand, choose all his clothes and the children's and keep them in order; to accompany him wherever he went socially, to cut him down to size, and to reassure him, every time she opened her mouth, that Ireland was not far away. Joyce never asked more of her, and nobody else dared.

Nora and Joyce, for their part, were astonished by the American energy, which bordered on foolhardiness. Kay Boyle recalled that, meeting them for the first time at a party, Nora looked at Kay and (as Kay heard it) said, "Isn't she the thrue picture of an Irish colleen, with her dark hair and misty blue eyes?"

Kay, embarrassed at the personal attention, said, "What about my broken nose?" She had broken it years before in a sledding accident in the Pocono Mountains in Pennsylvania.

The Joyces were fascinated. They listened with horror as Kay told how she was sliding down a hill and met a sleigh with two horses coming up. Swerving, she had plunged into a snowbank, which contained a telephone pole, and swallowed one of her front teeth.

"When I hear her talk," Nora said, "I can't help thinking, Jim, that our own lives haven't been very eventful."

"It's true," Joyce said, "but Americans are that way." Then, for the benefit of Kay and Nora, he added that Bach had led a very quiet life.[45]

The ceremoniousness and prudishness of the Joyces, just entering their forties, contrasted with the uninhibited behavior of the young expatriates around them. The Joyces were even prim in their speech. Wyndham Lewis said that Joyce's insistence on calling everyone "Mr." "Miss," or "Mrs." showed how middle class he was. All noticed. The phrase "Hi, Bob" could not pass Joyce's lips.

Hemingway enjoyed returning Joyce's exaggerated politeness with American breeziness. He was even rumored to have called Joyce (whom he revered for the spareness of his prose style) "Jim." One day Hemingway was minding the bookshop for Sylvia when Joyce came in to look for "Miss Beach." "Sylvia's not here," said Hemingway. "Oh, you mean Miss Beach," Joyce corrected. Hemingway, undeterred, went on: "And Myrsine is not here either." "Oh . . . you mean Miss Moschos." Thereupon Hemingway extended the offense to Myrsine's younger sister: "Hélène is not here either."[46]

Nora flaunted her rights under this convention proudly. She was the only one who could call Joyce "Jim," and she did so to all and sundry. When guests came to see him and Joyce would emerge from his study, wearing the white working coat in which he looked a cross between a band leader and a dentist, Nora would say disgustedly in front of the awed guest, "For God's sake, Jim, take that coat off you."[47]

Those who put Joyce on a pedestal were shocked, but others, like Sylvia Beach, who came to know them well, saw that Joyce enjoyed Nora's teasing. To Irish friends, their banter had an intimacy about it as if they were speaking a private language while playing public roles. Arthur Power felt that there was perfect understanding between them.[48]

Nora always made friends easily. One of her good friends was Myron Nutting's wife, Helen, a writer. The Nuttings had a studio near the Gare Montparnasse, and Nora would come over frequently to visit. Nora had worries, they knew — money, Joyce's drinking, her unsettled children. "She wasn't a complaining woman at all," said Nutting. "She didn't come to weep on my wife's shoulder, but she liked to have somebody to confide in. She liked Helen very much, and for that reason, she'd be over quite a lot." The Nuttings believed that the Joyces were very hard up and took them on excursions to Fontainebleau in their little Citroën. The two couples had dinner together once a week, and Nora said she had a special reason for being fond of Myron: when he brought Jim home, he remembered to bring Jim's coat.[49]

Joyce himself expected to make good money from the publication of *Ulysses*, but by late 1920 it was obvious that this time would not come soon. In February 1921 in New York the Society for the Suppression of Vice won its lawsuit against the *Little Review* and its editors, Jane Heap and Margaret Anderson. The scene of Bloom's masturbation on the beach was judged obscene, in spite of a vigorous defense by John Quinn, lawyer for the case. The news was doubly bad: it meant *Ulysses* would not find an American publisher and that it would not be protected by copyright. Instead of the one-thousand-dollar advance (Quinn had suggested this sum) on royalties Joyce was expecting from America, there would be none; worse, an illegal edition could appear, as Joyce rightly foresaw, siphoning off the American earnings of the book into a pirate's pockets. So the chances of reaping the reward for his years of hard labor since he began *Ulysses* in 1914 looked dim, and the receipts from *A Portrait* did not cover costs by 1921. (Miss Weaver obscured the book's losses with odd sums marked "proceeds from remainders" and other bogus receipts.[50] The money in fact was her own.)

When the news arrived from New York, Joyce wandered disconsolately into Shakespeare and Company, where he had become both an habitué and a prime attraction. To Sylvia he declared, "My book will never come out now." Sylvia Beach later recalled saying (a bit like Mickey Rooney and Judy Garland deciding to do their own show, "right here, in the barn!"), "Would you let Shakespeare and Company have the honor of bringing out *Ulysses*?"[51] In reality, it was Joyce who took the initiative and suggested the idea. He knew that Adrienne Monnier had done some publishing under the imprint of her shop and suspected that Sylvia could be persuaded to follow suit. He probably also suspected the truth that Sylvia, for all her sapphic feminism, capitulated because she was captivated by him. That was quite true, but Sylvia had another reason, as she gushed to her sister, Holly:

> Ulysses is going to make my place famous — Already the publicity is beginning and swarms of people visit the shop . . . and if all goes well I hope to make money out of it, not only for Joyce but for me. Aren't you excited? [52]

Joyce wrote to Miss Weaver asking for more money. She was startled but unwilling to refuse him anything. She sent two hundred pounds as an advance on royalties from her "English" edition, which was to be published from the type set in France at some unspecified time after Sylvia Beach's "French" edition. In preparing for an "English" publication, he skirted the conflict that was building up between Miss Weaver's edition of Ulysses and Sylvia Beach's. He needed the money, he said, because he had been counting on a thousand-dollar advance from an American edition, money that he would now not get. More as an excuse for helping him than to set up a rival to Sylvia Beach's Paris edition, she sent him the money.

How poor were the Joyces? The picture of their finances is clouded by their transactions in five currencies (British, American, French, Swiss, and Italian), by Joyce's habit of translating money sums into their value in the currency of the person to whom he was writing, and by the inflation that followed World War II. Between the wars exchange rates were fairly stable. Joyce's main income during his life in Paris was in pounds sterling: it came in the form of the interest on the war bonds Miss Weaver had given him and on the capital she had turned over to him. He received the interest quarterly and drew on capital by writing a request, either to Miss Weaver or to her increasingly worried solicitors.

Americans came to Paris in the early 1920s not only because it was the vibrant center of all that was new in art and literature, but also because it was cheap. The photographer Berenice Abbott sailed from New York with six dollars in her pocket. The Hemingways were well-off with $3,000 a year (about £500) of Hadley Hemingway's money. Ernest was so eager to stay in Europe as long as possible that they practiced every sort of economy, from living in a cold-water, five-flight, walk-up flat to searching out the cheapest cafés. Eliot in London was earning a substantial £500 a year at Lloyds Bank; true wealth was Peggy Guggenheim's $22,000 (£4,500) a year. [53]

When he first came to Paris, Joyce had only £62 a quarter income from Miss Weaver's first big gift. But he was also selling the manuscript of

Ulysses as he wrote it to John Quinn and soon was receiving McAlmon's £30 monthly "loans." Miss Weaver's second gift of £200 should have given him enough to last for a good stretch (the Hemingways' rent was about £48 a year), and by the time she gave him access to £2,000, he had no reason to think himself indigent.

Nora, by no means sure that Paris was the right place to set up house-keeping — it was expensive and offered the children no future — none-theless wanted a settled home. Even more, she wanted Joyce to give up drinking. She was doomed to disappointment on both counts. Once McAlmon brought Joyce in at ten in the morning after a night of drinking, dumped him on the bed, and fled to avoid Nora's tirade: "Jim, you've been doing this to me for twenty years . . ." and so forth. McAlmon was fit only "to sleep, to die, to know agony, to curse Joyce, life, myself."[54] Just as he got to sleep, at three o'clock in the afternoon, a telegram arrived from Joyce, summoning him to tea at four thirty, without fail, in the name of friendship. When McAlmon, scarcely able to walk, duly arrived, Joyce said earnestly, in front of Nora, "And, McAlmon, what have you been hearing today about the apartment the man said we were to have?"

McAlmon thought fast. He knew that Nora was intent on moving out of their temporary accommodations and into a flat but that Joyce was rather hoping that friends would find one for him. "Oh, he's seeing about it now," McAlmon lied to Nora. "I'm to meet him at six o'clock."

Joyce was immune to Nora's anger about his drinking, but he was terrified that he might incur Miss Weaver's wrath. She knew nothing of it until May 1921 when Wyndham Lewis broke the news. Miss Weaver was his publisher too, and calling on her in London, Lewis merrily recounted what a stupendous drinking companion the Irish writer was, how he drank until dawn or beyond, quite often ending up dancing by himself, and how he picked up the bill for everybody.

Miss Weaver was stunned. She knew how hard Joyce was working on his book and assumed that other Calvinistic virtues accompanied his industriousness. It would have been uncharacteristic for her, however, to fret silently and make furtive inquiries. She instantly wrote Joyce, told him what she had learned, and gave a polite lecture on the evils of drink. Nevertheless, the news shook her. She had been brought up to believe that drink was one of the great pitfalls of life, and a quiet, gentle woman, she was frightened of drunken people.[55]

Joyce was equally shattered by her reproof. Although he was not careful with Miss Weaver's money, he prized her esteem. And he knew as well as anyone that, although he enjoyed his bad habit, he was not an alcoholic. He never drank during the day. The celebrated inebriation came from a regular consumption of several bottles of white wine between, roughly, eight in the evening and two in the morning. He rarely drank spirits. (Just as Joyce's spending was related to his excretory cast of mind, so was his drinking. He often compared his favorite Swiss white wine to urine — an archduchess's urine, to be sure. He loathed red wine because to him it tasted of blood.)

How, he wrote and asked Budgen, should he defend himself? Budgen, to whom he had boasted of his nights on the town with Wyndham Lewis — "uproarious allnight sittings (and dancings)" — suggested that Joyce laugh it off.[56] Joyce followed Budgen's advice. He sent Miss Weaver a long and witty catalogue of all the other vices of which he had been accused since he had gained a modicum of fame.[57]

Joyce's efforts to whitewash his reputation did not stop there. He besought McAlmon to write a defense of his character to Miss Weaver. More cunningly, he sought to retrieve the physical evidence of the criticism against him. As an initial precaution, he asked Budgen to return Miss Weaver's letter by registered post. But one telltale item was still outstanding: his own letter to Budgen. He did not know how to ask for that back without appearing foolish.

When Budgen was next in Paris, Joyce saw his chance. The incriminating letter lay in Budgen's wallet. Joyce saw to it that they had one of their convivial evenings together but that Budgen had more to drink than he. Then, depositing the reeling Budgen back at his hotel, Joyce took the wallet. Back home, he extracted the letter, put the bar bills in its place, and had a messenger return it next day with a note saying he had taken the wallet for safekeeping. Budgen was furious at the deception, and their friendship was ruptured for about three years.[58]

That Joyce, even in 1921, should take such care to protect his good name raises the question of the whereabouts of his and Nora's obscene correspondence of 1909. Did they think it was safe from prying eyes? Leaving Trieste, Joyce had packed one box of papers to go to Paris and later requested a bundle of papers that he had left in a briefcase in Stanislaus's bedroom. He needed the papers to complete *Ulysses*. But most of their archive was left behind. The sense of danger in leaving erotic letters lying around entered Joyce's writing about that time, and also entered his dreams. When, upon the publication of *Ulysses*, Stanislaus complained about its obscenity, Joyce must have wondered if Stanislaus had dipped into the secret store.[59] Some dreams that he recorded around the time of the publication of *Ulysses* include this one: "A young woman tells me with less and less indignation that I have written a compromising letter to her. The contents do not shock her much, but she asks me why I signed it 'Ulysses.' "[60]

·   ·   ·

In June 1921, as their lease on the luxurious if Dostoevskian flat came to an end, they had the kind of luck Joyce felt was his due. The French literary critic Valery Larbaud lent them his elegant and spotless bachelor flat on the rue du Cardinal-Lemoine in the fifth arrondissement. Joyce claimed that Larbaud had had it redecorated expressly for them. Larbaud may well have done so. As France's foremost exponent of English literature, Larbaud described himself as "raving mad" over *Ulysses* and had promised to give a lecture at Adrienne Monnier's bookshop to introduce Joyce to the French literary public. In *Ulysses,* Larbaud claimed, Joyce had returned Ireland to world literature.

Giorgio did not make the move with them. After several abortive attempts to begin a career in business, he had returned to Zurich to spend a month with some friends; he was to escape the claustrophobia of the family circle much more easily than his sister could. Lucia did, however, go to summer camp for a time, with a niece of Helen Nutting's. Later she attended a lycée briefly and also studied typing. Lucia had trouble finding friends. Nora was always on the lookout for new acquaintances with teenage daughters because, as Joyce observed, Lucia found every afternoon boring.[61]

Nora and Lucia were delighted with their new surroundings. They loved the flat with its polished floors, antique furniture, and collection of toy soldiers. The view was so green that they felt they were in the heart of the country, an impression heightened by the entrance through a courtyard with a big iron gate. The only thing that could have pleased Nora more was a flat of their own. Even Joyce became nostalgic for his family portraits and other knickknacks of sentimental value.

The flat even had a special writing room, with a low, rounded ceiling and a long table where it was possible to work in total silence. Joyce, however, preferred noisy surroundings[62] and found Larbaud's flat like a tomb.

While there, writing the last episode of *Ulysses,* Molly Bloom's monologue, Joyce was struck with another eye attack so painful that he rolled on the floor weeping. Nora sent the children rushing to fetch Sylvia Beach while she stayed at Joyce's side, dipping a cloth into ice water and applying it to his eyes.

Nora was also furious. Joyce had been drinking heavily even though he had been advised of the risk to his eyes. She blamed him even for leading his friends astray. "Jim, you've been bringing your drunken companions home to me long enough," she said, "and now you've started McAlmon the same way." But McAlmon liked Nora for her dignity and reassuring manner, and understood the dual role Joyce forced her to play as punishing wife and loving mother. One night, out with Joyce, McAlmon saw a rat and cried out, whereupon Joyce fainted dead away.

When McAlmon bundled him home and explained to Nora what had caused the collapse — fear, not drink — she "turned tender at once." [63] The next night the three of them were in a café when Nora suddenly called a taxi. She had spotted Joyce's contorted face and, realizing that he was in terrible pain, immediately took him home.

For six weeks Joyce was ill, in such pain that his doctor injected cocaine into his eyes and cut down his working hours (from ten a day to six). The pain was nothing to the threat to his work. Fate, with cruel precision, struck Joyce, like Beethoven, in the very organ necessary for the practice of his art. Although the iritis flared up again, he managed to complete "Penelope" and the penultimate episode, "Ithaca," by October. *Ulysses* was done. [64]

The drink did make the eye pain worse, and Nora tried vainly to tell his professed admirers that, by encouraging his drinking, they harmed his sight. But they tended to dismiss her warnings as those of a nagging wife and, like Budgen, listening underneath her window, paid more attention to the rhythms than the substance of her speech:

> Jim, do you hear me? You've had enough. Jim, I'm telling you, this has been going on for twenty years and I'll have no more of it. It's me that has to tend you when your eyes are giving you trouble and raising a nuisance for all of us. Jim, I'm telling you, I'll take the children and go back to Ireland. [65]

Nora understood the pressure of Joyce's deadline. Writing to Katherine Sargent (wife of Louis Sargent, an English painter with whom they had become friendly through Budgen), Nora said that the eye trouble was most unlucky because Joyce had so much work to do in writing the ending of *Ulysses* and correcting the proofs. It was bad luck for her also because otherwise they might have been able to join the Sargents on holiday at Thun in Switzerland. Nora recommended to them a pension where they might stay. [66]

Correction of the proofs was work indeed. The book was being set by the printers in Dijon who printed Sylvia's bookshop stationery; they did not know ordinary English, let alone Joyce's. Joyce also had much to change and to add. He wrote as much as one-third of the final text of *Ulysses* in the form of corrections or additions in the margins of the proof sheets.

In October 1921 the idyll at Larbaud's came to an end. Giorgio having returned from Zurich, they moved back to the *maison de famille* on the rue de l'Université, into two rooms as before. Giorgio was on his own; Lucia with her parents. She was thus sharing her parents' bedroom at an age (fifteen) when she was almost certainly menstruating and subject to the occasional embarrassment of finding that her period had started in the night. Amid all the voluminous detail on the Joyces' personal lives, there is no hint of how the three of them protected their personal privacy under such conditions.

From necessity as well as convenience, Shakespeare and Company, now in new quarters at 12 rue de l'Odéon, had become their business address. Joyce expected to make about £1,500 from *Ulysses*. But to finance publication, Sylvia Beach needed to raise money. To this end, she put out a prospectus announcing the publication of the already notorious masterpiece and sold "subscriptions" to those who wanted to order copies. Many admirers of avant-garde literature (among them T. E. Lawrence, Winston Churchill, and Havelock Ellis) accepted the offer and sent in their money (150 francs, 300 francs for a deluxe edition), some flattered to be asked. George Bernard Shaw was not among them. "In Ireland," he wrote Sylvia, declining her invitation, "they try to make a cat cleanly by rubbing its nose in its own filth. Mr Joyce has tried the same treatment on the human subject." He hoped Joyce would succeed if only because the book was an accurate representation of the "slackjawed blackguardism" of the Dublin of his youth.[67]

As the subscriptions poured in, all the Joyces dipped regularly into the bookshop's till for petty cash. Giorgio usually performed the errand, drawing out 600 francs on July 12, 200 on September 12, and ten days later 200 more. On November 29 Nora herself came to the shop and borrowed the not small sum of 100 francs (about $20, or £5) from the advance sales of tickets to the reading on Joyce by Valery Larbaud scheduled for December 7.[68]

Joyce occasionally did pay some of the money back — 300 francs in December — but began borrowing again, and by July 1922, five months after the appearance of *Ulysses*, he owed Sylvia 40,565 francs. Sylvia, to be fair, had paid him no advance on royalties, and he had been working on the book for at least seven years. She kept all her expenses in a little black notebook: taxi (8 francs) to fetch an order for 150 envelopes (15 francs).

The Joyces' Christmas in 1921, in spite of their confined hotel life, was festive as usual — the children ate lots of chocolate, and they enjoyed boxes of fruit from the Sargents. There was a party at which Lucia dressed up and did a Charlie Chaplin act, but Nora could not come.

A week or so before, she had been waiting at a bus stop by a gas lamp when an approaching bus swerved, mounted the footpath and pinned her to the lamp. As superstitious as her husband, Nora took it as an omen. She needed as long to recover from the fright as from the minor injuries. In describing it to Stanislaus, Joyce declared, "It was hardly an accident."[69]

Lucia was old enough at fifteen to take over the duty Nora hated — writing letters — and she tackled the Christmas thank-yous on her mother's behalf. She did them, however, in a disjointed rambling childish prose that suggests (with hindsight) emotional difficulties beyond those of learning to write in a third new language.

Joyce soon received an ill omen of his own. The day before publication of *Ulysses,* with their nerves on edge, Nora and Joyce went for a walk in the Bois de Boulogne with the young American author Djuna Barnes. Brushing against Joyce, a man muttered, "You are an abominable writer!" It was a dreadful portent for his book, Joyce, white-faced, told the two women.[70]

On Joyce's fortieth birthday, February 2, 1922, although the final page proofs had been returned only two days before, the first two bound copies of *Ulysses* were ready. Sylvia Beach got up to meet the 7:00 A.M. train from Dijon so that Joyce could have a copy on his breakfast table. Joyce was deluged with telegrams all day. The bookshop was under siege by those wanting a glimpse of the other copy, which was on display. And Joyce, in gratitude, adapted a Shakespearean song to recognize the American quality in her courage:

> Who is Sylvia, what is she
> That all our scribes commend her?
> Yankee, young and brave is she
> The West this grace did lend her
> That all books might published be . . .[71]

But although he and Nora had entertained Sylvia and Adrienne, he did not invite them to a celebration dinner on January 20. That night they took a group of personal friends to Ferrari's, an Italian restaurant: the Nuttings; their niece, Helen Kieffer (and a daughter of John Quinn's law partner), who had been at camp with Lucia; the Wallaces; and Giorgio and Lucia. They toasted the author, the waiters admired the book, and even Nora had a good word for it. Jim had spent sixteen years thinking about the book and seven years writing it, she said proudly. At the end of the evening, after the party had moved on to the Café Weber, Nora called a taxi. Joyce did not want to get in. She bundled him into it. To Richard Wallace, Joyce cried, as Nora pushed him from view, "I must be saved from these scenes."[72]

Nora knew she was cast as shrew. McAlmon tried to tell her how essential she was to Joyce's work, that if she had not put up with Joyce and brought him down to earth, he would have remained like Stephen Dedalus, the posturing martyr to art, and never matured and mellowed into the family man and great artist.

"Go along with you!" Nora answered. "People say I have helped him to be a genius. What they'll be saying next is that if it hadn't been for that ignoramus of a woman what a man he would have been! But never you mind. I could tell them a thing or two about him after twenty years . . ."[73]

When Joyce presented Nora with her copy of the first edition of *Ulysses*, she weighed it in her hand and tilting her head toward Arthur Power, who was watching, said, "How much will you give me for this?"[74] In later years her remark was interpreted as a sign of her ignorance, but Power, who liked her very much, took it as the taunt of a strong, confident woman cutting her man down to size. Joyce, however, did not laugh. Nora's indifference to his work saddened and tantalized him. It was part of her desirability and unattainability that his genius was of no interest to her. She loved him for his ordinariness.

Fame was lifting all four Joyces to the circles of international café society. In March 1922 they attended the wedding breakfast of Laurence Vail, a dashing young American writer, and Peggy Guggenheim, the American heiress. Joyce did not know why they had been invited, but he believed that Vail had met Nora or the children somewhere.[75]

Also in March their standard of living received another boost. Miss Weaver bestowed upon Joyce a new unrestricted gift of £1,500 in capital. He had told her that he was again out of funds, and she loyally felt bound to respond. She agreed with him that after his labors on *Ulysses* he needed money to be able to rest and take a holiday.

The good news from London did nothing to make Joyce soften to a bitter request from Stanislaus for repayment of a loan of £10 made when Joyce left Trieste:

> Dear Stannie, My solicitor will send you a check for 10£ [sic] on the 25 instant. I am sorry to hear you are pressed for money. How do you manage it? Living in a furnished apartment without a family, of exemplary habits and giving all the lessons to all the pupils. . . .[76]

Joyce in the same letter went on to describe his own hardship, living in a cramped, costly hotel, having to write in the bedroom where three of them slept . . . He could not refrain from adding to his brother that Miss Weaver's latest tribute had made her total gifts to him £8,500, plus, he added patronizingly and misleadingly, "the reversion of a country house somewhere."

Yet he had been feeling so impoverished earlier in the month that he asked McAlmon, who was in the south of France, to send him a nice necktie if he had any castoffs (and professed to be appalled when McAlmon bought him some new ones and sent an episcopal-looking ring as well).[77]

When Miss Weaver's news arrived, he believed that at last he had the money he needed — enough, he hurried to tell Sylvia, to support him and his family for the rest of their lives.

At last, Sylvia said to herself, a little loan while waiting for Miss Weaver's gift to arrive, and I can go on with my job.

At last, Nora told Joyce, she could go home on a visit to Ireland.

Arthur Power was one of the few people who appreciated how homesick Nora was. He understood her disdain for the artificiality of Parisian life. Nora was more stoical than Joyce was, and, in Power's view, far readier to accept the worst with the best; a down-and-out lodging house or the table of honor in a three-star restaurant — it was all the same to her. What Nora could not bear, Power observed, was deception or insincerity. From Joyce she was learning the art of public silence, but with a fellow countryman, such as Power, she would speak spontaneously. One evening she was next to Power at a party at which a few self-conscious couples began dancing in a desultory way. "If this was happening in Galway," Nora said in disgust, "we'd all be out in a minute on the road kicking up our heels in the dust."[78]

Following the receipt of Miss Weaver's largesse, Nora kicked up her own heels. With *Ulysses* published and their money problem solved, Jim could look after himself. Nora had not seen her mother since before the war, and her father, Tom Barnacle, had recently died. Annie Barnacle had nursed her husband, their estrangement notwithstanding, through his last illness in July 1921, and the following spring, with only two daughters left at home, she longed to see Nora again.[79]

There was an enormous row. Joyce implored Nora not to go. Ireland was on the verge of civil war, he reminded her, showing her the latest dramatic headlines from Irish newspapers. For once Nora did not give in. She ordered Giorgio and Lucia to pack, and they walked out of the hotel. She did not care if she never saw Paris — or another drunken writer — again.

11

In a
Free State

THE CROSSING of the dreaded Channel went smoothly. Nora and the children arrived in London on April 2, 1922, and checked into the Bonnington Hotel on Southampton Row, not far from where they would catch the boat-train for Ireland once they had had the good look they wanted at London.[1] Nora liked the city very much and began to consider that, instead of pursuing an elusive flat in Paris, she might persuade Joyce to switch to London. They had so many friends in and around it — the Sykeses, Frank Budgen, and the Sargents — and to hear English on all sides was a relief.

Giorgio and Lucia found little difficulty in accompanying Nora. They had not made lives of their own in Paris and had nothing to do most of the time. Besides, as Sylvia Beach had observed, "Joyce's children had early taken the decision not to allow themselves to be enslaved by Babbo." (A wise decision, Sylvia thought: "Alas for me — I got trapped but it was interesting.")[2] Giorgio, Sylvia noticed, was very protective toward his mother; he severely disapproved of drinking, especially his father's.

While in London, they wrote to "Caro Stannie" in Trieste to tell him how much they were enjoying their trip, although they found the ways of the English very different from those on the Continent, and to request a favor: when he was packing up the family portraits in Trieste for shipping to Paris, could he include their reproduction Pompeian masks?

The one person they did not look up in London was "Saint Harriet," as Lucia referred to their patron. Harriet Weaver was in the north of England, visiting her other protégée, Dora Marsden; Miss Marsden, a writer of philosophy, was nearly as demanding as Joyce, without the compensatory genius. From Paris they received a fusillade of messages from Joyce, trying to dissuade them from crossing the Irish Sea. They delayed a few days beyond their planned week but no more.

Ireland in April 1922 was not the Ireland Nora had left in 1912. There had been two years of terrible violence as Irish revolutionaries fought the British and the despised Black and Tans. ("There's nothing but raids and murders here," Aunt Josephine had written to Joyce in 1920.)[3] Since signing a treaty with Britain in December 1921, Ireland had become a Free State, a self-governing dominion, like Canada, within the British Empire. For four months, British troops and police had been pulling out of Ireland, handing over their barracks and installations to the Free State authorities and the Irish Republican Army. The hope was that the treaty would bring peace and stability and long-awaited self-government to Ireland.

However, many in Ireland saw the treaty as a victory only for perfidious Albion. The treaty partitioned Ireland into the twenty-six counties of the mainly Catholic south and the six counties of the Protestant-dominated north. And it in no sense granted Ireland the status of an independent nation. It obliged members of the Irish Parliament in Dublin to swear allegiance to the British Crown — hardly the free Irish Republic declared by the rebels of the Easter Rising in 1916 before they died.

In consequence by 1922, the people of the twenty-six counties of southern Ireland were divided into those who favored and those who opposed the treaty. The army itself, the IRA, was split into pro-treaty forces — the Regulars — and anti-treaty forces — the Irregulars — who were prepared to fight on for an independent and united Ireland even if it meant Irishman killing Irishman. With a general election coming up in June 1922 to find out how the Irish voters themselves felt about ratifying the treaty, the new state was divided against itself.

Unafraid and probably uninterested, Nora headed home. Her uncle, Michael Healy, still working for the customs service, met them in Dublin. With a fine annual income equal at least to Joyce's in Paris, he took Nora, Giorgio, and Lucia to dinner with Joyce's father and John Joyce's old crony Tom Devin, the man who had spotted the eloping couple at the North Wall in 1904. The next day Nora and the children went on to Galway.

The minute they stepped from the train they were in the midst of the conflict. The railway hotel in Eyre Square was the headquarters of the Regular IRA, while the Irregulars occupied the former Connaught Rangers' Renmore barracks along the rail line about a mile out of town. Even within the town, individual buildings were recognized to be held by one side or the other. The Regulars held the Masonic Hall, the Irregulars the Customs House. The newspapers were full of stories of robberies of post offices, banks, and liquor stores and of trains being stopped and boarded. Civilians were dragged from their beds and shot in the streets (as they were in other Irish cities from Cork to Sligo). Galway was so tense that priests feared to go out at night to give last rites to the dying. The only consolation was the knowledge that in Belfast things were much worse.[4]

Nora, with the children, took rooms at Mrs. O'Casey's boarding house on Nun's Island. Her worries were more personal than political. She did not want to return to Paris and had asked Jim to send her an allowance to support her while she stayed as long as she liked, in Galway or London. And she found that her children, now seventeen and fifteen and accustomed to Continental sophistication, no longer found Annie Barnacle's little terraced house as charming as they had ten years earlier. In fact, they loathed the smell of boiling cabbage so much that they refused to go in and lounged outside, sitting on the window ledge, in full view of all the neighbors. Nora had to take them to a café for meals.[5]

Nora enjoyed herself, all the same. She took the children to visit the Presentation Convent. She gossiped with the two sisters remaining at home: Delia, who was thirty-six, and Kathleen, who was twenty-six. Nora found high-spirited Kathleen especially amusing. She saw the sights, sent a postcard to Helen Nutting,[6] praising the bracing air, and posed for photographs with her good hat on.

Back in Paris, on his own for the first time in five years, Joyce could barely get through the routine of living. He refused a dinner invitation from the Nuttings, collapsed in Shakespeare and Company, and besieged McAlmon, in letters and telegrams, to come and reassure him. "And do you think they're safe then?" he kept asking McAlmon. "You don't understand, McAlmon, how this is affecting me. I am worried all the day, and it does my eye no good."[7]

He wrote frequently to Nora. The letter that has survived shows an intensity of longing and dependence far more like the letters of 1904, 1909, and 1912 than the laconic notes he sent to her in Locarno in 1917:

> 8.30 a.m.
> Thursday [n.d.]
>
> My darling, my love, my queen: I jump out of bed to send you this. Your wire is postmarked 18 hours later than your letter which I have just received. A cheque for your fur will follow in a few hours, and also money for yourself. If you wish to live there (as you ask me to send two pounds a week) I will send that amount (£8 and £4 rent) on the first of every month. But you also ask me if I would go to London with you. I would go anywhere in the world if I could be sure that I could be alone with your dear self without family and without friends. Either this must occur or we must part forever, though it will break my heart. Evidently it is impossible to describe to you the despair I have been in since you left. Yesterday I got a fainting fit in Miss Beach's shop and she had to run and get me some kind of a drug. Your

image is always in my heart. How glad I am to hear you are looking younger! O my dearest, if you would only turn to me even now and read that terrible book which has now broken the heart in my breast and take me to yourself alone to do with me what you will! I have only 10 minutes to write this so forgive me. Will write again before noon and also wire. These few words for the moment and my undying unhappy love. Jim[8]

The image is out of Thurber: the cowering male and the masterful female. Joyce, in the letter, linked his book and his body: he wanted Nora to touch both supine objects. He knew her weakness for fur and was eager to indulge it, but he revealed a curious wish to have Nora "without family and without friends." Perhaps this was another motive for taking her from Trieste.

As Joyce's discussions about Nora's monthly allowance suggest, he was resigned to a lengthy separation. And Nora was in no hurry to return; she wrote to Helen Nutting on April 29, and Joyce himself gave Helen Nora's address so that she could write back. But Joyce had counted without the help of the IRA.

Nora had chosen the most emotion-laden time of year in the Irish calendar — Easter, the sixth anniversary of the Rising — to return home. Tension mounted as Eamon De Valera himself, the erstwhile president of the republic, the only survivor among the leaders of the 1916 insurrection (he was saved from execution only by the fear of American public opinion, for he had been born in the United States), appeared in Galway on Easter Day, April 23. De Valera refused to accept the treaty. The Irish people should maintain the republic they had proclaimed in 1916.

There was no doubt, however, about where Galway's sympathies lay. It was pro-treaty, just as it always, like Michael Healy, had been pro-Crown. The crowd listened to Dev in silence. But the atmosphere was tense, and Giorgio, of the age and height to be a soldier, was eyed hostilely by the troops in the streets. A drunken officer once blocked his path, demanding, after looking at his foreign, elegant clothes, "How does it feel to be a gintleman's son?"[9] The boy could not sleep at night for fear that "the Zulus," as he called the troops, would come to get him.

And one afternoon the IRA Regulars were at the door of Mrs. O'Casey's — not looking for Giorgio, but rushing in to use the Joyces' bedroom windows for mounting their machine guns in order to fire at the Irregulars, who had occupied a warehouse across the street. That was enough for Nora. She surrendered. Jim had been right after all.

Packing up, she and the children boarded the train with relief to return to Dublin. Their brush with war was not over, however. As the train passed the Renmore barracks, sniping began between the Free State troops on the train and the Irregulars in the barracks. Nora and Lucia dived to the ground, although Giorgio (advised by a native to ignore the sound of gunfire) remained upright.[10]

The shooting was absolutely routine, a daily occurrence — nothing like the main event of the week, which was the retaking of the Customs House by the Regulars. People in Galway were so used to leaving town to the accompaniment of gunfire that when one young couple left on their honeymoon, their friends placed firecrackers under the train as a going-away joke.[11] So when the shaken trio of Joyces reached the relative safety of Dublin and poured out the tale of their experience to Michael Healy, he laughed so hard that he nearly fell off his chair.[12]

But tourists take a different view of terrorism than natives do, and so do their relatives. Joyce did not underplay the incident. He told everyone that his family had escaped assassination in Ireland, and he even began to believe that it was directed at them because they belonged to him. When he carried on in front of his Dublin friend, the lawyer Constantine Curran, who was visiting Paris, Curran told him he was being preposterous.[13]

Curran could not have realized how useful the incident was to Joyce. At very least it gave Joyce an excuse with which to appease Aunt Josephine. After waiting ten years to see her grandnephew, grandniece, and Nora, she found that, without stopping to see her, they had left Ireland. She was deeply hurt. "No doubt you will see Nora again when she revisits her native dunghill," Joyce wrote his aunt archly a few months later, although he doubted that Giorgio and Lucia would accompany her. "The air in Galway is very good but dear at the present price."[14]

Joyce thus wove the IRA's fusillade into the family mythology; it became a snare to prevent Nora from ever leaving his side again, a colossal "I told you so."

The episode marked the end of Nora's most determined break for freedom. She surrendered to the truth: she had no existence except as Mrs. James Joyce. The sad part of it was that she never revisited "her native dunghill again" and that from then on she hardly had a good word to say about Ireland.

12

Molly

WAS NORA Molly Bloom? Joyce never said so. Often asked after *Ulysses* appeared, he suggested that there were other models. He used to invite friends in restaurants to guess which woman in the room was Molly.

Nora also grew used to being asked if she were Molly. "No," she would answer. "She was much fatter."

Molly, who was born in Gibraltar of a Spanish mother, did not look like Nora. Her black hair came from Joyce's Triestine pupil Amalia Popper, her Spanish-Irish looks from the daughter of a friend of Joyce's father. Her singing voice came from a matron in Dublin, her *embonpoint* from another in Trieste. Her famous last word, "Yes," came from Nora's friend Lillian Wallace. One afternoon Joyce was dozing in the Wallaces' garden in Chatillon and heard Lillian talking to a friend and saying "yes," over and over. He then realized how he wanted to end his book.[1] And her name was fashioned from *moly,* the herb Odysseus or Ulysses, to give him his Latin name, gave his men to save them from Circe's spells.

Nora can be seen in all the main women characters in Joyce, from Lily the serving girl in *Dubliners* to Anna Livia Plurabelle in *Finnegans Wake.* She even appears, through the meaning of her surname, in *A Portrait,* the only one among Joyce's books with which she is not usually associated. In *A Portrait* Stephen Dedalus finds his muse in a beautiful girl wading on the beach "whom magic had changed into the likeness of a strange and beautiful seabird." Even in *Ulysses* traces of Nora can be found in characters other than Molly Bloom; Joyce worked Nora's aggressive de-

rision, which he so enjoyed, into the character of Bella Cohen, the broth-
elkeeper.

Yet it is with Molly that Nora is most identified. Sylvia Beach thought
of them as one and the same.[2] Many Joycean scholars also have taken
the connection for granted and seen it as Joyce's tribute to Nora for
anchoring him to reality. In *James Joyce: Common Sense and Beyond,*
Robert M. Adams said that the gush of Molly's vitality makes much of
the book that precedes it look contrived and mechanical. Joyce, said Adams,
had misgivings about the artificiality of art: "Only Nora knew what he
was like behind his literary facades — and it is fitting that in writing of
Nora he came, finally, to cast some of them aside."[3] His relationship
with Nora, says Adams, "with its astounding depths, contradictions, and
ambivalences, was in many ways a model for the one which Joyce imagined between Bloom and Molly."

There are many ways in which Nora was not Molly. Molly *was* fatter:
eleven stone nine (163 pounds). Nora herself, to judge from photographs, was not as heavy as that in her prime, except perhaps when nursing. (Molly, *Ulysses* says, put on nine pounds after weaning her daughter,
Milly.) Molly also lacks Nora's modernity, propriety, practicality, close
friendships with women, and love of Wagner.

The customary misgivings about hunting for biographical information
in works of fiction, however, must give way in the face of the many
obvious parallels between the real woman and the fictional creation in
Joyce's text. The links are strengthened by Joyce's detailed notes for *Ulysses,*
where he makes many of the connections explicit, often repeating some
of the references to Nora he had made in the notes to *Exiles:* the girlish
pinafore, the buttoned boots, the grief over the girlhood friend who went
off to America.[4] Joyce, of course, embroidered, expanded, and com-
pressed his raw material, but in Molly much that appears to be Nora
remains visible and often little altered.

Molly's monologue forms the "Penelope" episode that ends *Ulysses.*
Even in its appearance on the printed page it mimics Nora's writing style,
consisting, as it does, of eight very long, rambling, unpunctuated sentences. In this episode, Molly lies in bed, reclining on one elbow, thinking
silently to herself at two o'clock in the morning of June 17, 1904, about
the events of the preceding day. She thinks of her adultery with Blazes
Boylan in the afternoon and of her life with her husband, who is asleep
beside her. (Bloom, her Odysseus, his wanderings completed, lies in his
usual position with his feet on the pillow and head at the other end of
the bed.) Molly muses about the young poet, Stephen Dedalus, whom
Bloom has befriended; she hopes he will become a lodger and perhaps
her lover. She thinks too of her other lovers, of her now adolescent
daughter, Milly, of her infant son, Rudy, who died when he was eleven

days old. She ruminates on her childhood in Gibraltar, on her friend who
went to America, and on a great jumble of things, from the price of
oysters to the origin of the universe. Because Molly is communing with
herself, she has no need to make it clear about whom she is talking. *He*
refers in the same sentence to Mulvey and to Bloom. During her rumi-
nations her menstrual period starts, and she sits on the chamber pot. She
ends with a memory of lying with Bloom among the rhododendrons on
the Hill of Howth overlooking Dublin Bay. Her final words are the best
known lines of *Ulysses,* the set piece of Bloomsday broadcasts everywhere:

> . . . and then he asked me would I yes to say yes my mountain flower and
> first I put my arms around him yes and drew him down to me so he could
> feel my breasts all perfume yes and his heart was going like mad and yes I
> said yes I will Yes.[5]

In the thirty-six preceding pages, the reader learns a great deal about
Molly and, it is tempting to suppose, about Nora as well — particularly
the way she sounded. Nora was not a silent woman. She talked all the
time. Her speech was vivid and profane; on intimate matters, she was the
only woman to have Joyce's ear. Joyce the scavenger would not ignore
such domestic gems as a wife's complaint about the maid:

> . . . her face swelled up on her with temper when I gave her her weeks
> notice . . . better do without them altogether do out the rooms myself quicker
> only for the damn cooking and throwing out the dirt . . .[6]

Each reader of *Ulysses* who knows the biographical details of the Joyces'
lives will find certain of Molly's lines that seem to be pure Nora. Molly's
private opinion of her husband's sleeping position (the same one that
Joyce and Nora used in Rome) could well have been Nora's, and it includes a hint on the way Joyce and Nora may have passed rainy afternoons during their courtship:

> I suppose there isnt in all creation another man with the habits he has look
> at the way hes sleeping at the foot of the bed how can he without a hard
> bolster its well he doesn't kick or he might knock out all my teeth breathing
> with his hand on his nose like that Indian god he took me to show one wet
> Sunday in the museum in Kildare street all yellow in a pinafore lying on his
> side on his hand with his ten toes sticking out that he said was a bigger
> religion than the jews and Our Lords both put together all over Asia imitat-
> ing him as hes always imitating everybody I suppose he used to sleep at the
> foot of the bed too with his big square feet up in his wifes mouth . . .[7]

In the same spirit, on the supposition that Nora would have had plenty
to say for herself in Trieste and in Zurich when Joyce scolded her for

flirting with Prezioso and Weiss, Molly's views on jealousy take on added interest: "Stupid husbands jealousy why cant we all remain friends over it instead of quarrelling . . ."[8]

That Joyce considered the day he fell in love with Nora the most important day in his life is one of the most agreeable things we know about him. That he modeled the most famous woman character in twentieth-century literature on her shows how rich an inspiration she was.

The correspondences between Molly's life and Nora's are striking. Both had the same "espousal" day: the eighth of October. Both were in their early thirties (Nora turned thirty in 1914 as Joyce was beginning the book), and each, not quite sure precisely how old she was, lopped two years off her age. Both could boast of sexual experience at fifteen and were jealous of adolescent daughters with whom they lost their tempers and whom they sometimes slapped.

Their names have the same vowel and stress pattern. To Joyce's acute ear, different vowels suggested certain personal characteristics. He linked *o* with boldness.[9]

Each relished the privilege of calling her husband by his nickname. In *Ulysses* only Molly calls Bloom "Poldy."[10] By the time of their Paris years few even thought of calling Joyce "Jim." (Djuna Barnes tried but drew a very stony reaction.)

Molly and Nora shared a hectoring tone of voice. "Scald the teapot!" says Molly. Nora used to bark at Joyce. One of his nieces recalled how Joyce, meeting them in a station in Paris, tried to carry his sister Eileen's bags. "Put those down!" Nora ordered. "Get a porter!" And her "Jim, you've had enough!" often echoed around Montparnasse. Both real and imaginary husbands were henpecked, but, it is clear, both took all the big decisions affecting their wives' lives.

Molly, like Nora, had an admirer who said "the sun shines for you" and when young had a boyfriend named Mulvey who initiated her into one or another of the sexual practices. Molly's memory — "Mulveys was the first" — is hardly different from Nora's own. Joyce may not even have known that his dreaded rival in the Galway mineral water factory actually spelled his name Mulvagh.*

Both women could boast of stage appearances but no career. Molly Bloom is a concert singer, but she does not take it very seriously (apart from a way to attract lovers); on June 16, 1904, she had not sung in public for over a year. At the time Joyce was writing "Penelope," three

---

* "Mulveys was the first" is one of the important editorial changes incorporated in the new corrected text of *Ulysses* (p. 624). The more familiar version, now known to be inaccurate, is "Mulvey was the first." The new version implies both that Mulvey's was the first love letter Molly received and also that Mulvey's was the first penis she had touched — much more appropriate to Nora's likely experience with the real Mulvagh.

years had passed since Nora's brief hour on the English Players' stage.

Both women hated umbrellas and liked roast chicken, read pornography and believed in God. Both tried to learn from their husbands but did not try very hard, asking naive and not very interested questions about intellectual matters.

Each had a curious marriage, with Molly's husband, like Nora's, interested in the possibility of sharing her with other men. (Bloom dreams of "offering his nuptial partner to all strongmembered males.")[11] Frustrated and vain, both found pleasure in the role of artist's model. Nora had posed for Silvestri and Budgen and knew how well she served Joyce, visually as well as verbally. Both knew the erotic possibilities of the role. Nora refused to have an affair to please Joyce. Molly is more obliging and dreams of how she will seduce and inspire the young writer Stephen Dedalus, and get her reward:

> Ill make him feel all over him till he half faints under me then hell write about me lover and mistress publicly too with our 2 photographs in all the papers when he becomes famous . . .[12]

Each husband remained unsure of how many lovers his wife has had. Bloom imagines more than two dozen for Molly, but scholars in recent years have dismissed most (apart from Blazes Boylan, about whose act of penetration there is no dispute) as fantasies or flirtations. "By post-1959 consensus," according to Hugh Kenner, "the number of Molly's lovers other than Boylan swings between 0 and 1."[13] The same score could well have been Nora's, if the possibility is considered that at least one of her suitors made a full sexual conquest.

Yet neither Nora nor Molly was entirely straightforward in matters of sex. They shared a prostitutional attitude toward the act itself (Molly expects a present "after what I gave") and wheedled for money for underclothes. Yet something about their personalities made masculine attire not inappropriate. When Molly appears in "Circe" she wears trousers — as did Nora as a girl on her Galway nocturnal escapades.

Both Molly and Nora received obscene letters from their husbands that drove them to masturbation. Molly thinks back to

> his mad crazy letters my Precious one everything connected with your glorious Body everything underlined that comes from it is a thing of beauty and of joy for ever . . . that he had me always at myself 4 and 5 times a day sometimes and I said I hadnt . . .[14]

Each was not the only recipient of her husband's erotic correspondence.

Each had lost a baby and feared having another.

Each made unashamed use of the chamber pot.

Neither understood what had happened to the sexual drive in the man to whom she said yes.

In *Ulysses* Molly and Leopold Bloom have not had complete carnal intercourse since little Rudy died. The book's unseen narrator knows the length of time precisely: ten years, five months, and eighteen days; Molly knows the dangers to her looks:

> Im young still can I its a wonder Im not an old shrivelled hag before my time living with him so cold never embracing me except sometimes when hes asleep the wrong end of me not knowing I suppose who he has any man thatd kiss a womans bottom Id throw my hat at him after that hed kiss anything unnatural where we havent 1 atom of any kind of expression in us all of us the same 2 lumps of lard . . .[15]

There is no comparable information, letters being lacking, about the marital relations of the Joyces.

But *Ulysses* is not so much a book about impotence and cuckoldry as it is about love: married love. Bloom's mind wanders too as he drifts off to sleep, and in the "Ithaca" episode, before Molly's soliloquy begins, the narrator answers a catechistic question:

> What advantages were possessed by an occupied, as distinct from an unoccupied bed?
> The removal of nocturnal solitude, the superior quality of human (mature female) to inhuman (hotwaterjar) calefaction, the stimulation of matutinal contact, the economy of mangling done on the premises in the case of trousers accurately folded and placed lengthwise between the spring mattress (striped) and the woollen mattress (biscuit section).[16]

What Bloom and Molly are left with is comfort, trust, companionship and solicitude. It is a deeper, less conflict-laden form of love than married love but one welcome to Molly because she grew up without a mother's care. Molly, brought up by her father, says, "Where would they all of them be if they hadnt a mother to look after them what I never had . . ."

Nora, reared by her grandmother and disciplined by her uncle, had a similar background, with the same consequences for her personality: maternal deprivation led to coquettish ways. Nora put up with Joyce and stuck to him, spurning the Preziosos and Cosgraves who presented themselves, because he could give her unquestioning, unconditional love — the love that Stephen Dedalus calls *"amor matris* . . . the only true thing in life." The maternal qualities that Nora saw in Joyce are the same that Molly saw in Bloom. By making Molly a motherless girl who had been reared by a man and who turned early to pleasing the opposite sex in search of affection, Joyce shows that he understood why Nora was the way she was, even though it drove him to frenzies of jealousy. It would not have escaped Joyce's notice that the unsatisfactory mothers of his two heroines had alliterative names: Lunita Laredo and Honoraria Healy.[17]

Nora's refusal to read *Ulysses* is one of the best-known facts about her. There are many reasons why she did not — chiefly because, like many and perhaps most who open the book, she found it too difficult. However, it is also true that, as she told Frank Budgen and August Suter, what she had read she found obscene. For Nora some passages were worse than obscene, they were shameful, revealing things she cannot have believed Joyce wanted to reveal. Why would Nora want to read the brothel scene in which Bella Cohen changes into a male and humiliates Bloom?

> What else are you good for, an impotent thing like you? *(he stoops and, peering, pokes with his fan rudely under the fat suet folds of Bloom's haunches)* Up! Up! Manx cat! What have we here? Where's your curly teapot gone to or who docked it on you, cockyolly? Sing, birdy, sing. It's as limp as a boy of six's doing his pooly behind a cart. Buy a bucket or sell your pump. *(loudly)* Can you do a man's job?[18]

Nora's aversion to the book could also have sprung from recognition. Too many of the lines were her own. She may even have written some of them.

The ease with which Joyce wrote the "Penelope" section in the summer and autumn of 1921 was assisted by the delivery in March that year of the briefcase that Joyce had left in Stanislaus's bedroom in Trieste. Ettore Schmitz personally retrieved it after receiving Joyce's meticulous description and brought it to Paris, locked, according to Joyce's instruction. It is more than likely that the case contained Nora's obscene letters of 1909. Joyce did not need his own letters, for he knew very well their contents, but for his portrayal of the hidden workings of a woman's mind he needed his notes — or rather, Nora's.[19] (Joyce's original intention, according to Ellmann, was to write "Penelope" in the form of a series of letters from Molly.)

If so, Nora had an even greater influence on "Penelope" than has been imagined, contributing not only to the style but the substance of what Molly was saying.

Joyce intended his book to be the Irish *Faust*. He described Molly as "the flesh that always affirms," or, as he wrote it to Budgen in imperfect German, *"Ich bin der Fleisch der stets bejaht."* That line is a deliberate travesty of the boast of Mephistopheles in Goethe's *Faust: "Ich bin der Geist der stets verneint"* ("I am the spirit that eternally negates").[20]

Molly's famous last line ("yes I said yes I will Yes") is a conversational translation of "I am the flesh that always affirms." In using it for the finale of his great book, Joyce was counterbalancing the cynical, rational,

Unidentified photograph found in Trieste, taken by R. W. Simmons, considered Galway's finest photographer, appears to show Nora, in her buttoned boots, with either her mother or, more likely, to judge from the way she is dressed, her well-to-do grandmother, Catherine Healy, c. 1895–1900.

Presentation Convent, Galway, where Nora went to work as a porter
when she left school at the age of twelve in 1896.

"At the fish-market in Galway town"; a photograph taken by J. M. Synge in
Nora's time. It shows the docks area near Whitehall where she lived with her
grandmother.

Willie Mulvagh, Nora's 1904 Galway boyfriend, an accountant in Joe Young's Mineral Water Factory. Joyce was still so jealous of Mulvagh in 1912 that he wrote Nora, "Can your friend in the sodawater factory . . . write my verses?" (August 19, 1912, *Letters II*, 304).

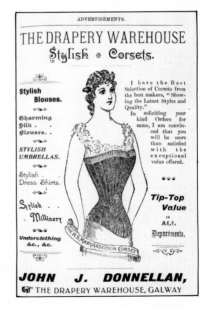

Left: Nora's successful uncle, Michael Healy, a customs officer in His Majesty's Civil Service.

Right: A Galway advertisement of 1902 suggests that Joyce had genuine grounds for complaint when he wrote to Nora during their courtship, *"Please* leave off that breastplate. I do not like embracing a letter-box" (July 12 [?], 1904, *Letters II*, 43–44).

Grafton Street, Dublin, at the turn of the century.

The Finn's Hotel sign can still be seen overlooking
the park of Trinity College, Dublin.

Nora, Giorgio, and Lucia in Zurich.

Left: Joyce's sister Eileen, with her banker husband Frantisek Schaurek and daughters Eleanora and Bozena in Trieste, several years before Schaurek's suicide in 1926.

Right: Roberto Prezioso, editor of the *Piccolo della Sera,* shown here as a young officer in the Austro-Hungarian Navy, in a photograph whose affectionate inscription to Aldo Meyer caused talk in Trieste.

Number 30 Universitätsstrasse, Zurich, where the Joyces lived in 1918–1919 in a flat that, at the back, overlooked that of Marthe Fleischmann.

Lucia with her classmates at the Huttenstrasse School in Zurich, c. 1918–1919.

James Joyce in 1904. Asked what was in his mind when his friend Constantine Curran took the photograph, Joyce replied, "I was wondering would he lend me five shillings."

Nora as Cathleen in the English Players' production of Synge's *Riders to the Sea*, Zurich, 1918.

Left: Portrait of Nora done in Trieste by Tullio Silvestri, who said she was the most beautiful woman he had ever seen.

Right: Portrait of Nora by Frank Budgen in Zurich in 1919.

Left: The Joyces patronized the best photographers. Berenice Abbott, an American in Paris in the 1920s, was an apprentice of Man Ray. For his sitting, Joyce posed without his usual spectacles but with a bow tie—daring daytime wear for the 1920s.

Right: Portrait of Nora done in Paris in the early 1920s by Myron Nutting, whose wife Helen, a writer, was one of Nora's close friends.

Joyce in Trieste, c. 1919–1920.

Harriet Shaw Weaver.

The Joyce family in 1924, following the publication of *Ulysses* and Harriet Shaw Weaver's gift of £12,000.

Nora and Giorgio, c. 1926.

Square Robiac, Paris, seventh arrondissement: the Joyces' happiest home.

James Joyce and Sylvia Beach at Shakespeare and Company.

Left: Adolph Kastor, patriarch of the New York Kastor family, with his adored daughter, Helen Kastor Fleischman; her son, David Fleischman; and his daughters-in-law: left, Mrs. Alfred Kastor; right, Mrs. Robert Kastor. The photograph appears to have been taken when Helen was about thirty, the time when she fell in love with Giorgio Joyce.

Right: Helen and Giorgio in France, probably at Cauterets, the Kastor home in the Pyrenees, in 1928.

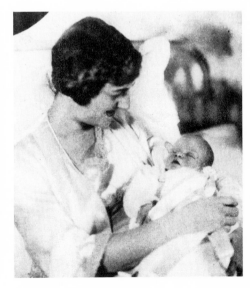

Even as a grandfather James Joyce preferred tennis shoes.

Helen Joyce and newborn Stephen in the society section of a French newspaper.

Kathleen (Mrs. René) Bailly, Nora's best friend in Paris. In 1934 the wealthy Baillys took the Joyces on their first long trip by motorcar and drove them to the south of France and Zurich.

Wedding day in Kensington, July 4, 1931. Nora is less dismayed
by the photographers than is her husband or solicitor.

Harriet Shaw Weaver with Lucia at Reigate in 1935 shows the strain of trying to help the girl recover from her mental breakdown in Ireland.

Lucia, photographed by Berenice Abbott, is the height of fashion, in a long cardigan, a blouse with an Eton collar, and short bobbed hair.

Lucia Joyce, seventy-one in 1979, at St. Andrew's Hospital, Northampton, England.

Nora by Berenice Abbott, c. 1928.

Nora, Hollywood-style, with low neckline and fox fur, a photograph she apparently had taken after Giorgio requested one and she pronounced all the existing ones bad. Joyce wrote his son, "When I find a lady who is content with her own picture I will send a bouquet to the Pope" (June 3, 1935, *Letters III*, 360).

Nora in Zurich in 1948.

Nora and Giorgio in Zurich in 1948 pose for a photograph
taken by Robert Kastor's daughter.

male opening of the book, personified by Buck Mulligan, the Mephisto-phelean medical student, who scoffs at everything. That Buck Mulligan had a real-life counterpart in Oliver Gogarty is beyond dispute. In *Ulysses*, as in his youth, Joyce chose Nora over Gogarty.

Is Joyce Bloom? In part, yes. According to Richard Ellmann, Joyce saw himself as having escaped the fate of Faust: the unmarried, arrogant, doomed, pointless rebel. He liked to think of himself instead as Ulysses, and, Ellmann says, "It is not surprising that Joyce's description of Ulysses as pacifist, father, wanderer, musician, and artist, ties the hero's life closely to his own."[21]

Bloom, in spite of his Christian baptism, is a Jew. He does not get drunk or into debt. Joyce admired the Jews, he told Budgen, for the strong family life they maintained in the face of persecution. Jews, he said, are "better husbands than we are, better fathers and better sons."[22]

More difficult to disentangle are the entwined images of Milly Bloom, the Blooms' fifteen-year-old daughter, and Lucia Joyce. Scholarly forays into this thicket have discovered, not too deeply buried, the theme of incest, and textual evidence has been produced to suggest that Milly has been sent away from home (she is in Mullingar as a photographer's apprentice) because Bloom has three times committed sexual improprieties with her.[23] "Bloom," A. Walton Litz of Princeton has written, "like Earwicker after him [in *Finnegans Wake*], is unconsciously in love with his own daughter as a young reincarnation of his wife, and for this reason he is attracted to the 'seaside' girl Gerty."[24] *Ulysses* contains references to the kind of eye defect, a "turnedin eye," about which Lucia and her parents were increasingly worried as she reached adolescence. In his notebooks for *Finnegans Wake* Joyce wrote: "turn in her eye rather taking.")[25]

If *Ulysses* is, in any sense, a Joyce family album, where is Giorgio? He does not appear even in the notes for the book. It is odd that Joyce, who seemed to write about every scrap of his experience, made so little use of his son in his work, apart from the unreal little Archie in *Exiles*. Little Rudy in *Ulysses* seems to be drawn more from Joyce's reactions to Nora's miscarriage of 1908, the son who might have been. It is possible that by the time he wrote *Ulysses* Joyce had dismissed his actual son as intellectually and emotionally uninteresting for literature, or that his jealousy of Giorgio's closeness to Nora was so intense that he could make no direct artistic use of it. The biggest difference between Molly and Nora may be that Molly's son lives only eleven days.

More relevant to the comparison of Molly with Nora is the question, why Gibraltar? Why should a book so faithful to fact, with every physical detail so accurate that Joyce boasted that if Dublin were destroyed it could be rebuilt from his book, end with a long reverie about a subtropical city where neither Joyce nor Nora had ever set foot?

Joyce constructed his Gibraltar accurately after loving research with maps, travel guides, history books, and genealogies, yet he left scholars puzzled. James Card, in his book *Penelope,* postulates that for Joyce Gibraltar represented the antithesis of Dublin and also the city guarding the Pillars of Hercules, the gateway separating Odysseus's known world, the Mediterranean, from the abyss beyond. Card also saw in Gibraltar the symbolic geography of female organs.[26]

Useful as these interpretations are, it seems far more likely that Joyce had such a strong sense of "Gibraltar" because it was Nora's hometown. Galway and Gibraltar have more in common than meets the eye: sea, somnolence, an uncomfortable British connection, and (in Nora's day) British soldiery. Galway is Gibraltar without the sun. Its Spanish pretensions were known to Joyce, as his 1912 Triestine newspaper article showed. Joyce's reference notes to the "muros and fenestras" of sunny Gibraltar can be applied very readily to the Spanish-style windows and walls of windswept Galway, and the Moorish Wall where Molly allowed Mulvey to be the first sounds like Galway's Spanish Arch, an old landmark down by the docks, not far from Nora's grandmother's home.[27]

Certainly for nineteenth-century emigrants, Galway was a gateway to the western world from which few travelers returned. And what Gibraltar was to Molly Galway was to Nora: a childhood place hallowed by memory and lonely exile.[28]

Interpretations of Molly Bloom have progressed since the 1930s when *Ulysses* was finally allowed into the United States and Britain and found its way into the English literature curriculum. Her early critics were preoccupied with her amorality, her slovenliness, her supposed promiscuity, her laziness, ignorance, and foul mouth. Rebecca West, an early feminist, perceived Molly as a Great Mother, but Mary Colum condemned her as a "female gorilla." Virginia Woolf loathed the whole book.

Ulysses used to be taught as the Son's search for the Father. Stephen Dedalus and Leopold Bloom go about their day, wandering through Dublin, nearly meeting but always missing each other until Bloom helps Stephen to his feet outside the brothel, where he has been knocked down by the British soldier, Private Carr. Bloom, with his lost infant son never quite out of his mind, picks up the motherless Stephen, takes him to a cabman's shelter, then home to his "Ithaca," 7 Eccles Street. The two men, father and son for a brief time, eventually part, but with a sense of reconciliation. Climbing into bed, Bloom tells Molly of his meeting with Stephen and then falls asleep, his thoughts petering out into a black dot, printed as a large period, on the page.

In that interpretation of the book, Molly is only a minor character and her soliloquy a meandering irrelevance tacked on after the book proper ends.[29]

Joyce himself said that "Ithaca" ended the book and that "Penelope" was the coda, with no beginning, middle, or end. But he himself also told Budgen that Molly was the *clou* of the book, the axis upon which it all revolved.[30] That statement, along with the words of the soliloquy itself, make it seem as if he, writing early in the twentieth century, with his chambermaid wife at his side, saw feminism coming and fashioned his text to greet it.

In his personal social prejudices, Joyce was as misogynist as any man of his time, and his remark to Mary Colum, "I hate women who know anything," shows that he wanted them kept in their place. But to Arthur Power, Joyce voiced a more considered view. Ibsen, Joyce said, was animated by a belief in the emancipation of women, which had caused "the greatest revolution in our time in the most important relationship there is — that between men and women; the revolt of women against the idea that they are the mere instruments of men."[31]

Late twentieth-century feminism has offered a new perspective on Joyce to Joycean scholars, male and female. David Hayman has seen Molly Bloom as a manly woman in balance to Bloom's womanly man. Hugh Kenner has observed that Bloom never notices how desperately lonely Molly is; Bloom prefers to think of his wife as a hot-blooded Spaniard. Colin MacCabe sees in the formless reverie and lateral thinking of Molly's soliloquy "a shattering of phallic male modes of discourse." Carol Shloss sees *Ulysses* as a long journey into women's speech.[32]

Feminists have taken the lead even over Marxists in finding new ways to read Joyce. (Marxists tend to be drawn to *Finnegans Wake*.) Works such as *Women in Joyce*, by Suzette Henke and Elaine Unkeless, and *Joyce and Feminism*, by Bonnie Kime Scott, place a feminist filter over Joyce, revealing a substructure that looks suspiciously like the basic foundation.

Scott has described the feminist discovery as one of "an alternate female order" in which women disdain male authority, as she believes they did in the prehistoric, prepatriarchal world. By this analysis, women in Joyce are conspicuous by their absence or their silence when they are in masculine company. They serve men, as mothers, maids, or whores. Those who do speak up are disagreeble. In general, the men, self-important, blather on; the women think their own thoughts and keep family life and the social order together.

Feminists value Joyce for his otherworldly, lyrical voice. Scott has argued that unlike D. H. Lawrence, the phallus worshiper, Joyce moved into bisexual language: ruminative, associative, infantile. Shloss has read a double meaning into the famous passage in *A Portrait* in which Stephen Dedalus reflects upon the words of his dean of studies, an English Jesuit:

The language in which we are speaking is his before it is mine. How different
are the words *home, Christ, ale, master,* on his lips and on mine! I cannot
speak or write these words without unrest of spirit. His language, so familiar
and so foreign, will always be for me an acquired speech. I have not made
or accepted its words. My voice holds them at bay. My soul frets in the
shadow of his language.[33]

The resentment of Stephen Dedalus, an Irishman, toward the conqueror's
language is analogous to that of today's feminist toward the structures
of language reinforcing the male claim to superiority. Like Joyce, when
English lets them down, feminists invent new words: *spokesperson, her-
story.*

Feminists like Bloom better than Molly. Leopold Bloom, whom the
Dublin males of *Ulysses* ridicule, emerges as perhaps the twentieth century's first specimen of the new womanly man, who wants an equal role
in caring for his children. Bloom suffers from womb envy. "O, I so want
to be a mother!" he cries, changing sex in "Circe."

Molly, in contrast, seems, in Scott's words, a caricature, "a male attempt at the female." That, as far as is known, was Nora's view. Told
that people congratulated her husband on his portrayal of the inner
workings of a woman's mind (Jung told Joyce, "Maybe the devil's grandmother knows as much about women. I don't"), Nora scoffed. "That
man," she declared to Samuel Beckett, "knows nothing about women."[34]

Molly possesses all the qualities of the male's fantasy woman. She is
lethargic, illogical, unreasonable, vain, self-preoccupied, passive, and always in bed. The first sound she is given to utter in *Ulysses* is not even a
proper word. Bloom says:

> — You don't want anything for breakfast?
>   A sleepy soft grunt answered:
> — Mn.[35]

With these qualities, Molly fits comfortably into the stereotype described
by the pioneering postwar feminist writers. In *The Second Sex,* Simone
de Beauvoir wrote that, to men, woman never comes to grips with anything but words and mental pictures; therefore, contradictions give her
no uneasiness. Her head is filled with a strange jumble. And Mary Ellmann, in *Thinking About Women,* pointed out that in literature women
are associated with bed.

If today's feminists see Molly as a caricature, they do so with some
sympathy. Women of Molly's time, and Nora's, tried to live up to this
caricature. According to Henke,

> Like most women in turn-of-the-century Ireland, Molly has been thoroughly
> conditioned to think in terms of male identification. Raised to believe that a

woman's worth is determined by physical beauty and social status, she uses marriage and motherhood to bolster a faltering self-image, then turns to Blazes Boylan for verification of fading sexual charms.

Molly sees all other women as rivals and disparages her sex — "a dreadful lot of bitches." She also hates her broadening belly and envies her daughter's slimness. Molly is dependent, in Henke's phrase, "on male valorisation": "Even her adultery is part of the prescribed pattern in her society for the way a woman might escape the boundaries of her marrige."[36]

Yet there is much of the radical feminist in Molly Bloom. She thinks the male sex may be superfluous. She fondles herself and has homosexual fantasies: "The smoothest place is right there between this bit here how soft like a peach easy God I wouldnt mind being a man and get up on a lovely woman . . ." She criticizes the physiology the deity gave women ("we have too much blood in us . . ."), dislikes her male gynecologist, and even more than her own sex distrusts the other: "Id rather die 20 times over than marry another of their sex . . ." The feminist critics dismiss (as male exaggeration) Joyce's portrayal of Molly's protracted orgasm with Blazes Boylan (or, rather, her memory of it) as a male fantasy:

> Coming for about 5 minutes with my legs round him . . . O Lord I wanted to shout out all sorts of things fuck or shit or anything at all . . .[37]

They noticed that Molly admits that she gets no satisfaction from intercourse with her husband: that, with Bloom, she says, she found "no satisfaction in it pretending to like it till he comes and then finish it off myself."[38]

In his notes for *Ulysses,* Joyce sounded even more like a crusading feminist. He foresaw the rule of women coming, and he allowed Molly to be a spokesperson for the female revolution:

> I dont care what anybody says itd be much better for the world to be governed by the women in it you wouldnt see women going and killing one another and slaughtering when do you ever women see rolling around drunk like they do or gambling every penny they have and losing it on horses yes because a woman whatever she does she knows where to stop . . .[39]

From seeing Molly as a true subversive of male authority, it is a short step to Molly-worship. To some she will remain the earth goddess, Gea-Tellus. Robert Adams has pronounced Joyce's creation a tremendous imaginative achievement, a vision like Blake's:

> Molly's mind, spinning in planetary majesty on its self-centered axis, calmly accepts him [the sensitive reader] within itself, enveloping him in her indif-

ference to everything which has made and kept him a reader, as the book literally becomes the world.

She has become the motion of life itself, self-befouling, self-purifying, an enormous imago in which to be drowned and devoured, born and reborn, cherished, corrupted, deceived and blessed.[40]

The debate has not ended. Molly is at the same time a caricature, a revolutionary and a goddess, a fat, lazy housewife and a testimony to the superiority of the female view of the universe.

The contradiction in Molly's character — life-affirming but male dependent — was present in Nora's. How could strong woman be so passive? The answer lies in the character of the women of Galway and tradition-bound women everywhere: they use their strength to bear their fate, not to shape it.

Yet their vision of life is at best, like Joyce's own, comic, not tragic. Molly, in her plain speaking and humor, rivals the Wife of Bath. She gives her own sex the beauty prize. As for the opposite sex's proudest possession, she ridicules it with a mockery unsurpassed in literature:

what a man looks like with his two bags full and his other thing hanging down out of him or sticking up at you like a hatrack no wonder they hide it with a cabbageleaf . . .[41]

Did Joyce make that up? Or did he hear it from his wife?

13

Fame

FROM IRELAND Nora returned to fame. They had become The Joyces. Within three months of its publication, *Ulysses* was recognized as a masterpiece and as a dirty book. If *A Portrait* had made Joyce's reputation, *Ulysses* turned him into a celebrity. People clambered on chairs to get a look at him. They sent notes in restaurants asking him to join them, they rang his doorbell. Journalists crowded in at parties. Expecting a rake, a roisterer, a teller of ribald stories, they were disappointed to find a thin, scholarly Irishman who peered at them from behind thick glasses, hid behind his wife, and blushed scarlet if anyone said a rude word.

To Nora, after the years of hunger and humiliation Jim had suffered at the hands of language students and publishers, the adulation was ridiculous. "We should put him in a cage," she said, "and feed him peanuts through the bars."[1]

Grudgingly, she had come to accept that her husband's crazy book had some value and importance, but her acceptance was always tempered by her dismay at its obscenity. By those years, she had resumed going to church (and perhaps to confession). When a priest asked her, "Mrs. Joyce, cannot you stop your husband from writing those terrible books?" Nora replied, "What can I do?"[2]

More than ever she became Nora the quotable. One night at a party at Les Trianons, one of Joyce's favorite restaurants, held to introduce Joyce to William Carlos Williams, someone asked Nora if she read her husband's work. "Sure, why would I bother?" she replied. "It's enough he talks about that book and he's at it all the time. I'd like a bit of life of my own."

Joyce still longed for her to read *Ulysses*. To Aunt Josephine, who would not read it either, he complained, "Nora has got as far as page 27 counting the cover."[3] To Nora, in a moving little note in January 1924, he said,

Dear Nora the edition you have is full of printers' errors. Please read it in this. I cut the pages. There is a list of mistakes at the end Jim.[4]

Nora did not oblige him any more than he obliged her. She still yearned to give up hotel life and have a place of their own, especially since Giorgio and Lucia were getting older and needed a settled home, but she could get no sense out of Jim. All he cared about was his work.

The developing malaise in their family life went deeper than housing. Joyce boasted long and loud about the supremacy of his family, but his efforts to look after them were pathetic. Sylvia Beach, observing them all, felt that Joyce had no idea how bizarre his home life was or of the torments of those sharing it with him. He could not see how his children reacted against his obsession with his work and his constant eye illness. Yet in the months after Nora returned with the children from Ireland, Sylvia blamed his family for preventing him from embarking upon a new book. What Mr. Joyce needed, she wrote to Harriet Weaver, was space, quiet, and outdoor exercise:

All this past year while he was finishing *Ulysses* and quite overstrung with the adventures attending the publishing of his book he was sharing a noisy hotel room with his wife and daughter and obliged to go out to a restaurant for every one of his meals. I tried my best to find an apartment but they required six rooms at least. . . . Mr. Joyce insisted on being in the Odeon quarter . . . [but] there is never an apartment to be had in this quarter . . .

I know it is not my business and in strictest confidence I would like to tell you that I think Mr Joyce's son George ought to begin at once to learn some profession or business . . . He is seventeen and owing to the abnormal existence his family has had, has had no training of any kind to enable him to earn his living one day. George is a fine big fellow but he has nothing to do all the time but loaf. (He teaches Italian one hour a week.) . . . Joyce is so absorbed in his work that he is quite unable to cope with any such situations.[5]

Sylvia feared she had gone too far. She wrote asking forgiveness for having passed on the burden of the Joyce family's difficulties when Miss Weaver was too distant to do anything about them. Sylvia felt she should add, however, that Mrs. Joyce was still talking of moving to London.

Harriet Weaver replied almost immediately:

I have been thinking over the problem you mention but so far am at a complete loss as to a solution. It is such an extremely difficult problem, particularly so to me who have never seen Mr. Joyce or his family. I doubt whether any of them would like London and comfortable accommodation is still very difficult to obtain here. I find it impossible to make any suggestion about Mr. Joyce's son until I know something as to his temperament and aptitudes. If Mr. Joyce [were to come to London] it would be easier to make practical suggestions. At present I can only worry about them to no purpose.[6]

Miss Weaver had never met Sylvia Beach either but felt increasingly close to her owing to their common cause. She thanked Sylvia for writing so fully about "the family difficulties." Like an intelligent mother, she preferred to know the truth, however unpleasant. For nearly a decade of assisting Joyce's literary work, she had hesitated to intrude in his private affairs, but, she told Sylvia, "it seems necessary to do so now."

Miss Weaver soon had ample opportunity for active duty. In August 1922 Nora and Joyce arrived in London. They had packed Giorgio off to the Tyrol and Lucia to summer camp in Deauville and, delegating Sylvia to look for a flat for them in Paris, headed for a holiday in England. After their first two summers in Paris, when Joyce was finishing *Ulysses,* they never made the mistake of staying in Paris through the *congé annuel.* Nora would have preferred to have gone to Germany with the Nuttings, but Joyce was determined to see the English south coast. It was their first visit to London together since their one-day stopover in 1904, and they checked into the Euston Hotel, next to the terminus for the boat-trains for Ireland. (In London Euston Station suggests Ireland, just as Paddington does Wales and King's Cross, Scotland.)

When Miss Weaver first saw her Mr. Joyce, her expectations were more than fulfilled. She saw, say her biographers, a mature Stephen Dedalus, with charm, wit, great dignity, a slow, soft, very Irish voice, and an unexpected but engaging waywardness in his manner.[7]

To Nora in 1904 Joyce had made excuses for himself by saying, "There is something a little devilish in me that makes me delight in breaking down people's ideas of me," and he did not spare Miss Weaver the shock treatment. Within hours she witnessed "her" money flying in all directions — to waiters, porters, taxi drivers. He tipped proudly and wildly. In three weeks, he boasted to Aunt Josephine, he spent two hundred pounds.[8] The sum, Miss Weaver, who lived frugally, must have quickly calculated, was equal to nearly half his yearly income in interest from her capital.

Miss Weaver got firsthand experience of Joyce's illness as well. Hardly had he and Nora settled in than he was laid low with a new attack of conjunctivitis. The trip to the coast was canceled. With Nora leading him up the stairs, Joyce managed to visit Miss Weaver's walk-up flat on Gloucester Place, but most of the time he lay in bed in a darkened room or rode about in taxis with his patron, visiting one London eye specialist after another. When one of them advised an operation for incipient glaucoma, Joyce decided to return to the ophthalmologist he knew, Dr. Louis Borsch, an American in Paris whom Sylvia Beach had found for him the previous year.

Miss Weaver liked Nora enormously. Not for one minute did she entertain the thought that Nora should have controlled Joyce's spending or organized their domestic affairs more economically. She saw at once how impossible that was. Both women had their hands full the entire time looking after the invalid.[9]

When they returned to Paris from London, Nora found 9 rue de l'Université dingier than ever. Leaving Joyce indoors, working with his right eye closed and the left one clouded, Nora and Giorgio went out flat hunting. They found a pleasant furnished flat on the avenue Charles Floquet, in the less bohemian, more bourgeois environment of the seventh arrondissement, near the École Militaire yet only a quick taxi ride from Sylvia's bookshop on the rue de l'Odéon. (Arthur Power later judged it the nicest apartment they ever had.) They took it — Joyce signed and paid for a six-month lease — and immediately departed for Nice to avoid the cold, damp Parisian winter. In Nice they settled in at the Hôtel Suisse on the quai des États-Unis. Lucia was with them. Giorgio had stayed behind with his singing teacher, who encouraged parental hopes that the boy might make an opera singer. Nora and Joyce toyed with the idea of putting Lucia in school in Nice and perhaps settling in through the spring. As Nice seemed cheaper than Paris, Joyce took out a lease on another flat (and asked Miss Weaver for more money, which she duly sent),* but soon he fell ill again, and Nora grew bored.

As Nora neared forty and Joyce turned into a semipermanent invalid, her old penchant for flirtations disappeared. In its place was a new restlessness, which Joyce willingly indulged. Nora wanted a flat; he took a flat. She wanted to winter in Nice; they went to Nice. She wanted to go shopping; they went shopping.

In Nice, as in all their travels, and eye problems notwithstanding, the Joyces were diligent tourists, seeing the sights, buying souvenirs, and writing

---

* The money — £250 — was a payment of royalties on Miss Weaver's own edition of *Ulysses*, the "English," or Egoist Press, edition, which was also advertised as the second edition. The public and booksellers were naturally confused, as the "English" edition had been printed in France, for fear of seizure by the British censors. (When her stock of books was delivered to London, Miss Weaver consigned it to a mailing agency and kept only a few copies at her office. The rest she kept hidden in the large Victorian wardrobe in her bedroom and often delivered them to shops herself.) Joyce's loyalties were thus divided between his two publishers, but he favored Miss Weaver, his patron, and he feigned innocence when Sylvia Beach was hurt and angry about the rival edition.

postcards to all their friends. One day they went from Nice to Menton and on the border between France and Italy bought cameos from old women on the bridge. Joyce had one mounted on a gold ring. In Nice Nora and Lucia amused themselves by going out to tea at cafés on the promenade. Back at their hotel Nora evaded secretarial duty, but Lucia was not so lucky. Joyce found plenty for her to do. Although Lucia's English was better than Giorgio's, it was full of mistakes in spelling and punctuation, for which she had to take down his dictated apologies. Joyce also apologized to Miss Weaver, through Lucia's hand, for Lucia's failure to put the number of the house on the London street address: "She is more absentminded than ever since she met the King of Spain" (a reference to the royal visitor to Lucia's camp in the summer).[10]

Soon Nora demanded a return to Paris. Joyce had no difficulty in acquiescing. The move south had failed to work its magic; his eyes were no better, and the doctors in Nice were advising, as a possible cure, having all his teeth extracted. But Nora had no doubt that her wishes were paramount. She certainly did not want to settle in "Niece," as she described it to Helen Nutting:

Today is beautiful people are all out in cotton dresses. But when everything is said and done I find the place too uninteresting. Now I suppose you will think I am very difficult but one cant live only for the sun and the blue Mediterean [sic] sea.[11]

Back they went to Paris and confronted again the problem of Lucia's education. She was now over fifteen. They found a school for her outside Paris. She left after a week. They sent her instead to a nearby lycée, hoping she would continue music and gymnastics; she was very strong, and she was playing the piano very well. But they were worried about her.

Nora was set for her first winter season as a Parisian hostess. One night they had dinner with the Yeatses and the Pounds. With Yeats Nora had at least one thing in common: he had never finished *Ulysses* either. Now also they were able to give dinners of their own and resume the home entertaining they had so enjoyed in Trieste. For their first dinner party they invited Larbaud, asking if he wanted a special diet as he had been ill, and also asked Sylvia and Adrienne, who accepted, even though they had been refusing all other social engagements because of the pressure of work. Sylvia wrote home to tell her father about the impending event.

Invitations to the Joyces' parties were much prized. Nora's friend Helen Nutting agonized over the right thing to wear, as she confided to her diary:

I ready to cry over my made-over dress, black lace with red rose, paste straps. Many compliments for it, M. [her husband, Myron] saying after I was the best dressed there & none of them had such shoulders. Great relief.

Joyce all smiles. Pound, come from a big dinner, refused to eat. Suddenly dumped on my plate his chicken & ham. Later, as suddenly seized them, back again, & ate. Pound danced with me, vy well, great rhythme. Also Joyce, but jigging. Danced a solo, with pulling of coattails & fell at the end . . .

Mrs. Joyce perfectly happy, walking about continually, singing music hall songs, continually handing about more "eats" & drink. . . . About 2 a lull in the gaiety, then Pounds left. And then a sudden intimate feeling, of being left, drawing together, & then fun beginning again . . .[12]

Nora was at ease among the women of the Left Bank, with the exception of Gertrude Stein. Stein not only hated Joyce as a rival, but she also disliked any of the wives of any of the writers she cultivated. She delegated her companion, Alice B. Toklas, to keep the boring spouses out of her way. As a feminist, Sylvia Beach disapproved:

This was not the way Adrienne and I treated wives. Not only did we always make a point of inviting Mrs. Writer and her husband, but we found them quite as interesting. Many a time a wife will be more enlightening on the subject of writers than all the professors in the classroom.[13]

One of the woman writers who particularly liked Nora was Djuna Barnes. Djuna, tall, glamorous, full-bosomed, and hard-drinking, was proud of her Irish blood and vastly admired Joyce, about whom she had written a profile for *Vanity Fair*. Djuna had gained notoriety in New York in 1915 when she published an underground book of shockingly homoerotic poems, *The Book of Repulsive Women*. She and Nora became friends. They shared a philosophy of life — that women are no good but men are much worse — and were not dissimilar in appearance with their height, red hair, deep voice, and confident laugh. Perhaps Nora, with the trace of lesbianism that Joyce had detected, recognized Djuna's bisexuality. Djuna was deeply involved in the lesbian subculture of the Left Bank and was, at the time of her friendship with the Joyces, the lover of Thelma Wood, a sculptress. Later Djuna, in her Rabelaisian feminist epic, *Nightwood* (now a cult text of high modernism), named one of her main characters Nora, and it has been assumed that she took the name from Joyce's wife.[14]

In the Paris of the 1920s, Nora, for so long a sexual rebel, found herself a bourgeois among the bohemians. The younger women around her flaunted their promiscuity and joked about their abortions and venereal disease. Peggy Guggenheim, the New York heiress and arts patron, boasted that she had been to bed with every man she had ever met. (In her memoirs, however, she denied the rumor that the actual count was about a thousand.)[15] Lesbians met and courted at the Friday afternoon literary salons of Natalie Barney. The English aristocrat Nancy Cunard sported a black lover and covered her long white arms with primitive African ivory bracelets. To that crowd, flamboyant decor was as important as outrageous behavior. The Joyces failed on both counts.

Even Djuna Barnes could not resist a jibe. One day she was with Peggy Guggenheim as Peggy was puzzling over an enormous, ugly Victorian tea set that had arrived in a trunk of her mother's silver from New York. "What shall I do with it?" Peggy asked Djuna. "Give it to Nora Joyce," said Djuna. "It's just her style."[16]

The Joyces were not puritans in the usual sense, nor were they hypocrites. They simply let it be known that they respected stable relationships and frowned on sleeping around. As Arthur Power, a frequent visitor to the flat, learned, "One could expect a very cold reception from both Joyce and Mrs Joyce if one brought to their flat a casual girl friend. Your *belle amie,* yes! — provided it was always she — but a casual piece, no."[17] Just as they never blinked at Sylvia Beach's relationship with Adrienne, the Joyces invited regularly to their dinner table Valery Larbaud's mistress, Maria Nebbia. Nora often met Signora Nebbia for tea, finding an affinity perhaps in the Italian woman's irregular status as well as her language.

One reason they feigned not to notice the Roaring Twenties was a wish to shield their children. In no way did they prepare Giorgio and Lucia for even the ordinary rituals of courtship. Yet both young people responded to the atmosphere around them, and Lucia wrote happily to Stanislaus about how busy life was when you swanned around Paris.[18]

In such an atmosphere, Sylvia Beach was conscious that her boundless devotion to Joyce caused comment. Arthur Power said, "She gave the impression that she was willing to be crucified for him on the sole condition that it was done in a public place." Others inevitably suspected that there was a sexual relationship between her and Joyce. So there was, although of the most unconscious kind. When an English woman visitor archly asked Sylvia about the men who were her lovers, Sylvia unhesitatingly answered that there were none.

"My dear, that is not your reputation in London," the friend smiled.

Sylvia thought to herself that it should be obvious that all intercourse between herself and Mr. Joyce took place in her shop. It was also obvious to anyone who knew the Joyces, Sylvia believed, that he could not bear to be separated a minute from "his Nora" and was incapable of any infidelity. If Joyce's woman publisher had been seductive instead of "the business type," she shrewdly surmised, Joyce would have run away.

Sylvia believed that the Joyces' marriage (as she thought of it) was one of the best pieces of luck that ever befell him, in spite of Nora's views on writers. "Look at him, leeching on the bed!" Nora would say to Sylvia. (*Leeching* is an Irish expression for loafing or lounging.) "If only I had married a ragpicker or a farmer or anything but a writer . . ." Her lip would curl in scorn. *He* was no company for her; first thing in the morning he reached down for the pencil and paper beside his bed. *He* never knew what time of day it was. How could she keep a servant for a man who left the house just as lunch was put on the table?[19]

Nora and Joyce lived now, thanks to Miss Weaver, in some comfort. At last Nora was able to keep the kind of household she liked and was relieved to be free of the squalid family hotel. One of the rare outsiders to see their living quarters there had been a doctor who treated Joyce for an attack of glaucoma just after Nora returned from Ireland. The doctor was shocked. He had found the two Joyces sitting on the floor with a pan of chicken between them, with trunks open and combs, towels, and soap strewn around the room.[20]

On the occasions when they had a settled home with their own furnishings around them, however, Nora and Joyce were fastidious, and their visitors were struck by the gleaming brass, the well-laid table, the smell of furniture polish, and overall bourgeois orderliness.[21]

The troubles of householding were not far away. The maid stole, they believed, a ring and a brooch and "God knows what else," Joyce wrote to Ford Madox Ford, asking Ford, who was in the south of France, to buy some more cameos if he went to Menton.

The Joyces' housing problem lay mainly in their demands. Nora was fussy and did not like a bad address or an ugly neighborhood. However, she also had to live with Joyce's mountains of books and papers and often despaired of finding anywhere in Paris they could afford that was big enough. Their children, of course, meant an extra expense. But although the Joyces had brought their nomadism with them from Ireland, they were not alone in moving from place to place. "We all did," said Arthur Power. Parisian landlords often sublet their flats for short periods, and the expatriates themselves traveled a great deal and did not want to be burdened with paying double rent.

News of his son's changed circumstances reached John Joyce in Dublin. Jim had written to Aunt Josephine to say that the second edition of *Ulysses*, selling at two guineas, had sold out in less than a week. The old man wrote to ask his successful son, not unreasonably, if he would send his father some money.

Joyce answered with the weariness of the householder. Life at 26 avenue Charles Floquet was not cheap. He lived in Paris, Joyce told his father, only for Nora's sake; he would have preferred less expensive Nice. He and Nora were not enveloped in luxury. True, he had been given a munificent sum by an English lady but it yielded an income of only £450 a year. Of that, £300 went on rent, £100 for medical bills, and £36 for the cleaning woman. Nora had to do her own shopping and cooking.

Joyce himself every morning made two of the four beds and stoked the stove with wood and coal. Still, he said, the rooms were so dark he could not find his clothes in the morning. All in all, John Joyce, living in Dublin on a pension of £150, was far better off than his son.[22]

Joyce did not tell his father the whole truth. In addition to his regular interest income (tax free because he was a British subject abroad), he had received in 1922 £650 in royalties from Miss Weaver's edition of *Ulysses* alone. Also, the capital she had given him was invested in Canadian Pacific Railway stock and other securities. Whenever he needed more cash, he had only to ask Miss Weaver to instruct her solicitors to sell some stock, and, braving their disapproval, she always obliged.

One night Nora and Joyce were dining at their new haunt, the Café Francis at the Place d'Alma, when a startlingly good-looking young couple walked in. They were Americans, the man tall and fair, the woman small, dark, vivacious, and extremely elegant. Her costume was from the Lanvin spring collection — a suit of warm brown, with a collarless wide neck which showed off her blouse of yellow and orange print. Her hat was of a matching print. As the pair looked round the restaurant, the man recognized Joyce and led his wife to the Joyce table.[23]

He was Leon Fleischman, Paris representative of Boni and Liveright, a New York firm that had published most of the best expatriate and avantgarde writers, including Ernest Hemingway and Djuna Barnes. Fleischman had been one of the original subscribers to *Ulysses*. His wife, Helen, was a close friend of Peggy Guggenheim and like Peggy used New York wealth to back an enthusiasm for art and for artists. She had paid Djuna Barnes's way to Europe.

Nora was struck with admiration. Everything about Helen Fleischman's costume was perfection; her jeweled earrings were stunning. Nora, without reserve, confessed her envy. She herself never wore earrings because she felt they made her look common.

The two women looked each other over carefully as they chatted about the difficulty in finding flats in Paris. Helen liked Nora's attractiveness and clear skin, and she was fascinated by Joyce. Nora, of course, did not appreciate Helen's sophistication, and may not have realized that in Helen's wardrobe she was admiring the best Paris had to offer.

The two women could hardly have been more different. Helen was the archetypal Jewish princess. She was the daughter of Adolph Kastor, a New York cutlery manufacturer. Her doting father, a German-Jewish immigrant to New York, indulged her every whim and had given her the earrings that caught Nora's eye. In Manhattan, where she was born, Helen belonged to the circle of wealthy New York German Jews that called itself "Our Crowd." It was a group not accepted by New York's gentile society, yet just as rigid in its own parallel standards as it strove to distance itself from the new wave of poorer Jews coming into the United States from Russia and Eastern Europe.[24] Helen's dress sense epitomized the standards of the Crowd: superb fabrics, elegant cut, quiet colors, everything in perfect taste.

After their meeting that night, the Fleischmans walked the Joyces home, delighted to be on speaking terms with Paris's greatest literary celebrity. Friendship grew, and soon the Fleischmans were invited to the Joyce home and presented to the "children." Helen privately thought that Lucia's squint marred her looks but otherwise judged the girl pretty. Mrs. Joyce, Helen noticed, favored the boy.

As the summer of 1923 drew near, the lease on the flat was up and Nora and Joyce prepared to move out in order to take the English seaside holiday that had eluded them the year before. Nora packed three hatboxes and four suitcases of clothes, and Joyce assembled ten cases of books, three sacks of newspapers, and four trunks. They left Sylvia Beach behind with Giorgio to look for a flat for their return. Giorgio, Joyce wrote to Sylvia airily, not wanting to be troubled with the details, was "the best living authority on the manners, customs, institutions, privileges, perquisites hereditary and acquired domestic characteristics of the Joyce family abroad."[25]

Sylvia offered Giorgio the flat above her bookshop for the family. When he refused it, she was cross. "He had very high-falutin' ideas," she said. What she meant was that he had rejected it because it had no bathroom.[26]

Joyce had had a miserable year with his eyes and teeth. In April he had gone into hospital to have all his teeth out, the extractions being followed by three small operations on his eyes. The pain was very great, from his gums as well as his eyes, and the result was disappointing. He flatly denied to Miss Weaver, however, an American newspaper report that he was "a tragic blind figure" trapped in his Eiffel Tower apartment.

To accompany them on their holiday, Nora invited her sister Kathleen in Galway to join them. It was the first time in nineteen years with Joyce that Nora had had any of her relatives to stay. In London, she and Kathleen tried to find their sister Peg, who had left home for London during the First World War to do hotel work, but they failed. Peg (the sister with the squint like Lucia's) had to be numbered among Mrs. Barnacle's lost brood. Nora's brother, Tom, who had been badly wounded in the leg during the war, had also gone off to England and lost contact with his family.[27]

In the seclusion of their seaside boarding house in Bognor, and without her children to eavesdrop, Nora unburdened herself to her youngest sister and allowed herself to complain about her husband's passivity. It was then that she compared Jim unfavorably with their father.[28]

But a baker like Tom Barnacle would not have taken Nora into an international world, or indulged her passion for clothes. Nora and Jim, Kathleen noticed, having last seen them in Galway in 1912, had become very concerned with their wardrobe. Jim in fact had become a dandy and Nora a confident shopper. When one of a pair of suede shoes she had bought for Kathleen cracked, Nora marched back to the shop, threatening in front of Kathleen, "My husband is a writer and if you don't change them I'll have it published in the paper."[29]

The two sisters bought much else. Kathleen returned to Bowling Green wearing high fashion such as was rarely seen in Galway and make-up on her face, something Mrs. Barnacle did not allow. Parcel after parcel from Paris followed her return. Joyce was happy to indulge Kathleen. He had been pleasantly surprised by her table manners and affability and even escorted her to Sunday Mass, telling her, "You know what they'll be saying at home if I don't."[30]

Soon Nora was able to banish thoughts of modest boarding houses and humble pensions from her mind. Miss Weaver had come into a new and larger sum of money — £12,000 — and in the summer of 1923 made it all over to Joyce. She still told herself that she was buying him a quiet and restful place in which to work.[31]

Did she do him more harm than good? Mary Colum later blamed Miss Weaver for much of the trouble that beset the family; access to so much money, without strings, had a bad effect on them all, she judged. Sylvia Beach felt the same way and, needless to say, so did Miss Weaver's solicitors. The total amount of capital she had transferred to James Joyce, £21,000, was a small fortune — her own. It was the equivalent, in 1988 values, of £438,000, or $825,000.

Had Joyce husbanded this gift, he could have been free of money worries for life. He did not. He squandered it, not least on his children, removing from Giorgio whatever weak incentive he had to build a career. (Giorgio did work briefly at a bank in 1923.) Joyce, having been so poor as a youth, gave his children everything they asked for and demanded nothing of them (except that they do his errands). Miss Weaver's largesse, some have argued, also impoverished world literature by allowing James Joyce to waste his lyrical gift on the bad joke of *Finnegans Wake*. The effect of her philanthropy, however, was not for Miss Weaver to judge. She could no more control it than Joyce could control his spending. "Harriet could not be naughty," said her goddaughter. "She needed James Joyce to be naughty for her."[32]

Back in Paris Nora and Joyce talked endlessly about finding a home. "We chase flats, we are worn to exhaustion," Joyce wrote to T. S. Eliot,[33] but fortified with a suddenly doubled income, they moved instead into the Victoria Palace, one of the larger hotels on the rue Blaise-Desgoffe in

Montparnasse. Katherine Mansfield had lived there shortly before she
died the previous year, and Joyce had visited the hotel to take tea with
John Middleton Murry. The tenor of life at the Victoria Palace was described by Katherine in her journal:

> The weeks pass and we do less and less, and seem to have no time for any-
> thing. Up and down in the lift, along the corridors, in and out of the restau-
> rant — it's a whole complete life. One has a name for everybody; one is
> furious if someone has taken "our table," and the little gritty breakfast-trays
> whisk in and out unnoticed, and it seems quite natural to carry about that
> heavy key with the stamped brass disk 134.[34]

But the Joyces liked it. In spite of their protestations, they found a
curious security in playing Grand Hotel and remained for nearly a year.
Joyce did his writing, using for a surface a green suitcase bought in Bognor and hearing in the background the sound of the vacuum cleaners in
the corridor and the voices of American tourists calling to each other.[35]

The search for a place of their own continued when Joyce was well
enough. Giorgio went to the Scuola Cantorum, and the Joyces hired Arthur Power to improve his English, which Power tried to do by reading
the boy *Tess of the D'Urbervilles*. Lucia improved at the piano.

At the Victoria Palace, they had many visitors: from Dublin, Charlie
Joyce, now a night clerk in the General Post Office, and from Trieste,
Eileen's husband, Frank Schaurek. (Frank, Stanislaus had written Joyce,
had been borrowing money for trips to Czechoslovakia and Venice.) Also
from Trieste came Ettore Schmitz, to whom Nora delivered her summary
view of James Joyce's talents: "I've always told him he should give up
writing and take up singing."[36]

One aspect of their life had not changed: Jim's drinking and Nora's
fury at it. One night, as she tried to wrestle him into a taxi, Joyce broke
loose and went hopping down the street shouting, "I'm free, I'm free."
Nora pushed aside offers of assistance. "I'll handle him," she said. On
other nights, she did not bother and, abandoning him at the café, went
home by herself. She poured scorn on his drinking companions, all the
more so now that some of them, like Joyce, were becoming recognized.
When Hemingway carried Joyce home one night, Nora looked at the
disheveled pair and greeted them, sneering, "Well, here comes James
Joyce the writer, drunk again, with Ernest Hemingway."[37] She still
threatened to take the children and go back to Ireland, but her threats
rang hollow.

After more than a year of hotel life, a time during which Nora had her
teeth replaced by dentures and Joyce had two more eye operations (his
sight *would* come back, Dr. Borsch promised, but it didn't), and a holiday in Brittany, they had another new home, on the avenue Charles Flo-

quet as before, but at number 8, where they had the whole fifth floor to themselves.[38]

Nora had a servant once more, and to Miss Weaver she wrote proudly, "I am fairly well myself and my maid continues to be a great success which of course makes it much easier for me."[39]

Too much of Nora's time was spent at Dr. Borsch's eye clinic. Joyce's operations seemed endless. Why so many? Stanislaus asked from Trieste — a question that remains difficult to answer. The problems were real: glaucoma, a succession of cataracts, compounded by inflammation. Joyce often wore an eye patch or a bandage and at times had to write with charcoal or colored crayons in large childlike letters in order to see anything he wrote at all. When he had to stay overnight at the clinic, Joyce, as usual, insisted that Nora stay and sleep beside him. She complained that no one came to see them and that they sat there "cooped up like old hens." When Sylvia Beach did visit one day she came upon Nora, with a nurse, trying to pick up leeches from the floor. The doctor had decreed that leeches be applied around Joyce's eye to draw off the excess blood, but "the creatures," as Nora called them, would not stay put.[40]

At the avenue Charles Floquet, Nora and Joyce became quite domesticated, with a biscuit-colored cat that according to Joyce "eats a lot of bread and butter and the *Daily Mail.*" Giorgio was taking a new interest in developing his physique with a muscle-stretcher. Joyce found the gadget in his room and tried it gingerly but, fatigued as always, quickly put it down.[41] Soon, however, their lease expired, as they knew it would. Joyce nonetheless put on his best evicted-tenant's face and invited Larbaud and Signora Nebbia to dinner "before they throw us out."

Nora solaced herself by having her portrait done yet again. Myron Nutting was the painter; he also did Joyce and Lucia. As before, Nora's qualities as a sitter and her calm self-possession shone through. Nutting confessed that of the three Joyce portraits, the one of Nora was most successful, one of the best he did during that period in Paris, even though he had used in its composition a daring contrast of geometric shapes and curved planes.[42]

Nora, at thirty-nine, was about to serve as the model for Joyce's final great portrait of Woman: Anna Livia Plurabelle in *Finnegans Wake.* It was to Kathleen in the summer of 1923, just a year after being rid of the misery of *Ulysses*, that Nora confided the dismal news: "He's on another book again."[43] She also knew the book's secret title, *Finnegans Wake* (although Joyce probably did not bother to tell her that he was omitting the apostrophe so that the title would contain, among other meanings, the command to all the Finnegans of the world to wake). The title, Nora could certainly see, also carried the stamp of Finn's Hotel, the place that effectively gave her to James Joyce.

Nora knew the rollicking Irish ballad about Finnegan the hodcarrier who is killed by falling from his ladder but who wakes at his wake when he gets a whiff of whiskey. But she was hardly prepared for what Joyce was putting down on paper this time. In April 1924 the first excerpts appeared in the *transatlantic review* (lower case was all the rage) under the title "Work in Progress." The passage was about seabirds, or appeared to be:

> Overhoved, shrillgleescreaming. That song sang seaswans. The winging ones. Seahawk, seagull, curlew and plover, kestrel and capercallzie. All the birds of the sea they trolled out rightbold when they smacked the big kuss of Trustan with Usolde.[44]

As he worked on the book in 1924, because of the state of his eyes Joyce appears to have asked Nora to help. Notes for *Finnegans Wake* having to do with *The Divine Comedy* exist in Nora's handwriting, the only evidence of her active part in his literary work. In her hand too is this comment appended to the notes: "To day 16 of June 1924 twenty years after. Will anybody remember this date." Nora too recognized the importance of the date in their lives.[45]

Even if she had grasped that Joyce was writing another hidden tribute to the barnacle goose in his life, Nora would not have liked the book any better. She referred to it as "that chop suey you're writing." "Why," she implored him, "don't you write sensible books that people can understand?"[46]

She was not the only one dismayed. Stanislaus found it unbearably wearisome. Ezra Pound (somewhat later) wrote that only "a new cure for the clapp can possibly be worth all the circumambient peripherization." Miss Weaver maintained a tactful restraint, yet Valery Larbaud, whose enthusiasm for experimental literature was boundless and who loved the first sixty pages, said he could not understand it.[47]

If any further proof were needed of Nora's loyalty to Joyce it lies in her keeping the title of *Finnegans Wake* to herself for seventeen years. Joyce's desperation, according to Ellmann, shows the magical power he attached to names.[48] The only one who could use his first name was the only one who could be entrusted with the powerful code. Angry as Nora grew about Jim's drinking and throwing money away, unintelligible as she could see the book was, she never used the weapon of revenge that was always to hand.

Haute couture is one way Joyce repaid her loyalty. He had always taken her clothes seriously and gladly gave her a signed copy of *Ulysses* for her milliner, Suzie, a fan of his. He himself was not shy of setting styles. He wore bow ties in the daytime long before it became generally fashionable to do so.[49]

With their new money, Nora discovered the Paris fashion houses. Helen Fleischman encouraged her, suggesting that the woman who was Mrs. James Joyce should smarten herself up. To Nora, clothes-mad all her life, the advice was galling, but Helen was right. In her hair and clothes Nora had not moved with the times nor had she dared to brave the inner sanctums of the couturiers. Until they had real money, she could not afford to do so and on her trip to Galway in 1922 had worn the clothes she had been wearing in Zurich during the war.[50]

The result of Nora's conversion is preserved in the best-known photograph in the Joyce archive: The Joyce Family in 1924, taken by Wide World Photos, shows the four of them proud as a family of Spanish grandees and dressed from top to toe in new clothes (and, for Joyce and Nora, new teeth) bought with Miss Weaver's money.

Nora wears a black and white Chinese print of embossed velvet, probably from the Lucien Lelong collection of 1923 or 1924. Lucia wears a similar outfit; obviously bought by Nora, it is much too old for a girl of seventeen: a straight, waistless coat, which had to be held across the body without a belt. Both women sport fashionable, fur-trimmed cuffs and collars. Joyce shows his cufflinks and is wearing one of his bow ties, while Giorgio looks every inch "a gintleman's son," standing pompous and stiff, with wing collar and nipped-in waist.

Yet shoes steal the picture. Lucia wears elegant, so-called bar shoes, and Nora an even more dazzling pair, fastened across the instep with a Byzantine-style diamanté buckle. Giorgio wears spats.

The photograph well expresses the state of the Joyce family in 1924. Poverty is gone; so are Edwardian corsetry and subservience. Three of the family are preoccupied, gazing off center, Joyce the formal paterfamilias, Giorgio the tense son and heir, and Lucia, expressionless, lost in a world of her own. Only Nora, confident, triumphant, looks the camera straight in the eye. A line of Molly Bloom's would serve well as a caption:

> Sure you cant get on in this world without style all going in food and rent when I get it Ill lash it around I tell you . . .[51]

But this splendid manifestation of family unity was illusory. Giorgio had been seduced by Helen Fleischman, and the seduction was turning into a full-blown love affair, which was nothing new for Helen. She had had many love affairs, including one with Laurence Vail that her husband had encouraged. Peggy Guggenheim, who married Vail in 1922, boasted, "I guess I took him away from her." Peggy had previously been in love with Leon Fleischman, but it was a small matter between friends. "Helen didn't mind," said Peggy. "They were so free."[52]

Nora and Joyce were shattered. They were not that free. Their son was twenty, Helen thirty-one, married, and the mother of a young son. Forgetting their own youthful pride in sexual precocity, they had blindly expected their children to remain children. They were totally unprepared for their son to succumb to the atmosphere around him and break several taboos at once. For Nora losing Giorgio to Helen came as a double shock. "But she was *my* friend!" she said sorrowfully.[53]

14

Square Robiac

IN MARCH 1925 Nora succeeded in persuading Joyce to do something they had not done since Trieste — to take an empty flat and furnish it themselves. She had strong ideas about their needs: three bedrooms, a study for Joyce, and a dining room for dinner parties. Bohemian squalor was not for her. After visiting the studio in which a friend worked, she declared, in one of her remarks that convulsed Joyce, "That place isn't fit to wash a rat in." [1]

After much searching Nora found a sunny flat on the third floor of an apartment building in the Square Robiac, a quiet cul-de-sac off the north side of the bustling rue de Grenelle. The flat was, like their other residences of the past three years, in the heart of the bourgeois Seventh, convenient for their friends, and near Les Trianons, still their favorite restaurant, and the Café Francis. Joyce signed a lease in March, agreeing to a rent of twenty thousand francs a year, plus five thousand francs for charges. [2] Soon they were installed, with their family portraits, their cat, a piano, and gray writing paper in three sizes bearing their new address and telephone number (Ségur 95-20). They had invested in two wardrobes, a dining table and chairs, a dinner service, a soup tureen, and the canvas awning essential for the balcony of a Paris apartment. At the invitation of their friend Léon-Paul Fargue, they visited his glassware factory and chose *coupes*, presumably for champagne. They had the walls repapered, the floors carpeted, and six windows and three doors draped in brocade. They paid the concierge, the insurance company, and the electrician. "The house so far is all right," wrote Joyce the householder

to Miss Weaver, "but it seems to have cost a lot of money." He passed
on to her a bill for 15,000 francs. The total reached 125,000 francs —
equivalent to a year of Joyce's interest income. Miss Weaver may or may
not have been consoled to learn that the Joyces had decorated three of
the rooms in "her" colors, blue and yellow.[3]

Their friends all crowded in for a look and privately found it dreadful.
The kindest verdict was the painter Myron Nutting's: "comfortable and
not untasteful." Helen Fleischman regretted that it was so unattractive,
and even Miss Weaver, once she had braved the ordeal of a Channel
crossing to come to inspect the new settled working environment she
wanted Joyce to have, found it bare looking. To Sylvia Beach she confided the hope that the Joyces would furnish the flat more fully (although
she knew at whose expense this would be done).[4]

These critics, like most of the Joyces' visitors, were aesthetic sophisti-
cates who expected Joyce, as leader of the avant-garde in writing, to be
equally adventurous in his personal surroundings. Arthur Power, at that
time art critic for the *Paris Herald,* had tried to interest Joyce in the
Braques or Modiglianis they saw in the gallery windows of the Left Bank
but to no avail. Joyce preferred his family portraits (women in big bon-
nets and men in red hunting coats) and his reproduction of a Vermeer
view of Ghent.[5]

The Joyces' indifference to design puzzled their friends all the more
because Nora and her husband took an interest in modern music. Nora
pursued her interest in Wagner, even when she had to go to the opera
alone, and they did what they could to encourage the work of their friend,
the young American composer George Antheil. All four Joyces granted
Antheil the honor of their presence at the first performance of his *Ballet
Mécanique,* with its score for nine grand pianos, saws, hammers, and an
airplane propeller. (When Nora, Joyce, and their children filed into their
box in the celebrity-filled Théâtre des Champs-Élysées, Sylvia Beach cat-
tily remarked that it was as if the royal family had arrived. "You expected to hear the Irish National Anthem strike up.")[6]

What none of their Parisian friends understood was how much Nora
and Joyce each cherished the ideal of bourgeois family life. It was part of
their buried vision of the life they might have led had they remained in
Ireland. Joyce, in his notes for *Exiles,* pictured Bertha as "Mrs. Robert
Hand . . . ordering carpets in Grafton Street."[7] In fact, their home at
the Square Robiac was furnished just the way they wanted, and they
loved it. "At least I have a house now," Joyce wrote Stanislaus and offered to pay his way to Paris to see it.[8]

The moving-in accomplished and with his sight "queer but not bad,"
the Joyces, like good Parisians, left town after Bastille Day in July. Their
new style of life saw them spending nearly two months away every summer; they seldom returned before mid-September. Joyce used these trav-

els to investigate places whose names and associations he was weaving into *Finnegans Wake,* and in spite of severely curtailed vision, he loved all the tedious detail of poring over guidebooks and train timetables; he liked to say that he had the mind of a grocer's clerk. He and Nora sought out first-class hotels, usually right on the seafront, where they would settle in for weeks at a time. The names of the establishments they favored in their Paris years reads like a selection of Best of Baedeker between the wars.

In the summer of 1925, for example, as they made their way down the French Atlantic coast, they began at the Grand Hôtel des Bains et de Londres at Fécamp (where they celebrated Lucia's eighteenth and Giorgio's twentieth birthdays), moved to the Grand Hôtel de la Poste in Rouen, from there to the Grand Hôtel du Raisin de Bourgogne at Niort, then on to the Hôtel de Bayonne at Bordeaux, and finally to the Regina Palace Hôtel et d'Angleterre at Arcachon. Joyce always paid cash on these trips. To stock up before they set out, one or other of the family paid a visit to Shakespeare and Company. If he needed more money en route Joyce wired Sylvia Beach (never Miss Weaver).

Nora having become nearly as afraid of thunder as he was, Joyce plotted their itineraries as if they lived in the tropics rather than in temperate Western Europe. They clung to their faith that electrical storms, like air raids, could be avoided with foresight and considered it extraordinary bad luck if they ran into one. In 1925 after they had left for Normandy Joyce wrote to Miss Weaver that they had suffered terrifying downpours in the Bois de Boulogne and had fled Paris, only to be met in Normandy by "rain, hail, thunder, lightning, etc." He hoped she was safe from the "wild weather" in the English Lake District. Joyce, marveling that Italian men seemed to be entirely free of fear of thunder, attributed the increase in storms around London and Paris to "all this wireless" (radio broadcasting was then becoming widespread).[9]

Their circle of sophisticated friends in no way cut Nora and Joyce off from their families. From Trieste Stanislaus, now forty, wrote to say that he had become engaged to a young Triestine student. His fiancée, Nelly Lichtensteiger, was the same age as Lucia. From Galway, Nora learned that her younger sister Annie, the twin sister to Peg, had died. So had her Uncle Tommy, whose blackthorn stick had driven her into Joyce's arms. From Dublin also came the news of Aunt Josephine Murray's death. They had been estranged from Joyce's aunt ever since Nora had failed to visit her in 1922, and also since the publication of *Ulysses.* Aunt Josephine had been deeply shocked and called it a book unfit to read. (To which Joyce retorted to his cousin, Mrs. Murray's daughter, who relayed the complaint, "Then life isn't fit to live.") Fortunately, Joyce's brother Charlie had warned him that Aunt Josephine was dying, and Joyce had time to write her a beautiful letter of reconciliation:

You attached me to you in youth by so many acts of kindness, by so much
help and advice and sympathy, especially after my mother's death, that it
seems to me as if your thought of me now is one of reproach . . . but if I
am estranged in that I am still attached to you by many bonds of gratitude
and affection and of respect as well . . .[10]

As in so many of his relationships, Joyce was able to heal, with the power
of his words, the hurt caused by his actions, and in this case, by Nora's.

About the time they moved into the Square Robiac, Nora and Joyce had
to accept that Giorgio was passing out of their control. He continued his
singing lessons and also took a job in an accountant's office, but his main
occupation was keeping company with Helen Fleischman. In 1925 the
Joyces met some of Helen's American relatives. They were Helen's older
brother, Alfred Kastor, and his young Danish wife, Ellen, who were on a
trip to Europe. The Kastors knew about Helen's affair with Giorgio, as
Leon Fleischman had returned to New York alone, and they saw it in
quite a different light than did Nora and James Joyce. They knew that
Helen had a predilection for artists. They all assumed that Helen must
have set her sights on James Joyce and when she failed to snare him
turned to his son instead.[11]

Ellen, who later divorced Alfred Kastor, did not like Helen. "Her
brothers adored her," Ellen recalled. "She got away with murder. They
worshipped the ground she walked on. To me she was a sexual vampire,
a bloodsucker.

"When we met them the affair was fresh and very hush-hush. When
we were with them, Helen was so jealous — Giorgio was just my age —
she wouldn't let us alone together — even though I was pregnant. I felt
sorry for Giorgio. He didn't have a Chinaman's chance."

Nora apparently thought much the same, for although she received the
Kastors she did not speak a single word during the visit. Joyce was hardly
more welcoming, sitting in a chair, silent and huddled in a shawl.[12]

It is unlikely that the Joyces ever realized the full extent of the attraction their name held for Helen Fleischman.

Helen's group, and particularly her generation, was highly ambivalent
about its Jewishness. As described by Stephen Birmingham in *Our Crowd*,
this New York German Jewish aristocracy considered it highly desirable
to "assimilate" — that is, to marry into a gentile family.[13]

Girls in these families had a particularly difficult time. Indulged by
their fathers but handed over by their busy mothers to the care of strict
and unsympathetic nurses, usually German or Irish, they were seldom
accorded the first-rate education considered essential for Jewish sons.
(Helen's younger brother, Robert, had graduated from Phillips Andover
Academy and Harvard. Helen had not gone to college.) Given such a

combination of indulgence, neglect, and idleness, girls from such families not infrequently became sexual rebels. Peggy Guggenheim, Helen's good friend, was a classic example. Yet Peggy — and, to a lesser extent, Helen — also displayed another, less self-destructive consequence of such an upbringing, her interest in art.

Helen's father, Adolph, an immigrant to America from Germany, had made his fortune through the Camillus Cutlery Company in Camillus, New York. It was not so large as to place them among the richest of Manhattan's German Jews, but it did provide the Kastor children with independent means and won Adolph Kastor a listing in *Who's Who in American Jewry*.

Helen was the only one of Kastor's four children to marry a Jew. Alfred's wife was Danish, while Robert and their older sister, Edna, had married American gentiles. (When Edna moved to Washington and dropped completely out of touch, the family said it was because she did not want people to know she was Jewish.) Helen had married Leon Fleischman in 1916 in a ceremony held at the family home at 14 West Seventieth Street and performed by a Protestant minister. She had given birth to a son, David, in 1919. After her marriage Helen had many affairs, yet her brothers never reproached her. Their philosophy toward Helen's behavior was "Don't let Grandpa [Adolph Kastor] know." [14]

One reason that Alfred and Robert Kastor hesitated to restrain their sister was that Helen's vivacity could turn to manic excitability. A worrying strain of mental illness ran in the family, as it did through much of "Our Crowd." Alfred himself suffered from manic depression, and their mother, Minnie Danzer Kastor, had long been confined to a home on the Hudson.

Helen, however, was happier in Paris than in New York. It was less anti-Semitic and provided the perfect backdrop for her beauty and taste. She had a wide circle of friends, including many from the New York and international art worlds. She knew how to entertain and had the money with which to do it. Her sister-in-law marveled that every detail of Helen's dress was always perfect and every handkerchief taken from her drawer carried her personal perfume. Helen patronized the very latest designers, particularly Elsa Schiaparelli, who had just emerged as the boldest of them all.

Self-centered as Helen was, she was not ungenerous. She would give away clothes as freely as she bought them. "Help yourself," she would say to friends, opening her wardrobe doors. She gave Lucia Joyce dresses and sweaters, and gave Djuna Barnes the black cloak that became Djuna's trademark. Seeing beautiful Djuna typing away one day, dressed in some old frayed underwear, Helen told Peggy Guggenheim to give Djuna some of her excess lingerie. Peggy, however, unlike Helen, had a miserly streak and gave Djuna some that had been mended. When Helen found out, she was furious. So was Djuna, who never wore the cast-off step-ins.[15]

For Joyce his son's sexual initiation by a Jewish beauty must have been deeply distressing. Since Trieste, his dream women, real and literary, had been Jewish, or Jewish-looking. As parents, Nora and Joyce feared that Helen was just toying with Giorgio and using his name for social climbing, although they did not appreciate its possibilities for cloaking Jewishness.

By and large their friends did not like Helen. Anti-Semitism, so rife between the wars, cannot be ruled out. Stuart Gilbert, for example, found her "vulgar." Others found her nervous and aggressive.[16] As for Nora, she would have been hostile to any woman who got close to Giorgio, who, with his deep blue, almost violet eyes and long black lashes, was so clearly her own. But to surrender him to a former friend, as near to Nora's own age as to Giorgio's, was insupportable.

Giorgio's escape only served to tighten the Joyces' hold on Lucia. In November 1925 some old friends from Trieste, the Trevisani family, invited Lucia to come and stay. Lucia was eager to go. She liked the Trevisani girls, Letizia and Gioconda, very much, and she had not been in Trieste since they all had left in 1920. Joyce refused to allow her to make the trip. To Ettore Schmitz, who had relayed the invitation, Joyce explained that he had to have his seventh eye operation in December and then had to go to London for the premiere of *Exiles;* Lucia, Schmitz would understand, had to be with him for both events. He promised that Lucia could go to Trieste the following year.

But Lucia did not go in 1926, nor in any year after that. The time was never right, and Lucia never saw the city of her birth or the blue Adriatic again.[17]

When they went on their summer holidays, Nora and Joyce always took Lucia with them and took Giorgio too, until he refused to accompany them any longer.

At the time of the move to Square Robiac, Giorgio and Lucia seemed set for artistic careers. Nora and Joyce were very proud of their accomplishments. Lucia, already proficient at the piano, had made a good start in modern dance and performed with *Ballets de Rythme et Couleur,* led by the Scottish dancer Lois Hutton. Lucia's tall angular frame suited itself well to the choreographic counterpart of abstract art, and she gave a number of public performances (although some were merely pupil recitals), which her parents attended. Lucia designed her own costumes as well — another drain on the family purse.

Yet the Joyces treated her as a child. In 1928, when Lucia was twenty-one and went with her dance group to the Isadora Duncan school near Salzburg, Nora and Joyce chose to take their holiday in Salzburg. Their clinging undoubtedly contributed to Lucia's immaturity but was a response to it as well. As their friends had begun to notice, there was something odd about the Joyces' daughter.

Their settled home attracted their far-flung relatives. The Joyce procession was constant. In the spring of 1926 Eileen came from Trieste with her three children for three weeks. Stanislaus followed for a two-week visit; he was disgusted to see Joyce drinking more than ever and surrounded by flatterers. From Galway Nora's uncle Michael Healy got up the courage to travel to the Continent. The Joyces, like many Parisians, had no spare bedrooms in their flat and put up visiting relatives in small hotels in the *quartier*. For the devout Mr. Healy, Nora dispatched Joyce and an Irish friend to scout the neighborhood and find a hotel near a Catholic church so that her uncle could keep up his practice of daily communion.

As Nora had had a good reunion with Eileen in the spring, she was surprised, in November 1926, to receive a letter from Eileen written not from Trieste but from Oughterard in Ireland. Why had Eileen chosen to go straight from Trieste to Ireland, traveling through Belgium and not stopping in Paris? Nora could make no sense of Eileen's trip.[18] Nonetheless, Eileen's letter was cheerful; she was having a pleasant time and would give Nora all the Irish news when she stopped in Paris on her return. A few days later Nora and Joyce were shaken to receive a frenzied telegram from Eileen, sent from Ireland but written in Italian for secrecy. "Frank *rovinato*," the telegram said ("Frank ruined"), or rather implied that he would be if Joyce did not send the sum Eileen had demanded to Trieste. "*Salveci*," she begged ("Save us"). Joyce had no idea what sum Eileen was talking about and was, as usual, short of cash. They had just come back from Belgium and he had paid five thousand francs in rent, five thousand in taxes, ten thousand for clothes for Nora and the children, and had sent Stanislaus six thousand. Just as he wired Eileen that no funds were available he received a letter from an acquaintance in Trieste giving some blunt, bad news.

On Monday morning, just after his bank opened, Frank Schaurek, Eileen's husband, had shot himself.[19] A wire from Stanislaus also arrived to relay the dreadful news.

Joyce told none of the story to Nora. Frank, the model of the successful Triestine businessman, paterfamilias, and antique collector, had been discovered to have embezzled seventy-five thousand francs (about £500 or $2,425), and had been given one month to repay at least half the funds. Unable to do so, he killed himself. Just as Joyce was trying to decide how to break the news to Nora, the situation became almost farcical. Wires from Eva in Dublin announced the impending arrival of Eileen in Paris on her way back to Trieste. "Is there anything wrong with Frank?" asked Eva.[20] Eileen obviously was unaware that she was a widow.

Throughout his life Joyce was unable to face bad news. His usual defense was that he was protecting nervous women. On this occasion, he decided not to tell Nora of Frank's death and not to tell Eileen either. For nearly three days in Paris, therefore, he endured the company of an agitated Eileen and a mystified Nora without blurting out the truth. Instead, in order to prepare Eileen for the absence of Frank when she arrived at the station in Trieste, he told her that Frank had gone back to Prague until the affair at the bank blew over.[21] This lie left Stanislaus with the task of meeting the train and telling their sister that her husband was dead. It was perhaps the meanest trick Joyce ever played on Stannie.

To cushion the blow for Eileen, Stannie removed his black arm band and black hat before meeting her. By the time Eileen arrived in Trieste, the funeral had been held and Frank's body had already been buried. (He was such an avid collector — perhaps the cause of his indebtedness — that the Triestine antique shops closed for the day in his memory.) Eileen was so dumbfounded by the news and by the sight of her children in black and her servants weeping that she could not take it in. She demanded that Frank's body be dug up before she could surrender her hope that Joyce had been telling the truth and that Frank was really in Prague. The shock caused her to lose her memory for months.[22]

For Nora, Jim, and Stanislaus, Schaurek's suicide meant a new financial burden, as the brothers contributed to the support of Eileen and her children. Stanislaus's own marriage was delayed for a further three years.

Nora and Joyce at that time enjoyed an income of two thousand pounds a year, derived almost equally from Harriet Weaver's trust and from royalties on *Ulysses* paid him by Sylvia Beach. They had no bank in Paris. Instead they used Sylvia's bookshop, taking as petty cash advances on royalties *Ulysses* was expected to earn. Sometimes they left notes in the till, sometimes not. At the time of Stanislaus's visit to Paris, Nora herself withdrew fourteen thousand francs ($400 or £80).[23] According to her biographer's study of the books of Shakespeare and Company, Sylvia made no profit whatsoever from *Ulysses*. For the whole family, Shakespeare and Company was far more than a bank or petty-cash box. It was a ticket agency, post office, secretarial service, and customs house. When Joyce wanted Harriet Weaver to send him some gramophone records from London, he told her to address them to Miss Beach, as she was so much better than he at dealing with the official forms. Such was the daily flow of business between the rue de l'Odéon and the Square Robiac that Sylvia employed a special messenger as go-between. (The messenger was the sweet-tempered, mentally retarded sister of her shop assistant, Myrsine Moschos.)

Sylvia dealt not only with Joyce's considerable correspondence with publishers, agents, translators, and readers, but also with many of his and Nora's personal bills. Once while on holiday he wired Sylvia to pay their florist and to give Giorgio money to pay the electricity bill and the maid. At one point he was borrowing money not just from Sylvia but also from her mother.[24]

Joyce, exploiting everyone around him while convinced that he was being persecuted, had much to feel persecuted about. His eye doctor continued to assure him that the next eye operation would restore his sight. By late 1925, he had had about ten operations. The pain of piracy hurt even worse. An American magazine publisher, Samuel Roth, had begun in 1925 printing *Ulysses* in serial form, pretending that Joyce had authorized it. Joyce received no payment or copyright protection. As the pirating continued (and Roth changed the name of his magazine to avoid prosecution for obscenity), Joyce despairingly saw all his potential American sales disappearing, even those from the tourist market. A stop at Shakespeare and Company to buy the banned dirty book was, for many Americans, an essential part of a trip to Paris. Much of Sylvia's and Joyce's combined efforts went into an attempt to stop the pirating of *Ulysses* in the United States.[25]

Nora by then was a settled and confident Parisian. Her French never reached the standard of her Italian or even her German, languages in which she could communicate with close friends who could not speak English. Nevertheless, she had mastered enough French to make herself understood by her fellow tenants, her maids, her hairdressers, and her hatmakers. One day, sharing a taxi with Arthur Power, the driver could not find the address she gave him. *"Vous ne savez aucune rue!"* Nora told him.[26]

Her wit and composure were unnoticed by many of Joyce's literary admirers. As their adulation grew, so too did the belief that his consort was not worthy of him. Thomas Wolfe found himself in the summer of 1926 on a tourist bus at Waterloo with the Joyces, who were holidaying in Belgium. Wolfe silently observed the family: Joyce, wearing an eye patch, with a humorous mouth and a red nose pitted with scars and boils; Giorgio and Lucia, looking like an American college boy and a flapper; and with them a woman with "the appearance of a thousand middle class French women I've known — a vulgar, rather loose mouth; not very intelligent looking."[27]

That sums up fairly well the view of Nora of many of the transatlantic scholars and writers who came to gaze at Joyce. Joyce himself was partly to blame, for he never relaxed with worshipers and remained a silent and forbidding figure. However, some saw through his defense, and Nora's. Margaret Anderson, who, with Jane Heap, as the American publishers of the *Little Review* had been found guilty of obscenity on his behalf, said after meeting them:

I have seen no contemporary comment that does justice to Mrs. Joyce. She is charming. She is good drama. Her Irish mockery and personal challenge furnish Joyce with a continual, necessary and delightful foil. She teases and tyrannizes him. There is an undercurrent in her voice that makes her mockery at once exasperating, exciting and tender.

She must be at ease to show her quality. She has a feeling of inferiority before "intellectuals," though she would not mince words in expressing her scorn of them. She was quickly at ease with Jane and me, seeing our appreciation. Norah Joyce is one of those women a man loves forever and hopes one day to take effectively by the throat. She has spirit and independence which she has been willing (one feels not without rebellion) to subordinate to her devotion to a man she considers great in spite of "his necessity to write those books no one can understand."[28]

Irish reaction to Nora was different. Among their friends from Ireland, even the most intellectual, Nora was well liked; she made their home, and Joyce himself, very accessible. A member of the Irish rugby team in Paris for an international match, for example, was called to the telephone one morning and found James Joyce at the other end of the line, inviting him to tea. Of course for Irish men of letters Joyce was a mandatory port of call, and they found when they arrived "an ordinary quiet man living with his family who liked to meet friends in the evening at a restaurant and drink wine."

Those were the words of Thomas McGreevy, who was appointed *lecteur d'anglais* at the École Normale Supérieure in 1926. As soon as he was installed in his fine rooms on the rue d'Ulm, he wrote a letter to Joyce to introduce himself. At half past nine the next morning Joyce was on the telephone. Could McGreevy come to tea at the Square Robiac? McGreevy duly presented himself and knocked on the door, to be dazzled when the door opened and the light streamed from behind "a beautiful halo of gold hair."

"Miss Joyce?" McGreevy inquired. But it was Nora, not Lucia, and she roared with laughter. That began a friendship between them that, for McGreevy, a witty bachelor and brilliant conversationalist, was closer than his with Joyce. Joyce had no need of friends, said McGreevy; all that mattered to him was whether they were prepared to help him with *Work in Progress*.

Nora was fun. One day shortly after their meeting McGreevy was walking near the Gare Montparnasse on his way to the laundry, struggling with a large and awkwardly shaped bundle and hoping he would see no one he knew. Suddenly someone shouted his name. There was Nora Joyce in an open-backed taxi, laughing and waving at him. "She was my kind of Irish," he said. Joyce used to concede that his wife and McGreevy knew more about Ireland than he did. "Thirty miles outside

Dublin and I am lost," Joyce would say. To McGreevy Nora mocked Joyce's habit of assigning tasks to everyone in sight. "Don't mind him, Tom," she said. "If God Himself came down from Heaven that fellow would find something for Him to do. You ought to be ashamed of yourself, Jim." Joyce, McGreevy noticed, smiled at her teasing and always put his hand up in front of his face when he did. There seemed to be, McGreevy thought to himself, perfect understanding between them.[29]

Another Irish literary friend, Mary Colum, was put off at first by Nora's lack of education, but she also came to find Joyce's devotion quite understandable. Nora was "not only beautiful but vivacious and humourous," and Mary could see that "her personality was full of interest for him." He loved her swift summing-up of people and her sharp retorts. Moreover, Nora had natural aptitudes, among them a love and understanding of music, through which she and Joyce drew close.[30] Maria Jolas, who came to know the family, and the marriage, very well, in later years defended Nora against her critics: "Nora was always carefully dressed, carefully groomed, and he was proud to take her out. It is idle speculation to think that she was anything else than what he wanted her to be."[31]

There were many parties at the Square Robiac. Whether the guests enjoyed them or not depended upon how grateful they were to be invited. Helen Nutting found Nora a warm and gracious hostess. Helen Fleischman was more critical. Nora was better at feeding her guests — there was always a buffet with a turkey or a ham — than at making them feel at ease. Sylvia Beach found the parties dull. "Himself sang Irish songs accompanied by himself," she wrote her father.[32]

There was a predictability about the guest list: the Nuttings, William Bird, an American journalist and editor, and his wife, Sally, Sylvia and Adrienne, McGreevy, and the Joyce children and their friends. Not so frequently seen at the Square Robiac were McAlmon, Kay Boyle, and other friends of their early stay in Paris. McAlmon was fed up with "James Jesus Joyce," and Pound (also tired of Joyce's demands) had moved to Italy.

Around him Joyce was gathering a new circle. Stanislaus distrusted them as sycophants, and perhaps they were. They were also hard-working sycophants, deeply committed to helping him with the preparation and publication of his difficult new book. Chief among them were Maria Jolas and her husband Eugene, an energetic American couple who were publishing extracts from *Work in Progress* in their cosmopolitan literary journal, *transition*. Another important recruit was Stuart Gilbert. Gilbert (whose name Joyce pronounced with three syllables: *Gi*-la-bert) was an Oxford-trained lawyer who had served as a judge in Burma and who was devoting himself to explicating and translating *Ulysses*. Gilbert's French wife, Moune, a small lively woman, was active in publishing. She soon became one of Nora's best friends.

The Joyces' guests would arrive at nine. Nora would greet them alone. Then they would all wait awkwardly (without a drink) until their host appeared. Although his blindness was by no means total ("Joyce could see as well as anyone when he wanted to," Sylvia Beach thought), Nora would lead him around the group, instructing him, as if he were a child, to say good evening to each of his guests, supplying their names in turn. Then the drinking and the singing would begin. Giorgio would sing arias, Lucia light folk songs, and Joyce his favorite ballad, "The Brown and Yellow Ale," with words that might have struck home with Nora if she had been reading *Work in Progress,* where the publican, H. C. Ear-wicker, is full of incestuous thoughts about his "daughter-wife": "He asked was the woman with me my daughter . . . And I said that she was my married wife."

Sylvia and Adrienne usually left early, as did Miss Weaver if she was in Paris. Then the dancing would begin, crowned by Joyce's solo dance: long spidery legs (inside trouser-leg measurement thirty-two and a half inches) and long arms waving, always about to keel over, twirling and pirouetting, lost in himself.[33] Nora, who drank some wine but never a great deal, would enjoy it all for a while and then as the hour grew late became visibly impatient for the guests to go home. If Jim started another song, she would stick her fingers in her ears. "There he goes again," she would say. "Will the man never learn?"[34] Nora herself would end the wild dancing. She would order Maria Jolas to stop playing the piano and, flushed with anger (like Bella Cohen in *Ulysses*), would push Joyce into a chair from which he would beam wickedly at having prolonged the evening so long.

Nora was at her best at the post mortem that took place at teatime the next day. With the inner circle around her — Giorgio and Lucia, Joyce, perhaps McGreevy — she would go down the guest list and, like Molly Bloom, criticize all the women. Giorgio would encourage her. He liked wicked gossip as much as his mother did, and Joyce silently would listen and smile, sprawled in his chair. Nora loved the tea hour. The ritual had great importance for the whole family, a daily ceremony linking their lives in Ireland and France, with Nora as celebrant. She took great care with the food: the sandwiches were delicious and cut very thin; there were always two kinds of cake, usually sweet biscuits as well, and often something hot, perhaps scones. Nora was proud of her tea, brewed strong and served hot. (References to tea in Joyce's work would fill a good-sized doctoral dissertation.) Those who were invited to tea at the Joyces' could truly count themselves among the Joyces' inner circle. Joyce would come out of his study, Giorgio would come home from wherever he was, Irish visitors to Paris would turn up. Elizabeth Curran, the daughter of Joyce's Dublin friend Constantine Curran, was a frequent guest. Needless to say, Nora, a Joyce if not a Joycean, did not make any of her food if she could buy it and was a steady patron of Richaud's and Rumpelmeyer's, expensive Parisian pastry shops.[35]

When Miss Weaver came, the tea ritual went onto a higher plane. "Earth knows which side her bread is buttered," Joyce had observed in his notes for *Ulysses* (*Earth* being his equivalent for Molly, and by extension, Nora). Nora liked Miss Weaver very much and once bought her a fine handbag, which Miss Weaver always treasured. But Nora nonetheless regarded a Weaver visit as a command performance and was glad when it was over. Miss Weaver would appear on the dot of four. Tea was served with the finest linen napkins, the choicest cakes, and the most interesting literary guests who could be summoned. The Joyces rarely, if ever, took Miss Weaver out to dinner in Paris. Miss Weaver too was not at ease on these visits. She would sit on the edge of her chair and reply to "Mr. Joyce" only with a "Yes, Mr. Joyce" or "No, Mr. Joyce."[36]

Those settled years, from 1925 to 1931, gave Nora her only real chance to display her skills as hostess and homemaker. Maria Jolas observed that the household was always spotless. The finest compliment of all came from the admiring McGreevy. In those years, he said, "the domesticities ran on wheels for [Joyce]" and he was free to dedicate himself to the work with which he was obsessed.

One reason for Joyce's eagerness to please Miss Weaver in those years was her reaction to his new book. She had written to him, politely but honestly, in February 1929:

> I do not care much for the output from your Wholesale Safety Pun Factory nor for the darknesses and unintelligibilities of your deliberately-entangled language systems. It seems to me you are wasting your genius.[37]

Shyly, the good woman added that she was probably wrong. She did not want to discourage him. She came to Paris personally to assure him of her unqualified support in whatever he chose to write. Miss Weaver had no idea of the emotional role she played in Joyce's life. Nora neither could nor would play mother to his writing. Miss Weaver's disapproval was so intolerable, however, that Joyce felt quite ill until she withdrew it. Nora knew perfectly well what Joyce was attempting. *Finnegans Wake* was written in a new language so obscure that Joyce had sent a glossary to Miss Weaver so that she could understand merely the first page. Nora asked Sylvia Beach worriedly if Jim were not making things difficult for himself in writing the way he did.[38]

Joyce composed the book by writing on large cards on a table. He would reach to the chair beside him and pick up a card of a particular color, hold it close to his eyes, and write. "What are you doing with all those cards?" Nora would ask, to which he answered, "Trying to create a masterpiece."[39]

In 1929 he published one of the more accessible parts of *Work in Progress,* the fable of the Ondt and the Gracehoper. The Ondt — the ant, or plodder — was a caricature of Wyndham Lewis, to whom Joyce had taken a dislike. The identity of the sprightly Gracehoper, "always jigging ajog, hoppy on akkant of his joyicity," was hardly a mystery.[40]

Joyicity was in short supply one afternoon at the Square Robiac when Nora wanted to go out by herself and Joyce wanted her to accompany him on an errand. Nora telephoned McGreevy to come and be her stand-in. (Because of his eyes, Joyce could not get around by himself.) She had an invitation to an afternoon party at the Ritz for which she had bought a new hat. She was not going to sacrifice her afternoon for Joyce's sake.

When McGreevy arrived, Nora tried to make her escape, but Joyce kept calling her back on one pretext or another. Finally she told him in exasperation, "For heaven's sake, Jim, let me go to my party and you mind your Ondts and Gracehopers till I get back." She then swept off in her finery.[41]

Mary Colum, fond as she was of Nora, disapproved of her extravagance on costly clothes, especially on hats — a sign, Mary thought, of the corrupting influence of Miss Weaver's money.[42] Nora did spend exuberantly. She did not like to be even one year out of style. On their holiday to Ostend and Waterloo, for example, the couture houses having decreed "the sporting look" for daytime, Nora outfitted herself in the then-fashionable beige, although she did nothing more athletic than watch Joyce skip stones on a beach.

By 1928 Nora had totally transformed her appearance. She had her long hair fashionably shingled and marcelled. As "separates" had come into vogue, for herself and for Lucia (whom she never allowed to do her own shopping) Nora bought skirts and long waistless tops, with which they wore costume jewelry. In 1927 when fashion dictated polka dots, Nora chose a spotted skirt and tunic top, in which she was photographed by Berenice Abbott, assistant to the American Dadaist Man Ray.

Miss Abbott thought Nora was beautiful and loved her voice. She took excellent portraits of all three: Lucia, in a long cardigan and blouse with an Eton collar, and Joyce himself, posed like a matinée idol, in white jacket and bow tie, with his hands clasped on a raised knee. Once again among family portraits, Nora's was the most successful because she so openly revealed herself to the camera.[43]

Joyce, satisfied to be seen to be keeping his wife and daughter in the latest styles, had not surrendered his nostalgia for the kind of clothes Nora had worn when he met her. Meeting the sculptor Brancusi, he found they got along well after discovering that they both deplored modern feminine fashions.[44]

Joyce's own interest in the symbolic importance of clothes bordered on the superstitious. He had begun, he joked in a letter to Miss Weaver, to dress to ward off blindness. In other words, he had assembled his costume in the colors of gray, black, and green, and he described it to her in detail. Because of his poor sight, he had begun dictating the letters he wrote Miss Weaver, with the result that these grew not only longer but more familiar. Exceedingly formal with Miss Weaver in person, he began to sound in letters like a boy writing home from boarding school, or like the Nora of 1904 writing to him.

> So I had a jacket made in Munich of a green stuff I bought in Salzburg and the moment I got back to Paris I bought a pair of black and grey shoes and a grey shirt; and I had a pair of grey trousers and I found a black tie and I advertised for a pair of green braces and Lucia gave me a grey silk handkerchief and the girl [the maid] found a black sombrero and that completed the picture.[45]

Immortalizing your enemies does not mean forgiving them. More than two decades after he had last laid eyes on his old rival, Vincent Cosgrave, and paid off his old score by naming Cosgrave "Lynch" both in *A Portrait* and in *Ulysses*, Joyce was still nursing a grievance about whatever had passed between Cosgrave and Nora in 1904. He was not displeased to learn, sometime after September 1926, that Cosgrave had been found drowned in the Thames. In dealing with Cosgrave as Lynch in *Ulysses*, Joyce had Stephen Dedalus darkly predict that Lynch would kill himself as Judas had done.[46]

The only friend who knew how Cosgrave had shattered Joyce's trust in Nora came to visit the Square Robiac in November 1927. J. F. Byrne had not seen Joyce since the famous day at 7 Eccles Street in 1909, and he had not seen Nora since 1904 when he had encouraged Joyce to elope with her. Nora and Joyce had invited Byrne to Paris, met him at the train, took him to the opera, and introduced him to their friends. During the visit Joyce told Byrne of Cosgrave's fate.[47] Joyce took care, Byrne noted, to deliver the news "in the presence and audition of Nora." Byrne knew very well how much Joyce wanted Nora to hear of the sorry end of her old admirer, but she did not give him the satisfaction of a reaction.

The Joyces persuaded Byrne to extend his visit, Joyce writing to Byrne's wife, as if she were his mother, to ask if Byrne might stay a few days longer. When Byrne returned to Ireland, the Joyces loaded him with gifts and with copies of Joyce's work, as well as a gramophone record of Joyce's readings from the "Anna Livia Plurabelle" section of *Work in Progress* and *Ulysses* for Joyce's father. They put him on the train and said they hoped he would visit them again. Then Joyce sat down and wrote out of the other side of his mouth to Miss Weaver:

> The latest Irishman to ring my bell is "Cranly" of the *Portrait* etc! The "Lynch", he tells me, of the *Portrait* and *Ulysses* was fished up out of the Thames some months ago. He seems to have come from Ireland to see me, has never been on the continent before, can't speak any French, has seen nothing in Paris and returns to Ireland after a stay of three days.[48]

Years later, after Joyce's death, when this letter was published, Byrne was livid. He had not "rung Joyce's bell," he fumed; he had been expressly invited, and the Joyces had been (he thought) graciously hospitable. Joyce, he said, never could resist the chance to prove himself a "smart-Alec." To Byrne, the crowning insult was that, contrary to Joyce's statement to Miss Weaver, it had not been he, Byrne, who told Joyce about Cosgrave but the other way round.[49]

By 1926 when he drowned at the age of 48, Cosgrave was beyond question a failure. He had squandered the legacy from his mother and was living in rooms in the Bloomsbury district of London. He never took his medical degree and the death certificate pathetically gave his occupation as "former medical student." Yet there was no evidence that he had taken his own life. His body was found on the Bermondsey bank of the Thames in September 1926 after a night of violent storms; he may have drowned himself, but he may have fallen in, possibly while drunk, or even been pushed. The coroner delivered an open verdict.[50]

Nora made her own use of Byrne's visit. She offered to take Byrne shopping, to save him from being cheated, she said, but while they were out, she took advantage of their privacy to confess, "There is only one fly in the amber of my happiness." Byrne politely pretended not to understand what she meant. Nora pressed, "Don't you know what it is?"

Byrne spared her feelings by answering obliquely. Had she ever talked to Jim about it? Nora said no. (The following dialogue, taken from Byrne's memoirs, is not to be taken literally. Joyce's Irish friends were, in many ways, as inventive as he was; as his fame grew, so too did the pivotal importance of what they could remember saying to him.) Thus Byrne's recollection:

> Nora, . . . whatever may have been the case in years gone by, I am certain that now Jim would not have the slightest objection to doing what you want. I'll ask him about it this very night.[51]

Byrne said he later put the question to Joyce, "who assented warmly." However, Joyce did not remove the fly from the amber of Nora's happiness for four more years — and then only for reasons of his own. That

Nora herself could not tell Joyce that she wanted to be a married woman shows what a sensitive issue it was between them.

Whatever Joyce's objections to marriage, they did not include his former sweeping aversion to the Catholic Church. In April 1928 Joyce consented to serve as godfather at the Catholic baptism of the infant daughter of Ford Madox Ford. The man who would not pray at his dying mother's bedside consented to stand beside the font and assist the removal of the devil from a baby girl. Joyce said he did it "as an act of friendliness," although he supposed she could remove it herself.[52]

After the ceremony, Joyce and Nora accepted the loan of Ford's house in Toulon for a spring holiday.

In 1928 Tom McGreevy introduced a new Irish member to the Joyce circle. He was Samuel Beckett, a twenty-three-year-old scholar from Trinity College, Dublin, who had recently come to the École Normale. A tall, gaunt, and broodingly silent young man, Beckett warmed to McGreevy's spirited conversation, and he soon found himself in thrall to Joyce as translator and general literary factotum. Beckett's biographer, Deirdre Bair, maintains that Joyce was happy to have an upper-middle-class Irish Protestant as an unpaid helper, especially one who soon idolized him to the point of imitation.[53] Beckett revered Joyce as a mentor, a rebel, a fellow Irish explorer into new ways of using language. He also responded, in a way that is easy for later generations to overlook, to Joyce's severe handicap. Joyce, semi-blind and suffering the constant itching, burning, and throbbing of eye pain, was a pathetic figure; people wanted to help him carry on the work he felt he had to do. Beckett loyally went to the Joyces' flat every day. Yet he was under no illusion that the attachment would be reciprocated. To Beckett, as to McGreevy, Joyce had confided, "I don't love anybody but my family."

Beckett, like McGreevy, also enjoyed Nora's company, and liked the Irish atmosphere she had created in her home and the authority with which she ruled the family. (It is interesting to see how, in Beckett's novel *Molloy*, the word *chambermaid* floats about the hero's mind, associated with sexual initiation.)[54]

Another new element in their lives was Nora's ill health. In the spring of 1928 Nora for the first time in many years complained of feeling unwell.[55] Joyce was poorly too: his weight had dropped to eight stone (112 pounds), and he tried to regain the weight by stuffing himself with the candy he and Nora both loved — Turkish delight, toffees, and cream sweets. It was the summer that Lucia was in Salzburg, and, taking the Gilberts for company, they left Paris on a marathon swing that took them through Frankfurt, Munich, and Strasbourg, ending up back on the French coast at Le Havre. The Gilberts enjoyed their role as the Joyces' traveling companions but never adopted their style of life. They always stayed in cheaper hotels, meeting Nora and Joyce at their grander establishments for meals and excursions.

They all stayed in Salzburg six weeks. For Lucia Nora brought the piano music for Brahms's *Lieder*. Lucia was worried to observe her mother's state of health.[56] While there, they met Stanislaus and his bride, who, after a three-year engagement, had married on August 13. The meeting was very much that of the great author with his young brother. The two couples met only twice during the visit and on both occasions at lunches with many people present. Lucia entertained the group with a little dance. Nora and Joyce hardly spoke to Nelly, the new Mrs. Joyce.[57] The cool reception must have been a bitter experience for Stanislaus. His years of sacrifice were so ignored that he was obliged to order his own copies of installments of Joyce's new work from Sylvia Beach's shop, where he had an account. Added to the insult was Stanislaus's utter disgust at what he read. He could see no merit whatsoever in *Work in Progress*.

At this family reunion in 1928, Giorgio was conspicuous by his absence. Joyce had taken care to explain this in advance, twice writing to Stanislaus that his son was in the Pyrenees. He did not say with whom.[58] In fact, Giorgio was with Helen at the Kastors' family villa, Cauterets, in southwestern France. His affair with Helen showed no signs of abating. In fact, the odd couple seemed genuinely in love. The previous November Helen had become officially separated from Leon Fleischman, winning an *ordonnance de non-conciliation* from her local *mairie*.[59] By this time the Joyces were so distressed by the liaison that they had broken off relations with Helen and did not speak to her if they passed her in the street.[60]

Their worries took a new direction, however, when Nora underwent a gynecological examination and was found to have a tumor. An operation was urgently recommended. Nora flatly refused to consider it. Nothing Joyce could say would persuade her. Distraught, Joyce looked around for friends who might have some influence on his wife, and his distress was so great that he even turned to Helen Fleischman for help.

Nora's diagnosis had come from a new young woman doctor to whom both Joyce and Nora had entrusted themselves upon Sylvia Beach's advice. Dr. Thérèse Fontaine was thirty-one and beautiful, a feminist and a member of a distinguished scientific family. (That Joyce should have accepted Dr. Fontaine so readily is yet another sign of the comfort he found in being looked after by strong women.) For Nora, Dr. Fontaine was a welcome change from the stuffy kind of male gynecologist whom Molly Bloom ridicules in *Ulysses*.

The prospect of Nora's operation frightened the whole family. Nora had refused for months to see a doctor, saying that one patient in the family was enough. It was obvious to them all that she might have cancer, but Dr. Fontaine held out the possibility that a slight operation (probably a dilation and curettage), followed by radium treatment, might be sufficient. Nora duly went into a clinic in Neuilly, and Joyce went in with her. On the day of her admission, Joyce kept a lunch date with H. G. Wells. Wells had just sent Joyce the perceptive and subsequently famous letter about his obsession with lavatories and obscenity.* Joyce was looking forward to the conversation; he found the British writer friendly, but he himself could not rise to the occasion because he was too upset.[61]

After the operation Joyce telephoned Miss Weaver (he was an intrepid user of the long-distance telephone service from which many others still shied). He also wrote cheerfully to Valery Larbaud and Signora Nebbia, "We go home in a day or so and then, after 15 days auto-vaccine treatment return here for 4 days more radium."[62]

Sylvia Beach had had different news from her friend Dr. Fontaine. In her car she drove Nora and Joyce back to the Square Robiac, but as soon as she returned to her bookshop she wrote grimly to Harriet Weaver. There was a distinct possibility that the disease would return — in six months or a few years' time.

The truth was that if the cancer had spread, Nora's life could not be saved, unless, of course, some new cure were discovered in the meantime. Neither of the spinsters, as they exchanged worries, could see how their Mr. Joyce could continue living, let along writing, without his Nora. They pledged each other to protect Joyce from facing the possibility of Nora's death for as long as possible. In one of the many letters that flew between them back and forth across the Channel during those weeks, Harriet Weaver promised Sylvia,

> I will certainly say nothing whatever to Mr. Joyce of such a possibility. I am sure it is far far better that he should know nothing whatever about it, but that he should believe that the trouble was completely cured, once and for

---

* Wells wrote to Joyce on November 23, 1928, to explain why he saw Joyce's experimental way of writing as a "dead end":
> You began Catholic, that is to say you began with a system of values in stark opposition to reality. Your mental existence is obsessed by a monstrous system of contradictions. You really believe in chastity, purity and the personal God and that is why you are always breaking out in cries of cunt, shit and hell. As I don't believe in these things except as quite provisional values my mind has never been shocked to outcries by the existence of waterclosets and menstrual bandages — and undeserved misfortunes. And while you were brought up under the delusion of political suppression I was brought up under the delusion of political responsibility. It seems a fine thing to you to defy and break up. To me not in the least.

all. If it does come, it would be far far better for the truth to dawn upon him gradually and not a moment before it was necessary. Does Giorgio know of the possibility? I hope not.[63]

The two women took some consolation in Giorgio's attentiveness; Miss Weaver allowed that he was really a very nice boy, although somewhat spoilt.[64]

In January Joyce wrote Miss Weaver cheerful news. Three doctors had pronounced Nora cured; the radium treatment had worked, and his wife's was one of the swiftest and most successful recoveries in the history of the disease (whose name no one ever mentioned).[65]

Joyce was entirely wrong. Miss Weaver already had contradictory information from Dr. Fontaine via Sylvia Beach: malignant cells were still present. Nora would have to return to hospital for a full hysterectomy (or, as they guardedly described it, "a much more serious operation"). But they kept the secret to themselves. Dr. Fontaine did not tell Joyce for about three weeks. Then all sides conspired to keep the truth from Nora. Giorgio, Miss Weaver, Sylvia, Stuart Gilbert — all were sworn to secrecy. Even Stanislaus in Trieste was asked not to mention the subject in his letters in case Nora read them. Joyce, who as husband needed to give his consent for the operation, hesitated to do so. Even when he had talked himself into it and finally broken the news to Nora, Joyce managed to postpone the operation until after February 2, his birthday ("to cheer his wife," Miss Weaver concluded). Miss Weaver herself came to Paris to be with Joyce; no mother could have done more. She believed, as she wrote Sylvia, that Mr. Joyce would need her more after the operation than before:[66]

> For after such a serious operation there will be a long weary period in the clinic while the wound is healing and Mr Joyce will not have anything to do whereas now he is distracted with worry.[67]

If Miss Weaver imagined that Joyce would be bored alone at home while Nora lay in hospital on the other side of Paris, she was mistaken. Joyce still could not spend a night alone without Nora at his side. When she re-entered the clinic at Neuilly for the operation on February 5, 1929, he went with her. One consequence of his dependency was the abandonment, by both Nora and Joyce, of any attempt to boycott Helen Fleischman. They needed her. Not only Giorgio but Lucia too moved over to Helen's flat on the rue Huysmans while their parents were in hospital. There, it was as if Joyce were the patient. He moved into a large room next to Nora's. He sat or lay on a couch, with his books around him, and his friends coming to visit every day. Samuel Beckett came daily with the mail. Joyce left the hospital only to buy cigarettes and newspapers and to visit a nearby church, where he would sit silently in the darkness.[68]

Did this manifestation of total adoration and dependency move Nora? Not in the slightest. Every time Jim came into her room, she scolded him. "Go home!" she told him. "Let me recover in peace!" He did not. He remained and suffered wakeful nights listening to "the groaning of the lift mingling with the howling of the blast and the shrieking of the trees," not to mention the groans of the patients and the "frenzied shouts of the French staff."[69]

Within two weeks, however, Nora was ready to come home. She looked much better and had shed some of the excess weight she had put on. Lucia and Giorgio were much relieved. They had really thought their mother was going to die. Helen capably organized the kind of homecoming that Nora would appreciate: a maid in to clean the flat, flowers, and a new china tea set in a rose pattern.[70]

Even in 1929 cancer could be cured. Nora made a complete recovery. But then, as now, the possibility of a recurrence was never far from the mind of the patient or her family. Two years later Joyce was writing to Miss Weaver, "My wife has gone to Dr. Fontaine on one of those periodic visits which make me nervous until she comes back. (No allusions to this, please, when you write.)" The very next day (a sign of the close contact he kept with his patron), he was able to write, "The report is all right, thank goodness, so that's that."[71]

In February 1929 the Joyces began openly to acknowledge Helen Fleischman as part of their family entourage. Their relations with her changed markedly when her French divorce became final and the proprieties could be observed.[72] From then on, she was seen often with them in public, at dinners and at Lucia's dance recitals. By June she was so established as a member of the entourage that she was included in the outing organized by Sylvia and Adrienne to a restaurant in the country to celebrate the French translation of *Ulysses* and the twenty-fifth anniversary of Bloomsday. In a new, light gray suit and clutching a red handbag, Helen thoroughly enjoyed herself. So too did McGreevy and Beckett — too much to suit Joyce and Nora, for the bachelors, the only Irishmen present, drank so much and sang so raucously that they disgraced themselves. The photographs of the *Déjeuner Ulysse* (to which the Paris English-speaking press corps was invited) show Nora looking if she wished she were back in hospital or anywhere but at the Hôtel Léopold, sandwiched between the French journalist Philippe Soupault and Édouard Dujardin, the putative inventor of the stream-of-consciousness technique. The one most at odds with the scene is Lucia. While everyone else looks at the cameraman, Lucia is, as in so many of her photographs, staring off in another direction.

Nora never stayed home from an occasion just because there would be only literary people present. If they felt "stuck" with her, she could not have cared less. If they were Irish, she talked about Ireland. If they were women, she talked clothes and flats. If they were French, she stared straight ahead and said nothing at all. She was often a silent wife but never an invisible one; sometimes Joyce may have wished that she were more silent. One evening at L'Avenue, a restaurant across from the Gare Montparnasse, where Joyce had been summoned to meet Ford Madox Ford, there was an uncomfortable silence between the two men of letters. Nora was exasperated. "Jim," she chided, "what is it all you find to jabber about the nights you're brought home drunk for me to look after? You're dumb as an oyster now, so God help me." [73]

In her teasing she never spared her husband. One night when they were dining with the Hemingways, Joyce marveled at Hemingway's African adventures and worried aloud that perhaps his books were too suburban. "Ah, Jim could do with a spot of that lion-hunting," Nora told Hemingway. The very thought terrified Joyce. He protested that he would be unable to see the lion. Nora replied, "Hemingway'd describe him to you and afterwards you could go up and touch him and smell of him. That's all you'd need." [74]

That summer Nora was subject to fits of weeping. In July Joyce took her to England, a place she always enjoyed. Theirs was a large traveling party, including Lucia, Giorgio and Helen, and Stuart and Moune Gilbert. Their first stop was London, where they spent several weeks, staying at the Euston Hotel, going to Italian restaurants in Soho, and visiting their many friends. These included James Stephens, the Irish writer, and his pretty wife, Cynthia, who lived in Highbury, a suburb of London. The Joyces liked to go out to the Stephenses' on a Sunday and sit in the garden, talking and having tea; Lucia liked the Stephenses' son and daughter, who were also in their early twenties. During that same visit Joyce invited the Irish playwright Sean O'Casey, whom he had never met, to come for a drink at the Euston Hotel. But O'Casey had a heavy cold, and the two of them had a long and excited conversation over the telephone, sure there would be another opportunity to meet. It never came. [75]

Next, the Joyce party moved southwest, to Torquay in Devon, and into its best hotel, the Imperial. Nora was delighted with the place, as was Helen, who loved touring the town and hunting for treasures in antique shops, while Joyce, nattily dressed in a blazer, white trousers, and straw hat, walked around the hills above the town. All would meet for tea at the hotel, then part to dress for dinner, when they would reassemble and dine as a group.

Miss Weaver came to visit them in Torquay, and Joyce thoughtfully negotiated a reduced rate for her with the Imperial Hotel's management so that she would not have to stay, as the Gilberts were, in more modest surroundings. Helen and Giorgio tactfully left for France before she arrived. In the afternoon Stuart Gilbert came over from his boarding house, and the two men worked on Gilbert's study of *Ulysses,* which was to become for many readers an indispensable, if humorless, guide to the difficult book.

Nora was cheered up by the holiday but not by her return to Paris. Her "girl" let her down by getting married. (Complaints about domestic help *chez* Joyce had succeeded the old complaints about shoes.) Besides, Nora had developed an increasing fondness for London. Joyce dubbed it "lotusland." "My wife," he joked to Miss Weaver, has "to be held down from assaulting different types of French civil and uncivil servants and we have to ring a bell every quarter of an hour to stop her from talking about London."[76]

Nora's more serious worry was Lucia. Upon their return Lucia had decided to give up dancing. She was not strong enough, she said, but wept and wept over her lost career. Joyce told Miss Weaver about the "month of tears" when Lucia contemplated the three or four years' hard work she was throwing away.[77] By November nonetheless she had narrowed her sights to teaching and hoped that she might join Margaret Morris, an English modern dancer whose work she admired and who was coming to Paris.

Joyce insisted to Miss Weaver that the decision had been Lucia's, but one friend of Lucia's, Dominique Gillet, believed that Nora and Joyce had decided for her and put a stop to the dancing. Whatever the explanation, the fact was that by late 1929, with Giorgio twenty-four and Lucia twenty-two, the career prospects of both Joyce children had almost vanished.

Joyce liked to boast about their talents but hampered their careers. He marshaled all his friends, Beckett included, to hear Giorgio's singing debut, but Giorgio suffered from paralyzing stage fright and also from a nervous habit, probably related, of clearing his throat. Giorgio was also handicapped by Helen, who did not really want him to succeed. Her wealth, on top of Miss Weaver's, sapped any need he might have had to work for a living and catered to his dandyism. In any case, Giorgio was happy to spend time with friends of his own, including McGreevy and Beckett, both nearer his age than his father's.

Lucia's problem was quite different. She was neglecting her appearance. Her clothes were untidy, and she did not brush her hair. Nora tried the only tactic she knew. She scolded Lucia and compared her unfavorably with other young women of their acquaintance. Lucia argued back. She was nearly as tall as her mother and had large breasts, her mother's strong eyebrows, dark blue eyes, and thick, springy hair.

As if the family's internal psychological pressures were not enough, Joyce by late 1929, through an introduction from Stanislaus, met John

Sullivan, a Franco-Irishman who was resident tenor at the Paris Opera. Sullivan's real name was O'Sullivan, but Joyce persuaded the singer — and all his own followers — to use "Sullivan" instead "for the love of music."[78] In the beginning Joyce passed off his fixation with Sullivan as an extension of his concern for his son's voice. He invited Sullivan to a small concert of Giorgio's and told Miss Weaver that Sullivan, "a great admirer of mine," was going to assist Giorgio's career. But soon it was Joyce who was pushing Sullivan to the point of obsessive adoration. He identified Sullivan not with Giorgio but with himself. Sullivan, he believed, was also an underrecognized genius; soon he claimed that Sullivan was probably the most powerful dramatic tenor alive. He threw himself passionately and bizarrely into a Sullivan publicity campaign. His friends were dragged to Sullivan's performances; Miss Weaver, after a visit to Paris, dutifully commented how exciting it was to visit the Square Robiac because there was always something new to learn about Sullivan's progress. Nora had no use for the whole crusade. When McGreevy came to visit them, Nora whispered to him not to mention the name of Sullivan and to ignore it if Jim did.

It was as if Sullivan had become the son Joyce dreamed of having — a magnificent opera singer who caused him no pangs of rivalry. If Joyce had thrown behind Giorgio a fraction of the energy he devoted to Sullivan over the next few years — the full force of his international literary reputation went into rallying support for Sullivan, wooing critics, wheedling engagements, making all his friends buy tickets — Giorgio might have at least had a modicum of a working professional life. His voice, by all accounts, was splendid, fuller than his father's. But Giorgio, succumbing to despair over his stage fright and cough (for which Arthur Power blamed Nora and Joyce), had embarked upon a more ruinous path. He began to drink heavily — not the white wine to which his bibulous father restricted himself but the far more corrosive whiskey and cognac.

Lucia was in a similar double bind. Her parents were pushing her forward yet holding her back. Joyce and Nora seemed to encourage her dancing. They attended every performance. When in May 1929 Lucia failed to win a prize in a competition at the Bal Bullier, Joyce was enraged. He told Miss Weaver that half the audience had protested the injustice, calling for "l'Irlandaise!" ("the Irish girl"). Stuart Gilbert, like a courtier, told Joyce he agreed absolutely. Lucia would have won, Gilbert said, had it not been for the vogue for "negroid dancing." The performance was the last time Lucia danced in public, and Joyce's disillusion became one of the ingredients leading to her abandonment of her career.

Public appearances did cause Lucia great anxiety. She was immature (Stuart Gilbert said that she had the "inexperience of half her age").[79] Nora and Joyce may have been trying to forestall a breakdown. Yet Joyce had impressed upon her that it was unseemly for women to get on the stage and wave their arms about. He told Lucia, "As long as you know how to walk into a room properly, that is all that matters."[80] (It was an art at which her mother excelled.) In truth, he was quietly pleased that his children did not have to work for a living and could live a life of leisure, quite as if their father were a rich industrialist — which, in a sense he was. By 1928 Joyce had written two-thirds of what was to become *Finnegans Wake*.

Nora soon had new reason to become alarmed about Lucia. Lucia began to have an uncontrollable interest in young men. Sexual liberation was all around Lucia, and she saw herself as "sex-starved."[81] Her brother was traveling around Europe with his mistress, yet she dined almost every night with her parents. Nora tried to find suitable friends, like James Stephens's daughter, but it was difficult. Lucia had not attended school long enough in Paris to be fluent in French or to have developed many French friends. Besides, her father's reputation as the author of obscene books closed to her the doors of many of the bourgeoisie, in England even more than in France.[82]

Lucia was sexually inexperienced but also, unlike her mother at an earlier age, defenseless. She was, as one of her cousins later was to judge, "easy." Ellmann records one affair with an American writer, Alfred Hubbell, that was sexually consummated, but there were many others.[83] One afternoon at the Joyces' Arthur Power was approached by the writer Liam O'Flaherty, who had a triumphant gleam in his eye. "See that girl over there," said O'Flaherty, a womanizer who had considered himself a celebrity ever since the success of his novel *The Informer*. "I'm going to meet her at the Gare du Nord."

"Don't you know who that is?" replied Power, scandalized. "That's Joyce's daughter!"[84]

As she gradually lost control of herself, Lucia became promiscuous and was taken advantage of. Her father turned a blind eye, but her mother did not. Nora gave Lucia a tongue-lashing about her relationship with the American sculptor Alexander Calder.[85] But the relationship that caused the greatest grief to Nora and to Joyce was Lucia's fierce and unrequited passion for Samuel Beckett.

Beckett, born in 1906, was a year older than Lucia, a year younger than Giorgio, and at twenty-four in 1930 seemed unaware that he was devastatingly attractive to women. His charm was quite different from that of James Joyce. Unlike Joyce, Beckett exuded sexuality. His pale green eyes, high cheekbones, and brooding intensity excited women, and his shyness only inspired them to take the initiative. Peggy Guggenheim, who coaxed him into bed a few years later, said that he was in love with her for a few days but that it took her years to get over him. Lucia, who saw Beckett every day when he came to the Square Robiac to work with her father, became deeply infatuated. Beckett sensed that Joyce's daughter was getting the wrong idea when every day she showed him into her father's working room, but he felt he gave her no encouragement. It was inconceivable to him that he stop seeing Joyce.

Work in Progress was expanding Beckett's ideas about the use of language and about writing outside a framework of time. Beckett was one of those enlisted by Joyce to contribute to a series of essays explaining *Work in Progress* to a puzzled world. To those who protested that the *Work* was not in English, Beckett said,

> You cannot complain that this stuff is not written in English. It is not written at all. It is not to be read . . . It is to be looked at and listened to. His writing is not about something. *It is that something itself.*[86]

Beckett also helped with the translation into French of the "Anna Livia Plurabelle" episode of the book. Joyce finished this episode, which many find the most agreeable part of *Finnegans Wake,* early in 1924. He described it to Miss Weaver as a "chattering dialogue across the river [Liffey] by two washerwomen who as night falls become a tree and a stone. The river is named Anna Liffey."[87]

It was a passage that Nora loved to hear Joyce read aloud. In the only recording of his voice, Joyce chose this passage to read, along with one from the "Aeolus" episode of *Ulysses,* and he conveys the voice of the washerwomen washing the dirty linen of life in the river of life, the Liffey, Anna Livia herself, and gossiping about her in cadences and phrases that could well have been Nora's own:

O
tell me all about
Anna Livia! I want to hear all
about Anna Livia. Well, you know Anna Livia? Yes, of course, we all know
Anna Livia. Tell me all. Tell me now. You'll die when you hear. Well, you
know, when the old cheb went futt and did what you know. Yes, I know,
go on. Wash quit and don't be dabbling. Tuck up your sleeves and loosen
your talktapes. And don't butt me — hike! — when you bend. Or whatever
it was they threed to make out he thried to two in the Fiendish park. He's
an awful old reppe. Look at the shirt of him! Look at the dirt of it! He has
all my water black on me. And it steeping and stuping since this time last
wik. How many goes is it I wonder I washed it? I know by heart the places
he likes to saale, duddurty devil! Scorching my hand and starving my famine
to make his private linen public.[88]

How far was Anna Nora? Joyce's language in *Finnegans Wake* is so convoluted and strewn with fragmented biographical references that it is easy to find almost anything in it. The correlations are not nearly as obvious as those between Molly Bloom and Nora. As a woman Anna Livia is described as being very small, much smaller than her husband, H. C. Earwicker, but she is also a river and a bird. Not a seabird but a hen.

Yet in many ways she is more Nora than Molly could ever be. Anna Livia has lived through all the stages of womanhood, reaching disillusioned old age, and has worn herself out looking after her family. Some of the physical correlations with Nora are close. Anna Livia is both beautiful and ugly. She has or had red hair; she has it marcel waved.

The *Wake* scholar Margot Norris has pointed out how Anna loves clothes ("I am so exquisitely pleased about the loveleavest dress I have") and new shoes, her "goodiest shoeshoes." (Joyce in 1904 addressed Nora as Miss Goody Two-Shoes.) She worries about her increasing weight, like a river filling with stones "getting hoovier . . . fullends a twelve stone hoovier," shields her sensitive skin from the sun, or puts cosmetics on it.

Anna, by Norris's feminist interpretation, is lonely and can only restore her pride by being sexually desired by a man. The sexuality has gone out of her marriage (such as it is — Anna trapped Earwicker into wedlock after long cohabitation), but she is a strong, loving, and dutiful nurse to her elderly, invalid husband. She forgives him his past transgressions and his brutal and eccentric sexual practices. More vigorous and mobile than he, she pulls him up and out into life. "Rise up, man of the hooths, you have slept so long." She leads him by the hand, fusses over his clothes, and speaks to him as if he were a child: "And stand up tall! I want to see you looking fine for me."[89]

Beckett was not blameless in the matter of Lucia. He saw his literary future jeopardized by the unwanted attentions of the daughter of his idol. He allowed himself to be drawn into a family group of six — Helen and Giorgio, Nora and Joyce, and himself and Lucia. In fact, he was seen so often in Lucia's company that Paris literary gossip had them engaged. Beckett, for example, formed part of the family group on two important occasions: Giorgio's singing debut on April 25, 1929, and the dance competition in May that Lucia narrowly lost. As she shimmered in her silver fish costume, she had the pleasure of knowing that Beckett's piercing pale eyes were upon her.

Beckett was diverted by Lucia, who chattered volubly on many subjects, but he had no sexual interest in her whatsoever. He was, says his biographer, emotionally retarded. Not until he was twenty-three did he begin to take an interest in women; at the time of Lucia's infatuation, he was in love with a German-Jewish cousin. Yet before long he formed the suspicion, and confided to Kay Boyle, that Joyce's daughter was going mad.[90]

In May 1930, while her parents were in Switzerland, Lucia invited

Beckett to lunch at an Italian restaurant. She was expecting a magical private occasion and perhaps a proposal. But he, insultingly, brought a male friend along for protection. Lucia, although well dressed, behaved very strangely. She hardly ate, then suddenly and wordlessly got up from the table and moved out the door before the end of the meal. The symptoms were of schizophrenia, not of a broken heart, but Beckett finally felt he had to speak directly to her. He told Lucia in plain words that he was not romantically interested in her and that he came to their home every day as her father's helper, no more.

Lucia was distraught. Nora, when she returned from Switzerland, was furious. She blamed Beckett for leading the girl on in order to ingratiate himself with Joyce. Nora rounded upon Joyce and told him that his daughter's affections had been trifled with. Joyce (who, absorbed in his book, may not have noticed before) accepted his role as the outraged father. He delivered the message. Beckett's visits were to cease; he was persona non grata at Square Robiac.

McGreevy tried to console Beckett. In time, McGreevy told him, Joyce would have to face Lucia's instability. When he did, he would recognize that Beckett had behaved honorably. McGreevy was right, and Joyce and Beckett were eventually reconciled. But Joyce did not live long enough to appreciate that Beckett was to be one of the most loyal friends Lucia would have until the end of her days.

The break with Beckett was just one of the tremors that marked the close of their only period of real family life. Events would force them to leave the Square Robiac. Nora, describing those years to a Swiss friend, Jacques Mercanton, said wistfully, in a French as fractured as Anna Livia's English, *"Nous étaient si gais!"*[91]

15

Legitimate Interests

WITHIN A YEAR there were two Joyce weddings, one in Paris, one in London. If the first had not taken place — Giorgio to Helen on December 10, 1930 — the second — James to Nora on July 4, 1931 — would not have been necessary.

In March 1930 Harriet Weaver was astonished to learn that Joyce was thinking of giving up his flat in Paris and moving to London. His reason, he said, was economy. The pound had dropped; his money did not go far enough in Paris. Besides, he added, piling reason upon reason as he always did, his eyes were too bad for him to continue working. There was no point remaining in Paris if he could not write. He would give up the Square Robiac flat when the lease came due for renewal in May.[1]

Soon, however, Joyce revealed his real intention. He wanted to marry Nora, in England, under English law, and needed to establish English domicile to do it. Could their mutual solicitors, the firm of Monro Saw, look into what was involved? The request, according to Miss Weaver's biographers, almost floored Fred Monro, who had thought he was inured to shocks on the Joyce front.[2] Dutifully, however, he set about investigating the marriage and nationality laws of England, France, and prewar Austria.

The pressure to marry clearly had not come from Monro Saw. Nor had it come from Nora. Over the years Joyce had resisted her wish to marry — in 1904, in 1910 (when her sisters-in-law had raised the question), and in 1927, when Byrne visited.[3] Joyce had not even offered Nora marriage when her life was in danger from cancer. He clearly thought any ceremony superfluous; he believed himself to be as married as any-body else.

But Helen Fleischman did not. By 1930, after the three-year process of getting a French divorce was finally completed, she had decided to marry Giorgio and to try to have a child. But she did not want one by a man who was illegitimate and did not even have a true claim on his family name. Helen insisted, possibly on the advice of her younger brother, Robert Kastor, that Nora and Joyce should marry if she was to have a baby.[4] She was adamant on the point.

Before then Helen had not been bothered by the Joyces' irregular sta-tus. One day Giorgio had burst into the flat where he was a semiperma-nent resident and said in great distress, "I've just learned the most terrible thing! My parents aren't married!" Helen was amused that the irony of the situation escaped him. (Giorgio's total lack of humor, a quality he inherited from neither parent, may have come from his cultural rootless-ness.)[5] In any event, Giorgio's bastardy scarcely bothered Helen. Ap-proaching middle age and with a child of her own, she considered, when she took up with the Joyces' young son, that her own child-bearing days were over.

When she and Giorgio began to talk of marriage, however, it became clear, as Joyce delicately sounded out Helen's views, that Joyce very much wanted descendants who would carry on his family name. If they were not planning a family, he argued, there was no reason to marry. He con-fessed to Padraic and Mary Colum, when telling them in 1930 of the impending marriage, that "I hope they will give me a grandchild soon."[6]

Nora took the opposite view. She was utterly opposed to the match. On a primitive level, she was jealous of Helen, who outclassed her in style and sophistication, and whose company Joyce too clearly enjoyed. He was always livelier when Helen was in the room. But Nora, with her good judgment of character, could also see that the marriage was un-likely to last. Helen was unstable; she was too old for Giorgio and too rich. Maria Jolas later said, "He was practically — I don't like to use the word 'gigolo' — but he was absolutely at the beck and call of this spoiled, attractive, rich woman."[7] Others were not so reticent; Lucia, with her imperfect English, referred to Helen as the gigolo. Their reactions to Helen, on a small scale, were those that greeted Wallis Simpson a few years later: that she was a social-climbing American divorcée over-whelming a naive European with her elegance and gaiety. One difference, however, was that, unlike Mrs. Simpson, Helen had money.

But Joyce had begun, like Peachum in *The Beggar's Opera,* to see how he might turn the unsuitable match to his advantage. He had not, since John Quinn died, had a really vigorous representative on the New York scene, an environment entirely alien to him. The solid financial connec-tions of the Kastor family might be enlisted to help him secure what he most desired: a legal, copyright-protected American edition of *Ulysses,* from which he could derive the revenues appropriate to his long years of labor. In no social sense was Joyce a snob. He meant it when he said, as he frequently did, that he had never met a boring person. Rank did not impress him in itself, but in every city where he lived he was ever alert to how wealth and influence could help him reach his goals, and he was shameless in pursuing his interest once he had decided where it lay.[8]

Accordingly, Joyce took steps to accede to Helen's wishes. All during 1930 preparations for his own wedding proceeded in tandem with his son's. Also at the same time — Joyce may have been unaware how steadily he was moving himself into the protective embrace of Helen Fleischman and Robert Kastor — he began to cut his ties with Sylvia Beach.

In the same letter in which he began to talk of a move to London, Joyce confided to Miss Weaver that he was having trouble with the "rue de l'Odéon" — that is, with Sylvia and Adrienne. Sylvia blamed the tension on his Sullivan mania but also on his continual demands for royalties on successive editions of *Ulysses.* But as he had been making these demands for years, Joyce said airily, the real source of the difficulty must lie somewhere else.[9] It certainly did. Giorgio and Helen, pushed by Padraic and Mary Colum, and possibly by Robert Kastor, were telling him and Nora that Shakespeare and Company was no longer a fitting publisher for James Joyce. A world-famous author, they said, in effect, should cut free from the shabby, scatty, aging American Girl Abroad and the dusty bookshop that was more *poste restante* than publishing house.

Besides, Joyce's family had long and wrongly believed that Sylvia was making a lot of money out of *Ulysses* and not giving Joyce his due.[10] There was another reason why Joyce was susceptible to such arguments: by the spring of 1930 he had a new devoted servant, and a much more capable one than Sylvia. He was Paul Léon, a wealthy Russian-Jewish émigré, a lawyer, philosopher, and sociologist who had fled to Paris in 1918. Léon and his wife, Lucie, had known Helen when she was married to Leon Fleischman and become acquainted when Joyce wanted to learn Russian. The Léons' apartment on the rue Casimir-Périer was near the Joyces', just across the Place des Invalides from the Square Robiac. Eager and unpaid, Léon worked with Joyce daily and dealt with all his correspondence in meticulous if somewhat unidiomatic English. It was a highly professional and time-consuming service that Sylvia, stuck behind the cash register at 12 rue de l'Odéon, could not match. Nor could she match Léon's selfless gratitude for the sheer privilege of being allowed to observe Joyce's mind in operation.

Léon and his wife, along with the architectural historian Sigfried Giedion and his wife, the art critic Carola Giedion-Welcker, from Zurich, completed the new circle that both protected and isolated Joyce in the 1930s. They differed from the bohemian friends of the early 1920s by their blend of professional success, practical competence, and unstinting devotion. They also, with the possible exception of Eugene Jolas, drank less.

Nora had adapted herself to the new crowd. Their intellectuality did not faze her. She frequently went to the opera with Maria Jolas. She talked fashion with Lucie Léon (who was later, as Lucie Noël, a fashion writer for the *New York Herald Tribune*), and Moune Gilbert was a close personal friend. Only Carola Giedion-Welcker seemed to look down upon Nora, explaining the phenomenon of Nora to her daughter as "that little bit of Ireland Joyce always had to have with him."[11] Sylvia Beach, although she did not realize it, was on the verge of expulsion from the magic circle. Joyce, in 1930 and 1931, relied upon her and her shop for cash and practical assistance but had given the publication of *Work in Progress* to the Jolases' *transition,* not to Shakespeare and Company.

In the spring of 1930 Joyce told Sylvia nothing of his marriage plans, not even that he was contemplating a move to England. As he explained to Miss Weaver, Sylvia "knows nothing of my motives."[12] Miss Weaver, however, did; they were to legitimize his children under English law. He and Nora were still British subjects and remained so until the end of their lives.

A new English Legitimacy Act in 1926 had brought England in line with the Continent in allowing the legitimation of bastards when their parents married — provided that the father was domiciled in England or Wales at the date of the marriage. (Scotland had, and has, its own marriage laws.) To give Giorgio and Lucia legitimate status, therefore, Joyce had to make, or pretend to make, England his home. Joyce had persuaded the authorities in Trieste, when his two children were born, to certify them both as legitimate, but he had no wedding certificate with which to back up this claim. Also, Monro Saw had explained to him that it would be far easier for Nora to inherit from his estate if he established domicile in England and were properly married under English law. Hence an English marriage was doubly desirable.[13]

Nora's views on Joyce's plan to make her a legally wedded wife are not known. It is known that she did not want to break up their home at the Square Robiac. Happily for her, new plans of Joyce's in the late spring of 1930 postponed that disagreeable task. Joyce changed his mind about moving to London and decided instead to go to Zurich to try a new eye doctor. Harriet Weaver was relieved. She had feared that the Joyces were coming straight to London to marry before all the legal ramifications had been explored. Although Joyce's regular eye doctor in Paris, Dr. Borsch, had died, Miss Weaver was happy to learn that the Giedions had directed him to Dr. Alfred Vogt, a brilliant Swiss specialist whose reputation gave hope of putting an end to Joyce's recurring compound afflictions of cataracts, iritis, and calcification.

It was Nora's first visit to Zurich with money. With Giorgio and Joyce she checked into the St. Gotthard, one of the finest hotels in the city. She began to look up old friends and settled in for a long stay. Giorgio wired Helen to join them; he informed Helen that he too would be required in Zurich for some time as he had to be with his mother.[14] Lucia remained behind in Paris, in Helen's flat. (It was the time of the crisis with Beckett.)

Helen was taking great care to ingratiate herself with her future mother-in-law. In March, although she was crossing the Atlantic on the *Aquitania* at the time, she had sent a radiogram of good wishes on Nora's forty-sixth birthday — a grand gesture that pleased Nora very much, particularly since no one else but Joyce had remembered the day. Helen had great respect too for Nora's sharp tongue, although at times it made her laugh. When she and Nora had sat in Zurich and contemplated what they saw as the unattractiveness of the populace, Nora had remarked that when God created the human race, he must have made the Swiss first and just been practicing.[15]

Nora soon had Helen working for her as a stenographer. Dr. Vogt had performed an operation on Joyce's left eye for tertiary cataract; it was the first of two projected operations from which he optimistically (and accurately, as it turned out) hoped to restore to Joyce a measure of practical vision. Yet Joyce was such a celebrity by that time that any eye operation was news. In the Joyces' hotel suite at the St. Gotthard, the telephone rang constantly with inquiries from the press on the prognosis for Joyce's sight. Also, Miss Weaver wanted full medical reports.

Nora delegated these chores of responding to Helen, instructing Helen to explain to Miss Weaver that she herself had not written on the details of her husband's operation because she was a poor letter writer, because she was busy visiting Joyce at the clinic, and because, with so many old friends in Zurich, she had a great many social engagements.[16] Joyce found plenty of use for his son's mistress as a stenographer; confined for a month in his hotel, he was at his peak as a manipulator of women. Helen had to take long dictated messages to Sylvia Beach, sent via Lucia, about organizing free tickets for the press for a forthcoming performance by Sullivan in Paris (the man from *The Times* was to have four seats in the stalls, and so forth). She also had to copy Vogt's full medical report on the operation for Miss Weaver and to convey instructions on errands Joyce wanted Miss Weaver to perform: she was to buy and send him certain books, including a guide to Wales; to see a film of John McCormack's; to cut out all the press notices and send them to Zurich. Helen carried out her assignments cheerfully and efficiently. Like many American women of her time, regardless of rank, she typed very well.

When Helen returned to Paris with Giorgio, however, her duties fell to Nora. Nora had to spend a whole afternoon reading aloud *Samson the Nazarite,* by Vladimir Jabotinsky, the book sent by Miss Weaver as Joyce had requested. And she assumed the burden of the Weaver correspondence. By this stage in her life, Nora could write a gracious letter:

> My husband left the clinic on Wednesday. Giorgio has gone back to Paris
> . . . thank goodness the room in the hotel is very big and there are many
> quiet streets where he can walk . . . People are kind to him at the clinic,
> reducing the price without being asked and declining all tips and Professor
> Vogt himself refuses to accept any fee either for his attendance or the oper-
> ation.[17]

Nora also reported that Dr. Vogt had prescribed temporary glasses so that Joyce could return to Paris and be spared any more hotel bills in Zurich.[18]

Released from Zurich at last, they made their way to London. They arrived after the cancellation of John Sullivan's appearance singing Romeo at Covent Garden on June 20 — an unexplained cancellation that only deepened Joyce's conviction that there was a conspiracy against the Irish tenor as he believed there was against him. (However, on the occasion of Sullivan's only performance at the Royal Opera House, his debut in 1927, London critics were far from sharing Joyce's opinion about the greatest voice in the world.) Joyce called on Monro Saw and had the requirements for legitimization of the children explained to him, whereupon he and Nora took themselves to the Welsh seaside resort of Llandudno and spent a month at its Grand Hotel. They summoned friends to join them and enjoyed themselves in spite of the Welsh weather. Nora bought postcards, showing rough seas crashing onto the promenade, and wrote on the back, "It is raining Welsh cats and dogs."[19]

They returned to Paris earlier than usual to find the city, from their point of view, deserted, so they left again. "Paris was intolerable so we came here," Nora wrote to Miss Weaver from Étretat.[20] Giorgio and Helen were there at Les Golf Hôtels, near the camp where Helen's son David, then twelve, was spending the summer. So was Robert Kastor, Helen's brother.

Kastor, a New York stockbroker and Harvard graduate, listened with incredulity to Joyce's story of trying to stop the piracy of *Ulysses* in the United States and said he would have a word with his friend Bennett Cerf of Random House.[21]

When they did return to Paris for a second time, Nora resumed housekeeping, looked for a maid, and with her own hands provided a hefty tea every day for the troops of men who came to help Joyce translate "Anna Livia Plurabelle." But Joyce would not let her settle in. After his talk with Monro Saw, he was now fixed upon returning to London and getting married. On September 30 he informed the landlord that they were giving up their Square Robiac lease the following April.[22]

"My present plan," he told Miss Weaver on October 30, 1930, "is to have the ceremonies take place over the water."[23] He did not say when, nor specify what ceremonies he had in mind. Secrecy was uppermost in his mind. As if she did not already understand the need for it, Joyce spelled out for Miss Weaver that she was not to show anything concerning his marriage to the young American writer Herbert Gorman, who was preparing his authorized biography. "Do you keep any of my letters?" he asked Miss Weaver disingenuously. If she did, she had his approval to show Gorman all the others.

Joyce knew full well that Miss Weaver treasured every scrap of his correspondence and that in providing her with such a detailed version of the events of his private life, he was, in effect, writing his own biography. By the same calculation and acutely aware by 1930 of the durability of the written traces left by a famous man, he did not entrust his thoughts to paper when he really wanted something kept secret. Twice, when it was necessary to discuss actual legal details about the marriage, Miss Weaver traveled over to Paris so that they would not have to write.

While Joyce was preparing his legal maneuvers, Nora had begun a fresh campaign to stop the marriage of Giorgio and Helen. The good temper of their stay in Zurich had faded as the prospect of the wedding loomed. The strain in the family and the antagonism between the two women was so great that five times Joyce had to cancel the important return visit to Zurich so that Dr. Vogt could make a decision about the second operation. Joyce portrayed himself to Miss Weaver as the calm center of the storm:

> Excuse me for not having written but I have had a dreadful amount of worry all this last month about my son's projected marriage about which my wife is extremely pessimistic and concerning which I have to proceed like an aged old rat walking over broken bottles.[24]

When they did return to Zurich at the end of November, Nora was able to write to Miss Weaver, "My husband saw the doctor who says the eye has made progress."[25] Her good news, however, was followed by a letter from Joyce admitting to his patron that Giorgio had moved into Mrs. Fleischman's and "my wife and the bride-elect are not on speaking terms."[26]

Sylvia Beach little knew how the wedding would change her own life. She had written home about it, somewhat gushingly,

> Giorgio is marrying Mrs. Fleischman . . . a charming woman, older than him, and an old friend of the family and especially of Giorgio's . . . she is not much older than him.[27]

On December 9, 1930, the day before the ceremony, Joyce walked into Shakespeare and Company and presented Sylvia with a legal-looking piece of paper with a seal on it and asked her to sign. It was, eight years and eleven editions after the first publication, a contract for *Ulysses*, setting conditions for its publication in the future; Joyce was to own all rights in the book. Sylvia, however, as original publisher, would retain the right to name her own price for surrendering her own interests in the book if another publisher (that is, an American one) wanted to take it over.

Later, preparing her memoirs, Sylvia noticed the juxtaposition of the two events:

> Joyce and I never had a sign of a contract between us: he wouldn't hear of such a thing and I didn't insist until his son got married — and then he asked me to draw up a contract.[28]

Joyce did not give his reasons, she said, but after a time she discerned them: "Some of his friends in New York were urging him to cut loose from silly ties."

Giorgio and Helen were married the next day. The witnesses were Tom McGreevy and George Bodington, an English barrister from a highly fashionable Anglo-French law firm. Nora put her feelings to one side and, with Joyce, attended the civil ceremony at the *mairie* of the sixth arrondissement. But she and Joyce must have kept their identities secret. The *acte de mariage* records the parents of both the bride and the groom as deceased, even though all four were alive at the time.[29]

Considering the high quality of their legal advice and the presence of their lawyer at the wedding, the errors cannot have been accidental. They may have seemed the simplest way to forestall embarrassing questions about Giorgio's legitimacy. More important, the wedding certificates contained a potentially serious omission, failing to mention that Helen and Giorgio had signed a marriage contract — an agreement that presumably poteced Helen's money if the marriage broke up. Nine quick strokes of the pen, however, corrected the problem and Helen became Mrs. George Joyce.[30]

Miss Weaver soon had her full report. Joyce pronounced the mother-in-law problem solved — "My wife and daughter-in-law are at present on the most affectionate terms" — and indeed "my daughter-in-law" (never "Helen") became one of the characters to inhabit his letters.[31]

Joyce himself was increasingly fond of Helen. Bright, energetic, and devoted, she was a hard-working member of the *Work in Progress* team. Tirelessly, she read out long extracts from the *Encyclopaedia Britannica* from which Joyce gleaned place and street names to work into his text. "Aren't I the best helper you've ever had, Babbo?" she asked.[32]

Now Joyce had to keep his end of the bargain by marrying Nora. He discussed his situation in detail with Helen, who assured him that in the United States his relationship to Nora would be recognized as a common-law marriage, just as Joyce understood that it was in Scotland. Even in Ireland, he said, there was recognition of marriage "by habit and repute."[33]

One way and another, Joyce spent at least three years in the labyrinth of international family law. He watched and waited while Helen struggled from 1927 to 1929 to get a French divorce from her American marriage of 1916, and then began his own efforts to extricate himself and Nora from the ambiguity of their own situation. One sign of how hard Joyce worked on these problems is a book that has survived from his Paris library: a fourteen-hundred-page study, in Latin, of 497 decisions taken by ecclesiastical courts on questions of marriage, divorce, and incest. The book is by far the most heavily used of all the books in his collection. Joyce vehemently underlined many cases in which the Congregation of the Holy Office in Rome considered whether Catholic judges were permitted to dissolve the bonds of matrimony of couples joined under civil law.[34]

These years of research and anxiety were not wasted. They found a place in the mosaic of *Finnegans Wake,* the story of the universal family. Richard Brown, in *Joyce and Sexuality,* has observed that the married couple in *Finnegans Wake* are not clearly married in any strict sense. The name that Humphrey Chimpden Earwicker (HCE) gives his wife when he defends the legitimacy of their relationship is not his own but a variant of Anna Livia Plurabelle (ALP), Brown points out, "alerting us to the fact that though apparently married HCE and ALP do not share a surname." Earwicker admits, Brown observes, that "he harboured her [Anna Livia] when feme sole" (*feme sole* is an English legal term for an unmarried woman) and that she is "jackticktating." (Nora — as well as Joyce — was conscious from October 8, 1904, until her wedding day in 1931 of being guilty of "jactitation" — the false claim to be married.)[35]

One of the *Wake*'s best-known lines — "woo me, win me, wed me, ah weary me!" — has been interpreted as a cry of disenchantment, perhaps Joyce's, perhaps Nora's, with the ritual of love. Yet the line, taken in its context, contains a trace of the book's incest theme and of another of Joyce's preoccupations during those years; it suggests a father's wish that his beautiful daughter escape the whole sordid business:

> she is so pretty, truth to tell, wildwood's eyes and primarose hair, quietly, all the woods so wild, in mauves of moss and daphnedews, how all so still she lay, neath of the whitethorn, child of tree, like some losthappy leaf, like blowing flower stilled, as fain would she anon, for soon again 'twill be, win me, woo me, wed me, ah weary me![36]

In fact, the tangled language of the book suggests not only a writer trying to fashion a new language, but a father desperately trying to create a world in which his daughter's flying-apart thoughts would seem normal.

Nora's thoughts of marriage were concentrated on Lucia, and Lucia shared the anxiety. Turning twenty-three in 1930, she was becoming desperate to find a husband. Her parents had each other. Giorgio had Helen. Her lack of success she laid to the defects in her beauty, particularly the cast in her eye, with its fateful echo of her father's affliction, which dominated their lives. Nora had never pretended that the squint made no difference. McAlmon remembered an entire evening spent discussing it with the Joyces. Nora said, "It's twice as noticeable when she's nervous." [37]

Joyce encouraged her to seek a cure and wrote to consult a medical specialist in Barcelona. Lucia finally decided upon an operation in Paris, performed by Dr. Borsch's successor. Joyce pronounced himself well satisfied with the result. The problem, which had troubled her all her life, was corrected in twenty minutes, he reported with satisfaction to Miss Weaver: "She came home in a taxi and in a week both her eyes were straight." [38]

It was another example of his powers of wishful thinking, as later photographs show. That she had gone to such an effort to transform her appearance made her failure with Beckett all the more discouraging.

When Nora said that Lucia needed a nice young husband, she did not mean Beckett. She could spot the flaws in all the males who were presenting themselves. Beckett was clearly, at that time, not the marrying kind; McGreevy was a classic, pious Irish bachelor. McAlmon actually proposed to Lucia (having divorced Bryher, his British heiress wife), but he was homosexual. [39] Calder, of whom Lucia had been very fond, was engaged to be married to a grandniece of Henry James. And Alfred Hubbell, Calder's successor in the autumn of 1930, was a married man. [40]

Mary Colum gave Joyce some advice. (He admired her business sense, although he mocked her behind her back for earning more than her husband did — largely, he said, by accepting publishers' advances for books she did not write.) [41] Mary told Joyce to arrange a marriage, with a dowry, as the French did, in order to stop Lucia's chasing after unsuitable young men. As they talked about Lucia, Nora objected to the detachment in Joyce's voice. "You have never really known your daughter," she said. "Allow me to say that I was present at her conception," Joyce retorted, as if that counterbalanced all the time that Nora had spent bringing up the difficult child. [42]

In those two years Lucia's frail personality suffered shock after shock. She struggled to reorient herself. She had given up her dancing and was fitfully trying to develop a new talent, drawing. She had been rejected by

Beckett. She had lost her adored brother, the only continuous thread with her childhood. Upon all this came the devastating blow of learning that she was illegitimate. Far more than Giorgio, she was shattered. They both understandably had been misled by all the fuss Nora and Joyce made every year about celebrating their "anniversary." On the twenty-fifth anniversary of October 8, 1904, Sylvia Beach had even thrown a big party to celebrate. To Lucia the news was unbelievable and degrading.

Nora's sharp tongue did not spare her daughter. Losing her temper with Lucia one day, she shouted "You bastard!" at her.[43] "And who made me one?" Lucia shouted back. She then refused to speak to Nora for several days. Her father, therefore, bore the brunt of Lucia's fury. "If I am a bastard, who made me one?" she kept demanding over and over. Her frenzy made Joyce all the more determined to marry Nora.[44]

From the far side of the sexual revolution, it is easy to underestimate Lucia's distress — and Helen's — at being associated with illegitimacy. The legal status of illegitimate children was greatly inferior to that of legitimate children. The social stigma was considerable, and the practical difficulties real. Giorgio, for example, risked being conscripted into the French army if he could not prove himself British. The Italian army had already tried to claim him.

Living in sin — by standards prevailing in England and America — was also scandalous. It was precisely to escape the prying eyes and vicious tongues of Main Street that free-thinking Americans had fled to Paris.

Until 1931 Nora and Joyce believed they had concealed their nonmarriage very well. Everyone from Trieste to London took them as married. When in February 1931 Giorgio and Helen returned from their honeymoon in Germany, where they had visited some of Helen's relations, Nora and Joyce were still unmarried, but there was no reason to believe that this skeleton in the family cupboard would be revealed.

They had reckoned without Dublin. Their unwed elopement in 1904 was legend in literary circles as soon as their ship left the North Wall, and the subsequent scandal of *Ulysses* in the 1920s during the emergence of a new, highly puritanical Catholic nation had placed it in popular mythology.

In March 1931 the American readers of the monthly magazine the *Catholic World* were treated to a scathing exposé of Joyce's immorality. The author, Michael Lennon, was a Dublin judge whose company Joyce had much enjoyed one evening in Paris. The two men had sat up talking until the small hours. When he left, Lennon had asked for and received a signed copy of *Ulysses;* he later wrote to inquire if his wife might call on the Joyces when passing through Paris. The pleasure of the meeting did nothing to blunt his pen.

For his highly shockable American Catholic readers, many of them of Irish descent, Lennon related how the twenty-two-year-old James Joyce, sullen, moody, and weary of Dublin, went to teach in Trieste in 1904,

> taking with him a west of Ireland girl, a waitress in a Dublin restaurant. To her he did not grant the protection of even a civil marriage, protesting, at the time, that he would have no church ceremony or priest's work over his alliance, but that he would deal fairly by the girl, a promise which he has kept. She must have been strangely infatuated with him to enter into such a partnership. She has borne him a girl and a boy, each of whom is now over twenty years of age. Since this household went to France, Joyce, I am informed, has contracted a civil marriage, no doubt in the interests of his children, as French testamentary law makes the position of the mistress and of the spurious off-spring one of very great insecurity.[45]

Lennon's information on the civil marriage was four months premature but accurate — so accurate, in fact, as to suggest that he had questioned Joyce about his marital status as they dined together and elicited some genuine information that he then decided to put to use. The condemnation of the *Catholic World* article was so sweeping that the Colums kept Joyce from seeing a copy for some months, but he was very aware that it was being read in America, possibly even by the Kastor family, whose good opinion he valued.

In March 1931, as the article appeared, Nora had just begun to pack up the family portraits at Square Robiac and put them into storage along with the blue chairs and brocade curtains. She was by now hostile to the whole scheme. She liked London and their friends there; an annual visit and even a flat there would have been very welcome. But she was very reluctant to break up their settled home and routine. She did not think Joyce's health would stand rainy London, nor the fatigue of transplanting himself, and she must also have been uneasy about moving Lucia. Lucia did not want to go either. Her drawing teachers were impressed with her progress; she had begun writing a novel and — in her many friendly moments with her mother — enjoyed going to the fashion houses and sampling perfume in the shops along the rue St.-Honoré.[46]

But there was no stopping Joyce now. Like Lucia, he had been profoundly unsettled by Giorgio's marriage. He suffered from acute insomnia.[47] Like a child tipping over the whole game board because he is losing, Joyce took savage delight in breaking up his home. He wallowed in his self-inflicted homelessness; he described himself as selecting possessions to give to friends and going to live in a barrel. Sending Miss Weaver early drafts of *Work in Progress,* he described them as "some rubbish found in a sack, that lay in the house where Joyce leaves."[48] The *lares* and *penates* of the Joyces — the portraits, the piano, and the sofas — went to Giorgio and Helen. Let theirs be the new center of the family.

As in many ways it was. The hoped-for baby was already on its way, due early in 1932. Also, in Parisian social circles Helen and Giorgio had very much become, as Helen's formal cards announced, "Mr and Mrs George Joyce." (She insisted that his friends call him the less foreign-sounding "George," even though she never called him anything but Giorgio.) They were photographed by Man Ray, and their pose as a couple shows Helen girlish in size and manner, and Giorgio, tall and grave; the difference in their ages is not striking.

Depressed, Joyce began spending more wildly than ever, and to Monro Saw's dismay, he realized another one hundred pounds of his capital, bringing the total consumed out of Miss Weaver's original twelve thousand pounds to two thousand pounds. Fred Monro wrote to Joyce and advised him to live within his income.[49]

But Nora's standard of living had improved, now that Giorgio had entered what *Finnegans Wake* calls, in a merciless pun, "the ricecourse of marrimoney." She began to ride around Paris in a motorcar for the first time. Adolph Kastor had given the newlyweds a new Buick as a wedding present. Giorgio learned to drive and took his parents out for rides in the country, and Helen lent Nora the chauffeur to take her on errands in town.[50]

In April 1931 Nora and Joyce, with Lucia in tow, arrived in London. Harriet Weaver regarded the marriage scheme as madness; Joyce ought instead to have been returning to Zurich for a check-up with Dr. Vogt. Eyes were more important than marital status, she thought. But she soon was busy helping them settle into the small flat that, at her instigation, the Kensington estate agents Marsh and Parsons had found for them at 28b Campden Grove, on Campden Hill in Kensington.

The flat, unfurnished, was one of the dreariest the Joyces ever had. They made a stab at furnishing it but as usual did not buy enough. The flat itself was part of a terrace of charmless Victorian brick houses that were never meant to be divided into apartments. Its large, drafty windows looked out onto a stretch of the London Underground's Circle Line where trains surface briefly between Kensington High Street and Notting Hill Gate.

Still, Nora liked many aspects of life in London. She always liked her world within walking distance. She loved the food department of Barker's, the Harrods of Kensington, so much that Joyce dubbed the flat "Chicken from Barker's." But the kitchen was small. They quickly found a favorite restaurant nearby, Slater's, on Kensington High Street, and Joyce enjoyed strolling through nearby Kensington Gardens. For Nora there was the quiet satisfaction of speaking her native language and feeling herself somehow at home. She and Joyce were British in many ways, after all, and strongly averse, their friends apart, to many things Irish.

Their income was in sterling, and they relied on the strong English sense of duty of their benefactress and the reliable uprightness of her lawyers, Monro Saw, to keep their own chaotic lives in order.

It was particularly because of Miss Weaver's Englishness that Joyce hoped she would like his new book. Stuart Gilbert was the only Englishman among Joyce's literary retinue in Paris, and he had observed that, as he prepared his obscure new work, Joyce was surrounded by helpers — Russian, French, Irish, and American — who enjoyed the idea of breaking up the English language. Miss Weaver was, on the other hand, a guardian of the mother tongue, and it was vital to Joyce that she sanction his experiments.

Miss Weaver, in truth, had come to enjoy unraveling the verbal puzzles he sent her. He did not realize, however, that she searched them, with maternal anxiety, for signs of melancholy and distress. The following draft passage from *Work in Progress,* say her biographers, did not reassure her:

> What's my muffinstuffinaches for thease times? To weat: Breath and bother and whatarcurss. Then breath more bother and more whatarcurss. Then no breath no bother but worrrworrums. And Shim shallave shome.[51]

Joyce chose their wedding day: July 4, his father's birthday. He and Nora told almost no one in advance, not even Padraic Colum, to whom Joyce wrote two days before. Exceptions were Robert and Sylvia Lynd, Irish literary friends who lived in Hampstead. Joyce had known them since the days when he was struggling to get *Dubliners* published. Robert Lynd was also an ardent Irish nationalist — he had been a good friend of Roger Casement's and had written, in the midst of the First World War, a pamphlet arguing that if the English lost the war and were forced to speak German, they would only be suffering the fate of the Irish.[52] A night or two before the wedding Nora and Joyce took a taxi to Hampstead to have supper with the Lynds.

With such friends Joyce and Nora could discuss freely their hopes to keep the wedding ceremony secret. Joyce had taken the precaution of marrying by license — a procedure requiring only one day's notice — by which he hoped to avoid the attention of the press. As he had eloquently written to Harriet Weaver

> If twenty-six years ago I did not want a clerk with a pen behind his ear or a priest in his nightshirt to interfere in my matrimonium, I certainly do not now want a score of journalists with pencils in their hands intruding where they are not wanted . . .[53]

If Joyce had chosen to marry in a small English town (as Beckett was to do, for similar reasons, many years later), his stratagem might have worked. But in London reporters regularly scanned the notice of marriage books in the main register offices and on July 3 immediately saw that they had a story.

When the Joyces rose on their wedding day, a Saturday, they found that, under the headline "Author to Wed" and the subheading "Mr. James Joyce, Who Wrote 'Ulysses,' " the *Daily Mirror* had blown their cover:

> Notice has been given at a London register office of the forthcoming marriage of Mr. James Augustine Aloysius Joyce, aged forty-nine, of Campdengrove, W.
>
> The bride's name has been given as Nora Joseph Barnacle, aged forty-seven, of the same address.
>
> Mr. Joyce is the author of "Ulysses." According to "Who's Who," he was married in 1904 to Miss Nora Barnacle, of Galway.
>
> Mr. Joyce's solicitor stated yesterday: "For testamentary reasons it was thought well that the partners should be married according to English law."

The phrase "testamentary reasons" — high-sounding and vague — had been chosen by Joyce himself to shake inquiries off.[54] There was nothing to do but go through with the ceremony.

For her wedding day, although in her Catholic heart she knew it was no such thing, Nora put on the latest fashion, which had taken women away from the strident, tomboyish twenties to the more clinging feminine stance of the thirties. She wore a slim, dark, hip-wrapped coat, with a swirling, knee-length skirt that set off her legs. With it she wore her favorite fox fur, sleek court shoes, and a cloche hat pulled down so low that all Lionel Monro, Fred Monro's son, who had joined the firm and who accompanied his father to the ceremony, could see were "very dark eyebrows."[55] With their lawyers, the Joyces walked into the Kensington Registry on Marloes Road.

The dry little ritual, which normally takes fifteen minutes, was prolonged when Joyce, in spite of all Monro Saw's careful legal preparation, made a last desperate effort to pretend that they had been married in Trieste. His wife, he said, had given a false name.

Even under stress, Joyce did not invent false names lightly. The name Nora was said to have given was Gretta Greene, a play on the name of the border town in Scotland to which young lovers from England eloped to marry without the consent of their parents. But the name was a double pun: Gretta was the name Joyce had given Nora in "The Dead"; Greene carried satisfying associations with Ireland. (Until his death, Joyce continued to record in *Who's Who* that he had been married in 1904, but there has been no evidence to support his claim.)[56]

The pretense nearly ruined the day. If they were already married, the registrar pointed out with infuriating logic, he could not marry them. They would have to get divorced. Yet Fred Monro came prepared; he produced legal chapter and verse to argue that whatever marriage Joyce was speaking of could have no validity in English law.[57] The registrar duly went ahead and married James Joyce, bachelor, and Nora Barnacle, spinster, of the same address. Fred Monro must have winced when he saw what Joyce had put down as his profession: not "author" but "independent means." Mr. Monro had fought a losing battle to dissuade Harriet Weaver from putting Joyce in a position to make that claim.

When she emerged and saw the press waiting for them, Nora observed drily to Jim, "All London knows you're here." That afternoon the *London Evening Standard* carried the photograph that has served as the Joyces' official wedding portrait: Nora, clutching her hat and hiding her face but looking pleased, Joyce, looking appalled, and Mr. Lionel Monro exasperated. Joyce learned that one of the journalists involved was Irish. "I expected he would be," he said, with great bitterness.[58]

Their ordeal by press had just begun. With Sunday newspapers to fill, a full flock of Fleet Street paparazzi camped outside 28 Campden Grove, from which the only street exit is by the front door. Besieged, Joyce desperately telephoned the Monro Saw offices and found that Fred Monro had gone to the country for the weekend. He felt deserted and abandoned. Even Miss Weaver was in Guildford. To her he wrote a petulant letter:

> You will have seen the papers by now so it is useless to write. For two entire days the street was haunted by prowling islanders, one fellow even waiting till midnight. My wife wanted to leave today but I had not the means to do it. You were away and Miss Beach is running up and down France. I could get no advice as to how to handle the situation for Mr Monro was out of town all day Friday and all day Saturday after the event. So was his partner. Finally at about 8.30 pm I found him at his house and he telephoned the press association as you know. Please say nothing of all this to anyone till I see you. The street before this house [?] was occupied by a squad of cameramen . . .[59]

Joyce exaggerated. They were not prisoners. He and Nora managed to get out for a meal at Slater's, where Arthur Power, who was in London, tracked them down. Power said with amusement, "That's an interesting story I read in the papers." Nora giggled. "I felt such a fool," she said. But Joyce glowered and advised Power coldly to see his solicitors if he wanted more information.

Joyce, while complaining about the press attention, strove to get copies of any of the news accounts he had missed. He might have had reason to complain of the coverage he did not get. London's serious papers took no notice: there was nothing in *The Times* or the *Daily Telegraph*. The *New York Times,* however, obliged with a mention in its section on marriages, deaths, and births, headlined "Reweds Wife for Testamentary

Reasons." When she heard him on the subject later that year, Sylvia Beach thought he was delighted with all the fuss. She and Adrienne, who had not been informed in advance of the wedding, had hardly been "running up and down France" but rather were at their small cottage on Adrienne's parents' farm in Savoy.

News from London was not long in crossing the Irish Sea. In Galway, Annie Barnacle's neighbors in Bowling Green confronted her with the scandalous story about Nora and Jim. Annie Barnacle was furious and threatened to sue anyone who dared to suggest that Nora had not been married in 1904. The wedding certificate, she insisted, had been destroyed in Trieste during the war. But her neighbors believed the London papers instead, and Mrs. Barnacle vented her wrath in letters to Nora in London.[60]

For Nora, the civil marriage helped a little bit. Even if the civil ceremony made no difference to her standing in the eyes of the Church, she had always been self-conscious about her irregular status and was quietly relieved to acquire the recognition of the law.[61] In no way did the press publicity make the Joyces reclusive. On July 15, they went back to the Lynds' for an evening garden party to celebrate the new moon with a crowd of politicians and writers, among them Goronwy Rees and Douglas Jay. Joyce was the star attraction as he sat at the piano and sang beautifully.

Moira, one of the Lynd daughters, felt sorry for Joyce "because he could hardly see what he was eating, even though wearing two pairs of spectacles." She pitied also "the two silent grown-up children, whose feelings Joyce's wish for secrecy was presumably intended to spare."[62]

Hers is the only account that places Giorgio in London at the time of his parents' wedding. It is certain that Helen, then two months into a pregnancy proving difficult, did not accompany him.

That same month Nora and James Joyce were guests at a formal literary lunch given by the chairman of Putnam, the publisher. The occasion produced a vivid description of the physical contrast between the two Joyces as it appeared that summer of their marriage, for among the guests was the brilliant diarist Harold Nicolson, husband of Vita Sackville-West. Nicolson found himself in a drawing room with the other guests, nervously waiting for the celebrity to arrive. There was a sound on the staircase. All rose:

> Mrs. Joyce enters followed by her husband. A young-looking woman with the remains of beauty and an Irish accent so marked that she might have been a Belgian. Well dressed in the clothes of a young French bourgeoise: an art-nouveau brooch. Joyce himself, aloof and blind, follows her. My first impression is of a slightly bearded spinster: my second is of Willie King [an expert on porcelain] made up like Philip II; my third of some thin little bird,

peeking, crooked, reserved, violent and timid. Little claw hands. So blind that he stares away from one at a tangent, like a very thin owl.

Joyce was an awkward guest. He sharply contradicted the lady at his elbow who jabbered at him in Italian about Italo Svevo. Nicolson tried to draw Joyce into conversation by referring to an incident in the news and asking, "Are you interested in murders?"

"Not," Joyce answered (with, said Nicolson, the gesture of a governess shutting the piano), "not in the very least."

Joyce perked up only when Nicolson said he was going to give a talk on him on the BBC. Nicolson's verdict was: "not a rude man; Joyce manages to hide his dislike of the English in general and of the Literary English in particular. But he is a difficult man to talk to." [63]

After the marriage, Joyce notified Stanislaus and the Colums. To the Colums he made the stilted joke that while the king was signing the Marry-Your-Aunt Bill (the popular name for a new law dropping some of the prohibited categories of marriage to relatives) "he should now sign a Marry-Your-Wife Bill." The English wedding, Joyce told his brother, was necessary "to secure inheritance under the will," and even to Stanislaus he kept up the fiction that he and Nora had been married in Trieste (although he avoided stating it as an absolute fact):

> Having eloped with my present wife in 1904 she with my full connivance gave the name of Miss Gretta Greene which was quite good enough for il Cav. Fabbri who married us and the last gentleman in Europe il conte Dandino who issued the legitimate certificates for the offspring . . .[64]

Joyce lost no time signing the will that provided for his as yet unborn heirs. On August 5, 1931, he left the income for life from his royalties to Nora and thence to his children and their descendants. He left Harriet Weaver all his manuscripts — a recognition of her service to him — and made her his literary executor as well. He gave all his worldly goods to his son, but he gave nothing in the form of bequests, books, or pictures to Lucia — an omission that makes it clear that, although Joyce did not formally recognize Lucia's mental illness until the following year, he could see how unlikely she was to have an independent future. Nora did not make a will.

"Violent outbursts from my wife's family in Galway," as Joyce described them to Miss Weaver, did not prevent Nora's youngest sister, Kathleen, from coming to London for another visit. Kathleen was as mystified as ever about what Nora and Joyce saw in each other: "Nora all go and Jim all stand-still." During the visit, Kathleen heard Nora express herself unequivocally on the subject of sex: "I hate it, Kathleen," Nora said.[65] Kathleen had no way of knowing how much lay behind that very conventional (for those times) wifely complaint to a sister.

It is possible that Nora herself had broken off their sexual relations, if any there were, after her hysterectomy. Lucia Joyce later remembered that her mother was "less sensitive" after her operations. And Maria and Eugene Jolas, who had been close friends of the Joyces since *transition*'s first publication of *Work in Progress* in 1927, also speculated that the Joyces, by the 1930s, had a sexless marriage. Nora had told Maria, "My husband is a saint" — a remark that Eugene Jolas said to his wife could have only one meaning.[66]

Kathleen's presence made four in the small flat. Lucia, already mortified by the wedding publicity, grew jealous of her ebullient aunt, whom Joyce trotted around to the standard tourist attractions, of which he never tired. For Kathleen's benefit, Joyce gave a bravura display of overtipping. On a visit to the theater, Nora said as they went in, "Now don't tip the usher." (Ushers or usherettes in the English theater, unlike their Continental counterparts, were never tipped.) Nonetheless, Joyce gave the usher ten shillings (about $2.50) for showing them to their seats. Nora turned and walked out. It was her only punishment and one that wounded Joyce even if it did not deter him. At a dinner at Kettner's, with Miss Weaver as their guest, Kathleen saw Joyce tip the waiter five pounds. The sum was exactly equivalent to two weeks' rent at their flat. Kathleen could not believe her eyes. Nora could, all too well. "Oh, he's always doing that sort of thing," she said.[67]

Miss Weaver hoped she might succeed where Nora had failed in reforming Joyce. Two bottles of wine at dinner, she thought to herself, were too much. She politely advised Joyce to start each meal with a glass of water and to have another between each glass of wine. But Nora could have told her to save her breath.[68]

By August Nora and Joyce were restless again. They decided to return to Paris for the winter and to resume their English domicile at their Kensington flat in the spring. Lucia, in a fit of impatience, went first, escorted across the Channel by a hotel-keeper friend in Dover (to help her through customs, Joyce said, as if she was not twenty-four).[69] Lucia then bestowed her presence, which was hardly welcome, on Giorgio and Helen. Helen's pregnancy was presenting severe complications. She had an ovarian tumor (possibly a failed twin) that grew as the baby grew, and to avoid a miscarriage, she had to spend almost the whole pregnancy in bed.[70]

Joyce was in a despairing mood. He had no home in Paris in which to install his wife and daughter. He felt persecuted on all sides, particularly by the thought of his empty Kensington flat, whose lease and fire insurance had about five years to run.[71]

For an extravagant man he worried himself to distraction over small sums: without a tenant to sublet his place, he was paying out two pounds ten shillings a week, and the loss grated on his nerves. Scattering puns like arrows to punish all his London tormentors, he dubbed Campden Grove "Campden Grave" and Marsh and Parsons "Mashed Parsnips." The British prime minister Ramsay MacDonald (for devaluing the pound) became "Ramshead MacDullard," and Covent Garden (for failing to appreciate Sullivan) the "Kitchen Garden Opera."[72] He told Stanislaus he had been cheated out of six months' rent on the flat. And he believed he had been defrauded by a Frankfurt newspaper that had mistakenly attributed a story to James Joyce when it was by a Michael Joyce. (Over this matter, Joyce sent thirty-six letters and ten telegrams, and threatened legal action for forgery until Monro Saw advised him he had no case.)[73] Nora tried to cut through his paranoia. As they were having dinner one night in London with Padraic Colum, she said, "Well, Jim, here's a friend." Joyce conceded her point and relaxed.[74]

Back in Paris, Nora was busier than ever. She visited Helen every day, their hostility vanished under the circumstances (and she was relieved that Helen did not accept her brothers' suggestion that she return to New York to see an American gynecologist). Helen lent her the chauffeur to take her flat-hunting, but when he fell ill, Nora had to use a taxi. Nora finally acceded to Joyce's suggestion that they take a furnished flat in Passy because, as he wrote Miss Weaver, his wife was exhausted "from trying to please everybody."[75] Joyce himself deluged Miss Weaver with letters, writing to her several times a week, sometimes once a day, showing, once again, an intimacy in correspondence that contrasted with the coolness and reserve that permeated their face-to-face relations.

For Joyce marriage was shortly followed by professional divorce from Sylvia Beach. The antagonism between Joyce and his most important publisher of *Ulysses* had worsened in May when Adrienne Monnier wrote Joyce a stinging letter, one she had meant to write for a long time. She accused Joyce of pretending not to be interested in success or money when, she said, he was obsessed with both. She further charged him with exploiting Sylvia ruthlessly to keep his family living in luxury, while she and Sylvia were scrimping to try to make ends meet.

Joyce was wounded, and angry. He denied that there was any truth in her accusations and got Miss Weaver to agree with him — thereby creating a rift between the two women, who had become close friends. Harriet Weaver was not a lesbian. She was a decidedly asexual woman who nonetheless warmed to the safety of women-only relationships. Until 1931 Sylvia was her best friend in the alien territory of Paris, one to whom she granted the rare privilege of using her private name, Josephine. But Miss Weaver believed that Joyce and his work should take precedence over all other interests, and when the choice came, she chose her genius over her friend.

When he returned to Paris in September 1931 Joyce was more determined than ever to secure an American publication of *Ulysses*. A number of offers had begun to come. Mary Colum assured him that an American edition would mean the Nobel Prize. What is more, news had reached him that Samuel Roth in the United States was not only getting away with his pirated edition but had recently printed ten thousand copies. There would be no American buyers left if Roth were not stopped.

The obstacle was Sylvia. Since the previous December, she had been holding a contract giving her the right to name her price for surrendering her rights, and she was not at all eager to do so. She had been taking in about one thousand pounds a year from selling *Ulysses* to American tourists. If they could buy the book at home, she would be forced (Sylvia never lacked for a homey American phrase) to "give up my shop and raise chickens."[76]

Accordingly, Sylvia set what she considered a large but justifiable demand for releasing her rights: twenty-five thousand dollars, a fortune in those days. The size of her demand caused the chief publisher then in the bidding to withdraw his offer. At the same time Sylvia began to receive almost daily visits from Padraic Colum, who argued with her to reduce her demand. Also, she had become, as Miss Weaver never did, a figure of fun *chez* Joyce. Nora came home from the bookshop one day and reported, "Lo and behold! There was Miss Beach nursing a headache and looking like a wild Elektra."[77]

Nora was referring to Sylvia's chronic migraine headaches, which contributed to Joyce's doubts about whether she had the intelligence or the competence to handle his American affairs. He recoiled from her problems, which he detailed in a frank letter to Miss Weaver. In it he allowed himself for the first time to refer openly to Sylvia's lesbianism and revealed that in his canon, suicide, mental illness, and migraine were far more shameful than homosexuality. His reasons for distrusting Sylvia were that

> in spite of her many kindnesses to me and her many charming qualities, of late years she has become an automaton under the influence of her more intelligent partner (in many ways a remarkable and charming woman too) . . . that both are abnormal (which doesn't matter much) but chiefly that Miss Beach is the daughter of a suicide, that her sister has been in an asylum and that she herself suffers periodically from very queer headaches.[78]

For Sylvia, the daily visits from Colum continued. He pressed her to lower her price. With Adrienne's backing, Sylvia refused. She had her contract. That contract, Colum brusquely informed her, was meaningless. She had no ground for demanding anything at all. Hammering home his point, Colum accused Sylvia of selfishness. As she recalled them, his final words to her were: "Ya're standing in Joyce's way!"[79]

Stricken, Sylvia reached for the telephone. Joyce answered. He could have *Ulysses,* she told him. She was surrendering all her rights, without compensation.

But at the end of 1931 family problems were uppermost. Because they both recoiled from the stigma of mental illness, Nora and Joyce refused to have Lucia seen by a psychiatrist. They had lived for many years with suppressed worry about their daughter. Indeed, Joyce's tender poem "A Flower Given My Daughter," written in Trieste when Lucia was six, seems almost prophetic in its perception of the "wonder wild" in the eyes of his child. Lucia had genuine artistic talent. When she became agitated, Nora would suggest that she go and do some of her drawing.[80] Then to boost Lucia's morale, Joyce persuaded her to design elaborate initial letters for the poems in his 1927 collection called *Pomes Penyeach.* Lucia complied, producing letters Joyce thought beautiful. He then contrived to have her paid ten thousand francs, ostensibly from a publisher.

Nora, helpless to stop Joyce from this folly, soon had to help him through a new crisis. Joyce's father, John Joyce, died on December 29, 1931, in a room filled with pictures and newspaper cuttings of the son he had not seen since 1912. Joyce was overwhelmed with guilt. The old man had been begging to see him before he died, and Joyce had never faced the truth that he was too terrified to go back to Ireland. Especially after Lennon's attack in the *Catholic World,* he feared he might be assassinated by a religious fanatic or, like Parnell, have quicklime thrown into his eyes. Yet he had continued to lead his father to believe that he would come home to see him. "I knew he was old. But I thought he would live longer. It is not his death that crushed me so much but self-accusation," Joyce said, pouring out his heart to Harriet Weaver.

In his grief, Joyce explained to Miss Weaver why he so persistently and defiantly threw money to the wind: the characteristic was linked with his creativity, qualities he had inherited entwined from his father. "I got from him his portraits, a waistcoat, a good tenor voice, and an extravagant licentious disposition (out of which, however, the greater part of any talent I may have springs) . . ."[81]

Joyce's remorse was so great that he had to resurrect, in a letter to T. S. Eliot, the old story of Nora and the children being shot at in a railway carriage as a reason for his failure to go to see his father.[82] His friends did what they could to console him. From Galway Nora's uncle Michael Healy traveled to Dublin for the funeral, and Harriet Weaver sent £100 to pay for the expenses of the illness and the funeral.[83] Old John Joyce had reciprocated his son's extravagant affection. He bequeathed none of his small estate of £665 to any of his other children — the widowed Eileen, the sad spinsters Eva and Florrie, the hard-pressed married children, Stanislaus, Charlie, and May — instead he left it all to his favorite son, the author.

When Sylvia surrendered her rights in *Ulysses* she had no idea that, in the words of one of the Kastor family, "Robert Kastor and Bennett Cerf had cooked it all up between them."[84] They had decided on a clever tactic whereby they could be bold where others feared to tread. Cerf (or Serf, as Joyce first spelled it) at Random House had decided to brave the costs of a court test of the book's obscenity. Joyce's former publisher, Viking, dropped out because of the cost. B. W. Huebsch had already bought for Viking, in 1931, the rights to the still untitled *Work in Progress*.

Cerf was interested because he had known Leon Fleischman when Leon was at Boni and Liveright and because he was publishing *A Portrait* and *Dubliners* under his Modern Library imprint. As soon as Sylvia had climbed down, in December 1931, Cerf wrote immediately to the well-known lawyer Morris Ernst and invited him to fight the *Ulysses* case on a contingency basis: nothing if he lost, 10 percent of the royalties from sales if he won.[85] Ernst agreed.

Less than two months into 1932, Joyce's two longed-for results of the Kastor connection had arrived. In late January Robert Kastor arrived at Marseilles with a Random House contract for *Ulysses* in his pocket. On February 15 Helen gave birth to a son, Stephen James Joyce.

Five days later Bennett Cerf arrived in person. At first he offered only a miserly two-hundred-dollar advance on *Ulysses*. Robert Kastor, who outperformed Joyce's literary agent, shamed him into quintupling it and into paying top royalties — 15 percent — as well. Joyce could not resist going round to boast to Sylvia and Adrienne; from then on, he admitted Kastor to that tight circle of people he considered as family.

Sylvia was very bitter. She censored her anger out of the many drafts of her pollyannaish published memoirs, *Shakespeare and Company*, but she felt that she had been deprived of the fruits of a dozen years' labor. Although she had enjoyed a surge of income with each of the eleven editions of *Ulysses* she published, she could not forget the "advances" demanded by the Joyce family on the next edition and their expectation that she would pay for everything, even their medical expenses. Sylvia paid for Nora's hysterectomy.[86]

In later years, Stephen Joyce, arguing on his family's behalf, felt that Sylvia protested too much. Who would ever have heard of Shakespeare and Company had Sylvia not been fortunate enough to latch on to James Joyce?[87] By the time of the Random House deal, the Depression was well under way, and Sylvia's earnings from the book were virtually at an end in any case. What is more, only Kastor and Cerf had been clever enough to plan a strategy for a court challenge of the ban on *Ulysses* in the

United States. The whole moral climate was changing. Prohibition was on its way out. The sufferings of the Depression brought a new realism to replace the naive and xenophobic righteousness of the years following the First World War.

In early 1932, however, all Joyce had was the Random House advance and the hope that the company would win the court battle. He and Nora were more preoccupied for the moment with the birth of their grandson. The event gave them the happiest moments of their later lives, and Joyce wrote one of his most moving poems, "Ecce Puer," linking the loss of his father to the joy and hope of a new Joyce. He even took apart the first line of *Work in Progress* in order to squeeze in a hidden reference to the newest family member. (The Joyce scholar Hugh Kenner has observed that, by inserting the phrase "past Eve and Adam's" in the opening line, which then read "riverrun, past Eve and Adam's," Joyce managed to work in "st Eve an." Kenner also points out that if "past Eve and Adam's" contains "pa" as well as "Stephen," then we have the "Ecce Puer" theme: father dying, grandson born.)[88]

As luck would have it, the Joyce grandson was, and remained, extraordinarily handsome. Strangers stopped to comment on the baby when he was being pushed in his pram.

In New York, Adolph Kastor soon settled a sizable sum on his new grandson, while Helen, in lace and satin bedjacket, holding the baby, was soon pictured in the rotogravure of a bilingual Paris newspaper:

> Mrs. George Joyce, daughter-in-law of the noted Irish author and formerly Miss Castor of New York, with her son, Stephen James Joyce.[89]

The caption gave the baby's father scant credit. It also gave no recognition to the baby's other grandfather, Adolph Kastor. Helen, in any event, was determined that Stephen should be a Catholic, and she enlisted Padraic and Mary Colum to act as godparents and had the baby baptized.[90] The Colums conspired with Helen and Giorgio to keep the ceremony secret, believing Joyce to be positively hostile to the Catholic Church, unaware that he had stood as godfather for Ford Madox Ford's child.

Joyce, on the other hand, was pleased with his grandson's heritage — mixed, like Leopold Bloom's, of Irish and Jewish — and joked that they didn't know whether to baptize or circumcise his grandson, without knowing that the joke was on him. He (and probably Nora) did not learn of the furtive ceremony for several years, but whenever she heard of it Nora would have been pleased. In her later years she worked hard to keep the boy practicing his religion.

For Lucia the strain of Giorgio's impending parenthood was the last straw. On February 2, 1932, Joyce's fiftieth birthday, her sanity collapsed spectacularly: she picked up a chair and hurled it at Nora. Joyce was so upset by the scene that he poured all his grief into a letter to Miss Weaver which was so painful that she destroyed it.[91] When word got around, the common view was that Lucia blamed Nora for breaking up her relationship with Beckett. However, those who knew Lucia well saw the true cause as Giorgio's marriage. It had been a personal catastrophe for her, putting him permanently out of reach. He had always been very hard on her, because she adored him, and, Maria Jolas noticed, "It made her feel that she was of little importance in the family and that only the brother had counted." Iris Stephens, James Stephens's daughter, who had come to know Lucia, felt that her breakdown had been caused by the illegitimacy trauma.[92]

Giorgio, whatever the complex reasons behind the event, lost patience. He believed his sister was mad. He did what Joyce could not; if only to protect his mother, he took Lucia to a private clinic for mental illness, leaving Nora to escort a dismal Joyce to the fiftieth birthday party the Jolases had arranged in his honor.

Nora too feared Lucia was mad. But she could face it if she had to. Her favorite saying was "We must put up with it."[93] Joyce, in contrast, could not accept the possibility. He was so distraught that he barely reacted to the first of Miss Weaver's birthday gifts, the cancellation of his outstanding debt to her. And the second — an offer to find a tenant for the Campden Grove flat — he refused so curtly that Miss Weaver once again scolded herself for having revealed herself to be a meddling busybody. (She went to Paris to apologize to Joyce in person for her lack of tact.)

Lucia stayed in the clinic only a very short time. Joyce would not let her remain, and as she was over twenty-one she could leave whenever she chose. Soon she was back at home and, for the most part, calm. Nora was nonetheless terrified of her from then on.

As spring approached, Joyce and Nora tried to keep to their plan of returning to London. Nora was homesick, Joyce said, for their Kensington flat. They had no alternative but to take Lucia. She was too nervous to stay in a hotel by herself or to try to live with friends; she could not move in with Helen and Giorgio, for their flat now contained Helen's son, the baby, and a nursemaid. Early in April 1932 they said goodbye to Sylvia Beach, packed the hatboxes, trunks, boxes of books, and valises, and left for the boat-train.

The scene — how Nora and Joyce both hated scenes — took place in the Gare du Nord. All the Joyce luggage was piled onto the train, and the porters were filling up the Joyces' reserved compartments when Lucia became hysterical. She said she did not want to leave Paris. She hated England, she cried. And she did not just cry. She howled and howled.

Her strong voice echoed through the station. The three of them, and attendant porters, were paralyzed for forty-five minutes, during which time Lucia could be neither silenced nor budged.[94]

Standing there, with the train about to leave, Nora and Joyce were panicked thrice over. They faced incontrovertible evidence of Lucia's insanity. They feared the press might get wind of a new Joyce scandal. Worst of all, they were threatened, by not returning to England, with losing their claim to English domicile.

Finally, with even the porters joining in the scene, Nora was convinced that Lucia could neither be forced onto the train nor left behind in that condition. All the luggage came off the train. She and Joyce checked into a hotel, and Lucia, at her own insistence, went to the Léons' (and stayed in bed for nine days).

There was to be no London residence for them, even if staying in Paris were to invalidate the legitimacy of the Joyce children — legitimacy being what he aimed at, Joyce wrote in an agonized letter to his lawyers, when he married their mother according to English law.[95]

He asked the lawyers to draw up a codicil to his will to say that if his children's legitimacy were ever disallowed, they should inherit from him on the condition (he almost apologized for insisting upon it) that they assume his surname.[96]

Yet Fred Monro's view was that the name requirement could have been added to a will, as a codicil, even if Joyce had not married.[97]

The lawyer's letter made it sound as if perhaps the whole disastrous marriage adventure had been unnecessary. All Joyce said, however, when the codicil procedure was explained to him, was the dry comment, "It is a pity I did not know that two years ago."[98]

But he did trace the origin of all his subsequent troubles to "the London adventure." Stanislaus had already written to scold him for it. Reviewing all the disasters that followed his marriage, Joyce protested to Miss Weaver that he had acted from the best of intentions. But all he had achieved, he said forlornly, was to disrupt his home and bring misery upon misery into the lives of those he loved.[99]

That was not entirely true. He had made Nora legally Mrs. James Joyce, and he was about to see a legitimate edition of *Ulysses* published in the United States.

PART IV

Anna Livia

I done me best when I was let.
Thinking always if I go all goes . . .

—*Finnegans Wake*

16

Madness in Progress, I

LUCIA'S ILLNESS drove Nora to the breaking point. She blamed Joyce for giving her and Lucia an unbearable life. She was fed up with the tedious obsession with Sullivan, the ludicrous tipping, the drunkenness every night ("tumbling about," she called it),[1] and, above all, the lack of a settled home. One afternoon in May 1932 she announced she was leaving him.

Joyce desperately telephoned Stuart Gilbert and asked him to come right over. Gilbert, seeing no sign of Nora, tried to calm Joyce down by taking him to a matinée and to tea. Together they went back to the hotel, and Gilbert waited while Joyce went up to see if Nora was there. Soon Gilbert was asked to come upstairs. He found Nora alone and packing. "It's all over," she said. "I won't live with him any more." She had no money but she would survive, she told Gilbert, by passing the hat among her friends, the Irish custom that Annie Barnacle had described to her in 1916 and that Joyce had used in *Ulysses*.

Joyce reappeared. He sat in a chair, watching Nora and, so upset that he shed his usual reserve, told Nora in front of Gilbert that he could not look after himself; he needed her. Would she relent if he took a year's lease on a flat? Would she like to go away with him on a trip? Nora's reply was succinct. "I wish you would go drown yourself," she said.[2]

No one else talked to Joyce that way. Nora's brusqueness made her all the more indispensable to him, as did the precision of her jibe. She knew that Joyce knew that death by water was the fate that had claimed his worst enemy, Vincent Cosgrave.

But Nora's break for freedom was doomed. She had no way of supporting herself. When Gilbert telephoned later to see what was happening, it was Nora who answered. "I've given in again," she said. She had tried before and always failed. Eugene Jolas and Paul Léon had also heard her forlorn cry, "I wish I had never met anyone of the name of James Joyce."[3]

As Gilbert's private diaries, in which this scene was recorded, give the date only as May 1932, there is no way of knowing whether Nora's rebellion preceded or followed Joyce's foolhardy effort that month to encourage his daughter to become engaged. Nora was utterly opposed to the engagement: Lucia was in no state to marry. Since the black day at the Gare du Nord the month before, Lucia had had three more hysterical attacks.

Nora lost that battle as well. Paul Léon, as if to prove his boundless devotion to Joyce, talked his wife's brother, Alex Ponisovsky, into proposing to Lucia. Ponisovsky had been escorting Lucia occasionally to dinner and the theater. Léon argued that this had led her to think Ponisovsky's intentions were serious. Ponisovsky agreed, in part perhaps because he was a passive and correct young man, and an admirer of Joyce, to whom he had taught Russian. Lucia accepted him. Joyce gave his consent because he was sure that he could cure Lucia by finding out what she wanted and then giving it to her. And what she wanted, she insisted, was to be married before she turned twenty-five, an event due in July. If she did not, she was convinced, she would never marry. Giorgio sided with Nora. He rushed back from the south of France to tell his father that Lucia was in no condition for such a step. Lucia herself vacillated. She became engaged on a Tuesday, broke it off on Saturday, became re-engaged on Sunday. She spent hours on the telephone. She stormed that she hated all Jews; Ponisovsky was a Jew.[4] Joyce was more concerned that the fiancé was a Russian; Russians of all kinds, he said, gave him the shivers. All that Nora could say in favor of the match was that Ponisovsky was at least good enough for Lucia, unlike some of the men (that is, Beckett and Calder) with whom Lucia had taken up.[5]

To celebrate, or perhaps to cement, the engagement, Joyce gave the couple a party at the Restaurant Drouand near the Opéra. But the festive mood scarcely survived the party. As soon as it was over, Lucia went back to the Léons', lay down on a couch, and stayed there in a catatonic stupor.[6]

The engagement was all the more unrealistic considering that Lucia was under doctor's orders to spend her days lying down near an open window and to get up only for meals. She was under medication, including Veronal and phosphate of lime, to calm her down.[7] In his copious correspondence to Miss Weaver, Joyce never made it clear how he expected Lucia to make the transition from virtual house arrest to married life.

Everybody around the Joyces was shouting advice on what Lucia needed: rest, religion, work. Nora, crushed by the enormity of the problem, was consoled by various visitors who told her stories of cases that were similar, only worse.[8] It is unlikely that in her anxiety she blinded herself, as Joyce did, to the sexual content of Lucia's bizarre behavior.

Joyce prettied it over. Perhaps, he wrote to Miss Weaver, Lucia had done some of the things she was alleged to have done and perhaps some of the young men had, in his words, "unnerved her"; he himself did not give a damn, and all the young men, with the exception of Ponisovsky, were worthless.[9] When Lucia accused all the men around her of seducing her, he responded by banning them all from the house, even the pious McGreevy.

And when in that troubled summer of 1932 an American etymologist hired Lucia to perform some of the translation and office work that friends had thought might prove therapeutic, Joyce angrily believed that the scholar had presumed upon Lucia's innocence by dictating to her stories full of bad language and sexual innuendo — things, he insisted, she could not possibly take in.[10]

It is not the protest that one would expect from the author of "The Ondt and the Gracehoper." Joyce completed the fable, part of *Work in Progress*, in 1929, when Lucia was beginning her own courtship dance. It is modeled on "A Frog He Would A-Wooing Go," and, as Joyce complained about Wagner, it reeks of sex — and in this case of incest (or "insects"). The Gracehoper

> was always making ungraceful overtures to Floh and Luse and Bienie and Vespatilla to play pupa-pupa and pulicy-pulicy and langtennas and pushpy-gyddyum and to commence insects with him, there mouthparts to his orefice and his gambills to there airy processes, even if only in chaste, ameng the everlistings, behold a waspering pot. He would of curse melissciously, by his fore feelhers, flexors, contractors, depressors and extensors, lamely, harry me, marry me, bury me, bind me, till she was puce for shame . . .[11]

But author and father wore different faces.

The betrothal charade ended after Lucia, having moved herself from the Léons' to the Colums', grew even worse. Strong-minded Mary Colum, convinced she could cure Lucia, slept in the same bed with her and pinned their nightdresses together so that Lucia would not escape. She nonetheless escaped during the daytime. She was strong, sly, and capable of lightning-quick disappearances. It was clear that she could not remain at large. Giorgio once again was the agent of her confinement. With Mary Colum (and with Joyce's approval) he tricked Lucia into a taxi, which took her to a *maison de repos* at l'Hay-les-Roses outside Paris. The doctors there recommended that Lucia have some real repose — a regime that banned all telephone calls and contact with either parent.

Once again Lucia discharged herself, as she was still entitled to do, not having been legally certified insane. When she swiftly suffered several more hysterical attacks, however, including one in the middle of a street, she had to go back. The diagnosis of the doctors carried various labels of the day, most of which translate into schizophrenia. The form it took was hebephrenia — overexcited, speeded-up reactions and disjointed thinking. The clinic's doctors joined with the Joyces' own Dr. Fontaine in suggesting that Lucia be placed in solitary confinement, to be observed through a peephole. That was too much for Joyce. Lucia to be left with not even a nurse for company? He decided to countermand the doctors and take her treatment into his own hands, and he enlisted Maria Jolas to help him. Mrs. Jolas was well to the fore as the latest strong woman in Joyce's life. Even more than Sylvia Beach and Harriet Weaver, she idolized Joyce. Unlike them she never made the mistake of crossing him. This appearance of total acquiescence, combined with a strong managerial temperament, enabled her — almost uniquely — to influence him.

The Jolases had been planning to go with their children for a holiday to Feldkirch, a small resort in the Austrian Alps. At Joyce's behest, Mrs. Jolas hired a competent nurse named Mathilde and led Lucia to believe that the nurse was a young woman eager for a holiday in Austria and paying for her trip out of her own savings. Patient and nurse would not live in the Feldkirch hotel where the Jolases were staying but in a chalet nearby, with their own cook. Joyce hoped to see if Lucia would benefit from the nonclinical atmosphere and from the various artistic assignments, mainly continuing with her alphabet designs, that he would set her. He and Nora would follow on at a safe distance — that is, they would stay in Zurich, two and a half hours from Feldkirch. Mrs. Jolas agreed, even though it meant a great intrusion into her own family's summer.[12] She nonetheless quietly believed that Lucia should be left in the clinic.

So did Nora. So did Helen and Giorgio. So, needless to say, did all Lucia's doctors. Even Lucia (whose conversation was, for the most part, rational) declared that her father was pushing her around. None of their objections carried the slightest weight with Joyce.

The atmosphere of drama and crisis had two families in an uproar. Helen and Nora began quarreling again. The Joyces fell out with the Léons, and Lucie Léon with her husband. He, she believed, had been trying to push her brother into a disastrous marriage.[13] Giorgio quarreled with Ponisovsky.

Joyce determined to smuggle Lucia out of the clinic and, with the new nurse, onto the train for Austria. The worry over Lucia had only intensified his drinking. He still abstained during the day, but come dinner time, he would drink white wine, bottle after bottle, until he was oblivious to the cigarette burning his fingers. Eugene Jolas often took him home and helped him to bed, removing the charred ash and paper from his hands.[14]

The night before Joyce and Nora themselves were to leave for Zurich, they were with William Bird in a restaurant in the middle of the Bois de Boulogne. The usual argument started. If he ordered one more bottle, Nora warned him, she would leave. He did, and she did.[15]

Nonetheless, they reached Zurich. "I seem always to be coming back here," Joyce remarked. They checked into the Carlton Élite, still making no economies in their accommodation, even though extracting Lucia from her French clinic had cost ten thousand francs and establishing her, plus nurse, in Feldkirch another four thousand. There was good news from London; the public trustee somehow still held five thousand pounds in unspent capital on Joyce's behalf, ostensibly for his children's education. There was also somber news from Dr. Vogt. By postponing his visit for two years, Joyce had allowed his right eye to calcify beyond saving. To retain any sight in his left eye (the only one really left, Joyce joked), possibly two operations would be necessary.[16]

The news of a possible operation on her father sent Lucia into violent fits of weeping. She said she should come to Zurich to be with her mother. This was enough to impel Nora into the almost unprecedented step of leaving Joyce and going to her daughter.[17] Time and again, when forced to choose between her husband and her children, Nora had chosen (or been clutched by) Jim. This time was different. Lucia had asked for her. Furthermore, Lucia's condition would determine what Nora had to do next. As Joyce explained to his benefactress:

> My wife has gone to see if any plans can be made ahead. She does not think Lucia wants to leave us definitely yet and thinks we should prepare a Paris home. I will tell you more when she comes back.[18]

There was also the worry of Lucia's being in politically turbulent Austria. In Germany the Nazis had emerged as the largest party in the elections of 1932, and Nora was unhappy at having her daughter outside the safety of the Swiss border. Nevertheless, both Joyces strongly wished to prevent Lucia from coming to Zurich. Nora had literally fled when Lucia staged one of what Joyce called her "King Lear scenes."

Left alone in Zurich, Joyce felt abandoned, especially at night, and had his rooms moved down to the ground floor near the courtyard. Nora did talk to him on the telephone, but she could not speak freely, as Lucia stood listening right by her elbow. He overcame some of his nervousness by writing almost daily long and emotional letters to Miss Weaver. His daughter had said, he wrote plaintively, that he should not be left alone and that she wanted to see him too.[19] To Stanislaus, however, Joyce wrote affectedly that Lucia was "summering" in Feldkirch.

Joyce would have accompanied Nora but for an embarrassing problem: he could not leave the hotel without settling the bill, and he needed money from London in order to do it. Because he owed sixty-nine pounds to his solicitors, Monro Saw, he feared the firm might hold back his monthly check, and he wanted far more money than that: he wanted to sell one thousand pounds of stock.[20] For once, Miss Weaver put her foot down. The routine monthly payment would be paid, but under pressure from Monro Saw, she refused to condone further selling. She went so far as to scold him for squandering his money along with neglecting his eyesight.

It was her last major stand against his throwing away his (that is, her) money, to use her bitter phrase, "like a drunken sailor." Joyce reacted by listing all his troubles and the money they were costing him and reminding her that Dr. Vogt had said he needed peace for his eyes' sake. Once again Miss Weaver, like Nora, gave in. She reproached herself for troubling him, approved the release of the money so that he could join his wife and daughter in Feldkirch, and she vowed never to cross his wishes again.[21]

When Joyce reached Feldkirch, he was so relieved to see that Lucia had continued her letter designs that he was able to resume his *Work in Progress,* the next installment of which the Jolases were waiting to publish. Lucia was relieved to see him too. As she wrote to Miss Weaver (in a lucid and charming letter that shows how her parents could cling to the hope of her sanity), she and Giorgio felt that the doctors operated too much on their father. They both were genuinely fond of him, even though he was on occasion hard to get along with.[22]

During those weeks, Lucia did work hard at her illustrated letters. Some were published two months later in an edition of Joyce's *Pomes Penyeach* and two years later as an accompaniment to an excerpt from *Work in Progress* known as "The Mime of Mick, Nick and the Maggies." She also at that time had the good sense formally to break off her engagement. She spent hours in front of the mirror trying on a dress that Helen had given her. Her father thought it was a good sign.

It was not. Maria Jolas joined Dr. Fontaine and Miss Weaver in believing that Lucia suffered from severe mental illness. Nora by then agreed, although she could not say so openly without angering her husband. Joyce tried frantically to breathe life into Lucia's career as a designer of *lettrines.* He pretended that she was, as he saw himself, an unappreciated artist whose brain was afire. He pressed his friends to praise, then to buy her *Chaucer ABC* with her illustrations. When they declined or hesitated, he broke with them. When her "publisher," paid by himself, was late with the proofs, Joyce fumed that he had missed the Christmas market for her book.[23] With all the worry, he lost sleep and weight.

From Feldkirch he and Nora took Lucia and the nurse to the French resort of Vence. They installed themselves in Nice — once again near but not too near. Then it was back to Paris, first to a hotel, then to yet another furnished flat in the rue Galilée, off the Champs-Élysées. To Nora fell the burden of Lucia's care. The girl had the single-mindedness of a psychotic. At any minute she could strike a blow, throw something, or run out the door and disappear. No form of nursing is more exhausting. Joyce closeted himself in his study, working seven hours a day to complete the second section of *Work in Progress.*

Yet Nora needed free time to look for the new flat that Miss Weaver, quite as much as she, wanted them to have. It was essential for Joyce to have his books and papers around him. Nora lit upon the idea of hiring Myrsine Moschos, whom Sylvia Beach had sacked after a row, and who was well acquainted with the Joyce family. With Miss Moschos in the morning and another nurse for three hours in the afternoon, Nora could get at least six hours a day away from Lucia.

Joyce, with his family-mindedness, thought Giorgio ought to help out. He persuaded Giorgio to take Lucia into his home for a week to relieve Nora, but he had counted without Helen. She, not surprisingly, refused. Looking after Lucia was a round-the-clock job, Helen said, and she would have none of it.[24] The general tension was compounded by arguments with the doctors. Joyce was hurt that the doctors were cross with him. No wonder, Nora told him, considering that he had taken the case out of their hands. Their lives were also darkened by new hostility from Sylvia Beach. She was furious about their hiring Miss Moschos. The Joyces, she felt, had taken into their household a discredited employee whom she and Adrienne never wished to see or hear of again in their lives.[25] And the unhappy Lucia was not immune from grievance. She was hurt to find that Helen's son, David Fleischman, was allowed to hold baby Stephen in his arms and she was not.[26]

Joyce marveled at Lucia's ability not only to antagonize the women around her but to set them against each other: Nora against Helen, Helen against the nurses. He considered himself well out of these imbroglios. To Miss Weaver he joked that she would be alarmed to learn that Lucia was thinking of going to London to pay her a visit.

Nora's strength was taxed to its limits. As Lucia's condition deteriorated, so did Joyce's health. While much of the time Lucia was passably well behaved, attending museums with Miss Moschos during the day and dining in sullen silence with her parents in the evening, Joyce became prey to attacks of colitis, nervous weeping, and acute hypochondria. It was as if Joyce, resenting Nora's attention to Lucia, increased his own claim on her. In January 1933 Joyce showed Nora how little able he was to get along without her.

Nora had promised to accompany him on an overnight trip to Rouen to hear Sullivan sing. When the time came she did not feel she could leave Lucia. At her suggestion, Joyce found another companion, an Indo-Chinese medical-student prince. The morning after the performance, when Sullivan was seeing the two men off at Rouen station, Joyce began to feel ill, and when the train was a quarter of an hour into its journey, he had one of his "collapses." He was certain he had fallen victim to the current epidemic of grippe, caught from sitting in the "coughing booth of the theatre," even though his companion told him that he had neither a temperature nor symptoms of flu.[27]

Two nights later he had a worse attack. Joyce would not allow himself to fall asleep because Nora had gone to hear *La Traviata* with Maria Jolas. She did not come in until half past one in the morning. At that hour, he swallowed his usual six sleeping pills and fell into a troubled sleep. Nora (his letter to Miss Weaver revealed) was in a separate bedroom. He passed a night of horrors and hallucinations, hearing menacing noises outside his door, and when it was morning he grabbed his overcoat and ran out into the snowy street and thence to the Léons to tell them that he was in danger.[28]

What had happened to him? The medical diagnosis from Léon's doctor (Dr. Fontaine being away) was an "abuse of somniferents." At home Nora blamed the noises on Miss Moschos, who said she had been tiptoeing up and down the corridor in the night thinking she heard Joyce calling for help. Nora said sarcastically to Joyce, "If you take something to make you sleep, apparently she takes something to keep her awake." But Joyce concluded that one good effect of his collapse was to make that "subtile et barbare person," his daughter, solicitous about her father. Lucia was sincerely worried about his health, and she and Nora had another scare when Joyce went to Dr. Fontaine with acute internal pains, but Dr. Fontaine pronounced him in better health than ever and blamed the pain on nerves.

One result of all the alarms was that Joyce gave both mother and daughter money for new clothes: four thousand francs to Lucia for a fur coat, which Joyce said would do her more good than any psychoanalyst, and two thousand to Nora. Watching the dispensation of this largesse, Myrsine Moschos strongly disapproved. She could see that Joyce, trying to give his children everything they desired, had determined that they would never go without, as he had, but any money he gave Lucia she spent instantly and foolishly. The spectacle of waste, however, did not stop Paul Léon from writing to Miss Weaver on Joyce's behalf to say that Joyce was running low on funds.[29]

Joyce indeed was so drained by these events that he delegated the task of writing to Miss Weaver to Paul Léon. Cruelly, through Léon, he requested that she stop writing to him. True to form, Miss Weaver responded with a visit to Paris, assuring him that he could count upon her help to pay Lucia's bills. Yet her visit was a failure. It did not restore their former closeness, partly because she visited her old friend Sylvia Beach, which put her in Joyce's black books, and partly because he could sense her unspoken conviction that Lucia was incurable. Their closeness was shattered. The next year Miss Weaver was in Paris on February 2 and Joyce did not even invite her to his birthday party.[30]

Come spring 1933, Nora was torn between her two dependents once again. Joyce had to return to Zurich for an eye examination. As the meticulous Léon conveyed to Miss Weaver:

> I do think that both materially and morally he needs Mrs Joyce to accompany him and the problem then is limited to the fact what to do with Miss Joyce during the week or fortnight that her parents will be away.[31]

In April, and again in July, when they visited Zurich, they resolved the conflict by taking Lucia with them. On the second visit they regretted it. Carola Giedion-Welcker encouraged Joyce's hopes by presenting suitable young men for Lucia to meet, but Lucia herself extinguished them. She threw another railway station scene. There was no alternative but to put her in an institution, so Joyce bought the best.

Les Rives de Prangins at Nyon near Geneva was Europe's foremost sanatorium for the well-to-do mentally ill. Patients were made to feel like guests in a luxury hotel; there were hundreds of acres of landscaped grounds in which they could wander. They dressed for dinner in the evening. The atmosphere of Prangins is captured in F. Scott Fitzgerald's *Tender Is the Night;* his wife Zelda had been a patient there in 1931. Lucia entered Prangins in July. Yet Joyce did not allow Lucia to taste the comforts of the place for very long. Within a week he had taken her away.

Nora again had pleaded, "Leave her there," but Joyce held out against her and Helen and Giorgio, and soon had Lucia back in Paris with a nurse-companion. Every day brought a new explanation for her disease, wrote Paul Léon: "The only thing which does not vary is the fact that he is the culprit."[32]

As news of Lucia's illness began to get out, people began, in Arthur Power's words, "to say a lot of things that don't bear repeating." Rumors of incest, in plain words. It seemed not improbable that the author of such a corrupt book as *Ulysses* might have corrupted his own daughter. And the book was still regarded as very dirty. In 1932 a young lecturer at Cambridge University who put *Ulysses* on his students' reading list found himself investigated by the Director of Public Prosecutions.

Joyce was hardly oblivious to the incestuous fantasies built into *Ulysses* and *Work in Progress,* and even as Lucia's illness progressed to the stage where she was unlikely to attract anybody at all, Joyce remained jealous of her supposed suitors. His daughter was, to him, "mignon-esque," and he did not mind being seen as a "vieillard" against the "strip-lings." But his offense as a parent, insofar as can be judged from the evidence, was malignant self-absorption — it ruined Nora's life and forced his children to subordinate their lives to his — rather than anything as crude, criminal, and uncharacteristic as child abuse. In its intensity, the fixed observation he trained upon Lucia during puberty may have been sufficient to unsettle her. Ellmann, Joyce's biographer, was often asked about the possibility of incest between Joyce and his daughter; his view was that Joyce was "not that highly sexed" and would not have carried any such thoughts into action.[33]

Joyce was more shaken by the open accusations, hurled at him by Nora and by Stanislaus, that the rootless life he had given his family had harmed Lucia. He knew that his wife and brother were only voicing what was being said behind his back by countless others, and that the constant shift from country to country, from language to language, and the continual rupture of ties with friends and relatives created textbook conditions for a confused identity. Their way of life had hit Lucia hardest. Joyce and Nora were wrapped up in each other. Giorgio, who always made friends effortlessly, was scooped up early by Helen. Nothing came easily to Lu-cia: friends, career, or lovers.

Joyce had another reason for denying Lucia's schizophrenia. The causes of the disease are still hidden in a blend of nature and nurture, but today tranquilizing drugs give many schizophrenics a seminormal life. In the 1930s, however, a diagnosis of insanity was a sentence of banishment from society. It condemned the victim to a life of barred windows, sur-veillance, and straitjackets. From Lucia's early years, when Joyce began to make jokes about her "absent-mindedness" and perhaps earlier — one report traces her first symptoms to 1914 when she was seven — he was resisting the terrible thought that his daughter would spend her days in an institution. When this prospect moved nearer and she began to be confined for brief periods, Joyce always described the institutions with pretty French euphemisms, *maison de santé* and *maison de repos,* or homey English ones such as *clinic* and *nursing home.*

A man wracked with guilt does not want to share it. As he reproached himself for his daughter's state, Joyce does not seem to have considered that Nora might have been responsible. The possibility would appear not to have occurred to Nora either. She was guilt-free to a fault — one of her main attractions for Joyce.

Lucia, in growing up, may have been deprived of mothering. Nora, who felt cheated of mother-love herself, was wrapped up in her husband and son and may have failed to establish that bond that passes a mother's experience and intuitions on to her daughter.

There was also, although Joyce never spoke of it in his letters, mental illness on Nora's side of the family. Nora received many letters from Galway, as Joyce's own make clear, and an event that troubled Annie Barnacle deeply during the 1920s was the breakdown of her daughter Dilly, Nora's sister, whom Joyce had liked and put into *Ulysses*. In 1925 she was admitted "in a highly disturbed condition," say the medical reports, to the dreaded lunatic asylum at Ballinasloe and kept there for eighteen months. She never fully recovered. With Dilly's experience on their minds, Annie Barnacle and her brother Michael Healy kept advising Nora about Lucia: "No doctors, no sanatorium, no blood examination."[34]

There remains also the sorry fact, which Joyce seems not to have wished to take into account, of Ireland's very high rate of schizophrenia, three to five times as high as that for most Western countries, with the rural west of Ireland having a higher rate than the east.[35] That Lucia should have been stricken was just part of the bad luck of the Irish. Nora knew what mental illness was. Her acceptance of Lucia's fate no more signified indifference than Joyce's stubborn denial signified love, and her reaction had the virtue of realism.

Back in Paris, embarked on a brave attempt to simulate normal family life, Nora, Lucia, and Joyce went out with the Jolases one night to the theater to watch a comedian. But for Nora the evening was ruined when, as they took their seats, she learned that Lucia's latest psychiatrist, a Dr. Coudet, whom she had never met, was sitting behind them. Nora turned around and found herself staring at one of the ugliest faces she had ever seen. The thought that this ogre was treating her daughter so upset her that she had to leave the theater. Joyce and Lucia stayed until the end of the performance. What Nora said when they returned home is echoed in Joyce's letter to Miss Weaver: "I am sorry he [Coudet] is not more beautiful but it is not my fault."[36]

As parents, the Joyces labored to find friends for Lucia. They enlisted Louis Gillet's daughter, Dominique, to accompany them to the theater. They invited Elizabeth Curran, Constantine Curran's daughter, to stay with them for a week to get to know Lucia. Elizabeth Curran was very excited about being granted the rare privilege of being a Joyce house guest in the flat on the rue Galilée, but she found Lucia, who was slightly older, offhand, unfriendly, and totally self-preoccupied. The Joyces took Elizabeth out to dinner several times, and she was just beginning to enjoy herself when a letter came from London saying that Curran was mildly ill. Joyce assumed instantly that Elizabeth would start packing. "Your father is ill," he told her. "Of course, you're going to be with him." Elizabeth had no intention of rushing to her father's side. Nora sensed this. "Oh, let her make up her own mind," Nora said. To no avail. Joyce virtually ordered Elizabeth out of the flat to perform her filial duty.

Curran's wife, who was often in Paris, was a friend of Nora's. Mrs. Curran had been an actress and had created the part of Maurya in the original Abbey Theatre production of *Riders to the Sea*. Nora loved to talk about the theater to her. Nora also confided, although she never unburdened herself in any detail, that she had no influence over Jim about Lucia. "I just can't make Jim see sense," she said. She wished he would stop changing the girl's treatment. "I keep telling him Miss Weaver knows best," Nora would say, and Mrs. Curran agreed. But Nora accepted her defeat. "Nora was never a person to moan and groan," said Elizabeth. "She was a buoyant character. She never looked back. That was part and parcel of why she went away with him in the first place." [37]

Their lives in those tormented years were not quite the unrelieved tragedy that Joyce and Paul Léon led Harriet Weaver to believe. Their gloom-laden letters to London were aimed at Miss Weaver's pocket as well as her heart. In fact, Nora and Joyce had an active social life. They went regularly to the opera, always in formal dress — Joyce in silk-lined evening cloak, silk hat, and iron-tipped cane — and they dined out and saw friends. Nora enjoyed scouring the smart sections of Paris for a flat, escorted on occasion by their friend the Italian composer and musician Count Edgardo Carducci. The need was upon them again, for the lease on their rue Galilée flat ran out in the summer of 1934.

Nora's great outlet remained clothes. She would take Mrs. Curran and Elizabeth with her to Lelong couture showings at 16 avenue Matignon and to fittings if she were having something made. She could be very cruel, they noticed, about what other women wore. Privately they thought that Nora always looked well turned out but erred on the side of dark colors and severity.

Nora had not lost her sense of humor. Bennett Cerf in Paris had dinner with Joyce one night and found his author becoming "completely potted." When they got back to the Joyces' flat, Joyce, according to Cerf, decided he was going to sing some Irish ballads and Mrs. Joyce decided he was *not* going to sing some Irish ballads. Undeterred, Joyce went to the piano, whereupon Nora grabbed one end of the bench and Joyce the other, and they tugged it between them. Suddenly Nora let go, and Joyce tumbled over.

Cerf decided to retreat. Nora took him down and put him in a taxi, apologizing for the domestic scene and laughing. "Sometime *I'm* going to write a book," she said, "and I'm going to call it, *My Twenty Years with a Genius — So-Called*." [38]

Both Nora and Joyce derived great pleasure from taxiing out to Enghien near Paris to visit some good friends, Kathleen and René Bailly. The Baillys had no literary connections whatever. For Nora, Kathleen — trim, blonde, slightly over-dressed — was the ideal best friend; she was a

Galway woman married to a Frenchman. Both women appreciated the absurdity of fate that had brought them to high life in the French capital. Kathleen enjoyed cutting a fine figure at Irish embassy receptions in Paris, and she also, like Nora, liked a joke.

René Bailly was a businessman, wealthy enough to own an imposing villa surrounded by a small park, set just at the end of the town of Enghien. Goats grazed in the park, and Kathleen one day decided to have all their hooves and horns painted gold. Nora roared with laughter when she saw them.

The Joyces were such regular visitors that Joyce had his own study on the ground floor overlooking the gardens. For loyal friends like the Baillys the effort of treating Lucia as normal for the Joyces' sake was a great strain. Lucia was an annoying guest. She would position herself next to her father, monopolizing his full attention. Everybody fumed as Joyce would bend to catch her every word and would indulge her every whim. At night she had to sleep in her parents' room (as she had had to do as a teenager). Giorgio, as if in compensation, would be very attentive to his mother when he was there. He would sit on the arm of Nora's chair, murmuring solicitous questions: Did she need her sweater? Would she like to walk around the garden?

Nora always relaxed when she walked into the Baillys' house. She would go into the kitchen at the back and say, "Show me what you're making, Kathleen." Both women loved cooking, although Kathleen had plenty of staff. Sometimes Nora would turn a hand herself and make her favorite chicken dish or a rhubarb pudding with meringue topping. She was very good at simple baked apples wrapped in pastry.

In fashion, however, Nora could no more keep up with Kathleen than with Helen. She would wander through Kathleen's mirrored dressing room, which lay between the Joyces' bedroom, in the guest wing, and the Baillys', and admire the racks and racks of clothes. Nora would have loved such a wardrobe, but although Joyce never complained about her clothes bills — an outfit from Lelong ran to between 750 and 1,450 francs — she did not have that kind of money to spend.[39]

It was Nora, of course, who prodded Joyce into making the most of his natural elegance. He was too blind to shop for himself. An Irish visitor, James Stern, brought to the rue Galilée by Robert McAlmon in 1934, was struck by the contrast between the man and his clothes. Joyce had the hand of a recluse, Stern said — bony yet soft to the touch; he had a tired, whispery voice and held his head like a blind man's, chin raised, head tilted slightly back, "and almost incongruously the smart peacock-blue velvet jacket and dark trousers."

As Stern remembered the visit (he was struck, like so many, by the drab impersonality of the rooms, not realizing that they were furnished accommodations), he began to tell Joyce an anecdote about a Cork man with a passion for hunting, when Joyce interrupted him. "A dreadful thing has happened," Joyce said. "I have to be fitted." His wife, he explained, insisted that he have a new suit. He kept glancing at the door. Then, "a woman, tall, grey-haired and dignified filled the doorway. 'Come on, Jim. He's here.' " Joyce let out a groan. Stern tried to continue. "Jim," Nora cut in. "Did you hear what I'm after saying? The tailor's here. Another week, and you'll not be fit for the street!"

As Joyce strained to hear the rest of the story, Nora said, "Ah, come on out of that," and drew him shuffling from the room. Joyce returned a little while later, and the conversation continued, until Nora reappeared and announced it was "time."

> For an instant Joyce seemed to pretend not to hear. Then he slowly raised his head towards her, and, as his thin lips parted in what might have been wonder, annoyance, anxiety — or a combination of all three — I remember how his whole attitude struck me as that of a child.[40]

In December 1933 the family had Christmas as usual, with Nora making four plum puddings, and Lucia designing the family Christmas cards and spending money at a rate that astonished even her father. Yet Lucia was increasingly hard to handle; she had attacked her attendants, and the bizarre treatments her various doctors were recommending (injections of seawater was one) did not help.

They did have something to celebrate that year. On December 6 John M. Woolsey, the federal district court judge in New York, after hearing the *Ulysses* case, found after a careful reading that *Ulysses* might be "somewhat emetic," but "nowhere does it tend to be aphrodisiac." The book, in his view, was a serious attempt to devise a new literary method for the description of mankind. As such, it might legally be published in the United States. Random House hurriedly printed one hundred copies to secure copyright, and *Time* celebrated by putting Joyce on its cover. The magazine (always good on Joyce) posed the question about the book, "Is it dirty?" and answered in a one-word sentence, "Yes." *Ulysses* was also, *Time* judged, "one of the most monumental works of the human intelligence." Such a profile required a *Time*-style description of the author's home life:

> In his early 20's he left Ireland and the Church for good, took himself and his sleek blonde Galway wife, Nora Barnacle, to Italy. . . . Some three years ago he made newshawks wild by remarrying his wife at the London Registry office without offering explanations.

Time pronounced Joyce, at fifty-one, a resident of Paris, a shy, proud, private citizen with a worldwide reputation and periods of virtual blindness. Posterity would have to decide, it concluded, whether Joyce would be remembered as an invigorator and inventor of language or as the man who made the term *unprintable* archaic.[41]

Time did not mention the man's daughter. The Joyces must have been thankful. Keeping Lucia out of the newspapers was a constant worry. The scene at the Gare du Nord in April 1932 had been noticed after all. A Paris paper that reported it, however, had gushingly interpreted Joyce's agony on that day, when his baggage was piled on, then off the train, as a reluctance to leave, *"car le grand poète aime Paris."*[42]

In January 1934 Lucia ran away from home and was absent for three days before she was brought back by the police. Joyce did not know what to do. He thought hopefully of sending Lucia to visit Stanislaus and Nelly in Trieste. But events took any further decision out of his hands. On February 2, as telephone calls poured in to celebrate his fifty-second birthday and to congratulate him on his victory in the United States, Lucia, angry at being ignored — *"C'est moi qui est l'artiste,"* she insisted — cut the telephone wires, not once, but twice. Then she marked the day, as she had done two years earlier, by striking Nora.[43]

Back Lucia went to Geneva, to Prangins, for a prolonged and turbulent stay. That left Nora, as she turned fifty in March 1934, with her first breathing space in nearly three years.

With great pleasure and relief she and Joyce accepted the Baillys' invitation to take a long motor trip, heading to the south of France and Monaco and finishing in Zurich. Nora and Joyce were never shy of a crowded car. The Baillys' two nieces were on the trip as well, and they were amused to see that Joyce was too prim to observe the French custom of stopping to pee by the side of the road. He insisted upon diving into hotels when need arose. Like all of the Joyces' wealthy friends, the Baillys picked up all the bills when they were together, and Evelyne Shapero, one of the nieces, understood that Joyce's account at Fouquet's was also paid for by an admirer. Her uncle, however, paid his own share when he and his wife dined there with the Joyces.[44]

The trip was marred by the news that an old and good friend, George Borach from Zurich, had been killed in a car accident. He had been a pupil and friend since before the English Players days during the Great War. Joyce once again kept the bad news from Nora for several days — with good reason. When Nora learned of it, she was so upset that she could not enjoy Zurich. She found the city haunted, she said, by Borach's memory. The sight of the grieving parents of Borach, a bachelor, touched her — but not so deeply that she could not remark that old Frau Borach, supposedly a wealthy woman, used to bring broken biscuits from home in her handbag when she met Nora at a café for tea.[45]

They were back at the rue Galilée in April. Joyce boasted that they had done 2,500 kilometers: "my first motor trip." He had taken to writing light, bantering letters to Lucia and sent her Nora's advice to put on weight if she could. He also wrote,

> Mamma is chattering on the telephone with the lady above who dances the one-step so well and fished my note of a thousand lire out of the lift. The subject of the conversation between them is the lady on the fifth floor who breeds dogs . . . Now they have finished with dogs and are speaking of me.[46]

The lady in question, who had indeed traced to Joyce a lost banknote (then worth about forty dollars), became their friend when Joyce out of gratitude sent her an enormous box of roses. She in turn invited the Joyces to tea. Joyce was so blind that he had to feel for the seat of his chair before sitting down. Nora had to put the milk and sugar in his tea and tell him what was on his plate.[47]

Instead of being able to relax, however, Nora soon had a new blow. Helen was taking Giorgio and Stephen to live in New York. The move would help Giorgio's career, Helen said. That was no consolation to Nora or to Joyce. Both had a dread of America, Nora because she thought of it as a place from which people did not return, Joyce because he had a fear of crossing so much water. ("We nearly persuaded him once," said Bennett Cerf, "but he was afraid of boats. At the last minute he welshed."[48]) If Joyce had been willing to go to America, as his friends Gogarty, Byrne, James Stephens, and the Colums had done, he could have solved his financial problems. As Gogarty observed, "America would have been his happy remunerating exploiting ground."[49] But Joyce disdained doing anything to make money except to write.

But there was more to his fear than mere distance. It began to look as if the Joyce family was going to have a second case of madness on its hands. Helen was showing signs of restlessness and agitation. For a time she and Giorgio threatened to pack up the family portrait gallery (which by then included one of her done by Marchand) and move to Vienna. Then she hit upon returning to America. Giorgio was to enter under the preference quota allocated to spouses of American citizens, a procedure that required him to ask Stanislaus to obtain copies of his Triestine birth certificate. When Helen typed Giorgio's letter, in which he apologized for troubling his uncle, she added a furtive postscript. Would Stannie please forgive her for the overexcited letter she had sent him previously? The letter was unimportant, she said; she had written it when she was upset. Giorgio did not even know she had done it.[50]

Helen was still beautiful. A snapshot taken on the beach at Le Touquet with Bennett Cerf and a younger woman shows Helen in a bathing suit, laughing, with her dark hair streaming down her back. (In his memoirs Cerf claimed that Joyce had offered his son and daughter-in-law as chaperones when Cerf wanted to take "a darling little girl from a very respectable, very rich Westchester family" to Le Touquet for the weekend.)[51]

There was no stopping the departure. Helen and Giorgio sold their car (a Rolls-Royce) and left on May 19. For the first time in nearly thirty years Nora and Joyce were together without their children. As they had always split parentally on oedipal lines, Nora and Giorgio versus Joyce and Lucia, they were equally bereft.

The absence of the children gave Joyce a new excuse for writing letters. The deliberately light tone he used in them contrasts sharply with Paul Léon's letters to Miss Weaver portraying a man cut off by blindness, lack of money, and "exclusion from the rue de l'Odéon," from the social and literary circles in France and England.[52]

Miss Weaver would have had a more balanced picture if she had received Nora's version of life *chez* Joyce. On a June day in 1934 after getting back from the races, Nora wrote to Giorgio and Helen,

> We seem to have taken your place here as far as late hours is concerned we have been to see many things . . . I spend most of my time flat hunting. Carducci took me out to Neuilly to see some wonderful ones but they were all let Mrs Dyer invited us to an evening party I must say it was very smart she had the most wonderful buffet everything on the table was from the colonies I must tell you the funniest part of that was when I was getting into the new evening dress Jim thought the back was a bit too decolleté so he would have to stich [sic] up the back of the dress can you imagine the result? of course he stiched it all crooked so I had to undo the stiches again I decided it was better [to] have a bare back I wish you could have seen him stiching my skin [and] back bone altogether.[53]

Joyce's continuing interest, even with his clouded sight, in the details of women's clothes was not confined to Nora's. The novelist Jean Rhys always liked James Joyce because at a party in Paris he had tactfully told Nora to fasten the open zip of Jean's new black dress — a kind gesture she had not expected from the august (and nearly blind) famous author.[54]

Nora had lost none of her Mollyish eye for the imperfections in the appearance of her sex. She reported to Giorgio and Helen that Stephen's former nursemaid looked unhappy in her new job:

> I did find her not looking so well as a matter of fact when she came in through the door she looked very dishevelled her hair was hanging around her she had a bunch of flowers in her hat and another at her waist and if I dont mistake she had a bunch in her bosom . . .[55]

Nora added how much she missed her grandson. Whenever she saw other little boys running around, she thought of Stephen.

That month Nora had found two suitable flats, one near the Parc Monceau and a slightly cheaper one at 7 rue Edmond Valentin, in their old neighborhood in the seventh arrondissement. They chose the latter, which had five rooms on the fourth floor — much more elegant than the Square Robiac, Joyce thought. Nora was delighted with it. They called in the carpenters and decorators and congratulated themselves on being settled for the first time in forty months, and then set off with the Gilberts to Belgium, so that Nora could "repair her nerves" with a cure of baths.

Lucia was never far from their minds. Joyce kept Giorgio's emigration from her — to spare her feelings, he said. He worried when Beckett published his book *More Pricks Than Kicks* because one of the characters in it was named Lucie. However, he wrote Miss Weaver, "it is quite different. She [Beckett's Lucie] is a cripple or something. He has talent, I think."[56]
The news from Prangins was not encouraging:

> Lucia seems to have fallen for some undesirable gent in the Nyon shop [Prangins] who either lives in Dublin or London. They are being kept apart and he is going away. This has for the moment upset her. but they say it will soon pass. I see nothing crazy in that, as women go.[57]

Lucia also scribbled an eight-page letter in pencil, of which Nora could decipher only bits but from which she was unhappy to learn that Lucia seemed to be saying that she spent her days sitting by the window. They decided that, after Belgium, they would head for Switzerland. Lucia's doctor had said they might risk a visit — though they were not to burst in upon their daughter but to come to his private villa first.
As Nora and Joyce walked up the path to the villa, however, Lucia was standing there waiting for them. "Quick!" said Nora to Joyce. "Let's go in before she sees us." She slipped in. But not soon enough. Lucia had seen them, and with loud cries of "Babbo!" and "Mama!" she fell upon her parents, weeping and kissing them. Someone on the staff had told her that they were coming, and she had deduced where they would arrive. She was very affectionate to Nora. Joyce, relieved, wrote it all instantly to Giorgio when they got back to their hotel.[58]
His optimism was premature. The doctors threw up their hands at the case. "The only hold she seems to have on life is her affection for us," Joyce wrote to Carola Giedion-Welcker. And a poor hold it was. Kept under restraint in a room with barred windows, Lucia set fire to her room in four different places. She was not mad, Joyce insisted. He took her to a blood specialist to see if a physical cause to her illness could be discovered:

> The poor child is just a poor girl who tried to do too much, to understand too much. Her dependence on me is now absolute and all the affection she repressed for years pours itself on both of us. Minerva direct me.[59]

Joyce's next decision — again against Giorgio's advice — was to move Lucia to Burghölzli, a mental hospital near Zurich. Joyce recognized it as the Swiss equivalent of Bedlam but chose it for a blood specialist whom he wished to look at Lucia. But when the psychiatrist there diagnosed her as incurable, Joyce took her away a week later and moved her to a private sanatorium at Küsnacht, also outside Zurich, where the star of the staff was the same C. G. Jung he had so successfully avoided in 1919. Joyce liked Jung this time, especially when Jung hesitated to psychoanalyze a schizophrenic.[60] For his part, Jung had already recognized the greatness of *Ulysses* and tried to help Joyce with his overwhelming problem.

Because he witnessed both father and daughter closely that year, Jung was able later to give the definitive answer to the question that many still ask. Was Joyce himself not schizophrenic? The language of *Finnegans Wake* is very odd. It might even be described as *word salad* — the term used for the new words and private language often coined by schizophrenics. Jung's answer was no. Joyce and his daughter, Jung said, were like two people going to the bottom of a river — one falling, the other diving. Lucia herself was not impressed with Jung's sensitivity. She ridiculed him as "a big fat materialistic Swiss man try[ing] to get hold of my soul."

Nora was caught in the worst triangle of her life with Joyce. Because she had the burden of Lucia's care, over and over again she had the thankless task of bearing bad tidings. Joyce was angry once day when Nora came home from a visit and reported that Lucia had painted her face with black ink. On another visit Nora found her daughter in full evening dress at eleven o'clock in the morning. Reporting this to Joyce, she told him there was only one conclusion: Lucia was mad. Joyce did not agree.[61]

A disordered time sense, Joyce chose to ignore, is one of the main symptoms of schizophrenia. Lucia had many others. She worried obsessively about two physical problems — the small scar on her chin and a vaginal discharge. She was still prone to pyromania (or, as Joyce called it more elegantly, incendiarism). She sent telegrams by the dozen to people she admired (not all of whom were alive), and, in an echo of her Triestine childhood where she heard much about the *malocchio,* she muttered that Harriet Weaver had put the evil eye on her.

Once, when Lucia had the common paranoiac fantasy that people in the hospital were stealing her things, she complained to Joyce that a pen he had given her had disappeared. He eagerly suggested what the culprit's motive might have been: envy of him. Nora's view was that Lucia might have thrown the pen into the lake.[62]

Lucia had her own theories. Her father's generosity to her and Nora made others envious. Joyce persuaded himself that Küsnacht was doing

Lucia good. She seemed livelier, playing billiards and going for drives in a motorcar, entirely free from the restraint that the ordinarily permissive Prangins sanatorium had felt obliged to impose upon her. But Jung did not come cheap: 3,600 francs a month, and the clinic's bill of 7,000 francs on top of that. Joyce wrote to Helen and Giorgio thinly disguised appeals for money. Giorgio was to hurry up with his career, as his father wanted to borrow a million dollars. They were to inform all their rich relatives about his forthcoming birthday; he was getting tired of starched collars and would prefer a diamond necklace.[64]

He also begged Helen to ask "all the Jews in America to get up a subscription for me as I am planning to enter the poorhouse on St. Patrick's Day," and he reminded them, with eight underlinings, that his birthday was COMING.[65]

Joyce was in no way anti-Semitic, but he was exceedingly conscious of Jewishness. Nora probably was too and is unlikely to have held her tongue on the subject. Jews were a curiosity in the Ireland in which they grew up, as *Ulysses* makes abundantly clear. And Joyce at least (there is no record of Nora's views) unashamedly associated Jewishness with money. Another odd feature of Joyce's jokey correspondence with his very rich daughter-in-law lay in the curious caricature of American lingo he affected. After Helen apparently had scolded him about a mistake and also said some words in praise of Roosevelt, Joyce replied (putting the blame for the error on Paul Léon),

> Le Hon very nice chap but he not know the englisch grammatick like me and you, missus. Also why for you make me big speechstaff about Frankee Doodles? . . . But, say, you's grown to be a swell orator, missus, I'll tell the woyld you is.[66]

Part of his jollity was to cover Giorgio's failure in New York. Joyce thought his son's trouble was his odd accent. People expected a singer with the name of George Joyce to have an Irish brogue. Giorgio, however, spoke with a European accent, yet even then he had problems. Singing in Italian, he appended a very English *h* sound before vowels, so that, according to Joyce, words like *"cuore"* (heart) came out as "cuo-h-ore."[67] Helen's family, watching the couple, quietly thought the difficulties lay elsewhere. Helen did not seem to want Giorgio to succeed. She preferred him as a puppet to show off to her friends. She demanded that he go everywhere with her; she even kept him with her when she was having her legs waxed.[68] And Giorgio was lazy.

In any event, Giorgio's career was unlikely to be enhanced by his spending the summer at the Kastor summer home at Long Branch, New Jersey. Long Branch was along the stretch of coast then known as "Jewish Newport." To Peggy Guggenheim it was "the ugliest place in the world" — a barren world of hydrangeas, rambler roses, turreted Victorian mansions, and nursemaids in starched clothes, a separate nurse for each child.[69]

Part of Giorgio's own alarm at the news from Europe was his growing fear that any money his father might earn from *Ulysses* was all going to be poured into expensive mental hospitals for the care of his sister. He might need that money. His marriage was in trouble — as Joyce and Nora knew, to judge from guarded phrases in letters to New York — and the Kastors were worried about Helen. The strain of manic-depressive illness, which they believed to run in the family, had already broken up the marriage of Helen's older brother, Alfred, and his Danish wife.

In Zurich as in Paris, the Joyces were no stay-at-homes, in spite of their misery about Lucia. They remained assiduous operagoers; that summer they heard *Die Meistersinger* and a new opera by Respighi. They dined often with the Giedions and spent a whole day at the university, attending a lecture and having lunch and dinner with the rector.

They remained in Zurich for four months to be near Lucia. Every time they mentioned returning to Paris where the new flat lay empty and waiting, Lucia grew frantic. Yet they knew their visits did her no good. For a whole month they stayed away entirely.

Together they decided that Lucia was clairvoyant; they both enjoyed superstition and marveled that Lucia knew, without their having told her, that Joyce's sister, Eileen Schaurek, who had been living in Dublin, had moved to Bray. (Lucia probably heard it from Eileen.)

Christmas found them still in Zurich, for the first time with no family or friends. They were like "two godforsaken gipsies on the roadside," Joyce wrote Budgen (assuming that Budgen would take the Carlton Élite in Zurich as equivalent to a campsite).[70] Joyce also told Miss Weaver of his gloom:

> We shall not have a soul to join us. Jolly after 30 years. And word comes from U.S. that Giorgio and Helen are not coming back till summer, perhaps till etc. And to crown all I have yesterday and today the start of a colitic attack. Yet what I am trying to write is the most absurdly comic thing in the book . . .[71]

Lucia did join them on Christmas for dinner. Then in January she left the clinic and moved into an annex of the hotel with a nurse. Jung approved the move. He could make no headway with her treatment. As Joyce and Nora despairingly wondered what to do next, Lucia suddenly took charge. She decided that her aunt Eileen (whom she remembered fondly from Trieste days) should come to Paris. "Eileen is a bit loony but so am I, they say," Lucia told her father. "I think it would do me good to be with her."

At that point in their lives, what Lucia wanted Lucia got. She profited, Joyce believed, from his indulgent character. Very soon, therefore, Eileen, in spite of a job and three children in Ireland, was installed in Paris in the new flat with Lucia and her parents.

This development dismayed Miss Weaver. She believed all the doctors had been right when they said that Lucia needed separation from her parents. What is more, with Lucia around, Mr. Joyce would be unlikely to get much work done — the main purpose, she thought, of taking the new flat. Yet Lucia was not to be settled so easily. Swiftly she decided that Paris made her nervous, whereupon Miss Weaver summoned up her courage to do the last thing she would have dreamed of back in 1922 (when she hesitated even to be informed about Mr. Joyce's private life). She invited Lucia and Eileen to come to London to be her guests.[72]

Nora did not try to hold her daughter back. She could not face looking after her again herself. As if she were helping Lucia prepare for a luxury cruise, Nora went on a shopping spree and sent Lucia off on her travels with two trunks full of wonderful clothes, including a new opera cloak trimmed with fur.[73]

17

Madness in Progress, II

REASONING WITH MADNESS never works, but there are always people willing to try. Eileen Schaurek — in 1935 a thin, high-strung widow of forty-six, with a sharp tongue and a penchant for card reading — thought she could handle Lucia. Joyce paid her two pounds a week. When after they had arrived in England Lucia asked for a gun, Eileen offered to buy two in case the first one did not go off. Harriet Weaver thought Eileen was very quick witted. Miss Weaver herself had an attack of shingles from the apprehension of looking after Lucia. She had bravely installed Lucia in the spare room in her small flat on Gloucester Place and put up Eileen at a nearby small hotel. The young woman had to have two warm baths a day — the advice of a Parisian gland specialist whom Joyce consulted in the hope that Lucia's trouble was fundamentally glandular. Also, according to instructions from Paul Léon, her every move had to be reported back to her father.

Easier said than done. At first Lucia was very tractable, and Miss Weaver wrote to Paris that it was a mistake to consider her insane. This declaration soon rang hollow. Eileen suddenly announced she had to return temporarily to Ireland, where her children were. Miss Weaver was left alone with the patient, who took to her bed. When Miss Weaver brought her to a doctor and spent too long talking to him privately, Lucia grew angry and walked out — to visit Piccadilly, she said. She did not come home until the next morning. She was a grown woman, she announced, and did not need looking after.[1] Miss Weaver dutifully relayed the incident to Paris and got a rebuke from Joyce; far from healing the breach with him, she was only widening it by her efforts.

Lucia did have friends in London. Beckett took her to dinner a few times. There were various cousins (children of Joyce's brother Charlie who had moved to London), there was James Stephens's daughter, and Paul Léon's niece, a young actress.[2] Lucia could have visited any of these on her night away, but she insisted (and Miss Weaver believed her) that she had spent the night sleeping rough in Gloucester Place.

She was not easy to shepherd. One day, after Eileen's return, they were walking along the street when Lucia suddenly leaped upon a bus marked for Windsor. Eileen jumped in after her, and soon was on the telephone from the Star and Garter Hotel in Windsor asking Miss Weaver to come down and bring them some clothes. Miss Weaver, of course, obliged and sent them. She was rewarded with a thank-you note from Lucia, in a wildly erratic hand, questioning if perhaps Miss Weaver were not excessively kind. Lucia also ventured the hope that Miss Weaver did not find her too revolting a person; her problem, she volunteered, perhaps was being Irish.[3]

Lucia was in a messianic mood. She determined to reconcile her father to Miss Weaver and — much more ambitiously — to his native land.[4] By mid-March 1935 she was well on her way to producing his final alienation from both.

It is hard to reconcile Harriet Weaver's great intelligence with her blindness to the situation she was dealing with. There was no way in which, inexperienced with children or mental illness, she could win Joyce back by caring for his daughter. If she tried to pretend that the young woman was not seriously ill, this was belied by events. When she told Joyce the truth, as she had about the Piccadilly escapade, he was sarcastic and cruel. In a letter, he charged her with boasting that she could handle Lucia by herself — the last claim Miss Weaver would ever have made. He accused her of conspiring with his sister and — worse — of not liking Lucia.

Joyce believed only Lucia. He took her disjointed thoughts as imaginative wisdom akin to his own. He marveled when she uttered inanities such as (while in a restaurant) "Strange to think we are all sitting down and in a few hours we shall all be lying down." Joyce gossiped to Lucia candidly about his and Nora's friends: Kathleen Bailly was flighty, he said, and Carola Giedion-Welcker slightly hysterical. And he took her version of events. When she told him in a letter that Miss Weaver had stolen a bottle of cognac, Joyce commented to Eileen, "Perhaps the strain is driving her to drink."[5]

Having wrecked her father's relationship with the woman who had made her life of luxury possible, Lucia then set off for Ireland. Nora agreed that Lucia should go there but not to Galway. As Joyce explained it to Eileen,

> She [Nora] is not very keen on Lucia's going to Galway as she anticipates trouble when her people find out that she doesn't go to holy mass, holy confession, holy communion and holus bolus. However she thinks the air will do her good. Also Irish eggs are famous all over the world.[6]

However, Nora undoubtedly had other reasons for wanting to keep her daughter clear of the gossips in Galway.

Joyce could see one advantage in his daughter's removing herself even farther from home. In a veiled reference to Lucia's sexual vulnerability, he told Miss Weaver that he would be glad to see Lucia away from London, a wicked city where every other man was a criminal. Puritanical Ireland, by implication, was safer.[7]

For Nora, Lucia's absence was a tremendous relief. It gave her in February 1935 the peace to settle into the rue Edmond Valentin flat, on which they had held the lease since the previous September. The flat, with large, high-ceilinged rooms, was much grander than their previous one at Square Robiac, as was the whole building, with mirrors on each landing. Nora chatted happily with the workmen in her broken French and tried to shut her ears to the sound of children on the floor above, although Joyce didn't mind that kind of noise.[8] She had six large and five small mirrors put up. She let down all the blue curtains, which had been in storage, and she reclaimed the family portraits, which had been with Giorgio and Helen. She commissioned Budgen to do a mural of the Thames for her new drawing room. When her work was done, she put up her feet and read the *Irish Times.*

Nora lived for news of Giorgio. She expected a letter whenever one of the transatlantic liners docked at Le Havre. In May she went to meet the boat-train from the *Bremen* in order to get news in person from John McCormack, who had been in New York and seen Giorgio, but McCormack had left the station before she could find him, and she went home disappointed.[9]

Giorgio missed her too and asked her to send a photograph. Nora looked round the house, decided they were all bad ("When I find a lady who is content with her own picture," said Joyce, "I will send a bouquet to the Pope") and immediately went off to have a new one taken. She told Joyce that she wanted Giorgio to find her "blooming" (Joyce loved her choice of word).[10] The result was astounding: Nora as Marlene. She sent it off by the next boat. With its Hollywood touches — the white fox fur dramatically draped over one shoulder, the marcelled hair, the body

held in profile — the photograph portrays a lady of middle years pleased
with herself and her looks, proud to show herself off to her son. It is not
the portrait of a defeated woman.

Nora also took great pleasure in organizing their lives. Joyce said, "I
continue to write five words a day while Mamma runs about like a hare."
She went to a textile exhibition of work by Adrienne Monnier's sister, a
weaver, who wove them a rug design representing the Liffey for their
drawing room. And she found them, temporarily, a new pet. Coming out
of the Café Francis one night, she spotted a fine stray black cat — her
good-luck symbol — and took it home.[11] The cat had other ideas, however, and soon wandered off.

The opera was a continuing pleasure. One night at Les Trianons Nora
said to their friend, "Last night, Mr Sullivan, you sang like a god." He
replied gallantly, "Madame, next to your husband, I am an insect!"[12]
Maria Jolas marveled at the knowledge of opera Nora had gained from
the years in Trieste:

> It was extraordinary the number of operas and the words from them —
> Italian words, of course — that she remembered . . . operas that no one
> even knows the names of anymore. Nora would sing, and I would say, "What's
> that from?" and she would give me some name I had never heard of before.[13]

Nora continued to long for Giorgio's return, especially as he had been
unwell, but in this she was matched by her husband. Joyce's greatest
distress, Paul Léon observed in June 1935 (and probably accurately), lay
not in the problems but in the sheer absence of Giorgio and Lucia. "They
were, both of them," he wrote Constantine Curran, "such a part of his
life that their separation has left him in loneliness and despair which are
greater than we could suppose."[14]

Yet Helen did not want to return. She took Giorgio and Stephen off
for a second summer at the Jersey shore. A family photograph taken at
Long Branch shows Giorgio scowling behind a proud Adolph Kastor,
beaming Helen, and lively Stephen. Giorgio looks bored, discontented,
and, in his beautiful sports clothes, like the kept man that many people
thought him to be.

In his letters, Joyce tried to respect their right to a separate life. He
remarked that his little grandson was growing ever handsomer and how
moved he was to see his son showing the same paternal pride that he and
his father before him had done. Yet he was stepping up the pressure to
get them back to Paris. To Helen he was quite cool when she explained
that her father was ill and required them in New York.[15] Joyce was puzzled. In America Giorgio was having a disastrous time; his career prospects and his health were poor, he was at Helen's beck and call, yet he
seemed to want to stay there.

What had gone wrong? "Some strange malady," he wrote to Miss Weaver, "is creeping over both my children."[16] Yet he disclaimed responsibility. Doctors, he said, traced the troubles of both to the exile to Zurich during the war. He wrote to Giorgio, telling him to stay in America, even though "I know nothing of the country which may seem very beautiful to many," and also to keep his independence of spirit, a belated warning against Helen's influence. At the same time he arranged for a friend, Philippe Soupault, who was in the United States that summer, to go to the Jersey coast and to advise Helen and Giorgio to return to Paris. If they did not, Soupault warned the couple, Mr. Joyce, who was already suffering in Paris from severe stomach pains and was unable to eat or sleep with them so far away, would become seriously ill. The campaign was also taken up by Maria and Eugene Jolas and Thomas McGreevy.[17]

Lucia's Irish visit is still talked about with amazement by those who witnessed it. She arrived on Saint Patrick's Day 1935 and was taken to Bray, the pleasant seaside resort twelve miles south of Dublin, where Eileen's two teenage daughters, Bozena and Eleanora, were living in a bungalow. Joyce had lived in Bray as a boy in the house where he was to set the famous Christmas dinner in *A Portrait*.

Nora and Joyce seem not to have grasped (perhaps not wanting to), having taken Eileen away from her children for several months, that she was scatty and irresponsible. She herself was not living in Bray at all. She had a flat in Dublin in Mountjoy Square, where she lived with her young son, Patrick, and a job at the Irish Sweepstakes Office. From time to time, Eileen would go down to Bray, stock the larder with food, and then forget about the girls for weeks. They were left at times on the verge of starvation. When Eileen went to Paris, her daughters had to pawn the silver to buy food.[18]

The Schaurek sisters were beautiful girls of nineteen and seventeen, with strong Slavic features. Although they knew Lucia from visits to Paris (and she remembered them fondly as tiny children in Trieste), they were hardly equipped to look after their older, stronger, richer, worldlier, and utterly unpredictable cousin.

At that time there was open hostility between Nora and Lucia. Joyce tried to heal it by instructing Lucia to write reassuringly to her mother. Instead Lucia sent a letter that, according to Joyce, drove Nora half-mad. "Doubtless that was your intention," he wrote to Lucia, in one of his rare rebukes. He also scolded Lucia for forgetting her mother's birthday. Nora herself obliged with one letter, which has not survived, but which prompted Lucia after that to address her letters to them both. "Mama and I are always thinking of you," Joyce then assured her, adding wrily, "it seems that in certain cases absence is the highest form of presence."[19]

For Joyce Nora's exhaustion justified the folly of leaving Lucia in a household where nobody was in charge. Joyce had to mollify her as well as Lucia, and she needed her daughter out of the way. As Joyce explained to Miss Weaver,

Instead of running around from one scruff to another (of course I don't mean you) she [Lucia] should be in this house which was set up for her. But you can think in what a state my wife's nerves are after four years of it. And that is the problem, the whole problem, and nothing but the problem . . .[20]

Exporting schizophrenia is a common practice. Desperate for some respite, families in which there is a schizophrenic young adult all too easily persuade themselves that a trip abroad or a change of air will drive the symptoms away. Nora and Joyce kept toying with plans to go to London to see Lucia, but in the end they never did. Nora also considered going to Ireland by herself; she wanted to see her mother. Joyce conceded that it was only right, as Annie Barnacle was over seventy, but he drew out his well-worn reminder to Nora that in 1922 she had left lying on the floor of a railway carriage, and once again he managed to prevent her from leaving his side.[21]

To a quite conscious degree, Joyce favored Nora over his children. In a letter to Miss Weaver that spring, he referred explicitly to "My wife who personally is probably worth both of her children rolled together and multiplied by three."[22] Insofar as Nora had extraordinary resilience and shrewdness, he was correct. The truth, however, was that he needed her more than he needed them, and that although he parted from them with the greatest difficulty, he could not part from her at all.

In Bray the Schaurek girls lived in one side of a two-family bungalow on Meath Road. For Lucia they rented a flat on the other side. The night Lucia arrived, their friends flocked in to meet Joyce's daughter. "Bring them in! Bring them in!" Lucia shouted. She was lying on the floor in front of the gas fire wearing a kimono with nothing on beneath it.

To young Irish eyes, Lucia was an exotic and fascinating personality. She would never travel in anything but a taxi and would telephone maniacally to people she admired; Maude Gonne MacBride was one. In her extravagance she resembled her father, but she had her mother's carriage. Patrick Collins, the Irish painter, one of those who met her at the start of her visit, marveled at the way she walked, wearing a camel's hair coat and carrying a stick, "as if she owned the whole bloody world." He found her strange but great fun. He met her once when she was carrying a bottle of champagne, and she offered him a drink. Her voice was lovely: "It bubbled up as if from a deep country well. She had great scope to her."[23]

Her cousins found her very pretty; the squint in her eye made her look like Norma Shearer, they thought. She had lots of spending money; Joyce sent her postal orders for about four pounds a week — twice Eileen's weekly salary. He also sent medicine (Veronal, to slow her down) and books (carefully selected not to be depressing — Tolstoy, but not Dostoevsky). Lucia lavished the money on champagne and fruit, which she bought from the best fruiterers in Bray. She ate other things as well. Doing her own shopping and eating whenever she wished, she soon put on weight and began to look quite fat.

Many of the things Lucia did made the cousins laugh. One day while making stew she put porridge in it. She used to try to make sandwiches out of raw meat; she also ate sausages uncooked. She was never sick, was strong as a horse, and sometimes slept on a bench outside. At the bungalow next door there was an ornamental pond. Lucia went fishing in it with a pin for goldfish.

The girls did not interpret these acts as madness. "I thought she was being bold," said Bozena. And they looked with envy at her clothes — more appropriate for Baden-Baden than for Bray — especially a cocktail dress made of blue and white taffeta ribbons.

Her behavior with young men embarrassed them. As convent-educated Catholics and at an age when they were trying to keep their boyfriends at a distance, the Schaurek sisters were dismayed by their cousin's lack of inhibition. "She was so easy," said Bozena. "We didn't dare to leave her alone with our boyfriends; she would sit on their laps and try to undo their trousers." She never wore underwear and would swim naked in the sea. At the top of her voice, she would sing songs in four languages and keep it up around the clock. Her favorite song was "You're the Cream in My Coffee."

One night there was a break-in at the bungalow. Details are hazy, but it was clear that Lucia had left the door open to both houses. The girls and Eileen were very upset, and Lucia wrote to her father about the incident.

Yet Joyce made light of it, once again draining the sexual element from her behavior. Perhaps, he wrote to her, the ruffians who entered her bungalow wanted all the art treasures and cases of gold coins it contained.[24]

During her several months in Bray, Lucia's behavior turned from the bizarre to the dangerous. Her cousins simply coped with each event as it happened. Lucia painted her room black, stuck a row of black phonograph records over the curtain rails, and bought black and gold covers for the chairs. They thought the effect was pretty. She had a predilection for turning the gas jets on; they opened the windows. She swallowed a whole bottle of aspirin; Bozena gave her a glass of mustard water to make her sick. Lucia lit a fire in the middle of her room; the girls decided that the landlady, to whom she had already given a ring, had encouraged her in order to claim a new rug from Joyce.

As all this went on, Joyce protested that no one wrote to Nora and him. That was not true. Eileen had wired him of her alarm, but Joyce brushed her off: "The scenes that scared you and Miss Weaver are nothing to speak of. Her mother stood four years of very much worse than that."[25] Nonetheless, he asked Constantine Curran, with his wife and daughter, to drive down to Bray to see what was going on. It did not take them long to see that Lucia was living in squalor and was incapable of looking after herself. Mrs. Curran and Elizabeth sorted out Lucia's beautiful clothes, which were in a terrible heap. Even as Lucia, who was a heavy smoker, watched them, her tweed jacket caught fire from a box of matches in her pocket.[26]

Alarmed by what they had found, Curran wrote at length to Nora rather than to Joyce. He recommended taking Lucia to see an American-trained psychoanalytic doctor in Dublin. Joyce, annoyed because Curran had not reported directly to him and distrustful of psychoanalysts, cabled immediately that no such appointment was to take place. Joyce was resolved to continue with his strategy of allowing Lucia total freedom, seeing that all medical attempts at restraint had failed. The one thing Lucia hated, he knew, was being under surveillance.

Unfortunately Lucia was not being watched. She put an advertisement in a local paper for "Chinese lessons" and soon after disappeared, only to be found in a ditch in Kilmancanogue, a village near the summit of the Great Sugar Loaf Mountain near Bray. She was drugged, her cousins were told, although they did not know with what. Perhaps, they speculated, the newspaper advertisement had been a code for obtaining drugs. Lucia did return home with them, but then she vanished. This time she could not be found.

Bozena wrote it all to her Uncle Jim. Lucia had left the bungalow and, she added, had got very fat. Bozena mentioned also that she herself had been coughing and spitting blood. Joyce was enraged. His daughter in the company of a tubercular![27]

By then Joyce had begun to mobilize his battalions. He sent Kathleen Bailly, who was in Ireland, to Bray to investigate. He also requested Nora's uncle, Michael Healy, then seventy-five, to go from Galway. The briefing Joyce gave Mr. Healy can hardly have reassured him or Nora's mother, who was undoubtedly reading over her brother's shoulder:

> In the form of mental or nervous malady she is subject to, i.e., schizophrenia, the real trouble is not violence or incendiarism or hysterics or simulated suicide attempts. . . . The real danger is torpor.[28]

Joyce issued one other instruction to the Galway crew: not to tell Constantine Curran he was sending Lucia four pounds a week. (Curran, at that point, was in effect the Joyces' lawyer in Ireland.)

Healy found, when he arrived in Bray, that no one knew where Lucia was. He spent six days trying to catch up with her and only then relayed the information to Nora and Joyce that Lucia was wandering by herself around Dublin. He got a cold reply from Joyce for his pains. Why was this so undesirable? Mr. Healy, Joyce said, had seen his grandniece in a bad light; there was another side to her. Joyce then rewarded Mr. Healy, his former benefactor, with an icy dismissal.[29] However, he accepted the accuracy of Healy's letter and passed it on to America so that Giorgio and Helen could see how bad things were — and how wrong he had been to reassure them that she was getting better.

Nora had her own opinion. She did not keep it from her husband. What he was really worried about, she said, was what Lucia's behavior might do to his reputation in Ireland. Joyce told her she was wrong — "as far as I know." But he need not have worried. Curran, a zealous guardian of Joyce's honor, had had a word with the Irish police, to see that whatever Lucia did, when she fell into their hands, nothing would get into the papers.

It might well have done. Lucia was at great risk during her days on the run. Patrick Collins, who had met her in Bray, bumped into her in Dublin. She was filthy and hungry, so he took her into a café "to give her a feed" and saw a sinister, moon-faced man looking at her. The man, reeking of Jameson's, breathed, "I've been following that girl for hours."

Since Collins had last seen her at Bray, Lucia had slipped deeper into a private world. "Look at the name of that house!" she exclaimed, gesturing toward an ordinary Dublin house with a banal name. Yet the name bore a meaning of oppressive significance to her, and she became wildly excited.

She would not be detained. She continued her aimless meandering through Dublin, once walking into Trinity College — or so she wrote Nora — offering to make a present of Joyce's letters. She slept in the college park. When, back wandering in the streets, she was picked up by the police, her maiden aunts, Eva and Florrie Joyce, had to collect her at the station — the same quiet sisters who for years had tried to pretend that they were not related to *that* James Joyce. (Joyce, however, had been sending Eva some money every month.) Finally, Lucia had had enough. At her own request, Constantine Curran found a nursing home to take her. Lucia, relieved to be looked after at last, became less agitated and wrote a loving letter to Nora. She seemed, for the first time in months, settled and healthy.

From Paris Maria Jolas arrived, Joyce's personal emissary. She too saw the situation at a glance. She could not understand how Eileen could have assumed so much responsibility for her seriously ill niece.[30] Eileen, Maria believed, had been writing cheerful evasions to Paris. "It was neither friendly or kind to withhold the truth about Lucia's movements and condition from her parents. . . . Neither parent," said Mrs. Jolas to Curran, "'is at all taken in by such documents." Their only uncertainty, she said, was where to move her next.

Why not let her stay where she is? Nora asked. Joyce overruled her. Lucia had to be taken out of Ireland as soon as possible. Maria Jolas regretted the decision; she too thought Lucia seemed happy in Dublin. She also gave Constantine Curran her own theory of the origin of Lucia's mental breakdown — Giorgio's marriage, an event that "made her feel that she was of little importance in the family and that only the brother had counted."[31]

Had Joyce taken Nora's and Maria Jolas's advice, Lucia's whole future might have been different. She might even have spent the Second World War years in the peace of Ireland. But Joyce was uneasy with her there among his enemies. Besides, he had heard of a new cure. Mrs. Jolas, while on board a boat from Ireland to France, had learned of the miraculous results achieved with mental patients by a bovine serum dispensed by a doctor in London, W. G. Macdonald. Through Paul Léon Joyce suggested that Miss Weaver reinvite Lucia to be her guest in London, and once again his wish was Miss Weaver's command.[32]

By mid-July plans to wrench Lucia from Ireland and get her back across the Irish Sea were laid with military precision. On the appointed day the Currans would escort Lucia on the boat to Holyhead. That same day at four o'clock in the afternoon Miss Weaver would leave her flat on Gloucester Place and board the Irish boat-train, arriving at Holyhead at half past eleven. There at the station she would meet Lucia, waiting with the Currans. Miss Weaver, with Lucia, would then immediately board the midnight sleeper headed back to Euston.

With her methodical mind, Miss Weaver even conveyed a fall-back plan to the Currans:

> If you do not arrive I shall take it that Lucia has refused in the end to travel and I will spend the night at Holyhead and ring you up from there Sunday morning.

If all went according to plan, as she hoped, she would let the Currans know of her safe return with Lucia to her flat, where a friend who was a trained nurse, Edith Walker, was already waiting.[33]

Lucia in the end gave no trouble. Docilely she crossed the Irish Sea and accompanied Miss Weaver to Gloucester Place. Little did she know what awaited her. Far from resuming her English holiday, Lucia found herself a prisoner. The small flat had been transformed into a nursing home. Miss Weaver and Miss Walker had nailed up all the windows so that they could not be fully opened. The very next day Dr. Macdonald arrived with his cow serum to administer the first of what was to be a long series of injections. Lucia put up a struggle and lost. The injection was not the worst part of the treatment. Even though it was a hot summer, Dr. Macdonald ordered her to bed for seven weeks. Lucia passed the time by singing loudly in all her languages and by throwing books out of the partly opened window. When one book struck a passer-by, Harriet Weaver gave Lucia her own bedroom overlooking the mews at the back. Within a matter of weeks, however, Lucia had grown so violent that she required two nurses during the day and one at night. From Paris Joyce encouraged her to be patient. He held out the hope that Dr. Macdonald would do for her what Dr. Vogt had done for him — succeed where all the others had failed:

> The cure is short and seems certain. It is divided into two periods of approximately 4 and 3 weeks. Altogether 25 injections divided in 15 and 10. Between the two I suppose you will go to the country.[34]

Once this regime was organized, Nora and Joyce went on holiday to repair their nerves. They weighed London against Copenhagen and settled on Fontainebleau. Herbert Gorman, Joyce's biographer, and his wife went along as their companions. Holiday snapshots reveal that three decades of effort by Nora had been in vain; Joyce was still wearing white tennis shoes.

There seemed no limit to Miss Weaver's self-sacrifice for Mr. Joyce. When Dr. Macdonald pronounced Lucia ready to convalesce in the country, Miss Weaver rented a furnished cottage, with a garden and the ironic name of Lovelands, in Surrey near Reigate. She hired a strong-armed Scottish practical nurse named Mrs. Middlemost, and also a cook.

Joyce wrote a poignant letter to Lucia, holding out hope once again: "Ora si tratta semplicemente di cambiare ambiente ed aria . . . eppoi di lasciare tempo al tempo" ("Now it is simply a question of changing environment and air . . . and then of letting time take its course").[35]

Nora never deceived herself with false hope. In no way did she feel singled out by fate. Kathleen Bailly's son had died a tragic death from drugs. The scandal had unsettled the Baillys' marriage — the reason why Kathleen Bailly had taken herself off to Ireland, with her husband chasing after her. To Nora, life was like that.

When Joyce sent Lucia a camera, photographs were taken in the Reigate garden and the prettiest one of Lucia sent to Paris. It showed a sullen but attractive girl in a hammock reading a book. Joyce wrote Lucia gaily, wishing that all the inhabitants of the world might look as tranquil. But other photographs taken that day show a very stern Miss Walker, an unsmiling Miss Weaver (obviously under great strain in loco parentis), and a very unhappy young woman with a mass of wavy hair.

Miss Weaver had disliked Dr. Macdonald from the start. He had begun treatment without examining his patient, and, as a doctor's daughter, she knew that was wrong. And by prohibiting sedatives, Dr. Macdonald had made their task far more difficult. Lucia was a strong young woman who could be both suicidal and violent. Miss Walker, who as nurse in charge bore the responsibility for Lucia's day-to-day care, had to hide all the knives and at night turn the gas off at the main. In the morning she would find that Lucia had opened the gas jet in her room, half hoping to kill herself in the night. In a more cheerful mood, she threw a tub of water over Miss Weaver. None of these details reached Paris. Joyce received from Dr. Macdonald the news he wanted to hear — that her progress was encouraging.

Lucia retained her sharp tongue. When Miss Walker and the Scottish nurse organized their days off, Lucia said that next would come her turn "for two days away from you both." When Miss Walker retorted smartly that perhaps Miss Weaver too might need a respite, Lucia replied, "She does not do anything so she does not need a holiday."

A vivid description of how the two women tried to cope has been given by Miss Weaver's goddaughter:

> When Lucia went on hunger strike, Edith would get Mrs. Middlemost to sing a Scottish song and dance a Highland fling and would pop in a mouthful of food when Lucia, amused, forgot for a moment her determination not to eat.[36]

When neither of them could handle their charge, they enlisted the local people to give a hand.

Treating a deranged twenty-eight year old like a two year old was the service of a saint, but it was doomed to fail and to be unappreciated. When Lucia's behavior did not alter, Dr. Macdonald, ever resourceful, asked that Lucia be sent for some tests to a private mental hospital, St. Andrew's in Northampton, about a hundred miles north of London. Joyce agreed.

As they sat in the doctor's office waiting for Lucia, however, Miss Weaver and Miss Walker saw Lucia's medical record lying unattended on a desk. They gave in to the temptation, as who would not, to read it. They instantly were punished by seeing the dreaded word *carcinoma* with a question mark in front of it. Miss Walker had been worried that a chronic problem of Lucia's, a vaginal discharge, might be a symptom of cancer. Miss Weaver, accordingly, obeyed her conscience. What would happen to Mr. Joyce's unfinished book if an even worse tragedy were to strike his beloved daughter? She felt she had to convey the possibility to someone and chose Maria Jolas. Mrs. Jolas obeyed her own conscience and passed the information straight to Joyce.

The result was uproar. Dr. Macdonald himself had to cross to Paris to tell Joyce that the suspicion had proved unfounded, and he added to Miss Weaver's guilt by forbidding her to visit Lucia. Joyce himself wrote Miss Weaver a letter — one of the very few she chose not to leave to posterity.

Her duties toward him and his daughter were by no means over. He suggested that Lucia be cheered up with a fur coat, but this was countermanded by a letter to Lucia from Nora:

> And what about your hair do keep it well brushed and I hope you will be able to find a warm coat in Reigate as apparently a tweed coat will be the more serviceable for the moment Miss Weaver thinks and I agree.[37]

In December of that turbulent year, with Lucia still at Northampton, Joyce put new frames around the portraits of "Messieurs my ancestors." Those worthies, he wrote a friend of his father's, had seen quite a lot of Europe and looked at each other as if to say, where next?

It is as well that neither he nor they knew how soon they would be back in their packing cases, not to emerge until after his own life and a new world war had ended.

That same month they got more sad news. Michael Healy had died in Galway of a heart attack; he had slumped over one morning while attending Mass. Had the exhausting chase across Dublin for his mad grandniece shortened his life? The suspicion did not seem to cross Joyce's mind. He said that Healy, a devout Catholic, could not have wanted a better way to die.

The last traces of Lucia's Irish journey remained. Joyce angrily complained that there was no sign of Lucia's two trunks, let alone her opera cloak; he implied that the crass natives of Ireland had stolen them. He had also to deal with the damage Lucia did at her bungalow. In August he received an angry letter from Mrs. E. Nicoll of Meath Road, Bray, asking £100 compensation for burned carpets, rugs, and bedding, and other breakage.[38]

Her list of damages bears silent witness to the violence that Nora and Miss Weaver had both confronted at close quarters in the cause of assisting Joyce to deny the reality of his experience. By February 1936 he too had to reconcile himself to accepting the truth. Lucia had to leave Saint Andrew's, Northampton, because Nora and Joyce would not certify her as mad, forcing her compulsory detention. Yet she could not go home, because of the danger to Nora. Maria Jolas escorted Lucia out of Northampton, back to Paris, and into her own home. The result was inevitable. After three weeks, the straitjacket appeared. Lucia was carried out of the Jolases' house, and institutional doors closed behind her forever. There is no record that Nora ever saw her daughter again.

The friendship between Joyce and Miss Weaver proved equally irreparable. He did see her once after that and wrote sporadically, but formally, never with his old filial frankness. Her sin, in his eyes, was not so much the cancer incident but her belief that Lucia was incurable and that *Work in Progress* was a waste of his talent. The latter charge was unjust. Miss Weaver had come to admire the experiment. But she did not waste her time in vain regret. She had already found a new and even more insatiable claimant for her devotion and funds: the Communist party.

18

Madness in
Progress, III

THE SPRING of 1936 dispelled any illusions that Hitler would respect the Treaty of Versailles as he ordered German troops into the demilitarized zone on the west bank of the Rhine. This threat to France's security made other expatriates in France begin to think of returning home, but the Joyces were anchored to Paris by a daughter in a closed institution. Lucia, because of her outbursts of physical violence, had been transferred to a new clinic with staff more able to handle her: the *maison de santé* run by Dr. Achille Delmas in Ivry, a suburb of Paris.

Nora's personal world was for the moment tranquil. War clouds were visible but distant. *Work in Progress* progressed to the point where Viking and Faber and Faber were talking about publication dates (although they were still in the dark about the book's real title). She and Joyce received many visitors from Ireland. Brian Coffey, poet and Old Clongownian, twice brought homemade Irish bread at Constantine Curran's request. Kenneth Reddin, an Irish district judge, brought a black pudding from Olhausen's, Dublin's well-known pork butcher.[1] Irish visitors fortified with an introduction would telephone nervously and find themselves directed to the rue Edmond Valentin by the Great Joyce himself: they were to get off the Métro at La Tour–Maubourg. Once arrived, they looked around them very closely. Brian Coffey decided upon one of the best descriptions for the famous head: "the shape of a kidney bean." Eileen O'Faolain and Nancy McCarthy, wife and friend respectively of the short story writers Sean O'Faolain and Frank O'Connor, were intrigued by the Joyces' caged birds. The young women were honored to be invited to tea and were also very conscious of knowing "the whole story" — that Nora and Joyce had lived together unmarried for many years and that Nora had had a terrible time with Lucia because Joyce had refused for so long to put her in an asylum. Eileen and Nancy were pleasantly surprised to see how friendly and attractive Nora was but were really unprepared, as were all Irish visitors to the Joyces', for the meticulous inquisition they were about to be put through about every detail of life in Ireland, from the sequence of shops in Dublin streets down to the price of butter. Nor did they expect to be scrutinized so closely themselves. "There's no doubt where you come from, Miss McCarthy," said Joyce, hearing Nancy's Cork accent. Staring at Eileen intently, he asked, "Tell me, Mrs. O'Faolain, are you by any chance Jewish?" Eileen little knew what a compliment, coming from Joyce, the question was.[2]

Ireland was much on Nora's mind. Her mother and her sister Kathleen had been begging her to come home and help sort out Michael Healy's affairs. The old man, with a carelessness inconsistent with his civil servant's temperament, had died without making a will. Local rumors were rife that, during a frugal and pious life, Nora's uncle had amassed a fortune of eight thousand pounds. Mrs. Barnacle turned to her son-in-law, the famous writer, for guidance. Joyce thereupon shipped the whole problem back to Ireland, to the long-suffering Constantine Curran:

> I would prefer to keep out of the affair if I could because my mother-in-law (who has always been a kind of worshipper of mine and thinks I am a miracle-worker) wants now to give all the money to my wife. In a former letter she said she wanted to keep it all so as to have a proper funeral, something rivalling that of the late Queen Victoria, I suppose. Like her son-in-law she is a great spendthrift. Did you ever hear of such a funny inheritance.[3]

The total of the estate was only £1,662 — a small fortune nonetheless in Galway at that time. Mrs. Barnacle did not intend to "give it all" to Nora or anybody else; she needed it to keep herself and Dilly.

In the late summer of 1936, while waiting impatiently for Giorgio's return, Nora and Joyce made their long-intended trip to Copenhagen. As was their habit on holiday, they settled into a good hotel for several weeks, taking in all the big tourist attractions — in Denmark this meant Elsinore, the ballet, and the red-uniformed soldiers — and sending a flurry of picture postcards to all their friends. Joyce could not have seen much of the sights. His sight was so poor that when, on their way home, they stopped in Bonn to visit Helen's German cousins, Wilhelm and Grete Herz, the Herzes found Joyce so blind that Nora had to cut his food for him and bring his plate up to his face so that he could eat.[4]

Nora, as was her way with strangers, went into her silent mode. The Herzes, observing the dark elegance of her clothes, thought, "Helen has taught her a lot." They decided further, perhaps summing up the feeling of the Kastor clan, "Helen has done a lot for James Joyce."

Helen was to do much more. Returning to Paris in September 1936, she, Giorgio, and Stephen moved to 17 Villa Scheffer, a small street off the avenue Henri Martin in the sixteenth arrondissement; they had a lovely spacious flat with French doors opening onto a garden. Soon their chauffeur was once again at the disposal of Nora and Joyce. Helen became their official hostess. Giorgio had recovered his voice after a throat operation, and Joyce still nurtured hopes that at thirty-one his son was on the threshold of a career as a singer.

Nora resumed her role as mother-in-law. She visited Helen's cook, who was in hospital, and hunted for a veterinarian for the dog. She also, as before, made new and wealthy friends, such as Mrs. Victor Sax, through Helen. But the old hostility was still there. Helen found Nora a less satisfactory grandparent than the gentle Joyce, who told the boy stories and even wrote one especially for him. Neither of the women could know how soon Nora would take over from Helen as the mother-figure in the boy's life.[5]

Helen, to the Joyces, did not look well, although Joyce politely called it tiredness. Strains were apparent. Helen took a house in the country to get some rest. She was also suspicious when the Joyces used Italian when speaking or writing to Giorgio; she thought they were trying to conceal something from her. The age difference between her and Giorgio was more apparent than before. Helen, in her early forties, had a nervous facial tic, and she worried acutely about Giorgio's roving eye for younger women. Those who never liked her liked her less.[6]

In the troubled world of the 1930s irrevocable personal gambles had to be made in the face of uncertainties. The Herzes, shortly after the Joyces' visit, decided not to stay in Hitler's Germany any longer and moved to St. Gallen in Switzerland, east of Zurich. It was to them, therefore, that Joyce turned to help Stanislaus, who had fallen victim to the rise of fascism in Italy. Stanislaus had been dismissed from his post at the University of Trieste and threatened with expulsion from Italy — an ironic turn of events, considering that he had paid for his loyalty to Italy during the First World War with four years in an Austrian prison camp. Stanislaus hoped for a teaching job in Switzerland. He was bitter at the way life had worked against him. He told Joyce that he and Nelly had been in debt for a long time following Schaurek's suicide. In the event, the post Stanislaus was offered in Switzerland was so uninteresting to him that he returned to Italy. He and Nelly and their only child (James, born in 1942) were to spend the war in Florence under difficult conditions.

Nora and Joyce gave no thought to leaving Paris, partly because they wanted to remain near Lucia but also because they were not great forward-planners, even on the smallest matters. Joyce explained this very clearly in the spring of 1937 to Mrs. Sisley Huddleston, the wife of the English critic who had been one of the first to declare *Ulysses* a masterpiece. She had invited him and Nora to come and spend a day in the country. "We are the sort of people who decide everything at the last possible moment so we could always ring up in the morning to find out if you were in residence," he replied. "I think that is the best plan."[7]

Lucia was rarely out of Nora's mind. Because she had aroused Lucia's most florid schizophrenic reactions, Nora was not allowed to accompany Joyce on his ritual Sunday afternoon visits to Ivry. Not only did this exclude her from any contact with her daughter, it also required her to spend much of each week arranging for someone to accompany Joyce, who could not easily go alone. Occasionally family friends, like Mrs. John Sullivan, would visit. Helen never went, Giorgio seldom. Nora kept in touch with presents and worried if Lucia did not write to her.[8] The visits were painful for Joyce. He tried to cheer up Lucia by bringing her Italian cakes or by teaching her Latin. Sometimes they would play the piano and sing together, but a strong nurse was never far away.[9]

Joyce liked to portray himself as safe from Lucia's violence, as if he was the only other permitted inhabitant of her private world. Yet once when Giorgio went with his father, Lucia saw them and cried *"Che bello! Che bello!"* then lunged and tried to strangle them.[10]

When Joyce came home from Ivry, he would be utterly drained. He and Nora dined with the Jolases on Sunday evenings, and none of them could pull him out of his gloom. "And I'm supposed to be writing a funny book," he would say. As for Nora, she kept her feelings locked inside herself. "You didn't ask her about it," said Elizabeth Curran. "She didn't want to discuss it. That was the way she lived with it."

By the late 1930s the relationship between Nora and Joyce was strained by Joyce's drinking and by their children's disastrous lives, yet it rested on a base of trust and satisfaction in what they had achieved. They often seemed bored with each other. Nora complained to one of their friends, "There sits a man who has not spoken one word to me all day," to which Joyce replied, "What is there left to talk about when you have been married thirty years?"[11] The boredom was genuine, but it was far from the whole measure of their marriage. Nora and Joyce found a delight in each other's company which, even after thirty or more years, marked what even a younger generation could recognize as love. One night in Paris Arthur Power left a restaurant just behind the Joyces, who did not know he was there. As the noise of the crowd faded and they felt themselves alone on the dark street, Nora and Joyce turned to each other and smiled. "A look of such affection passed between them," Power said. "Nora wasn't putting on an act. She wasn't capable of it."[12]

Over the years Joyce had put aside his irritation at Nora's continued religious faith and had come to accept it. Visiting Lausanne, Nora went to Mass every Sunday with Jacques Mercanton, a young literary scholar and a deeply devout Catholic. She was open and comfortable in her religious practice. Joyce made no attempt to stop her. It was simply understood that she would go and he would not. He was never the rabid anti-Catholic that Stanislaus was; indeed, he could not have remained a life-long friend of Constantine Curran's had he been. Nora, for her part, never dreamed of nagging him about his lack of religion. In those years, she was not the most zealous of Catholics and did not always attend Mass. When with Mercanton, she did not take Communion.

In many ways, Nora was more anti-Irish than Joyce was. Joyce, Mercanton felt, romanticized the place upon which he had built his art, but Nora would have none of it: "A wretched country, dirty and dreary, where they eat cabbages, potatoes, and bacon all year round, where the women spend their days in church and the men in pubs." But, Joyce protested, Dublin was the seventh city of Christendom, while the Liffey . . . "Wretched, muddy little stream," said Nora.[13]

Mercanton, like Power, was impressed with their devotion to each other. Nora talked "with incredible tenderness of nothing but Jim." All the Irish were difficult, she explained to Mercanton. Even so, Mercanton could see why Nora put up with the many difficulties Joyce presented. With her he was utterly gentle and (on small matters) attentive to her slightest whim. Mercanton recalled a discussion of how to spend an afternoon. " 'What do you want to do, Nora?' he would ask. 'I want to walk to Vevey,' Nora said. So we began to walk to Vevey. About a quarter of the way there, Joyce was tired. 'Tell Nora we are at Vevey,' he begged me."[14]

Joyce was happy if Nora was happy. "My wife has fallen in love with your countryside. Look at her!" Joyce said to Mercanton. She, in spite of her teasing, treated him as a sacred, fragile object. Joyce that summer looked even more schoolboyishly helpless than usual, for he was wearing a Swiss jacket of shiny cloth, flannel trousers that were too short, white shoes, and a yellowed straw hat pushed back above his ears.

Nora, smiling and relaxed at the thought of a vacation and of *Work in Progress* reaching its end, went off to do something by herself one afternoon, saying to Mercanton, "Watch him. I leave him in your care. He must not be left alone for a minute." A moment later, Mercanton had to grab Joyce's arm to keep him from being hit by a car.[15]

During that trip to Switzerland Joyce suffered, as Nora had predicted before they set out, from severe stomach pains. An x-ray was recommended, but he refused it.

Nora enjoyed her role as the approachable side of the deity. She was a welcome guest at the Giedions' house in Zurich. She greeted husband and wife, as was her custom, with a kiss and brought presents for the children. "There was a wonderful feeling of warmth when she came into the garden," the Giedions' daughter Verena recalled. "We would run and show her our new kittens. But we kept away from *him*, with his black glasses."[16]

Nora (even though she had pronounced it "chop suey") was more tolerant of *Work in Progress* than she had been of *Ulysses* and liked its musicality, especially when read aloud. She also liked the book because it amused Joyce. "I can't sleep any more, I can't sleep any more," she told Mrs. Giedion-Welcker, who asked why not. "Well, Jim is writing at his book. I go to bed and then that man sits in the next room and continues laughing about his own writing. And then I knock at the door, and I say, 'Now, Jim, stop writing or stop laughing.' "[17]

Nora was still not sure whether "that man" was the genius everyone told her he was. "I'm sure of one thing," she told Mrs. Giedion-Welcker. "There is nobody like him."[18]

She and Joyce still traveled constantly, Nora by then an artist at packing and settling into hotel rooms. Joyce needed frequently to visit Zurich to consult Dr. Vogt (who found his sight improved), but their travels were complicated by the need to deceive Lucia into thinking they were where she thought they were. From Lausanne in the summer of 1938, for example, they crept to Dieppe for some sea air, leaving behind letters to be posted by Mercanton.

Such deceptions did not spring merely from guilt. Joyce loved his daughter deeply and dreamed that her mind might suddenly be cured. For her twenty-ninth birthday he placed in her hands at last a bound copy of her own book, the illustrated alphabet poem by Chaucer. The publication cost him fifteen thousand francs, he told Miss Weaver, but he wanted to fight her feeling of worthlessness and to convince her that her life had not been a failure. What was more, he intended to pursue every possible hope of a cure, no matter how unreasonable or expensive the attempt. It would be cheaper, he said with bitter eloquence, to confine Lucia to an "economical mental prison," but

> I will not do so as long as I see a single chance of hope for her recovery, nor blame her or punish her for the great crime she has committed in being a victim to one of the most elusive diseases known to men and unknown to medicine.[19]

The sarcasm was directed not only at Miss Weaver (who responded by covering half the book's cost), but also at Giorgio, who resented this form of his father's extravagance above all. In fact, the clinic at Ivry was not as expensive as those in Switzerland had been, and the director, Dr. Delmas, said that Lucia did not have dementia praecox (as schizophrenia was then often called) and thought that "there was something to be saved." Even so, Joyce did not let the case rest there. He also wrote to Wilhelm

Herz in St. Gallen to ask for information about the sanatorium where Nijinsky, he had been told, had been transformed miraculously by an insulin treatment. It is unlikely that Nora shared his hope for a miracle.

By late 1936 Joyce had spent three-quarters of the portion of Miss Weaver's capital upon which he could draw. There was still coolness between them, however, after Lucia's disastrous visit. Paul Léon advised Miss Weaver to come to Paris, to put right, face to face, little things that should not have been magnified. Once more she braved the ordeal of the Channel, which she hated fully as much as Nora and Joyce did, and at the end of November they met. "Not a word, not a syllable survives to cast light on their meeting," say her biographers. Miss Weaver promised Joyce the money he needed to finish his book and assured him of her faith in it. As always, he coolly accepted patronage as no more than his due. They never saw each other again.[20]

Nora had a more realistic view of Giorgio, as well as of Lucia, than Joyce did. She adored her son, but he often exasperated her. Giorgio's addiction to drink was becoming incapacitating as his father's was not. Yet Joyce could no more see flaws in Giorgio than in Lucia. If Giorgio had not been able to build a career upon a fine bass voice, in Joyce's mind the fault must lie elsewhere. Joyce went so far as to blame Michael Lennon's attack on him in the *Catholic World* for ruining Giorgio's singing prospects in America. And he was furious when the BBC turned down Giorgio after an audition with the verdict: "Below the level of Great Britain in the art of fine singing."[21] His son, he said, was too ready to accept criticisms of himself.

It was inevitable that when Giorgio's marriage began to go on the rocks, Joyce should take his son's side. Unfortunately, Paul Léon sided with Helen, believing Giorgio to be unsympathetic to Helen's problems. The dispute further soured Léon's relationship with Joyce, which had never fully recovered from the Ponisovsky engagement fiasco. Nonetheless, Léon continued to serve as scribe and continued to send letters to Miss Weaver describing Joyce as listless, despondent, seeing almost nobody. Léon did admit, however, that he saw Mr. Joyce very seldom.[22]

Depressed as Joyce may have been, he and Nora kept up their social rounds as before. They dined as regularly as ever at Fouquet's, where Joyce was, as always, very popular with waiters, giving them "millionaire tips" and asking their opinions, not only on the menu but also on their preference for Racine or Corneille. Nora enjoyed the pleasure of eating on these evenings far more than Joyce did. He liked plain food, mushrooms, oysters, lobsters, and Nora liked fancy desserts such as *omelette norvégienne*. She herself was a presence to be contended with. Nancy Cunard, who was summoned to dine with them at Fouquet's, could not find the Joyces amid their usual clutter of lobster shells and wine bottles. As she searched the noisy rooms, wondering why the Joyces patronized a place favored by racing people and smart society, Nancy worried that "Mrs. Joyce would be furious with her for being late."[23] Nora kept a careful eye on the other patrons, as she always did in restaurants. One night she was delighted to recognize Marlene Dietrich (who, like Nora, bought her clothes at Lelong). Nora nudged Joyce, who then presented his compliments to the actress and said that he had admired her in *The Blue Angel*. "Then, monsieur," Dietrich said, "you saw me at my best."[24]

They were eating at home, however, one evening late in 1937 when the telephone rang. It was Samuel Beckett, to say that he had returned to live in Paris after years in London and Dublin. Beckett was apprehensive of being snubbed by Joyce. He had put off looking him up until he summoned the courage one night, bolstered by a good dinner with friends and much wine. He was greatly relieved when he got Nora on the telephone instead of Joyce. Nora quickly put him at his ease, chatting to him about friends and Dublin while, she said, Jim finished his dinner. When Joyce took the receiver, he was distant at first but livened up when he remembered a small favor that Beckett might perform for him.[25]

The favor kept Beckett at Giorgio's house for the next three days. Beckett and Giorgio were good friends from years past. Together, they labored through proofs of the difficult galleys of *Work in Progress*. (The many criticisms made against Giorgio for never working a day in his life should be balanced against the years of unpaid labor he gave his father.) Beckett was content to be unpaid. It was only out of politeness that he accepted the patronizing handout that Joyce gave him: 250 francs, a cast-off overcoat, and five worn neckties.[26]

Beckett, drawn into the family once again, sympathized with Giorgio's efforts to keep his home together in the face of Helen's disintegration. He himself had determined to write no more at Joyce's request, certainly not the new explication of *Work in Progress* that Joyce wanted in advance of the book's publication. If there were another rupture, Beckett told McGreevy, "At least this time it won't be about the daughter." The only thing that Beckett disliked about rejoining the magic circle was Maria Jolas's know-it-all domination of the Joyces' affairs — a resentment that Nora shared in part. Beckett used to refer to Mrs. Jolas as "Jolases-Molases."[27]

Maria Jolas dominated Nora as well as Joyce. Nora was strong but in no way managerial. Like Joyce, she always leaned passively and heavily on the organizational ability of the protectress of the hour. In the late 1930s, what Mrs. Jolas planned, they followed, and before long young Stephen was enrolled in her École Bilingue in Neuilly. But Mrs. Jolas never interfered between Nora and Joyce; she marveled, as all did, how Joyce never said a cross word to Nora.

One night Nora and Joyce took Helen, Giorgio, Beckett, and Helen's friend Peggy Guggenheim out to dinner, following which they all went back to the Villa Scheffer. Beckett, who had been staring at Peggy, asked if he could see her home. Home, Peggy later recounted, led to the sofa, and then "we soon found ourselves in bed where we remained until the next evening." Peggy left only because she had a dinner engagement. Beckett thanked her and said, "It was nice while it lasted."[28]

As 1937 ended Nora suffered a new blow. Helen had talked Giorgio into returning to New York because her father was ill. She had booked passage for January 8. Nora was so hurt and angry that she refused to join Helen and Giorgio for their planned New Year's Eve party. Beckett, who came to collect them, found Joyce begging Nora to go. She adamantly refused. Since Joyce would not leave Nora, he dispatched Beckett to join Helen and Giorgio, and the Joyce couples spent the evening apart, in equal gloom.[29]

As Nora had no Paul Léon to record her state of mind, her anxieties can only be imagined. She had thought her son and grandson firmly in Paris, only to have them snatched away. With all the talk of war, any separation might be a long one. Then there was the matter of Helen's stability. Nora and Joyce had seen trouble coming for a long while.[30] If anything went wrong with Helen in America, Nora could do nothing to help Giorgio or Stephen. The Kastors were a harrowed family at that time. In August 1937 Helen's older brother, Alfred, had tried to kill himself. Joyce wrote old Adolph Kastor a kindly but circumspect letter of condolence in which he suggested without going into detail that

> the actual physical disfigurement might be much worse as a result of a train or a machinery accident and it may prove to be only a tribute which he had to pay in order to buy off a demoniac possession.[31]

Private crises continued to mimic public traumas, as if to underline the message of Joyce's new book: that the history of a family is the history of the world. The night before Giorgio and Helen were to set sail, Beckett, on the way home from a Left Bank café with two friends, was stabbed by a pimp whose aggressive importuning he had roughly brushed off. The knife nearly penetrated his heart, and his life was in danger.

Joyce was one of the first to find out about the attack; he had been telephoning Beckett's hotel because he wanted to see Beckett. From then on, the Joyces, as favorite and most important friends, took charge. Joyce had Beckett moved to a private room at his own expense. Their Dr. Fontaine was put on to the case. At their flat Nora manned the telephone, which rang constantly — "like the stock exchange," Joyce reported in a letter to Helen and Giorgio, who had left for America.[32] Even Peggy called Nora to see how Sam was. Nora sent a custard pudding to the hospital, giving Beckett a taste of Irish home cooking to help his recovery.

. . .

Beckett had hardly recovered when the political climate grew darker. In March 1938 Hitler annexed Austria — the Anschluss, his first move outside German territory. The same day the French government fell. There was tea as usual at five o'clock at the Joyces'. Friends had gathered, but the atmosphere was more like a wake. Joyce was in a black depression. He saw the approach of war as a terrible personal tragedy. If it came, no one was going to be reading his book. That day the group included Beckett and Elizabeth Curran. No one was speaking. The silence was terrible. Then Nora cut into the gloom, saying briskly, "We can do nothing about it." Her calm fatalism brought them out of themselves, and they began to talk to each other, the ordinariness of life restored.

Nora's intervention struck Elizabeth as very Irish. Maria Jolas and the Paris literary set (Beckett and McGreevy apart) never understood her Irishness, Elizabeth felt. They always carried "that sense of coming to see The Master." They liked Nora but did not comprehend how Joyce *liked* being pushed around by Nora. "She could laugh him out of his depressions by her plain down-to-earth humour," Elizabeth said. "He never shut her up, not for a minute. The others had him on a pedestal. Nora didn't fit on the pedestal. They came to worship. But people from home [Ireland] could see their closeness. He would start a conversation with Nora, intentionally shutting all the others out. They had a kind of running banter between them on a very intimate level. She was a relief and an outlet for him. It made a wonderful impression — this utter understanding between two people." [33]

One way Nora teased her husband was to threaten to divulge the magic words of the real title of *Work in Progress*. Joyce, like Rumpelstiltskin, enjoyed daring his friends to guess what it was. Nora joined the game one night, playfully humming the tune of an Irish ballad about a Mr. Flannigan and Mr. Shannigan.

As Ellmann recreated the scene,

> Joyce, startled, asked her to stop. When he saw no harm had been done, he very distinctly, as a singer does it, made the lip motions which seemed to indicate F and W. Maria Jolas guessed "Fairy's Wake." Joyce looked astonished and said "Brava! But something is missing."

It took Eugene Jolas the whole night (he had, after all, published many extracts from the work) to solve the riddle, and the next night at Fouquet's he said it aloud: "Finnegans Wake." Joyce said, "Ah, Jolas, you've taken something out of me." But he paid up the reward he had offered — in a bag of small coins — the next morning. [34]

Beckett, whose first novel, *Murphy,* had just been published, still revered Joyce. When he recovered, he was content to follow Joyce around as a Giorgio-substitute. He was disappointed when the Joyces did not invite him, as he had expected, to Zurich with them when he came out of hospital. He was convinced that they had not entirely forgiven him for inspiring their daughter's hopeless passion. When Joyce began to confide in Beckett his latest theory about Lucia — that all her mental disorientation might have been caused by an infection in her teeth — Beckett listened patiently, grateful to be a confidant. And his appreciation of Nora, which had always been strong, only deepened when she gave him some of their large pieces of unwanted furniture for his new flat. (Unlike the Joyces, Beckett preferred working-class districts and a simple style of life.)

Their social life continued lively. Joyce declined one dinner invitation, however, since the invitation was for 7:30 P.M., an hour he continued to find uncivilized for dining. Nora represented them both at the five-hour Russian Orthodox funeral for the great bass Chaliapin.[35] Then their lives brightened in April when against Nora's foreboding, Giorgio and Helen returned.

In May 1938 Nora and Joyce presented themselves at the Villa Scheffer for three days of photographs to accompany the publicity for *Finnegans Wake*. The book was nearly finished, although it would not be ready in time to be published, as Joyce had hoped, on his father's birthday, July 4. The photographs taken at that time by Gisèle Freund (who had replaced Sylvia Beach as Adrienne Monnier's companion) are among the finest, most relaxed, and happiest ever taken of Joyce. He is shown smiling, even in proximity to a dreaded dog. Helen, Giorgio (also shown with a rare smile), and Stephen are also in the photographs. Yet there is no sign of Nora. She, who liked so much to be photographed, absolutely refused to join in, saying, in traditional grandmotherly fashion, that no one wanted to look at her. Perhaps she felt overshadowed by her daughter-in-law. Helen appears, as in almost all her pictures, beaming with pleasure.

Two months later Helen was a patient in a mental clinic in Montreux, suffering from deep depression. As if, Joyce wrote to his friend the French academician Louis Gillet, the similar tragedy of their daughter were not enough.[36] Nora had the bleak satisfaction of seeing her pessimism about the marriage in 1930 all too well borne out. Helen's illness split the family just as Lucia's had. Neither Nora nor Giorgio could believe that Helen would get a great deal better. Joyce professed himself optimistic. He was very fond of Helen. On the Fourth of July he sent Helen flowers, urging kindly, "Cheer up for the love of Giorgio."[37]

In those closing months of 1938, with both his daughter and daughter-in-law lost to him and Europe on the edge of war, Joyce wrote the close of *Finnegans Wake*. After he finished it, he was so exhausted that he sat a long while on a street bench, unable to move, yet, rarely for him, satisfied. These were the last pages he was ever to write and they were among his greatest. However obscure much of the rest of the book, these pages justified Joyce's insistence, "If anyone doesn't understand a passage, all he need do is to read it aloud."[38]

The closing passage of *Finnegans Wake,* as of *Ulysses,* is delivered in the voice of a woman — an Irishwoman. She is Anna Livia Plurabelle, the book's main female character, the universal mother. But in the symbolic shorthand of the *Wake,* the woman is also a river, the Liffey, and she speaks as she flows to extinction in the icy arms of Dublin Bay.

Anna Livia's reverie shows a woman at the end of her life, just as Molly's monologue in *Ulysses* shows a woman at the end of her day. Anna, looking back on the long years, from girlish beauty to exhausted age, quietly accepts the futility of all the sorrows of raising a family and of devoting her life to an impossible man:

> I done me best when I was let. Thinking always if I go all goes. A hundred cares, a tithe of troubles and is there one who understands me? . . . All me life I have been lived among them but now they are becoming lothed to me. And I am lothing their little warm tricks. And lothing their mean cosy turns. And all the greedy gushes out through their small souls. And all the lazy leaks down over their brash bodies. How small it's all! . . .[39]

The family that Nora and Joyce created was the *Wake*'s family — a family out of any cultural context, as poor Giorgio learned, with his mongrel accent. Today Marxist scholars among the Joyceans observe that in the *Wake,* Joyce wrests English from its colonial past; they remark also that Ireland's two greatest prose writers of the twentieth century chose to shun the language of the conqueror, Joyce by inventing his own language, Beckett by writing in French.

Yet the universal language that Joyce created is really English with foreign touches and a strong Irish accent. That is how Nora spoke. All her life her speech retained the rhythms of Ireland: "I pray to God, I pray to God every night for rain."[40] If the polyglot language of the *Wake* is Joyce's triumphal answer to Stephen Dedalus's complaint against the English spoken by his dean of studies in *A Portrait* — "The language in which we are speaking is his before it is mine" — it is also true that the words of Molly Bloom and Anna Livia Plurabelle were Nora's before they were Joyce's. In using a female voice to utter the universal truth — that all things die and are born again — Joyce was making women's speech the universal tongue.

But above all it was upon Nora's temperament — the calm if mocking submission to whatever life sent: love, unreasoning, sometimes obscene passion; drunkenness, disappointment, madness, luxury, and poverty — that Joyce drew for the *Wake*'s epilogue, a great final hymn to the acceptance of death because of the permanence of life.

As Anna Livia nears the "therrble prongs" of Dublin Bay and her extinction in the great father, the sea, she moans,

> I am passing out. O bitter ending! I'll slip away before they're up. They'll never see. Nor know. Nor miss me. And it's old and old it's sad and old it's sad and weary I go back to you, my cold father, my cold mad father, my cold mad feary father, till the near sight of the mere size of him, the moyles and moyles of it, moananoaning, makes me seasilt saltsick and I rush, my only, into your arms.[41]

Still fresh in Anna Livia's memory are the days of her early love, of her children as infants, of her own father, of yielding to an overpowering man who obliterated her. She disappears with a ripple of the waters as day breaks:

> So soft this morning, ours. Yes. Carry me along, taddy, like you done through the toy fair! If I seen him bearing down on me now under whitespread wings like he'd come from Arkangels, I sink I'd die down over his feet, humbly dumbly, only to washup. Yes, tid. There's where. First. We pass through grass behush the bush to. Whish! A gull. Gulls. Far calls. Coming, far! End here. Us then. Finn, again! Take. Bussoftlhee, mememormee! Till thousands-thee. Lps. The keys to. Given! A way a lone a last a loved a long the[42]

All things pass away but life renews itself. Ends are beginnings. The river becomes the sea which becomes cloud which becomes rain which falls on rivers which flow to the sea. Everything circles round, just as the last incomplete phrase of the *Wake* circles round to rejoin the beginning of the book:

> riverrun, past Eve and Adam's, from swerve of shore to bend of bay, brings us by a commodius vicus of recirculation back to Howth Castle and Environs.[43]

On February 2, 1939, a bound copy of *Finnegans Wake* was ready, although the book would not be published until May. The event called for a celebration, all the more because Helen, out of her depression and her clinic, was back in Paris in fine form, vivacious and charming. She organized a banquet, to which Joyce invited all his close friends, to honor his birthday and his book. Helen employed her talents to the full. For her table she assembled symbols of Joyce's work and life: silver paper to stand for the Liffey and the Seine, a mirrored tray to represent the English channel, a bottle in the shape of Nelson's Pillar in Dublin, and a decanter in the form of the Eiffel Tower. She had also commissioned a baker to make a cake in the form of all Joyce's books in a row, from *Dubliners* to the *Wake*. Others might have found the display embarrassing, but Joyce adored it.[44]

Joyce indulged in his own symbolic celebration. He gave Nora a ring containing a large aquamarine, the symbol of the Liffey and of herself: the river of life. Nora wore the ring proudly to the dinner. "Jim," she said in front of them all, "I haven't read any of your books but I guess I'll have to seeing how well they sell." Nobody laughed. All felt the weight of the years of hunger, poverty, and illness that the two Joyces had come through together.[45]

Joyce, reconciled through his daughter-in-law to the American accent, asked Helen to read the last pages of the *Wake*. As they sat and listened, only Nora, of all in the room, knew that the Liffey flowed to the sea past Ringsend where she and Jim had first walked out together, and that Jim had ended his book with the very words with which he had asked her to come away with him in 1904: "Is there one who understands me?" No wonder that Nora would say in years to come, "What's all this about *Ulysses? Finnegans Wake*. That's the important book."[46]

O bitter ending. The party was Helen's last performance as Mrs. George Joyce. By April their Parisian family life was shattered. Helen had broken down again and had been sent back to Montreux. The lease was up on the rue Edmond Valentin flat, and many of their friends were leaving Paris. Hitler had completed the occupation of Czechoslovakia, and there was talk of invasion. Dr. Delmas made plans to evacuate his clinic and patients to La Baule in Brittany. Still, Nora and Joyce made no plans to leave but instead moved into a new and smaller flat at 34 rue des Vignes, not far from Giorgio in the sixteenth arrondissement. As they packed up, Joyce gave Paul Léon eight packages of proofs of *Finnegans Wake* to send to Miss Weaver in London. Nora tried to tidy up her own papers. "I've just spent the most awful day," she said to Maria Jolas, "tearing up Jim's letters to me. They were nobody's business. There weren't many anyway — we've never been separated."[47] Her remark was not strictly accurate, as the emergence of the correspondence of 1904, 1909, and 1917 left behind in Trieste was later to reveal. What Nora herself chose to censor by destruction remains her own secret.

Nora's political views on the war were less ambiguous than her husband's. Just as she was never anti-British, Nora was never neutral. Joyce used to tease her about her royalist fondness for "King Giorgio," and Nora made Maria Jolas laugh when she gazed at the two little Jolas daughters and said, "Tina and Betsy always make me think of Elizabeth and Margaret Rose."[48]

Joyce, although not as outspokenly pro-German as he had been during the First World War, never denounced Hitler in the ringing terms that many of his later admirers might have wished. He did sympathize intensely with the sufferings of the Jews and used all his influence to help a number to escape from Germany. He uttered occasional phrases, how-

ever, that ring hollow in the postwar ear. Of Hitler he once said scorn-
fully, "Give him Europe!"[49] Insensitively, one night at the Léons' he remarked how impressed he was with Hitler's immense force and powers
of leadership. That was too much for Nora. She picked up her dinner
knife and jumped up, threatening, "Jim, one more good word about that
devil, and I'll murder you!"[50] Her response had such a strange mixture
of genuine anger and acting that Mrs. Giedion-Welcker thought of Char-
lotte Corday: "I suddenly wished I could see this high-spirited Irishwoman, who was now standing at the head of the table with her drawn
knife, confronting Hitler not Joyce." Joyce, Mrs. Giedion-Welcker observed, accepted Nora's outburst with admiration and fascination, as he
always did when she spontaneously expressed herself upon matters to
which he had given long and inconclusive thought.

In 1939 Joyce, who had almost ceased to communicate with Harriet
Weaver, wrote her an account of Helen's breakdown. His son's home
life, he said, was ruined. Miss Weaver wrote back sympathetically but
once again managed to choose the wrong words. Joyce replied by accusing her of improper curiosity in his family affairs.[51] Miss Weaver destroyed his letter and the previous one about Helen, perhaps her last
great service to Joyce the man. His letter to her is unlikely to have done
him credit.

Helen spent most of the summer of 1939 in the Montreux clinic while
Stephen was at summer camp in Étretat. Nora and Joyce visited him
there. Helen reappeared in Paris in September — not an ideal time for
peace of mind. War was beginning. In the first few days of September
Poland fell, Britain and France declared war on Germany, and the invasion of France was expected at any time. Eugene Jolas had returned to
the United States. Maria had evacuated her school to a village near Vichy
with the promise to her husband that she would take their daughters and
leave Europe if the situation worsened. A few stuck it out in Paris: Sylvia
Beach and, for a time, Gertrude Stein and Alice B. Toklas. Helen Joyce
was in no condition to stand the daily increase of tension. Having retrieved Stephen from his summer camp, Helen sent the Joyces a postcard
at La Baule. On the front was a photograph of Stephen, looking like a
pensive angel, and on the back a message scribbled in such frenzy that
they must have known, from sad experience with Lucia, that Helen's
mind had snapped.
    Indeed it had. The Currans thought of Helen's final collapse as "a
menopause thing" (Helen was forty-four in 1939). The tragedy for them
all was that it took the form of a spectacular burst of bizarre behavior
that finally put her in the hands of the police. Peggy Guggenheim described the event unfeelingly in her memoirs, opening a chapter called

"My Life During the War" with a description of Helen's last free hours in Paris:

Giorgio Joyce was in great trouble. His wife Helen had gone mad and was rushing around Paris with two blue Persian kittens which she took everywhere in order to attract attention. She was having an affair with a house painter in the country, and also tried to seduce every man she met. Giorgio had retired to Paris and was living with our friend Ponisovsky. He came to get me hoping I would console him and give him some advice. He was very worried about his child, and wanted to get [it] away from his wife. One night, when we were in a restaurant his wife came in with the nurse who was supposed to guard her. She made an awful scene and I left at once. The whole thing was painful and Ponisovsky and I were terrified that Giorgio was going to have her locked up. We did not realize how ill she was and we tried to prevail upon Giorgio to leave her in freedom. She was going about incurring debts with all the dressmakers, as she had the *folie de grandeur*. She went to the police and denounced as spies her friends Elsa Schiaparelli, James Joyce and some other people. She really was getting dangerous, but I hated the thought of her being locked up.[52]

As the exodus from Paris gathered force in September 1939, Nora and Joyce were in La Baule, waiting for Lucia's removal. She arrived, with her clinic, in midmonth. They remained to be near her. Giorgio, no longer living at the Villa Scheffer, was somewhere in Paris. He wanted Helen taken back to New York. Joyce asked Paul Léon to write to Robert Kastor, relaying Giorgio's request. Léon refused. Joyce then brutally severed relations with the man who had for ten years been his closest helper.[53]

Giorgio, worried about Stephen, decided to act. He enlisted a friend to come with him out to Helen's villa on the outskirts of Paris as witness to the fact that she would not let him into his own house. As they approached the house (named, by Helen, Shillelagh) she emerged and told them not to come farther. She bent and began flinging stones from the gravel path at them until they retreated.

The final parting between husband and wife took the form of a physical tug of war over Stephen. In broad daylight Giorgio virtually kidnapped his son and, with Helen clutching at the boy, bundled him into a taxi. Giorgio telephoned his mother and father in La Baule. They agreed to rush back to Paris to help him. Joyce assured Lucia that they would return soon but he was wrong. One madwoman took them away from another. He was never to see his daughter again.

Nora was left with the task of trying to make a home for four in the rue des Vignes flat meant for two. Normal life was impossible. Bitter cold set in early in October, and there was no heat in the apartment building. They decided to move together into the Hôtel Lutétia on the boulevard Raspail. Even as they did so Helen's condition grew worse. After Stephen was taken away, she went on the wild spending spree described by Peggy and ran up debts of half a million francs. What happened next was described with sorrow and dignity by Joyce in a letter to Mercanton on January 9, 1940: "My unfortunate daughter-in-law, after having spread about her an indescribable ruin both material and moral was interned by the French authorities as dangerous to herself and others."[54]

Helen was confined, in fact, to the Maison de Santé at Suresnes, a mental hospital outside Paris which had many well-known patients. Robert Kastor flew over in early November to try to take his beloved and once elegant sister back home to Manhattan, but Helen was too agitated to be put on a plane. For the time being he had no choice but to leave her in Suresnes. He returned by himself to New York by Pan American clipper.[55]

Nora and Joyce decided to send Stephen to join Maria Jolas's school in its evacuation quarters in a village near Vichy. In November, Stephen, just seven, having been shunted from nurse to nurse and from school to camp almost from birth, traveled to the school at St.-Gérand-le-Puy. He was in a highly nervous condition and was given a room by himself, away from the noisy dormitory. Some of the staff, who felt sorry for him, used to smuggle him sweets, hoping that Madame Jolas would not learn of it.[56]

Perhaps his grandson's lonely exile reminded Joyce of the homesickness and loneliness of a small boy who was delivered, aged six, to Clongowes Wood boarding school in Ireland in 1888. He promised Stephen that he and Nonna, as Stephen called Nora, would join him for Christmas. Left in the abnormal atmosphere of Paris, with its curfew and daily expectation of bombardment, Joyce had a kind of collapse himself, spending and drinking wildly. He depended childishly on Beckett and took him back to the rue des Vignes to collect some things. Everything was still there, even the piano. Joyce sat down and played and sang loudly for half an hour, with shaking voice and hands. "What is the use of this war?" he asked Beckett.[57] Beckett, a younger man and a confirmed Francophile, saw the war against Hitler as something more than a personal intrusion and later was active in the French Resistance.

Two days before Christmas, Beckett put Nora and Joyce on the train for St.-Germain-des-Fossés, the nearest train stop to St.-Gérand-le-Puy. Except for their clothes, they left everything they owned at their flat. Giorgio went too but planned to return immediately after the holiday. Nora and Joyce did not seem to know where they would go next or care. Joyce was frail and exhausted, Nora was suffering the onset of arthritis. As they turned their backs on Paris, uprooted once again, they needed their grandson as much as he needed them.

19

Flight into Zurich

S T .- G É R A N D - L E - P U Y I S a small village nearly two hundred miles southeast of Paris. Its lattice of gray streets and shuttered houses lies between the golden farmlands of the Allier and the main truck route from Clermont-Férand to Paris. Arriving there just before Christmas in 1939, the Joyces found that the Hôtel de la Paix, into which Maria Jolas had booked them, was little more than a café, with rooms overlooking the square and the noisy highway.

Nora persuaded Joyce to settle there until their next move was clearer. Although they both disliked the tedium of village life, there was no point going back to Paris. At least in St.-Gérand they did not have to strain every nerve to hear whether the bombardment had begun. Also Stephen could join them every Sunday on his free day from the Jolas boarding school. Since they were cut off from their possessions, their flat, and their friends, it hardly mattered where they were. Nora's immediate worry was Giorgio. He had returned to Paris after Christmas and had not written even to let them know his address. (Giorgio had, in fact, moved back into the Hôtel Lutétia and had begun an affair with Peggy Guggenheim.)[1]

Nora adapted herself to village life better than Joyce cared to do. He appeared as a solitary silent figure as he walked through the village with his pockets full of stones to drive away the dogs that nipped at his heels. Occasionally he was seen to slip into the church, where he would sit silently in a chair at the back. Nora, in contrast, soon greeted everyone she passed by name and made some friends among the wives. They knew she was the wife of a famous writer and saw her as *"une dame distin-*

guée, agréable et calme," with superb posture and a splendid astrakhan coat.[2]

Their lives were in a state of paralysis. They were far more fortunate than many in Europe as 1940 began, but they could not see their way ahead. Nora had never known Joyce in a blacker mood. In 1912 he had written her that he was like a man looking into a dark pool, yet none of the frustrations of his early career could compare to the abyss he faced in 1940. His personal world was shattered, and the book over which he had labored for seventeen years had created nothing of the impact of *Ulysses*. Worse, for the first time in his life, he had no work in progress. Like Othello, his occupation was gone.

The remarkable thing is how well, considering the distractions of war, the first critics of *Finnegans Wake* understood the book and Joyce's intention. The American critic Edmund Wilson had already given readers a useful key long before the book was finished. Although some of today's critics disagree with Wilson's contention that the book is the story of a dream and that its action takes place in the sleeping mind of H. C. Earwicker, Wilson explained as well as Joyce could have wished the working of Joyce's new language. A single one of Joyce's sentences, Wilson said, combined two or three different meanings. A single word might combine two or three:

> Without the complications of his vocabulary, Joyce would no doubt never be able to paint for us with so sensitive and sure a hand the turbid life of that mental half-world where the unconscious is merged with the conscious — as without his machinery of history and myth, he would not be able to give his subject any poetic freedom of significance beyond the realistic framework which holds it firm. We are to see in H. C. Earwicker Everyman (he imagines his initials standing for Here Comes Everybody). We are to find in his dream all human possibilities. . . . And what humor, what imagination, what poetry, what psychological wisdom, Joyce has put into Earwicker's dream![3]

Time had once again given Joyce a cover story, accompanied by another model of popular literary criticism. It explained the many-layered meanings of the title:

> Besides reminding readers that they are in for an Irish evening, his title might be taken as a simple declarative sentence meaning that Finnegans wake up. Hence the implication: ordinary people (such as his hero) do not; the nightmare existence of Everyman ends merely in deeper sleep.[4]

Time once again did well by Nora too. It ran a stately photograph with the caption "In Galway she was a Barnacle," and quoted her as remembering Zurich as a place of poverty and cramped quarters, "long on mice, short on kitchen utensils."

Geoffrey Grigson in the British *Picture Post* described the plot as "the adventures of primal man and primal woman, H. C. Earwicker (or Haveth Childers Everywhere) and Anne [sic] Livia Plurabella [sic], who is Eve and all the rivers of the world, just as H. C. Earwicker is all the mountains in the world." The book, Grigson judged, was "an Irish stew with passages of real beauty" and its "new" language basically English but "mixed up with everything from Irish to Iceland."

As if to justify Joyce's self-indulgence in inventing his own language, Grigson said that Joyce had become a king in Paris, worshiped by writers as painters worshiped Picasso. Adulation, Grigson implied, had not done Joyce any good.[5]

There was little adulation for a displaced artist in a Burgundian village. Nora, unlike her husband, was busier than ever. She worked to divert him, to find him friends, to make a semblance of a routine. She found him a barber, where he went every morning to be shaved, bringing his own razor, and herself a hairdresser, where she went every week to have her thick, now gray, hair washed and arranged in a chignon. One day Joyce decided that Nora's hairdresser, a Madame Bouboule, should cut his hair as well. Madame Bouboule was shocked and refused. She cut only women's hair, she protested. But Joyce, as disdainful of sexual boundaries in hairdressing as in language, grew stubborn and refused to leave her shop until she gave in.[6]

Frustrated and bored, Joyce spent much time drinking at the café of the Hôtel de la Paix. In such a small village, he had to work harder than ever to slip away past Nora's watchful eye. He took to entering the café by the back door for several glasses of Pernod before dinner, at which he would become quickly drunk. "Look at the man," Nora would say. "He can't stand a glass of wine" or "He's absolutely blithered!"[7] He could not stand food either, and Nora could find little to tempt his appetite except pastry for tea.

Even in tiny St.-Gérand, Nora and Joyce remained nomads. They moved four times within a year. (In 1982, when the village decided to put up a plaque to commemorate Joyce's year there, the authorities had difficulty deciding at which address to place it.) They remained at their first stop, the Hôtel de la Paix, until Easter. Then they moved to the outskirts of the town to Maria Jolas's school, a pleasant country house set in beautiful forested grounds. When pupils returned after the vacation, Nora and Joyce sought the more sophisticated environment of Vichy, not far away. There for eight weeks they lived at the Hôtel Beaujolais, enjoying the thermal springs, the parks, and fountains. Nora enjoyed visiting her good friend Maria Nebbia, who was living there with Valery Larbaud, who was by then nearly completely paralyzed from sclerosis. But then any semblance of normal life vanished as Hitler began his assault on the western front.

In April 1940 German troops occupied Denmark. Holland and Belgium fell in May. So did Norway, taking Chamberlain's government in Britain down with it because Britain had counted on retaining a foothold in Norway. Winston Churchill became the British prime minister, and with the evacuation from Dunkirk, the last British troops had withdrawn from the Continent by June 3. Then it was Paris's turn.

Helen Joyce remained locked in Suresnes in Paris. At the last moment before the German invasion, from New York Robert Kastor succeeded in prising his sister free. He had her taken under sedation, escorted by two doctors and two nurses, to Genoa and put on a liner for the United States. That Helen was at least safe (she spent the war in a sanatorium in Connecticut) was some consolation to Joyce, who was full of wistful and sad thoughts of her, of the marvelous banquet she had given on his birthday in 1939, of her moving reading of the epilogue of *Finnegans Wake*, and of her constant thoughtfulness. As he wrote, he told Constantine Curran, the little gold charm she had had made for him tinkled from the end of his fountain pen.[8]

The arrival in Vichy of the French wartime collaborationist government forced Nora and Joyce out of the Hôtel Beaujolais. As the French parliament met in the Grand Casino and the Gestapo established itself at the Hôtel Portugal, Vichy swiftly filled its fifteen thousand hotel rooms with politicians, diplomats, and secret police and was on its way to becoming an international byword for defeat, intrigue, and betrayal. One of the parliament's first acts was to give full powers to the eighty-four-year-old Marshal Pétain, whose government saved the French people from the full force of the German army but at the price, many felt, of France's honor.[9]

The Joyces took themselves back to St.-Gérand. The village was just a few miles south of the border between occupied and unoccupied France and was itself a place of confused allegiances. Thus Joyce found himself, in the Second World War as in the First, in an environment torn by both pro- and anti-German factions, and it was noticed in St.-Gérand that he was guarded about proclaiming his views.[10]

They settled into a flat of their own temporarily, and Nora hired a refugee to help with her housework. From there they moved into the Hôtel du Commerce, then back out to the Jolas school, where they lived in a lodge adjoining the main building.

By now they were hardly alone. The fall of Paris had sent some of their friends to join them. Paul and Lucie Léon arrived, and Joyce made a cool peace with his old friend. To Nora's great relief, Giorgio also arrived. Nora put him up on a bed in the dining room, as she had so often during his adolescence. This time there was no question of his leaving. He was trying to avoid being conscripted into the French army and tried to be as inconspicuous as possible. He did not register, as he should have done, at the town hall. However, if he was officially a nonperson, Giorgio soon became well known locally for his fondness for cognac and for the local girls.[11]

To Nora fell the task of enlivening their days. As usual, she entertained. No occasion for a celebration was missed, and Joyce joined in by buying all kinds of special foods that had sentimental or symbolic value for him. One evening, with friends gathered round the table, Nora had prepared a fine dinner with two roast chickens. The doorbell rang, and a boy delivered some dish Joyce had ordered. Nora added it to the menu. The bell rang again. More food. Nora did not get annoyed. She knew Jim too well. "Just look at the man!" was all she said. "Will you look at the man!" Joyce was proud of her adaptability. "My wife," he would say, "used to cook over an open turf fire in Ireland."[12]

Always on their minds was the abandoned Paris flat. All their things were there, and the rent was not being paid, since their main source of income, Miss Weaver's fund, was blocked — Britain had cut off diplomatic relations with France following the German occupation. The Léons were returning to Paris, and Paul Léon determined to do what he could to relieve the Joyces' anxiety.

Léon went around to the rue des Vignes, without a key, and found that he could get into the flat through a window. Bribing the concierge to silence, he spent two days sorting out Joyce's private letters and documents. He placed them into envelopes and had them carried back to his own flat. Léon knew how uncertain his own future was. The Germans had been rounding up Parisian Jews. "What are you doing here?" Beckett had asked him in alarm when he saw him. Léon hit upon the idea of sending Joyce's papers for safekeeping to the Irish legation on the Place Vendôme. Since Ireland was neutral in the war, its premises would not be attacked. He gave the papers to the Irish consul, Count Gerald O'Kelly, with two stipulations. If he were to die, the papers were to go to James Joyce. If both of them were to die, the papers were to go to the National Library of Ireland, not to be opened (because of their "intimate character") until fifty years after Joyce's death.[13]

The problem of the rest of the contents of the flat was not solved so neatly. The landlord, angry at being unpaid, illegally auctioned off some of the Joyces' pictures and furnishings. The Léons bought all they could on Nora's and Joyce's behalf. Then Léon decided that it was time for him to leave the city. However, his son, Alex, was due to be examined for the baccalaureate, and Léon postponed his departure until the day after the examination. That paternal gesture cost him his life. The Gestapo came to the flat and led him away. He was taken to a camp near Compiègne, then moved to Silesia. In 1942, probably on April 4, as he was being marched with some other prisoners, Léon was ordered out of line by a guard and shot in the head.[14]

By August 1940 Nora and Joyce knew that they had to move on. Maria Jolas, the pillar of their existence in St.-Gérand, was taking her daughters and returning to America. For the Joyces too America would have been a safe haven. They had many friends there, such as Padraic and Mary Colum; Joyce had many admirers, and Stephen Joyce had all his maternal relatives, who were willing to help look after him. But Nora was terrified of crossing water and still recoiled from the idea of America, and so did Joyce. Lucia was the determining factor. Her clinic in Brittany was in the German-occupied part of France, and her parents could not think of putting an ocean between them and her.

Switzerland once again seemed the appropriate refuge. They had sat out one war there; they might as well try again. The difficulty was that Swiss authorities, inundated by refugees on all sides, were restricting eligibility by demanding the deposit of a large sum as a financial guarantee.

Unfortunately, the Joyces' access to their money was blocked by the German forces. In St.-Gérand Nora and Joyce had lived on a subsidy paid through the American embassy in Vichy on behalf of the British government for British subjects trapped in France. Joyce's income, even if he had been able to receive it, was modest. It came from four sources: from Harriet Weaver; from his three London publishers, Faber, John Lane, and Cape; from two American publishers, Viking and Random House; and from Helen Joyce's father, Adolph Kastor, who gave a sum to support Stephen that was well in excess of the boy's school fees. It all added up to the equivalent of $4,300 a year, enough to support them in Switzerland, but in no way approaching the 20,000 Swiss francs ($7,500) that the Swiss wanted in the bank before the Joyce family crossed the border.[15]

Apart from trying to amass the guarantee, Joyce had the nightmarish task of trying to secure written permission for the move from the Germans in Occupied France, the French Vichy government, and the Swiss, and to get their British passports stamped with the appropriate exit and entry stamps. Giorgio bicycled back and forth to Vichy on the seemingly endless quest. Just when Joyce thought he had assembled all the necessary documents, two new obstacles arose. One was Lucia's outstanding bill at her clinic; Joyce had no money with which to settle it. The second was that the Swiss turned down his application on the grounds that he was a Jew.[16]

Joyce was outraged. "What next. Burglars, lepers?" [17] When the Swiss authorities saw his financial statements, Joyce said to friends, they would see how little Jew he was.

When Joyce was persecuted, as usual his realism deserted him. The Swiss authorities were undoubtedly aware of Joyce's Jewish relatives at St. Gallen. They probably concluded that anyone married to a Jew was likely to be Jewish. Joyce himself could have done more to acknowledge his indebtedness to Helen's generous father, as, for example, when he promised to Carola Giedion-Welcker that he would repay any contribution she and her husband made toward his guarantee: "If my son and I prepare to pay for the child in a school in Vaud and for my daughter in a *maison de santé*, I suppose we cannot be entirely destitute of the means to exist." [18]

The Giedions and the Brauchbar family, other old Zurich friends, came through with the money, personally making up the twenty thousand Swiss francs required and depositing the money in Joyce's name in a Swiss bank. For help with Lucia's bills, Joyce turned to another reliable Zurich friend: Gustav Zumsteg, the manager of the famous Kronenhalle Restaurant. [19]

There seemed no end to their bad news. In November 1940 Nora learned from Galway that her mother had died. There was no other information about why or how or what arrangements were made for the funeral. Stephen Joyce remembered the event because his grandfather broke down and wept like a baby. [20]

Almost simultaneously the Zurich authorities decided that the Joyces could take refuge there, and the German authorities withdrew Lucia's exit permit. That made a decision easier. They would go without her. Nora had had their trunks packed for weeks, and Joyce reasoned that from Switzerland, with the help of the Red Cross and with Count O'Kelly serving as intermediary in Paris, he could more easily negotiate the arrangements for Lucia to join them. The more immediate danger was to Giorgio. If he hung on in France, the army would surely claim him, and what is more, their own visas to enter Switzerland, already extended once, would expire.

On December 16, 1940, the Joyces left France, clutching documents, suitcases, and Stephen's bicycle. The only train they could catch to Geneva stopped at the station in a nearby village at three o'clock in the morning. As they made their way through the sleeping streets of St.-Gérand, steathily and with their dwindling pile of possessions, they were almost like the Joyces of Dublin forty years before, flitting by moonlight to a new and poorer address.

Three times Nora had marked momentous changes in her life by disembarking at Zurich's central *Bahnhof*. This time she was limping with arthritis, and Joyce was emaciated and wracked with stomach pain. As in 1915 they had two dependents with them, Giorgio, almost as helpless as he had been as a boy, and their grandson, calmly trusting the grandparents who had, in effect, become his parents. Stephen arrived without his bicycle. The Swiss guards had confiscated it at the border when Joyce could not pay the duty.

There was no question of the Carlton Élite or the St. Gotthard for this stay in Zurich. Mrs. Giedion-Welcker escorted them straight to the modest pension, the Delphin, where she had booked rooms. The Giedions and the Brauchbars were not able to extend to the Joyces largesse in the Harriet Shaw Weaver manner; moreover, they fully expected their money back as soon as Joyce had access to his money in London. Joyce, for perhaps the first time in his long history of accepting patronage, felt uneasy at being in debt to friends. Nora hated it.[21]

Less than one month later Nora was a widow. Joyce died on January 13, 1941, of a perforated ulcer, just short of his fifty-ninth birthday. The ulcer had gone untreated for seven years as Joyce, in other ways so resistant to Freudian theories, had accepted the reassurances of Maria Jolas and Dr. Fontaine that his pains were psychosomatic, caused by "nerves." "If Joyce had listened to Nora," Arthur Power later said, "instead of to Maria Jolas, he would not have died so young."[22]

The last evening he and Nora spent together was at the Kronenhalle on January 9. Nora was unhappy at having to go out to a restaurant on a wintry night. When she slipped on the stairs as they left, she scolded Joyce in Italian: *"Perchè m'hai fatta uscire una sera così?"* ("Why did you make me go out on a night like this?") In the middle of the night Joyce awoke with violent stomach pains. He was carried on a stretcher to the Roten Kreuz Hospital and given morphine.

The next morning Grete Herz arrived from St. Gallen to visit Stephen, only to be told by Nora and Giorgio that the doctors were going to operate on Joyce. Joyce was frightened. It was to be the first time (his countless eye operations notwithstanding) that he would be put under general anesthetic. When he awoke, he said to Nora with relief, "I thought I wouldn't get through it."[23] And to Giorgio he conveyed the fear that had kept him from having his pain investigated: "Is it cancer?" Giorgio said that it was not, but Joyce refused to believe him. He was weak but appeared to be recovering. "Jim is tough," Nora said.[24]

On Sunday night, January 12, Joyce asked Nora to stay with him through the night as he had done for her when she had been in hospital. The doctors, however, persuaded her to return to her pension to get some rest. In the night, however, peritonitis set in. Nora and Giorgio were telephoned and told to come quickly, but they arrived too late. To her sorrow, Nora learned that Jim had woken and asked for them. He had died alone.[25]

Stephen had to be cared for. Nora and Giorgio summoned Klara Heyland, their favorite waitress from the Kronenhalle, who came and took the boy to a playground. Then Grete Herz returned to take him to stay with his cousins for a few days. They could not keep him long. Stephen, only a few days before his grandfather died, had been enrolled in a new school in Zurich and had to return. The Herzes did what they could to comfort him. They found him strong and clever, less nervous, they thought, than in the past, but still restless. Their hearts went out to him as he had, not yet nine, suffered so much. "Nonno, Nonno!" he kept crying. He also spoke often of his mother, someone else who was lost to him.[26]

Nora bore the entirely unexpected blow with composure and fortitude. Her first task was to organize the funeral. The new professor of English at the University of Zurich, Heinrich Straumann, was to speak, and she provided him with all the biographical information he sought; he was impressed with her command of the situation.[27] Then there was the question of the character of the service. A priest approached her and asked if Joyce should not have a Catholic funeral. Nora did not hesitate. "I couldn't do that to him," she said.[28]

Nora's decision has raised the question of the depth of her religious faith. To non-Catholics, it is a mark of her integrity. She had promised Joyce that she understood him, and she knew he would not serve his Church; she would not be party to any posthumous subversion. To Catholics, it is a sign that her faith meant little to her.[29] Yet Nora is unlikely to have seen any contradiction; she was born Catholic and pragmatic. As Joyce had died unrepentant, without the last rites of the Church, she may well have said to herself, as she did over questions of punctuation, "What difference does it make?"

She took great care with the other funeral formalities, however. The day following Joyce's death, the Neue Zürcher Zeitung carried a black-bordered announcement of a death. Translated, it read:

> This morning at two o'clock in the Red Cross Hospital with unexpected suddenness our beloved husband, father and grandfather. In deep sorrow Nora Joyce George Joyce Lucia Joyce Stephen Joyce.

Nora also gave Mrs. Giedion-Welcker permission to have a Zurich sculptor make two death masks of Joyce's face. They show a kind and humorous face, a determined Irish chin, a bulbous, curved forehead, and a broad, straight hairline. The existence of the masks, whose ownership has been much disputed, helped to make the head of James Joyce an icon, one of the best-known faces of the twentieth century, an image recognized by far more people than have ever turned a page of Joyce's work.

Joyce always set great store upon funeral wreaths. For his, Nora chose a wreath of green leaves in the shape of a harp. *"Ho fatto questa forma,"* she told their friend Paul Ruggiero, *"per il mio Jim che amava tanto la musica"* ("I chose this shape for my Jim who so loved music").[30] Music was the art that had bound them.

It was cold and snowy on January 15 when the small congregation gathered for the funeral service at the chapel of the Fluntern Cemetery. Words at funerals are often sadly mischosen, but Joyce was fortunate in what was said at his. Professor Straumann's short address was followed by an eloquent tribute from Lord Derwent, the British minister to Bern. "Of all the injustices Britain has heaped upon Ireland," he said, "Ireland will continue to enjoy the lasting revenge of producing masterpieces of English literature."[31]

Nora added her own perfect valedictory. She stood, tall, erect, and dry-eyed, watching as the coffin was lowered into the grave. As she gazed for the last time on the bony face visible through the small *vitrine* in the coffin lid, she cried out in her low voice, "Jim, how beautiful you are!"[32] She had always loved his looks.

After the funeral Nora went back to the Delphin. The Giedions held a reception, but she did not go. She had the future to contemplate. She had a son with no career, no wife, no ability to make decisions; she had a grandson whose mother was in a mental hospital three thousand miles away. She had a daughter in another hospital in Nazi-held territory. Her mother had died. She had no money. She was cut off by a war of unprecedented devastation from the income and advice from London that had sustained her husband. All the calm self-possession she had summoned in her years with Joyce was nothing to the strength she would need without him.

20

⇥✳✳⇤

Staying On

HARRIET WEAVER learned of Joyce's death from the BBC eight o'clock radio news only hours after it happened on the morning of January 13, 1941. The words half floated in to her from the sitting room while she was making her bed. "Did he say Mr. Joyce was dead?" she asked Edith Walker, who was staying with her. She knew he had reached Zurich safely just before Christmas because of his Christmas greetings telegram asking for £300 to cover family debts, but she had no idea that he was ill. Stunned as she was, she immediately thought of Nora. As Joyce's £250 quarterly interest payment from her fund was due to be paid, she had the money cabled for speed, and soon had a wire from Nora: "Money received many thanks your wonderful help in our great sorrow kindest regards Nora Joyce." Nora paid the hospital bill of 300 Swiss francs by the end of the month.[1]

Nora, like most widows, had no time to grieve, as all the decisions that she had formerly left to her husband fell to her. Most of them concerned money. Extravagant as a wife, Nora as a widow took a different attitude toward debt. She wanted none of it and hoped everything could be paid quickly so that she would know where she stood. In this first crisis of her widowhood, Miss Weaver had appeared like an ever-hovering guardian angel.

But there were limits to Miss Weaver's powers. Nora was trapped in Zurich. As a widow, she was far poorer than she had been a month before as a wife, for although Stephen at least was provided for by Adolph

Kastor's regular remittances, every other bit of Joyce's income, even the American royalties from his books, went into Joyce's estate in London, where it could not be touched until the will was granted probate.[2] A long process at best, proving the will was slowed down by distance and a world war. Communications between London and Zurich were so disrupted that even letters sent air mail could take a month to reach their destination. Nora still had no information about what was happening to the place she considered home — the flat in Paris — and her disorientation at trying to live without the man whose side she had hardly left in thirty-seven years was worsened by the appalling plight of both her children.

Lucia was still in the Delmas clinic at Pornichet, south of La Baule, in Occupied France. Lucia, Nora heard, learned of Joyce's death from the newspapers. Nora did not know whether Lucia could remain at Pornichet if her bills were not being paid; she could not even ascertain how much Lucia's bills were. Her maternal nightmares were fed by unanswerable questions: Where would Lucia go if the clinic turned her out? What would the German authorities do with a mental patient holding an enemy passport? Nora dearly wanted to carry out Joyce's intention of shifting Lucia to a sanatorium in French Switzerland, but even if she could organize a new *permis de sortie,* she could see no possibility of paying for the expensive journey for Lucia and escort, let alone for institutional care in Switzerland, where costs were higher than in France.[3]

Giorgio's predicament was almost worse. He was unemployable, de facto and de jure. All he could do to earn money was to sing, but the limitations of his talents scarcely mattered, for the Swiss refused work permits to all refugees. Yet if he set foot outside Switzerland's borders, he was at risk of being pressed into one army or another. He was penniless too, any financial support he had been receiving from Helen having stopped with her return to the United States, and he was out of touch with her family in New York.[4]

Scarcely was Joyce in his grave than Nora suffered another blow familiar to widows: the defection of friends. Carola Giedion-Welcker, who had danced attendance on both Joyces for more than a decade, had no interest in or even sympathy for Nora alone. Before the month of Joyce's death was out, she had demanded that Nora repay the 15,700 Swiss francs that the Giedions had contributed toward the financial guarantee enabling the Joyces to enter Switzerland. Mrs. Giedion-Welcker might as well have demanded the British crown jewels. There was no way that Nora could get her money out of London before the estate was settled — as Mrs. Giedion-Welcker should have been aware. The debt weighed heavily on Nora's mind, and bitterness set in between the two families when Mrs. Giedion-Welcker followed her demand for repayment with a refusal to let Nora and Giorgio have either of the Joyce death masks. She had paid for them and would not relinquish them while the Joyces owed her money.[5]

Nora was deeply embarrassed and, although perhaps she did not fully realize it, weakened. As a refugee in Zurich, with hardly more than the clothes on her back, she could well have used the support of an influential Zurich family to help with the tangle of problems of money, health, and housing in which she found herself.

Giorgio struggled to help his mother. He wrote and asked Miss Weaver to let them know what income they could count on so that they could arrange their lives.[6] The question turned out to be very difficult for Miss Weaver to answer.

Nora's first plan, when she began to try to look ahead, was to make a home for the two uprooted males in her care. By the first week in February, she, Giorgio, and Stephen left the Pension Delphin and moved into a furnished flat at 30 Dufourstrasse.[7] But the dream quickly faded. Nora's arthritis prevented her from running about to do the necessary shopping and errands. She found her highly strung grandson difficult to handle, although she loved him dearly, and she felt responsible for his religious upbringing and shouted at him if he missed Mass. He had a great respect for her temper.[8] Giorgio, with his expensive tastes, gave her even more trouble. Then in the summer of 1941, Hitler's war opened upon the Russian front. When she and Giorgio heard that the Vichy government had ordered all British nationals to leave France, she could get no news of how this would affect Lucia. Her nerves gave out, and she had what she called "a kind of breakdown" for two weeks.[9] By December 1941 Giorgio was living at a different pension from his mother's, and Stephen was in a boarding school in Zug.

The future continued to darken. In December also the last direct link with the European branch of the Kastors snapped when Helen's cousins Wilhelm and Grete Herz finally took Robert Kastor's advice and left St. Gallen for New York. Giorgio wrote to Miss Weaver that his mother's way of life was very distressing. She spent most of her time, he said, visiting the cemetery.[10] Nora never complained about her fall from five-star living. Her new life in Zurich was passed in a succession of small rooms in austere pensions, with their low-watt lightbulbs, smell of soap, and all-seeing proprietresses. Even living on her own, Nora was restless and changed pension frequently. From Dufourstrasse she went to a pension on Irisstrasse, and then in 1943 she moved uphill to the Pension Fontana at the bend in the road of Gloriastrasse. One winter, thanks to the generosity of an American admirer of Joyce, she was able to spend eight months in a well-heated hotel and was much improved.[11]

Settling Joyce's estate was complicated by more than war. Exactly as Joyce had feared in 1932 when Lucia broke down at the Gare du Nord, the ambiguity of his domicile would come to haunt him and his family. Before deciding that it had the authority to administer the estate under English law, the High Court in London had to settle the point once and for all: Was James Joyce really to be considered a resident of England simply because he had lived there from May to August 1931? The dispute entered court, and the prospect of settlement receded.[12]

Not since looking after Lucia in 1935 had Harriet Weaver been so drawn into the Joyces' private lives. Nora, named in the will as executor, could not act from Zurich. Furthermore, the public trustee in London, who was also named, declined to act as executor. Miss Weaver, there-fore, became an administrator of Joyce's personal estate as well as exec-utor of his literary one.[13] Resuming quasi-maternal responsibilities helped to erase the bitterness of the break with Joyce, but Miss Weaver did so at great inconvenience. In 1941, she was living in Oxford. She had left London to escape the blitz, not out of cowardice — she had been an air raid warden in Marylebone — but because the building in which she lived on Gloucester Place had caught fire during a bombing attack. In Oxford, she was very busy with her work for the Communist party. She delivered the *Daily Worker* house to house in working-class neighborhoods and helped run the party's bookshop. To deal with the multifarious Joyce affairs required her to travel up to London on blacked-out trains that passed through blacked-out stations.[14]

The main problem was getting any money at all transferred to Nora. The British authorities were not at all happy about sending money over-seas. Miss Weaver visited the controller of the Trading with the Enemy branch of the Board of Trade to persuade him of the special circum-stances, but he was unrelenting. That Switzerland was neutral made very little difference. There was a shortage of Swiss currency in Britain, and the amount that any one family could withdraw was limited. The Joyces' case was complicated by the need to send money to two different places, Switzerland and France. How could British officials be sure that money intended for Lucia's clinic would not fall into the hands of the Germans? Endlessly, Miss Weaver filled out forms and put up with long delays, while Nora waited and never knew when her money was coming.[15]

As there was no "Joyce money" to be sent until the estate was settled, Miss Weaver, as so often in the past, filled the gap with money of her own, selling stock to raise it. This only put her further into trouble with the authorities, for there was a ban on sending gifts of money abroad.

In spite of the great distance between them, Miss Weaver tried also to help Nora with advice. She suggested asking Carola Giedion-Welcker to accept the repayment of only the interest on her loan until Joyce's estate was settled. She also reassured Nora (little knowing about the impatient landlord) that there was no need to worry about the Paris flat because the American embassy (the United States not yet having entered the war) was looking after the property of British citizens in Paris.[16] Miss Weaver was not the only one concerned with Nora's financial predicament. In February 1941 Mary and Padraic Colum sent a letter, signed also by Bennett Cerf, B. W. Huebsch, Robert Kastor, Eugene Jolas, Maria Jolas, J. J. Sweeney, Thornton Wilder, and Edmund Wilson, to American admirers of Joyce:

> Can you contribute to the support of James Joyce's dependents? If you cannot, will you speak to any persons you feel might want to do so? No sum would be too small. We have received many $1.00 bills sent by students; we feel sure that Joyce himself would have appreciated such spontaneous offerings.

There were heavy expenses, the appeal said, related to Joyce's death and Lucia's illness. "There is also his wife in Zurich to be taken care of, to be furnished, later on, with means of transportation either to Ireland or to this country."[17]

Somehow, whenever people thought of Nora's future, they thought of Ireland. It was if they assumed that nearly forty years' living on the Continent had left no trace and that Nora would be eager and able to revert to the Irish life she had left in 1904. They were quite wrong. America and Ireland were almost the last two places Nora thought of going. She recoiled from America as before, and as for Ireland, Nora said, when people brought up the subject, "They burnt my husband's books and I will never go back."[18] In any event, there was little to draw her back. The only person she cared about in Ireland was gone. It was part of Nora's anguish in 1941 that she had no details about the circumstances of her mother's death.[19]

Soon Nora had more news from Galway than she cared for, and about a subject she was tired of: wills. No one in Galway, it seemed, could find Annie Barnacle's will.

Nora's mother had died at eighty-two as something of a neighborhood character. Nearly six feet tall and white-haired, Annie Barnacle spent her days on a hard-backed chair outside her cottage, wrapped in a long black cardigan and taking snuff. Like many old people, Mrs. Barnacle liked to talk about her will, and as it was known locally that she had inherited the bulk of the tidy sum amassed by her late brother, Michael Healy, the customs officer, she did not lack for listeners. Chief among these was Nora's youngest sister, Kathleen, now married to a furniture polisher, John Griffin. Kathleen had counted on receiving most of her mother's money. She had been assured of it, because she, unlike the rest, had stayed in Galway to look after her old mother and invalid sister, Dilly (who was fond of spirits).[20] "Kathleen," Mrs. Barnacle would say, "the money is in the bank and Mr Concannon [her solicitor] has the will and all the papers and everything is in black and white for you and you'll be all right."[21] But Mr. Concannon did not have the will, and he remembered why not. Mrs. Barnacle had called at his office one day. She told him that her daughter, Mrs. Nora Joyce, who lived in Paris, and her husband, Mr. James Joyce, had always been so good to her that she wanted to send them her will to show them how generously they were to be rewarded when she died. Annie took the will away, according to Mr. Concannon, saying that she would return it to his office. She never did.[22] Could their mother's will be among Joyce's papers somewhere in Paris? Kathleen wrote and asked Nora, who telegraphed back that she did not know. Kathleen was unconvinced and desperate. The high-spiritedness that Joyce had so admired in his wife's youngest sister had turned, in middle age, to a fierce aggressiveness. Besides, Kathleen, like her brother Tom and her other sisters, was convinced that "Nora had done all right for herself" and that Nora, living in comfort on the Continent, knew little of the grinding poverty the rest of the Barnacles endured.[23] Kathleen, therefore, wrote straight to Nora's well-connected friend Harriet Weaver to enlist her help.

Miss Weaver always answered letters meticulously, within a day or two. Swiftly and sadly she informed Kathleen that if the original of Mrs. Barnacle's will was among the Joyce papers in Paris, it would be quite unobtainable because she had just learned from Giorgio the terrible news that the Nazis had interned Paul Léon. Mr. Léon was the only one who knew where everything was.[24] Naturally, she also wrote and told Nora of Kathleen's request.

Nora exploded. With all the rage of a woman who has made friends far above her sister's station, she once again demonstrated that when her passions were aroused she could express herself in writing in no uncertain terms. Using the stationery of her former grand residence, the Carlton Élite Hotel, she rounded on Kathleen:

8th 4 1942

Dear Kathleen. I have just received a letter from Miss Weaver and am very much upset that you should have bothered her with the matter of Mothers will She in any case knows nothing about it and as I telegraphed you many months ago neither do I. If at any time a copy of Mothers will was sent to Jim I know absolutely nothing about it but it seems to me that Mothers lawyer should be the possessor of it I mean the original of the will I hope once and for all you will be able to clear this affair up and please on no account write to Miss Weaver

I may remind you that I have plenty of worries myself Jim's death has been a terrible shock to me Lucia is in France I have no news of her hope you are well

Nora.[25]

The will was never found. Kathleen's counsel in Galway suggested that Mr. Concannon had actually lost the will and invented the story about James Joyce and Paris in order to shield himself. Mr. Concannon then sued Kathleen's lawyer because he had not been paid for his own work on the will, whereupon a legal battle raged between the two with a litigiousness that lost none of its ferocity just because the sum involved was less than four pounds.[26]

Payments from Annie Barnacle's estate were finally allowed late in 1943 on the basis of what Mr. Concannon remembered of its contents. Apart from Kathleen, Nora got the largest gift, £100. There was just £30 for Dilly, and for Tom, Mary, and Peg, £20 each. The money must have come to Nora as very late and welcome proof that her mother did value her highest among all her emigrant brood. The residue, which went to Kathleen, was the goodly sum of £1,467, well worth fighting over, and a strong reminder that Nora's family was by no means as poor as has been generally believed. In fact, Mrs. Barnacle, whose physical circumstances at the time of her death were officially described as "living in an artizan dwelling and . . . no furniture but the barest necessities," left an estate larger than that of her favorite son-in-law, the world-renowned author.[27]

Joyce's own estate, finally settled in 1945, amounted to just £1,212 gross, £980 net. The court case on the vexed question of his legal domicile was resolved in 1943 in Joyce's favor, but not without giving the press once again an opportunity to review Joyce's life saga and to retail small jokes at his expense. From the hearing the *Dublin Evening Herald* reported the following exchange:

MR. JUSTICE BENNETT — What sort of books did he write?
MR. VANNECK [for the administrators of the will] — I think his best-known book was called *Ulysses*.
MR. JUSTICE BENNETT — It sounds Greek to me. *(laughter)*.[28]

Probate was also delayed by the reluctance of Nora and Giorgio to answer letters. The English authorities could not understand why Nora could not return to the country of her husband's domicile. Nor could they grasp why the Joyces of Zurich needed so much money or why Mr. George Joyce, an able-bodied man of nearly forty, could do nothing for a living. In 1943 Nora gave her own answers in a letter to Miss Weaver that sounds as if she wrote it upon instructions from her London solicitors. In it she took the opportunity to defend Giorgio for what she knew were widespread attacks on his character:

> It is impossible for us to get along on the money you are kind enough to advance us, for it is very expensive living here. I have been under the care of doctors for the last two years, as I am suffering from acute rheumatism. Giorgio also has been under the care of doctors as he is suffering from very bad nervous headaches. In spite of all this he has been working at his music very hard and has managed with the permission of the police over here to give ten concerts in the last year. Needless to say, those concerts brought in no money whatsoever. I do hope that something will be arranged to ease this [?] very difficult situation.[29]

Giorgio suffered from severe migraine headaches, which were exacerbated by the Föhn, the disagreeable Alpine winds, and which may have been caused by a goiter operation in the 1930s. In a letter to Fred Monro Miss Weaver added her own analysis of what was wrong with Giorgio:

> Fortune has been against him. His education was poor, except as regards singing which Mr Joyce had expected him to go in for professionally. This latter project was interrupted by his marrying at a young age and against his parents' advice (or, rather, being married by) a wealthy American woman . . .[30]

Debts outstanding further delayed the will so that at the end of 1943 even the American royalties from Joyce's books still flowed to the estate in London and were blocked. "This must be maddening to you," said Miss Weaver in her Christmas message to Nora. "It seems a mockery to wish you a happy Christmas. I hope that 1944 will have better things in store."[31] (Nora's own greetings, sent through her preferred medium, the international telegram, arrived in their usual garbled form: to "Harriet MRaver from Jora Joyce.")[32]

Nora was deeply grateful for Miss Weaver's constant generosity, and even Giorgio seems to have been touched. As he wrote Miss Weaver at the end of their first year without Joyce:

> A few days ago we received a letter from Mr Monro in which he tells us you have been very kindly advancing the money he is sending us since my father died. It is useless for me to try and tell you how grateful both my mother and I am [sic] for all you are doing for us — I hate to think of the position we would have been in had it not been for you.[33]

Shortly after the war ended, the biggest change in their lives came with the decision of Stephen, then fourteen, to leave Zurich and go to the United States. Giorgio did not want to part with his son, but there was no holding the boy back. Stephen had not seen his mother at all during the war, and Helen, recovered from her mental breakdown and out of the hospital, wanted him near her. Also, Stephen was eager to begin his studies at Phillips Andover Academy in Massachusetts, where he had been enrolled. The news brought out Miss Weaver's anti-Americanism; she thought it a bad move — Stephen would be spoiled in America, she believed.[34]

In the summer of 1946 Helen's other son, David Fleischman, then stationed with the American forces in Germany, visited the Joyces in Zurich and wrote home to his mother that the son she had not seen for so long had grown strong and healthy, that he spoke English with a slight accent, and that he wanted to become an engineer.[35] On December 17, 1946, Stephen left by plane for the United States. It was a wrench for Nora, who had become used to her grandson's screeching his bicycle to a halt beside her on Seefeldstrasse. He would miss her too, the only mother he had had for many years. They would sit and talk to each other frankly, saying things they would not say to anybody else. As Stephen later recalled, "We'd sit down and she would tell me what was on her mind and I would tell her what was on my mind. Nonna was a very straightforward woman."

The end of the war brought increased austerity to Britain and with it new pressure on Nora from the Bank of England. The bank, imposing harsh postwar controls on transfers abroad of sterling, sent an ultimatum through her solicitor, Fred Monro: either Mrs. Joyce must return to England or obtain a doctor's certificate explaining why she could not. The authorities asked Monro to remind Mrs. Joyce that they had warned her two months earlier.

By this time Nora was able to delegate much of her correspondence to her old friend Evelyn Cotton. The actress, who had played in Joyce's production of *The Importance of Being Earnest,* had become a close friend of Nora's during the war years. She now undertook to act for her somewhat as Paul Léon had acted for James Joyce. Like Léon, Miss Cotton added her own gloss to what she wrote: how pathetic it was to see Mrs. Joyce, increasingly crippled, try to go up and down stairs from the small attic room where she was living and how she really needed a pension with a lift. But there was no question of Mrs. Joyce's wanting to leave Zurich. "Having lost her home," Miss Cotton said, "she would naturally rather stay here where she has some friends. It seems cruel not to let old people live in peace where they want to live."[36] T. S. Eliot added his influential voice to the cause. Many British people were returning to live on the Continent after the war. He felt that some dispensation ought to be extended to Mrs. Joyce, as, he argued (apparently unaware of the intense legal efforts to prove the contrary), she had never lived in England.[37]

Nora's Zurich doctor, Dr. W. Behrens, however, convincingly argued her case. He provided the required certificate in June 1946 and drew a sorry picture of Nora at sixty. (She was actually sixty-two; even to her doctor Nora apparently kept to the fiction that she had been born in 1886 rather than 1884.) He described how her joints — knees, knuckles, ankles, hips, and shoulders — were deformed with arthritis. She suffered from high blood pressure. She was in a depressive state of mind, he said, adding pointedly, "The uncertain future and the difficulties in transfer of money make the situation worse." [38] Nora was easily upset, it is true. She could not bear to speak of Lucia. With the war ended and his patients moved back to Ivry on the outskirts of Paris, Dr. Delmas sent reports from time to time and also her accumulated bills: 300,000 French francs were owing. In June, at Behrens's insistence, Nora entered hospital to try to get some relief from her arthritis. [39]

Nora endured her stay in the hospital for six weeks, including three weeks in bed. It did her good, but she found it too quiet and gloomy. As soon as she could she moved into a new hotel-pension, the Neptun, at 15 Seefeldstrasse. The pension was centrally heated, with a lift and telephones in the rooms, and its location was ideal, just a step from her favorite vegetarian restaurant, the Gleich. It was also very near the park by the lake, where she would go and sit in the afternoon sun. She made friends there and never moved again, remaining there longer than she had ever lived in one place since the Square Robiac. [40]

After she had recovered from Joyce's death, however, Nora was not depressed. Low spirits were not in her nature — a point missed by American Joyce scholars who, returning to Europe after the war, made a point of calling on Joyce's widow. Almost to a man they took home a picture of a sad, forlorn woman living on the edge of poverty. Leon Edel, for example, who noticed Nora's warmth and charm (and also her large, bony hands), found her face "lined and sad" and "her pride of carriage" such as to make it impossible for him to ask if she were short of money. [41]

But much of the poignancy was in the eye of the beholder or of those seeking money on Nora's behalf. Giorgio's letters to Miss Weaver in the 1940s are reminiscent of those sent her by his father in the twenties and thirties, written with the same object in mind. When Miss Weaver wrote to Nora's sister Kathleen in 1942, she reflected an unsubtle plea from Giorgio:

Mrs Joyce seems to be in a sad way — not at all well, suffering from rheumatism and very lonely, so Georgio [sic] said in his letter written on December 29 . . . I hope she will manage to arrange to take the cure of baths which Georgio said she ought to do in the spring. [42]

To her Swiss friends, of whom she had many, Nora did not appear gloomy. They saw her in quite a different light, almost as her Irish visitors in Paris had a decade earlier. Bertha Ruggiero loved meeting her for tea. Klara Heyland, the waitress, laughed with Nora about the customers at the Kronenhalle. Professor Heinrich Straumann, who often saw her in the Gleich, said that she always seemed cheerful. She never complained. She accepted the conditions of her existence with equanimity and always chatted quite pleasantly with him.[43] Her arthritis was severe, but as a writer from Dublin who met her observed, "Even that has not affected her serenity, her impeccable poise, her almost regal appearance."[44] And always there was Giorgio. Nora basked in his constant comfort and attention. It was a rare day when she did not see him, although he exasperated her in many ways. She hated the way he cleared his throat and spat. She was walking along a Zurich street one day with him and Stephen, and whenever the father stopped to spit, so did the small son. Nora came to a full halt and announced, "I'm not going to take one more step until you two stop spitting."[45] Even so, Giorgio remained very precious to her, her only reliable companion, just as he had been as an infant in Rome. Her attachment to him only deepened as he grew to look more and more like James Joyce, with the same high forehead, straight, wide hairline, and long, straight hair brushed back. One day Nora came into her room to find Giorgio sitting there in a silk dressing gown with the cat on his lap, and he looked so much like his father that she almost felt she had seen a ghost.[46]

The dispute with the Bank of England dragged on into 1947. Nora never knew when — or if — her supposed monthly allowance would get through. She described her predicament, without self-pity, in a warm letter to the Colums in New York:

> Dear Padraic and Molly,
>
> I really don't know how to thank you and your friends for your very kind gesture in sending me two remittances of 50 and 40 dollars. You can't imagine what a help it is for me to receive some financial aid as I have not received any money from England for seven months except £20. Luckily my solicitor was able to arrange that I get some of the royalties direct from America. It is very difficult for me because I have to support Giorgio who has absolutely not a penny of his own and can't work here. I am so glad that you saw Stephen and find him such a fine boy. Giorgio did all he could for him while he was here.
>
> I am afraid I shall sooner or later have to sell my manuscript of *Chamber Music* written in Dublin in the year 1909 and dedicated to me; it is written on parchment and bound in cream coloured leather with the Joyce crest on one side of the cover and our initials on the other side. If you know anybody who you think will be interested in buying such a work would you kindly let me know.

Please convey my best thanks also to Mr Sweeney [J. J. Sweeney of the Houghton Library, Harvard] and Mr Healy for the very welcome financial help.

With warmest thanks to you and Molly and with kind regards,

Sincerely yours,

Nora Joyce[47]

Soon after, pressed for funds, Nora carried out her threat and sent her copy of *Chamber Music* to Robert Kastor in New York, asking him to sell it. Almost at the same time, without warning or explanation, the Bank of England capitulated. It informed Monro Saw that it now regarded Mrs. Joyce as a resident of Switzerland and would approve the transfer of any income due her. "I do not quite know how it has happened," said Lionel Monro to Harriet Weaver.[48]

The bank's volte-face presented a new dilemma. Lionel Monro, who had taken over the Joyce affairs from his father, Fred, spelled it out for Miss Weaver (his second cousin). There now was no obstacle to Nora's withdrawing all the money that had accumulated in her royalty account. If she were to realize how much was there — about two thousand pounds — she might ask for it all, or what was more likely, Giorgio would talk her into asking for it all. Lionel Monro proposed not telling Nora that the total sum was accessible to her and instead paying her an allowance of fifty pounds a month, plus the Joyce royalties from America.[49]

"Excessive," replied Miss Weaver. Between thirty-five and forty pounds would be sufficient, she said, and recommended that American royalties be sent not to Nora but to London. Miss Weaver too feared Giorgio, who, she felt, had undue influence over his mother.

Their fears cannot be dismissed as condescension or overprotectiveness. Miss Weaver was too circumspect ever to refer, in her voluminous correspondence on matters Joycean with many friends and associates of the family, to the fact that Giorgio had become an alcoholic. Others were more candid. One of these was John Slocum, an American State Department official who had become one of the postwar leaders in collecting Joyce manuscripts and memorabilia. After meeting Giorgio in Zurich, Slocum described him as "a tragic dipsomaniac who lives in the shadow of his father and who lost a good voice through refusing to sing."[50]

Evelyn Cotton, as she conducted Nora's correspondence, confined herself to saying that Nora's position would be easier if she did not have to support her son, "who is no help at all."[51] A true picture of Nora's poverty in the years after the war must take into account the ever present but unspoken problem of Giorgio's drinking. Much of Miss Weaver's money disappeared down his throat. The fact is that even in the early wartime years, she managed to send to Zurich a very great deal of money by the British standards of the time, and none of it went to support Lucia, whose fees were paid directly from London. Between 1941 and 1943 Miss Weaver sent Nora about £1,200.[52]

In 1948, moreover, with the great surge of postwar interest in Joyce's work, the money began to roll in, and Nora's financial worries were gone. In August 1948 the balance in her royalty income account with Monro Saw stood at £1,937. Of this Lucia's fees took more than half, but Nora was left with £930 a year at a time when a British professor earned only £400 a year and a factory worker £350. Moreover, as a widow, Nora enjoyed some of the informal patronage upon which James Joyce had long relied to keep up a luxurious standard of living. She was welcome to dine without paying at the Kronenhalle, for example. The Zumstegs simply wrote the charges in a book and when the book was full tore it up.[53]

The same courtesy was not extended to Giorgio at the bar. He had to pay for his drinks, yet was such a fixture there that he gave his name to his favorite cognac with water. His cronies at the Kronenhalle used to enjoy calling out, as Giorgio did, "Cognac Joyce! Cognac Joyce!"[54] But his drinking was a constant drain on their income, as much a cause of their hardship as any currency restrictions of the Bank of England, and Nora knew from long experience that there was no point arguing about it.

Neither Nora nor Giorgio had the sophistication to see that their London protectors were keeping them deliberately on short rations of money, for their own good and Lucia's. (Nora had authorized the Monro Saw law firm to pay Lucia's bills directly.) By 1948, nonetheless, mother and son did understand that their worst days were over. Nora sent word to Robert Kastor to return her copy of Chamber Music; there was no need to sell it now.[55]

21

✢✳✳✢

The Sound
of Lions

As she came to play the part of the Widow Joyce, Nora began at last to believe in her husband's genius. She was interested in literary news and pleased to see the number of books appearing about Joyce's work. She asked for three copies of *The Portable James Joyce* to give as gifts, and for herself, she asked for a copy of Lucia's *Chaucer ABC*.[1]

She parried her literary inquisitors well. Ignazio Silone's wife asked her for her opinon of André Gide, and got it. "Sure, when you've been married to the greatest writer in the world," Nora said, "you don't remember all the little fellows." To John Slocum, on a European swing to collect Joyce papers and memorabilia and to prepare a definitive bibliography of all of Joyce's published writing, Nora said, "It is just as well my husband didn't have a literary wife. There had to be somebody to do the cooking and wash the dishes." She would, at times, idealize her marriage and say that she and Joyce had been blissfully happy. Giorgio, overhearing the remark, said, "I wonder what my father would have said to that." More usually, she kept to her familiar deflating tone: "They all tell me my husband was one of the immortals. I'd much rather be receiving some royalties from his books than be the widow of an immortal."[2]

Ever since Trieste days admirers of Joyce had taken a close look at Nora and tried to fathom what he saw in her. Painters such as Silvestri had caught her vibrancy in portraits, but no one, apart from Joyce, had seriously tried to capture the quality of her voice and speech. Fortunately for posterity, in 1948 a young American journalist named Sandy Campbell broke a train journey from Paris to Rome at Zurich to try to find

Mrs. James Joyce. It was at the best pastry shop in the city that he learned that Mrs. Joyce lived at the Pension Neptun in Seefeldstrasse near the lake.[3] As it was evening, he called in to leave a message to ask if he might see Mrs. Joyce the next day. The clerk, however, understood only the word *Joyce* and rang Nora's room then and there. Nora's own low voice answered. Yes, she would be delighted to see him, but she was an old lady and it was her bedtime. If he would come to see her the next day, any time would be convenient. They settled upon noon.

Campbell arrived early. Nora was waiting in the sitting room; it was small and crowded with cheap furniture. As Nora rose to greet him, he was struck "by the quietness of her tone and the beauty of her Irish voice — so different from the hard Irish accents of actresses I had become used to in New York."

Nora ordered them each a Dubonnet and said she hoped that Giorgio would join them. Her son had a fine singing voice, like his father before him, she said, but could not work in Switzerland because the Swiss refused to give him a work permit. If only Giorgio could go to Hollywood, Nora said, she was sure he would find work. "He isn't anxious to sing, though," she said, confiding intimately in a total stranger. "Something is wrong with him. Perhaps it is hard for him being Joyce's son."

Campbell suggested lunch. Nora accepted on the condition that they eat at the Gleich because that was where Giorgio would look for her. She was not a vegetarian, she said, but had learned that restaurants that did not serve meat were cheaper. To Campbell the cheese, fruit, and vegetables looked so good that he did not mind. As they ate and talked, Nora said, "Oh, Mr. Campbell, I am enjoying this. I was afraid when I spoke to you on the telephone that you would be one of those people who come to see me to ask what passages from *Ulysses* or *Finnegans Wake* mean, and of course I cannot answer them; I do not know."

Nora was never at the ease with scholars or *littérateurs,* but with the young journalist she was herself and spoke openly and easily. She told him that she did not really like Zurich but would prefer to be in Paris, with all Joyce's books around her. Joyce, she said, had loved to read.*

What authors? Campbell pressed for literary information. Nora smiled. "Well, as a matter of fact, he spent a good deal of time reading himself." (Her candid statement supports the argument that Joyce's myriad references to rare and specialized works give a misleading impression of the depth and range of his reading. In his later life, with his dimmed sight, he certainly was not a great reader.)[4] Nora claimed that often he relied on her: "When his eyes were bad, I used to read to him; all sorts of

---

* Campbell's interview has Nora referring to Joyce by his last name. Her usual practice, with those for whom "Jim" was too familiar, was to call him "my husband."

books. We had so many books in Paris. I should go back to Paris. Perhaps I will visit for a while anyway. I have friends there and I wouldn't have to go to the apartment."

Nora said her money worries had only just been eased. Until 1948, she said, she had been receiving only thirty pounds a month from which she had to support Giorgio "and Giorgio's sister who is in a home in France." Her life was quite different from when her husband was alive, she told Campbell. "We ate in the best restaurants and he loved to entertain his friends."

Giorgio suddenly joined them — nervously, as he had imagined for a moment that Campbell was Stephen, whom they were expecting to arrive from America. Campbell could see without being told that Giorgio was Joyce's son and thought that his voice was as pleasing as his mother's. Nora tried unsuccessfully to persuade first one man, then the other, to eat some strawberries. "Mother just can't understand that I don't like to eat much," said Giorgio.

After lunch Nora, with Giorgio, took Campbell back to her room to see the only book of Joyce's she owned: the copy of *Chamber Music* he had copied onto parchment for her in 1909 when she was in Trieste and he in Dublin. "I had others," she said, "but I have given them away or people have borrowed them and kept them. But I will not part with *Chamber Music* because Joyce made this copy in his own writing for me. Once, when I needed money badly, I sent it off to America to be sold, but I missed it so much that I wrote and said to send it back, that I would not part with it for any money."

Nora's room, to Campbell's eyes, was very small, very clean, and very bare. It had a big window; the bathroom was down the hall. "It was not a room that you would sit in for long even with people," thought Campbell, "and not a room that you would sit in alone at all." As Nora unwrapped her volume of poetry from tissue paper, she quoted particular lines she thought beautiful and seemed to know the poems by heart. With the agreeable Irish habit of frequently repeating the name of the person being addressed, she said, "You can understand, Mr. Campbell, why I could not sell this."

Nora spurned the thought that she might take a nap. Instead, she suggested that they visit Joyce's grave. When Campbell proposed taking a taxi, she was horrified at the thought of the extravagance. (Even today Swiss taxi fares are very high.) When he insisted she proudly told the clerk to call one. Giorgio said goodbye, promising to see her the next day. As they rode along, she poured out random reminiscences about Joyce: how he thought that Garbo walked like a duck, and how he would cross the street to avoid a nun ("which I thought unnecessary, Mr. Campbell"). Dogs he disliked, but cats he loved — of any kind.

Then, as they approached Fluntern, Nora said, "I often think he must like the cemetery he is in. It is near the zoo and you can hear the lions roar."

The image reveals the power of Nora's imagination. The woman whose memory of a dead lover in a lonely graveyard led to one of the most beautiful passages in English literature casually conjured up for a total stranger a vision of her husband lying in his grave, enjoying the sound of lions, perhaps chuckling to himself. It suggests that Nora herself may have evoked for Joyce the final scene in "The Dead," the snow falling on the grave of Michael Furey.

That the dead are very near — watching, listening, and judging the living — is the message of "The Dead." It is the message too of Ireland, whose dominant image on the world's television screens is the procession to the graveyard, with coffins carried by men who, like Gabriel Conroy, are overwhelmed by the presence of those who belong to the past.

The conviction that the dead are not really dead lay behind Nora's answer to Campbell's question, why did she not return to Ireland? "I guess it's because he's here," she said. "They wanted me to live in England so I can get the money that's there, but I have never lived there, and I'm not fond of the English so I won't do it. I'd like to have a cottage in Ireland, but the Irish don't like Joyce, so there you are."

As they left Joyce's grave, Nora drew Campbell's attention to a plant with green leaves. Joyce had not liked flowers, she said. She invited Campbell to take some of the leaves away with him. "It's a nice place, isn't it?" she said to him. "I'm glad we came. Thank you for bringing me with you, Mr. Campbell."

Nora remained an exile for Joyce's sake. She could not leave "him" — that is, his body. Her antagonism to Ireland was no greater — and no less — than Ireland's antagonism to him. An event in Ireland that same year only strengthened Nora's belief that the Irish did not like James Joyce. In 1948 the Irish government brought the body of W. B. Yeats back to Ireland from the south of France where he had died in 1939. Yeats had wished to be buried in the Drumcliff churchyard in his beloved Sligo and had reserved a plot for himself and his family. In 1948 Ireland repatriated Yeats's body with solemn homage. The coffin was taken from France to Galway Bay by a ship of the Irish navy; there the widow, her children, and the poet's brother were piped aboard. Then a funeral procession escorted them from Galway to Sligo, where Yeats was buried with a military guard of honor and representation from the Irish government.[5]

Why not the same for Joyce? Nora, backed by Giorgio, felt that the Irish government should do no less for its greatest writer of prose than for its greatest poet. Joyce's body, in any case, needed a more permanent resting place than the grave accorded him upon his unexpected death in Zurich. Swiss policy, unwelcoming to immigrants dead or alive, encouraged the repatriation of bodies of foreign visitors. However, neither Nora nor Giorgio was capable of the campaigning needed to organize an official request for the return of Joyce's body to Ireland. Such an arrangement, what is more, was almost certainly politically impossible. The Protestant ascendancy of Nora's youth had been superseded by a Catholic ascendancy and a puritanical and theocratic government that maintained a strict censorship over books and newspapers.

Joyce's books were never banned in Ireland because, as Mr. Deasy in *Ulysses* says of the Jews, Ireland never let them in. Customs officials simply seized any that were found entering the country. But Joyce the man was as unacceptable as Joyce the author. Unlike Yeats, who had served as a senator in the Irish Free State ("A smiling public man," Yeats had called himself),[6] Joyce remained in the Irish mind of the postwar years shocking, blasphemous, and arrogant. His boarding school, Clongowes Wood, did not acknowledge his work, apart from the schoolboy rumor that an Old Clongownian had let the school down by writing a book about a man who spent twenty-four hours in a public lavatory.[7] And when Joyce's brother Charles died a week after Joyce, Belvedere, their Jesuit secondary school in Dublin, accorded only one of the Joyce brothers an obituary in the school magazine, and it was not James. He was looked upon as "one of the bad boys."[8]

Nora, nonetheless, persuaded Miss Weaver to try to use her influence, and Miss Weaver accordingly approached Count O'Kelly and Constantine Curran to see if the Irish government or the Royal Irish Academy would consider requesting the return of Joyce's body. (If Joyce's body left Switzerland, Nora and Giorgio would leave too, Miss Weaver believed.) Maria Jolas added her support; she wrote an impassioned letter to O'Kelly to tell him that Joyce was beyond question a good Catholic and that his body should be brought back not only because his widow wished it but because Joyce was a towering figure of Irish literature.[9]

It fell to Count O'Kelly to make inquiries and relate to Maria Jolas the sad news that such a proposal would receive little popular support. Ireland had not forgiven James Joyce. Much of the Catholic academic world was as implacable in its resistance as the government and, needless to say, the Church.[10]

By 1948 Giorgio had begun to make changes in his own life. Not yet divorced from Helen, he had found a new love — Asta Jahnke-Osterwalder, a German eye doctor who was separated from her husband and who had two children, a son and a handicapped daughter. Nora was not pleased about the relationship, but she tolerated it. Jacques Mercanton, visiting Zurich, looked up Giorgio and found him living with Asta in a pleasant villa. When he rang the bell, he found not only Giorgio at home but also Nora. "You can't imagine who's here!" Giorgio called out to his mother, and when Nora saw their old friend, she took his hands and burst into a torrent of tears. Mercanton was distressed to see her arthritic state because otherwise she appeared to him still young.[11]

In the summer of 1948 Nora and Giorgio had visitors from New York: Giorgio's sister-in-law, Margaret Kastor (Robert Kastor's wife), and her teenage daughter, Enid. Margaret Kastor was a warm, friendly woman who had done much to make a home for Stephen in the United States. Enid, about Stephen's age, was visiting Europe for the first time and kept a journal in which she recorded her impressions of her travels and of the Joyces.

Twice Margaret and Enid dined with Nora, Giorgio, Stephen, and Asta at the Kronenhalle, which Enid found reminiscent of a German-American restaurant in New York with its high ceilings and dark paneling. Its food was plain if expensive, and she observed that the poorer customers came after dinner to linger over beer, and to chat and smoke Players, the English cigarette then popular.

Meeting Nora for the first time, Enid saw "a plain rosy-cheeked Irish woman with very white hair, lovely skin and a completely ordinary face."[12] It was "impossible to think of her that she was the mistress and then, right before Stephen's birth, the wife of such a man as James Joyce." Nora, Enid marveled, did not seem to think of her husband as a great writer. "To her," wondered Enid, "he remains a man with the faults and virtues that any man might have."

Enid took note of Nora's brogue as well as of the Irish phrasing of her sentences. Nora was ashamed that she had become "soused" on champagne the night that Stephen had returned on summer vacation from America and they had celebrated in grand style at the Kronenhalle. On both evenings with the Kastors, when offered wine, Nora was rather skittish, not wanting anything to happen "like the other night." And to them she exhibited her habit of the direct personal remark: "I don't know if I should say this," she said to Margaret Kastor, "but Enid is so glamorous, like out in Hollywood." Enid decided that Nora was happy in Zurich, "eating, sleeping, fussing over her arthritis, and putting the past behind her."

Enid had not seen Giorgio since he and Helen had lived in Manhattan. At forty-three, he looked older and not as handsome — "that is," she confided to her journal, "if one considers him handsome, which I never did." His hair was long and steely gray, his hands slender, with well-manicured fingernails, and he nervously broke his long silences with little fragments of deep basso humming. His English was accented and scrupulously enunciated, and he passed the time, having given up singing, in "drinking, smoking, eating only a little, and clowning with his girlfriend, a hale and hearty German woman, much younger than he, who played games kicking Stephen under the table." His companions at the Kronen-halle seemed to Enid "like himself . . . outcasts from life."

Enid found Asta "romantically enthralled" with Giorgio but was sure that "playing temptress-mother to him was a way of relaxing after a hard day at the eye clinic and not the prelude to marriage." Such a basically sensible woman would not undertake such a marriage, she and her mother were sure.

But the Kastors underestimated the attractiveness to the weak and hy-pochondriacal Giorgio of a strong, medically trained woman. Giorgio at that time still suffered from migraine headaches. These flushed his face a bright pink. Frau Doktor, as they all called her, diverted him, tried to get him to eat, and sometimes could reduce the headache before it peaked. She and Giorgio remained together and married in 1954.

Nora was used to hearing Giorgio complain about his headaches. When he did so in front of Margaret and Enid, she ventured that perhaps psy-choanalysis might be good for him. "Rubbish," Giorgio snorted. "If I want any of that sort of baloney I can always confess myself to a priest. It's the same thing."

Relations between the ex-relations were edgy. Giorgio knew that Ste-phen had enjoyed the family atmosphere at the Kastors' in New York, and observing his son and Enid together, asked Stephen if he was on such good terms with all his cousins. Enid made a special effort with Giorgio: "I really tried to be my most charming as I know Giorgio's hearty dislike of our whole family and wanted to amend it to some degree."

Before parting, Margaret and Enid took some photographs that con-firm other reports of Nora's poise and tranquillity in those years. Nora at sixty-four shows the same steady gaze that she had accorded the camera since girlhood, with eyes that take in a great deal and show her to be at ease with herself and the world's curiosity. She is portly but strong, erect and square-shouldered. Her large black fedora hat, geometrically pat-terned suit, and blouse with its soft tie at the neck proclaim that she has not lost her interest in style, nor her distinct androgynous air. Beside her on a Zurich street stands Giorgio, an aging roué, a man of whom by middle age the only kind thing that could be said was that he loved his mother.

In late 1948 and in 1949 Nora twice left Zurich to visit Paris. She was needed to help sort out the possessions retrieved by Paul Léon from the Paris flat and to play a small part in organizing an exhibition and sale of Joyce manuscripts, books, and pictures. This was to be at Librairie La Hune, a new bookshop and gallery on the Left Bank, and proceeds were to go to her and Giorgio.

Among the items for sale were all the family portraits, including those of Nora done by Silvestri and Budgen. For the exhibition but not for sale, Nora loaned her copy of *Chamber Music*. Giorgio was eager to raise as much money as possible, resentful as ever that much of the income from his father's books was going to meet the heavy expenses of keeping Lucia.

As Joyce material came up for sale, dissension broke out in the ranks of scholars and collectors. John Slocum, eyeing the La Hune collection, hoped to be able to buy everything and to present it to his alma mater, Harvard. He was bitterly disappointed when he found that somehow the University of Buffalo had outwitted him and had made a higher bid of ten thousand dollars, which had been accepted. In what was only the beginning of a struggle that would scatter Joyceana all over the American academic archipelago, Slocum looked for a culprit and blamed Maria Jolas for allowing him unwittingly to be outbid. She just as fiercely accused him of being more concerned with Harvard and Yale than with getting the largest possible amount of money into the hands of Mrs. Joyce. To those who would listen, she denounced John Slocum as an "s.o.b."[13]

Carola Giedion-Welcker too used the occasion of the La Hune exhibition to air her grievances against Nora and Giorgio. In loaning one of the controversial death masks, she complained to Sylvia Beach that Nora had turned Maria Jolas against her and that Giorgio had gossiped all over Zurich about how the Giedions had exploited the Joyces.[14] She herself had only intended that the masks be made so that they might go to a museum or a library, she said, and was waiting to hear from Ireland if postage, packing, and insurance would be paid if she sent one of the masks there.

While Nora was accessible in Paris, Harriet Weaver crossed the Channel to see her and the exhibition. As literary executor, Miss Weaver had the power to make all decisions about the publication and location of Joyce's papers, but she wanted to respect Nora's wishes. Two manuscripts were much on Miss Weaver's mind. One was a notebook for *Exiles* that had come to light among the papers taken from storage. The notes appended to the play would obviously be of great interest to Joyce scholars, but some of the comments had highly personal references and heightened the autobiographical nature of the play. (The notes, it must be remembered, referred to Prezioso's attachment to Nora and to Nora's girlhood memories and contained such highly specific comments as "at the convent they called her the man-killer.") The other was the disposition of the manuscripts of *Finnegans Wake*. Miss Weaver hoped to donate them to the National Library of Ireland: she had in fact promised the keeper of books that Ireland should have them.

Nora willingly consented to the publication of *Exiles,* notes and all. But she startled Miss Weaver with her implacable hostility to the idea of the *Wake* manuscripts' going to Ireland. If Ireland did not want her husband's body, Nora said, it should not have his manuscripts. The British Museum, Nora said, would be a more fitting repository.[15]

In fact, two years earlier, Nora had been extremely distressed to learn from a newspaper clipping sent by Kathleen that Count O'Kelly had handed envelopes containing several thousand letters by and about the Joyce family to the National Library of Ireland. Léon should have consulted her and Giorgio, Nora felt, before consigning them. She asked Miss Weaver to try to get them back. But there was nothing Miss Weaver could do. The papers were under seal, under precise instructions from Constantine Curran, obeying Paul Léon, not to be opened until 1991, the fiftieth anniversary of Joyce's death, and not even his widow and son had the power to undo the terms of the bequest.[16]

Miss Weaver let the matter rest but returned to England shaken to have found Nora "without a good word for the Irish."[17] She herself was without a good word for the Americans, even the well-meaning and well-heeled libraries eager to buy Joyce material. America, to her mind, had "become unbearably aggressive since Mr. Roosevelt's lamentable death," and she took no pains to conceal her own political allegiance. When John Slocum's wife politely inquired about it, Miss Weaver replied, "I'm redder than your dress, my dear."[18]

In Paris Nora had her first opportunity since the war to see Lucia. The visit never took place — Giorgio and Maria Jolas prevented it. Giorgio himself went out to Ivry and spent an hour walking with his sister on the grounds of the Delmas clinic and was so distressed by her state (he told Maria Jolas) that he decided that his mother should not go. He and Mrs. Jolas agreed that, as she wrote to Harriet Weaver, "It is so many years since [Nora] saw her that it hardly seems necessary now." Mrs. Jolas glossed over the decision in her report to Miss Weaver and undertook instead to talk with Nora a great deal about Lucia. "I have never been aware," she said, "how deep her maternal distress is and always has been."[19]

It is not possible to know, as Nora's own views were not recorded, whether she was disappointed or grateful at having been spared the stress of a reunion with her mad daughter.

Lucia had spent the entire war at Pornichet in occupied Brittany. The total isolation from any family or friends served to complete the institutionalization of her personality. Back in Paris, some of Joyce's old friends paid her visits, but they were prompted as much by curiosity as by concern. As Gogarty gleefully recounted to a friend in September 1949:

I met Colum last week. He had come from a visit to the asylum where Joyce's daughter is confined. He told me that she is gray haired and has a little beard. She talks of marrying and she suggests McGreevy because they both like food. Sad; but it goes to prove that which Slocum did not like to hear that her father transmitted the madness.[20]

The report was accurate insofar as Lucia did have hairs growing on her chin. The condition (possibly a response to hormonal medication), which remained with her until her death in 1982, only added to her sense of unloveliness and her obsession with defects in her appearance.

One reason why Mrs. Jolas had not wanted Nora to visit Ivry was that the physical surroundings were depressing. The damage done by the German bombardment had not been repaired. Another reason was that Lucia was still extremely violent. When Dr. Delmas died and Mrs. Jolas went to discuss Lucia's case with his successors, she found that Lucia had just broken six windows, attacked two patients, and been put for a time into a straitjacket. During her visit, Mrs. Jolas did not dare risk entering Lucia's room.[21] Reporting to Miss Weaver, who had been worried that — as Dr. Delmas had died — the clinic was now keeping Lucia merely for profit, Mrs. Jolas said that, to the contrary, the staff would not object at all if Miss Joyce were to be moved to another institution. About her prognosis they were very pessimistic. They saw no hope of any improvement in her behavior until "the cessation of certain physiological functions," Lucia then having reached the age of forty-one.

Maria Jolas, who tended to have a good word for everybody, except those whom she saw as rival custodians of the Joyce memory (notably Sylvia Beach), found Giorgio "of excellent counsel" and felt confident that he would become more and more helpful to his mother as time went on.[22]

She tried to help Nora by putting her on a diet to help her arthritis. Nora would have none of it. "I can eat like anybody else," she snapped. Arthur Power, who was in Paris, tried to cheer Nora up by taking her out to dinner. "Where would you like to go?" he asked. She did not hesitate: the Café Francis. But the evening was not a success. Old memories crowded in, and her arthritis had slowed her almost to a halt. As she moved painfully toward the taxi, Power heard her murmur wearily, "This too too solid flesh . . ."[23] She was glad to return to Zurich, a fine city for old ladies.

By this time Joyce scholars had become part of the Joyces' extended family and often acted as go-betweens. John Slocum went to Ireland and acquired from Kathleen some letters exchanged by Joyce and Michael Healy. It was to Slocum later that Kathleen wrote angrily to complain that Nora had abandoned her, refused to answer her letters, and did nothing to help with the problem of their sister Delia. When Nora and James Joyce needed financial assistance from Galway, Kathleen said bitterly, they were given all that they needed.[24]

Not only was John Slocum collecting letters for American libraries but other literary sleuths were on the trail, and Miss Weaver herself was trying to assemble what she could for a published volume of Joyce letters, to be edited by Stuart Gilbert. "Does Mrs. Joyce have the address of Mr. Stanislaus Joyce?" Harriet Weaver asked Evelyn Cotton. "He might have some letters he could contribute for the book."[25] Miss Weaver apparently did not know that Slocum was in touch with Stanislaus in Trieste and had in fact been buying Joyce manuscripts from him. It never occurred to Slocum that Joyce's papers in Trieste might be Nora's property and the proceeds due her, or that their sale should be reported to Miss Weaver, Joyce's literary executor.

Nora, in failing health, concentrated her energies on her immediate problems. She willingly assented to the collection and publication of the volume of Joyce's letters, stipulating only that she be allowed to review the selection first in order to rule out any that were too personal. She asked that little mention be made of the Joyces' financial difficulties, as these had been covered sufficiently in the Herbert Gorman biography, but she was not unduly sensitive to the invasion of her privacy. When Mary Colum published her book *Life and the Dream* in 1947, it was largely about the Colums' friendship with the Joyces and included passages about Lucia's illness. Nora shrugged it off and said she took it as simply a good joke.[26] Nora discouraged, however, the suggestion of a young American Joycean, Richard Kain, that he assemble a collection of reminiscences about James Joyce. She said firmly that she did not want to have "all sorts of silly stories published." Miss Weaver agreed with her.[27]

One controversial decision about publication was being made behind Nora's back. When Joyce died in 1941, Marthe Fleischmann, who was still living in Zurich, read the publicity attendant upon his funeral and approached Professor Heinrich Straumann with four letters Joyce had written her. She also had an autographed copy of *Chamber Music*. A glance was enough for Straumann to recognize that Nora would not be happy about the contents: they were love letters, although of a decidedly innocent nature. He urged Fräulein Fleischmann — she had never married — to wait until the end of the war when international buyers might be available. He promised her that whenever she was moved to sell them he would better the highest price she was offered. Astutely Marthe refused to let him copy the letters and departed.

In 1948 Straumann tried to trace the letters. He found that Marthe Fleischmann was in a hospital for elderly invalids but that her sister had almost all of what he had originally been shown — all, that is, except a postcard — and was willing to sell on her sister's behalf. Straumann bought them and showed the letters to Giorgio, who denied that they were authentic. His father did not make Greek *e*'s, Giorgio said. No great reader of his father's work, he appeared oblivious to the fact that in *Ulysses* Leopold Bloom conducts a similar clandestine correspondence, using Greek *e*'s as a clumsy disguise for his handwriting. Giorgio, with equal myopia, dismissed the possibility of the affair; he would have heard of it, he said, because his mother would certainly have found out and raised a tremendous storm.[28] Stuart Gilbert later agreed with Giorgio that the letters should not be published.

In Zurich Nora continued to see her friends — Frau Zumsteg of the Kronenhalle, Bertha Ruggiero, and Klara from the Kronenhalle. There was a dealer in Oriental carpets with whom she liked to chat. She passed her days in orderly routine. Because of her stiff joints, it took her a long time to get dressed ("a performance," she laughed), then she walked out with her stick and sat in the sunshine. Regularly she went to Mass at the Saint Antoniuskirche, a few streets away, where she had her personal confessor, a priest who became a good friend. At night she said her rosary, which she kept on her bedside table. Her health worsened, but she never, even to close women friends, complained about her health.[29]

Stephen Joyce, when he visited his grandmother from America and saw her through older and more experienced eyes, admired her courage. He could see the problems she had with his father and her fondness for him in spite of all. Stephen was on his way to becoming estranged from his alcoholic father but could see that whatever was wrong with Giorgio, Nora did not consider it her fault.[30]

John Slocum was another visitor from America. He formed the opinion that her condition was not being properly treated and organized a surprise gift from Ireland of the then wonder drug cortisone. When Nora first began taking it, she was euphoric. She thought her arthritis had gone for good. But the relief was only temporary and the treatment expensive. Harriet Weaver sent three hundred pounds of her own money (with the Bank of England's permission) to help Nora out until the ten thousand dollars from the sale of the La Hune collection to the University of Buffalo came through.[31]

In the summer of 1950, at Harriet Weaver's request, Maria Jolas visited Nora to raise once more the question of sending the *Wake* manuscripts to Ireland. Sean MacBride, then Irish minister for external affairs, had written to Nora to suggest that the work be lodged in the National Library and to tell her that the Irish government was proud to claim James Joyce, "one of the greatest Europeans of his time," as also a son of Ireland. These were not the official words Nora was waiting to hear. Maria Jolas's conversation with Nora and Giorgio lasted several hours and ended with Nora shrugging and saying that Miss Weaver must do as she wished.[32]

In the autumn of 1950, Nora's condition deteriorated rapidly. Giorgio scarcely left her side. One consequence was that he took over the correspondence with Miss Weaver and soon extinguished any possibility that Nora would endorse giving the *Wake* manuscripts to Dublin. Whether speaking only for himself or reflecting Nora's true views, Giorgio said that both he and his mother were "utterly hostile to Dublin." They preferred the British Museum.[33]

Late in 1950 Nora's joints grew so stiff that she could no longer walk. She entered the Paracelsus Clinic, run by nursing sisters, in Belvedere Park overlooking the lake. (It has now moved to the suburbs.) It was one of Zurich's finest hospitals and a sign that the Joyces had recovered some of their former standard of living. As the new year dawned, Giorgio wrote to Miss Weaver to say that that his mother was very seriously ill. There was, he said flatly, no hope.[34] He blamed the cortisone, which had been administered with such a free hand that, far from helping her, it only hastened her decline.

Giorgio visited her every day. Shaken by his mother's suffering, he even gave up drinking. Stuart Gilbert, when he saw him, believed Giorgio to be a totally changed character, and perhaps, for the moment, he was. It was touching to everyone to see the closeness between the mother and son who had spent much of their lives clinging together in the wake of James Joyce.[35]

In April 1951 Giorgio saw that Nora was dying. He called Frau Zumsteg from the Kronenhalle to come to say goodbye. Nora's confessor visited the clinic and gave her the last rites of the Church.[36] In her last weeks she slipped into unconsciousness. She developed uremia, and her heart weakened. On April 10, with Giorgio at her side, Nora unexpectedly opened her eyes. With a burst of strength, she reached up and touched her son's cheek. It was the last act of her life. The long journey from Galway was over. Giorgio wired the news to Miss Weaver: "Mother died this morning."[37]

Nora's funeral was small, attended by about forty people, mainly her Swiss friends and elderly ladies from the pension. Professor Straumann made it a point to attend, providing a link with Joyce's funeral. Maria Jolas and Stuart Gilbert came from Paris. All were dismayed that there was no room in the grave beside Joyce; Nora had to be buried in a new plot about fifty yards away. The priest assigned to the ceremony, Fr. Johann von Rotz, was not Nora's regular confessor but rather the man on duty that day, and he gave a perfunctory sermon. Stuart Gilbert thought it a pity that the priest spoke more of the great *Dichter* than of Nora, and that "only her intimate friends knew how lovable she was, and how devoted a wife."[38]

At Gilbert's side, Maria Jolas, straining to hear and to translate, caught two words that floated out over the morning air: *"grosse Sünderin."* Had the priest called Nora a great sinner? How unfair of him to expose poor Nora's secret shame — that she had lived as a mistress for twenty-seven years! Her own Episcopal religion, Mrs. Jolas thought to herself, was far more forgiving than the harsh Roman Catholic Church.[39]

In history and biography, the record is written by those who live the longest. Maria Jolas outlived almost every member of the Joyce circle; for many years until her death in 1987 at the age of ninety-four she reigned unchallenged as the authority on the events of the Joyces' later lives. She imposed, with the sheer force of her personality, her version of events on the clouded and contradictory record, and it was she, therefore, who inserted the *"grosse Sünderin"* epithet into Nora's legend. Neither Stuart Gilbert nor Professor Straumann caught anything like the offending phrase in the priest's remarks. Mrs. Jolas, however, was convinced that Nora's confessor had excused himself from the funeral out of embarrassment because of Nora's scandalous past, and that he had allowed the ceremony to be taken instead by a bumpkin of a priest. Later, after reflection, she did concede that the words she heard at Nora's funeral "may have been the customary rhetoric but I was shocked."[40] And she tried to console Giorgio, as they left the funeral, with an old Irish joke of Joyce's about a poorly attended funeral: "If he'd [referring to the deceased] been here, it would have been different."

If Joyce had been there, he might indeed have heard something different. The bucolic and unlettered priest was less likely to have been flinging Nora's past sins upon her grave than mouthing familiar phrases from Goethe's *Faust* — quotations from Goethe being as common cultural currency in German as quotations from Shakespeare are in English. The phrase appears (used in the plural) in the prayer to the Blessed Virgin:

> *Die du grossen Sünderinnen*
> *deine Nähe nicht verweigerst*
> *und ein büssendes Gewinnen*
> *in die Ewigkeiten steigerst,*
> *gönn auch dieser guten Seele,*
> *die sich einmal nur vergessen,*
> *die nicht ahnte, dass sie fehle,*
> *dein Verzeihen angemessen!* *

Although a literal reading might suggest that Father von Rotz could have been briefed on Nora's irregular past when he chose the well-turned phrases about great sinners and a good soul, he himself emphatically denied the possibility. "It was an absolutely routine funeral for me," he

---

* Thou who women greatly sinning/Grantest to come nigh to Thee/By sincere repentance winning/Bliss through all eternity./Grant to this good soul thy blessing,/Who but once herself forgot,/Who knew not she was transgressing,/Pardon meet refuse Thou not![41]

said.[42] In any event, it would have been theologically inconsistent to accuse Nora of sins of which she was absolved during her last years when she regularly took the sacraments.

This imagined slur at her funeral service was the final misjudgment of Nora by the literary world. The woman who had given her loyalty, her strength, and her wit to Joyce went down in literary history not only as a burden who contributed nothing to his work but also as a belatedly married mistress who was described as a Great Sinner at her burial. "Few epithets could have been less apt," Ellmann concludes charitably.[43]

If the words were from *Faust,* however, few epithets could have been more appropriate. Nora, like Gretchen, was a simple honorable soul who loved a man of Luciferian pride. And Joyce himself worshiped her as his rescuer from Faust's fate.[44] It was also fitting that Nora should have been accorded words from one of the masterpieces of European literature. She, like Joyce, was a true European at her death, a proud resident of the pleasant city that had three times given her refuge.

From her many visits to the cemetery, Nora was undoubtedly aware that there was no place for her beside Joyce, and she accepted it. The Joyces' many friends did not. In 1966, with considerable ceremony and no further thoughts of repatriation to Ireland, the Joyces' bodies became forever part of Zurich, reburied together in a permanent and well-landscaped grave in Fluntern overlooking the city. Joyce lovers in their thousands every year make their way to the grave site and, if they recall Nora's remarks, are pleased to find that to get to Fluntern Cemetery, they must take to the end the tram for the zoo.

22

Nora Speaking

Wherever thou art shall be Erin to me.

— James Joyce, Alphabetical notebook,
entry under "Nora" [1]

"IRELAND MUST BE IMPORTANT," says Stephen Dedalus to Bloom, "because it belongs to me." Nora is important because she belonged to Joyce and because she never did. She was the stronger of the two, an independent spirit who had far more influence on him than he upon her.

For a long time the only recognition she achieved was as her husband's portable Ireland. J. M. Synge, in order to capture the authentic Irish voice, had to lie on the floor of a rural farmhouse that his mother had rented for the summer and listen to the chatter of the maids in the kitchen below. Yeats and Lady Gregory sat in her stately home at Coole Park and talked about the rich experience of the peasantry. But Joyce married his Ireland. Nora's unremitting Irishness was for him a constant comfort and inspiration. When Joyce died, Kenneth Reddin wrote in the *Irish Times*, "I remember Mrs. Joyce's beautiful Galway voice, her hospitality and constant good humour . . . and the never-changing sense of a Dublin transplanted abroad." [2]

Nora never expected more recognition. Anna Livia's dying words could have been hers: "I'll slip away before they're up. They'll neither see. Nor know. Nor miss me." Yet her own death was noticed by the world's press: the *New York Times*, the *Herald-Tribune*, the *Times of London*, and, of course, *Time*, which gave her age as sixty-five rather than sixty-seven. *Time*, on April 23, 1951, warmly if not absolutely accurately accorded Nora some rare public credit for her part in her husband's achievement:

Died: Mrs. James Joyce (Nora Barnacle), 65, longtime confidante and literary midwife to her famed author husband; of a heart attack; in Zurich,
Switzerland, where Joyce died ten years ago. A practical woman, she helped
him settle down and get his work done, sighed after reading *Ulysses:* "I guess
the man's a genius, but what a dirty mind he has, surely!" After he reached
success and died, she long endured a genteel poverty, unwilling to live in
England, unable to get more than a fraction of his royalties out of the country.

Those who knew Nora at close hand had little doubt of her contribution. Elizabeth Curran believed that Nora, by her own efforts, had saved
Joyce from becoming alcoholic. Without her constant "Jim, you've had
enough," Curran's daughter felt, his habit would have overwhelmed his
ability to work. To Maria Jolas, Nora's insistence that Joyce have the
right conditions in which to work belied her supposed indifference to his
work; Nora, to Mrs. Jolas, cared about his work because he did — a
view supported by her enthusiasm for *Finnegans Wake*.[3]
In the memoirs of their friends, Nora emerges as a force to be reckoned
with, and if her comic side is emphasized by some of the more literary
figures, there were others, such as the Colums and J. F. Byrne, who laughed
with her. The Joyce marriage, for all its internal strains and mysteries,
looked unusually strong to those closest to them. Sylvia Beach called it
the happiest she knew. Stuart Gilbert later refused to publish the Marthe
Fleischmann letters when he was shown them because he saw Joyce as so
devoted a husband.[4] Stanislaus Joyce, in choosing to be brief in his comments on his brother's marriage, said a great deal:

I shall only say that he married his wife in a civil ceremony some years ago,
and that up until the time of his death . . . he was apart from her only for
a very few weeks, and then unwillingly.[5]

An eloquent appreciation in later years came from Arthur Power:

I can say in all sincerity that I do not believe James Joyce could have coped
with the difficulties of daily life had it not been for the great devotion and
courage of his wife Nora. Theirs was a constant companionship based on
love and congenial understanding. Anyone who knew Mr. and Mrs. Joyce
realized that no important move would be made one without the other. Unless one had seen them together one would not realize how much James
Joyce depended on his wife Nora. In all the blows that fate dealt Joyce
and his family, through all the trials and tribulations, they remained devot-
edly together.

It was Nora, Power asserted, who held the family together, "with her
courage, and rock-firm common sense":

It is true that she was not an intellectual in any sense; and why should she be? . . . She was a sincere and gallant woman, and his worthy companion and mate — this breath of Galway air in the intellectual hothouse of Paris.[6]

Perhaps the finest tribute of all came from her grandson. "Nonna was so strong," Stephen Joyce has said, "she was a rock. I would venture to say that he could have done none of it, written not one of the books without her."[7]

Nora would have been surprised to know that posterity would dismiss her as a slovenly illiterate who could not even cook. Over the years the jibes have accumulated: "She never mastered the languages of the countries in which they lived"; "His uneducated and unlettered wife (she was a chambermaid when he met her) . . . refused to read *Ulysses* or anything else by her husband"; "Nora was unable to supply a minimum of tranquillity or tidiness or system in their household"; she, "like Molly Bloom, kept a dirty house."[8] Nora would have shrugged off the bad press. She was never at ease with the kind of people who might have preserved her reputation and did not bother to court them. Those whom she cared about, her friends and family, knew that in performing her duty as she saw it — looking after James Joyce — she was flawless.

There is no doubt, however, that Nora did refuse to read *Ulysses;* it is her best-known fault, although she shares it with most of the human race. Her main accuser was James Joyce. He moaned, not only to Frank Budgen but to any number of visitors, "My wife has been complaining because there is no light literature in our flat. She has never read *Ulysses* which, after all, is light, humorous stuff." Not everyone took Joyce's side, even at the time, when he made fun of his wife in this way. "*Ulysses* amusing to read?" said C. R. W. Nevison, a British guest who heard Joyce make the remark when he and his wife had joined the Joyces' table one evening at Les Trianons and could not believe his ears. "As his book had shocked the world, I was dumbfounded."[9]

In the late twentieth century, when Joyce is widely regarded as a difficult, even unread author (especially in Britain where the Cambridge critic F. R. Leavis classified him as outside the Great Tradition), Nora's sin of omission seems less ignorant than self-protective. For Nora *Ulysses* presented special difficulty, partly because of its language, but also because of her efforts to distance herself from the character of Molly and because of her conviction that Joyce ought to be earning more money to support the family. That she did not despise Joyce's work as a totality was proved by her fondness for quoting his poems and by her enthusiasm for *Finnegans Wake.*

The Joyces' devoted and enduring marriage will always remain a mystery to those who insist upon looking at it as a match of intellectual incompatibles. There are more powerful forces for cohesion. Chief among these was Nora's uncomplicated sureness against Joyce's persistent uncertainty about everything except his genius. There was also the undeniable androgynous element in their relationship. That this mesh of qualities associated with the opposite sex was part of the bond that held them together is apparent from their letters to each other, their friends' comments, and Joyce's work.

Less obvious and far too often discounted is that they loved each other. They had a genuine delight in each other's company that can best be appreciated from photographs, such as the snapshot taken by Carola Giedion-Welcker in Lucerne in 1935: Joyce is beaming at Nora, and Nora is happily confident in herself and her man.

It is remarkable that so many people today know Joyce only for the lingering notoriety of *Ulysses* and assume that he was a womanizer. That was far from the truth. Stanislaus, in another bleak phrase, said that his brother, like many of his countrymen, married early as if to get it over with and was a faithful husband after that.[10] In fact, according to all the available evidence (and, taking all Joyce's letters and the great weight of memoirs of the period into account, there is a great deal of evidence) there is no sign that, with the exception of prostitutes in Dublin before he met Nora and possibly some in Trieste later, Joyce ever had full sexual intercourse with any woman but Nora.

Underpinning the loyalty of Nora and Joyce to each other was their deeper dependency. They gave each other, both deprived, *"amor matris . . . the only true thing in life."*

Apart from the real Nora there is another, the Nora Barnacle who saunters through the imaginations of the Irish male and those who know the life of Joyce: the carefree redhead who dared to say yes in an age when nice girls said no. As John Slocum wrote, after being taken out to Howth Head on his visit to Ireland in 1948, "I only wished at times that Constantine Curran had been a winsome young barmaid from Galway City so that the evocation of those last pages of *Ulysses* might have been complete."[11]

Nora Barnacle is as much a part of Irish mythology as Queen Maeve. Men confess to fantasies about her. A musical, *Nora Barnacle,* was performed in Phoenix Park in 1977, its songs bearing titles from Nora's imagined past: "Parc Monceau" (where Joyce briefly abandoned her in 1904) and "A Home of My Own." Sean O'Faolain wrote a short story about a Dublin literary bore who claimed to have a genuine portrait of Nora Barnacle, his image of a young, red-haired Irish beauty. O'Faolain himself in old age mused upon her personality during an interview:

She was a girl from crude animal Galway. Her spontaneous animal way attracted him enormously. A most suitable companion for this pseudo-intellectual. Joyce was a bit of a mug but she wasn't. She was commonsense to his no-sense but, mind you, she wouldn't have suited everybody."[12]

One man who never forgot Nora was "her Protestant," Willie Mulvagh, the accountant from Joe Young's Mineral Water Factory. Twice a widower, Willie lived on until the 1950s and in his last years made his home in England with his daughter. He was a silent man who never spoke about his past, never read books, and had not the faintest idea that he was in *Ulysses*. His daughter was all the more startled one day, therefore, when Willie looked up from his newspaper, his memory apparently jogged by something he had read, and asked, "James Joyce? Didn't he marry a Galway girl by the name of Barnacle?"[13]

Fantasies of Nora are giving way to recognition. The *Irish Times*, when the centenary of her birth was being planned, described her as "becoming almost as famous as the husband whose works she couldn't comprehend."[14] "In her native city," the newspaper said, "where once her name was only mentioned in disapproving undertones, Nora has been accorded the ultimate Irish accolade. A pub has been named after her." The Galway Tourist Board had also, the paper noted wrily, affixed a plaque on Nora's mother's house in Bowling Green, filled with harmlessly erroneous information.[15] There is another pub named for Nora in Dun Laoghaire, not far from the Martello tower at Sandycove, now known as the Joyce Tower.

More seriously, Nora is now seen to embody the continuing predicament of many young Irish women: passionate, eager, untrained, caught in a conflict between family and poverty, religion and sex. The Irish writer Edna O'Brien, who has turned the experience of such young women to literature, believes that she deals with "the world of Nora Barnacles," one of girls "in lonely, desperate and often humiliated situations, very often the butt of men and almost always searching for an emotional catharsis that does not come."[16]

That searching for catharsis well describes Nora's solitary nights at the opera in Paris. Sitting alone, basking in the love-death of the unfaithful Isolde, she drew back into herself and into that nostalgia for the romantic past which seems to possess the Irish above all other races:

> O the days of the Kerry dancers.
> O the lilt of the piper's tune.
> O for one of those hours of gladness!
> Gone, like the days of our youth, too soon.

To what extent Nora found satisfaction from knowing of her part in Joyce's literature can never be known because she said very little apart

from her rude references to Molly Bloom. She startled Eugene and Maria
Jolas one night when the four of them, dining at a restaurant in Paris,
drifted onto the subject of first love. Nora, who usually deferred to Joyce
in conversation, suddenly woke up:

> There's nothing like it. I remember when I was a girl and a young man fell
> in love with me, and he came and sang in the rain under an apple-tree outside
> my windows, and he caught tuberculosis and died.

Nora made her remark simply — not so much, Mrs. Jolas recalled, as if
she had never read "The Dead" but "as if *we* had not read it." [17]
  Whatever else it reveals, the anecdote shows that, quite without help
from Joyce, Nora was a romanticizer of her own past.

Scholarly interest has begun to focus on Nora. Now that women who
are "just wives" are seen to have value, Nora is recognized as the model
for all the main female characters in Joyce's work, and much more. Her
sensibility — what she noticed as important or annoying or funny —
weighed upon what Joyce chose to write just as her loose syntax, sentence structure, and indifference to punctuation lodged themselves in him,
to reappear and to alter the course of literature in the audacities of *Ulysses* and *Finnegans Wake*. More important, he took her view of life. It
does not require much straining to see Nora's calm stoicism in Anna
Livia's acceptance of death, or her unashamed tolerance of sexuality in
all its forms in Molly's "it didnt make me blush why should it either its
only nature." [18] Nora, Catholic, was a true protestant. She did not believe
that God would punish her for loving Jim any more than for refusing to
inflict a Catholic funeral upon him.
  There is much more to be learned about Nora's thoughts from Joyce's
work, but it can only be speculative. The bar between biography and
fiction must remain. Tempting as it is, for example, to hear Nora in *Exiles,* when Bertha angrily refuses to be humbled by her lover's sophisticated friends, the words must remain Bertha's:

> Humble me! I am very proud of myself, if you want to know. What have
> they ever done for him? I made him a man. [19]

Nora knew, because Joyce had told her, that he believed she had made
him a man. She told her sister that she had not made him man enough. [20]
She knew that she had rescued him from the corrosive and stultifying
sexual guilt of consorting with prostitutes and that she had written him
the letters he requested in order to keep him out of their clutches.

The tributes to Nora are scattered through Joyce's work: Woman, from
high-spirited youth to withered age.

Literary archaeologists will work for generations to tweezer out the hidden references to Nora: the "charmermaid" in *Finnegans Wake*, whose very title enshrines Finn's Hotel; the Blooms' Connemara marble clock, which stopped on March 21, 1896 (Nora's twelfth birthday, if the twenty-first is taken as her birthday). They will never find them all, for only Joyce knew where they were buried.

The homage to Nora's surname, and by extension to geese and sea-birds, can be found throughout Joyce's work. There are sixteen geese in *Ulysses*, there is the brown goose on the Christmas buffet in "The Dead," and seabirds in myriad forms all through the *Wake*.[21] Of Joyce's many references to the barnacle goose — his symbol of Nora, of metamorphosis, and of resurrection — perhaps the most explicit is contained in one of the most obscure lines in *Ulysses*. As Stephen Dedalus walks along Sandymount Strand "into eternity," his mind wanders from thoughts of a decomposing corpse to the continuity of all things living and dead. A phrase forms in his mind almost like a mathematical equation: "God becomes man becomes fish becomes barnacle goose becomes featherbed mountain."

In the hands of experienced translators, this code can be made to read: God descends to earth, becomes man who eats a kind of fish that turns itself into meat or a bird whose feathers are plucked to fill an eiderdown, which covers the marriage bed of domestic bliss, which enables the artist to rise to godlike heights of creation. Put another way, the line holds that just as God became man through the Incarnation, and Christ became a fish (the symbol by which he was known to the early believers), Joyce became a man in the hands of the woman who anchored him to the featherbed reality of married love and who opened his eyes to a new artistic vision: that the most important thing in life is love — the very opposite of "Force, hatred, history, all that."[22]

That Joyce should raise Nora to the status of his personal goddess is not surprising. That the ordinary is extraordinary is the meaning of Joyce. Nora was ordinary. That is to say, she accepted life, with its madness, drunkenness, poverty; its music, its comedy, and its sexual imperatives. Her tragedy was that Joyce never seemed to notice that their family life and her sexual appetite, which he so admired, were sacrificed on the altar of his art.

In every book except *A Portrait* the last words are spoken by a woman, the Nora character. In "The Dead" the words are Gretta's: "O, the day I heard that, that he was dead!"; in *Exiles*, Bertha's: "You, Dick. O my strange wild lover, come back to me again!" In *Ulysses* and the *Wake* the entire closing monologues down to the final utterances are in the female voice. Molly Bloom and Anna Livia Plurabelle, according to Adaline Glasheen, speak as "vessels of the cosmic secret . . . outside the moral and theological schemes that man erects to his torment."[23]

This shift to the female is a curious manifestation on the part of a young Irishman whose determination on going into exile, as declared at the close of *A Portrait of the Artist as a Young Man,* was "to forge in the smithy of my soul the uncreated conscience of my race." *A Portrait* is the only one of Joyce's books to end with a male voice. Why should the Irish conscience that Joyce created in exile be a feminine one?

A good answer has been offered by the critic Colin MacCabe. He has observed that Joyce rejected masculine structures — language as well as institutions — that rejected female desire. According to MacCabe,

> If the young Joyce was antipathetic to the national ideology which his generation did so much to promote, it was not so much to the specific claims of Gaelic . . . but to their service of a notion of Irish purity which linked a wholly false notion of the Gael to the equally false notion of the sexually and racially pure Irish person — to be more specific, the pure Irish woman . . .[24]

The continuing Irish struggle to believe in the exceptional purity of Irish womanhood and to remain more austere than other Western countries on matters of sexual morality shows that this ideology continues strong. So, it must be noted, does Irish violence.

Joyce related the repression of women to male brutality in the *Wake* when he wrote of "the vaulting feminine libido . . . sternly controlled and easily repersuaded by the uniform matteroffactness of a meandering male fist."[25]

Nora, in this light, was more than Joyce's Ireland; she was Irish Woman as he thought she should be. Just as *Finnegans Wake* creates on the page an Irish nation that history has never allowed to exist, Nora combined a mixture of Irishness with female libido, two qualities that Irish society still strives to keep apart. Joyce chose her to be his companion in a life of silence, exile, and cunning because she embodied the idea of the head-strong Celtic woman who trusts her intuition and her passions and is proud to be "worse than the men." She, like the peasant girl in *A Portrait,* was a guileless and bold young woman who offered herself to a timid stranger in the dark. Far more lightly than her conscience-tormented lover, she slipped the social bonds placed to hold her back.

Meeting Nora was indeed the most important day in Joyce's life. From their first walk to Ringsend, she changed his view of the world and of the driving force behind it. When Joyce made Leopold Bloom recall Molly's pleading, "Give us a touch, Poldy. God, I'm dying for it," he gave his country, and his century, the voice of female desire.[26] It was Nora's voice.

✦

Man of
Letters

Take. Bussoftlhee, mememormee!
Till thousendsthee.

— *Finnegans Wake*

NORA KEPT NO DIARIES. That her personality can be reconstructed is
owed largely to her brother-in-law Stanislaus Joyce. It was he who saved,
and his widow who sold to Cornell, the large collection of private letters
that reveal almost all that is known of Nora's family background, her
courtship, and her relationship to James Joyce.

Market forces also played their part in revealing Nora to the world.
With the end of World War II, the time had come for Joyce's papers to
set out on their journey westward. Fierce competition among American
universities drew anything connected with Joyce out of trunks and boxes
all across Europe, and into the climate-controlled security of special collections rooms of their libraries. The main collector in the immediate
postwar period was John Slocum. When word reached the press that this
young and wealthy Joyce enthusiast from the U.S. State Department had
paid Nora's sister Kathleen forty-five pounds for some of Michael Healy's letters and some pictures, Slocum found himself deluged with letters
from people all over Ireland with battered copies of Joyce's works to
sell.[1]

Had the papers not made their way to American academe, little would
be known of Nora except for a few anecdotes and her refracted images
in Gretta, Bertha, Molly, and Anna Livia. She would have remained a
cipher, a rough, if shadowy, figure to whose company Joyce was myste-
riously addicted. In 1957 Stuart Gilbert published his *Letters of James
Joyce,* a collection he assembled from Paris. In it there is no record of
Joyce and Nora's love, no letters of Nora's own except a polite note to

Miss Weaver in 1917 after Joyce's first eye operation in Zurich, and none at all from Joyce to Nora. Gilbert explained the omission, with the assurance of an old and trusted friend:

> No letters from Joyce to his wife are extant, so far as I can discover and this is not surprising. The two were literally inseparable; during all the years I knew him, Joyce never spent a night or even a full day away from his wife.[2]

Gilbert even censored important letters of Joyce's that he knew about — the 1919 love letters to Marthe Fleischmann. Friend first, scholar second, Gilbert was appalled at the thought that anything might be printed that would cast doubt on Joyce's "strong family feeling, deep love for his wife and a rare sense of personal dignity."[3] He also based his judgment upon what Joyce would probably have wished: no publication. Giorgio Joyce and Stephen, by then a Harvard graduate, heartily agreed. With Miss Weaver and T. S. Eliot sorely disappointed, the *Letters of James Joyce* were published as if they represented the most interesting of the known Joyce correspondence.[4]

In consequence, Joyce emerged as a dull, unfeeling man, concerned mainly with the printing and publishing of his work. Many reviewers concluded that Joyce was no more than the face he presented to the world in the 1930s: a desiccated, self-obsessed genius. "It is only with his daughter — and, at that, when she is on the edge of madness — that there is any intimacy," said Stephen Spender in the *New York Times Book Review*.[5]

Even Richard Ellmann, who was at the time writing his great biography of Joyce, to be published two years later, endorsed the idea that Joyce was an overcontrolled, mannered correspondent. "Joyce took from the beginning a special posture for his correspondence, and rarely relaxed it," Ellmann said, reviewing Gilbert's book for *Commonweal* in 1957. "The undisturbed ebullience that he displayed with his intimates in conversation is not notable in his letters."[6] Ellmann did not reveal that at that very time he was working with the great body of unpublished letters that had reached Cornell and that showed Joyce to be anything but unemotional as a letter writer.

Slocum began hunting about a year before the La Hune auction in 1949 in which he was outwitted by the University of Buffalo. He had embarked, with Herbert Cahoon of the Pierpont Morgan Library, on the preparation of a Joyce bibliography — a meticulously documented list of all of Joyce's published work, from the first reviews to the posthumous publication of *Stephen Hero*. The two men wanted to buy Joyce material as well as to catalogue it, and in 1948 they set out through Europe to gather what they could. "Don't for the Lord's sake," wrote Slocum to Cahoon, "omit Trieste from your itinerary."[7]

Slocum and his wife Eileen went to Trieste, and at the offices of *Il Piccolo* inquired for "Signor Joyce." Which Joyce did they want? asked the men at the newspaper, *il piccolo* or *il grande?* Slocum told them that *il grande* was dead and that it was the younger brother they sought.[8]

Stanislaus was not hard to find. In 1948 he enjoyed, at sixty-four, the status of professor at the Commercial University of Trieste, the former Scuola Commerciale. After the war, when he and his wife Nelly had returned from Florence with their small son, he had served as an interpreter for the Allied military government in Trieste in the long-running dispute in which Italy and Yugoslavia each claimed the city.[9] Slocum found Stanislaus unwilling to answer questions, probably, Slocum thought, because Stanislaus was writing his brother's life himself. Stanislaus was happy, however, to open negotiations on the sale of manuscripts in his possession.

Slocum had the money, the mobility, and the zeal to sustain his dream of gathering all Joyce's papers under one roof. From Stanislaus in 1948 he bought, among other things, the manuscript of "A Painful Case" with Nora's laundry list on the back. As Stanislaus offered items for sale, teasingly, bit by bit, Slocum began to sense that he had rivals. He was painfully learning a truth enunciated by Sylvia Beach when she was being pursued for her own Joyce material: "Well they are reglar Desparrados some of these businessmen scholars."[10]

The next year, before he saw his dream shattered by Buffalo, Slocum wrote to Stanislaus, thanking him for material received and promising swift payment:

> Concerning the possible sale of any manuscripts or other book material that you might be willing to dispose of, you have probably heard from a "Dr." Jacob Schwartz, an engaging rascal if there ever was one, but a rascal as I learned some ten years ago to my sorrow. Providing you don't mention my name to him or the conditions, I will top any offer he makes you for any material by twenty-five percent. Recently he has been getting hold of Joyceana all over France and England and scattering it all over the world, while I am trying to get it together in one place, catalogue it and then deposit it in the Harvard College Library where it will be available to students for all time. If you ever wanted to part with an appreciable amount of material by and about your brother, books or manuscripts, I would be happy to have them go into the library as a group identified and known as the "Stanislaus Joyce Collection."[11]

By the autumn of 1950, Slocum had learned that Stanislaus Joyce was a prickly character, about whom "I know less the more I correspond with him."[12] Three years later Slocum congratulated himself on realizing that Stanislaus was holding material back. When he and his wife visited Stanislaus in Trieste in 1953 they found him in a curious mood and [he] showed me an enormous batch of manuscripts material, mostly odds and ends which he will be willing to part with only after he has incorporated anything he needs in his books. I read a number of chapters of his book and it is a very curious document, combining fascinating biographical material with absolute nonsense. . . . He was charming and his wife and son most agreeable. Eileen and I spent the better part of a day with them and I am truly sorry for him, as he is still living in the shadow of the shadow of [sic] his brother. I suppose eventually we will be able to get all the rest of the material from him, but I have the feeling we have skimmed the cream off his library, unless he should find in a moment of economical need some extremely interesting manuscripts among his papers.[13]

Slocum's intuition was sharper than he knew. Stanislaus had indeed some extremely interesting papers left in his collection. He was sitting on a treasure trove of his brother's personal papers, dating from Joyce's school days, whose existence he had concealed from Herbert Gorman, Stuart Gilbert, and the Joyce trustees. There were about a thousand documents in all, including three hundred from Joyce himself, twenty-two from Nora, and a great number from members of the Joyce family. No one, except possibly Nora in Zurich, knew of Stanislaus's cache, certainly not Stuart Gilbert, who had approached Stanislaus for contributions to his volume of letters, only to be told that all the letters of any relevance had been given to Herbert Gorman, Joyce's first biographer, years before.[14]

Stanislaus wanted to keep his material to himself until he had finished his book about his brother. However, he was getting old, and his book, as Slocum saw, was proving difficult to write.

In 1953 Stanislaus met the man who was to solve his problems: Richard Ellmann. A tall, bespectacled specialist in Anglo-Irish literature, Ellmann was then thirty-five years old and a professor at Northwestern University. He had lived with his family in Dublin for a few years after the war and written excellent studies of Yeats. Now he was embarked upon a biography of James Joyce. As part of his research, he made his way to Trieste, and to this scholarly American Stanislaus revealed at last his secret store.

For Ellmann, it was like being led to the heart of Tutankhamen's tomb without having to dig. Stanislaus possessed an almost day-to-day account of Joyce's early life and innermost thoughts; even the letters Joyce wrote home to his mother from Paris as a starving twenty-one year old were in the collection, as was a chronicle of how Nora and Joyce fell in love in 1904. Stanislaus also had his own invaluable diaries, the first covering the years before he left Dublin for Trieste in 1905, and the second covering the turbulent years in Trieste until the brothers were separated by the First World War. With this rich material, quite apart from his own outstanding abilities as writer and critic, Ellmann was assured that his biography of Joyce would be extraordinary. It would totally eclipse Gorman's, published in 1939, and reveal it for what it was: an uninformative, obsequious, and lifeless sketch of the man who had authorized it.

For Stanislaus, nearing seventy, the opportunity was irresistible. Into the hands of a brilliant and sensitive scholar he could place his own version of the life of his brother, with particular emphasis on his own part in it. Through Ellmann he could give voice to his claim to have saved Nora and the children from starving and James Joyce for world literature. He could even reveal at last how he had saved his brother's marriage in 1909 (by defending Nora against Cosgrave's accusations).[15]

Stanislaus could glimpse also the way in which Ellmann could act as midwife to his own manuscript. In Trieste, living so far from the English literary scene, Stanislaus had been struggling against great difficulties to make his mark as a writer. Frustration dogged his endeavors, and old humiliations. For example, at the invitation of the BBC in 1948 he proudly recorded a talk on his brother, only to find that its transmission had been delayed because his sister Eileen had, from Dublin, approached the BBC to ask if she could record a talk as well. The BBC decided that the two interviews would make a pair and held up Stanislaus's. He was furious. Eileen, he stormed, was scarcely capable of writing a letter, let alone giving a talk for the BBC's most intellectual program![16] What is more, by her pushiness she had cost him money, he said. His talk would have been reprinted in *The Listener,* he said, thereby doubling the fee — three guineas — he was to receive for recording the talk at the studios of Radio Trieste.[17]

Underlying all was Stanislaus's bitterness. He saw himself (with some justice) as one of the worst-treated brothers in the history of genius. That he had sacrificed his own happiness only to be treated "with careless indifference"[18] was a recurring theme of his own book. His brother, Stanislaus was preparing to tell the world, was outrageously indifferent to needs other than his own. What Jim needed, Jim took. "He used to read my diary without permission," said Stanislaus, recalling his boyhood, "and be rather jocular about it." Because of the family's steep decline in the 1890s, Stanislaus's education had been inferior to his brilliant brother's, although he clearly had considerable intellectual ability. No Clongowes Wood College for him, which he described in later years matter-of-factly as "the best education the country had to offer a boy of his class and religion."[19] No University College, Dublin, either. Only Belvedere, the Jesuit day school to which Jim and Charlie had also been sent, and after that training as an accountant.

In his writing too Joyce had heaped humiliation on Stanislaus. He broke his promise to dedicate *Dubliners* to Stanislaus. Then, when turning *Stephen Hero* into *A Portrait,* Joyce removed the character of Maurice, the artist's sensitive brother, the better to display the artist standing "friendless and alone." Worse than the omissions were some of the lines Joyce put into his work: "A brother is as easily forgotten as an umbrella";[20] "My goldfashioned bother."[21] A story in *Dubliners*, "An Encounter," is based on an incident in their childhood when Joyce and Stanislaus had played truant together. In it the boy-narrator says about his companion, "In my heart I had always despised him a little." In the *Wake* Joyce created the twin brothers, Shem and Shaun: Shem (James) is "the Penman," the creative artist; Shaun (Stan) is "the Postman," the drudge, who prefers food to drink. These were all barbs meant to hurt, and they did.

These frustrations and slights (and especially the suffering of the Trieste years together) led Stanislaus to determine — well before he met Ellmann — to get what he could for himself and his family out of his memories and his brother's papers.[22]

The mountain of letters survived because both brothers were hoarders. Stanislaus had begun his Joyce collection as soon as he realized that his older brother was no ordinary mortal. It was he who, moving to Trieste in 1905, took with him the archive on Joyce's early life, as well as the letters Jim had sent home to Dublin from Pola and Trieste. He had even rescued from Aunt Josephine in Dublin, for example, the letters Joyce had written in 1905 about his disenchantment with Nora.[23] In Trieste Stanislaus added to his store all the letters that poured in from the family in Dublin and then from Rome. Later, when in his Austrian prison camp, he added the letters from Joyce and Nora in Zurich.

Joyce was a squirrel too. He threw nothing away — letters from all the sisters, from Charlie, from his father and Aunt Jo, from all the publishers and lawyers. Nora was not like that at all, no archivist in anticipation of future fame. Her correspondents were mainly women. She threw their letters away after reading, and they threw away hers (until the Paris years when Helen Nutting, Lillian Wallace, and Helen Joyce thought Nora's worth saving). None of Nora's letters to her mother has survived, for example. The fact that a few of the semiliterate ones her mother sent to her in Zurich found their way into Stanislaus's hoard suggests that Joyce snatched them for literary purposes and carried them from Zurich when the family returned to Trieste in 1919.

Nora's indifference to such matters makes it all the more extraordinary that she preserved the highly embarrassing correspondence of 1909. When Joyce instructed her, "Keep my letters to yourself, dear. They are written for you," she took both parts of the message: she was not only to keep the letters secret but to keep them.

One way or another, the obscene letters found their way into the collection of papers that traveled around Trieste as the Joyces changed ménage and that survived two world wars.

In 1920, when Joyce and Nora left Trieste for Paris, intending to return, they left all their papers behind at Eileen and Frank Schaurek's flat. Joyce gave his first sign of apprehension about them two years later. Just after *Ulysses* catapulted him onto the world stage and he began to taste the penalties of fame — he was deeply hurt by Francini's malicious lecture, "Joyce Stripped Naked in the Piazza," given in Trieste in early 1922 — Joyce wrote to Stanislaus that he was coming "to your hospitable city to collect a few odds and ends: pardon, to make a bundle of several things I could not put into my trunk on the occasion of my departure from Trieste." [24] He never did return but may have intended to do so after the war. He did not expect to die in 1941.

As early as 1921 he had taken precautions to have Ettore Schmitz bring certain confidential materials to him in Paris from Trieste. These may have included Nora's end of the pornographic correspondence of 1909, to be used in writing Molly Bloom's soliloquy. The wittily coarse Triestine slang in which Joyce instructed Schmitz as to where to find the documents shows that with what he derided as his "grocer's clerk mind" he remembered exactly where everything was stored in Trieste:

> There is in Trieste in the quarter [flat] of my brother-in-law . . . in the bedroom presently occupied by my brother . . . an oilcloth briefcase fastened with a rubber band having the colour of a nun's belly and with the approximate dimensions of 95 cm. by 70 cm. In this briefcase I have lodged the written symbols of the languid sparks which flashed at times across my soul. [25]

Joyce advised Schmitz to pack the briefcase in a suitcase locked so that nobody could open it — even telling him where to buy the case, adding characteristically that his brother, the professor, would pay. Joyce said at the time that he needed these materials to finish *Ulysses*.

It is possible that Joyce was protecting at least Nora's privacy. Conceivably, from the time he received them in Dublin in late 1909 until he and Nora left Paris in 1939, Nora's obscene letters to him never left his possession. What happened to Nora's letters? They may have been the letters Maria Jolas saw Nora tearing up in 1939. Stories, however, persist that they were among the papers rescued by Paul Léon and consigned to the National Library of Ireland, to be opened in 1991.

Did Joyce consider that Stanislaus must have read every word of the letters that remained behind? When in 1922 Stanislaus wrote scathingly, "Everything dirty seems to have the same irresistable [sic] attraction for you that cow-dung has for flies," he could well have been referring to his brother's personal letters as well as to *Ulysses*. [26]

It is clear that Joyce did not try to keep Stanislaus away from the papers that remained behind in Trieste. Far from it; he kept Stanislaus busy acting as his Triestine curator, rummaging for certificates and letters on literary matters. In 1931, after authorizing Gorman to write his biography, Joyce asked Stanislaus to wade through "that damn dreary correspondence."[27]

Stanislaus obliged and grumbled to Gorman:

> I enclose a small sheaf of letters representing, so far as I can judge, about one tenth of the letters to be copied. The work goes on very slowly. I don't type and have no typewriter myself, but a friend of mine, who has a fair knowledge of English, has kindly helped so far. As he finds my brother's handwriting difficult to read, I dictate and he types. In this way a rather long letter of 6–700 words takes an hour and a half, ten long postcards take three hours. I have given practically all my spare time to this job and to the far less pleasant one of sorting the letters out of a heap in a mouldy old packing-case.[28]

The letters fell into three categories, Stanislaus told Gorman: "matter of Rome, matter of Pola, matter of Trieste." That was not the whole truth. There was a fourth category: matter of Dublin. Among the letters were all of Joyce's early love letters to Nora, starting from "I may be blind. I looked for a long time at a head of reddish-brown hair . . ." to the despairing letters of 1912, when he wrote from Dublin to her in Galway, "thinking of the book I have written, that child which I have carried for years and years in the womb of the imagination as you carried in your womb the children you love . . ."

In making a selection for Joyce's biographer, however, Stanislaus did not try to flatter his brother. Some of the letters, said Stanislaus, handing them over, showed "my brother's inadaptability to average economic conditions, which was, and I think, still is incorrigible."[29] He included in his package for Gorman some surprisingly personal material — the letters about Schaurek's suicide, for example. He also offered Gorman excerpts from his own Trieste diaries to make his "life" real. Even in 1931, it seems, Stanislaus was looking for an outlet for his version of his brother's life.

Stanislaus also vented his bitterness to Gorman, as he later would to Ellmann. He had gone to Trieste in 1905, he said, because his brother "wished to have someone to talk to," and he had never managed to revisit Ireland. In 1909, Stanislaus told Gorman, he had been preparing for a trip home, taking with him his nephew, Giorgio, but

> at the last moment my brother wanted to go, as I had always inwardly suspected he would. He was met at the station of Westland Row in Dublin by a family group who asked him "Where's Stannie?" It's a question I have often asked myself. Yours very truly
>
> Stanislaus Joyce.[30]

In 1954, nearly half a century after he had left Dublin, Stanislaus crossed back over the English Channel. He made the trip as the leader of a group of Triestine students, but he got only as far as London. He refused an invitation to go to Dublin; he was too hostile to the Irish republic and its attitude toward his brother. While in London he met Harriet Weaver for the first time, and he also saw Richard Ellmann again. Ellmann observed that Stanislaus was tired and did not look well.[31]

Upon returning to Trieste, Stanislaus resumed his English teaching and continued into 1955, but his health deteriorated. In mid-June he was stricken with terrible pains in his chest, and after three days in agony he died. He was seventy-one. The day of his death was June 16, Bloomsday. At his funeral his adolescent son, Jimmy, wept bitterly. The rector of the university gave an address.

Yet the university could do no more to help Stanislaus's widow and child. Stanislaus was not entitled to a pension because he was a foreigner. Nelly Joyce, his wife, was in a desperate financial predicament. As she had acquired British citizenship, she too was a foreigner and found it difficult to get work.[32] With no money at all, there was only one possible source of income: selling the papers of the brother-in-law she hardly knew to the highest bidder among American libraries.

On December 5, 1956, William Mennen, the chairman of the after-shave company in Morristown, New Jersey, received a surprising invitation in his morning post. The library of his beloved alma mater, Cornell University in Ithaca, New York, was looking for donors to help it buy a collection of James Joyce letters — the largest collection of Joyce material in private hands, the richest source of material in the world on the life of Joyce until 1920. The collection also contained manuscripts, Joyce's early school essays, much family correspondence, photographs, and other documents. It was, Mennen was told, being "quietly offered" for sale by the widow of Joyce's brother, and Cornell had taken an option on it. The price of the "basic collection," said the librarian, Stephen A. McCarthy, was thirty thousand dollars. There was also the possibility of an additional group of letters becoming available. If so, it would add another six thousand dollars to the price.[33]

Cornell did not know, or care, that Harvard had spoiled Slocum's dream by declining to have the Joyce papers, for administrative reasons, or that Yale, which had acquired Slocum's papers and labeled them the "John and Eileen Slocum Joyce Collection," had turned down the new offer because of the high price. Cornell was more interested in getting ahead of the nearby University of Buffalo, which had its own impressive Joyce holdings but was also deterred by the price. Cornell's dean of the College of Arts and Sciences was determined to acquire the Joyce material from

Trieste. "This collection," he claimed, "is to the English Department what a cyclotron is to the Physics Department."[34]

Cornell planned the purchase with quasi-military secrecy. The confidentiality of the deal could not be overemphasized ("the availability of the collection is known to only a few people"), nor could the need for haste. The library was "quietly" turning to several of its friends in the hope that they might underwrite even a thousand dollars and if any single donor could do it by himself, "that would be wonderful."

On January 11, 1957, Stephen McCarthy got the letter he had been waiting for. From the office of the president of the Mennen Company, embossed with the Mennen cameo, came the welcome words: "I am your fall guy, as I am inclined to take up your proposition of presenting to the university the Joyce Collection." Mennen briskly said that his payment would be spread over three years, that he was leaving for South America for three months, and that Cornell should "get busy and locate another Santa Claus" for the extra money.[35]

There turned out to be several batches of additional correspondence, the more important of which consisted of James-Nora correspondence. It somehow had been packaged separately. The price of $7000 was set on this "secondary collection" and was met by gifts from Victor Emanuel and C. Waller Barrett. In her negotiations with Cornell, Nelly Joyce had the assistance of two go-betweens. One was Richard Ellmann, who was eager to help Nelly Joyce out of sympathy and out of gratitude for Stanislaus's help with the new biography of Joyce. Ellmann would have preferred that the letters go to Yale, his own alma mater, but knew the provision for Stanislaus's family took higher priority. The other could not have been more appropriate, more skilled. He was the Joyces' old Triestine friend from Zurich, Ottocaro Weiss.

By the 1950s Weiss was living in New York. He was a wealthy and successful businessman, with interests on Wall Street and also in Buffalo, New York, where he was chairman of the board of a large Italian insurance company, Assicurazioni Generali di Trieste e Venezia, operating in Europe and the United States, and also chairman of the board of the Buffalo Insurance Company, which had been bought by Assicurazioni Generali and which operated in Europe and the United States. Since he had been the one who alerted Buffalo to the sale of the La Hune collection in Paris in 1949 and knew of the existence of the far bigger collection in Trieste,[36] it was Weiss more than anybody who was responsible for tugging two of the world's most important collections of Joyce papers into the hinterland of New York State. Was Weiss still bitter about his break with Joyce in 1919? There is no way of knowing. The passage of time affected Joyce's old friends differently. Although many of them had become estranged from Joyce in their youth, most, as Joyce's reputation grew, forgave all in order to bask in the reflected glory.

The fact remains that, whatever his motives and however ignorant he was of the collection's contents, Weiss had nonetheless helped to arrange a sale that revealed to the world Joyce's most intimate sexual fantasies and descriptions of every secret crevice and odor of Joyce's wife's body.

On May 21, 1957, all of the Trieste papers had reached Ithaca, and it did not take long for Cornell to realize it had bought not a cyclotron but a bomb.

Quickly the university, describing the acquisitions, said that portions would be restricted, including some of the personal correspondence, because of references to people still living. Only the major part was to be catalogued and made available to scholars.[37]

However, events turned out differently. The whole collection was catalogued. A young graduate student in search of a dissertation topic, Robert Scholes, drew the assignment. The letters were already in rough chronological order. Scholes sat in the manuscript room, then two floors below ground, mastered all the handwritings — Aunt Josephine's and Mrs. Barnacle's were nearly illegible — and arranged all the other material in beautifully clear order, numbering from 1 to 1,450. To identify individual letters, he followed the simple formula of taking the salutation and opening phrase of a first line. The letter of December 9, 1909, began, "My sweet naughty little fuckbird"; Scholes used the exact quotation. The Scholes catalogue was published in 1961, with an introduction that referred to "an intimate and revealing correspondence between James Joyce and his wife Nora."

Word was not long getting abroad among Joyce scholars that Joyce had written letters to his wife that made *Ulysses* look bland. Those who had made the journey to Cornell told those who had not.

For the ordinary reader, however, relying only upon Ellmann's biography, there was little hint of the quantity or quality of the controversial correspondence. Ellmann, who had had full access to all the letters before they were sold to Cornell, quoted Joyce's most lyrical images of Nora — "Her soul! Her name! Her eyes! They seem to me like strange beautiful, blue wild-flowers growing in some tangled, rain-drenched hedge" — yet he touched very little on the coarse language in the letters, much less on what they revealed of the sexual practices of Joyce and Nora. "The style is Verlaine's, but the voice is Masoch's," he said, to convey the sense of Joyce's lines about longing "to feel you flog, flog, flog me viciously on my naked quivering flesh!!" He summed up the whole extraordinary correspondence with the brief and monumental understatement that Joyce and Nora "exchanged letters much more open than Bloom's and Martha Clifford's."[38]

That is the only direct extract in a nearly nine-hundred-page-long biography from the obscene letters that reveal so much about Joyce's relationship with Nora, about the rampant anal imagery and sexual guilt of

Ulysses and *Finnegans Wake,* and also about Nora's own character. Readers of the Ellmann biography thus had no way of appreciating the intensity and crudity of the demands Joyce made upon Nora or her willing compliance. Even allowing for the fact that intellectual biographies of the 1950s were not expected to concern themselves with their subjects' sexual lives, this discretion was nevertheless a form of distortion — as misleading to the reader as the omission by Sir Roy Harrod of any mention of John Maynard Keynes's homosexuality from his authorized biography in 1951.[39]

Ellmann was far from happy with such self-censorship. It was imposed on him by the Society of Authors, representing the Joyce trustees, who sought to minimize the notoriety surrounding the letters. They allowed Ellmann to publish an extensive selection from the obscene correspondence in the new edition of Joyce's letters that he was preparing, but permitted only a hint of the letters in the biography.

When his biography appeared in 1959 it was justly acclaimed as one of the best literary biographies of the time, the definitive work on Joyce, and a work of art in itself. Yet it was not unflawed. Even before its publication, J. F. Byrne had warned Ellmann about relying too much on the version of events given him by Stanislaus, "a bitter, frustrated, confused and inaccurate man."[40] "That the book is skewed from the start" by its dependence on Stanislaus made it, according to Hugh Kenner, "by no means 'definitive.' "[41]

It was noticeable that when Ellmann revised his biography for a new edition, which appeared in 1982, in a vastly different moral climate from that which prevailed in 1959, he chose once again to shy away from the dirty letters. Once again he offered his readers a very limited quotation from the salacious heap: "My prick is still hot and stiff and quivering from the last brutal drive it has given you when a faint hymn is heard rising in tender pitiful worship of you from the dim cloisters of my heart."[42]

However, the letters became available to the public in part in 1966 when Ellmann's volumes 2 and 3 of Joyce's letters were published. These incorporated the heart of the Cornell collection, vastly improving upon Stuart Gilbert's book, which became known as volume 1. Ellmann's volume 2 included the dirty letters of 1909, although with many large deletions.

In his introduction to it, Ellmann defended the inclusion of what he had reluctantly censored from his biography of Joyce by saying that literary considerations were overriding: the letters constituted an extraordinary record of Joyce's sexual feeling. "The editor has sought," he wrote, "to publish all the letters in their entirety, for a new generation does not confirm the privacy of a dead author's conjugal life."[43] Then in 1975 in a new book, *Selected Letters of James Joyce,* Ellmann published the 1909 correspondence in full, without a single ellipsis. Every foul word was there.

The Joyce trustees (not including Miss Weaver, who had died in 1961) had finally consented to publication in order to stop the letters' being pirated and quoted (and misquoted) widely. They had been read by many people. A French scholar had copied them in longhand and published them in France.[44] Scholars had discussed them in academic publications (a particularly valuable analysis being done by Mary T. Reynolds of Yale in 1964).[45]

But should they have been published? Few controversies can so readily be seen from both sides. Joyce's old editor from Viking, B. W. Huebsch, argued that since the dirty letters — for whatever reason — had survived, it would have been criminal to destroy them, and since they existed, it would be pointless to keep them from students of Joyce's work. What is more, as Joyce's genius had liberated modern literature by putting into print the taboo and ordinary thoughts of the human imagination, his private letters could not diminish his reputation in any way.[46]

Other have answered that even if he did want the letters to survive, Joyce never could have dreamed that the letters would ever see print. (Ironically, his own words could not be protected by the conventions he had smashed.) Many of the Joyces' close friends, Samuel Beckett and Kay Boyle, for example, were deeply offended.[47] So too was Arthur Power. Publishing the letters was, he said, shortly before his death in 1984, "a rotten thing to do."

Family sensibilities were considered, then overruled. Giorgio Joyce was still alive when *Selected Letters* was planned, but he was too ill and alcoholic to fight the decision of the trustees. Stephen Joyce was incensed but powerless. Miss Weaver, he believed, would never have permitted publication.

It is true that Miss Weaver did suppress letters on Joyce family matters she deemed sensitive. In giving many of Joyce's letters to the British Library, she candidly acknowledged destroying some "with my own hand."

One of these letters was the long one Joyce wrote on February 6, 1932 (after Lucia had thrown a chair at Nora). In his preface to the *Selected Letters* Ellmann says, "One must allow her conviction that three or four among Joyce's hundreds of letters to her, many of personally painful context, were unbearable."

If Miss Weaver found those letters unbearable, Nora's grandson, Stephen Joyce has speculated, how much more so would she have found the obscene letters? On the other hand, Jane Lidderdale, Miss Weaver's goddaughter and biographer, believes that her godmother would have favored publication because she was opposed to censorship and to inviting piracy by suppression. Miss Weaver, her prim appearance notwithstanding, was unshockable, and saw a clear distinction. The letters about Joyce's relationship to his wife were germane to Joyce's work; letters about Lucia's behavior were not.[48] It is a matter of record that she had been in favor of publishing the Marthe Fleischmann letters.

The question remains, why did Joyce not ask Stanislaus to return the pornographic letters? According to Moune Gilbert, Nora's close friend, Joyce did exactly that. "He begged for them!" Madame Gilbert stated vehemently in an interview.[49] Francis Evers, a friend of Beckett, also alleged (on the basis of conversations with Maria Jolas) that "the Joyce couple left [the letters] behind in wartime Trieste and tried later to recover [them], probably with the intention of destroying them," but that "these letters were never returned to him or his wife by those who retrieved them in Trieste."[50]

Perhaps Joyce did write to Stanislaus and ask for the return of his incriminating correspondence. One striking feature of the Trieste collection at Cornell is that there is nothing in it that shows Stanislaus in a bad light. In the long and bitter years in Trieste, when he saw his brother's world fame grow while he himself had to order some of Joyce's works from Sylvia Beach's bookshop, when he was mocked for asking for the return of the loan of £10 in the same letter in which Joyce boasted of Miss Weaver's new gift of £8,500,[51] Stanislaus had ample time to censor the papers to his own advantage. Conspicuous gaps in the collection suggest that he did. There is no sign of the anxious letter Helen said she had written Stannie without Giorgio's knowing. There is no letter containing Joyce's original instruction to Stanislaus to provide letters for the Gorman biography. The fact that no letter survived to reach Cornell showing Joyce asking for the return of his correspondence does not mean that Joyce did not write one.

The controversy has not gone away.

Stephen Joyce has passionately continued to fight against the violation of what is left of the privacy of his grandparents (whom he calls, by the names that he alone is entitled to use, Nonno and Nonna). He believes that no more need be said than Joyce's own advice to Nora to keep the letters to herself.[52] At the Ninth James Joyce International Symposium in Frankfurt in June 1984, looking straight at Richard Ellmann and other Joyce scholars, Stephen declared:

> Intimate very personal private letters, which were never meant for the public eye, have been sold, pirated and published. I condemn and deplore this intolerable shameless invasion of privacy, as would my grandparents, were they standing beside me here today.

In a letter to the *International Herald Tribune,* Stephen elaborated:

> My disapproval is directed at all who contributed to the publication of these letters: the person who sold the letters without ensuring adequate protection,

in fact Stanislaus Joyce's wife Nelly; the French journalist-author who pirated them from the Cornell University Library and the French periodical which first published them; and of course the publisher as well as the editor of the *Selected Letters*, Professor Ellmann.[53]

Stephen has contrasted the treatment of his grandfather's letters with the withholding from publication of Stanislaus's Trieste diary, to which Ellmann had access and which contains explicit passages about Stanislaus's sexual life. It was unfortunate, Stephen has said, that the same delicacy had not been extended to his grandfather's letters to his grandmother.[54]

The full publication of the letters demonstrated that there was no enforceable embargo upon them, whatever may have been promised at the time of the sale to Cornell.

Nelly Joyce, left to bear the responsibility of having released the intimate correspondence to the world, has denied that she had any knowledge of the contents of what was sold. Her husband was many years her senior, spent his evenings closeted with his books, and was interested only, as far as she knew, in "politics, politics, always politics." She nonetheless remained profoundly grateful for the sale of the letters. As an elderly woman, she said simply in an interview, "They were my fortune."[55] The Cornell money enabled her to move to England, to educate her son, and to buy a house.

It remains indisputable that if Joyce had not wanted the letters to survive, he would have destroyed them after returning to Trieste early in 1910. He never made any secret of the fact that the stuff of his literature was his own life and that, like Shem the Penman, he "wrote with the ink of himself over the skin of his body."[56]

Nora certainly would not have wanted her letters published. However, as so much is known of their contents, admirers of Nora have special cause for regret that her side of the notorious correspondence did not reach Cornell. As Peter Costello, an Irish biographer of Joyce, wrote to the *Irish Times*, the destruction — or concealment — of Nora's letters has "meant that a very one-sided view of the Joyce marriage has emerged and that the personality of Nora Joyce has been overshadowed by her husband."[57]

Nora's initiative in writing what Joyce dared not be the first to do showed great courage, erotic imagination, and loyalty for which she has been deprived of recognition by everyone except Joyce. When he wrote "your letter is worse than mine," it was praise indeed.

Stanislaus achieved his dream of being recognized as a man of letters, albeit posthumously. His book on his brother, *My Brother's Keeper*, was published by Faber in 1958, with a preface by T. S. Eliot in which Eliot said,

Possessed as he was by the subject of his memoir, Stanislaus Joyce, under the exasperation of this thorn in his flesh, became himself a writer, and the author of this one book which is worthy to occupy a permanent place on the bookshelf beside the works of his brother.[58]

It is also indisputable that Stanislaus had his reward and his revenge from beyond the grave. The approximately fifty thousand dollars his widow received in total from Cornell from the combined sales was more than Nora had ever received in royalties from Joyce's writings during her widowhood. With the sale of the letters to Cornell, Shaun the Postman had delivered his load.

In March 1951 just before Nora's death, Lucia Joyce was transferred from the Delmas clinic at Ivry to St. Andrew's Hospital in Northampton, England, where she had been a patient in 1935–36. The move to England placed her nearer Harriet Shaw Weaver, who was her legal guardian.

Lucia remained at St. Andrew's until her death in 1982. There she received many visitors, both old friends and Joyce scholars. Her guardian after Miss Weaver's death in 1961 was Miss Weaver's goddaughter, Miss Jane Lidderdale, a warm, vigorous, highly intelligent woman who had been a temporary member of the British civil service. Miss Lidderdale regularly visited Lucia and looked after her interests to the end.

Giorgio Joyce, who made his home in West Germany with his second wife, visited Lucia in 1967 when he was guest of honor, along with Frank Budgen, at the first International James Joyce Symposium, held in Dublin. After that, he suffered from deteriorating health and, after a severe stroke, died in Konstanz, West Germany, in 1976 at the age of seventy-one. He was buried in Zurich at Fluntern beside his parents.

Lucia was buried in Northampton, by her own choice, yet at Fluntern a place still awaits her. The inscription on the family tombstone there stops short, almost like the last page of *Finnegans Wake:* "James Joyce, Nora Joyce, Giorgio Joyce . . ." — with a blank left for one name more. The "whole Celtic crew," as Hemingway saw the Joyce family, which Joyce labored so hard to keep together, rests incomplete.

Giorgio left his estate to his wife. The net value of Lucia's estate, when it was granted probate in January 1985, was estimated at £176,105. Her will named as her heirs her brother (or his widow, as turned out to be the case) and her aunt by marriage, Nelly Joyce. Upon the deaths of these women, the income was to go to her nephew, Stephen Joyce, and Nelly's son, Jimmy Joyce.[59] Nelly Joyce, who with her son had moved to London, had kept in steady touch with Lucia at St. Andrew's.

Thus a large part of the income from the work of James Joyce was diverted permanently to Stanislaus's wife and son, giving Stanislaus further posthumous recompense for his years as his brother's keeper. Thus, too, Stephen Joyce, who had been estranged from his father, was quite justified in saying to the *Irish Times* in 1982 that, contrary to the popular supposition that he was living off his grandfather's books, he had never seen "a red cent of royalties."[60] He had, however, been one of the principal heirs of his mother, Helen Kastor Joyce, who died in 1963.[61]

Stephen is the only direct descendant of James and Nora Joyce. In Paris, where he lives with his wife, Solange, he holds a senior position at the Organization for Economic Cooperation and Development and interests himself increasingly in the management of the Joyce estate. Stephen remains handsome, irascible yet likable, solemn as his father, uxorious as his grandfather, a source of excitement and awe at gatherings in Joyce's name, for he so resembles his grandfather that, he has said, "People have come up to me in the street and told me who I am."[62]

Notes

To avoid repetition, I have kept citations in the notes short. Full citations appear in the bibliography. I have made certain abbreviations to frequently cited books, publications, libraries, and people. University libraries and special collections are denoted by the name of the university unless otherwise abbreviated. Further information on the location of specific collections appears in the acknowledgments. Unverified or speculative information is contained in brackets; uncertain dates indicated by ?. No date is indicated by n.d.

Letters of James Joyce, volumes I, II, and II, are cited as *I, II, III; Selected Letters of James Joyce,* as *SL.* Richard Ellmann's revised edition of *James Joyce* is cited as Ellmann, his first edition as Ellmann-I. Herbert Gorman's *James Joyce* appears as Gorman; Padraic O Laoi's *Nora Barnacle Joyce* as O Laoi; Stanislaus Joyce's *My Brother's Keeper* as *MBK; Dear Miss Weaver,* by Jane Lidderdale and Mary Nicholson, as Lidderdale; Sylvia Beach's *Shakespeare and Company* as Beach; Noel Riley Fitch's *Sylvia Beach and the Lost Generation* as Fitch. The *James Joyce Quarterly* is *JJQ.*

Frequent correspondents are cited in the notes by initials: NB for Nora Barnacle Joyce, GJ for Giorgio Joyce, LJ for Lucia Joyce, HKJ for Helen Kastor Joyce, JJ for James Joyce, SJ for Stanislaus Joyce, MH for Michael Healy, SB for Sylvia Beach, CC for Constantine Curran, MJ for Maria Jolas, JL for Jane Lidderdale, PL for Paul Léon, and BM for Brenda Maddox.

Page references to Joyce's work are those of the editions used in the preparation of this manuscript. These include *Exiles,* Penguin, 1973 and *A Portrait of the Artist as a Young Man,* Penguin, 1960. *Ulysses* references are to the Penguin edition of *The Corrected Text,* which follows the line divisions of the critical and synoptic edition (New York: Garland, 1984). The Random House and Bodley

Head editions of the corrected text also have identical pagination. All editions of *Finnegans Wake* have identical pagination.

No page references have been given for quotations from *Dubliners, Exiles, Chamber Music,* and *Pomes Penyeach.*

University libraries and special collections are denoted by the name of the university. The exceptions are: Texas, for Humanities Research Center at the University of Texas; Berg, for the Berg Collection at the New York Public Library. BL is the British Library; SIU is Southern Illinois University; TCD is Trinity College, Dublin; UCD is University College, Dublin; UCG is University College, Galway; UCL is University College, London; and UCLA is the University of California, Los Angeles. Papers and documents from the Cornell Joyce Collection are cited with their Scholes catalogue number.

1. Exit from Finn's

1. The costume in which Nora left Dublin and arrived in Pola is described by Alessandro Francini-Bruni in "Joyce Intimo Spogliato nella Piazza," translated in Willard Potts, ed., *Portraits of the Artist in Exile* (Seattle: University of Washington Press, 1979). Patricia Hutchins, in *James Joyce's World,* describes the family party at the quay.
2. JJ to NB, September 19, 1904, *II,* 55.
3. O Laoi, *Nora Barnacle Joyce,* and Galway records.
4. JJ, "The Holy Office."
5. JJ to NB, September 19, 1904, *II,* 55.
6. JJ, "Ireland, Land of Saints and Sages," *Critical Writings,* 170.
7. Nora's departure from Galway is described in Ellmann, 159.
8. JJ to NB, September 19, 1904, *II,* 55; JJ to SJ, November 19, 1904, *II,* 71.
9. Arthur Power in his unpublished draft for *Conversations with James Joyce* recounts Nora's remarks on Joyce's appearance as he came into the bar at Finn's Hotel and her doubts about entrusting herself to him.
10. Nora expressed her views on Joyce's profession to Sylvia Beach (*Shakespeare and Company,* 42) and to her sister Kathleen (Ellmann, 554).
11. JJ to NB, September 19, 1904, *II,* 55.
12. JJ to NB, September 16, 1904, *II,* 53.
13. J. F. Byrne to Ellmann, Jan. 23, 1958, Texas. Also, Joyce wrote many letters to Nora, doubting that she had told him the whole truth about her past.
14. JJ, "Eveline," *The Irish Homestead,* September 10, 1904; also in *Dubliners.*

2. The Man-Killer

1. Interview with Phyllis Moss Stein, June 16, 1985.
2. The history of Galway has been taken from *The Galway Year Book and Directory* (Galway: M'Dougall & Brown, 1902), and Eilis Dillon, "The Innocent Muse," 33–37. Also, Robert M. Adams, *Surface and Symbol,* 23, and *Ulysses,* 522.
3. *The Galway Year Book and Directory,* 1902.
4. O Laoi, 10, and Galway records.

5. This and subsequent details of Nora's immediate family are taken from O Laoi, unless otherwise indicated.

6. Maurice Beebe, "Barnacle Goose and Lapwing," 302–20, and Robert Adams Day, "Joyce, Stoom, King Mark," 244.

7. E. G. Quin of the Dublin Institute for Advanced Studies to BM, July 2, 1986. Also, Edward MacLysaght, *A Guide to Irish Surnames.*

8. Many scholars use the terms Irish and Gaelic interchangeably. Synge and most Anglo-Irish writers referred to the native language as Gaelic, but today's usage favors Irish, to distinguish it from the Celtic language of Scotland.

9. Thomas E. Connolly, ed., *James Joyce's "Scribbledehobble,"* 14.

10. Graham Smith, librarian and archivist, HM Customs and Excise, to BM, Oct. 8, 1985; *The Galway Year Book* of 1904 and letter to BM from the Irish Office of the Revenue Commissioners, February 14, 1986.

11. Ellmann, 159, and wedding certificate of Thomas Healy and Bedelia Connor. Galway Cathedral records.

12. JJ, notes to *Exiles,* 155. Nora's lasting resentment is described in Patricia Hutchins, *James Joyce's World,* 65.

13. Dillon, "The Innocent Muse," 38.

14. Nora's school record as shown in the Mercy Convent Register appears in O Laoi. Nora's recollections of her schoolmate Cissy Casey may have surfaced in the character of Cissy Caffrey, the friend of Gerty MacDowell, in *Ulysses.*

15. JJ to SJ, December 3, 1904, *II,* 72, and O Laoi, 5.

16. Ellmann, 554.

17. JJ to SJ, December 3, 1904, *II,* 72.

18. *The Galway Year Book,* 1902, shows that Simmons's business was so flourishing in Galway at the turn of the century that he had to turn his main establishment on Nun's Island into a branch office and move his main studios to Market Street. Eilis Dillon, a native of Galway, said in a letter to BM, February 22, 1986: "The Healys must have been better-off than we thought if they were photographed by Simmons." However, she added, "My family was too nationalist to have gone near them."

19. The original of the photograph is at Cornell.

20. Eilis Dillon to BM, February 22, 1986.

21. *Ulysses,* 26.

22. Harold Nicolson, *Diaries,* 83.

23. Interview with Patrick Henchy, October 1984, and Patrick Henchy to BM, January 8, 1986. Henchy, a native of Galway and former keeper of printed books at the National Library, learned of Nora's early romance with Feeney and of Nora's grief at his death from Nora's sister Kathleen.

24. Death certificate of Michael Feeney, Galway Cathedral records.

25. Death certificate of Catherine Mortimer Healy, Galway Cathedral records.

26. Census of Ireland, 1901.

27. Maria Jolas, interviewed by Eilis Dillon, "The Innocent Muse."

28. Death certificate of Michael Bodkin, Galway Cathedral records.

29. Interview with Rev. Mother Mary Doyle, August 6, 1984.

30. In his letter to SJ, December 3, 1904, *II,* 72, Joyce says that Nora had many

boyfriends when young, "including one who died." His notes for *Exiles,* however, written about 1913 after he had visited Galway, acknowledge more than one dead lover. Joyce appears not to have been comfortable with the name he chose for the boy in "The Dead" — Furey — for he spelled it Fury in the manuscript. See *The James Joyce Archive,* edited by Michael Groden, *"Dubliners" Drafts and Manuscripts* (vol. 4), p. 503.

31. JJ to SJ, December 3, 1904, *II,* 72.
32. Comments on Annie Barnacle's character from interviews with Evelyne Chardonnet, John Slocum, and Peter Heaney.
33. Ellmann, 158.
34. Leon O Broin, *Protestant Nationalists in Revolutionary Ireland.*
35. Ellmann, 158–159.
36. JJ to NB, December 3, 1909, *SL,* 183.
37. O Laoi, 42.
38. JJ to NB, December 9, 1909, *SL,* 186.
39. JJ to NB, September 7, 1909, *SL,* 170.
40. Ellmann, 158–159.
41. Joyce's letter to Nora of September 7, 1909, *II,* 251, asking her to get the cinders out of her hair, is the only jarring note in his descriptions of Nora's appearance. It was, however, written when she had two small children, no help, and no money.
42. Information on Willie Mulvagh comes from O Laoi and letter from his daughter, Eveline Mulvagh Odierna, to BM, January 25, 1985. Another descendant, Jane Mulvagh, who did the fashion research for this book, pronounces the name "Mul-*vah.*"
43. Power, *Conversations,* 70, and O Laoi, 19.
44. *Ulysses,* 624.
45. Stanislaus Joyce, *Recollections of James Joyce.*
46. *Reports of the Commissioners for Ireland,* 1905, vol. 17, p. 571.
47. *Ulysses,* 626.
48. JJ to SJ, December 3, 1904, *II,* 72–73, and Ellmann, 159.
49. Eveline Mulvagh Odierna to BM, January 25, 1985.
50. See note 10.
51. Eileen O'Connor to BM, May 2, 1986.
52. Christopher Murray, Notes to *Bailegangaire,* by Tom Murphy (Druid Lane Theatre production, London, February 1986). Murphy writes of "the sheer indecency" of the poor Mayo home and the persistence of a brutal environment that even today maims the young people in the region long before they can wrench themselves free.

3. The Summer of 1904

1. Jacques Mercanton, "Heures avec James Joyce," in Willard Potts, ed., *Portraits of the Artist in Exile,* 238.
2. *Stephen Hero,* 177.
3. Ellmann and *Stephen Hero* have the best of the many accounts of Joyce's views on Ibsen.
4. Many have tried to convey the color of Joyce's eyes. His passport of May 3,

1926, describes them as gray and that of June 19, 1935, as gray-blue. The passports, issued by the British consul general in Paris, are at Buffalo.

5. Biographical details taken from Joyce's letters and also from Ellmann, Gorman, *MBK*, and Patricia Hutchins, *James Joyce's Dublin*.

6. J. F. Byrne to Richard Ellmann, January 29, 1957, also January 19, 1957, Texas. Ulick O'Connor, in "James Joyce at University College," *Time and Tide*, January 21, 1956, also says that Cosgrave introduced Joyce to Nora.

7. Nora's recollections in Ellmann, 159; Jacques Mercanton, 238; and Arthur Power, unpublished draft for *Conversations with James Joyce*.

8. May Joyce to SJ, February 2, 1906, Cornell, Scholes 718.

9. NB to JJ, September 26, 1904, *II*, 57.

10. John Slocum to Herbert Cahoon, January 16, 1953, Yale.

11. Many of Joyce's letters to Nora in the summer of 1904 refer to her aches and pains, for example, JJ to NB, [about September 1, 1904], *II*, 51.

12. JJ to NB, August 7, 1909, *SL*, 158.

13. JJ to NB, June 15, 1904, *II*, 42.

14. Ellmann, 156. Sidney Feshbach, in "June 16, 1904: Joyce's Date with Nora?" *JJQ* 21:4 (Summer 1984), finds the evidence flimsy.

15. Herbert Gorman papers, SIU.

16. Herbert Gorman, *James Joyce*, 118.

17. JJ to NB, December 3, 1909, *SL*, 182–83. Ellmann's *Consciousness of Joyce*, 23, accepts that Joyce and Nora "touched each other's bodies" on the first evening at Ringsend. O Laoi, 47, also accepts this interpretation.

18. JJ, "Mr Mason's Novels," in *Critical Writings*, 130–31.

19. JJ to NB, December 3, 1909, *SL*, 183.

20. Flann O'Brien, in *At Swim-Two-Birds* (London: Penguin, 1967; first published in 1939 and written in the 1930s), refers to "Nassau Street, a district frequented by the prostitute class" (p. 47).

21. Interview with Joe O'Halleran, August 1984.

22. *Ulysses*, 41.

23. Revealed in corrected text of *Ulysses*. See Edwin McDowell, "New Edition Fixes 5,000 Errors in *Ulysses*," *New York Times*, June 7, 1984.

24. NB to JJ, June 23, 1904, *II*, 42–43.

25. JJ to NB, August 29, 1904, *II*, 49.

26. *MBK*, 247.

27. JJ to NB, August 29, 1904, *II*, 49.

28. JJ to NB, [about September 1, 1904], *II*, 51.

29. JJ to NB, [July 12, 1904], *II*, 43–44.

30. Thom's Directory, 1904 (Dublin: Alex Thom & Co., 1905).

31. JJ to NB, [about September 1, 1904], *II*, 50.

32. JJ to NB, [July 12, 1904?], *II*, 43.

33. JJ to NB, [late July 1904?], *II*, 44.

34. JJ to NB, August 15, 1904, *II*, 47.

35. Eileen Vance, a childhood friend, quoted in Ellmann, 27.

36. J. B. Lyons, *James Joyce and Medicine*, 60.

37. JJ to NB, August 31, 1909, *SL*, 165, and *Stephen Hero*, 103.

38. *A Portrait*, 241.

39. *MBK*, 231.

40. Annie Barnacle to NB, [1916–19], Cornell, Scholes 412.
41. *MBK*, 74.
42. JJ to NB, August 29, 1904, *II*, 49.
43. Ellmann, 135.
44. Hutchins, *Joyce's Dublin*, 36.
45. Ulick O'Connor, *Oliver St. John Gogarty*, 12.
46. Oliver St. John Gogarty, *Tumbling in the Hay*, 70.
47. Oliver St. John Gogarty, *It Isn't This Time of Year at All*, 73.
48. JJ to NB, August 21, 1909, *II*, 161.
49. Hutchins, *Joyce's Dublin*, 72.
50. SJ, "James Joyce: A Memoir."
51. George Healey, ed., *The Complete Dublin Diary of Stanislaus Joyce*, 14–15.
52. *MBK*, 85.
53. JJ to NB, September 2, 1909, *II*, 243.
54. Ellmann, 529.
55. JJ to SJ, [October 9, 1904], *II*, 173. See also Bonnie Kime Scott, *Joyce and Feminism*, chap. 7, and Padraic Colum and Mary Colum, *Our Friend James Joyce*, 12–13.
56. NB to JJ, August 16, 1904, *II*, 47.
57. J. F. Byrne to Richard Ellmann, January 29, 1957, Texas.
58. Ellmann, 168.
59. NB to JJ, September 16, 1904, *II*, 54.
60. Phillip F. Herring, "The Bedsteadfastness of Molly Bloom," 51.
61. Gogarty, *Tumbling*, 70.
62. Gogarty, *It Isn't This Time of Year*, 70.
63. Various reports reveal that Joyce sang a number of songs that night. Constantine Curran (see BBC's "Portrait of James Joyce") says the songs included "Whom the Lord Chasteneth" and Sullivan's "Come Ye Children."
64. JJ to NB, [about September 1, 1904], *II*, 51.
65. JJ to NB, August 29, 1904, *II*, 48–50.
66. *MBK*, 62.
67. Healey, *The Complete Dublin Diary*, 50–68.
68. Scheper-Hughes, *Saints, Scholars and Schizophrenics*, 176.
69. Colm O Lochlainn, ed., *Irish Street Ballads*, 10809, gives the words as: "So it's true that the women are worse than the men/For they went down to Hell and were threw out again."
70. Gogarty, *It Isn't This Time of Year*. J. B. Lyons, in *Thrust Syphilis Down to Hell*, argues that Joyce's courtship may have delayed the move to the tower.
71. O Laoi, 54.
72. JJ to NB, September 12, 1904, *II*, 52.
73. Gorman, 125.
74. NB to JJ, September 12, 1904, *II*, 52.
75. JJ to NB, September 19, 1904, *II*, 55. See also the preface to *Ulysses: The Corrected Text*, in which Ellmann discusses how Aquinas distinguishes *"amor vero aliquid alicui bonum vult"* ("love which wishes another's good") from *"ea quae concupiscimus"* ("sexual desire concerned only with self-satisfaction").
76. *Chamber Music*, XXI.

77. "The Holy Office," *Pomes Penyeach*.
78. JJ to NB, September 16, 1904, *II*, 53.
79. J. F. Byrne, *Silent Years*, 148.
80. Interview with Arthur Wall, grandson of Mrs. Josephine Murray, August 1986.
81. JJ to NB, [September 26, 1904], *II*, 56.
82. NB to JJ, September 26, 1904, *II*, 57.
83. Kathleen Behan, *Mother of All the Behans*, 50.
84. *Emigration Statistics (Ireland) for the Year 1904*, vol. 98, pp. 81–92. BL.
85. Among the references to the difficulty of the Joyces' name are Maria Zöbeli-Gerhardt, "Lucia: Die Tochter von Dichters," *Zürcher Tages-Anzeiger*, December 24, 1982; Bruno Chersicla's "È Tornato Joyce: Iconografia Triestina per Zois," in *Il Ritorno di Joyce*, 19; and many telegrams.

4. Signora Joyce

All quotations unless otherwise indicated have been taken from *Letters of James Joyce*, vol. II.

1. JJ to SJ, October 11, 1904, *II*, 66.
2. JJ to NB, August 7, 1909, *SL*, 158. Richard Ellmann to BM, January 1, 1986, held that Joyce's discovery of bloodstains was proof of Nora's virginity. See *Finnegans Wake*, 213.
3. *Ulysses*, 633.
4. JJ to NB, September 7, 1909, *II*, 251.
5. J. F. Byrne to Richard Ellmann, January 29, 1957, Texas.
6. JJ to SJ, December 3, 1904, *II*, 73.
7. Ibid., and LJ, "The Real Life of James Joyce by His Daughter," Texas.
8. JJ to Josephine Murray, December 31, 1904, *I*, 57.
9. Alessandro Francini-Bruni, "Joyce Stripped Naked in the Piazza." In Potts, 11.
10. JJ to SJ, December 3, 1904, *II*, 72.
11. George Healey, ed., *The Complete Dublin Diary*, 36.
12. JJ to SJ, November 19, 1904, *II*, 71, and February 7, 1905, *II*, 81.
13. Robert Scholes,"Further Observations on the Text of *Dubliners*," 111–13. Also, Donald Torchiana, *Backgrounds to "Dubliners*," 71, suggests that the words *Derevaun Seraun* are west of Ireland dialect for "Worms are the only end." William Tindall, in *A Reader's Guide to James Joyce*, p. 22, quotes Patrick Henchy as suggesting that the phrase is corrupt Irish for "The end of pleasure is pain."
14. JJ to NB, [December ? 1904], *II*, 74.
15. Clotilde Francini-Bruni to NB, [n.d.], Cornell, Scholes 513.
16. JJ to NB, [September] 2, 1909, *SL*, 167, refers to Nora's use of a "word of provocation." His letter of December 5, 1909, *SL*, 182, is more explicit. Joyce's poem, "A Prayer," *Pomes Penyeach*, also suggests that another of Nora's words of provocation was "Come!"
17. Ulick O'Connor, *Gogarty*, 89.
18. JJ to SJ, February 7, 1905, *II*, 79–80.
19. Charles Joyce to SJ, April 12, 1906, Cornell, Scholes 615.

20. JJ to SJ, March 15, 1905, *II*, 85.
21. JJ to SJ, [May 2 or 3, 1905?], *II*, 89.
22. Francini-Bruni, "Joyce Stripped Naked," 20.
23. Lina Galli, "James Joyce in Trieste."
24. JJ to SJ, July 12, 1905, *II*, 92.
25. Ibid., 94.
26. JJ to SJ, April 4, 1905, *II*, 87.
27. JJ to SJ, July 12, 1905, *II*, 96.
28. Ibid., 96.
29. Vincent Cosgrave to JJ, [about October 29, 1905], *II*, 125–28.
30. Nora's laundry list appears on the reverse side of page 1 of the manuscript of "A Painful Case," which is at Yale. Also in *James Joyce Archive*, Michael Groden, ed., *"Dubliners" Drafts and Manuscripts* (vol. 4), p. 96. See *Finnegans Wake*, 213, 277.
31. Stelio Crise to BM, April 14, 1987. Also, interview with Zora Skerk Koren, friend of Anny Schleimer, Trieste, March 12, 1987.
32. JJ to Josephine Murray, December 4, 1905, *II*, 128.
33. "A Little Cloud," the eighth story of *Dubliners*, was written in March 1906, when Giorgio was eight months old.
34. Birth certificates, Giorgio and Lucia Joyce, and related correspondence, Cornell, Scholes 1377 and 1378.
35. Charles Joyce to SJ, November 4, 1905, Cornell, Scholes 611.
36. Ibid.
37. Josephine Murray to SJ, January 22, 1906, Cornell, Scholes 913.
38. Ibid.
39. NB to [?; n.d.], Cornell, Scholes 742.
40. Ellmann, 268.
41. Josephine Murray to JJ, July 24, 1906, Cornell, Scholes 917.
42. Ibid.
43. Josephine Murray to NB, January [8?], 1906, Cornell, Scholes 912.
44. Francini-Bruni, "Joyce Stripped Naked," 11.
45. JJ to SJ, February 6, 1907, *II*, 205.
46. Margaret Joyce to SJ, September 26, 1906, Cornell, Scholes 707.
47. May Joyce to SJ, February 25, 1906, Cornell, Scholes 718.
48. JJ to Grant Richards, October 15, 1905, *II*, 122.
49. Josephine Murray to SJ, June 6, 1906, *II*, 138–39.
50. Ellmann, 312–13.
51. Charles Joyce to SJ, May 24, 1906, Cornell, Scholes 616.
52. Ibid.
53. Ibid.

5. Madonna and Child

Biographical information and quotations unless otherwise indicated come from *Letters of James Joyce II* or Joyce family letters at Cornell.

1. Carla de Petris, "Exiles or Emigrants," in Giorgio Melchiori, *Joyce in Rome*, 75.

2. Lorenzo Quaglietti to BM, May 13, 1985, and Pierre Leprohon, *Italian Cinema*, 12.
3. Notes to *Exiles*, 152.
4. NB to SJ, October 2, 1906, Cornell, Scholes 743.
5. NB to SJ, postscript to JJ's letter of October 4, 1906, *II*, 173.
6. JJ to SJ, [about August 12, 1906], *II*, 49.
7. JJ to SJ, [October 9, 1906], *II*, 172.
8. JJ to SJ, November 6, 1906, *II*, 185.
9. NB to SJ, November 14, 1906, *II*, 197.
10. JJ to SJ, December 24, 1906, *II*, 204.
11. John Joyce to SJ, February 5, 1907, Cornell, Scholes 667.
12. JJ to SJ, January 10, 1907, *II*, 205.
13. NB to SJ, January 10, 1907, Cornell, Scholes 744.
14. *Exiles*, act 3.
15. JJ to HSW, January 17, 1932, *I*, 312.
16. Richard Ellmann, *The Consciousness of Joyce*, 57.
17. JJ to SJ, January 10, 1907, *II*, 206.
18. Ibid.
19. *Exiles*, act 3.
20. *Exiles*, act 2.
21. JJ to SJ, November 20, 1906, *II*, 196.
22. JJ to SJ, November 13, 1906, *II*, 191–92.
23. Josephine Murray to JJ, June 4, 1907, Cornell, Scholes 921.
24. Josephine Murray to JJ, July 29, 1907, Cornell, Scholes 922.
25. Interview with Patricia Barnacle Hutton, London, December 20, 1983.
26. *Ulysses*, 273, and JJ to HSW, March 18, 1930, BL.
27. Margaret ("Poppie") Joyce to JJ, October 10, 1907, Cornell, Scholes 710.
28. Leon Edel, *Stuff of Sleep and Dreams*, 94.
29. Interview with Edda Ritson, July 1987, who heard the story in Palo Alto, California, from Mrs. Ada Ohrstiel, a native of Trieste.
30. Vitaliano Brancati, "Riccordo di Professor Joyce," *Nuova Stampa Sera*, August 30–31, 1948.
31. Ellmann, 268.
32. May Joyce to SJ, February 24, 1908, and September 7 [1907?], Cornell, Scholes 720 and 722.
33. John Joyce to JJ, December 14, 1908, Cornell, Scholes 672.
34. Josephine Murray to SJ, July 21, 1908, Cornell, Scholes 924.
35. Charles Joyce to JJ, July 24, 1908, Cornell, Scholes 626.
36. John Joyce to SJ, August 11, 1908, Cornell, Scholes 671.
37. Josephine Murray to NB, [c. early 1909], Cornell, Scholes 925.
38. The photograph, in the Croessmann Collection at Southern Illinois University, is wrongly described in Chester Anderson's *James Joyce and His World* as having been taken in Galway in 1912. In 1912 Giorgio was seven years old, and the little boy in the photograph is only about three.
39. Stanislaus's diary has never been published, apparently because of its references to his sexual life.
40. May Joyce to JJ, June 3, 1909, Cornell, Scholes 724.
41. SJ to Herbert Gorman, August 8, 1931, SIU.

6. Away Alone

Quotations unless otherwise indicated come from *Letters II*.

1. JJ to SJ, August 4, 1909, *II*, 230–31.
2. JJ to NB, August 6, 1909, *II*, 231–32.
3. JJ to NB, August 7, 1909, *SL*, 158.
4. Ibid., 159.
5. J. F. Byrne, *Silent Years*, 156.
6. Ellmann, 281–82.
7. Oliver St. John Gogarty to JJ, August 4, 1909, *II*, 231.
8. Oliver St. John Gogarty to JJ, August 2, 1909; Ulick O'Connor, *Oliver St. John Gogarty*, 91.
9. JJ, "Fenianism," *Critical Writings*, 190.
10. See chap. 3.
11. JJ to SJ, September 2, 1909, *II*, 244.
12. J. F. Byrne to Ellmann, January 29, 1957, Texas.
13. Leon Edel, *Sleep and Dreams*, 87–95.
14. Robert Adams Day, "Joyce, Stoom, King Mark," 228.
15. *Ulysses*, 31.
16. JJ to NB, August 9, 1909, *II*, 235.
17. JJ to NB, August 21, 1909, *II*, 237.
18. JJ to NB, August 21, 1909, *II*, 237, and JJ to SJ, August 21, 1909, *II*, 238.
19. JJ to NB, August 22, 1905, *II*, 239.
20. Ibid.
21. The contents of Nora's letter can be judged by Joyce's letter of August 31, 1909, in which he acknowledges that she has demonstrated that she has understood his craving for coarse words in writing, although he dislikes them spoken aloud; that of September 2, 1909, *II*, 241–43, in which he allows himself for the first time explicit sexual references; and that of December 3, 1909, *SL*, 182, in which he acknowledges that she led the way in the obscene correspondence.
22. JJ to SJ, August 28, 1909, *II*, 241.
23. JJ to NB, August 31, 1909, *II*, 242.
24. JJ to NB, September 2, 1909, *II*, 242–43.
25. Ibid.
26. JJ to NB, September 5, 1909, *II*, 248.
27. JJ to NB, September 7, 1909, *II*, 249.
28. Ibid., 252.
29. Ellmann, 300.
30. JJ to NB, [October 25, 1909?], *II*, 254.
31. JJ to NB, October 27, 1909, *II*, 254–55.
32. JJ to NB, [October 25, 1909?], *II*, 254.
33. NB to JJ, November 2, 1909, *II*, 259.
34. JJ to NB, November 19, 1909, *II*, 266.
35. JJ to NB, October 27, 1909, *II*, 255.
36. JJ to NB, November 1, 1909, *II*, 259.
37. JJ to NB, October 27, 1909, *II*, 255.
38. JJ to NB, December 3, 1909, *SL*, 182.

39. JJ to NB, December 2, 1909, *SL*, 181.
40. JJ to NB, December 3, 1909, *SL*, 182.
41. Ibid., 183.
42. JJ to NB, December 6, 1909, *SL*, 183–84.
43. JJ to NB, December 8, 1909, *SL*, 184.
44. JJ to NB, December 20, 1909, *SL*, 191–92.
45. JJ to NB, December 16, 1909, *SL*, 190.
46. JJ to NB, December 16, 1909, *SL*, 190–91.
47. *Ulysses*, 633.
48. *Ulysses*, 642.
49. Peter Gay, *Education of the Senses*, 122–24.

7. A House of Joyces

1. Ellmann, 309.
2. Arthur Power, *Conversations*, 70–71.
3. Interview with Bozena Schaurek Delimata, January 20, 1984.
4. JJ to NB, September 7, 1909, *II*, 251.
5. Brenda Maddox, "Could Nora Cook?" *New York Times Book Review*, June 16, 1985.
6. Ellmann, 311–12.
7. See chap. 5, note 39.
8. Josephine Murray to SJ, August 19, 1912, Cornell, Scholes 929.
9. John Joyce to JJ, August 23, 1910, Cornell, Scholes 676.
10. Lina Galli, "Livia Veneziani Schmitz and James Joyce"; E. L. Hughes, "The Mystery Lady of 'Giacomo Joyce' "; interview with Letizia Svevo Fonda Savio, March 1987.
11. JJ to SJ, March 29, 1932, *III*, 241.
12. Thomas Staley, "James Joyce in Trieste," 447.
13. Ibid., and LJ, "Autobiography," Texas, which discusses Lucia's childhood illnesses.
14. Mary Colum and Padraic Colum, *Our Friend James Joyce*, 227.
15. LJ to JL, March 19, 1974, UCL.
16. JJ to Maria Kirn, August 30, 1911, *II*, 293.
17. NB to JJ, [n.d.], Cornell, Scholes 752. Though the letter is undated, it is clear that it was written early in their lives as parents, for Nora refers to the children by the English rather than the Italian versions of their names.
18. Thomas Staley, "James Joyce in Trieste," 449.
19. JJ, "Lecture on William Blake," *Critical Writings*, 217–18.
20. JJ to NB, [Aug. 21, 1912], *II*, 309.
21. Interview with Stelio Crise, March 10, 1987, and photograph of Prezioso inscribed "affettuosamente" [lovingly] to Mayer. Ellmann's suggestion of homosexual overtones in the Joyce-Prezioso relationship appears in the first edition of his biography but was deleted in the revised edition after complaints from Prezioso's family.
22. Roberto Prezioso to JJ and family, August 26, 1913, September 13, and n.d. Cornell, Scholes 1081, 1082, and 1084.
23. Ellmann, 316.

24. Ellmann, 316, 773, n.75.
25. Ellmann, 437.
26. *Giacomo Joyce*, 11.
27. Ibid., 15, 16.
28. Dario De Tuoni, *Ricordi.*
29. Florence Joyce to Eileen Joyce, February 20, 1912, Cornell, Scholes 731.
30. Eva Joyce to SJ, May 12, 1912, Cornell, Scholes 653.
31. May Joyce to SJ, July 25, 1911, Cornell, Scholes 727.
32. Giorgio Joyce, report card from Civica Scuola Popolare e Cittadini, Trieste, July 15, 1912, Cornell, Scholes 1379.
33. James Stephens, "The James Joyce I Knew," *The Listener* 36 (October 24, 1946):565.
34. De Tuoni, *Ricordi.*
35. NB to JJ, July 11, 1912, *II,* 296.
36. Ibid., 297.
37. JJ's postal deposit book for Trieste, 1907–12, Texas.
38. Interview with Letizia Svevo Fonda Savio, March 11, 1987.
39. JJ to NB, [July 12, 1912?], *II,* 297.
40. NB to Eileen Joyce, August 14, 1912, *II,* 302.
41. Ibid.
42. Nathan Halper, "The Grave of Michael Bodkin," *JJQ* 12:3, 273–80.
43. JJ, "The City of the Tribes," *Critical Writings,* 229ff. Ellmann, 325, and O Laoi, 88, make it clear that Nora was the unnamed companion to whom Joyce refers in his article on the Aran journey.
44. Ibid.
45. Louis Berrone, *James Joyce in Padua,* xxii.
46. NB to JJ, August 17, 1912, *II,* 303.
47. JJ to NB, [August 21, 1912], *II,* 308.
48. Ibid., 309.
49. JJ to NB, [August 22, 1912?], *II,* 310, and August 21, 1912, *II,* 309.
50. JJ to SJ, [August 21, 1912], *II,* 307.
51. Josephine Murray to SJ, August 19, 1912, Cornell, Scholes 929.
52. NB to Eileen Joyce, August 14, 1912, *II,* 303.
53. Ellmann, 335.
54. Interview with Arthur Wall, August 1985.
55. Charles Joyce to SJ, September 24, 1912, Cornell, Scholes 634.
56. Charles Joyce to SJ, September 11, 1912, *II,* 319.
57. Italo Svevo, *James Joyce,* 5.
58. De Tuoni, *Ricordi.*
59. Ellmann, 316.
60. Alessandro Francini-Bruni, "Joyce Stripped Naked," 45.
61. Ezra Pound to JJ, January 17–19, 1914, *II,* 327.
62. Interview with Letizia Svevo Fonda Savio, March 11, 1987.
63. May Joyce to SJ, October 19, 1912, Cornell, Scholes 734.
64. Shipping bill at Texas.
65. *Exiles,* act 1.
66. *Exiles,* act 2.
67. *Exiles,* act 3.

68. Robert Adams, "Light on Joyce's *Exiles,*" 83–105.
69. Ellmann, 434.
70. Padraic Colum, introduction to *Exiles* (Penguin), 10.
71. English Stage Society report, July 11, 1916, Yale.
72. May Joyce to SJ, September 1, 1911, Cornell, Scholes 729.
73. John Joyce to JJ, May 5, 1914, Cornell, Scholes 685.
74. Bozena Schaurek Delimata to BM, April 4, 1986.
75. Delimata, "Reminiscences of a Joyce Niece," 45.

8. Second Exile

1. Ellmann, 390.
2. JJ to HSW, October 28, 1919, BL.
3. MH to JJ, June 29, 1915, Cornell, Scholes 570.
4. Zurich City Records, 1915.
5. Lidderdale, 222, and class record, Mühlebach School, 1915–16.
6. Maria Zöbli-Gerhardt, "Lucia: Die Tochter von Dichters," *Zürcher Tages-Anzeiger,* December 24, 1982, and Walter Ackermann, *Bordbuch.*
7. Frank Budgen, *Making of "Ulysses,"* 36.
8. Dr. Senta Frauchiger to BM, March 2, 1985, and Zöbli-Gerhardt, "Lucia."
9. MH to JJ, October 24, 1915, Cornell, Scholes 576.
10. O Laoi, 112.
11. JJ to MH, November 2, 1915, *I,* 84.
12. Ibid., 85.
13. Otto Luening, *Odyssey of an American Composer,* 187.
14. Annie Barnacle to NB, [1915?], Cornell, Scholes 412. Scholes suggests the letter was written c. 1916–19, but its contents discuss Nora's brother's enlistment in the British Army early in the First World War.
15. Annie Barnacle to NB, n.d., Cornell, Scholes 411.
16. SJ to JJ, September 16, 1915, Cornell, Scholes 777.
17. SJ to NB, February 18, 1915, Cornell, Scholes 772.
18. SJ to NB, November 15, 1915, Cornell, Scholes 782.
19. SJ to NB, January 11, 1916, Cornell, Scholes 785.
20. SJ to JJ, January 16, 1916, Cornell, Scholes 786.
21. Clotilde Francini-Bruni to NB, n.d., Cornell, Scholes 513.
22. Ellmann, 437.
23. Ibid.
24. Eileen Joyce Schaurek to NB, September 26, 1916, Cornell, Scholes 1219.
25. Eileen Joyce Schaurek to NB, June 13, 1916, Cornell, Scholes 1217.
26. Eileen Joyce Schaurek to NB and JJ, August 5, 1916, Cornell, Scholes 1218. Eileen Joyce Schaurek to NB, September 26, 1916, Cornell, Scholes 1219.
27. John Joyce to JJ, September 11, 1916, Cornell, Scholes 656.
28. J. B. Lyons, *James Joyce and Medicine,* 206.
29. Felix Beran to Herbert Gorman, February 12, 1931, SIU.
30. Luening, *Odyssey,* 196.
31. Ellmann, 412.
32. August Suter, "Reminiscences," 194, and Ellmann, 382 and 460.
33. Ellmann, 438.

34. Ellmann, 393.
35. Weiss's photograph appears in Ellmann, plate 25.
36. Lidderdale, 38.
37. JJ to HSW, December 6, 1915, *I*, 88.
38. Ellmann, 408.
39. Ibid.
40. Lidderdale, 165.
41. Gorman, 232.
42. MH to JJ, March 8, 1916, Cornell, Scholes 579.
43. William Blackmore to JJ, February 9 [or September 2], 1916, Cornell, Scholes 428.
44. Annie Barnacle to NB, July 20, 1916, Cornell, Scholes 410.
45. Ruth Bauerle, "A Source for Dignam," *JJQ* 15 (Fall 1987).
46. MH to JJ, March 8, 1916, Cornell, Scholes 579.
47. NB to HSW, August 28, 1917.
48. NB to John Quinn, April 30, 1917. *Bulletin of Research in the Humanities* (New York Public Library) 81:2 (Summer 1978).
49. John Quinn to NB, May 24, 1917. Ibid., 225.
50. NB to John Quinn, April 30, 1917.
51. John Quinn to NB, May 24, 1917. Ibid., 227.
52. JJ to John Quinn. Ibid., 229.
53. Mary T. Reynolds, "Joyce and Miss Weaver," *JJQ* 19:4 (Summer 1982).
54. JJ to HSW, July 18, 1917, *I*, 106. See also *Ulysses,* 154.
55. Ellmann, 436–37.
56. Paolo Brunetti, Locarno Official Tourist Board, to BM, February 14, 1986.
57. NB to JJ, [August] 15, 1917, Cornell, Scholes 761.
58. SB often commented on Joyce's pronunciation of the *oo* sound.
59. NB to JJ, [August 11, (?) 1917], Cornell, Scholes 754.
60. NB to JJ, [about August 4, 1917], *II*, 401.
61. NB to JJ, [about August 13, 1917], Cornell, Scholes 760.
62. NB to JJ, August 11, 1917, Cornell, Scholes 759.
63. Ellmann, 445. Neither Yale nor Cornell can locate the "Dear Cuckold" letter, and Ellmann in 1986 was uncertain of its whereabouts, although he had read it.
64. NB to JJ, [August] 15, 1917, *II*, 404.
65. NB to JJ, August [11?], 1917, Cornell, Scholes 758.
66. NB to JJ, August [10?], 1917, *II*, 402.
67. NB to JJ, August [11], 1917, Cornell, Scholes 758.
68. *Ulysses,* 45.
69. NB to JJ, August 15, 1917, Cornell, Scholes 761.
70. NB to Ezra Pound, August 28, 1917, *II*, 405.
71. Ellmann, 417.
72. Ellmann, 422.
73. NJ to JJ, August [12?], 1917, *II*, 403, and interview with Maria Jolas, October 26, 1983.
74. Ellmann, 418–19.
75. A. Walton Litz, *The Art of James Joyce,* and interview with BM, April 2, 1985.

76. JJ to Claud Sykes, September [23?], 1917, *II*, 416.
77. Ellmann, 421.

9. Artists and Models

1. NB to JJ, August 1, 1917, *II*, 400.
2. Otto Luening, *Odyssey of an American Composer*, 187.
3. Ellmann, 423.
4. Luening, *Odyssey*, 187.
5. See, for example, the short biography on the half-title page of *Ulysses: The Corrected Text*, Penguin.
6. Litz, 143; Luening, *Odyssey*, 186–87.
7. Arthur Power, *Conversations*, 74.
8. Interview with Mrs. Henry Carr, June 1985.
9. *Ulysses*, 488.
10. HKJ, "Portrait of the Artist by His Daughter-in-Law" [hereafter cited as HKJ memoir], Texas.
11. Claud Sykes to Herbert Gorman, "James Joyce and the English Players," March 1931, SIU; LJ, "The Real Life," Texas.
12. Luening, *Odyssey*, 186, Sykes to Gorman, "The English Players," LJ, "The Real Life," Texas.
13. JJ to Forrest Reid, August 1, 1918, *I*, 117.
14. Notes to *Exiles*, 158.
15. Frank Budgen, *Myselves When Young*, 188.
16. August Suter, "Some Reminiscences of James Joyce," *JJQ* 7:3, 191ff.
17. Frank Budgen, *Making of "Ulysses,"* 20.
18. Ibid., 37.
19. Ibid.
20. Budgen, *Making of "Ulysses,"* 186.
21. Budgen, *Myselves*, 191.
22. JJ to Marthe Fleischmann, December [?], 1918, *II*, 433.
23. Budgen, *Myselves*, 190.
24. JJ to Frank Budgen, June 11, 1919, *SL*, 238–39.
25. Budgen, *Making of "Ulysses,"* 36.
26. Sykes to Gorman, reply to questionnaire, p. 4, May 31, 1931, SIU.
27. LJ, "My Life," Texas. Lucia's remark about Joyce's jealousy of Weiss's attentions to Nora is noticed in Hayman's "Shadow of His Mind."
28. Ellmann, 451.
29. Ellmann, 462.
30. Budgen, *Myselves*, 198.
31. *Ulysses*, 277.
32. Ibid., 300.
33. Interview with Colin MacCabe, April 21, 1985.
34. Lidderdale, 157, and LJ bequest, UCL.
35. NB to JJ, May 8, 1919, Cornell, Scholes 763.
36. Lidderdale, 157.
37. H. W. Saw to HSW, November 19, 1918, BL.
38. Fred Monro to JJ, June 24, 1919, *II*, 444.

39. HSW to JJ, July 6, 1919; Lidderdale, 157–60.
40. Walter Ackermann, *Bordbuch*, 98–99.
41. Mary Colum and Padraic Colum, *Our Friend James Joyce*, 71.
42. JJ to SJ, September 8, 1919, *II*, 452.
43. Josephine Murray to JJ, August 12, 1919, Cornell, Scholes 933.
44. SJ to JJ, May 25, 1919, *II*, 442–43.
45. JJ to SJ, July 31, 1919, *II*, 446–47.
46. Edith McCormick to JJ, October 12, 1919, *II*, 454, Buffalo.
47. Ellmann, 467. Sykes, reply to Gorman's questionnaire, SIU.
48. LJ, "The Real Life," Texas.
49. Bill from Dr. Adalbert Panchaud, July 1, 1919, Texas. He is listed as Panchaud de Bottens in the Zurich directory for 1919.
50. *Ulysses*, 633.

10. "Circe" Goes to Paris

1. Ezra Pound to John Quinn, June 19, 1920, *SL*, 153.
2. JJ to John Quinn, November 17, 1920, in Myron Schwartzman, "Quinnigan's Quake" (Summer 1978), and JJ to Frank Budgen, May 18, 1920, *II*, 465.
3. LJ, "The Real Life," Texas.
4. NB to Frank Budgen, January 27, 1920, *II*, 457.
5. Phillip Herring, "Joyce's Notes and Early Drafts for *Ulysses*," 204.
6. Arthur Power, *Conversations*, 71.
7. JJ to Frank Budgen, May 18, 1920, *II*, 464–65, and JJ to Ezra Pound, June 5, 1910, *II*, 467–69.
8. JJ to Ezra Pound, June 5, 1920, *II*, 468.
9. John Joyce to JJ, January 17, 1920, *II*, 457.
10. Bill from M. Giaconi, 25 Corso, Trieste, June 12, 1920, Texas.
11. JJ to Josephine Murray, June 17, 1920, *II*, 472; JJ to Frank Budgen, May 18, 1920, *II*, 465.
12. Ludmila Bloch-Savitsky to Ezra Pound, July 9, 1920, Buffalo.
13. JJ to SJ, July 12, 1920, *III*, 8.
14. JJ to Claud Sykes, July 29, 1920, *III*, 11.
15. Ezra Pound to Jenny Serruys, July 20, 1920, *III*, 9.
16. JJ to SJ, July 25, 1920, *III*, 10.
17. JJ to SJ, August 29, 1930, *III*, 17.
18. Frank Budgen, *Myselves When Young*, 204.
19. Ezra Pound to John Quinn, *Selected Letters of Ezra Pound*, 251.
20. Beach, 35–40, and unpublished notes, Princeton.
21. Beach, 35.
22. Beach, 39; Fitch, 67.
23. JJ to John Quinn, November 17, 1920, "Quinnigan's Quake"; Herring, *Buffalo*, 192.
24. JJ to John Quinn, November 17, 1920, ibid.
25. Myron Nutting, *An Artist's Life and Travels*, vol. 2, 435, UCLA.
26. Wyndham Lewis, *Blasting and Bombardiering*, 272–74.
27. Interviews with Jane Mulvagh and Arthur Power.

28. JJ to John Rodker, September 29, 1920, *III, 23*.
29. JJ to HSW, November 16, 1920, BL.
30. Lidderdale, 174.
31. JJ to Jenny Serruys, November 5, 1920, *III, 29*.
32. NB to Lillian Wallace, August 15, 1922, *III, 66*.
33. JJ to John Quinn, November 17, 1920, "Quinnigan's Quake," 255.
34. Ernest Hemingway to Sherwood Anderson, March 9, 1922, and Jeffrey Meyers, *Hemingway,* 89.
35. Ernest Hemingway, *A Moveable Feast,* 53.
36. August Suter, "Reminiscences," *JJQ* 7:3, 191ff.
37. JJ to Frank Budgen, December 10, 1920, *I, 151*.
38. Arthur Power, unpublished draft for *Conversations.*
39. Robert McAlmon, *Being Geniuses Together.*
40. Fitch, 11.
41. Meyers, *Hemingway,* 89.
42. Nutting, *An Artist's Life,* vol. 2, 458.
43. Fitch, 60.
44. See Mary Reynolds, "The Indispensable Countersign."
45. McAlmon, *Geniuses,* 242.
46. Fitch, 171.
47. Power, *Conversations,* 30.
48. Interviews with Elizabeth Curran Solterer, November 29, 1984, and Arthur Power, January 19, 1984.
49. Nutting, *An Artist's Life,* vol. 2, 451.
50. Lidderdale, 176.
51. SB, *Shakespeare,* 47.
52. Fitch, 78.
53. Jacqueline Bograd Weld, *Guggenheim,* 54; Meyers, *Hemingway,* 64–65: Peter Ackroyd, *T. S. Eliot,* 122.
54. McAlmon, *Geniuses,* 117–18.
55. Lidderdale, 184.
56. JJ to Frank Budgen, [May 31, 1921], *III, 42*, and Lidderdale, 185.
57. JJ to HSW, June 24, 1921, *I, 165*.
58. Fitch, 138.
59. SJ to JJ, February 22, 1922, *III, 58*.
60. Ellmann, 548.
61. LJ to Katherine Sargent, [n.d.; 1921?], Harvard; also JJ to John McCormack, December 17, 1920, *III, 34*.
62. Power, *Conversations,* 91.
63. McAlmon, *Geniuses,* 32, 118.
64. JJ to HSW, September 9, 1921, *III, 49*, and JJ to Valery Larbaud, September 24, 1921, *III, 49*.
65. McAlmon, *Geniuses,* 276–77.
66. NB to Katherine Sargent, [n.d.; summer 1921?], Harvard.
67. George Bernard Shaw to SB, October 10, 1921, *III, 50*.
68. Sylvia Beach accounts, Buffalo.
69. LJ to Katherine Sargent, January 22, 1922, Harvard. Also JJ to SJ, March 20, 1922, *III, 61–62*.

70. Ellmann, 524.
71. Beach, 85.
72. Ellmann, 524–25.
73. McAlmon, *Geniuses*, 168.
74. Ellmann, 525, and interview with Arthur Power, January 19, 1984.
75. JJ to Robert McAlmon, March [n.d.], 1922, *SL*, 289.
76. JJ to SJ, March 20, 1922, *III*, 61.
77. JJ to Robert McAlmon, March 1, 1922, *SL*, 289.
78. Power, *Conversations*, 20.
79. O Laoi, 100.

11. In a Free State

1. LJ to SJ, April 6, 1922, Cornell, Scholes 653.
2. SB, notes, Princeton.
3. Josephine Murray to JJ, March 27, 1920, Cornell, Scholes 934.
4. *Galway Observer*, April 22, May 6, 1922.
5. O Laoi, 99.
6. NB to Helen Nutting, April 29, 1922, Northwestern.
7. Robert McAlmon, *Being Geniuses Together*, 249.
8. JJ to NB, [n.d.; April 1922?], *III*, 63.
9. JJ to Josephine Murray, October 23, 1922, *I*, 189.
10. Ibid.
11. Interview with Jim O'Halleran, August 1984.
12. JJ to Josephine Murray, November 10, 1922, *I*, 194.
13. Constantine Curran, *James Joyce Remembered*, 81.
14. JJ to Josephine Murray, October 23, 1922, *I*, 191.

12. Molly

1. Ellmann, 133n, 177, 291, 322n, and 342; Gorman, 123n.
2. SB, notes, Princeton.
3. Robert Adams, *James Joyce: Common Sense*, 168.
4. Phillip Herring, *Ulysses Notesheets*.
5. *Ulysses*, 644.
6. *Ulysses*, 609.
7. *Ulysses*, 634–35.
8. *Ulysses*, 639.
9. Herring, *Ulysses Notesheets*, 248, reveals that Joyce associated the vowel sounds as follows: *a* with frankness, *e* with what he called "enclosed," *i* with weakness, *o* with boldness, and *u* with misanthropy.
10. *Ulysses*, 50, 51, 79, 555, etc.
11. *Ulysses*, 533 and 561.
12. *Ulysses*, 638.
13. Hugh Kenner, *Ulysses*, 145.
14. *Ulysses*, 634, and *SL*, 191.
15. *Ulysses*, 639.
16. *Ulysses*, 599.

17. S. A. Henke, "Molly Bloom's Family Romance."
18. *Ulysses*, 441.
19. Peter Costello, "The Trieste Letters," *Irish Times*, July 2, 1976. JJ to Ettore Schmitz, January 5, 1921, *SL*, 275.
20. JJ to Frank Budgen, August 21, 1921, *SL*, 285; printed in *I*, 170.
21. Ellmann, 393, 416–17. See also *The Consciousness of Joyce*.
22. Ira Nadel, "Joyce and the Jews," *Modern Judaism* 6:3 (1986):301–10.
23. Jane Ford, "Why Is Milly in Mullingar?" *JJQ* 14:4, 436–49.
24. Litz, *Art of James Joyce*.
25. *Ulysses*, 273, and *James Joyce Archive*, Michael Groden, ed. Notebook VIA, 51.
26. James Van Dyck Card, "Penelope"; also unpublished dissertation, and letter to BM, December 20, 1985.
27. The Spanish Arch–Moorish Wall equation was suggested by Nathan Halper in "The Grave of Michael Bodkin."
28. Phillip Herring, "Toward an Historical Molly Bloom," *ELH* 45 (1978), "The Bedsteadfastness of Molly Bloom," and *Ulysses Notesheets*.
29. See Richard M. Kain, *Fabulous Voyager*, 98.
30. JJ to Frank Budgen, August 16, 1921, *I*, 170.
31. Arthur Power, *Conversations*, 35.
32. Hayman, in Henke and Unkeless, *Women in Joyce*, 157–58; Kenner, *Ulysses*; Colin MacCabe, *Revolution of the Word*, 131–32; and Henke and Unkeless, *Women in Joyce*, 185. Also, Carol Shloss, "The End of Molly's Exile," paper delivered at Ninth James Joyce International Symposium, Frankfurt, 1984.
33. *A Portrait*, chap. 5.
34. C. G. Jung to JJ, August [?], 1928, *III*, 253, and Ellmann (quoting Beckett), 629.
35. *Ulysses*, 46.
36. Suzette Henke, "The Conventional Molly Bloom," in Henke and Unkeless, *Women in Joyce*, 153.
37. *Ulysses*, 621.
38. *Ulysses*, 610.
39. *Ulysses*, 640.
40. Robert M. Adams, *Surface and Symbol*, 255–56, 42.
41. *Ulysses*, 620.

13. Fame

1. Interview with Maria Jolas, October 26, 1983.
2. Arthur Power, *Conversations*, 70; Myron Nutting, *An Artist's Life and Travels*, vol. 2, 466.
3. JJ to Josephine Murray, November 10, 1927, *III*, 193.
4. JJ to NB, [January 5, 1924?], *III*, 86.
5. SB to HSW, June 18, 1922, Princeton.
6. HSW to SB, June 24, 1922, BL.
7. Lidderdale, 201.
8. JJ to Josephine Murray, November 10, 1922, *I*, 194.

9. Interviews with JL and Phyllis Herriot.
10. JJ to HSW, November 8, 1922, *I*, 193.
11. NB to Helen Nutting, November 27, 1922, Northwestern.
12. Helen Nutting diaries, c. 1923, Northwestern.
13. Fitch, 83.
14. Andrew Field, *Djuna: The Formidable Miss Barnes*, 190; Jane Marcus, "Laughing at Leviticus: *Nightwood* as Woman's Circus Epic," 14.
15. Jacqueline Bograd Weld, *Peggy: The Wayward Guggenheim*, 52.
16. Peggy Guggenheim, *Out of This Century*, 180.
17. Power, *Conversations*, 71.
18. LJ to SJ, December 16, 1924, Cornell, Scholes 694.
19. SB, "Those Unfortunate Creatures," unpublished, Princeton, and Beach, 42.
20. Ellmann, 535–36.
21. Thomas McGreevy papers at TCD; Augustus John, "Fragment of an Autobiography," 60; Cowley, 131.
22. Ellmann, 540–41.
23. HKJ memoir, Texas.
24. Birmingham, *Our Crowd*, 383.
25. JJ to SB, July 12, 1923, *III*, 79.
26. Interview with Peter Lennon, December 22, 1985.
27. O Laoi, 112, and interview with Patricia Barnacle Hutton, December 20, 1983.
28. Ellmann, 554.
29. Ibid.
30. Ibid., and O Laoi, 105.
31. HSW to SB, July 28, 1923, Princeton.
32. Mary Colum, *Life and the Dream*, 1948 ed., and interview with JL.
33. JJ to T. S. Eliot, August 15, 1923, *III*, 510.
34. Middleton Murry, *Journal of Katherine Mansfield*, 397.
35. Ibid., 314 and JJ to HSW, May 24, 1924, *I*, 214.
36. Ellmann, 561.
37. Nutting, *An Artist's Life*, vol. 2, 441, and Jeffrey Meyers, *Hemingway*, 83.
38. JJ to HSW, *III*, 96, and JJ to Valery Larbaud, November 4, 1924, *III*, 108.
39. NB to HSW, November 29, 1924, BL.
40. Beach, 71–72.
41. JJ to HSW, March 7, 1925, *III*, 115.
42. Nutting, *An Artist's Life*, vol. 3, 1110.
43. Ellmann, 554.
44. *Finnegans Wake*, 383.
45. Thomas Connolly, "James Joyce's Manuscripts at the University of Buffalo," paper delivered at the 1985 James Joyce Conference, Philadelphia. The line is taken from Joyce's Buffalo Manuscript VI, B.5, p. 39.
46. Ellmann, 590.
47. Ellmann, 543, 552, and 584.
48. Richard Ellmann, *The Consciousness of Joyce*, 12.
49. Ellmann, 615, quotes Joyce disparaging D. H. Lawrence for not dressing properly. Also, interviews with Elizabeth Curran Solterer, November 27, 1984, and Jane Mulvagh.
50. See plate 36 in Ellmann, showing Lucia and Nora in Galway in 1922.

51. *Ulysses*, 618.
52. Guggenheim, *Century*, 24, 29; Weld, *Guggenheim*, 52.
53. Interview with Phyllis Moss Stein, June 16, 1985.

14. Square Robiac

1. Mary Colum and Padraic Colum, *Our Friend James Joyce*, 115.
2. Arthur Power, in *The Joyce We Knew*, 110, contradicts the view that Nora's incompetence forced the half-blind Joyce to do all the flat hunting, as do many of Joyce's Paris letters.
3. Details of their flat can be found in JJ to Léon-Paul Fargue, *III*, 121; JJ to HSW, May 26, June 17, 1925, BL; piano bill at Buffalo; HKJ memoir, Texas, and Myron Nutting's memoirs, UCLA; and Augustus John, "Fragment of an Autobiography," 56.
4. Myron Nutting, *An Artist's Life and Travels*, vol. 2, 444; HKJ memoir, Texas; HSW to SB, June 22, 1915, Princeton.
5. Power, *The Joyce We Knew*, 111.
6. SB, notes for *Shakespeare and Company*, Princeton.
7. *Exiles*, notes, 150.
8. JJ to SJ, September 28, 1925, *III*, 127.
9. JJ to HSW, May 12, 1927, *I*, 252.
10. Ellmann, 567–68.
11. Interviews with Ellen Bentley (formerly Kastor), June 16, 1985, and Enid Kastor Rubin, June 17, 1985; also Jacqueline Bograd Weld, *Peggy: The Wayward Guggenheim*, 49, 52.
12. Interview with Ellen Bentley, June 16, 1985.
13. Stephen Birmingham, *Our Crowd: The Great Jewish Families of New York*.
14. "Kastor-Fleischman," *New York Times*, October 26, 1915, and interview with Ellen Bentley. See also Weld, *Guggenheim*, 71, for a discussion of Peggy Guggenheim's wish to hide her Jewishness.
15. Peggy Guggenheim, *Out of This Century*.
16. Stuart Gilbert to CC, May 10 [?], 1951, UCD, and interview with Georges Belmont, September 23, 1984.
17. JJ to Ettore Schmitz, November 21, 1925, *III*, 133, and LJ, Texas.
18. JJ to SJ, November 10, 1926, SIU.
19. JJ to SJ, November 17, 1926, SIU.
20. Eva Joyce to SJ, November 9, 1926, SIU.
21. JJ to SJ, November 17, 1926, SIU.
22. Bozena Delimata, "Reminiscences of a Joyce Niece," and Ellmann, 585.
23. Fitch, 130, 230.
24. SB to Eleanor Beach, February 19, 1926, Princeton.
25. JJ to Bennett Cerf, April 2, 1932, *III*, 243, and JJ to HSW, June 8, 1932, *III*, 246.
26. Interviews with Arthur Power, January 19, 1985, and Klara Heyland, May 23, 1984.
27. Elizabeth Nowell, *The Letters of Thomas Wolfe*, 114–15.
28. Margaret Anderson, *My Thirty Years' War*, 246.
29. Thomas McGreevy papers, TCD, and Ellmann, 699.

30. Colum and Colum, *Our Friend,* 113–14.
31. Richard Kain, "Interview with Carola Giedion-Welcker and Maria Jolas," *JJQ* 11:2, 94–122.
32. Helen Nutting diaries, Northwestern; and SB to Sylvester Beach, [n.d.; 1923?], Princeton.
33. HKJ memoir and SB papers.
34. Ernest Kroll, "Mrs. James Joyce and Her Controversial Husband," 56.
35. Interview with Elizabeth Curran Solterer, November 29, 1984.
36. Interview with JL.
37. Ellmann, 590.
38. SB, notes, Princeton.
39. Myrsine Moschos to Noel Riley Fitch as told by Fitch in interview with BM, September 1987.
40. *Finnegans Wake,* 414.
41. Thomas McGreevy, "Paradise Lost?" unpublished memoir, TCD.
42. Mary Colum, *Life and the Dream,* 190.
43. Telephone interview with Berenice Abbott, June 1985.
44. JJ to HSW, May 27, 1929, *I,* 279.
45. JJ to HSW, September 20, 1928, *I,* 269.
46. Ellmann, 598–99.
47. J. F. Byrne to Richard Ellmann, January 29, 1957, Texas.
48. JJ to HSW, November 9, 1927, *I,* 261.
49. J. F. Byrne to Richard Ellmann, spring 1958 (unsent), Texas.
50. Vincent Cosgrave death certificate, September 7, 1926, St. Catherine's House (Office of Population Censuses and Surveys), London.
51. J. F. Byrne, *Silent Years,* 149–50.
52. JJ to HSW, April 16, 1928, *I,* 176.
53. Deirdre Bair, *Samuel Beckett,* 86.
54. Samuel Beckett, *Molloy,* 7, 62.
55. JJ to HSW, March 28, 1928, *III,* 173.
56. LJ, "The Real Life," Texas.
57. Interview with Nelly Joyce, February 1984.
58. JJ to SJ, June 26, July 31, 1928, *III,* 178, 180.
59. Bureau des Actes de Mariage, Sixth Arrondissement, November 30, 1927.
60. HKJ memoir, Texas.
61. JJ to Valery Larbaud, November 16, 1928, *III,* 183, and JJ to HSW, December 2, 1928, *I,* 276; also, SB papers, Princeton.
62. JJ to Valery Larbaud, November 16, 1928, *III,* 183–84.
63. HSW to SB, November 18, 1928, Princeton. Also Lidderdale, 284.
64. HSW to SB, November 25, 1928, Princeton.
65. JJ to HSW, January 10, 1929, *III,* 186.
66. JJ to SJ January 26, 1929, *III,* 186–87; also, HSW to SB, December 20, 1928, Princeton.
67. HSW to SB, January 21, 1929, Princeton.
68. Kevin Sullivan, *Joyce Among the Jesuits,* 58.
69. JJ to HSW, December 2, 1928, *I,* 278.
70. LJ, "My Life," and HKJ memoir, Texas.

71. JJ to HSW, October 26, 1931, BL; October 27, 1931, *III*, 232. Note 5 in *III*, 232, incorrectly attributes Joyce's concern to his own health.
72. Bureau des Actes de Mariage, Sixth Arrondissement, Paris, February 12, 1929.
73. Robert McAlmon, *Being Geniuses Together*, 222.
74. Carlos Baker, *Ernest Hemingway: A Life Story*, 671.
75. Interview with Iris Stephens Wise, April 1986; also, Eileen O'Casey, *Sean*, 93–94.
76. JJ to HSW, November 22, 1929, *I*, 286.
77. JJ to HSW, October 19, 1929, *I*, 285.
78. Arnold Goldman, " 'Send Him Canorious,' " *The Listener*, August 3, 1972, 142–43.
79. Stuart Gilbert, introduction to *I*, 34.
80. Interview with Arthur Power, January 19, 1984.
81. Ellmann, 649.
82. Louis Gillet, *Claybook for James Joyce*, 31.
83. Interview with JL.
84. Interview with Arthur Power, January 19, 1985.
85. MJ to May Joyce Monaghan, September 13, 1965, Ken Monaghan papers.
86. Beckett, *Our Exag*, 14.
87. JJ to HSW, March 7, 1924, *I*, 212; Bair, *Beckett*, 86–88.
88. *Finnegans Wake*, 196.
89. Margot Norris, "Anna Livia Plurabelle: The Dream Woman," in Henke and Unkeless, *Women in Joyce*, 197–213.
90. Bair, *Beckett*, 79, 83, 91–93, describes the Lucia-Beckett episode.
91. Interview with Jacques Mercanton, September 24, 1984, and Potts, 232.

15. Legitimate Interests

1. JJ to HSW, March 30, 1930, *I*, 292.
2. Lidderdale, 295.
3. Byrne, *Silent Years*, 149–50.
4. Interview with JL, August 2, 1985.
5. Kevin O'Sullivan, "An Irishman's Diary," *Irish Times*, June 22, 1972; HKJ papers, Texas; and interview with Gerard O'Flaherty, August 1984.
6. HKJ memoir, Texas; Mary Colum and Padraic Colum, *Our Friend James Joyce*, 190; and Ellmann, 638.
7. Stuart Gilbert to CC, May 1, 1951, UCD; Deirdre Bair, *Samuel Beckett*, 78; Eilis Dillon, "The Innocent Muse," interview with MJ and Georges Belmont, 1984.
8. See *III*, 204, where Joyce talks of wealthy patrons; also Nancy Cunard, "On James Joyce," in Oliphant and Zigal, *Joyce at Texas*, 83–86.
9. JJ to HSW, March 18, 1930, BL.
10. Fitch, 318.
11. Richard Kain, "Interview with Carola Giedion-Welcker and Maria Jolas"; and interview with Verena Giedion Clay, May 1984.
12. JJ to HSW, April 11, 1931, *III*, 215.
13. JJ to Mr. Monro, [n.d.; 1932?], BL. Also, Law Commission, *Illegitimacy*,

Report no. 118, HMSO House of Commons paper 98 and High Court of Justice Chancery Division, September 8, 1941, Doc. 1942 J, no. 456, p. 6, which says that Joyce first consulted Monro Saw in July 1930 about the legitimation of his children and that the need for an English or Welsh domicile was explained to him at that time.

14. SB papers.
15. Ibid.
16. HKJ to HSW, May 23, 1930, BL.
17. NB to HSW, May 29, 1930, BL; LJ to HSW, June 22, 1930.
18. NB to HSW, June 8, 15, 1930, BL.
19. NB to Helen Nutting, [n.d.], Northwestern.
20. NB to HSW, September 12, 1930, BL.
21. Bennett Cerf, *At Random*, and JJ to HSW, January 28, 1932, BL.
22. High Court Doc. 1942 J, no. 456.
23. JJ to HSW, October 3 and 28, 1930, BL.
24. JJ to HSW, November 22, 1930, *SL*, 354–55.
25. NB to HSW, November 25, 1930, BL.
26. JJ to HSW, November 27, 1930.
27. SB to [Holly Beach?], November 1930, and notes for *Shakespeare and Company*, Princeton.
28. Ibid.
29. Wedding certificate of Helen Kastor Fleischman and George Joyce, Paris, Mairie du 6e arrondissement, December 10, 1930.
30. Ibid.
31. JJ to HSW, December 21, 1930, *III*, 208.
32. Ellmann, 628n; Colum and Colum, *Our Friend*, 199.
33. Ellmann, 637.
34. Thomas Connolly, *Personal Library of James Joyce*, 25–28.
35. Richard Brown, *James Joyce and Sexuality*, 35–49.
36. *Finnegans Wake*, 556.
37. Robert McAlmon, *Being Geniuses Together*, 296.
38. JJ to HSW, March 18, 1930, *SL*, 347.
39. JJ to HSW, April 24, 1934, BL.
40. JJ to HSW, April 24, 1934, BL; Ellmann, 612–13.
41. JJ to HSW, March 11, 1931, BL (unpublished portion of published letter).
42. Ellmann, 649; Colum and Colum, *Our Friend*, 232–33.
43. Lidderdale, 449; Nora confessed to Miss Weaver that she had used "an unfortunate expression."
44. Interview with Iris Stephens Wise, April 21, 1985.
45. Lennon, *Catholic World*, March 1931.
46. JJ to HSW, March 11, 1931, and interview with Phyllis Moss Stein, June 16, 1985.
47. Stuart Gilbert to HSW, January 26, 1931.
48. Lidderdale, 301.
49. Ibid.
50. SB to Holly Beach, April 4, 1931, Princeton; JJ to HSW, Oct. 27, 1931, *III*, 232.
51. Lidderdale, 300, quotes from *Finnegans Wake* ms., 299–300, BL.

52. JJ to Padraic Colum, July 2, 1931, National Library of Ireland; Lidderdale, 305; and interview with Moira Lynd Gaster.
53. Ellmann, 637.
54. JL to BM, December 30, 1987.
55. Interview with Lionel Monro, July 1985.
56. According to D. D. C. Monro to BM, February 22, 1985, Monro Pennefather & Co., successors to Monro Saw & Co., have no documents giving evidence of any foreign marriage of James and Nora Joyce.
57. Lidderdale, 304.
58. Colum and Colum, *Our Friend*, 206–7.
59. JJ to HSW, July 5, 1931, BL.
60. O Laoi, 17.
61. Interview with Elizabeth Curran Solterer, November 29, 1986.
62. Moira Lynd Gaster to BM, [August 1?] 1987, and interview, September 17, 1986.
63. Harold Nicolson, *Diaries*, 83–84.
64. JJ to the Colums, July 18, 1931, *III*, 221; JJ to SJ, July 18, 1931, *III*, 221–22.
65. Ellmann, 554, 639.
66. Interview with Maria Jolas, April 23, 1985, and Kain, "Interview with Carola Giedion-Welcker and Maria Jolas."
67. Lidderdale, 307.
68. Ibid.
69. JJ to HSW, August 13, 1931, BL; Lidderdale, 307.
70. HKJ papers, Texas, and interview with Ellen Bentley, June 16, 1985.
71. High Court Doc. 1942 J, no. 456.
72. JJ to HSW, December 7, 1931, *I*, 308, and November 28, 1931, *III*, 234.
73. F. R. D'O. Monro to JJ, October 6, 1931, *III*, 230.
74. Colum and Colum, *Our Friend*, 197.
75. JJ to HSW, October 8 and 17, 1931, BL.
76. JJ to HSW, October 1, 1931, *III*, 230.
77. Colum and Colum, *Our Friend*, 115.
78. JJ to HSW, December 22, 1931, BL.
79. Fitch, 323.
80. LJ bequest, UCL.
81. JJ to HSW, January 17, 1932, *I*, 312.
82. JJ to T. S. Eliot, January 1, 1932, *I*, 311.
83. Lidderdale, 309.
84. Interview with Ellen Bentley, June 16, 1985.
85. Bernard Crystal, Butler Library, Columbia, to BM, July 29, 1986.
86. Fitch, 330.
87. Interview with Stephen Joyce, October 22, 1984.
88. Hugh Kenner to BM, April 27, 1987.
89. Newspaper cutting from the archives of Mrs. Grete Hartley.
90. Colum and Colum, *Our Friend*, 204, and Stephen Joyce.
91. HSW note to BL Collection, July 5, 1960; and Ellmann, 645.
92. Interview with Dominique Gillet Maroger, January 26, 1984; MJ to CC, July 21, 1935, UCD; and interview with Iris Stephens Wise, April 21, 1986.

93. Interview with Evelyne Shapero Chardonnet, April 23, 1985.
94. JJ to HSW, April 17, 1932, BL.
95. JJ to Monro Saw, [n.d.; 1931?], BL.
96. Ibid.
97. JJ to HSW, May 7, 1932, BL.
98. JJ to HSW, June 25, 1932, BL.
99. Ibid.

16. Madness in Progress, I

1. Ellmann, 687n.
2. Ibid., and interview with Moune Gilbert, January 25, 1984.
3. Ellmann, 687–88.
4. JJ to HSW, May 27, 1932, BL. Ellmann's biography says, based on a 1954 interview with Lucie Léon, that Lucia became engaged to Ponisovsky in March 1932. However, Joyce's letter to HSW of May 27, 1932, says that Lucia became engaged "on Tuesday week last," that is, on May 17.
5. LJ, "My Life," Texas.
6. Ellmann, 650.
7. JJ to HSW, April 24, 1932, BL.
8. JJ to HSW, June 25, 1932, BL.
9. Ibid.
10. Ibid.
11. *Finnegans Wake*, 414.
12. Interview with MJ, April 29, 1985.
13. JJ to HSW, June 25, 1932, BL.
14. Leon Edel, *Sleep and Dreams*, 88.
15. Ellmann, 657.
16. JJ to Ezra Pound, February 9, 1930, *III*, 415.
17. JJ to HSW, July 23, 1932, and many subsequent letters in July and August describe that summer.
18. JJ to HSW, August 6, 1932, BL.
19. JJ to HSW, July 21, 22, 23, 27, 29, and August 6, 1932, BL.
20. JJ to Monro Saw, July 21, 1932; JJ to LJ, Aug. 12, 1932, *III*, 255; Lidderdale, 317.
21. Lidderdale, 318.
22. LJ to HSW, August 8, 1932, BL.
23. JJ to HSW, July 28, 1932, BL.
24. Mary Colum and Padraic Colum, *Our Friend James Joyce*, 229.
25. JJ to HSW, October 21, 1932, BL.
26. LJ, "My Life," Texas.
27. JJ to HSW, January 18, 1933, *I*, 331.
28. Ibid., and unpublished portions of JJ to HSW, January 18, 1933, BL.
29. PL to HSW, January 4, 1933, *III*, 267.
30. Lidderdale, 331.
31. PL to HSW, March 23, 1933, *III*, 274.
32. PL to HSW, September 23, 1933, *III*, 287.

33. Interview with Richard Ellmann, March 24, 1984.
34. O Laoi, 112; Bernard Haddigan, St. Bridget's Hospital, County Galway, to BM, March 2, 1986; and JJ to GJ, August 13, 1935, *III*, 372n.
35. Scheper-Hughes, *Saints, Scholars, and Schizophrenics;* Henry Murphy, "Comparative Incidences of Schizophrenia in Ireland," in *Comparative Psychiatry,* 65–70.
36. JJ to HSW, November 11, 1932, BL.
37. Interview with Elizabeth Curran Solterer, November 9, 1984.
38. Cerf, *At Random,* 91–92.
39. Evelyne Shapero Chardonnet, April 23, 1985.
40. James Stern, "James Joyce: A First Impression," *The Listener,* September 28, 1961, 461.
41. *Time,* January 29, 1934.
42. *"La lecture a fait de la fille du poète James Joyce une danseuse,"* unidentified and undated cutting in HSW collection, UCL.
43. Ellmann, 667–68.
44. Interview with Evelyne Chardonnet, April 23, 1985.
45. JJ to HSW, April 24, 1934, *I,* 339.
46. JJ to LJ, June 15, 1934, *I,* 342.
47. Marcella Ecclesine to John Slocum, December 7, 1949, Yale.
48. Cerf, *At Random.*
49. Oliver St. John Gogarty, *As I Was Going down Sackville Street,* 288.
50. GJ to SJ, with postscript by HKJ, April 11, 1934, Cornell, Scholes 662. Helen's original letter to Stanislaus has never come to light.
51. Cerf, *At Random,* 96.
52. PL to HSW, March 11, 1934, BL.
53. NB to GJ and HKJ, June [15?], 1934, *III,* 307.
54. Ibid., and Diana Athill to BM, January 28, 1985.
55. NB to GJ and HKJ, June [15?], 1934, *III,* 307.
56. JJ to HKJ, August 9, 1934, *III,* 316.
57. Ibid.
58. JJ to GJ, August 28, 1934, *III,* 321.
59. JJ to HSW, September 22, 1934, *I,* 346 — a censored version of original in BL.
60. JJ to GJ, October 29, 1934, *III,* 327n.
61. JJ to HSW, December 21, 1934, BL.
62. JJ to HSW, October 10, 1934, BL.
63. LJ to JJ, October [n.d.], 1934, BL.
64. JJ to GJ and HKJ, November 20, 1934, *III,* 328–29.
65. JJ to HKJ, January 18, 1935, *III,* 342.
66. JJ to HKJ, August 9, 1934, *III,* 315–16.
67. JJ to GJ, October 29, 1934, *III,* 327.
68. Interview with Ellen Bentley, June 16, 1985.
69. Peggy Guggenheim, *Out of This Century.*
70. JJ to Frank Budgen, December 18, 1934, *III,* 333.
71. JJ to HSW, December 17, 1934, BL; Lidderdale, 338–39.
72. Lidderdale, 338.
73. JJ to CC, August 10, 1935, UCD.

17. Madness in Progress, II

1. Lidderdale, 342. Many of the details of Lucia's visit to London and Ireland come from this biography of HSW.
2. LJ to HSW, March 13, 1935, UCL, and Ellmann, 269n.
3. LJ to HSW, March 13, 1935, UCL.
4. JJ to HSW, May 1, 1935, *I*, 366.
5. Lidderdale, 343; JJ to HKJ, June 25, 1935, *III*, 363; and JJ to Eileen Schaurek, May 30, 1935. See note 25, below.
6. JJ to Eileen Schaurek, March 13, 1935, *III*, 349.
7. JJ to HSW, April 7, 1935, BL; abbrev. in *I*, 361.
8. Details of furnishing the flat are in JJ to GJ and HKJ, February 19, 1935, *III*, 345; JJ to HKJ, March [?], 1935, *I*, 360; and JJ to GJ, June 23, 1935, *I*, 371.
9. JJ to LJ, May 15, 1935, *III*, 356n.
10. JJ to GJ, June 3, 1935, *III*, 358–60, and June 25, 1935, *I*, 371.
11. Ibid., and JJ to GJ and HJK, April 1 1935, *I*, 360; JJ to LJ [May 9?], 1935, *III*, 355.
12. JJ to GJ, June 3, 1935, *III*, 360n.
13. Richard M. Kain, "Interview with Carola Giedion-Welcker and Maria Jolas," 102.
14. Giorgio's illness is referred to in *III*, 358–60 and *I*, 366. Also, PL to CC, June 19, 1935, UCD.
15. JJ to HKJ, June 17, 1935, *III*, 363.
16. JJ to HSW, June 9, 1936, *III*, 386.
17. JJ to GJ, May 15, 1935, *I*, 370, and Ellmann, 683.
18. The account of Lucia's visit to Bray is taken from Bozena Delimata, "Reminiscences of a Joyce Niece," published letters, unpublished letters in the Constantine Curran collection at UCD, and interviews in Ireland.
19. JJ to LJ, March 28, 1935, *I*, 359; JJ to HSW, April 7, 1935, *I*, 363; JJ to HSW, May 1, 1935, *SL*, 376; and JJ to LJ, May 29, 1935, *III*, 357.
20. JJ to HSW, April 7, 1935, *I*, 362.
21. Ibid.
22. JJ to HSW, May 1, 1935, *SL*, 376.
23. Interview with Patrick Collins, October 8, 1984.
24. JJ to LJ, April 27, 1935, *I*, 364.
25. JJ to Eileen Schaurek, May 30, 1935. The text of this undated letter, provisionally dated March 16, in *III*, 350, makes it clear that Joyce wrote it on the day before the birthday of her son, Patrick, which was May 31.
26. Interview with Elizabeth Curran Solterer, November 29, 1987.
27. JJ to MH, [June 15, 1935?], *III*, 362.
28. Ibid.
29. JJ to MH, June 28, 1935, *I*, 372–73 and July 1, 1935, *I*, 373.
30. MJ to CC, July 21, 1935, UCD.
31. Ibid., and MJ to CC, July [19?], 1935.
32. Lidderdale, 350–51.
33. HSW to CC, July 26, 1935, UCD.
34. JJ to LJ, July [?], 1935, *I*, 377.

35. JJ to LJ, September 15, 1935, *I*, 382.
36. Lidderdale, 353
37. NB to LJ, October 24, 1935, Lidderdale, 354n.
38. E. Nicoll to JJ, August 6, 1935, UCD.

18. Madness in Progress, III

1. Brian Coffey, "Joyce! 'What Now?' " 28.
2. Interview with Nancy McCarthy, October 19, 1986.
3. JJ to CC, October 4, 1936, *I*, 389. The Patricia Hutchins papers, at Trinity College, Dublin, quote an anonymous "Billy" from Galway who placed Michael Healy's worth at £8,000. The Entry of Grant, Michael Healy, Principal Registry, Public Record Office of Ireland, April 17, 1936, shows that Healy, who died intestate, left an estate worth £1,662/8/1.
4. Interview with Mrs. Grete Hartley, August 28, 1986.
5. HKJ memoir, Texas.
6. Interview with Georges Belmont, October 22, 1984, and Ellen Bentley, June 16, 1985.
7. JJ to Mrs. Sisley Huddleston, May 11 [1937?], Texas.
8. JJ to Mrs. John Sullivan, September 24, 1937, *III*, 407.
9. HKJ memoir, Texas.
10. Interview with Georges Belmont, October 22, 1984.
11. Ellmann, 730.
12. Interview with Arthur Power, January 19, 1984.
13. Jacques Mercanton, in Willard Potts, 205–52.
14. Interview with Jacques Mercanton, September 24, 1984.
15. Mercanton, in Potts, 205–52.
16. Interview with Verena Clay, May 1984.
17. Ellmann, 710, and Richard M. Kain, "Interview with Carola Giedion-Welcker."
18. Ellmann, 198, 377n.
19. JJ to HSW, June 9, 1936, *III*, 385–88.
20. Lidderdale, 363–65.
21. JJ to George Rogers, August 3, 1939, *III*, 450–51.
22. Lidderdale, 363, 372–73.
23. Nancy Cunard, "On James Joyce," in Oliphant and Zigal, *Joyce at Texas.*
24. Mary Colum and Padraic Colum, *Our Friend James Joyce,* 149.
25. Ibid.
26. Ibid., 233.
27. Bair, *Beckett,* 241.
28. Peggy Guggenheim, *Out of This Century,* 163.
29. Bair, *Beckett,* 233.
30. JJ to Louis Gillet, September 8, 1938, *I*, 401.
31. JJ to Adolph Kastor, August 30, 1937, *III*, 405.
32. JJ to HKJ and GJ, January 12, 1938, *SL*, 390.
33. Interview with Elizabeth Curran Solterer, November 29, 1984.
34. Ellmann, 708.
35. JJ to HKJ, April 20, 1938, *III*, 420.

36. JJ to Louis Gillet, September 8, 1938, *I*, 401.
37. JJ to HKJ, July 4, 1938, *III*, 425.
38. Ellmann, 590.
39. *Finnegans Wake*, 627.
40. Ellmann, 710.
41. *Finnegans Wake*, 627–28.
42. *Finnegans Wake*, 628.
43. *Finnegans Wake*, 3.
44. Ellmann, 715, and Vivian Mercier, "Joyce in Gotham," *Irish Times*, March 11, 1953.
45. Interview with Georges Belmont, October 22, 1984.
46. Robert Adams, *James Joyce: Common Sense and Beyond*.
47. Ellmann, 721.
48. Interview with MJ.
49. Ellmann, 711.
50. Carola Giedion-Welcker, "Nachtrag," (Appendix) to Herbert Gorman, *James Joyce: Sein Leben und Sein Werke*, 362.
51. Lidderdale, 377.
52. Guggenheim, *Out of This Century*, 207.
53. Ellmann, 728–29, and JJ to Jacques Mercanton, September 8, 1939, *III*, 454–55.
54. JJ to Jacques Mercanton, January 1940, *SL*, 402.
55. Interview with Enid Kastor Rubin, June 17, 1985.
56. Interview with Anne-Marie Pacquet, August 8, 1986.
57. Ellmann, 728.

19. Flight into Zurich

1. Jacqueline Bograd Weld, *Peggy: The Wayward Guggenheim*, 191.
2. Interview with Mme. Marcel Bouboule, Anne-Marie Pacquet, and Juliette Rouchon Bernard, August 6, 1986.
3. Brenda Maddox, "Wakers of the World Unite!" *New York Times Book Review*, August 1987; Edmund Wilson, *Axel's Castle*, 188.
4. "The Finn Again Wakes," *Time*, May 8, 1939.
5. Geoffrey Grigson, *Picture Post*, May 13, 1939.
6. Interview with M. and Mme. Marcel Bouboule, August 6, 1986.
7. Eilis Dillon, "The Innocent Muse," 57, and interview with Maria Jolas.
8. Interview with Enid Kastor Rubin, June 17, 1985, and JJ to CC, February 11, 1940, *I*, 408.
9. David Marsh, "Wartime Ghosts Still Haunt the Streets of Vichy," *Financial Times*, May 9, 1985.
10. Interview with M. and Mme. Marcel Bouboule, August 6, 1986.
11. Ibid.
12. Interview with Maria Jolas, April 23, 1985, and Patricia Hutchins, *James Joyce's World*, 205.
13. CC's copy of typed notes accompanying the boxes describes PL's instructions to Count O'Kelly on handing over the boxes in 1940. When JJ died,

PL amended the instructions in a letter to Count O'Kelly, January 17, 1941, UCD.

14. Lucie Noël, *Story of a Friendship.*
15. Paul Ruggiero papers, Zentralbibliothek, Zurich.
16. JJ to Carola Giedion-Welcker, November 1, 1940, *III,* 494–95.
17. Ibid.
18. Ibid.
19. JJ to Gustav Zumsteg, November 22, 1940, *III,* 500n.
20. Ellmann, 737.
21. High Court Doc. 1942 J, no. 456, discusses Nora's unhappiness over the debt.
22. Interview with Arthur Power, January 19, 1984.
23. Ellmann, 741.
24. Ibid.
25. Ibid.
26. Wilhelm Herz to Robert Kastor, January 14, 1941; part is published in *III,* 507n; full text, Mrs. Grete Hartley.
27. Interview with Heinrich Straumann, September 1984.
28. Ellmann, 742.
29. Interview with Gerard O'Flaherty, August 1984.
30. Ruggiero papers, Zentralbibliothek, Zurich.
31. Stephen Spender, "James Joyce: 1882–1941," *The Listener,* January 23, 1941, 124–25.
32. Carola Giedion-Welcker, "Les Derniers Mois de la Vie de James Joyce."

20. Staying On

1. Lidderdale, 379–80, and Ruggiero papers, Zentralbibliothek, Zurich.
2. HSW to NB, December 7, 1943, BL.
3. GJ to HSW, February 8, 1941, BL.
4. Ibid., and HSW to Fred Monro, June 23, 1946, BL.
5. HSW to GJ, March 23, 1949; NB to HSW, September 23, 1943; and MJ to HSW, October 18, 1947, BL. Also, High Court Doc. 1942 J, no. 456.
6. GJ to HSW, February 8, 1941, BL.
7. Ibid.
8. Interview with Stephen Joyce, October 13, 1983.
9. HSW to CC, August 1, 1941, UCD.
10. Interviews with Grete Hartley, August 28, 1986, and Stephen Joyce, October 13, 1983; also GJ to HSW, December 17, 1941, BL.
11. Evelyn Cotton to HSW, March 24, 1946, BL.
12. High Court Doc. 1942 J, no. 456.
13. Lidderdale, 389.
14. Lidderdale, 386–92.
15. Lidderdale, 386, and HSW to GJ, March 23, April 13, 1941, BL.
16. HSW to GJ, April 30, 1941, BL.
17. Mary Colum and others, February [n.d.], 1941, Berg.
18. Interview with Arthur Power, January 19, 1984.
19. GJ to HSW, December 27, 1941, BL.

20. Affidavit from William Concannon to Eire High Court of Justice, Probate, January 1943, and Decree of Probate for Mrs. Annie Barnacle, UCD; also, Kathleen Barnacle Griffin to John Slocum, September 24, 1950, Yale.

21. Kathleen Barnacle Griffin papers, UCG, and JJ to CC, October 4, 1936, *I*, 389–90.

22. See note 20, above.

23. Interview with Patricia Barnacle Hutton, December 20, 1983.

24. HSW to Kathleen Barnacle Griffin, March 13, 1942, UCG.

25. NB to Kathleen Barnacle Griffin, April 8, 1942, UCG.

26. Decree of Probate for Mrs. Annie Barnacle; affidavit of Kathleen [Barnacle] Griffin to Eire High Court of Justice (Probate), May 7, 1943, UCG, Ms. 76.

27. The Manager, Munster and Leinster Bank, Galway, to Anon., September 7, 1943, UCG.

28. Undated clipping from *Dublin Evening Herald* among HSW's clippings in Lucia Joyce bequest, UCL.

29. NB to HSW, September 22, 1943, BL.

30. HSW to Fred Monro, June 23, 1946, BL.

31. HSW to NB, December 7, 1943, BL.

32. NB to HSW, December [?], 1943, BL.

33. GJ to HSW, December 17, 1941, BL.

34. HSW to Evelyn Cotton, March 19, 1946, BL.

35. David Fleischman to HKJ, September 4, 1946. Interview with Enid Kastor Rubin, June 17, 1985.

36. Evelyn Cotton to HSW, March 25, 1946, BL.

37. T. S. Eliot to HSW, May 20, 1946, BL.

38. Medical certificate of Dr. Med. W. Behrens, June 5, 1946, BL.

39. Evelyn Cotton to HSW, August 22, 1946, BL.

40. Ibid.

41. Leon Edel, *James Joyce: The Last Journey*, 85, and *Stuff of Sleep and Dreams*, 87.

42. HSW to Kathleen Barnacle Griffin, March 13, 1942, UCG.

43. Interviews with Bertha Ruggiero, May 22, 1984; Heinrich Straumann, May 21, 1984, and Klara Heyland, May 23, 1984.

44. Kees van Hoek, "I Met James Joyce's Wife," *Irish Times*, February 17, 1948.

45. Interview with Stephen Joyce, October 13, 1983.

46. Van Hoek, "I Met James Joyce's Wife."

47. Mary Colum and Padraic Colum, *Our Friend James Joyce*, 238–39.

48. Lionel Monro to HSW, July 31, 1947, BL.

49. Ibid.

50. John Slocum to Dr. H. K. Croessmann, September 13, 1950, Yale.

51. Evelyn Cotton to HSW, March 15, 1946, BL.

52. High Court Document J 1942, no. 456, and JJ's will, U.K. Principal Probate Registry.

53. Interview with Hulda Zumsteg, May 22, 1984.

54. Interview with Klara Heyland, May 23, 1984.

55. Lionel Monro to HSW, July 31, 1946, BL; HSW to Lionel Monro, August 1947, BL; and Sandy Campbell, "Mrs. Joyce of Zurich."

21. The Sound of Lions

1. Evelyn Cotton to HSW, Dec. 15, 1946, BL.
2. Ellmann, 743; John Slocum, quoted by David Dempsey, "In and Out of Books," *New York Times Book Review,* January 21, 1951, 8, and Mary Bancroft, *Autobiography of a Spy.*
3. See Sandy Campbell, "Mrs. Joyce of Zurich," for this and subsequent references to this excellent interview.
4. Ellmann, in "Joyce as Correspondent," *Commonweal,* June 14, 1957, 280–81, comments on Joyce's curtailed reading in his later years.
5. Allan Wade, ed., *The Letters of W. B. Yeats,* 933.
6. W. B. Yeats, "Among School Children."
7. Brian Coffey, "Joyce! 'What Now?' " 29.
8. Patricia Hutchins, *James Joyce's World,* 37; and Michael L. Sheil, S.J., to BM, January 12, 1988.
9. HSW to CC, October 31, 1947, UCD.
10. MJ to HSW, January 1, 1948, BL.
11. Interview with Jacques Mercanton, September 24, 1984.
12. This and subsequent material relating to the Kastor visit was provided by Enid Kastor Rubin from her private diary.
13. Interviews with MJ, April 23, 1985; Bernard Gheerbrandt, January 1985; and John Slocum, March 8, 1986; also, Fitch, 410, 436.
14. SB to HSW, November 2, 1949, BL.
15. Lidderdale, 410–13, 421.
16. "Joyce Documents for National Library," *Irish Independent,* August 21, 1947, and Evelyn Cotton to HSW, August 27, 1947, BL.
17. Lidderdale, 413.
18. HSW to Evelyn Cotton, August 29, 1947, BL, and interview with Eileen Slocum, March 8, 1986.
19. MJ to HSW, January 5, 1949, BL.
20. Oliver St. John Gogarty to J. S. Healy, September 9, 1945, Stanford.
21. MJ to HSW, December 6, 1948, BL.
22. MJ to HSW, January 5, 1949, BL.
23. MJ to CC, [n.d.; 194?], UCD; Arthur Power, "The Joyce We Knew," 70.
24. Kathleen Griffin to John Slocum, September 24, 1950, Yale.
25. HSW to Evelyn Cotton, August 29, 1947, BL.
26. Evelyn Cotton to HSW, [?] 1946, BL.
27. Evelyn Cotton to HSW, September 25, 1947, and HSW to Evelyn Cotton, September 28, 1947, BL.
28. *II,* 426–30, and interview with Heinrich Straumann, May 21, 1984.
29. Interviews with Heinrich Straumann, May 21, 1984; Bertha Ruggiero and Hulda Zumsteg, May 22, 1984; and Klara Heyland, May 23, 1984.
30. Interview with Stephen Joyce, October 22, 1984.
31. Walter [?] to John Slocum, November 7, 1950, SIU; Lidderdale, 417n.
32. Lidderdale, 417–18.
33. Lidderdale, 421.
34. GJ to HSW, [January ?], 1951, BL.

35. Stuart Gilbert to CC, May 1, 1951, UCD.
36. Ibid.
37. Interviews with Solange Joyce, October 22, 1984; Hulda Zumsteg, May 22, 1984; also, Lidderdale, 422.
38. Stuart Gilbert to CC, May 1, 1951, UCD.
39. Interview with Maria Jolas, October 26, 1983.
40. Richard M. Kain, "Interview with Maria Jolas."
41. Translation by George Madison Priest, *Encylopaedia Britannica*, "Great Books of the Western World," vol. 47, lines 12,060–67. While other translations are often better, Priest's at least preserves both *grosse* and *Sünderin[nen]*. I am indebted to Walter Engel of Bethesda, Maryland, lecturer and broadcaster on German literary history, for the initial observation and selection of translations.
42. Johann von Rotz to BM, September 16, 1984.
43. Ellmann, 743.
44. *Faust,* part I, Insel Goethe, 6 vol. ed. (1965), vol. 3, p. 43, l. 80.

22. Nora Speaking

1. JJ, "Alphabetical Notebook," in *JJ Archive,* ed. Michael Groden, vol. 7, p. 144.
2. Kenneth Reddin, obituary of James Joyce, *Irish Times,* January 14, 1941. Repr. in John Ryan, *A Bash in the Tunnel.*
3. Interview with MJ, April 1985.
4. Beach, 20, and Stuart Gilbert to CC, May 1, 1951.
5. SJ, "James Joyce: A Memoir," 506.
6. Arthur Power, *The Joyce We Knew,* 121–22.
7. Interview with Stephen Joyce, October 13, 1983.
8. Fitch, 125; Tom Gallacher, *Mr. Joyce Is Leaving Paris,* 58; Mary T. Reynolds, "The Indispensable Countersign"; Mark Schechner, "A Psychoanalytic Inquiry into *Ulysses.*"
9. C. R. W. Nevison, *Sunday Dispatch,* undated cutting in HSW papers, UCL.
10. SJ, "James Joyce: A Memoir," 509.
11. John Slocum to Oliver St. John Gogarty, December 10, 1948, Stanford.
12. Maureen Charlton, *Nora Barnacle,* 1977; Sean O'Faolain, "The Mole on Joyce's Breast," *London Review of Books,* November 20, 1980, and interview in January 1984.
13. Interview with Evelyn Mulvagh Odierna, August 1984.
14. Michael Finlan, "An Irishman's Diary," *Irish Times,* November 30, 1987.
15. Ibid.
16. Philip Roth, "A Conversation with Edna O'Brien," *New York Times Book Review,* November 18, 1984, 1, 39.
17. Eilis Dillon, "The Innocent Muse." Unpublished transcript of an interview that appeared, shortened, in the *JJQ,* 20:1 (Fall 1982), 33–66.
18. *Ulysses,* 639.
19. *Exiles,* act 3.
20. Ellmann, 554.

21. Robert Adams Day, "Joyce, Stoom, King Mark: 'Glorious Name of Barnacle Goose,' " 211–50.
22. *Ulysses*, 273.
23. Adaline Glasheen, *"Finnegans Wake* and the Girls from Boston, Mass.," 96.
24. Colin MacCabe, "James Joyce: Concepts of Race and Nation," address to the Tenth International James Joyce Symposium, Copenhagen, June 1986.
25. *Finnegans Wake*, 123.
26. *Ulysses*, 74.

Appendix

1. John Slocum to Patricia Hutchins Greacen, October 27, 1950, Yale.
2. Stuart Gilbert, introduction to *I*, 35.
3. Lidderdale, 433.
4. Lidderdale, 433–44.
5. Stephen Spender, *New York Times Book Review*, May 26, 1957.
6. Richard Ellmann, "Joyce as Correspondent," *Commonweal*, June 14, 1957.
7. John Slocum to Herbert Cahoon, September 21, 1948, Yale.
8. Interview with John Slocum, March 8, 1986.
9. *Picture Post*, February 2, 1946.
10. SB to Oscar Silverman, February 16, 1960, Buffalo.
11. John Slocum to SJ, May 25, 1949, Yale.
12. John Slocum to Dr. H. K. Croessmann, September 13, 1950, Yale.
13. John Slocum to Herbert Cahoon, July 22, 1953, Yale.
14. Richard Ellmann to John Slocum, December 7, 1953, acknowledges that Stanislaus was hoarding unseen materials essential for Joyce's biography; Yale.
15. Richard Ellmann to J. F. Byrne, February 2, 1957, Texas.
16. SJ to Eithe Monaghan, October 3, 1948, Ken Monaghan papers.
17. Ibid.
18. SJ to JJ, February 26, 1922, *III*, 59.
19. *MBK*, 62.
20. *Ulysses*, 173.
21. *Finnegans Wake*, 276n.2.
22. John P. Wickser to Charles Abbott, October 17, 1951, Buffalo.
23. Charles Joyce to SJ, November 4, 1905, discusses the saving of letters and sending papers on to Trieste. Cornell, Scholes 611.
24. JJ to SJ, March 20, 1922, *III*, 62.
25. JJ to Ettore Schmitz, January 5, 1921, *SL*, 275–77.
26. SJ to JJ, February 26, 1922, *III*, 58.
27. JJ to SJ, August 22, 1931, *III*, 227.
28. SJ to Herbert Gorman, August 8, 1931, *III*, 225.
29. Ibid.
30. Ibid.
31. Ellmann's introduction to *MBK*, 25.
32. Stanislaus had taken out Irish citizenship during the Second World War, to try to avoid being treated as an enemy alien, but the tactic failed. Nelly Joyce remained British. Nelly Joyce to May Joyce Monaghan, December 6, 1955.

33. G. Marvin Tatum, "The Joyce Collection at Cornell University," quotes the letter from W. G. Mennen to Stephen McCarthy. Letter at Cornell.
34. Ibid.
35. Ibid.
36. John P. Wickser to Charles Abbott, October 17, 1951, Buffalo.
37. Robert E. Scholes, preface to *The Cornell Joyce Collection*, and interview with BM, June 15, 1986.
38. Ellmann-I, 317.
39. Roy Harrod, *The Life of John Maynard Keynes* (London: Macmillan, 1951).
40. J. F. Byrne to Richard Ellmann, May 26, 1958, Texas.
41. William Empson, "The Joyce Saga: Before Bloomsday and After," *New Statesman*, October 31, 1959, 585–86; Hugh Kenner, "The Impertinence of Being Definitive."
42. Ellmann, 307.
43. Ellmann, introduction to *II*, xxix; *SL*, xxiv–xxv.
44. Hélène Berger, "Portrait de Sa Femme par l'Artiste," 44–67.
45. Mary T. Reynolds, "Joyce and Nora: The Indispensable Countersign"; Darcy O'Brien, *The Conscience of Joyce* (Princeton, 1968).
46. Richard Ellmann, in "B. W. Huebsch: A Memorial Volume."
47. Kay Boyle to BM, April 12, 1984.
48. Interviews with JL, June 22, 1987, and January 1, 1988.
49. Interviews with Moune Gilbert, January 25, 1984.
50. Francis Evers, "The Trieste Letters," *Irish Times*, June 30, 1976, and interview, 1985.
51. JJ to SJ, March 20, 1922, *III*, 61.
52. JJ to NB, [October 25, 1909?], *II*, 254.
53. Stephen Joyce, letter to editor, *International Herald Tribune*, July 23, 1984.
54. Unpublished portion of letter written to the *International Herald Tribune*, July 10, 1984.
55. Interview with Nelly Joyce, April 13, 1984.
56. *Finnegans Wake*, 185–86.
57. Peter Costello, "The Trieste Letters," *Irish Times*, July 2, 1976.
58. *MBK*, 13.
59. Probate certificate no. 331 and will of Lucia Anna Joyce; Family Division of High Court of Justice, Somerset House, London. In a letter to BM, January 19, 1988, D.D.C. Monro of Monro Pennefather and Co. said that the public record on the size of Lucia's estate and on her beneficiaries was substantially inaccurate. He was not permitted, however, to give further information.
60. Fergus Linehan, "It's an Accident I'm His Grandson. I'm Proud of It but He Wrote the Books, I Didn't," *Irish Times* supplement, February 2, 1982.
61. Helen Joyce in her will left a bequest to the psychiatry department of the New York University–Bellevue Medical Center. Inventory of the estate of Helen K. Joyce, New Milford, Conn., Probate Court, vol. 116, p. 562.
62. Interview with Stephen Joyce, October 13, 1983.

Bibliography

Ackermann, Walter. *Bordbuch eines Verkehrsfliegers*. Zurich: Fretz & Wasmuth, n.d.

Ackroyd, Peter. *T. S. Eliot*. London: Hamish Hamilton, 1985.

Adams, Robert M. *James Joyce: Common Sense and Beyond*. New York: Random House, 1966.

———. "Light on Joyce's *Exiles*." *Studies in Bibliography* 17 (1964):83–105.

———. *Surface and Symbol: The Consistency of James Joyce's "Ulysses."* New York: Oxford University Press, 1967.

Anderson, Chester G. *James Joyce and His World*. London: Thames and Hudson, 1967.

Anderson, Margaret. *My Thirty Years' War*. New York: Covici Friede, 1930.

Antheil, George. *Bad Boy of Music*. Garden City, N.Y.: Doubleday, Doran, 1945.

Attridge, Derek. "Finnegans Awake, or the Dream of Interpretation." Paper delivered at Leeds University Symposium on *Finnegans Wake*, July 1987.

Attridge, Derek, and Daniel Ferrer, eds. *Post-structuralist Joyce*. Cambridge: Cambridge University Press, 1985.

Bair, Deirdre. *Samuel Beckett*. New York: Harcourt Brace Jovanovich, 1978. London: Picador, 1980.

Baker, Carlos. *Ernest Hemingway: A Life Story*. New York: Scribner's, 1969.

Bancroft, Mary. *Autobiography of a Spy*. New York: Morrow, 1983.

Barnes, Djuna. "James Joyce." *Vanity Fair* 18 (April 1922).

———. *Nightwood*. London: Faber and Faber, 1936. New York: Harcourt, Brace and Company, 1937.

Bauerle, Ruth. "Bertha's Role in *Exiles.*" In *Women in Joyce,* edited by S. A. Henke and Elaine Unkeless. Urbana: University of Illinois Press, 1982.

――――. "Date Rape, Mate Rape, and the Death of May Joyce: A Reinterpretation of 'The Dead,' " in Bonnie Kime Scott, ed. *New Alliances in Joyce Studies.* Newark, Del.: University of Delaware Press.

BBC. *Portrait of James Joyce.* Unpublished transcript of broadcast on the BBC's Third Programme, March 17, 1950. Edited by W. R. Rodgers for the James Joyce Society, New York, 1950.

Beach, Sylvia. *Shakespeare and Company.* New York: Harcourt Brace, 1959.

Beckett, J. C. *The Making of Modern Ireland.* London: Faber and Faber, 1966.

Beckett, Samuel. *Molloy.* Paris: Olympia, 1955. London: John Calder, 1959.

――――, and others. *Our Exagmination Round His Factification for Incamination of "Work in Progress."* London: Faber, 1972.

Beebe, Maurice. "James Joyce: Barnacle Goose and Lapwing." *PMLA 81* (June 1956):302–20.

――――. "Joyce and Stephen Dedalus: The Problem of Autobiography." In *A James Joyce Miscellany, Second Series,* edited by Marvin Magalaner. Carbondale, Ill.: Southern Illinois University Press, 1959.

Behan, Kathleen. *Mother of All the Behans.* London: Hutchinson, 1984.

Beja, Morris. "The Joyce of Sex: Sexual Relations in *Ulysses.*" In *Light Rays: James Joyce and Modernism,* edited by Heyward Ehrlich. New York: New Horizon, 1984.

Benco, Silvio. "James Joyce in Trieste." In *Portraits of the Artist in Exile,* edited by Willard Potts. Seattle: University of Washington Press, 1979.

Benstock, Shari. "The Genuine Christine: Psychodynamics of Issy." in *Women in Joyce,* edited by S. A. Henke and Elaine Unkeless. Urbana: University of Illinois Press, 1983.

――――. *Women of the Left Bank.* London: Virago, 1987.

Benstock, Shari, and Bernard Benstock. *Who's He When He's at Home — A James Joyce Directory.* Urbana: University of Illinois Press, 1980.

Berger, Hélène. "Portrait de sa Femme par l'Artiste." *Lettres Nouvelles* (March–April 1966):44–67.

Berrone, Louis. *James Joyce in Padua.* New York: Random House, 1977.

Birmingham, Stephen. *Our Crowd: The Great Jewish Families of New York.* London: Longmans, Green, 1968.

Blamires, Harry. *The Bloomsday Book.* London and New York: Methuen, 1966.

Boone, Joseph Allen. "A New Approach to Bloom as 'Womanly Man': The Mixed Middling's Progress in *Ulysses.*" *JJQ* 20:1 (Fall 1982).

Bowen, Zack, and James C. Carens, eds. *A Companion to Joyce Studies.* Westport, Conn.: Greenwood Press, 1984.

――――. "Annotated Bibliography." Colum Collection, State University of New York at Binghamton.

Boyle, Kay. "Letter from Joyce." *Triquarterly* (Winter 1967), 195–97.

Brown, Richard. *James Joyce and Sexuality.* Cambridge: Cambridge University Press, 1985.

Bryher. *The Heart of Artemis: A Writer's Memoirs.* London: Collins, 1963.

Budgen, Frank. *James Joyce and the Making of "Ulysses."* Bloomington and London: University of Indiana Press, 1960.

——. *Myselves When Young.* New York: Oxford University Press, 1970.

Burgess, Anthony. *Here Comes Everybody.* London: Faber, 1964.

Byrne, J. F. *Silent Years.* New York: Farrar, Straus and Young, 1953.

Campbell, Joseph, and Henry Morton Robinson. *A Skeleton Key to "Finnegans Wake."* London: Faber and Faber, 1947.

Campbell, Sandy. "Mrs. Joyce of Zurich." *Harper's Bazaar,* October 1952.

Card, James van Dyck. *An Anatomy of "Penelope."* London and Toronto: Associated University Presses, 1984.

——. "A Gibraltar Sourcebook for 'Penelope.' " *JJQ* 8:2, (Winter 1971):163–75.

Cerf, Bennett. *At Random.* New York: Random House, 1977.

Chisholm, Anne. *Nancy Cunard.* New York: Alfred Knopf. London: Sidgwick and Jackson, 1979.

Cixous, Hélène. *The Exile of James Joyce.* Trans. S. A. J. Purcell. New York: David Lewis, 1972.

Clarke, Austin. *Twice Around the Black Church.* London: Routledge and Kegan Paul, 1962.

Coffey, Brian. "Joyce! 'What Now?' " *Irish University Review,* 1952.

Colum, Mary. *Life and the Dream.* Garden City, New York: Doubleday, 1947.

Colum, Mary, and Padraic Colum. *Our Friend James Joyce.* London, Gollancz, 1959.

Colum, Padraic. Introduction to *Exiles,* by James Joyce. New York: Viking, 1951.

Comitato per l'Anno Joyciano. *Il Ritorno di Joyce.* Trieste, 1982.

Connolly, Thomas E. "James Joyce's Manuscripts at the University of Buffalo." Paper delivered at the 1985 James Joyce Conference, Philadelphia.

——. *James Joyce's "Scribbledehobble."* Evanston, Ill.: Northwestern University Press, 1961.

——, ed. *The Personal Library of James Joyce.* Buffalo: University of Buffalo Monographs in English, no. 6. 1955.

Costello, Peter. *James Joyce.* Dublin: Gill and Macmillan, 1980.

——. *Leopold Bloom: A Biography.* Dublin: Gill and Macmillan, 1981.

Cowley, Malcolm. *Exile's Return.* London: Cape, 1935.

Crise, Stelio. *— And Trieste Ah Trieste.* Milan: All' Insegna del Pesce d'Oro, 1971.

——. *Epiphanies e Pedographs: James Joyce à Trieste.* Milan: All' Insegna del Pesce d'Oro, 1967.

Crosby, Caress. *The Passionate Years.* London: Alvin Redman, 1955.

Cunard, Nancy. "On James Joyce — For Professor Ellmann." In *Joyce at Texas,* edited by Dave Oliphant and Thomas Zigal. Austin: University of Texas Humanities Research Center, 1983.

Curran, Constantine. *James Joyce Remembered.* New York: Oxford University Press, 1968.

Curtayne, A. "Portrait of the Artist as Brother: An Interview with James Joyce's Sister." *Critic* 21 (1963):43–47.

Davies, Stan Gébler. *James Joyce: A Portrait of the Artist.* New York: Stein and Day, 1975.
Davis, Isabel. "The People in Djuna Barnes's *Nightwood.*" Ph.D. diss., State University of New York, Stony Brook, 1978.
Day, Robert Adams. "Joyce, Stoom, King Mark: 'Glorious Name of Barnacle Goose.' " *JJQ* 12 (Spring 1975):211–50.
Delaney, Frank. *James Joyce's Odyssey.* London: Paladin, 1983.
Delimata, Bozena. "Reminiscences of a Joyce Niece." *JJQ* 19:1 (Fall 1982):45–62.
Deming, Robert H. *A Bibliography of James Joyce Studies.* Boston: G. K. Hall, 1977.
De Tuoni, Dario. *Ricordi di James Joyce à Trieste.* Milan: All' Insegna del Pesce d'Oro, 1966.
Dillon, Eilis. "The Innocent Muse: An Interview with Maria Jolas." *JJQ* 20:1 (Fall 1982):33–66.
Dilworth, Thomas. "Sex and Politics in 'The Dead.' " *JJQ* 23:2 (Winter 1986):157–71.

Edel, Leon. *James Joyce: The Last Journey.* New York: Gotham Book Mart, 1947.
———. *Stuff of Sleep and Dreams.* London: Chatto and Windus, 1982.
Eglinton, John. *Irish Literary Portraits.* London: Macmillan, 1935.
Ehrlich, Heyward, ed. *Light Rays: James Joyce and Modernism.* New York: New Horizon, 1984.
Ellmann, Richard. *The Consciousness of Joyce.* London: Faber, 1977.
———. *Four Dubliners.* London: Hamish Hamilton, 1987.
———. "The Grasshopper and the Ant." *The Reporter,* December 1, 1955.
———. *James Joyce.* London: Oxford University Press, 1959. Rev. ed., 1982.
———. "Joyce as Correspondent." *Commonweal,* June 14, 1957.
———. "Joyce's Aunt Josephine." In *Joyce at Texas,* edited by Dave Oliphant and Thomas Zigal. Austin: University of Texas Humanities Research Center, 1983.
———. *Ulysses on the Liffey.* London: Faber, 1972.
———, ed. *Letters of James Joyce,* vols. II and III. London: Faber, 1966.
———, ed. *Selected Letters of James Joyce.* London: Faber, 1975.
———. Introduction to *Ulysses: The Corrected Text,* edited by Hans Walter Gabler, with Wolfhard Steppe and Claus Melchior. New York: Garland, 1986.
———. Contribution to *B. W. Huebsch, A Memorial Volume,* December 20, 1956. Berg Collection.
Empson, William. "The Joyce Saga: Before Bloomsday and After." *New Statesman,* October 31, 1959, 585–86.

————. *The Theme of "Ulysses."* Kenyon Review 18 (1956):26–52.

————. "The Ultimate Novel." *London Review of Books,* September 2, 1982, 3–5, September 16, 1982, 6–9.

Ernst, Morris L. *The Best Is Yet.* New York: Harper, 1945.

Feshbach, Sidney. "June 16, 1904: Joyce's Date with Nora?" *JJQ* 21:4 (Summer 1984):369–71.

Field, Andrew. *Djuna: The Formidable Miss Barnes.* Austin: University of Texas Press, 1985.

Fifield, William. "Joyce's Brother, Lawrence's Wife, Wolfe's Mother, Twain's Daughter." *Texas Quarterly* (Spring 1967):49–71.

Finneran, Richard. *Anglo-Irish Literature: A Review of Research.* New York: Modern Language Association, 1976.

Fitch, Noel Riley. *Sylvia Beach and the Lost Generation.* New York: W. W. Norton, 1983.

Ford, Jane. "The Father, Daughter, Suitor Triangle in Shakespeare, Dickens, James, Conrad and Joyce." *Dissertation Abstracts International* 36:7 (1976).

————. "Why Is Milly in Mullingar?" *JJQ* 14:4 (Summer 1977):436–49.

Francini-Bruni, Alessandro. "Joyce Stripped Naked in the Piazza." In *Portraits of the Artist in Exile,* edited by Willard Potts. Seattle: University of Washington Press, 1979.

Frank, Nino. "Souvenirs sur James Joyce." *La Table Ronde* (Paris) 23 (November 1949):1671–93.

French, Marilyn. *The Book as World.* Cambridge: Harvard University Press, 1976.

Freund, Gisèle. *Three Days with Joyce.* New York: Persea, 1985.

Gallacher, Tom. *Mr. Joyce Is Leaving Paris.* London: Calder and Boyars, 1972.

Galli, Lina. "Livia Veneziani Svevo and James Joyce." *JJQ* 9:3 (1972), 334–38.

Galway Year Book and Directory. Galway: M'Dougall & Brown, 1902.

Garvin, John. *James Joyce's Disunited Kingdom and the Irish Dimension.* New York: Barnes and Noble, 1977. Dublin: Gill and Macmillan, 1976.

Gay, Peter. *Education of the Senses: The Bourgeois Experience, Victoria to Freud.* New York: Oxford University Press, 1984.

Gheerbrandt, Bernard. *James Joyce, Sa Vie, Son Oeuvre, Son Rayonnement.* Paris: La Hune, 1949.

Giedion-Welcker, Carola. "Les Derniers Mois de la Vie de James Joyce." *Le Figaro Littéraire,* May 28, 1949.

————. "Meetings with James Joyce." In *Portraits of the Artist in Exile,* edited by Willard Potts. Seattle: University of Washington Press, 1979.

————. "Nachtrag," (Appendix) in Herbert Gorman's *James Joyce: Sein Leben und Sein Werke.* Hamburg: Claasen Verlag, n.d.

Gifford, Don. *Joyce Annotated: Notes for "Dubliners" and "A Portrait of the Artist as a Young Man."* Rev. and enlarged ed. Berkeley: University of California Press, 1982.

————, with Robert Seidman. *Notes for Joyce.* New York: E. P. Dutton, 1974.

Gilbert, Stuart. *James Joyce's "Ulysses."* Rev. ed. London: Faber.

Gillet, Louis. *Claybook for James Joyce.* London and New York: Abelard-Schuman, 1958.

Glasheen, Adaline. *"Finnegans Wake and the Girls from Boston, Mass."* *Hudson Review* 8 (Spring 1954):89–96.

Gogarty, Oliver St. John. *As I Was Going down Sackville Street.* London: Rich and Cowan, 1937.

———. *It Isn't This Time of Year at All.* New York: Doubleday, 1954. London: MacGibbon and Kee, 1954.

———. "They Think They Know Joyce." *Saturday Review of Literature* 23 (January 25, 1941).

———. *Tumbling in the Hay.* London: Constable. Toronto: Macmillan, 1939.

Golding, Louis. *James Joyce.* London: Thornton Butterworth, 1933.

Goldman, Arnold. " 'Send Him Canorious.' " *The Listener,* August 3, 1972.

———. "Stanislaus, James and the Politics of Family." In *Atte del Third International James Joyce Symposium, 1971,* Nini Rocco-Bergera (ed.). Trieste: Università degli Studi Facultà di Magistero, 1974.

Goll, Claire. *La Poursuite du Vent.* Paris: Olivier Oban, 1976.

Goll, Ivan, and Claire Goll. *Briefe.* Mainz: Florian Kupferberg.

Gordon, John. "In the Arms of Murphy." Chap. 7 of *James Joyce's Metamorphoses.* New York: Barnes & Noble, 1981. Dublin: Gill and Macmillan, 1981.

Gorman, Herbert. *James Joyce.* New York: Farrar and Rinehart, 1939.

———. *James Joyce: His First Forty Years.* New York: B. W. Huebsch, 1924.

Groden, Michael, et al., eds. *The James Joyce Archive.* 63 vols. New York: Garland, 1977–79.

———. *James Joyce's Manuscripts: An Index.* New York: Garland, 1980.

Grosskurth, Phyllis. "Search and Psyche: The Writing of Biography." *English Studies in Canada* 11:2 (June 1985).

Guggenheim, Peggy. *Out of This Century.* New York: Doubleday, 1980.

Halper, Nathan. "The Grave of Michael Bodkin." *JJQ* 12:3 (1975):273–80.

Hart, Clive, and David Hayman, eds. *James Joyce's "Ulysses."* Berkeley: University of California Press, 1974.

Hayman, David. "On Reading Ellmann's Edition: Notes on Joyce's Letters." *JJQ* 12:2 (Winter 1967):56–61.

———. "Shadow of His Mind: The Papers of Lucia Joyce." In *Joyce in Texas,* edited by Dave Oliphant and Thomas Zigal. Austin: University of Texas Humanities Research Center, 1983.

Hedberg, Johannes. "Jubilee Jingle and Nora Joyce." *Martello Magazine* (Dublin) 2 (Summer 1983).

Hemingway, Ernest. *A Moveable Feast.* London: Cape, 1964.

Henke, S. A. "Molly Bloom's Family Romance." Paper delivered at the Ninth International James Joyce Symposium, Frankfurt, June, 1984.

———, and Elaine Unkeless, eds. *Women in Joyce.* Urbana: University of Illinois Press, 1982.

Herring, Phillip F. "The Bedsteadfastness of Molly Bloom." *Modern Fiction Studies* (Spring 1969):49–61.

———. "Toward an Historical Molly Bloom." *ELH* 45 (1978).

———, ed. *Joyce's Notes and Early Drafts for "Ulysses."* Selections from the Buffalo Collection. Charlottesville: University Press of Virginia, 1977.

———, ed. *Joyce's "Ulysses" Notesheets in the British Museum.* Charlottesville: University Press of Virginia, 1972.

Hogan, Patrick. "The Joyce of Sex." Paper delivered at the 1985 James Joyce Conference, Philadelphia.

Huddleston, Sisley. *Paris Salons, Cafés, Studios.* Philadelphia: Lippincott, 1928.

Hughes, Eileen Lanouette. "The Mystery Lady of 'Giacomo Joyce,'" *Life,* February 19, 1968.

Hutchins, Patricia. *James Joyce's Dublin.* London: Grey Walls Press, 1950.

———. *James Joyce's World.* London: Methuen, 1957.

Jolas, Maria. "The Joyce I Knew and the Women Around Him." *The Crane Bag* 4:1 (1980).

———, ed. *A James Joyce Yearbook.* Paris: Transition Press, 1949.

Joll, James. *Europe Since 1870.* London: Weidenfeld and Nicolson, 1973.

Joyce, Helen. "Portrait of the Artist by His Daughter-in-Law." Unpublished. Texas.

Joyce, James. *Chamber Music.* London: Jonathan Cape, 1980.

———. *The Critical Writings.* Edited by Richard Ellmann and Ellsworth Mason. London: Faber, 1959. New York: Viking, 1959.

———. *Exiles.* London: Penguin, 1973.

———. *Finnegans Wake.* New York: Viking, 1957.

———. *Giacomo Joyce.* London: Faber, 1968.

———. *Pomes Penyeach.* London: Faber, 1968.

———. *A Portrait of the Artist as a Young Man.* London: Penguin, 1960.

———. *Stephen Hero.* Panther, 1977.

———. *Ulysses: The Corrected Text,* edited by Hans Walter Gabler, with Wolfhard Steppe and Claus Melchior. New York: Garland, 1984.

Joyce, Lucia. "Autobiography. My Life." Unpublished. Texas.

———. "My Dreams." Unpublished. Texas.

———. "The Real Life of James Joyce Told by Lucia Joyce." Unpublished. Texas.

Joyce, Stanislaus. *The Complete Dublin Diary.* Edited by George Healey. Ithaca, N.Y.: Cornell University Press, 1971.

———. "Early Memories of James Joyce." *The Listener* 41 (May 26, 1949):896.

———. "James Joyce: A Memoir." *Hudson Review* (1949–50).

———. "The Joyces," *New Yorker,* January 12, 1935.

———. *My Brother's Keeper.* London: Faber, 1958.

———. *Recollections of James Joyce by His Brother.* New York: The James Joyce Society, 1950.

Kain, Richard M. *Fabulous Voyager: James Joyce's "Ulysses."* Chicago: University of Chicago Press, 1947.

———, ed. "An Interview with Carola Giedion-Welcker and Maria Jolas." *JJQ* 11:2 (Winter 1974):94–122.

"Kastor, Adolph." *Who's Who in American Jewry, 1926.* The Jewish Biographical Bureau, Inc.

Kavanagh, James. *A Modern Priest Looks at His Outdated Church.* London: Hodder and Stoughton, 1968.

Kaye, Julian B. "A Portrait of the Artist as Blephen-Stoom." In *A James Joyce Miscellany,* series 2, edited by Marvin Magalaner. Carbondale, Ill.: Southern Illinois University Press, 1959.

Kelly's Directory of Ireland, 1900–1905. London: Kelly's Directories, 1905.

Kenner, Hugh. *A Colder Eye.* Penguin, 1983.

———. *Dublin's Joyce.* Bloomington: Indiana University Press, 1956. London: Chatto and Windus, 1955.

———. "The Impertinence of Being Definitive." *Times Literary Supplement,* December 17, 1982.

———. *Ulysses.* London: Allen and Unwin, 1980.

Kiell, Norman, ed. *Blood Brothers: Siblings as Writers.* New York: International University Press.

Kimball, Jean. "James and Stanislaus Joyce: A Jungian Speculation." In *Blood Brothers,* edited by Norman Kiell. New York: International University Press.

Kroll, Ernest, ed. "Mrs. James Joyce and Her Controversial Husband. Interview with Victor Llomas." *Cimarron Review* (January 1986).

Leavis, F. R. *The Great Tradition.* London: Pelican, 1972.

Lennon, Michael J. "James Joyce." *Catholic World* 132:792 (March 1931):641–52.

Leprohon, Pierre. *The Italian Cinema.* New York: Praeger.

Levin, Harry. *James Joyce: A Critical Introduction.* New York: New Directions, 1960.

Levitt, Annette. "Mothering in Djuna Barnes, Jean Rhys and James Joyce." Paper delivered at 1985 James Joyce Conference, Philadelphia.

Lewis, R. W. B. *Edith Wharton.* New York: Harper and Row, 1975.

Lewis, Wyndham. *Blasting and Bombardiering.* London: Eyre & Spottiswoode, 1937.

———. *Time and Western Man.* London: 1927.

Lidderdale, Jane, and Mary Nicholson. *Dear Miss Weaver.* New York: Viking, 1970.

Liddy, James. *Esau, My Kingdom for a Drink.* Dublin: Dolmen Press, 1962.

Linehan, Fergus. "It's an Accident I'm His Grandson." *Irish Times* special supplement, February 2, 1982.

Lister, Raymond. *William Blake.* London: Bell, 1968.

Litz, A. Walton. *The Art of James Joyce.* New York: Oxford University Press, 1961.

Luening, Otto. *The Odyssey of an American Composer.* New York: Scribner's, 1980.

Lyons, F. S. L. *Culture and Anarchy in Ireland 1890–1939.* London: Oxford University Press, 1979.

Lyons, J. B. *The Enigma of Tom Kettle.* Dublin: Glendale Press, 1983.

———. *James Joyce and Medicine.* Dublin: Dolmen Press, 1973.

————. *Thrust Syphilis Down to Hell and Other Rejoyceana.* Dublin: Glendale Press, 1988.

McAlmon, Robert. *Being Geniuses Together.* London: Michael Joseph, 1970. Revised, with supplementary chapters and new afterword by Kay Boyle. London: Hogarth, 1984.

MacCabe, Colin. *James Joyce: New Perspectives.* Bloomington: Indiana University Press, 1982. Brighton, Sussex: Harvester Press, 1982.

————. *James Joyce and the Revolution of the Word.* London: Macmillan, 1979.

————. "Joyce: Concepts of Race and Nation." Address delivered at the Tenth International James Joyce Symposium, Copenhagen, June 1986.

McCarthy, Michael. *Priests and People in Ireland.* Dublin: Hodges, Figgis, 1902.

MacDonald's Irish Directory. 1899–1900 through 1903–1904. Dublin, Edinburgh, and London: Wm. MacDonald.

M'Donough and Brown. *Galway Guide and Directory.* Galway: 1902, 1904.

McDougall, Richard. *The Very Rich Hours of Adrienne Monnier.* London: Millington, 1976.

McGreevy, Thomas. "James Joyce." *The Times Literary Supplement,* January 25, 1941, 43, 45.

————. "Paradise Lost." Unpublished memoir written after Joyce's death. Trinity College, Dublin.

McHugh, Roland. *The Sigla of "Finnegans Wake."* London: Edward Arnold, 1976.

MacLysaght, Edward. *Guide to Irish Surnames.* Dublin: Helicon, 1964.

MacNicholas, John. *James Joyce's "Exiles": A Textual Companion.* New York and London: Garland, 1979.

Maddox, Brenda. "Could Nora Cook?" *New York Times Book Review,* June 16, 1985.

————. "Wakers of the World Unite," *New York Times Book Review,* August 15, 1987.

Magalaner, Marvin, ed. *A James Joyce Miscellany.* First Series: New York: James Joyce Society, 1957. Second Series: Carbondale: Southern Illinois University Press, 1959. Third Series: Carbondale: Southern Illinois University Press, 1962.

Magalaner, Marvin, and Richard M. Kain. *Joyce: The Man, the Work, the Reputation.* London: John Calder, 1957.

Mahaffey, Vicki. "Giacomo Joyce." In *A Companion to Joyce Studies,* edited by Zack Bowen and James C. Carens. Westport, Conn.: Greenwood Press, 1984.

Marcus, David, ed. *Irish Short Stories.* Vols. 1 and 2. London: Bodley Head, 1980.

Marcus, Jane. "Laughing at Leviticus: *Nightwood* as Woman's Circus Epic." Paper delivered at Tenth International James Joyce Symposium, Copenhagen, 1986.

Martin, Augustine. "The Education of a Gentleman." *Irish Times* special supplement, 1882–1928.

Mathews, James. *Voices: A Life of Frank O'Connor.* New York: Atheneum, 1983.

Melchiori, Giorgio. *Joyce in Rome*. Rome: Bulzoni, 1984.

Mercanton, Jacques. *Les Heures de James Joyce*. Lausanne: Éditions l'Age d'Homme, 1967.

Mercier, Vivian. *Beckett/Beckett*. London: Oxford University Press, 1977.

Meyers, Jeffrey. *Hemingway*. New York: Harper and Row, 1985. London: Macmillan, 1986.

Moscato, Michael, and Leslie Le Blanc, eds. *The United States of America v. One Book Entitled "Ulysses" by James Joyce: Documents and Commentary — A 50-Year Retrospective*. Frederick, Md.: University Publications of America, 1984.

Murphy, Henry. "Comparative Incidence of Schizophrenia in Rural Ireland." In *Comparative Psychiatry,* edited by Henry Murphy. Springer Verlag.

Murry, John Middleton. *The Journal of Katherine Mansfield*. New York: Knopf, 1927; Constable, 1927.

Nadel, Ira B. *Biography: Fiction, Fact & Form*. London: Macmillan, 1984.

———. "Joyce and the Jews." *Modern Judaism* 6:3 (1986):301–10.

Nichols, Ashton. "JOYCEZSEASIDEGIRLS: Gretta, Bertha, Molly and Nora — All from Gibralway?" *Biography* 8:4 (Fall 1985).

Nicolson, Harold. *Diaries and Letters 1930–1939*. London: Collins, 1966.

Noël, Lucie. *James Joyce and Paul L. Léon: The Story of a Friendship*. New York: Gotham Book Mart, 1950.

Norris, Margot. "Anna Livia Plurabelle: The Dream Woman." In *Women in Joyce,* edited by S. A. Henke and Elaine Unkeless. Urbana: University of Illinois Press, 1982.

———. *The Decentered Universe of "Finnegans Wake."* Baltimore: Johns Hopkins University Press. 1976.

Nowell, Elizabeth, ed. *The Letters of Thomas Wolfe*. New York: Scribner's, 1956.

Nutting, Myron. "An Artist's Life and Travels." Vols. 1–4. Oral History Program, University of California, Los Angeles, 1972.

O'Brien, Edna. *James and Nora: Portrait of Joyce's Marriage*. Northridge, Calif.: Lord John Press, 1981.

O Broin, Leo. *Protestant Nationalists in Revolutionary Ireland*. Dublin: Gill and Macmillan, 1985.

O'Casey, Eileen. *Sean*. London: Macmillan, 1971.

O'Connor, Ulick. *Oliver St. John Gogarty*. London: Granada, 1981.

———, ed. *The Joyce We Knew*. Cork: Mercier, 1967.

O'Faolain, Sean. "Nora Barnacle: Pictor Ignotus." *London Review of Books,* November 20, 1980.

O Laoi, Padraic. *Nora Barnacle Joyce: A Portrait*. Galway: Kennys Bookshops and Art Galleries, 1982.

Oliphant, Dave, and Thomas Zigal, eds. *Joyce at Texas*. Austin: University of Texas Humanities Research Center, 1983.

O Lochlainn, Colm. *Irish Street Ballads*. New York: Corinth, 1960.

Paige, D. D., ed. *Selected Letters of Ezra Pound, 1907–1941*. London: Faber and Faber, 1950.

Parrinder, Patrick. *James Joyce*. Cambridge, England: Cambridge University Press, 1984.

Paulin, Tom. "The British Presence in *Ulysses*." In *Ireland and the English Crisis*, edited by Tom Paulin. Newcastle upon Tyne: Bloodaxe Books, 1984.

Potts, Willard. "Joyce's Notes on the Gorman Biography." *IcarbS*, 4:2 (Spring–Summer, 1981):83–99.

———, ed. *Portraits of the Artist in Exile*. Seattle: University of Washington Press, 1979.

Power, Arthur. *Conversations with James Joyce*. London: Millington, 1974.

———. Untitled essay in *The Joyce We Knew*, edited by Ulick O'Connor. Cork: Mercier, 1967.

Quick, Jonathan R. "The Homeric *Ulysses* and A. E. W. Mason's *Miranda of the Balcony*." *JJQ* 23:1 (Fall 1985):31–43.

Quinn, John. "Shem's Progress: James Joyce and the Making of *Finnegans Wake*." BBC Radio 3 broadcast, 1984.

Reynolds, Mary T. "Joyce and Miss Weaver." *JJQ* 19:4 (Summer 1982):373–403.

———. "Joyce and Nora: The Indispensable Countersign." *Sewanee Review* (Winter 1964), 29–64.

Rice, Thomas Jackson. *James Joyce: A Guide to Research*. New York: Garland, 1982.

Rodgers, W. R. *Ladies Bountiful*. New York: Harcourt Brace, 1968. London: Gollancz, 1968.

Ruggiero, Paul. "James Joyce's Last Days in Zurich." In *Portraits of the Artist in Exile*, edited by Willard Potts. University of Washington Press, 1979.

Ryan, John, ed. *A Bash in the Tunnel*. Brighton: Clifton Books, 1974.

Scheper-Hughes, Nancy. *Saints, Scholars and Schizophrenics: Mental Illness in Rural Ireland*. Berkeley: University of California Press, 1979.

Scholes, Robert E. *The Cornell Joyce Collection*. Ithaca, N.Y.: Cornell University Press, 1961.

———. "Further Observations of the Text of *Dubliners*." *Studies in Bibliography* 17 (1964):107–22.

———. "Some Observations of the Text of *Dubliners*: 'The Dead.'" *Studies in Bibliography* 15 (1962):191–205.

Schwartzman, Myron. "Quinnigan's Quake." *Bulletin of Research in the Humanities* (New York Public Library), 81:1 (Summer 1978), 83:1 (Spring 1980).

Scott, Bonnie Kime. *Joyce and Feminism*. Bloomington: University of Indiana Press, 1984.

Schechner, Mark. "A Psychoanalytic Inquiry into Ulysses." In *Joyce in Nighttown*. Berkeley: University of California Press, 1974.

Sheehy, Eugene. *May It Please the Court*. Dublin: C. J. Fallon, 1951.

Shloss, Carol. "The End of Molly's Exile." Paper delivered at the Ninth James Joyce Symposium, Frankfurt, West Germany, 1984.

Slocum, John J. *New York Times Book Review*. January 21, 1951.

Slocum, John J., and Herbert Cahoon, *A Bibliography of James Joyce*. New Haven: Yale University Press, 1953.

———. "A Note on Joyce Biography." *Yale University Library Gazette* 28:1 (July 1953):44–50.

Soupault, Philippe. *Souvenirs de James Joyce*. Paris: Charlot, 1945.

Spender, Stephen. "The Daytime World of James Joyce." *New York Times Book Review*, May 26, 1957.

———. "James Joyce: 1882–1941," *The Listener*, January 23, 1941, pp. 124–25.

Spielberg, Peter. *James Joyce's Manuscripts and Letters at the University of Buffalo: A Catalogue*. Buffalo, N.Y.: University of Buffalo, 1962.

Staley, Thomas. "James Joyce in Trieste." *The Georgia Review* (October 1962):446–49.

Steinberg, Erwin R. *The Stream of Consciousness and Beyond in "Ulysses."* Pittsburgh: University of Pittsburgh Press, 1973.

Stern, James. "James Joyce: A First Impression." In *A James Joyce Miscellany*, Second Series, edited by Marvin Magalaner. Carbondale: Southern Illinois University Press, 1959. A longer version of this piece appeared originally in *The Listener*, December 28, 1961.

"The Story of Adolph Kastor." In *Camillus Cutlery Company*, Camillus, New York, 1951.

Sullivan, Kevin. *Joyce Among the Jesuits*. New York: Columbia University Press, 1958.

Suter, August. "Some Reminiscences of James Joyce." *JJQ* 7:3 (1970):191–98.

Svevo, Italo. *James Joyce*. New York: New Directions, 1950.

Tatum, G. Marvin. "The James Joyce Collection at Cornell University," *Gazette of the Grolier Club*, N.S. no. 33–34 (1981–82), 78–83.

Thom's Official Dublin Directory and Calendar. Dublin: Alex Thom & Co., 1900–1905.

Time, "*Ulysses* Lands," cover story, January 29, 1934.

Time, "Night Thoughts," cover story, May 8, 1939.

Time, "Milestones," April 23, 1951.

Tindall, William York. "Joyce's Chambermade Music." *Poetry* 80 (1952): 105–16.

———. *A Reader's Guide to "Finnegans Wake."* New York: Farrar, Straus & Giroux, 1969.

A Reader's Guide to James Joyce. New York: Farrar, Straus & Giroux, 1959.

Torchiana, Donald. *Backgrounds to "Dubliners."* Boston: Allen and Unwin, 1986.

Townsend, Kim. *Sherwood Anderson*. Boston: Houghton Mifflin, 1987.

United Kingdom Official Publications. *Reports from Commissioners for Ireland. Statistics on Emigration and Immigration for the Year 1904.* Vol. xcviii, 88–92. *Statistics on Marriages, Births and Deaths, 1905.* Vol. XVII, 571.

Unkeless, Elaine. "The Conventional Molly Bloom." In *Women in Joyce,* edited by S. A. Henke and Elaine Unkeless. Urbana: University of Illinois Press, 1982.

Van Hoek, Kees. "The Way of the World." (Interview with Nora Joyce) *Irish Times,* February 17, 1948.

Wade, Allan, ed. *The Letters of W. B. Yeats.* New York: Macmillan, 1955.

Watson, G. J. *Irish Identity and the Literary Revival.* New York: Harper and Row, 1979. London: Croom Helm, 1979.

Weaver, Harriet Shaw. Papers and correspondence, vols. 1–8. British Library manuscripts 57345–52.

Weld, Jacqueline Bograd. *Peggy: The Wayward Guggenheim.* New York: Dutton, 1986.

Wilson, Edmund. *Axel's Castle.* New York: Scribner's, 1931.

Wilson, Mona. *The Life of William Blake.* London: Hart-Davis, 1948.

Index

453